The WORLD
ENCYCLOPEDIA OF
CONTEMPORARY
THEATRE

VOLUME 5
ASIA/PACIFIC

The **WORLD ENCYCLOPEDIA** **OF** **CONTEMPORARY THEATRE**

VOLUME 5
ASIA/PACIFIC

DON RUBIN

LONDON AND NEW YORK

First published in 1998
by Routledge
11 New Fetter Lane, London EC4P 4EE
29 West 35th Street, New York 10001

Typeset in 9/10$\frac{1}{2}$ pt Sabon and Optima by MCS Ltd, Wiltshire
Printed in Great Britain by Biddles Ltd, Guildford and King's Lynn
Printed on acid-free paper

This encyclopedia is a project implemented with the support of Unesco and at the request
of four non-governmental organizations. The opinions expressed in the various articles are
those of the authors themselves and do not necessarily reflect the point of view of the
sponsoring organizations.

British Library Cataloguing in Publication Data
A catalogue record for this book is available from the British Library.

Library of Congress Cataloging-in-Publication Data
A catalog record for this book is available on request.

ISBN 0–415–05933–X

INTERNATIONAL EDITORIAL BOARD

This volume was made possible through the generosity of many benefactors but would not have been able to be realized without the financial support of the Japan Foundation (Asia Centre), Tokyo and its affiliated offices in Toronto (Masamichi Sugihara, Director) and Bangkok. A special thank you is offered here for their willingness to risk with the WECT vision.

The World Encyclopedia of Contemporary Theatre would like to acknowledge with sincere thanks the financial contributions of the following:

REGIONAL SPONSORS

Canadian Department of Communications
Ford Foundation
Japan Foundation (Asia Centre)
Ontario Ministry of Citizenship and Culture
Rockefeller Foundation
Routledge
Social Sciences and Humanities Research Council of Canada
Unesco
York University

NATIONAL SPONSORS

Autonomous National University of México
Cameroon National Unesco Commission
Canadian National Unesco Commission
Cheik Anta Diop University, Dakar
Cultural Ministry of France
German Centre of the ITI
Higher Institute of Dramatic Arts, Damascus
Mexican National Unesco Commission
Joseph S. Stauffer Foundation
University of Bordeaux
Herman Voaden
Woodlawn Arts Foundation

STATE SPONSORS

Apotex Foundation
Austrian Ministry of Education and the Arts
Samuel and Saidye Bronfman Family Foundation
Floyd S. Chalmers
Faculty of Fine Arts, York University
Finnish Ministry of Education

FIRT
Georgian Ministry of Culture
Greek Ministry of Culture
Calouste Gulbenkian Foundation
International Theatre Institute (Paris) and National Centres in Bangladesh, Belgium, Bulgaria, Canada, Czech Republic, Finland, Hungary, India, Netherlands, Poland, Romania, Slovak Republic, Switzerland, United States and Venezuela
Israeli Ministry of Foreign Affairs, Division of Cultural and Scientific Relations
Japan Foundation Cultural Centre, Bangkok
Japan Foundation, Toronto
Henry White Kinnear Foundation
Ministry of the Flemish Community (Cultural Affairs)
Moldovan Theatre Union
Organization of American States
Polish Ministry of Culture
Republic of Macedonia Ministry of Culture
K.M. Sarkissian and the Zoryan Institute
Conn Smythe Foundation
Turkish Embassy in Canada

LOCAL SPONSORS

Marion Andre
Arts Development and Promotions
Australian Council
Mariellen Black
Lyle B. Blair
Canadian Theatre Review
Centre de Recherches et de Formation Théâtrales en Wallonie
Max Clarkson Foundation
Joy Cohnstaedt
Freda's Originals
H. Ian Macdonald
John H. Moore, FCA
Erminio G. Neglia
Farouk Ohan
Ontario Ministry of Skills Development
Peter Perina
E. Marshall Pollock
Rodolfo A. Ramos
Calvin G. Rand
Lynton Reed Printing
Don Rubin and Patricia Keeney
St Lawrence Centre for the Arts
Storewal International Inc.
Anton Wagner

Special thanks to:

Margrethe Aaby (Norway), Eric Alexander (Netherlands), Ebrahim Alkhazi (India), Ina Andre (Canada), Gaida Barisone (Latvia), Curtis Barlow (Canada), Isabelle Barth (France), Alexei Bartoshevitch (Russia), Shaul Baskind (Israel), Jean Benedetti (United Kingdom), Eric Bentley (United States), Don Berkowitz (Canada), Mariellen Black (Canada), Lyle B. Blair (Canada), Gaston Blais (Canada), Monica Brizzi (Italy), Robert Brustein (United States), John Bury (United Kingdom), Judith Cameron (Canada), Richard Cave (United Kingdom), Katarina Ćirić-Petrović (Serbia), Martin Cloutier (United States), Joy Cohnstaedt (Canada), Martha Coigney (United States), Communications Committee (International Theatre Institute), Leonard W. Conolly (Canada), Robert Crew (Canada), Renée L. Czukar (Canada), Esther A. Dagan (Canada), Gautam Dasgupta (United States), Donna Dawson (Canada), Susan Frances Dobie (Canada), Francis Ebejer (Malta), Krista Ellis (Canada), John Elsom (United Kingdom), Claes Englund (Sweden), Debebe Eshetu (Ethiopia), Martin Esslin (United Kingdom), Alan Filewod (Canada), Stephen Florian (Malta), Joyce Flynn (United States), Mira Friedlander (Canada), Julia Gabor (Hungary), Bibi Gessner (Switzerland), Madeleine Gobeil (Unesco), Mayte Gómez (Canada), Sevelina Gyorova (Bulgaria), René Hainaux (Belgium), Bartold Halle (Norway), Peter Hay (United States), Ian Herbert (United Kingdom), Nick Herne (United Kingdom), Frank Hoff (Canada), Eleanor Hubbard (Canada), Huang Huilin (China), Djuner Ismail (Macedonia), Jasmine Jaywant (Canada), Stephen Johnson (Canada), Sylvia Karsh (Canada), Naïm Kattan (Canada), Ferenc Kerenyi (Hungary), Myles Kesten (Canada), Valery Khasanov (Russia), William Kilbourn (Canada), Pierre Laville (France), George Lengyel (Hungary), Henri Lopes (Unesco), Meredith Lorden (Canada), Paul Lovejoy (Canada), Margaret Majewska (Poland), Lars af Malmborg (Sweden), Georges Manal (France), Suzanne Marko (Sweden), Bonnie Marranca (New York), Vivian Martínez Tabares (Cuba), Ruth R. Mayleas (United States), Giles R. Meikle (Canada), Paul-Louis Mignon (France), Ian Montagnes (Canada), Mavor Moore (Canada), Richard Mortimer (Canada), Judi Most (United States), Julia Moulden (Canada), Irmeli Niemi (Finland), Farouk Ohan (United Arab Emirates), Louis Patenaude (Canada), Oskar Pausch (Austria), André-Louis Perinetti (International Theatre Institute), Natasha Rapoport (Canada), Donald S. Rickerd (Canada), Roehampton Hotel (Canada), Charles-Antoine Rouyer (Canada), Mr and Mrs Irving Rubin (United States), Marti Russell (Canada), Raimonda Sadauskienė (Lithuania), Suzanne Sato (United States), Willmar Sauter (Sweden), Richard Schechner (United States), Petar Selem (Croatia), Małgorzata Semil (Poland), Mary Ann Shaw (Canada), Neville Shulman (United Kingdom), Mikhail Shvidkoi (Russia), David Silcox (Canada), Phillip Silver (Canada), Singer Travel (United States), Ron Singer (Canada), Mike Smith (Canada), Prince Subhadradis Diskul (Thailand), Anneli Suur-Kujala (Finland), Péter Szaffkó (Hungary), Carlos Tindemans (Belgium), Graham Usher (Canada), Indrassen Vencatchellum (Unesco), Janusz Warminski (Poland), Klaus Wever (Germany), Don B. Wilmeth (American Society for Theatre Research), Claudia Woolgar (United Kingdom), Yoh Suk-Kee (South Korea), Piet Zeeman (Netherlands), Paul Zeleza (Canada).

DEDICATION

This series is dedicated to the memory of Roman Szydłowski of Poland (1918–83), a former President of the International Association of Theatre Critics. His vision for all international theatre organizations was truly world-wide and his tenacity in the service of that vision was genuinely legendary. It was Dr Szydłowski who first proposed the idea for a *World Encyclopedia of Contemporary Theatre*.

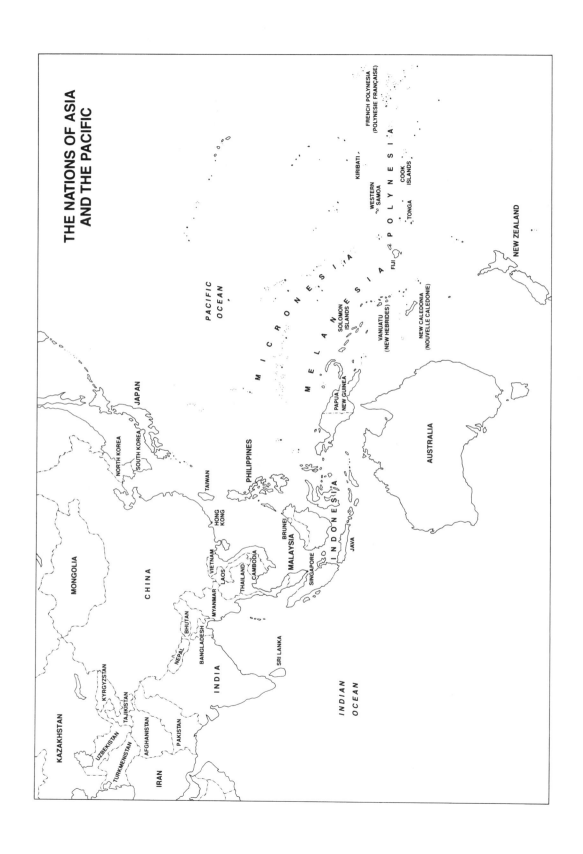

THE NATIONS OF ASIA
AND THE PACIFIC

CONTENTS

VOLUME FIVE • ASIA/PACIFIC

Contents • The Nations and Their Theatres

VOLUME FIVE

ASIA/PACIFIC

AN INTRODUCTION

OF NATIONS AND THEIR THEATRES

The encyclopedia has been with humankind since the ancient Greeks. Aristotle's works are certainly encyclopedic in nature; that is to say, they encircle particular aspects of knowledge, some extremely specialized, some more general. Pliny the Elder (AD 23–79) compiled a thirty-seven-volume encyclopedia of natural science. The largest encyclopedia seems to have been edited by the Emperor of China, Yung Lo, in the fifteenth century. Called the *Yung Lo Ta Tien*, it required 2,169 scholars to write it and ran to 917,480 pages in 11,100 volumes.

The *World Encyclopedia of Contemporary Theatre* (*WECT*) is a somewhat less exhaustive encyclopedia than Yung Lo's. When complete, we expect it to run to only 3,000 or so pages in a mere six volumes. However, Yung Lo sought to cover a much wider range of subjects than *WECT*. His goal was to examine nothing less than all of Chinese literature from the beginning of time.

WECT makes no such claims about its comprehensiveness. *WECT* is specifically an encyclopedia of nations and their theatres. The starting point is 1945, the end of World War II, a time of change politically, socially and culturally for much of the world. Sketching out a social and political context for each of the countries being studied, *WECT* seeks to explore in a comparative fashion each country's theatrical history since that time. The assumption from the beginning has been that theatre is an art form which grows from its society and which feeds back into it through reflection, analysis and challenge.

No other international theatre encyclopedia has attempted such a comparative, broad-based, cross-cultural study. The fact that virtually every one of our writers is from the country being written about adds still another level of authority and uniqueness to this work, which is attempting to present each nation's view of itself, a view not of politicians or propagandists but of each country's theatrical scholars and theatre artists.

It should also be made clear here that *WECT* is not intended as a guide to individuals, companies, festivals or forms. One will not find here analyses of Stanislavski, Brecht, Craig, Brook, Grotowski or Artaud. Nor will one find biographies of Soyinka, Fugard or Havel. *WECT* is also not the place to look for a history of the Comédie-Française or the Stratford Festival, Venezuela's Rajatabla or Japan's Tenjo Sajiki. Nor will readers find extensive documentation on the Carthage Festival or Edinburgh, on BITEF or Adelaide, on the Cervantes Festival or even Avignon.

The world of theatre is far too large and has become far too specialized for that. Information on the lives of everyone from playwrights to puppeteers, choreographers to composers, directors to designers can be readily found in a wide range of reference works available in every major language. There are book-length analyses and histories – some critical, some just documentation of all the major companies and festivals that one could ever want to know about. There are also dictionaries available that focus on virtually every specialized theatrical subject from semiotics to cultural anthropology. Many fine theatre journals around the world maintain a valuable and continuing dialogue and documentation of current issues.

What has not existed before – and what *WECT* has attempted to create – has been a theatrical reference work looking at a wide range of *national* theatrical activity on a country-by-country basis from a specifically *national* standpoint. As we near the end of the twentieth century, as nations in many parts of the world finally shed their colonial pasts, and as new nations emerge in the aftermath of the collapse of the Soviet Union and Yugoslavia, such a gap in our cultural knowledge may seem curious. What, for example, does Romanian theatre look like to a Romanian in this post-modern world? Canadian theatre to a Canadian? What is of import to an Australian about his or her own theatre? To a Senegalese? A Brazilian? A Vietnamese? An Egyptian? And what of all the individual republics that once made up the Soviet Union, Yugoslavia and Czechoslovakia? What is the self-perception of theatre professionals in the new Germany, where two totally different systems were uncomfortably reunited as the 1990s began?

To allow the reader to draw conclusions and to allow comparability, each of WECT's writers was given the challenge of bringing together just such a national impression in a very specifically structured essay which would include not lists of names and dates but rather a context – in some cases, contexts – for international comprehension. That is, each of WECT's extensive national articles – ranging from 3,000 to 30,000 words per country (small books in some instances) – has been written so as to provide theatrical professionals and those concerned with research on the profession with not only the basic material they would need if they were going to work in or visit a particular country for the first time, but also the basic material necessary to identify international trends and movements in the decades since the end of World War II.

Those who already know their own or some other country's theatre very well, no doubt, will find the information contained on those countries useful but probably too basic. Even at 30,000 words, these articles cannot possibly replace the library that would be needed to completely cover the theatre of any one country. In any event, encyclopedias historically have been intended only as introductions. Indeed, it is difficult to imagine them being anything more than that on any given subject. The philosopher and encyclopedist Denis Diderot (1713–84) argued that encyclopedias should be seen as basic libraries in every field but the reader's own. In this case, it is a theatre library for every country but the reader's own. To this end,

we have asked writers to think of their ideal reader as a sophisticated professional from abroad.

In this light, we believe that WECT will be most important to readers for the breadth of its coverage; in this case, for the distance from home that each reader can travel through these articles. This is not in any way to suggest a lack of depth but rather honestly to recognize given limitations. WECT is therefore providing extended and extensive articles on every theatre culture in the world, more than 160 countries by the time the project is concluded. Looked at as a whole, they will be more than able to help theatre professionals in every part of the world put plays, companies, policies and productions into a national context, and in our complicated world this seems an important and unique contribution.

WECT material can be accessed in one of two ways: by either reading vertically (from beginning to end in any particular country) or horizontally (focusing on only a single subject such as Puppet (and Mask) Theatre or Dramaturgy across several countries). Having suggested earlier that this is not an encyclopedia of individuals, companies, festivals or forms, the fact is that one *can* identify individuals, companies, festivals and forms by referring to the index at the back of each volume or to the comprehensive multi-volume index planned for the final volume. By going to specific pages, the reader will then be able to follow the influence and development of particular figures or groups both within their own countries, within regions and ultimately in the world.

Whichever approach one is using, whether professionally focused or casual, it is probably useful at this point to understand the many section headings in each of the national articles and what each section is intended to include.

How To Use This Volume

Each national article in this volume is divided into fifteen sections: History, Structure of the National Theatre Community, Artistic Profile, Companies, Dramaturgy, Directing and Acting, Music Theatre, Dance Theatre, Theatre for Young Audiences, Puppet (and Mask) Theatre, Design, Theatre Space and Architecture, Training, Criticism, Scholarship-Publishing, and Further Reading. These sections are intended to provide the following information.

History: Each national article opens with basic geographical, historical and/or socio-political material. In the case of countries whose histories may not be well known outside the immediate region, we have encouraged writers to provide a more extrensive background than might be normally found. Included as well is a history of the country's major theatrical movements and events since 1945, treated on a decade-by-decade basis or treated thematically. In each case the intent has been to give the national writer flexibility in interpreting the material being discussed.

Structure of the National Theatre Community: This is essentially a demographic section intended to offer information on the types of theatres (commercial, state-supported, regional or municipal) and the numbers of theatres operating in a particular country, their geographical distribution and relative sizes (both in terms of employees and budgets). One will find in this section information on the various infrastructures that have developed (national associations, national and international linkages), unions, as well as information on the major festivals in the country and national awards.

Artistic Profile: A look at the major artistic trends and styles in music and/or dance theatre which have evolved within each country with particular emphasis on significant indigenous forms and their relation to cultural and religous practice. Where a significant spoken drama has emerged that too is discussed within this section.

Companies: An identification and discussion of the major professional troupes as well as an examination of those non-professional troupes (often connected with educational institutions) which have influenced national cultural practice in the performing arts.

Dramaturgy: Initially called 'Playwriting', this section heading was changed to its current title to allow *WECT* to recognize the many collectively created productions which have been done across the many continents as well as to acknowledge the significant role of the director in script development. In no way is this intending to demean the importance of the playwright whose work, we believe, still remains central to the process of theatrical creation and is at the centre of this particular section.

Music Theatre and Dance Theatre: In this volume, music and dance theatre are usually discussed in the opening, historical section and under **Artistic Profile**. It is only in the national articles of such 'western' countries as Australia

and New Zealand that these areas are discussed in separate sections.

Theatre for Young Audiences: Professional theatre companies for young audiences have a long history in Asia with many groups – particularly in east Asia – dating back to the early decades of the twentieth century. Information on this important area has been provided in this section by all our national writers. By including this separate section, *WECT* is acknowledging the importance of this very special area of contemporary theatrical practice and its long-term effect on theatrical art world-wide since 1945.

Puppet (and *Mask*) *Theatre*: Sometimes linked with the **Theatre for Young Audiences** section but most often recognized on its own, puppetry has been rediscovered by contemporary theatrical practicners. Within this section we have asked writers to trace developments in the form from its theatrical mimetic roots (imitation of actors) to what has come to be known as Object Theatre in which things take on a dramatic life of their own thanks, very often, to black light techniques that emerged during this period in eastern Europe. We have also asked our writers to look at experiments involving the interrelationship between live actors and puppets or live actors and objects. This is a fascinating and important area which theatre professionals ignore at their own imaginative risk. As for the inclusion of masked performances, its presence within this section seemed both appropriate and useful for the light it sheds on the development of puppetry and its links between the world of the living artist and other worlds which theatrical art clearly has the possibility to reach.

Design: this section examines the work of each theatre community's visual artists. In some cases this has been done thematically; in other cases, on a decade-by-decade basis since 1945. Again, we have asked our writers to avoid lists. Instead of just naming names, we have asked them to choose a small number of representative designers and discuss their individual work.

Theatre Space and Architecture: When we began, this section was simply titled 'Theatre Architecture'. The words 'Theatre Space' were added as the articles began to arrive. Many of our writers originally interpreted this section as being only about buildings created specifically as theatrical venues. Clearly this would have eliminated many of the experiments relating to theatrical space which began in the 1960s and are still with us today, experiments which seem to have begun in North America out of sheer desperation and which evolved in many parts of the world to the total breakdown of proscenium theatre with its visual accoutrements as an a priori requirement for theatrical events.

Training: This section discusses the most important theatre schools and other professional training programmes in each country, their types of curriculum and the traditions they follow.

Criticism, Scholarship and Publishing: The most important theatre research and documentation centres in each country, major performing arts museums, positions being taken by leading critics and theatre scholars are identified in this section. The discussions here range from journalistic reviewing to more analytical philological, anthropological, semiological, and/or other types of structural approaches. In some cases historical context is provided; in others, contemporary developments are emphasized. As well, writers have been asked to identify the most important theatre journals and magazines along with the major theatre publishing houses in their countries.

Further Reading: Most national articles conclude with a brief bibliography identifying the major works available within the national language as well as the most important works about the country's theatre that the authors are aware of in other languages. We have tried to follow the bibliographical form recommended by the University of Chicago Press but in some instances writers followed their own scholarly form leaving us with certain Chicago-style omissions. Through we attempted to fill these gaps it was not always possible. In general, however, enough information has been provided to allow the diligent reader to find the works mentioned.

To some, this structure may seem overly complicated and perhaps even contradictory in terms of allowing each writer or team of writers to identify and define their national theatres. But in every instance, the key was to maintain comparability country-to-country and ultimately region-to-region. It is our belief that as interesting and informative as each national article may be, the real value of *WECT* will ultimately lie in its ability to provide comparability of theatres world-wide, in its ability to allow directors, playwrights, dramaturges, designers, critics, scholars and even those in government to look across a wide range of theatre communities.

Certainly this structure was not arrived at quickly or casually and it continued to be refined almost until publication. When this project was first conceived by the Polish theatre critic Roman Szydłowski (1918–83) in the late 1970s, it was seen simply as an opportunity to provide accurate and up-to-date documentation for theatre critics who were being confronted more regularly than ever before with theatre from all over the world as part of their daily reviewing duties. Visiting groups were no longer rare and exotic events on a critic's schedule. They were appearing with amazing regularity and the best critics simply wanted to do their homework.

But where could a working critic go to find quickly information on Turkish *karagöz*, on Thai *khon* or South Africa's Market Theatre? Critics just seemed expected to know everything and everyone. Even when some information did exist, the sources were too often out of date or existed only in a language not widely spoken.

Most scholars would probably point to the nine-volume *Encyclopedia dello spettacolo* as the standard reference in the field. Available, however, only in Italian, the vast majority of the documentation included there was gathered before World War II and was, to say the least, Eurocentric. Published after the war, this encyclopedia of world theatre history was certainly strong the further one went back in time. But despite the fact that non-European theatre generally and the twentieth century specifically were not especially well served, the *Enciclopedia dello spettacolo* did become a standard. Most libraries found it essential for their reference sections. By the 1970s, however, it was clearly out of date even in its approaches to some of its early material.

Through the years, less ambitious attempts were made. Along with specialized individual volumes, these were very useful but, because of their specificity or, in some cases, their purely academic approach, they were not always useful to theatre professionals. It was at this point in time that Roman Szydłowski proposed a new type of world theatre reference work to the International Association of Theatre Critics, one of many international theatre communications organizations that had sprung up in the wake of two world wars.

At this organization's Congress in Vienna in 1979, Szydłowski, its president, received wide support for the proposal but no clear directions on how to proceed. Within eighteen months, however, he had convinced the International Theatre Institute's (ITI) Permanent Committee on Theatre Publications – a loose association of editors of theatre magazines and journals – to take up the challenge. The ITI, it was felt, being affiliated with the United Nations Educational, Scientific and Cultural Organization (Unesco), at a higher level than the other international theatre associations, seemed to be the right agency to bring the idea to fruition on the world stage. At its 1981 Congress, this committee (subsequently to be called the Communications Committee) endorsed the idea and recommended it to the organization as a whole. It was the ITI's new secretary-general, Lars af Malmborg from Sweden, who decided that the project would be a concrete contribution to world theatre communication.

Malmborg, with the support of the ITI Executive Committee, brought the idea forward and in early 1982 called a meeting of interested international theatre organizations and individuals who might be able to help realize the project. It was from this meeting, held under the aegis of the Fine Arts Museum in Copenhagen, that specific plans began to be made. Four organizations – the ITI, the International Association of Theatre Critics (IATC), the International Federation for Theatre research (FIRT) and the International Society of Libraries and Museums for the Performing Arts (SIBMAS) – agreed to combine efforts towards the realization of what was now being called the *World Encyclopedia of Contemporary Theatre.*

By 1983, with the support of the Faculty of Fine Arts at York University in Toronto and with the initial interest of a major Toronto publishing house, *WECT* was incorporated as an independant not-for-profit project under Canadian law. Initial grants came from York University, Unesco and, the largest grant to that time, from the American-based Ford Foundation (thanks to a willingness to risk on a project that did not fit neatly into any previously established programme by its Theatre Officer, Ruth Mayleas). During 1984, representatives of the four sponsoring organizations met in Toronto (courtesy of Canadian philanthropist Floyd S. Chalmers) to set up parameters. Without this initial support and all the faith it implied in an unprecedented vision, *WECT* would never have gotten off the ground.

The year 1945 was established as a starting point through it was agreed that nothing ever really starts or ends neatly in the world of theatre. It was agreed that television and radio would not be dealt with but that music theatre and dance theatre would be included. It was agreed that a socio-cultural approach would be taken and that the relationship between theatres and the nations from which they grew would be explored. It was agreed that comparability would be emphasized and that writers should be chosen from within each country.

During 1984 an outstanding international team of editors was selected to coordinate the work and to advise in such speciality areas as theatre for young audiences (Wolfgang Wöhlert), music theatre (Horst Seeger), dance theatre (Selma Jeanne Cohen) and puppet theatre (Henryk Jurkowski) among others. Over the years the International Editorial Board would expand and contract as needs appeared or as particular individuals found themselves unable to continue the work. But throughout, the notion of self-identification for each national article was maintained and continued to be the primary reason why *WECT* searched for leading writers, critics, scholars and theatre professionals within each country.

The first full International Editorial Board meeting was held in Toronto in 1985 during the twenty-first World Congress of the ITI. There were five people present from North America, another five from Europe (including *WECT*'s two associate editors, Péter Nagy of Budapest and Philippe Rouyer of Bordeaux) and another six from Latin America, Africa, the Arab countries and Asia/Pacific. It was one of our Asian editors who put the first question to the gathering. 'What exactly do we think *we* mean when we use the word theatre?' he asked. 'I'm really not sure there's a definition we can all agree on. And if we can't come to an agreement on this basic question, how can we possibly agree on anything else?'

The apparently simple question led to an enormously involved discussion about the various types of spoken drama that had evolved in Europe and North America. Objections were quickly raised that we were ignoring musical theatre forms and forms involving movement. Others objected that we were locked into text while our puppet theatre editor was concerned that we were leaving out everything from *wayang kulit* to Punch and Judy. Our African colleagues suggested that our preliminary definition seemed to be ignoring the social relationships in much African theatre, from wedding ceremonies to circumcision rituals. And what of traditional forms in Asia such as *kathakali, noh, kabuki,* Chinese opera, or even the Vietnamese *hat boi*? What of folk forms in so many parts of the world? What of contemporary experiments?

What had appeared to be a rather innocent question in the beginning quickly turned into a life-or-death debate on the whole future – not to even discuss the international credibility – of the project. During the next few days, we turned to various standard texts on theatre in search of a suitable, internationally acceptable definition. It was a fascinating, though ultimately frustrating, exercise. To our amazement, we couldn't really find such a definition. Examinations of standard dictionaries – including the *Oxford English Dictionary* – were of even less help. Most simply defined 'theatre' as a building.

So we created our own international, intercultural working definition of the word. It is offered here not as a conclusion but rather as a starting point for a continuing consideration of what those of us working in the field mean when 'theatre' is spoken of in a contemporary global context.

> *Theatre*: A created event, usually based on text, executed by live performers and taking place before an audience in a specially defined setting. Theatre uses techniques of voice and/or movement to achieve cognition and/or emotional release through the senses. This event is generally rehearsed and is usually intended for repitition over a period of time.

By the time *WECT*'s International Editorial Board next met, it had become clear from discussions with the various international organizations that *WECT* would have to respect various national differences in approaching this work and would have to take, as the American poet Robert Frost once said, 'the road less travelled by' in seeking its writers; that is, it would go to source for its information and interpretation in every instance. Indeed, *WECT* has through the years taken pride in this unique approach, slow and costly though it has been. But it has also been an approach which has led the project to develop close working relationships with theatre people *in* each of the more than 160 countries now involved in what has become the largest international cooperative venture in the history of world theatre, and certainly the largest international publishing venture in world theatre today.

In focusing the work this way, it was obvious that the *WECT* project was taking many risks. The approach was clearly going to make this a lot longer project than anyone had ever dreamed of. By the time this work is concluded, it will have taken about fifteen years.

But we believed when we started – and still believe – that our approach was one which

would afford the best opportunity to ensure both the long-term goals and the highest standards of international scholarly excellence and accuracy. This approach was also one of the key reasons why Unesco decided to support the project and why Unesco ultimately named *WECT* as an official project of its World Decade for Cultural Development (1988–97). Such recognition is unusual for a scholarly work and we feel with some pride that it is an important model for future intercultural, interdisciplinary arts research.

A few words are needed here about world politics and its effect upon our work. For most people, political change is simply interesting newspaper fodder or the stuff to support opinions – pro or con – on particular subjects. The closer that politics gets to home, however, the more directly it impacts on one's reality and the more it affects how one goes about one's daily business. Political change has constantly impacted on *WECT*'s reality and profoundly affected its already complicated work.

To give but one key example, when work began on our European volume, there were only two dozen or so countries to deal with, and those in eastern Europe were guaranteeing they would cover all our writing and translation fees for the region. That was 1985. By 1990, the two Germanys had become one (requiring a significant restructuring of our German material) while the USSR, Yugoslavia and Czechoslovakia went from three separate national entities to twenty-three separate countries (fifteen individual republics from the Soviet Union, six from Yugoslavia and two from Czechoslovakia). Not only did the already completed major articles on the USSR, Yugoslavia and Czechoslovakia have to be completely revised and turned into what we decided to call 'historical overviews' but also new writers needed to be found and new articles had to be commissioned on each of the republics, republics that were, in many instances, in the midst of social, political or armed revolution. With such changes swirling around us, we read the newspapers each day with genuine trepidation. By the time of publication, the volume had expanded to some forty-seven articles. Suffice it to say here that trying to keep up with this ever-changing political landscape continues to be *WECT*'s greatest challenge, a challenge we are trying to meet through computerization and the establishment of *WECT* as an international theatre database.

It was precisely these political changes which Martha Coigney, president of the ITI, was referring to when she said, perhaps optimistically, at the opening of the ITI's 1993 World Congress in Munich that in the future it would no longer be wars between superpowers that people of peace would have to be concerned about, but rather confrontations between cultures. If this is so then we believe that *WECT* may well be able to make a real contribution in at least introducing those cultures to one another. *WECT*'s goal from the beginning has been nothing less than that.

In helping the project to achieve this end, many organizations, many theatre and government agencies, many foundations and individuals have played important roles. A list of the financial sponsors and those who have worked with us appears elsewhere but we would like to acknowledge specifically the ongoing help of Unesco, the Ford and Rockefeller Foundations (Rockefeller came to *WECT*'s aid at precisely the moment the recession and the enormous political changes in Europe threatened to kill the project), the Faculty of Fine Arts and the Office of Research Administration at York University, the Canadian and Ontario governments, the German Centre of the International Theatre Institute and particularly Rolf Rohmer, who has long served as president of the project's International Executive Board. This project would not have survived without the help of the Canadian Centre of the ITI (especially Curtis Barlow in the early years of the project) and the various members of the Canadian-based Board of Directors who worked to find funds to realize this work. The support of our two recent Board presidents has been particularly appreciated – Calvin G. Rand (founding president of Canada's Shaw Festival) and Professor Leonard W. Conolly, former president of Trent University in Ontario.

This project could also not have survived without the ongoing support of the Faculty of Fine Arts and the department of theatre at York University, its deans and its chairs (including Lionel Lawrence, Joyce Zemans, Joy Cohnstaedt, Seth Feldman, Ron Singer, Phillip Silver and Robert Fothergill) and especially the sponsors of the Walter A. Gordon Fellowship, York University's highest research award, which allowed me the time to bring the first volume to fruition.

This project would not have succeeded had *WECT* not had the active support and understanding of all the members of its International Editorial Board, particularly the wisdom and advice of Péter Nagy, whose diplomacy in the face of *WECT*'s own political struggles was never less than brilliant. Nor would it have succeeded without the stubborn belief in this project of its Managing Editor and Director of Research, Anton Wagner, whose work was long funded by the Canadian Social Science and Humanities Research Council, and the project's indefatigable administrators Donna Dawson and Catherine Matzig. Our editors at Routledge – Samantha Parkinson, Alison Barr, Michelle Darraugh, Robert Potts and Mark Barragry – and our copy-editor, Christine Firth, have been most understanding in working with us on what must have appeared to them a mad dream at times. Without their personal commitment and the corporate support behind them, *WECT* would still be in the planning stages.

If I have personally been seen through the many years of this project as its architect, I can only say that the building would never have stood without the strength, determination and belief of my wife and too rarely recognized co-visionary, Patricia Keeney. Against all her writerly instincts and sometimes against all logic, she bravely sat through meeting after meeting of every one of this project's boards, a duty she took on because she believed in the work. Without her faith and goodwill, *WECT* might well have foundered.

There are far too many people to thank here by name. It would be remiss to try, for too many would be left out. But to all of them, particularly to all our editors, writers, national editorial committees, ITI Centres and translators, to all the sponsoring and other organizations which supported this work, thank you for believing with us and in us. We trust that your patience and support will have proven to be worth all the time, the pain and the effort.

Don Rubin
December 1997

THE BLOOMING OF A THOUSAND FLOWERS

AN INTRODUCTION TO THEATRE IN ASIA AND THE PACIFIC

Asia

The extraordinary richness of Asia's theatrical traditions are well known and well documented. From Indian *kathakali* and *chaau* to Chinese *jing ju* (Beijing Opera), from Iranian *ta'ziyeh* to Japanese *noh* and *kabuki,* from Vietnamese *hat boi* and water-puppets to *bunraku* and shadow-puppets, the theatrical arts of Asia have excited and enriched world theatre traditions for thousands of years. But what of Asia's lesser-known and less well-documented modern traditions and their relationship with theatre practice in other parts of the world? What role do the traditional arts play now?

These questions and many others were brought up in discussions among the many national and regional editors who were involved through the years in the planning of this volume, perhaps the most complex yet in the *WECT* series. Of particular concern was the role of traditional theatre practice. In an encyclopedia of contemporary theatre should writers be asked to deal at length with traditional forms? Early debates by our editorial board and by the sponsoring organizations suggested that they be left out but as the actual work moved on, it became clear that one of the key goals of this series – self-definition – would not be properly served with a global answer. Indeed, the debate intensified with some writers insisting that traditional theatre needed to be dealt with in detail to understand the contemporary while others insisted that contemporary forms needed to be studied on their own. What the reader will find therefore in this volume is a mix of approaches to this question – in some cases significant space has been given to traditional forms while in others the forms are sketched or discussed only briefly. The choices made by the writers from each country are as revealing as what is actually said. For the record, it should be noted that *WECT* finally asked that all major traditional forms be identified at least briefly.

What has become clear as a result of this work is that theatre in Asia and the Pacific is a far more complex entity than many from other parts of the world might anticipate or appreciate. It is, as perhaps no other, a brilliant mosaic mixing old and new, east and west, indigenous and colonial, rooted and technological, communal and individuated. It is at once connected to traditions that date back 5,000 years and as avant-garde as any in the world in the 1990s. Whether one is discussing Indian dramatist Rabindranath Tagore and his links to sanskrit drama or the multimedia experiments and happenings of Japanese director Terayama Shuji, whether one is looking at the stark stagings of Indonesian director Rendra or the deeply influential work of a Moscow-trained director such as Azerbaizhan Mambetov in Kazakhstan, there is a pattern to be discerned that stretches from the Asian republics of the former USSR to the Philippines, from northern China to Singapore.

This richness is palpable and it is being studied both within the region and at places such as the East–West Center at the University of Hawaii where the traditional arts, the contemporary arts and the many crossover experiments between them are being examined by scholars such as James Brandon, an adviser to this volume and probably one of the west's most respected scholars in this area. But early on in this work it became clear both to Professor Brandon and to me that if this work were to succeed it had to be the Asian and Pacific scholars themselves who took the lead. The final version of this volume is very much the result of work by Asian and Pacific theatre professionals, unapologetic scholars all ranging from Nicanor Tiongson in the Philippines to Arby Ovanessian from Iran, from Solehah Ishak and Nur Nina Zuhra in Malaysia to Saini K.M. in Indonesia, from Rong Guangrun in China to Senda Akihiko in Japan.

What all the writers represented here have articulated in one way or another is that theatre in Asia and the Pacific is a microcosm of theatre in the world. One can see connections to religion and the supernatural in countries as far apart as Iran and the Philippines and one can see its non-mimetic and often avant-garde instincts in experiments from Japan to Indonesia. Between these extremes one finds traditional sung forms and European spoken forms, masked theatre and puppet theatre, danced theatre and shadow theatre, each with its own energy and each with its own committed following. In many cases, the communities overlap. In some, they barely speak to or acknowledge one another. This region has its political theatres and its street theatres and traditional artists at the root of it all continuing to revitalize their art even as the millennium approaches.

The aesthetic patterns are identifiable and visible to all. Sung and danced forms emerged early in this part of the world, some connected to religion and others supported by feudal courts. Growing from India (with perhaps the oldest and most complicated theatrical history of any country) and from China, theatre of this region spread across Asia and the Pacific utilizing, in later incarnations, not only tales from *Mahabharata* and *Ramayana* for inspiration but also more local stories and legends. Colonial and/or trading contacts introduced western forms of theatre practice in the nineteenth century and, in a few cases, even earlier. Where western forms were not rejected for political or religious reasons, new theatrical communities emerged and by the beginning of the twentieth century two clear styles of theatre could be differentiated in many countries in the region: the traditional ones rooted in the musical and movement skills of the actor and the modern one involving texts that were spoken rather than sung, texts more often than not mimetically interpreted rather than symbolically danced. The traditional theatre was dominated by great actors who handed their skills down generation by generation in direct and often familial lines while the spoken theatre privileged text and textual interpreters who often had social or political agendas.

In some Asian countries, the twentieth century was a period of dialectical debate between these forms. The intensity of such debate – both on-stage and off – deeply affected the respective theatre communities. Traditional forms changed, some modestly, some significantly and spoken forms adapted. Perhaps most ironic to the dispassionate viewer is how many theatre artists in the last two or three decades of the twentieth century sought to bridge the gap between the two forms, ultimately easternizing western aesthetics (with Artaud and Brecht as the avant-garde in this movement) while allowing strong western elements into the often ancient arts of Asia.

'Let a thousand flowers bloom' said Mao. Indeed, a thousand or more theatrical flowers are blooming in Asia and the Pacific in the 1990s. The number attests to a vibrant theatrical culture, one clearly connected now to both east and west, past and future. Asia's theatre particularly, as one will see by reading even just a few of the many thoughtful and revealing articles here, is not an easy one to understand. It is complicated and it is pluralistic. But for anyone willing to make even a modest effort, the journey will prove a rich one, and one that will make it impossible for anyone to say blithely that theatre is a western growth or that it developed fully only from Greek roots.

For the record, this volume would never have come together without the hard work of our regional editorial board: the indefatigable and always accurate Katharine Brisbane in Sydney, our deeply committed Central Asian editor Ravi Chaturvedi in Jaipur, our ubiquitous Southeast Asian dance and theatre scholar Chua Soo Pong in Singapore, Tanokura Minoru in Tokyo and Ramendu Majumdar in Dhaka. I would also like to acknowledge the work done during the early stages of this project by the far-sighted Indian director and designer Ebrahim Alkazi. To all these volume editors, to James Brandon, to our international editorial board (and particularly to our specialty editors Selma Jean Cohen, Henryk Jurkowski and Wolfgang Wöhlert) as well as to my editorial co-worker and administrator Catherine Matzig special thanks and appreciation for the time committed to this work.

Finally, I would like to acknowledge the financial support of two international agencies without whose very real financial help this volume would never have been completed: the Rockefeller Foundation in New York and the Japan Foundation in Tokyo. The former has been behind this project almost from the beginning and its many officers have never been less than supportive in what must have seemed at times to be a crazy vision. The latter through its visionary Asia Centre helped *WECT* to organize planning meetings in Bangkok and Tokyo, bringing together many of our writers and members of our Asian editorial team. Members of the Japan Foundation's Toronto office – most especially Sugihara Masamichi, Honda Osamu and Aoyagi Toshi – have helped in too many ways to acknowledge properly. To both these agencies, *WECT* offers a deep bow and its sincerest thanks.

Don Rubin
York University, Toronto

The Pacific

The geographical and historical legacy of the South Pacific is not only rich, wide and varied but much of it inaccessible both in time and space. This enormous area of the globe, spreading laterally from Western Australia to Easter Island, comprises volumes of ocean surrounding a myriad of tiny islands and atolls – Tonga has 170, Tahiti-Polynesia 118, Papua New Guinea 800 – and a few land masses with modern metropolitan centres of substantial population. Each inhabited island has its own ancient culture and language, to which has been added the hybrid cultures that travel and colonization have brought. Within each, theatre, dance and music have been as much part of community life as in any culture, though visitors may see little of them and continue to retain in their imagination the legend of the South Seas gained from western literature and films.

The largest land mass is Australia, whose indigenous culture is ancient but whose modern nationhood is barely a century old. A migrant culture imposed from 1788 upon widely dispersed and singular tribal institutions, Australia's 18 million population has been built in the aftermath of the wars of America, Europe and Asia. It is now the most heterogeneous of all the nations in the region. To the north is Papua New Guinea, with a population of 4 million deeply divided into island communities and separated by the steep highlands in the centre. Dutch, British and German colonization was replaced after World War I by Australian trusteeship until independence was declared in 1975.

To the southeast of Australia is New Zealand, colonized in 1840 by the British and with a similar history to Australia, but differing significantly in geographical dimension and the resistance of its Polynesian Maori people. New Zealand's population is now approximately that of Papua New Guinea. Archaeological evidence has shown that Papua New Guinea and Australia were colonized from Southeast Asia over 50,000 years ago by what became the Melanesian people. Polynesians, intrepid seafarers, came from the north from 1500 BC to settle much of the rest of the Pacific, reaching New Zealand about AD 850. The two races are distinct in appearance and cultural practices: the Melanesians, who make up the great majority of the population, are dark, their skin sometimes blue-black and their hair densely curly; the Polynesians have golden skin and a taller build. The Melanesians have hundreds of local languages: New Guinea alone has 720; Polynesians have one homogenous language, Tagalog, with local variations.

European exploration and trading began in the sixteenth century but it was not until the settlement of New South Wales which followed Captain James Cook's exploration of the South Seas that France went in pursuit, settling Tahiti in 1842 and New Caledonia in 1853. The British took control of Fiji in 1877. This haphazard exploration and settlement, initially by lawless commercial interests, created territorial divisions which were often alien to the natural divisions of race and culture and compounded the cultural complexities created by the haphazard nature of the original settlements. The consequence has been a history of warring neighbours and civil strife. Recent examples have been the military *coup d'état* in Fiji which reconstructed the government along racial lines and the long-running guerrilla war over the copper mine in Bougainville, a Papua New Guinea territory with a greater affinity to the Solomon Islands. Fiji, originally Polynesian, now has a population largely made up of the descendants of Melanesians kidnapped to work the early plantations and Indians, indentured as labourers between 1879 and 1916, following the banning of the 'black-birding' practice, which involved the kidnapping of plantation workers.

In the twentieth century, the Pacific War, following the fall of Singapore in 1942, disrupted the pattern still further as the Japanese colonized Micronesia in the north and the United States became the major force in the Pacific. The Solomon Islands were a major theatre of war. The peace brought further damage to the region as isolated atolls became sites for the explosion of nuclear bombs, a practice stopped by treaty in 1985. France detonated its last bomb in 1996. The 1960s and 1970s saw most Pacific nations achieve independence. Only French Polynesia continues to be governed by metropolitan France. Cultural independence and revival in the face of material advancement remains a struggle to be fought and won.

Distances between these Pacific settlements are so vast that it is only since the 1970s that the touring of theatre and other cultural ventures has become viable. This is for the main part limited to the four-yearly Pan-Pacific Arts Festival and specific occasions of cultural diplomacy. Public funding in the more populous areas has enabled small troupes to travel extensively. Between the existing companies in Australia and New Zealand there is still surprisingly little traffic despite their relative proximity, common ancestry and substantial cross-migration. They do, however, share a sense of humour and New Zealand is known for producing notable comedians who contribute to Australia's comedy festivals, radio and television. In the 1990s, government export incentives have encouraged Australian performers – mainly in the non-lingual fields of dance, puppetry and acrobatics – to expand their horizons and tour abroad. Asia and the Pacific have become major destinations.

Despite this regional diversity, the process by which contemporary theatre has developed has been remarkably similar among the nations of the region. Three factors have in sequence been responsible for this: the diversity of languages which encouraged the use of music, dance and mime in traditional forms of storytelling; the importation of European forms of theatre which provided a model for change; and since the 1960s the conscious re-examination of past practices, led by the academies, in the search for a new means of expressing and reflecting a national identity.

Until the development of Melanesian Pidgin (Tok Pisin) as a common language from Papua New Guinea to Fiji, performance was a local affair derived from ritual: strictly traditional in form and content but introducing parody of local authorities and political allusions. They were highly elaborate productions, the mask-making occupying the time and skill of the whole village, some in great secrecy. The coming of European work practices put an end to the more time-consuming celebrations, but the spread of variations of Pidgin enabled the formation of travelling troupes.

Melanesian Pidgin was a language devised by 'black-birding' traders who kidnapped Melanesian men from Papua New Guinea, Vanuatu and the Solomons to work on plantations in Queensland and Fiji. It was adopted also by the church. The coming of missionaries to the islands from the early nineteenth century was, in Professor Andrew Horn's words, a powerful social force for imperialism and political interests. On some islands and on Australian missions, performance of traditional rituals and parodies was discouraged. In others the missionaries adapted their moral messages to these existing forms, particularly through the intervention of women villagers. In Professor Horn's view, the church introduced western moral principles based on ignorance of the prevailing culture, something which amounted to indoctrination of the idea that people of colour were endemically inferior to whites.

The Melanesians of Papua New Guinea, Vanuatu and New Caledonia in the nineteenth century received much harsher treatment than the Polynesians of French Polynesia. Gauguin's picturesque account of village life and the popular doctrine of the noble savage prevented immediate assaults by governments on the traditional way of life; instead it fell victim to the strictures of the Catholic church. In consequence the major political theatre in the South Pacific has come from the Melanesians.

Principal among these companies are Vanuatu's Wan Smolbag, established in 1989 by

Peter Walker from London's East 15 Acting School, and Papua New Guinea's Raun Raun Theatre, founded in 1974. They have been of vital importance in disseminating information about hygiene, AIDS and sexually transmitted diseases and developing debate on domestic violence, deforestation and other social issues. Performers with these companies have formed new groups in other parts of the region.

From the 1970s writers for the theatre have begun to deal in more complex ways with national character and the quest for cultural identity. At first their models were the epic and the social realist play. With growing experience they have begun to explore their familiar forms of language and action and to look for inspiration to the rituals of the past. The work of theorists such as Poland's Jerzy Grotowski, Indonesia's W.S. Rendra and Brazil's Augusto Boal have been influential. The universities and training institutions have taken a lead in these developments and many of the pioneering writers and directors have been and still are academics.

Australia and New Zealand have followed this pattern and undergone equally radical social change but without the enforcements of colonialism that still prevail in some parts of the region. In the nineteenth century Australia and New Zealand, like Africa, India, Hawaii and Fiji, were on a circuit travelled by performers from all over the world. By the end of World War II, Australia had a well-developed commercial theatre which even toured American musicals like *South Pacific* around the South Pacific.

In the 1920s an amateur theatre had evolved, middle class in its aspirations for cultural expression. Out of this in time came a concern with creating a wholly Australian theatre and writers began to seek subjects that dealt with the great issues of bush survival, isolation, political injustice and change. The movement made only occasional impact upon the fabric of society until the student revolution of the late 1960s introduced an iconoclastic new group of writers and actors who, in fact, succeeded in changing their worlds in great measure because of government subsidy.

The pattern was similar in New Zealand, even more deferential to its British origins than Australia, and burdened with a sober-living Scottish heritage which in Australia was loudly outsung by a larrikin Irish voice. In both countries the injection of government funding into the arts transformed forever the level and variety of performance.

Early writers emerged, particularly from the universities, and later theatre practitioners embraced the theories of the Actors Studio, the Living Theatre, Peter Brook and later Grotowski's Poor Theatre. Found spaces used for performance were by degrees converted into major venues. More importantly, the indigenous cultures and minority groups also found their voices in this period of social change and began to use the theatre as a platform. New plays, polemical at first and gradually more substantial, began to shed light on the diversity of Australian life. In Australia the most important new voice in the 1990s is that of the Aboriginal and Torres Strait islander; particularly in dance and music they are drawing young artists from the South Pacific to join them.

Similar patterns can be seen in the larger population centres of Papua New Guinea and Fiji, for example. Influential drama from the University of Papua New Guinea in the 1960s was reinforced in 1974 by A\$5million from the Australian government to support a National Cultural Development Act. It provided funds for training schools and travelling theatre troupes and set about addressing social issues, researching the past and affirming a cultural identity. In Suva since 1967 the University of the South Pacific has undertaken that role and introduced several culturally important playwrights through the Fiji Arts Club. Lacking organized government support, the movement of necessity remains an amateur one. Both countries, however, have provided training facilities for the South Pacific region, as has the National Institute of Dramatic Art and other institutions in Australia. Vanuatu's Wan Smolbag company was established with finance from Britain and Australia.

An area of professionalism ideally designed to overcome the vast distances, isolation and small population is radio, a major influence in the dissemination of new work, traditional storytelling and cultural theory and practice. It remains the best opportunity for writers and actors in many parts of the region. Plays and stories were being written for radio in New Zealand and Australia from the 1930s and from the 1960s in the rest of the South Pacific. Serials became popular, sometimes carrying social and political messages. In the 1970s the Solomons' Opposition Leader, Mamaloni, was the author of a long-running political comedy called *Aedo*. In the 1980s Fiji's University of the South Pacific contributed radio drama training workshops. In Australia, where radio drama had lost status with the coming of television, Koori Radio, the Aboriginal broadcasting service, serves to reinforce traditional values and spiritual and political awareness.

Australia and New Zealand, the more prosperous and 'advanced' countries of the region, have moved ahead of other parts of the South Pacific in discarding the cultural conditioning of the colonial years. To achieve this, they have invested nearly half a century of funding, both government and, increasingly, sponsorship from major corporations. The dilemma which the arts now face amid these countries' budgetary restraints and growing conservatism is that they find themselves suddenly in a culture of dependence, one in which creation must wait upon funding and funding guidelines. This in itself is a new form of colonialism for which countries with small populations and large distances have no solution.

Radio and television communication, together with increasing travel and the drain of populations from the villages to the metropolitan centres, are inevitably breaking up community life and destroying languages and common memory. Theatre practitioners have played, and continue to play, a part both on stage and in the political arena in addressing these problems, reassembling the cultural identities of races long ago torn apart by migration and invasion.

The articles from this region in the volume give a new and valuable insight into these issues and into the growth of the fragile cultural forms of the South Pacific. I am deeply indebted to the writers – especially David Carnegie (New Zealand), Andrew Horn (South Pacific) and Esohe Omoregie (Papua New Guinea) – for their immense primary research and the wisdom of their interpretation.

For the Australian article I wish to acknowledge the Australia Council, the Federal Government's arts funding and advisory body, for financial assistance in the early stages of this work and my invaluable team of specialists: Jill Sykes and John West (music and dance), Michael FitzGerald (theatre for young audiences), Richard Bradshaw (puppetry), John Senczuk and Derek Nicholson (design), Ross Thorne (architecture) and Richard Fotheringham (scholarship). I am also very grateful to Joanne Tompkins of the University of Queensland, Geoffrey Milne of La Trobe University, Melbourne and Helen Thomson of Monash University, Melbourne for their careful reading and improvement of the final work.

Insurrections in Papua New Guinea made the completion of this article particularly problematic and we are deeply indebted to Don Niles of the Institute of Papua New Guinea Studies, Yasmin Padamsee of the Awareness Community Theatre and George H. Ulrich of the African and Pacific Ethnology section of the Milwaukee Public Museum for information and corrections.

Katharine Brisbane
Sydney

ASIA'S MODERN THEATRES

ENCOUNTERS WITH TRADITION

In the modern theatres of Asia there converge a number of forces including the impulse to modernize the claims of tradition and the endeavour to create alternative traditions. The tension among these forces gives an experimental character to theatre, and while these confrontations with the past are now for the most part halting and tentative, they will no doubt grow surer and steadier. But the results of such encounters with tradition will depend not only on individual talent, but also on social developments within the countries and in Asians a whole. It is likely that, as happened in the west, realistic modes centring on contemporary social themes will become typical of mainstream Asian theatre.[1]

That Asia represents the confluence of several distinct streams of theatre is widely recognized. Predictably, the major boundary follows a historical configuration, blocking off theatres between the modern and the pre-modern (or traditional). This broad division is, for the most part, chronologically justifiable since modern theatres are of fairly recent origin in most Asian countries while the pre-modern theatres claim a very old ancestry, and often an unbroken continuity.

On the whole, the pre-modern theatres of Asia (which range from the ritualistic and the folk to the classical) appear to have monopolized scholarly research and exegesis. These theatres have elicited copious study and minute analysis, notably from western scholars and researchers who have been drawn to the field in large numbers. This academic tilt towards pre-modern theatres has, to some extent, deflected

interest from the modern theatres of Asia, for these have not attracted similar scrutiny either from a dramaturgical or socio-political perspective.

The promptings behind the foregrounding of the pre-modern theatres are clear. Pre-modern theatres exhibit distinctive and unique lineaments which set them apart. Their generic properties quite naturally intrigue and engross scholars and practitioners. Asia's modern theatres, however, seem to be clones, offshoots or poor imitations of well-known western genres and styles.

For western scholars, Asia's pre-modern theatres are a storehouse of dramaturgical and performance resources that either are totally unknown to their own cultures or have vanished from their theatrical landscape. The traditional theatres of Asia have become a pathway to the occasionally obscure roots of theatre and performance. Asia's pre-modern theatres have been happy hunting grounds for practitioners seeking new acting techniques and presentational modes. For questing minds seeking alternatives to western dramaturgy, Asia has been providing exciting models. Anthropologists and sociologists too have been drawn to the study of pre-modern theatres as both literal and symbolic articulations of value schemes and social formations. As for the typical traveller to this part of the world, the pre-modern theatres are 'tourist attractions', cultural exotica and ethnographic oddities.

Such 'readings' of Asia's pre-modern theatres, whatever their degree of sensitivity, learning and appreciation, are of course perfectly legitimate on their own terms. None the less, the impression that they project of the topography of Asian theatre does not fully accord with the actualities observed and experienced by Asians themselves. The pre-modern sector of Asian theatre is not, generally speaking, in a robust or stable condition. In certain parts of Asia, in fact, pre-modern theatres find themselves in a pitiable state, ravaged by forces outside their grasp while in other territories they seem to retain some vitality and sense of purpose. Meanwhile, the modern theatres demonstrate signs of growth by expanding in volume, reach and scope.

The decline of Asia's pre-modern theatres, and the ascendancy of modern theatres, are not phenomena that demand much explanation once it is acknowledged that theatre is *par excellence* a social activity dependent on the contributory role of society. The dynamics of any given theatre are determined principally by the performance context.

In Asia in the late 1990s, the performance context is defined by the irreducible fact of change – change on a scale unprecedented in the annals of Asian societies and national entities. This change is neither casual nor fortuitous; often, it is methodically planned and implemented from the centre. Necessarily, the pace and the magnitude of change differ from country to country, and from culture to culture. Yet every single Asian society, irrespective of its operative social philosophy and political ideology, is in a state of mutation. This is the context in which theatre, both modern and pre-modern, has to be located.

What is the essence of this process of change? Within the Asian framework, the term modernization generally glosses the ongoing transformation. Modernization, a highly complex and overarching process, has generated a plethora of disputes, theorizations and critical terminologies. Nevertheless, the core elements of modernization can be established without too much controversy.

At its most basic level, modernization implies a critique of the past. The impulse to modernize stems from the assumption that, in order to meet the challenges of the emerging world, certain values, attitudes, social structures and other aspects of the inherited culture have to be either discarded or suitably modified, otherwise new elements have to be introduced into the existing culture. For example, it is often stressed that people and societies in Asia should distance themselves from superstition and adopt the

rational, scientific values that are essential for development. The modern is equated with the scientific. [2]

Modernization's impact on theatre is potentially multifaceted. First, modernization may negatively affect those culture formations, socio-economic structures and value schemes that support and sustain pre-modern theatres. Likewise, modernization creates new needs, and introduces previously unknown imperatives into the domain of theatre. Such interlinked developments have been witnessed in Asia at different times during the past 150 years.

The thesis of *differentiation* employed in social science helps to clarify the primary structural ways in which modernization determines the destinies of theatre. Broadly speaking, differentiation denotes a separation or compartmentalization of the constituent elements which together build up the spiritual and material universe of the human being.

Scott Lasch states the matter in the following terms in his sociological study of postmodernism:

> In primitive societies, culture and the social are as yet undifferentiated. Indeed religion and its rituals are part and parcel of the social. The sacred is immanent in the profane. Further, nature and the spiritual realm are undifferentiated in animism and totemism. The magician's role underscores the ambiguity of distinction between this-worldly and other-worldly, and the priests' functions have not yet become separate and specialized. [3]

In other words, early (or traditional) societies did not distinguish between the cultural and the social, natural and spiritual, sacred and profane, secular and religious, in the manner of modern societies. What the transition from tradition to modernity does is to eliminate these continuities and close-knit, mutually supportive relationships, replacing them with boundaries and demarcations.

As it progresses, differentiation promotes the autonomization of the different spheres of cultural activity and cultural experience. Each medium of art becomes an activity primarily subject to its own aesthetic laws. Differentiation also brings about a crucial shift from the symbolic to the representational in the arts. This summary crudely simplifies a non-linear process of transformation. However, it suggests why pre-modern theatres are waning while the modern theatres are gaining ground in tandem within the ethos of modernization.

The pace of modernization in Asian societies has of late been vastly enhanced and even radicalized by the impact of globalization. Without any notable exception, Asian countries have accepted global transformation as the reality of the late twentieth century. This means, in empirical terms, the opening up of societies and the lowering of national barriers on trade and commerce, on manufacture and foreign investment, on communication and cultural exchange. This liberalization is implemented on a scale that makes the world an increasingly interdependent agglomeration of national units. The issue of globalization in respect of individual Asian countries has generated a great deal of debate and discussion in such fields as economics, social science and cultural studies. But the forces unleashed by global transformation intensify the negative impact of modern on the socio-economic structures, lifestyles, culture formations and value schemes which legitimized and sustained the pre-modern theatres.

Most if not all pre-modern theatre activities have been woven into the fabric of traditional life. They formed an organic and necessary part of the rites, ceremonies and rituals associated with such primary concerns as worship, agriculture, healing; in sum, with the material and spiritual well-being of the community in a unified system. This close and integral bond between life and theatrical performance is either disappearing or weakening, for the obvious reason that the structures, contours and rhythms of life are themselves changing.

To be sure, the foregoing observations are among the commonplaces of cultural history. However, it would appear that they are not given adequate attention in theatre scholarship. The reality that needs to be taken into account is that the pre-modern theatres have ceased to serve the functions they once performed; they are outside the emerging scenario. Indeed, influential opinion in modern societies no longer perceives many of those previous functions as rational or meaningful.

The actuality, then, is that pre-modern theatres are not accorded any major instrumental function within the agenda of Asia's concerted thrust towards modernization and globalization. Asia's pre-modern theatres are unquestionably in their waning phase, their validity and vitality being drained away by the forces of modernization. In most regions of Asia, the survival of pre-modern theatres now requires artificial sustenance through the injection of nativist fervour and nationalist self-esteem. They are being turned into cultural icons or marks of identification. They are now being given a symbolic function.

Paradoxical as it may sound, the survival of pre-modern theatres in Asia seems to depend upon their ability and willingness to accommodate themselves in the *modern* performance context. This requires, for instance, shortening of performance. Yet, when a pre-modern theatre which requires a whole night or several consecutive days and nights for its complete enactment is cut down to a two- or three- hour 'show', it has already sacrificed its true being. In short, the emerging conditions of production and conditions of reception in the domain of Asia's pre-modern theatre are such as to favour the modern. What is now happening in most parts of Asia – indeed, what has been happening over the past 150 years – is similar (if not identical) in essence to what occurred in Europe some 200 years ago. As Raymond Williams states:

> What we actually find, as we examine this period in its long and slow lines of development towards our own century, is one of the two major transformations in the whole history of drama (the first was that of the Renaissance).
> We can identify five factors of an immensely influential kin in all subsequent drama. First, there was the radical admission of the *contemporary* as legitimate material for drama. … Second, there was an admission of the *indigenous* as part of the same movement; the widespread convention of an at least nominally exotic site for drama began to be loosened, and the ground for the now equally widespread convention of the *contemporary indigenous* began to be prepared. Third, there was an increasing emphasis on *everyday speech* forms as the basis for dramatic language. … Fourth, there was also an emphasis on social extension: a deliberate breach of the convention that at least the principal personages of drama should be of elevated social rank. … Fifth, there was the completion of a decisive secularism: not, in its early stages, necessarily a rejection of, or indifference to, religious belief, but a steady exclusion *from the dramatic action* of all supernatural or metaphysical agencies. Drama was now, explicitly, to be a human action played in exclusively human terms.[4]

With certain modifications, these words could have been written about Asia since the middle of the nineteenth century. We can identify the same five factors within Asian theatrical cultures, but with one very significant difference. Whereas in Europe, it was a case of modifying or transforming existing dramatic forms, in Asia it became necessary to fabricate entirely new forms. This was because the existing forms were either resistant (or not amenable) to change or because they were too closely enmeshed in the sacred and the ritualistic and therefore not available. Whatever the reason, the few attempts at modernizing traditional forms in line with the factors highlighted by Williams has on the whole proved a dismal failure in Asia.

In the creation of new forms, it was inevitable that Asia should have been inspired by western dramaturgical and theatrical models.

The central features of Asia's modern theatres can be conveniently identified. As in the rest of the world, Asia's modern theatres are an urban phenomenon. Furthermore, Asia's modern theatres are the direct offspring of European theatres. The nature of the far-reaching structural alterations brought about by the contact with western theatres has been stated by Girish Karnad, one of India's outstanding actors, playwrights and stage directors:

> Two features of the new theatre borrowed from the west were to set it totally apart from anything that preceded it and to qualify it for the adjective *modern*.
>
> The first feature was the proscenium stage, which radically altered the traditional player–audience relationship. The audience was separated from the stage, which discouraged active participation and response. The wings and drop curtains led to an emphasis on illusionism and other stage tricks.
>
> The second innovation, far more important in its impact, was the sale of tickets which changed the relationship of the theatregoers to the theatre itself. Until then, acting groups in India had depended on patronage of temples, princes, and high officials. ... Once it has to pay to see a show, an audience begins to demand its money's worth. Performances become pre-packaged goods sold in endless replications. The run of the play in the competitive market decides its worth and freezes it in a shape it cannot change without affecting its saleability.[5]

What Girish Karnad has to say about the advent of modern theatre in India, and about the fundamental outcomes of that advent, applies in a general sense to the whole of Asia. These modifications relate to the specific histories of separate countries, and to the activities of the numerous amateur, experimental and avant-garde theatre groups spread all over Asia. Needless to say, India and other Asian countries that once belonged to western colonial empires naturally demonstrate a variant chronology from that of countries such as Japan and China pertaining to new formations in modes of production and modes of reception.

However, the basic structural aspects of modern theatre are the same all over Asia. Enclosed auditoriums, proscenium stages, admission fees, reserved seats, specified timeframes, advertising, reviews and so forth are features evident in all urban centres. To be sure, they differ from place to place on such matters as scale, proficiency, specialization and so forth. Nevertheless, they are practically identical in spirit and intention. All makers of modern theatre in Asia, like their counterparts in the west, offer their productions to the public at a price. There are many exceptions to this basic contract, but they prove the rule.

As important – or probably more important – is the fact that the modern theatres of Asia have firmly adopted the 'realist' aesthetic of verbal meaning and formal signification that is integral to the modern dramaturgy of the west. From an Artaudian perspective, this is practically a total reversal of the unique forms of articulation found in Asia's pre-modern theatres. We might recall here the valuation that Artaud gave to the use of speech in pre-modern theatres – theatres he esteemed for their ritualistic substance. In his view, speech in these theatres 'functions primarily not as a conveyor of meaning, but as incantation – in which voices have, so to speak, a magical effect independent of the meanings of words'.[6] For Artaud, such use of speech indicated the centrality accorded to actors' bodily movements in certain pre-modern theatres of Asia.

Now one might dispute at length the pros and cons of Artaud's prescriptions for the use of verbal and body language in theatre. That, however, is not the issue before us. What should strike us is the fundamental manner in which Asia's modern theatres have moved away from the pre-modern and the traditional. This must not be regarded as a mere act of imitating the west. It is, on the contrary, a response to a felt and palpable need. Incantation and chant did not, and probably cannot, meet the demands of a theatre which sets out to explain the world in dialectical terms rather than to portray it symbolically.

This brings me to my closing argument, which is that modern theatres are more alike than different all over the world. They share many features in conditions of production and conditions of reception. They are, almost as a rule, driven by instrumental rationality and follow a broadly realist or non-symbolic aesthetic. They address similar if not identical themes. Their audiences too are similar if not identical. Modern theatres everywhere speak, by and large, to an urban middle-class audience which is a fairly homogeneous entity. This suggests why dramatic works of the modern repertoire travel so widely, either in their original form, or in translation and adaptation.

Global transformation has fuelled the dispersal and dissemination of modern theatres across national and cultural boundaries. What is being developed in the late 1990s is an international language of modern theatre. To be sure, the idioms, tropes and formulae employed in modern theatre differ from country to country, as indeed they must because of cultural specificities.

Mainstream modern theatres, along with the economies, are flowing in parallel directions throughout the world. Their convergence and continuity are acquiring greater significance than their variations. Modern theatres are globalizing into an 'international dramaturgy'. The constant cross-flows in texts, techniques, crafts and in personnel are in some ways analogous to the processes that have been occurring in the sphere of the moving image. To my mind, these are inevitable developments, given that individuals and societies are now wrestling with globally shared tensions, conflicts, contradictions and dilemmas, economic and political problems. In Asia (as previously happened in Europe) theatre is separating from religion and ritual, and turning more and more into an activity predicated upon secular compulsions and experiences.

Asia's modern theatres, and in some few instances, modernized versions of traditional theatres, are growing, sometimes vibrant, buoyantly articulate, innovative and experimental but always alive in many (though not all) parts of Asia. Modern theatres are casting out, broadening their reach, and consolidating themselves to form the mainstream of theatrical activity in Asia. This is reason enough to pay more attention to them than they have hitherto received.

There is another, and perhaps more immediate reason as well. This is the often disregarded fact that in Asia the modern stage is a prime site of negotiation between the modern and the premodern; tradition and modernity meet on the contemporary stages of Asia. And this confrontation takes place, as it were, along two major fronts.

The first of these, most obviously, is the thematic front concerned primarily with values and structures of feeling. That the issues, problems and conflicts thrown up by modernization, and latterly by globalization, should figure in contemporary drama is to be expected. It could not have been otherwise, given the dialectical anatomy of the dramatic medium. Most if not all of Asian modern drama is thematically shaped by the complex process of change subsumed under the terms modernization and globalization. The modern drama can therefore be approached as texts of modernization.

Second, the pre-modern and the modern meet on the stage in aesthetic territory. And it is this meeting on contested ground, together with its outcomes, that should be of great interest to theatre research. Theatre as a site of the complex negotiations that occur as a matter of course between tradition and modernity is a pan-Asian phenomenon. Certain salient features of this phenomenon may be illustrated with reference to one concrete theatrical example drawn from Sri Lankan theatrical history.

In 1956, a Sinhala play entitled *Maname* was staged. It was based on a *Jataka* tale familiar to all Buddhists. During his journey through *samsara* (the cycle of births and rebirths), the *Bodhisatva* (aspirant to Buddhahood) is born into a royal family and is named Maname. His father, the king, sends Prince Maname away to a reputed guru to complete his education. Having excelled above all the others, the prince is rewarded with the hand of the guru's beautiful daughter. The marriage is duly solemnized and the young couple journey back to the kingdom of the prince. On their way, the prince and the princess pass through a jungle and are accosted by a gang of wild men. The king of the wild men promises safe passage to Maname on condition that he leaves the princess behind. Maname spurns this offer. In the action that ensues, Maname overpowers his antagonist in single combat. He then asks the princess for his sword to slay the wild man. The princess gives the sword to the wild man, not to her husband. The wild man then kills Maname, collects the princess's jewellery, and departs. Thus abandoned, the princess dies, mocked even by jungle animals for a fate which she has brought upon herself.

The purpose of the *Jataka* tale is to show the evils of lust and excessive attachment. The modern treatment moves away from this traditional-religious value scheme without effecting substantial alterations to the story itself. In the dramatization, the princess ceases to be the faithless woman who is the object of outright condemnation. Rather, she becomes a human being to be pitied. The play drives towards a critical yet sympathetic understanding of human behaviour, and articulates moral and ethical issues dormant in the original story.

In the play, the princess pleads on behalf of the wild man when the prince asks her for the sword. She argues that the wild man was brave enough to take on the prince single-handed, when in fact he could have easily mastered him with the aid of his followers. The wild man behaved honourably; hence his life should be spared. This unexpected argument disorients the prince and he releases his hold on his opponent. The wild man seizes his opportunity, grabs the sword, drives the prince through the heart, and then woos the lamenting princess, telling her that he fell in love with her the moment he set eyes on her. The princess, for her part, admits to similar feelings towards him. She confesses that she was of two minds about giving the weapon to the prince. The wild man's response to this revelation is instant and brutal rejection: he will have nothing to do with such a treacherous and scheming female. The abandoned princess pleads for divine mercy and dies heartbroken in the forest. The play ends with the choric comment that it is not easy to apportion blame on any single person for this turn of events.

The dramatic structure and performance mode of the play derive from a traditional theatre called *nadagam*. While the *nadagam*'s exact origins are subject to some scholarly dispute, the consensus is that it came into being in the eighteenth century as a cross-fertilization between South Indian folk theatres and concepts and practices of drama brought in by Catholic missionaries from the Iberian peninsula. Initially devoted to the enactment of biblical stories and, as it became more popular, to romances, *nadagam* is a highly formalized, sung form of theatre where the musical idiom itself has a dramatic structure. Loose and episodic in structure, it employs a *sutradhara* (presenter) and a chorus to introduce the story and the principal characters and to provide a linking narrative. The players move in rhythmic fashion, and speech is rhythmically intoned. Conventionally, a *nadagam* open-air performance lasts an entire night, and often several nights in succession. Widely performed until the 1930s, the *nadagam* never left the arena of folk theatre.

The modern dramatization of the *Maname* story, first performed in November 1956, had an instantaneous and sensational impact. A crude folk performance tradition, disdained by critics and the elites, had been effectively transformed into a refined, sparkling and totally successful piece of theatre, the like of which had not been seen on the Sri Lankan stage before. The play was complete in itself, but its total running time was less than two hours.

But *Maname* was more than a profoundly satisfying theatrical experience; it became a model for the Sri Lankan theatre. In less than two hours on the stage, it achieved a felicitous blending of theatre craft assimilated from the west with the aesthetic substance and cultural values of native traditions. Combining the best of both worlds, it charted and illuminated a pathway for the modern theatre. The author of the production himself declared that his objective was to create a distinctively and identifiably theatrical idiom for Sri Lanka.

To critical Sri Lankan eyes, then, it appeared in 1956 that the negotiation between tradition and modernity in theatre had reached an eminently satisfactory conclusion. The contradictions and tensions between the two polarities had been resolved; the divergences had been bridged; the *nadagam* had 'grown up', matured and become modern without sacrificing its identity. *Maname* was regarded by all as compelling evidence that modern theatre could be fashioned out of traditional material.

Shortly afterwards, however, *Maname* sparked off an acrimonious and prolonged debate centring on the utility and suitability of highly stylized forms such as the *nadagam* for the task of addressing contemporary experience in a rapidly modernizing society. Those who were critical of *Maname* took up the position that the modern stage required less formalized, less codified and more 'realistic' forms which could deal with characters and situations from daily life, employing an appropriate language. The modern stage demanded more freedom than was available within the *Maname* model.

Significantly, it was not the artistic legitimacy of *Maname* that was challenged, but, rather, its ability to accommodate or articulate the extensive range of social, cultural and political concerns exercising a post-colonial society in the throes of modernization. This controversy surrounding *Maname*, though inadequate, voiced most of the principal issues at stake in the theatrical encounter between tradition and modernity. It seems to me that the following generalizations are possible, taking off from the historical example of *Maname* and the numerous theatrical experiments that came up in its wake.

First, the modern in theatre does not necessarily imply the rejection, disavowal or total exclusion of the traditional. On the contrary, the traditional forms are seen as a useful resource in so far as the performative aspects are concerned. The traditional domain contains 'raw material' that can feed and enrich the modern. It appears essential, however, that care be exercised in the selection process.

Second, rigidly codified performative modes such as *Maname* may prove restrictive as regards subject matter, particularly with reference to character and situation. At the same time, certain traditional forms may be so close to the sacred as to rule out their usage on the modern stage.

Third, the traditional has other uses for the modern which are not strictly motivated by dramatic or performative dictates. Elements of the traditional may be imported into the modern to impart flavour, to embellish and decorate, and above all, to add cultural identification marks. Thus the practice of clothing the modern in traditional garb is in part of an 'extra-theatrical' need.

Fourth, on most modern stages of Asia, the contest between the representational and performative dimensions of theatre is a central motif. As Raymond Williams observed, 'the most fundamental cultural history is always a history of forms'.[7]

A.J. Gunawardana
Professor, University of Sri Jayawardenepura,
Sri Lanka

(*This article first appeared in* Theatre International *Volume 22, no. 1 (Spring 1997). Reprinted with permission.*)

Notes

1 A.J. Gunawardana, *The Drama Review* 15 no. 3 (Spring 1971): 62.
2 The ongoing problematic of this aspect of modernization was evident in the range of reactions elicited by the total solar eclipse seen in India in October 1995. While astrologers predicted dire effects on the nation and the world, and cautioned people to stay under cover, national television carried the whole astral event 'live'. There was no country-wide panic and newspaper editorials commented the next day that the 'scientific spirit' had triumphed over 'superstition' in India.
3 Scott Lasch, *Sociology of Postmodernism*. London/New York: Routledge, 1990: 6.
4 Raymond Williams, *The Politics of Modernism*. London/New York: Verso, 1989: 83–4.
5 Girish Karnad, 'Daedalus', *Journal of the American Academy of Arts and Sciences* (fall 1989): 334–5.
6 Lasch, *Sociology of Postmodernism*, pp. 182ff.
7 Williams, *Politics of Modernism*, p. 83.

ASIAN IDENTITY AND MODERN THEATRE

The borderline of the twentieth century is not far away and the modern theatre of central Asia finds itself struggling to re-establish roots in the great traditions of the past, roots which were brutally cut during colonial upheavals, which in some instances lasted several hundred years. This area – surrounded by the Hindukus and the great Himalayas and Pamir plateau at its northern borders and by the Arabian Sea, Bay of Bengal and Indian Ocean in the south – has given the world some of its great civilizations, civilizations that developed in the Indus valley and on the banks of the Ganges, civilizations that attracted the barbaric 'kabilas' of the north and west to attack and loot and finally to settle here in the course of history.

The Aryan community from Iran to the far east along with Mongols and Dravids from the south created not only special worship methods but also codes of socio-religious conduct, which regulated these societies through the ages and gave immense protection to civilized society. The fusion of Iranian art with Indian epics and philosophical sects created beautiful works of art, enriched already well-established ritualistic performances and led to the codification of many streams of artistic activities.

The *vedas*, the *Upanishads*, the great epics of *Ramayana* and *Mahabharata*, religions such as Buddhism, Jainism and the *Natya Shastra* (*The Science of Theatre*), written by Bharatmuni and predating Aristotle's *Poetics*, have all influenced theatre of this huge subcontinent. *Ramayana* tales still run as a main nerve for theatrical activities not only in India, Bangladesh and Pakistan, but also into Thailand, Indonesia and other countries across Southeast Asia. A devotional art in its strictest sense, 'traditional' theatre activities at the same time have provided countless opportunities for experimentation in a multicultural, multi-religious and multi-ethnic context.

Burma, for example, projects Rama as an incarnation of Buddha, while traditional Siamese (Thai) theatre projects Rama in a totally different way. In some countries Ravana is a pathetic character while in others he is seen as a comic character. But in all versions, at the end of war, Rama remains a symbol of good and always wins over Ravana, the symbol of evil. The *Mahabharata*, a more idealistic work, nevertheless reflects harsh realities and even practical aspects of socio-political philosophies while guiding the psyche of the region's most modern sensibilities.

Yet despite this region's many wars, riots and ethnic and communal clashes over the past 300 years, the area has not been directly involved in the mainstream of world wars during the twentieth century, although it has certainly suffered the wounds. There have also been military coups in Pakistan, Bangladesh and Burma, brutal and heinous political assassinations, freedom struggles, the evolution of non-violence as a political strategy, a decade-long war between Iran and Iraq, a civil war in Afghanistan and the dissolution of the Soviet Union (which added more independent nations to the Asian family). The theatre, passing through such diversity, has reflected this chaos while successfully projecting instant images of the community's unifying ideas as well as helping to maintain its unique identity.

One can argue that there are three main types of theatre communities in the region. The first are those countries that have been colonies and war grounds and, through contact with western culture and its theatre, have adapted such forms for their own needs, becoming somewhat westernized in the process. Second, there are those countries, also colonies and battlefields, which did not ultimately mix their own arts in with the west but accepted western art as a separate tradition. Third, there are those countries that have simply maintained their own art and never allowed alien cultures to interfere in their rituals and traditional identity.

The theatre of these countries in the first category had led in the late twentieth century to a severe identity crisis in cultural matters. In those countries where ritual, classical, devotional, folk and popular theatre are being practised simultaneously with western-style theatre, the two have found a synthesis of tradition and modernity with western plays not only being done with their original sensibilities but also being adapted to the typical forms and situations of the local experience.

The theatre in many countries has also enriched the society. Burma, for example, produced Prime Minister U Na, who was a widely recognized playwright, one who even had a play performed on Broadway. It should be noted here that Burma was the first Asian country – perhaps the first in the world – to establish a Ministry of Culture as early as the nineteenth century.

Rabindranath Tagore is perhaps the best known playwright, poet and painter from the region. Nobel Prize-winner for Literature in 1913, he created a number of inspiring plays in the Indian theatre and was, later on, equally popular in Bangladesh. His plays *Rakt Karbi* (*Red Oleander*), *Dakghar* (*The Post Office*) and *Muktadhara* (*Free Stream*) still fascinate audiences and directors in the region.

More recently – aside from the continuing struggles for democratic freedoms that continue to haunt the psyche of the entire region – this part of the world is concerned about the invasion of the Asian sky by the western world through electronic media, an invasion led by the United States. This invasion particularly has started to swallow the region's traditional way of living and has disturbed the most sensitive of social relations – the extended family, which has been the root of Asian life for millennia and is now rapidly disappearing. Asia, basically an agrarian society, has been radically affected by the new single-family system. Social disintegration and degeneration is now clearly visible.

Women's issues have also come to wider attention through theatre, especially issues connected to birth control. Strong feminist and *dalit* (downtrodden) movements have emerged even in very conservative societies like Pakistan. Feminist groups there have taken to the streets with various types of protest theatre. *Chador*-clad or *Burqua*-clad (a black gown covering the whole body) women in Iran's Muslim society have shown their displeasure with authoritarian and arbitrary fundamentalism. During a presidential election, a former Minister of Culture became head of government despite liberal leanings and despite bans. This has also been the main subject of many theatre productions, especially after the fall of the shah and his reformist but feudal government in 1979.

Those countries that were until the 1990s under the protection of the Soviet Union – Uzbekistan, Tajikistan, Kyrgyzstan, Turkmenistan and Kazakhstan – suddenly found themselves standing under their own sky and with their own land under their feet. Struggling with serious socio-politico-economic problems in this changed situation, these countries also started thinking seriously about their cultural identities. In the past, though their ethnic identities were clear to them, the very question of identity within the USSR was never one that could be broached. In the new atmosphere, the question became essential and the theatre of these countries took on a new urgency both in terms of modernity and to make the nature of their ethnicity more apparent in the indigenous dance and drama. Uzbek and Kazakh experiences are particularly remarkable in this respect, while Turkmenistan is still under the trauma of its former system.

Indian theatre too, despite its deep-rooted traditions of some 5,000 years, was also facing critical problems. During the 1990s, few significant original plays were seen and translations and adaptations of western plays were being performed in greater and greater numbers.

Although traditions of folk and popular theatre still dominate in this region, the actual numbers of traditional performers is decreasing for want of employment and regular income, hence affecting the vitality of these forms. Younger actors, who have neither university training nor the western-oriented training of the National School of Drama in New Delhi, have certainly not produced original works to match the quality of these traditional forms. Moreover, most young artists are now migrating to film and television, as are many Indian directors and playwrights. The seriousness of the situation throughout the region has brought modern theatre in this area ever nearer to the essential question of re-establishing and redefining both local and regional identities within a rapidly globalizing world.

Ravi Chaturvedi
University of Rajasthan
Jaipur, India

THEATRE FOR YOUNG AUDIENCES

HISTORY AND HOMOGENIZATION

Theatre productions mounted specifically for young audiences still do not exist in many countries in the Asia/Pacific region. Rather, most tend to be either performances by children for children or marginal events barely acknowledged by the public. There are several cultural and historical reasons for this.

Until the development of a modern industrial society, the various generations of a family or group lived together and communally shared all the essential experiences of life: birth and death, hunger and war, joy and suffering. Childhood was perceived as only a very brief period, the stage in which the very young could not survive without adult assistance. Once children were able to communicate and walk independently, they learned all the things they had to know by imitating and assisting adults. Depending on their physical strengths, young people engaged in the same tasks as grown-ups, wore the same clothes, played the same games, and heard, saw and experienced the same things as adults.

This also applied – whether as audience members or actors – to their participation in ceremonies, festivals and theatrical events staged for worship or entertainment. In countries such as China, Japan, India and Korea – in which high levels of theatrical culture were developed very early – the necessary musical, pantomimic, verbal and dance skills as well as the preparation and use of costumes, masks and props required a high level of artistic skill from performers which could be acquired only through extensive training from early childhood. Such skills were passed on from one generation to another, as in the Indian *kathakali* or the Japanese *noh*, primarily within families of artists or, as in Japanese *kabuki*, in schools especially established for this purpose. But even when young boys and girls appeared on stage, such performances were still aimed at an audience composed of all generations.

Between the end of the nineteenth and the late twentieth century, an abrupt and rapid industrialization occurred in many Asian countries which radically altered traditional family and social structures. This led to efforts in some countries to establish a professional theatre for children and young people based on western models in an attempt to help them to become part of adult society. These theatres tried to preserve peoples' nearly lost cultural roots, to create awareness and tolerance for other cultures, to address the actual problems of young people or to convey relevant information regarding political, social, hygienic or medical problems.

Japan had actually begun this process in the last third of the nineteenth century after a self-imposed 300-year-long period of isolation. It opened up to western influences, transformed its political system along European models, introduced general mandatory education and stimulated industrialization. Takahiko Kurushima and Sadayakko Kawakami's theatre company staged one of the first public performances for children as early as 1903, the European fairytale *The Gay Fiddle* and an adaptation by Goethe, *Fox Reineke*.

During this period, the literary scholar Sazanami Iwaya became a catalyst and passionate advocate for children's theatre. Having lived in Germany for a time, he had witnessed many performances of fairytales and made these plays known in Japan. A few years later, Kurushima founded the first theatre company to perform specifically for children, a group which also toured the country. The influence of western culture increased after Kaoru Osanai brought the production experience and plays from Natalia Satz's Central Children's Theatre (Moscow) to Japan at the end of the 1920s.

Theatre for young people in Korea, performed by children for children, had its beginnings in the 1920s and was undoubtedly influenced by Japanese developments. For Korea had been occupied by the Japanese since 1910 who significantly industrialized the northern part of the country. Surprisingly, a remarkable number of authors wrote for this new theatre form. *Dong Ah*, one of the largest daily newspapers, initiated the first competition for children's plays in 1925 in which Yun Suk Jung won first prize for *An Owl's Eye*.

Because these playwrights had little experience with dramatic writing, their plays reportedly were of inferior quality and dealt primarily with political issues. The authors probably used the medium of children's theatre to write about themes forbidden by the Japanese censorship in other literary forms. The stricter censorship introduced by the Japanese colonial government in 1940 greatly reduced such writing, however. Only after the liberation of the country in 1945 could a new beginning in the field be made.

The first really significant professional theatre for young audiences in Asia was founded in 1928 in Tashkent, the capital of Uzbekistan. It consisted of two separate ensembles, one of which performed in Uzbek, the other in Russian. In 1950 the company was given its own theatre building and the two ensembles were merged. Later they once more separated when each was given its own performance space and independent artistic and administrative staff.

Theatre for young audiences in the four other former Asian Soviet republics experienced a similar evolution as Uzbekistan, though much later. Natalia Satz, exiled to Kazakhstan by Stalin, founded the first Kazakh theatre for children and young people in Alma-Ata in 1945. Victor Rozov, later famous as a playwright, initially was a member of her company. With a staff totalling 180, the theatre's sixty-five actors and fifteen musicians were divided into ensembles performing in Kazakh and in Russian. Similar large and structured theatres for young audiences were established in Tajikistan (1958), in Turkmenistan (1965) and in Kyrgyzstan.

The repertoire of these companies in the first years followed exactly the European theatre for children and young people as established in the rest of the Soviet Union. Even the indigenous playwriting that eventually emerged was dogmatically oriented towards the Soviet model for many years. In the mid-1960s it was possible to detect attempts by the Asian Soviet republics to break through these artistic restrictions and to establish closer contact with the cultural traditions of their own peoples.

Dramatization of early works by the Kyrgyz writer Chingis Aitmatov began to be staged, for example. This now famous author repeatedly combined contemporary events with myths and legends of the various peoples in this region in many of his stories and novels. Filled with poetry and drama, his works brought to life the controlling influence of past and present on the existence of individuals today. The later international recognition of Aitmatov's works undoubtedly also encouraged other writers to dramatize traditional stories and to utilize national performative elements to make theatre available to young people from an early age. These performances also attracted a large adult audience to children's theatre productions.

In China, theatre for young audiences also began in the 1920s when companies composed of young people and children performed in cities and villages for audiences composed of not only young people but also the population as a whole. Their productions addressed primarily the country's civil war and the fight against the Japanese. A professional theatre aimed specifically at young audiences came into being only with the founding of the People's Republic in 1949.

In countries dominated by the British such as Australia and Malaysia occasional school productions, primarily of Shakespeare, were the norm in the 1920s and 1930s. A professional theatre for young audiences emerged, as virtually in the whole region, only after World War II, and developed in many different forms.

In those Asian countries once part of the Soviet Union, the government instituted and financed large professional theatres following the Russian model of the Moscow and Leningrad children's and young people's theatres with their own buildings and permanent ensembles. Similar developments began in the

Mongolian and Chinese People's Republic at the beginning of the 1950s but, because of the Korean and Vietnam wars, such ensembles emerged even later in North Korea and North Vietnam. Initially these productions consisted of adaptations of Soviet plays for children and young people. Particularly in China, indigenous patriotic subject matter, national myths and legends quickly followed.

But the theatres of these countries turned away from European theatrical models, though at varying speeds. Using music, dance, pantomime, acrobatics, storytelling and design to develop their own national theatre culture, they also staged major works from the international dramatic repertoire, including productions of Shakespeare and Schiller in the Children's and Youth Theatre of Ulan Bator (Mongolia) and of Shakespeare, Molière and Anouilh at the Tuoi Tre theatre in Hanoi.

Between 1930 and 1950, the evolution of theatre for young audiences in Japan was interrupted by World War II and the US occupation of the country. Only with the subsequent rapid rise of Japan as one of the world's leading industrial countries could theatre for young audiences flourish once more. This occurred despite the fact that theatre received virtually no government assistance and that Japanese theatre artists to this day work for extremely low wages. The number of theatre companies nevertheless has risen steadily, from seventy ensembles at the beginning of the 1980s to over two hundred by the mid-1990s. The great majority are touring companies which perform in schools.

This impressive growth was made possible not only through the great enthusiasm on the part of theatre for young audiences artists, parents and teachers but also by effective collaboration through special cultural associations. Parents-Children-Theatre, the marketing association to build theatre audiences, was founded in 1966. A merger of all these theatres into the Japanese Union of Theatrical Companies for Children and Young People (JIENKYO), occurred in 1974.

The diversity of the Japanese theatre for young audiences is most impressive and includes, as in many parts of Asia, puppet and shadow theatre. Some companies have only five, others more than a hundred members. The variety in the artistic means of expression used is also unusual. Specific mixed forms of live and puppet theatre have emerged as in the Kaze-no-ko Theatre's production of *Animain* using hands and props. Techniques from *kabuki* are also used as well as

western dramatic forms from the classic and realistic theatre, ballet and opera.

No other country in the Asia/Pacific region has to this day developed a theatre for young audiences comparable to Japan in size and variety. There are only three other countries – China, South Korea and Australia – in which the discipline has been able to establish itself as such a growing and permanent part of the national theatre culture.

In China, in addition to numerous professional puppet theatres, there are approximately twenty-five large state-subsidized ensembles performing for young audiences. Resident in the capitals of the provinces and in Beijing, they also tour in their home provinces. Programming at these theatres is designed for different age groups and consists primarily of Chinese works. There are also occasional western plays, particularly translations from Russian.

Pushed aside during the Cultural Revolution, theatre for young audiences did not become revitalized until about 1980. Supported from this point and led by a Children's Art and Culture Committee of the Ministry of Culture, these theatres have made special attempts to reactivate traditional theatre forms and to familiarize young audiences with the diverse traditions of the many peoples and cultures existing in the country. Performances by children themselves are also greatly promoted in the classroom, and through competitions. Cultural centres specifically for children exist in almost every larger city in China.

In South Korea, theatre for young audiences evolved in quite a different manner. Following the country's liberation from Japanese occupation, the partition of the country and the end of the Korean War, a number of efforts were made to create a Korean theatre for young audiences. These included the publication of play texts, the creation of a children's theatre festival, the establishment of a Children's Drama Association as well as an institute for Korean children's plays. But stage productions consisted almost exclusively of children performing for other children in schools and churches. A separate professional theatre for young audiences emerged only in the 1970s to join the existing professional puppet theatre.

Into the 1990s, however, theatre for young audiences remains heavily dependent on audiences at daycare centres and in primary schools. Productions consist most often of western fairytales and legends, including works from the well-known Grips Theatre in Berlin. Plays which address political and social problems affecting young people in the country, such as the 1985 Dong-Rang Theatre production of *The Wandering Star* by Dai Sung Youn, are still rare. Because of the influence of television and the country's orientation towards western culture, attempts to incorporate traditional Korean theatre styles and subject matter remain in their infancy.

In Australia, theatre for young audiences has taken still another form. Numerous professional children's theatre companies were founded in the 1960s and 1970s following European models. They performed for young people in schools and rented halls, and went on tour. Their numbers decreased in the 1980s as theatres for adults and semi-professional independent companies also discovered this new public and marketed it for financial reasons. A strong movement towards Theatre-in-Education (TIE) as well as youth theatre – that is young people performing for their own age groups under the leadership of professional artists – nevertheless emerged at the same time, influenced by developments particularly from English-Canada. Such TIE and youth theatre groups are not only assisted financially by the authorities but also promoted in a relatively generous manner by institutions such as the Carclew Youth Performing Arts Centre and the Come Out Youth Performing Arts Festival.

Theatre for the young in Australia therefore consists of a mixture of professional, semi-professional and amateur companies. Rather than addressing the completely different cultural traditions of immigrants from Europe, Asia and South America, theatre companies dramatize and develop an understanding for the problems common to all immigrants in their new country. Productions are primarily of Australian plays and dramatic talent is already developed at the school level through young playwrights' workshops. There have been attempts to rediscover and incorporate the traditional performance styles of Australia's Aboriginal peoples.

There are almost another dozen countries in the region that also boast some professional theatres for young audiences. The influence of these companies on their national theatres, however, is not significant and their organizational structures and thematic and aesthetic concerns are similar to those of countries already discussed.

New Zealand, for example, as a former British dominion, is moving in a direction similar to theatre for young audiences in Australia. Vietnam, North Korea and Mongolia still follow Soviet and Chinese theatre models. Malaysia, Singapore and the Philippines are most comparable to South Korea in initially imitating the European and American children's theatre before discovering their own national performance styles and subject matter. In Thailand, one of the few countries in the region that never became a western colony, the children's and young people's theatre company MAYA has developed a creative fusion between traditional theatre forms and contemporary social issues.

On the Indian subcontinent, commercial theatre for young audiences from the middle and upper classes, based on European models, as well as theatre performances by children themselves, predominate. An engaged theatre for young audiences with socially relevant content is still rare although there have been attempts in this direction in Calcutta and especially in Bombay, stimulated by many productions from the Berlin Grips-Theatre repertoire. In Pakistan the sole professional theatre for children and young people is, in fact, named the Karachi Grips Theatre. The twelve Grips plays, staged since the 1980s initially in English and shortly thereafter in Urdu by the company's artistic director, the actress and journalist Yasmin Ismail, have become the standard for a national theatre for young audiences. The highly political plays of this theatre also assumed a great relevance for adult audiences at several points. Government censors, one assumes, failed to perceive the political content of the 'harmless' children's plays.

Sri Lanka sought to establish its own theatre for young audiences in the 1960s by inviting a variety of western advisers in the field and by encouraging TIE and an emancipatory children's theatre. Artists not only dramatized western fairytales such as *Red Riding Hood* and *Snow White* and children's plays such as *Tom Sawyer* but also began to adapt Sri Lankan stories and deal with contemporary issues. Such activities are now promoted by the Sri Lankan Children's and Youth Theatre Association and the affiliated Playhouse for Children and Youth. These developments have sadly been interrupted by the bloody ethnic conflicts in the country since the end of the 1980s.

In all these countries, even in Japan and Australia, theatre for young audiences receives only limited attention from the media and public authorities. While there are considerable differences from country to country, artists and other workers in the field invariably receive very low wages and are often required to support themselves and their families with other employment. Theatre for young audiences clearly exists in Asia primarily due to the enthusiasm and belief of its theatre artists and co-workers.

Only occasionally has Asia's youth and children's theatres been able to engage prominent artists, thereby elevating the artistic quality and prestige of their performances. Graduates from visual art schools too use theatre for young audiences mainly as a means for gaining practical experience. Educational and training institutions are the most important financial support sources for productions but they too look at theatre primarily as a tool for instruction rather than as art.

On a commercial, for-profit basis, theatre for young audiences succeeds only when it entertains children and their parents, not when it attempts to go further and certainly not when it attempts to question the existing order and provoke social or political change. As in most regions, theatre criticism – whether on an academic level or in newspapers – has not yet found the criteria to evaluate performances in other than a condescending or pedagogically prescriptive manner.

In Asia, theatre and performing arts have many old, rich and different roots. Therefore, in the future, theatre for young audiences in this region could grow to be the most varied, innovative, creative and stimulating of anywhere in the world. Because of the predominant influence of European and North American culture, however, it will become clear in the not-so-distant future whether traditional culture, perceived by most young people as hopelessly old-fashioned, will be able to survive. The global influence of television may result in such homogenization that no substantial cultural differences will be able to be detected between Kapstadt and Murmansk or between Tasmania and Seoul. Theatre for young audiences will have a future in Asia only if it can escape such a scenario.

Wolfgang Wöhlert
Berlin
Translated by Anton Wagner

PUPPET THEATRE

TOUCHING THE SACRED ROOTS

The world of puppetry in Asia and the Pacific has a history that is both rich and diverse partly due to the vast size of the region and partly due to its importance as an art form in this part of the world. In all of these countries puppetry grew out of magic and religion; in some it remains connected to these while in others it has become simply an art of entertainment. In some countries – such as the Maori islands – puppet figures reveal their original forms as manipulated representations of religious idols. In others, puppetry remains part of a continuing exchange of cultural values. In the countries on which European colonialism was imposed, puppetry was simply one more addition and simply became another part of the community's complex cultural fabric.

Many scholars have argued that puppetry was born in Asia and was taken from here to other parts of the world. It is certainly not beyond the realm of possibility to think of ancient peoples carrying puppets with them as easily as tools. We are obliged in this sense to look at puppetry as one of the earliest autochthonic manifestations of human culture, both essential and archetypal at certain stages of a community's religious and perhaps even socio-psychological development. Perhaps it is this which makes the puppet so recognizable in so many otherwise different parts of the world.

Religious aspects are still important features of Asian puppetry, especially in such countries as Japan, India, Korea, the Tibetan region of present-day China and in many other areas of Southeast Asia, especially Indonesia. Religious origins did not survive as long in central Asia where the art took a turn towards popular entertainment. In other parts of Asia, puppetry was submitted to the pressures of local rulers, to

economic exploitation by colonial powers and, in some countries, the ideological control of communism during much of the second half of the twentieth century.

There are at least three models of development for the puppet traditions that can still be seen. The first – the natural transformation of sacred traditions into more secular and populist forms – occurred most clearly in China, Japan and Korea. The second – the petrification of an early populist puppet tradition – can now be found mainly in rural sections of India. A third model – a maintenance of earlier traditions often in opposition to foreign influences – can be seen most clearly in Indonesia.

In all these instances, puppetry linked as well into more general currents of theatre practice. In China and Japan, for example, puppetry's links with local mythological narratives can still be observed in the Chinese *Story of the Three Kingdoms* and the popular *Travel to the West*. Such myths appear commonly in both puppet forms and in the many forms of Chinese Opera. Even when Chinese puppetry broke with religious practice, the stories remained. It was not so long, in fact, before they were considered suitable entertainment for the nobility.

In Japan, though the forms secularized, the sacred roots remain in such spectacles as *ningyo joruri* whose stages are still to be found near most Shinto temples. Religious ceremonial qualities are still felt in the on-stage actions of those who create *bunraku* even when it is bourgeois pieces or samurai plays being performed. This may be part of the reason why *bunraku* – along with *kabuki* and *noh* is considered as a Japanese national treasure and is officially protected by the state.

In Korea, puppetry – though it never achieved the popularity of Chinese and Japanese forms – grew from shamanistic rituals and Buddhist teaching. Replaced eventually by more populist forms (some of which no longer survive) certain puppet styles are also considered Korean national cultural treasures, among them the *kkokto-geuk*.

In many parts of Asia, nomadic lifestyles led to an active exchange of cultural values as well. New forms travelled not only from east to west and from north to south but also from west to east and from south to north, sometimes reaching distant territories on the edges of Europe. Forms of Chinese puppetry, for example, can be found right across central Asia as well as in certain parts of Russia. Forms of Indian mime tradition were incorporated into Persian (modern-day Iranian) puppetry and can be seen in Turkmenistan as well. Nomadic puppeteers from central Asia in their turn clearly took the idea of permanent comic characters from Persian puppetry. A popular Persian puppet figure such as Ketchel Pahlevan was the obvious model for similar characters in lands as far away as Uzbekistan. It is probably the puppet character called Vidusaka – whose name can be found in Sanskrit manuscripts – which was the first continuing comic character. From the early Vidusaka figure comes a long list of such characters ranging from Indonesia's Semar to Vietnam's Teu. Interestingly, many of these comic figures were of divine origin but most evolved in their secular forms into parasites or buffoons. These were also the beginnings of the mythological buffoons that became profane in such forms as Turkish *karagöz* and in European figures from Pulcinella to Punch and from Hanswurst to Kasperle.

In spite of its recognized ancient origins, perhaps the most difficult puppet history in Asia to reconstruct is that of India. Neglected both by Indian scholars and by the British raj (under colonial rule virtually every Indian art form was intentionally ignored), Indian puppetry seems to have emerged from nowhere, disappeared for a time and then re-emerged. Contemporary Indian scholars have identified a wide diversity of historic puppet forms and have documented their use in religious ritual. Indeed, virtually every Indian state has its own puppet and shadow theatre tradition, each with its own scripts and each with its own style. We know now that early Indian puppeteers copied classic or popular forms of traditional theatre, clearly the case in the puppet form called *pava kathakali* which even imitated the costumes and mask expressions of classical *kathakali*. Most of those who created the puppet figures found visual inspiration in paintings from local temples, sacred reliefs and other forms of sculpture. As well, there are clear links to religious roots in their performances of episodes from *Mahabharata* and *Ramayana*. Puppeteers would also perform in and around the temples using as their texts well-known *vedas* and *puranas*. These puppeteers – known as *pulavars* in some states and as *bhāgavatas* in others – were often believed to be sages or even priests and were alleged to have powers that could fight disease and drought. Some performed exorcisms, held social position and undertook sacred functions similar in nature to the revered Indonesian puppeteer, the *dalang*. In northern India, a more secular puppetry tradition developed closer in style and feeling to those of central Asia and Persia.

As Hindu culture spread through Southeast Asia, Indian and Chinese puppet forms emerged in such countries as Burma (now Myanmar), Malaya (now Malaysia), Cambodia (also known as Kampuchea), Thailand and Indonesia. Each new manifestation of the art was accompanied by new forms, interpretations, styles of manipulation, manufacturing and even patterning (usually taken from local religious sculpture and painting). Although the stock of religious subjects remained essentially the same, significant variations began to be seen in their treatment. One can find this even in Vietnam where Chinese forms were adapted to local traditions resulting in a unique form of puppetry which was performed in the waters of rice paddies. The presence of religious stories in puppet form – from Rajastan to Bali – represented an important element in establishing some form of cultural unity for people who belonged to many different races and linguistic groupings. In Burma and Thailand, these puppet traditions were freely adapted and enjoyed a long and popular life among upper-class audiences (particularly in the courts) until the twentieth century when changing political and social conditions affected them once again.

One country where the earlier traditions were essentially kept was Indonesia where puppetry became one of the main religious and cultural manifestations of the nation as a whole from rural villages to aristocratic courts, from large urban communities to modern politics. In Indonesia, *wayang* is the art of public storytelling and it is utilized in many areas of community life: as religious ceremony, as an instrument of magic healing or simply as entertainment. Puppetry is one of the major forms of *wayang* and it ranges from *wayang purwa* and *wayang kulit* (forms of shadow theatre using leather figures) to *wayang topeng* (mask theatre). All are of continuing interest to the communities themselves, to religion, to rulers, to visitors and, of course, to theatre scholars. The splendour and spectacle of *wayang* performances has also long been a point of pride for local and national authorities.

During the period of Dutch colonization – a period when indigenous styles were discouraged – the staging of a *wayang* performance was itself a political act as well as a reaffirmation of the past. It became almost impossible therefore to change the character of *wayang* as Christian missionaries quickly learned. Nor did those who sought to make *wayang* performances into political propaganda succeed any better. Still the main cultural expression of the Indonesian people even in the late 1990s, *wayang* has clearly helped to preserve the country's religious, familial and even national character. Even new trends towards the commercialization of theatrical art have resulted in little more than the addition of a satirical spirit in some of the *wayang* performers.

It is also important to recognize here that at the root of virtually all Asian art is a powerful symbolic language. Such symbolism can be found in all aspects of Asian puppetry as well: shapes, colours and ornamental qualities correspond to specific functions and representations of gods, demons and heroes. The tradition also allows Asian theatre to avoid for the most part realistic descriptions of both character and scenery. In countries where realism entered, such performances tended towards the satirical, the lightweight and the profane.

In those places where puppetry has flourished, it has been partly because of respect by political leaders for both the religious roots of the art and its continuing connection to the community. Where it has not flourished, the decline can often be traced to colonization and a failure by the colonists to recognize and support indigenous cultural achievement. No doubt, in some instances the art also deteriorated because of the secularization of communal life which deprived puppetry of its sacred character and relegated it to the oblivion of regional folklore.

As well, much devastation was caused by the smothering influence of the two dominant political/economic orthodoxies of the twentieth century: communist doctrine and US commercialism. Communism imposed on many countries in Asia – among them Mongolia and several former USSR republics – a Soviet model of culture and within that a specifically Euro-Soviet model of puppetry. Despite being taken seriously as an art form and despite being protected by socialist cultural policy, the imposition of European style and even European-style theatre buildings led to a situation where Asian puppeteers found themselves being trained by European teachers, many from the Soviet Union. The latter ensured that performances would be done following a state-approved ideology and this would be particularly important in areas where Russian settlers were arriving since the shows could often be performed in the Russian language. This said, the new European style of puppetry certainly found receptive audiences especially in central Asia where a number of professional groups emerged representing an important and interesting addition to indigenous culture.

Chinese Communism wiped away many ancient cultural traditions as well, particularly during Mao's Cultural Revolution in the 1960s. Traditional pieces disappeared from the repertoires of established companies at the time and were replaced by propagandistic revolutionary works dealing with such subjects as Japanese and US imperialism and the exploitation of earlier regimes. The new subject matter also brought with it a new, more realistic style of performance in puppetry although the extraordinary traditional skills of the Chinese puppeteers were carefully preserved. It was ultimately the much smaller communities of the Republic of China (Taiwan) and Hong Kong which best preserved the earlier styles of Chinese puppetry. After the death of Chairman Mao and the cultural liberalization that followed, traditional puppets and the old repertory cautiously re-emerged from hidden shelters where the ancient art had awaited better times.

Throughout the 1960s, puppeteers in Asia and especially in the Pacific began to get in touch with newer trends in European and North American puppetry through increased participation in world festivals and through international tours. Australia and New Zealand had fallen behind newer trends by simply maintaining the old British models, which often went back to the 1930s. Among the innovators that the new puppetry began to model itself on were the realistic experiments of Sergei Obratzov from Moscow and of the Central Puppet Theatre from Prague, the animated figures of Walt Disney's films and particularly Jim Henson's Muppet creations from US television. The result was the development of various crossover forms in which the newer cultural overlays began to be seen alongside the more traditional forms. The results of such experiments could be seen throughout the 1980s and 1990s especially in Japan, India and Australia.

It was most often the younger generation of Australian and New Zealand puppeteers who were the keenest to invite European masters to work with them in exploring new modes of expression including the imaginative blending of human actors and puppets on the stage. These forms joined with traditional puppet styles, bringing about the birth of a common cultural spirit across this region.

What is the effective balance between the preservation of tradition and the exploration of non-traditional forms? In Asia and the Pacific in the late 1990s, the question is being explored. Interestingly, it is tradition which still remains dominant, tradition that is regularly supported by government policy which tends to see puppetry as an inheritance of a national treasure (which these traditions certainly are) and as part of a search for national identity within a world that is becoming more and more culturally homogeneous. Such homogeneity tends to ignore national traditions in favour of art which is thought more capable of reaching across industrial or post-industrial societies wherever they may be. To some this may seem a sophisticated cosmopolitan ideal but it is also one which ignores the soil from which truly original art emerges. For young artists this means at times having to make a choice between their own art or someone else's, between government-sponsored art or no sponsorship at all.

In the end, it can be said that for most states in this region, puppetry remains important because of both its religious and populist roots. Only in the more industrialized countries – and one must include the post-communist countries in this grouping – does puppetry seem determined to have a more secular face. This is not always a problem. For example, in Iran puppet festivals have been used to help break the country's cultural and political isolation. But government awareness of the potential of puppetry as an art is balanced by the many calls there are on limited state funding. Only the richest and most industrialized countries in the region have a clear infrastructure in place which supports puppetry as a living and growing art with training programmes for puppeteers, educational programming in schools, national organizations, journals and festivals. Such support networks are beginning to spread in Asia and the Pacific and are making life more exciting and communal for its thousands of puppeteers. Such growth clearly bodes well for the future of puppetry in this culturally diverse part of the globe.

Henryk Jurkowski
Warsaw

THE NATIONS AND THEIR THEATRES

AFGHANISTAN

(Overview)

A rugged, mountainous country of some 650,000 square kilometres (250,000 square miles), Afghanistan is located in southwest Asia. Surrounded by Turkmenistan, Uzbekistan and Tajikistan to the north, China and Pakistan to the east, Pakistan to the south and Iran to the west, Afghanistan is one of the poorest countries in Asia with an estimated annual income of only US$220 per person. The population, as of 1995, was estimated at 21 million people, including some 2.6 million nomads.

The majority of Afghanis live in rural areas and can be divided into four main ethnic groupings – Pathans, who make up 50 per cent of the total population and can be further divided into Durani and Ghilzais; Tajiks, who represent about 25 per cent; and Uzbeks and Hazaras, who each comprise 9 per cent. Other ethnic minorities include Charar Aimaks, Turkoman and Baloch. The official and most commonly spoken languages in Afghanistan are Pashto and Persian (Dari). Pashto has an extensive literary tradition while Persian is used more in business and governmental realms. The truly unifying element in the country is religion. More than 99 per cent of Afghans are Muslim, the majority being Sunni Muslim. Most of the remaining Muslims, including the Hazaras, belong to the Shiite sect.

The history of Afghanistan has been shaped by its geography and topography. Lying between the central Asian plains and the fertile lands of India and Iran, the country has long provided routes for invasion and conquest. Some of these invaders, however, remained in Afghanistan and settled the country. The name 'Afghanistan' dates from about the mid-eighteenth century. Prior to this, the region was part of the great Empire of Aryana. The first mention of Afghanistan in recorded history occurs in about the sixth century BC when it was included in the Persian Empire of the Achaemenids. By about 330 BC the entire region was conquered by Alexander the Great.

After the death of Alexander, the country was ruled by a progression of smaller kingdoms, in particular Bactria and Parthia. In AD 2, Buddhism was introduced to the area but when the Arabs invaded in the seventh century, they brought Islam with them. It was several centuries, however, before Islam became the dominant religion. About 1220, the Mongols, under Genghis Khan, overran Afghanistan, which then remained under Mongol control until the end of the fourteenth century.

Until about the seventeenth century, the country was traded within the empires and dynasties of several conquerors. In the early seventeenth century the area was again united into one country under Ahmad Khān Abdālī. After his death, the country fell into anarchy due to recurring tribal and family loyalties and the political designs of Russia and Britain. Fearful of a Russian encroachment into India, the British attempted to establish authority in Afghanistan. This led to two Anglo-Afghan wars (1839–42 and 1878–80).

In 1907 the British and Russians agreed that Afghanistan should act as a buffer state and by 1919 a third Anglo-Afghan war was being fought. The British, faced with growing unrest in India, finally negotiated a peace treaty with Afghanistan that recognized the country as an independent nation. Amanullah Khan, the original emir at the time, changed his title to king and implemented a series of political, social and religious reforms that proved unpopular. This led to a rebellion in 1926 that saw Amanullah Khan abdicate and go into exile.

Afghanistan became a socialist republic in 1973 but reliance on Soviet support angered Islamic groups and led to the threatened collapse of the new government. Daud was ultimately killed in a coup in 1978 and replaced by Soviet-supported Noor Muhammad Taraki. Still unhappy with Soviet ties, Islamic groups took up arms against the government. In an attempt to bolster the regime, the Soviets launched a coup against Prime Minister Hafizullah Amin. In a counter-coup Taraki was killed and Amin seized power.

In 1979, Soviet troops invaded Afghanistan but, in the war that followed, Afghan guerrilla groups mounted a successful resistance by taking advantage of the country's mountainous terrain. Millions of Afghan refugees, however, fled to neighbouring Pakistan and Iran. Although the Soviets invaded the country, Kabul was kept generally protected from destruction. The outlying provinces, however, remain some of the most heavily mined areas in the world.

With the departure of Soviet forces from the country in 1991, political and cultural life became fractured. Major factions soon included the Jamiet-I-Islami (mainly ethnic Tajiks), the Hezb-I-Islami (mainly ethnic Pashtun from the east and southeast) and the Taliban (described as Islamic students). Each of these political parties ranged from moderate to extreme and all were heavily Islamic. Each believed that once Kabul was claimed, Afghanistan would be rid of the evils of the past. Alliances and power, however, shift quickly in Afghanistan. In the late 1990s, the Taliban had taken over Kabul and thus Afghanistan, and invoked a severely repressive Islamic fundamentalism. As of early 1997, the Taliban had banned dancing, music, videos and photographs.

Despite such responses to culture in the 1990s, the country retains its rich cultural heritage spanning more than 5,000 years, a history linked in many ways to the cultures and theatres of modern Iran and eastern India. Due to an exceedingly high illiteracy rate for most of this time however, the tradition is mostly an oral one. Novels as a result are a rarity with poetry considered the highest form of artistic expression. Most Afghan scholars are, in fact, poets; each valley has its own stories and songs along with poems by well-known poets of the past which have found their way into daily life. This oral culture is transmitted through fathers, mothers, *mullahs* (religious leaders) or by professional minstrels and/or circus players who travel throughout the country entertaining villagers in teahouses with their songs and improvisations.

Street storytellers are referred to as *madahs* in Afghanistan and are very similar to the ancient Greek storytellers. Their costumes consist of a *chapan* (long outer coat), a walking stick and a turban, which is compulsory for any *madah*, regardless of age. Found mostly in crowded bazaars of old Kabul and places where people gather and meet on occasions, these are professional storytellers and they do so to earn money for survival. *Madahs* recite, in a singing tone, poems about religious heroes and their heroic deeds; they can attract large audiences. Songs that convey news or ridicule well-known persons are highly valued entertainment. Such heroic tales and love songs, proverbs and folk wisdom, fairytales and ghost stories feed the imagination of the people and it is these theatrically performed songs – as opposed to the lengthy verses of learned poets – which comprise the true literature of Afghanistan. The theme of the most popular ballads – not surprisingly given the history of the area – is war.

Parents and teachers often begin teaching children tales from the *Kalilah wa Dimnah*, a collection of animal stories. As they mature, children are exposed to the legends of the *Shah Namah* (*The Book of Kings*) and stories of spiritual and romantic love. *Adam wa Durko*, an ancient version of the *Romeo and Juliet* story, is one such example. As they become more mature, young Afghans learn classical poetry.

Afghans regularly celebrate religious and national feast days and particularly weddings with theatrical manifestations, especially public dancing. The performance of the *attan* dance in the open air has long been customary in the culture. Formerly a Pashto ethnic dance, it is now considered the Afghan national dance. Performed in a large circle to the accompaniment of drums and pipes, the dancers are always male – women are not encouraged to participate for religious reasons – and the dance begins slowly but grows in momentum for two or three hours without a break except for changes in tempo or changes in song.

Theatre, in the western sense, was introduced to Afghanistan (specifically in Kabul) in the late 1920s and early 1930s during the reign of Amanullhah Khan, a man who was trying to westernize Afghanistan. He had a theatre built that was similar in structure to the arena theatre of ancient Greece. Located in the park of Pagnaman, plays were enacted by high-ranking government officials among whom were Kohgadai and Sarwar Goya, two renowned poets and writers. Adaptations of western classics such as Shakespeare and Molière were early features of the theatre experience, but plays in Persian or Pashto which dealt with modern Afghan life soon became favourites.

In the early 1940s government support led to the creation of the Afghan Nanderi (National Theatre), a proscenium house that has staged works from Turkey, the United States, the United Kingdom, France and the Soviet Union. Preference, however, has been given to Afghani writers and the company works works in both national languages. It has also performed in provincial centres and at country fairs in an effort to bring drama to those in rural areas. It has also toured to neighbouring countries.

A second troupe of note is the Municipal Theatre of Herat and a third is the state-sponsored Kabul Nanderi (Kabul Theatre) which also presents plays by local playwrights as well as European plays in translation. In all these groups, men played all roles until the 1950s when women first appeared on their stages.

Renowned modern dramatists are Ustads Burishna, R. Latifai, S.M. Nigab, M. Nohmat and M. Danagoi among others. Most of their plays are calls for freedom and demands for retaliation against official dishonesty.

A School of Fine Arts was established in Kabul in the 1930s. The Department of Fine Arts in the Ministry of Information and Culture subsidizes the school and maintains cultural relations with several countries and international organizations in order to develop, modernize and enhance cultural effort undertakings.

One of the first acts of the country's republican regime was to reinstate annual state awards to writers, artists and craft workers. Such awards provide an important supplement to the incomes of people holding jobs not directly related to the arts. As well, they publicly recognize significant contribution to the arts and a state fund now exists to assist professional artists in times of need. The families of musicians, singers or artists, in the case of death or long-term illness, are given a monthly stipend.

In 1979, all printing houses were nationalized and the Government Printing Press is now the printer of all newspapers, magazines and professional periodicals. The Education Ministry's publishing agency, Baihaqi, publishes and markets books selected by a committee of scholars as well as books that have been awarded state prizes.

The Academy of Sciences of Afghanistan was established in 1979 and included, under its auspices, the Afghanistan Historical Society and Pashto Academy. Both institutions publish literary magazines and generally encourage new writers. *Aryana*, published by the Afghanistan Historical Society, is a monthly magazine available in both Pashto and Dari. In addition, the society arranges for the publication of research works on subjects of Afghani interest. The Pashto Academy's monthly magazine, *Kābul*, promotes Pashto literature among the non-Pashto speaking population.

In 1992, fourteen newspapers were appearing regularly in Afghanistan. *Zhowandoon*, one of the most widely read, was established in 1948. It appears weekly and is written in both Dari and Pashto. *Zhowandoon* regularly carries stories on the arts. Radio Afghanistan broadcasts news, music and educational programming in local languages. Due to the high rate of illiteracy, it has become the country's most important vehicle for cultural communication.

WECT staff with Khan Agah Soroor
Translated by Waheed Amad Soroor

Further Reading

'Afghanistan' in *Travellers' Reports*. www.lonelyplanet.com.au/letters/meanst/afg_pc.htm

'Afghan Poetry' www.gl.umbc.edu

Jakimovič, Leonid. 'V centre Kabula' [In the centre of Kabul. *Teatr* 42 no. 12 (December 1983): 133–8.

Rahel, Shafie. *Cultural Policy in Afghanistan*. Paris: Unesco, 1975.

Wilber, Donald N. *Afghanistan: Its People, Its Society, Its Culture*. New Haven, CT: Hraf Press, 1962. 320 pp.

AUSTRALIA

Australia is the largest island and the smallest continent in the world; its cultural history owes much to both definitions. In pre-western history, the days of Gondwanaland, the land was believed to have been attached to Indonesia and the Malaysian peninsula and the Aborigines walked, or travelled by canoe, from the north to what is now Australia.

Approaching the year 2000, it is a country of 7,683,900 square kilometres (2,955,300 square miles) with vast climatic variations – from the tropical north to the central deserts, from the snowfields of the southeast to the green fields and wilderness of Tasmania. In 1901 the colonial settlements of the nineteenth century were federated into six self-governing states, with a central commonwealth government – situated in Canberra since 1927 – responsible for national issues such as trade, defence, finance, immigration, communications, arts and sciences, and health. The population of 18 million – made up of some 34 per cent first and second generation immigrants from Europe, Asia and the Middle East – is largely congregated in the capital cities on the green verges which cling to the seaboard.

The historical mindset of isolation from European civilization and fear of the enormous distances that make up the country's interior have contributed more to the imagination of non-indigenous Australians than it has to the economic development of the country. Since the first merino sheep arrived in 1797, Australia has been a major trader of primary produce: in the 1850s a drop in wool production brought about by the gold discoveries in eastern Australia caused a major economic depression in the north of England. But while culturally the population still looked to Britain and Europe – and later North America – financial stability relied on exports to Asia including horses to India, wool and minerals to Japan and China, and grain to the rest of the world. More recently exports in uranium, diamonds, wine, television drama and movies have begun to make an impact, along with skills like dry-land farming, engineering and new technology transfers to the Middle East and developing countries.

The country's modern history began with the founding of Australia as a penal colony of Britain in 1788. Botany Bay in New South Wales was 20,000 kilometres (12,000 miles) from Britain and notorious for its tyranny and oppression. Distance, however, also meant the absence of supervision and at times a freedom which allowed for enterprise and self-reliance. Many among the early settlers, both free and convict, saw the opportunities and quickly became wealthy merchants and landowners, providing by the 1830s a gentry of mixed lineage.

A proportion of the convicts had some skills in entertainment gained in the 'free and easy' pubs at home. Within twelve months of the colony's establishment in Sydney British-style performances began to be seen. The first recorded performance was of George Farquhar's *The Recruiting Officer* played in a convict hut on 4 June 1789 to celebrate the birthday of King George III. In 1796, Robert Sidaway (1757–1809) sentenced to transportation for housebreaking in 1782, and now baker to the colony, set up the first theatre in Sydney. Early audiences often paid in produce since coin was scarce. Both garrison soldiers and convicts took part in these occasional performances until the first purpose-built theatre, the Theatre Royal, was opened by the stage-struck merchant Barnett Levey in 1832.

The gold rush that began in 1851 brought sudden astonishing wealth and multiplied the population many times. The substantial disposable incomes attracted international stars. They came, often stayed for long periods and made enormous fortunes. They left behind legacies – fellow-actors, pupils and legends.

The plays presented were those acting editions carried in the actors' baggage, or distributed by publishers who controlled the copyright. Many were locally translated or adapted. Original writing was discouraged by censorship, imposed by authority in the uneasy atmosphere of a penal and post-penal colony, who feared the encouragement of anything blasphemous, immoral or seditious. Enterprising dramatists persisted, however, and became skilled in the metaphors of pantomime and travesty as an outlet for social criticism. Official censorship retreated with prosperity and the 1860s ushered in the golden age of melodrama for which the scenic painter and mechanist created scenes of heroism and disaster amid the forces of nature at its wildest.

Apart from rivalries established early between the Currency youth (those born in Australia and regarded as rough and free-spirited) and the more genteel, English-bred Sterling youth, the Australian colonists were not burdened with questions of national identity. Culturally they saw themselves as a suburb of the northern metropolitan centres: an integral part of a great empire. But by the 1880s the Currency was in the majority and thoughts turned towards federal unity. The first Australia-wide census was taken in 1881. Land scandals and a depression in the 1890s accelerated change from a cosmopolitan culture of free-enterprise individualists to an Anglo-Celtic population of owner and worker. The introduction of the cinema in the 1890s began a decline in popular theatre: commercial theatre became middle class, the actor-managers gave way to commercial management.

The profession was now dominated by J.C. Williamson Ltd, known as JCW or the Firm, founded by James Cassius Williamson (1844–1913), a Pennsylvania-born actor who first came to Australia in 1874. Run by the five Tait brothers (Charles, E.J., Frank, John and Nevin) it was the largest theatre chain in the world, covering Australia and New Zealand with North American comedies and European operetta, British farces, Gilbert and Sullivan and occasional opera seasons; and touring further abroad to Asia and South Africa. The two principal vaudeville chains, the Tivoli and Fullers', had competed strongly until knocked

out by the 1930s Depression. Garnet H. Carroll (1902–64), the last of the actor-managers, controlled the Princess Theatre in Melbourne from 1955 but his sudden death left the field to the Taits.

From 1908 news of fresh theatre forms and theories began to spread through the amateur theatre: of the Repertory Movement stemming from London's Royal Court Theatre, Dublin's Abbey Theatre and Manchester's Gate Theatre. In the 1920s to this was added the North American Little Theatre movement, which provided an additional structure upon which to build: a company of unpaid artists supported by a professional management. Aspirations for an Australian intellectual theatre were fuelled. While Henrik Ibsen was not unknown in Australia (Janet Achurch, who premièred the first English-language production of *A Doll's House* in London in 1889, brought it to Australia the same year), it was the amateur theatre that developed social and poetic realism and introduced expressionism and later theory. The works of Anton Chekhov, the writings of Mayakovsky, Stanislavsky, Gordon Craig and the *noh* theatre were introduced by immigrants in the 1930s. With rare exceptions the Australian playwright's stage experience between 1920 and 1950 was amateur. It is to the amateur theatre that Australia owes its contemporary structure and diversity.

Increasingly, actors thrown out of work by the Depression and Jewish immigrants escaping German oppression set up drama studios and ancillary theatre groups. By the late 1930s actors were working by day in radio and by night voluntarily in theatre; and the daily press was making little distinction between professional and amateur productions. This pattern was wiped out by World War II. The armistice again opened Australia to the world market and to a world of new ideas.

The 1940s and 1950s were marked in the commercial theatre by a sequence of hugely successful reproductions of Broadway hits that began with *Annie Get Your Gun* in 1947, followed by *South Pacific* and *Oklahoma!* in 1949. Throughout the 1950s this carbon-copy formula gave audiences the illusion of being part once more of the sophisticated world of international entertainment. But for JCW's shareholders it was an Indian summer which ended with *My Fair Lady* in 1959. The winds of change were blowing. Television arrived in 1956, signalling the end of live vaudeville and revue. Resentment brewed among the post-war generation of actors, singers and dancers who found them-selves forced to defer to often less talented imports. The Firm was now owned by a group of New Zealand retailers and a succession of managers failed to establish a new direction. In 1976, two years after the company celebrated its centenary, it sold its entrepreneurial arm and became a theatre landlord. Other entrepreneurs by that time, backed by new social forces, had arrived. The indigenous had taken control.

These social forces had their source in the new perspectives brought into Australia by returning service personnel and shiploads of dis-placed persons from Europe. The old belief in the arts as a uniting influence for peace had spread across the world, disseminated by arts councils, municipal authorities, the British Council, and private foundations. In 1943 the *lieder* singer Dorothy Helmrich (1889–1983) founded what became in 1948 the Arts Council of Australia and received the first government subvention to take performances to country areas and assist in the restoration of community arts. The British Drama League in New South Wales, the Victorian Drama League and the Theatre Council of Western Australia set up net-works of friendly competition; university stu-dents began inter-varsity drama festivals. The nation-wide socialist New Theatre Movement, active in the 1930s, reasserted itself. By 1948 this evangelism had achieved a wide conversion of the middle classes to the view that if Australia was to be seen as a country of some maturity, it must have its own arts and compete for 'world standards'.

The resurgence of energy for change was gal-vanized at this point by three events that reflect the conflicting drives in the push towards a cul-tural maturity. Two were 'imperial' theatre events, marking the degree to which Australian sentiment was still colonial. The third was an 'indigenous' incident signalling that an Australian native theatre would draw its strength from the grassroots amateur move-ment.

The three events were the triumphant British Council tour of the Old Vic Theatre Company, which began on the west coast in 1948; the première of the Australian war comedy *Rusty Bugles* later the same year; and a report to Prime Minister Ben Chifley by the Irish theatre director Tyrone Guthrie following a visit in 1949. Behind all three lies the symbolism of the war. World War II had first rallied Australians' unquestioning loyalty to the British Empire; then, after the shocking fall of Singapore in

1942, Australia found itself abandoned to its own resources.

For Australians, worn out by the grey, point-less, isolated war years, the Old Vic tour was magical. Led by the golden couple Laurence Olivier and Vivien Leigh, the company brought elegance, artistic economy and new standards of performance to Australia. Crowds queued overnight for tickets and lined the streets as the glamorous couple swept by like royalty. The *School for Scandal* sets, by London's most fash-ionable designer, Cecil Beaton, had a radical impact upon both amateur and professional stages for the next decade. For a generation of theatre workers these performances were the ultimate to which one might aspire.

Concurrently, in a rambling old vaudeville theatre in unfashionable North Sydney, an unpaid cast was performing *Rusty Bugles*. The author, Sumner Locke Elliott (1917–91), was already the author of several Shaftesbury Avenue-style comedies and radio plays. But this play was grounded in his own experience as an ill-suited army recruit trapped in an isolated ordnance depot in the extreme tropical condi-tions of Northern Australia.

The play was an instant success, the more so because a public complaint about the army ver-nacular led to police intervention. The produc-tion was bought for a lengthy professional tour – the first Australian work to achieve such popular acclaim since the days of the actor-man-agers. Locke Elliott, however, did not see his play. He had emigrated to New York in 1948 where he became a successful novelist and scriptwriter.

These events were in the public mind when Tyrone Guthrie arrived in Australia, charged with reporting on the establishment of a National Theatre. He saw a great many amateur productions but nothing which he perceived as 'distinctly Australian'. He recommended that government abandon any current attempt to build an institution and instead send its native talent abroad for experience and then wait for it to return. In the mean time audience taste could be improved by the importation of classical companies.

Guthrie's understandable failure to grasp the local culture in the space of two weeks naturally antagonized the artistic community. The report was shelved but it achieved two things: first, it gave public recognition to the notion that Australias' 'growing national consciousness and growing self-respect demand further means of expression' and that subsidy would be needed to achieve this; second, it galvanized interest groups into action.

In 1954 a public subscription was launched to establish an Australian Elizabethan Theatre Trust in honour of the young Queen's first visit to Australia. Endorsed by the Commonwealth Bank, the appeal raised £100,000, one-third from the Commonwealth government. The mission statement aimed to 'make the theatre in Australia the same vigorous and significant force in our national life that it was in the reign of Queen Elizabeth'. Donations were tax deductible.

The structure of the Trust, as it came to be known, was that of a private company, headed by a board drawn from the financial world and society. The businesslike façade was a necessary reassurance; but the ways of business are not the ways of art and the Trust's aim to 'establish native drama, opera and ballet which will give professional employment' could not be achieved without specialist support, training and administration. Inevitably, the Trust board fell back upon the overseas expert and appointed the British theatre director Hugh Hunt as its first executive director.

Following the example of the Old Vic in working-class south London, the Trust took over the old Majestic Theatre in Newtown, an inner Sydney suburb, and renamed it the Elizabethan. In July 1955 the doors opened on imported productions of two Terence Rattigan plays, *The Sleeping Prince* and *Separate Tables* with a cast led by Sir Ralph Richardson, Dame Sybil Thorndike, Sir Lewis Casson and Meriel Forbes.

The next grand tour, which opened in Canberra in October, was Hugh Hunt's production of Euripides' *Medea* in which the expatriate Judith Anderson (1898–1992) repeated her Broadway success. In 1918, as Frances Anderson-Anderson, she had left the Australian stage for New York at the age of 20. The cast contained other luminaries: John Alden (1907–62; who had his own Shakespeare company) as Creon; Doris Fitton (1897–1985; director of *Rusty Bugles*) as the Nurse; James Bailey (who had left the Old Vic tour and settled in Perth) as Aegeus; the young Zoe Caldwell (b. 1933; soon to follow in Anderson's footsteps) as a chorus member; and as a slave the young Peter Kenna (1930–87), soon to become one of Australia's foremost playwrights. The gathering of talent would have continued in this laborious way but for the timely arrival of *Summer of the Seventeenth Doll* (1955).

When the *Doll*, as it came to be known, first came to the attention of the Trust, its author Ray Lawler (b. 1921) was a young actor-director working with the Union Theatre Repertory Company (UTRC). This was a small company established in 1953 by John Sumner (b. 1924), an Englishman who had been appointed manager of the Union Theatre at the University of Melbourne. The play drew an immediate response from audiences, was taken up for a national tour, was brought to London by Laurence Olivier where it won the *Evening Standard* award for the best play of 1956, and played (though less successfully) on Broadway.

The story of two middle-aged Queensland sugarcane cutters who for sixteen years have spent their off-season in Melbourne with two faithful barmaids, *Summer of the Seventeenth Doll* became the watershed from which the flood of contemporary Australian theatre is measured. No other play has yet been able to match its success abroad. In London the admiration of the rebellious theatre critic Kenneth Tynan, who found in it the novel virtue of 'respect for ordinary people' assured its season; it arrived at a fortuitous moment on the English stage when the drawing room was invaded by the ironing board and the kitchen sink. Lawler played Barney, one of the cane cutters, in the première and on its tour abroad. He then settled in Ireland and most of the cast remained to work in British theatre.

The Trust began to seek bases for development among the amateur companies in each state and in 1958–9 established Australia's first National Institute of Dramatic Art (NIDA) on the campus of the University of New South Wales. Between 1956 and 1960 it launched three 'national' companies, the Elizabethan Trust Opera, the Australian Ballet and the Trust Players. The Australian Ballet subsumed the members of the Borovansky Ballet, following the death of Eduard Borovansky (1902–59) and like the Opera grew and developed on conventional lines. Despite its nominal dependence on the Trust, the Ballet was more or less autonomous from the start. In 1969 the Opera declared its independence and became the Australian Opera.

The fate of the Trust Players differed. A number of award-winning plays followed the *Doll* and they attracted a wide audience. But to some the new drama appeared to dwell too much on the disreputable; these anxieties, combined with the burden of touring demanded by the contributing states, led the Trust to abandon the Players after three years.

Hugh Hunt returned to Britain in 1960 and under succeeding directors the Trust embarked upon a series of ill-advised investments with commercial producers. The decline of credibility was rapid and nationalism gained momentum. In 1968 when the Australian Council for the Arts was set up by the Commonwealth government, the Trust was relieved of its entrepreneurial role and became a service institution. During 1984–7 under new management it resumed entrepreneurial activities, mounting and touring major productions of musicals. It failed spectacularly and ceased trading with a deficit of A\$900,000. It then restructured and continued to provide banking and other corporate services, including a conduit for tax deductibility. In 1991 it went into liquidation, carrying with it A\$470,000 in private arts funding.

The 1960s signalled, as they did in the rest of the world, dynamic social change. In Adelaide, 1960 was the summer of its first biennial Festival of the Arts, aimed at becoming the southern hemisphere Edinburgh Festival. History recalls the event chiefly because of the board of governors' rejection of *The One Day of the Year*, now a regularly revived classic. It portrayed a family conflict over the observance of Anzac Day (Australia's national day of remembrance). The play was presented the following year by the Adelaide Theatre Group and toured Australia and to London. Its author, Alan Seymour (b. 1927) went abroad with the play and remained to become a prominent TV writer and editor.

In 1961 the festival compounded its error by refusing a place to *The Ham Funeral* by Patrick White (1912–90). Written in 1947 but until then unperformed, the play is an expressionist work about a young poet coming to terms with the real and imagined worlds in a London boarding house. The amateur-based Adelaide University Theatre Guild mounted this play professionally in late 1961 and it transferred to Melbourne.

The centrepiece of the 1962 Adelaide Festival was Bernard Shaw's *Saint Joan*, starring Australian-born Zoe Caldwell, whom the Trust had assisted to Stratford-upon-Avon in 1957, and who by 1959 had made the British best actor lists. Her outspokenness created further controversy. These quarrels marked Adelaide early as a contentious environment for the arts and it has continued to live up to its reputation.

In Sydney, satirical revue had become reinvigorated in the 1950s by the amateur theatres, particularly the socialist New Theatres and

university campuses. In the profession the leader was William Orr (b. 1924), a Scotsman who gathered the talents from university revues into his Phillip Street Theatre (1954–61) in Sydney. Some of its savagery was revived briefly by a live television revue, *The Mavis Bramston Show* (1965–8) which had a major influence upon the workers in the infant TV industry.

It was out of a similar climate that the comedian Barry Humphries (b. 1934) emerged in Melbourne. A teenage dadaist, he joined the Union Theatre Repertory Company and in 1955 invented his alter ego, Dame Edna Everage, to entertain his fellow actors on a country tour. Edna and the lugubrious Sandy Stone soon moved into revue, radio and television. From 1959–62 Humphries was in London, where he became an associate of the *Beyond the Fringe* team and the Goons; he returned in 1962 with the first of his one-man shows and has since commuted between Britain and Australia. The enormous impact which Humphries made, with his mock-serious curiosity about his audience's suburban routines and his ridiculing of audience members on stage, reinforced in a still immature country fears of appearing colourless, humourless and naïve. At the same time he pioneered a uniquely Australian style of comedy which broke through the territorial contract between actor and audience. From the 1970s to the 1990s stand-up comics with names like Norman Gunston, Elle McFeast, H.G. Nelson and Raging Roy Slavin have used the TV interview barbarically to invade the real-life space of celebrities, politicians and sports figures.

The year 1960 saw the arrival of two new styles of theatre. The pioneers in Sydney were the in-the-round Ensemble Theatre and the Music Hall Theatre Restaurant. The Victorian-style Music Hall (1960–80) produced parodies of English melodrama and Italian grand opera, and then farces based on Australia's convict past. Its success led to a rash of such entertainments across the country, reinvigorating burlesque and variety. By the 1970s the vogue had run its course; but it served to remind the new generation that vaudeville and melodrama had long contributed to the process of decolonization from British gentility and American marketing.

The Ensemble Theatre, which settled in a converted boat shed at Milson's Point in Sydney's inner north, grew out of classes started in 1958 by Hayes Gordon (b. 1920), an American whom J.C. Williamson's had brought to Australia in 1952 to play Fred Graham/Petruchio in *Kiss Me Kate*. He was a disciple of New York's 'Method' teacher Lee Strasberg and introduced a muscular new bare-faced super-realism to a 'middle-class and middle-aged' theatre community. Gordon attracted a new kind of pupil from less privileged backgrounds than the elocution teachers of the previous generation. Many of his students in the following years became leaders in the nationalist arts movement.

In Melbourne a similar drive was underway with the four brief years of the open-stage Emerald Hill Theatre (1962–6), created by the young Brechtian Wal Cherry (1932–86) and the actor George Whaley, who advocated that only through ensemble work could one begin to develop an indigenous theatrical style. Local writing was central and the style was passionate, tough and political, prefiguring the work of La Mama and the Australian Performing Group a year or two later.

Experimental companies began to proliferate. In Perth, the principal amateur group, the Perth Repertory Society, had with the encouragement of the Trust determined upon a path to professionalism in the 1950s, first employing a director, then building its own theatre, the Playhouse. The disruption created in 1965 a breakaway group called the Hole-in-the-Wall Theatre, experimenting in the new drama and theatre-in-the-round.

Perth's most innovative contribution, however, was in outdoor theatre. The annual summer Festival of Perth (founded 1953) was an initiative of the Adult Education Board centred upon a variety of auditoriums in the extensive landscaped gardens at the University of Western Australia, used by students for summer performance. The New Fortune Theatre quadrangle, built in 1964, is used for research into Elizabethan acting style and has been influential in encouraging a movement away from naturalism. Later, these venues were to be a significant factor in the pioneering of Aboriginal theatre.

Following the impact of the first Adelaide Festivals, the Trust in 1964 funded the director John Tasker (1933–88) to form the nucleus of a South Australian Theatre Company (later the State Theatre Company of South Australia). Despite some notable successes it was not until a reformist Labor government in 1968 endorsed the company's existence by statute and set about building a Festival Centre that the company was able to consolidate. In Adelaide, as elsewhere, the theatrical heartland was the community theatres.

In Hobart, the Trust contented itself with supplying productions to the Bijou Theatre Royal and was unable to establish a foothold with the

three prosperous amateur theatres in Brisbane, founded by drama teachers on the Little Theatre principle. The pattern was to be shattered in 1969 with the imposition by government statute of the Queensland Theatre Company.

The late 1960s were a time of extraordinary ferment and optimism in Australia. The country had had a conservative Liberal–Country Party coalition government since the time of Tyrone Guthrie's report in 1949. The prime minister, Sir Robert Menzies, retired in 1966 after winning an election fought for the first time by the Australian Labor Party (ALP) on foreign policy: Australia's involvement in the Vietnam War. It was a turning point in public conscience. The battle was fought again in 1969 and finally won in 1972 when Gough Whitlam led the ALP to victory with the slogan 'It's Time'. That election was much more than a struggle for government, it was a gathering of energies by a nation which for a generation had left politics to the politicians. As in other parts of the world, the postwar baby-boomer generation's arrival at majority had much to do with these campaigns.

In the event, the new government moved too fast and was too inexperienced in the *realpolitik* of economics and administration. In 1975 the governor-general dismissed the prime minister and the coalition swept back for a further six years. This turmoil had a profound effect upon Australian artists and their work and established a strong rapport between the arts and the ALP.

The groundswell of social change from the mid-1960s, expressed by peace marches, youth culture, the contraceptive pill and the music industry, was reflected in the theatre and motivated successful campaigns for direct federal subsidy (achieved in 1968) and to challenge oppressive censorship practice in the states. No longer middle class and middle aged, groups set up performance spaces in warehouses and deserted factories in the major cities, the majority with campus connections.

In Melbourne in 1967 Betty Burstall, a high school teacher, opened La Mama, a tiny space in Carlton, a bohemian university area of Melbourne, as an experimental performance centre. The move was inspired by the New York namesake which, with its policy of free expression, had nurtured a new kind of playwright and the experiment proved of equal significance in Australia. Playwrights like Jack Hibberd (b. 1940), John Romeril (b. 1945), Alex Buzo (b. 1944) and David Williamson (b. 1942) had their early work presented by La Mama and by its offshoot, the Australian Performing Group,

Phil Thomson's 1990 Marli Biyol Company and Western Australian Theatre Company production of *In Our Town* by Jack Davis at the Playhouse, designed by Tolis Papazoglou.
Photo: David Dare Parker.

which set up nearby in a derelict pram factory in 1970. A similar rough theatre was established the same year in Sydney in an old stage-coach stable in Kings Cross, which became the Nimrod Street Theatre.

The most significant further development from the civil rights movement of the 1960s was Aboriginal theatre. Aboriginal and Torres Strait islander culture is one of songs, story-telling and dance; until the 1960s literary figures and performers, in the audience-oriented sense, were rare. Social justice protests had been rural, scattered and tribal-based until freedom rides drawing attention to the living conditions on country reserves, and the growing power of the mass media to disseminate news of protest action, gave strength for the first time to the notion of national unity. Fired by the need for a public platform, acting groups from 1970 began to work with the Australian Performing Group and Nimrod Street; the 1970s saw black theatre groups start in every capital city and in northern country centres. The arrival of the writer-activist Jack Davis (b. 1917) in the theatre in 1979 led to the growth in Western Australia of a core of black

performers who have profoundly influenced the development of theatre and dance in Australia. Modern dance was also seized upon as a way in which natural abilities could find expression. Actors now work in their own and mainstream theatre; both classical dancers and black dance troupes are at the forefront of new work.

The structure of the Australian theatre changed irreversibly from 1968 with the introduction of government subsidy on a practical scale. Until that time, as already indicated, the theatre consisted of commercial entrepreneurs, based in Melbourne or Sydney, and a variety of semi-professional and amateur community theatres groups with their own premises. Federal funding quickly established strong local production and the rise of these companies in turn encouraged the consolidation of state arts ministries.

In the commercial world, the J.C. Williamson empire was replaced by the late 1960s by younger producers like Harry M. Miller (b. 1934). Miller shook up the status quo with productions of Mart Crowley's *The Boys in the Band* (1968), which caused three of the cast

Gordon Chater as the Man in Richard Wherrett's 1976–7 production of *The Elocution of Benjamin Franklin* by Steve J. Spears at the Nimrod Theatre. Photo: Peter Holderness.

to be arrested in Melbourne for using obscene language, *Hair* (1969) and *Jesus Christ Superstar* (1972). He was also the first to take up the local product, notably David Williamson's *The Removalists* in 1973 and *The Elocution of Benjamin Franklin* by Steve J. Spears (b. 1951) in 1976. After national tours the former was mounted at the Royal Court in London and the Nimrod Theatre production of *Elocution* had long seasons in London and then Off-Broadway, where it won three Obie awards. Miller's run of luck ended in 1978 when his electronic ticketing agency went awry and led to his being convicted of fraudulent misappropriation of funds. On release from jail he returned to promotion but has not regained his original flair.

By that time the British producer Cameron Mackintosh had entered the field, his first productions being *Cats* (1981) and *Les Misérables* (1985). His presence brought about the extravagant restoration of lyric theatres in Sydney and Melbourne and revived a taste for the musical which smaller promoters have exploited. He has also invested modestly in local developmental work. His shows have disadvantaged the indigenous industry by excluding major venues from use by others. Australia has a variety of smaller enterprises such as the Adelaide Festival Centre Trust and the Perth Theatre Trust, agencies which control the government-owned theatre spaces in their cities and act as producers and tour managers.

The first initiative of the Council for the Arts in 1968 relating to theatre was to groom one organization in each capital to be the official state company. In Melbourne, the dominant Union Theatre Repertory Company had already expanded its activities from its tiny Russell Street theatre and changed its name to the Melbourne Theatre Company. Its only rival was the semi-professional St Martin's Theatre in South Yarra, which closed in 1973 but reopened in 1978 as a youth theatre.

In Sydney there were three contenders: the Independent, which showed its mettle by turning fully professional and introducing a European repertory; the Ensemble Theatre; and Old Tote Theatre Company, then only six years old and working out of a tiny university house holding barely a hundred people. The latter had, however, opened the Jane Street Theatre in 1966 – an even smaller house – to develop local work, and was in partnership with NIDA, also on campus at the University of New South Wales.

The Old Tote won hands down. The Independent returned to semi-professional status and closed in 1977. The Ensemble survived and in 1984 opened a new open-stage theatre and restaurant on its waterfront site.

In Adelaide, the state government endorsed the South Australian Theatre Company; in Brisbane a similar statute established the Queensland Theatre Company. In Perth support was offered to the *de facto* state company, the National Theatre at the Playhouse. In Hobart the small population continued to militate against supporting a resident ensemble. The Tasmanian Theatre Company, established at the Theatre Royal in 1971, had a fitful life and quickly resorted to importing productions.

Short-term funding was offered by the council for special projects; but most of the Little Theatres found they were ineligible under the new non-profit company guidelines, and died. Of all the groups that flourished before the introduction of subsidy, only a handful in Sydney, with its population of 4 million, survive as professional theatres: the Ensemble and Marian Street Theatres (founded as the

Queensland's Popular Theatre Troupe's 1976 production of *The Millionaire's Handicap*.

Community Theatre in 1965), both serving the populous dormitory suburbs of Sydney's North Shore, and the Q Theatre, begun as a city lunch-hour theatre in 1963 and later at Penrith, on the outskirts of Sydney, serving a further wide conurbation. Brisbane's in-the-round La Boite Theatre has survived through its strong local focus.

However, with federal assistance a host of new groups soon emerged from the ferment of nationalist activity. The most significant included the Australian Performing Group (1970–80) in Melbourne; the Nimrod Theatre (1970–87) in Sydney and the political Popular Theatre Troupe (1974–82) which toured nationally. From 1979 community theatres began to proliferate in suburbs and regional centres, initiated in the first instance by graduates of the Victorian College of the Arts. They were supported in the initiative by the addition of a Community Arts Board to the Australia Council in 1978; but most of the experiments were short lived. The principal legacy is the work of some playwrights and a number of skilled community artists.

The Council for the Arts began in 1968 with a modest budget of A$1.7 million which grew to A$14 million by 1974. In 1975 Prime Minister Gough Whitlam brought all federal funding for the arts together as a statutory authority renamed the Australia Council and since then funding has been well maintained, though subject to repeated scrutiny, controversy and the manoeuvrings of a succession of arts ministers and the country's economic crises. Its structure has been through several metamorphoses but its basis is a set of staffed boards, including the Performing Arts Board which funds music, drama and dance; and basic principles of arm's-length funding (that is, the right to subsidize without political interference) and peer assessment of applications. As the arts have grown the competition has increased and the choice of peers and methods of assessment remain contentious.

State arts ministries have kept pace, providing buildings and infrastructure. The increased attention by government in turn has encouraged corporate business to support the pursuit of excellence and to acquire naming rights to major venues.

In 1994 Prime Minister Paul Keating announced his 'Creative Nation' policy, with funding totalling A$252 million to the arts over four years. The Australia Council's allocation of A$59.2 million was boosted by a further A$25 million over four years. The statement ensured triennial funding for the first time to the Council and in turn to the major theatre companies and other arts organizations, who until then had been hampered by annual applications. 'Creative Nation' also made provision for new training initiatives, quality improvement and touring within Australia and overseas. The statement was strongly market-oriented and endorsed the arts as a means of asserting the independence and maturity of Australian nationhood.

The Liberal–Country Party coalition has long been a critic of the Australia Council and had vowed to abolish it in favour of ministry management. Keating lost office in 1996 but his statement assured the temporary survival of the Council. The Howard government endorsed support for the arts in principle but introduced strong measures to reduce debt and many of the programmes were by degrees dismantled.

Structure of the National Theatre Community

Melbourne and Sydney are Australia's theatre capitals and most theatre is still concentrated in these cities. Historically, the business of show business has been conducted from Melbourne; but present-day film producers, casting directors and agencies tend to congregate in Sydney. Melbourne is still regarded as the intellectual capital and Sydney as one of more physical attractions. Melbourne admires thought while Sydney admires action, it is commonly said. While this is only an approximation of a more complex truth, it has some bearing on comparisons between the styles of Melbourne and Sydney theatre companies.

Beyond these cities, each regional capital has its major subsidized company and alternatives, and some country centres have working theatres; but the erosion of funding which began in the 1980s has left some states starved of funds and encouraged the importation of productions at the expense of the local industry. In the late 1990s it has become increasingly difficult for practitioners to remain at home in any state beyond New South Wales and Victoria.

Major entrepreneurs are the producers of the arts festivals which now promote every mainland capital. Like much of Perth's entertainment, its festival has an English bias, but Aboriginal work has also made it distinctive. Adelaide's biennial festival remains the biggest and most avant-garde event in the public mind, and has an equally influential fringe festival; more recent but now rivalling Adelaide is the spring Melbourne International Festival, which also has its fringe and Comedy Festival. The winter Brisbane Festival was formerly a community-based arts and crafts occasion called Warana (Blue Skies) but now aims at direct competition. Canberra's October festival of Australian Theatre (Australian Opera from 1997) includes a 'performing arts market' at which performers can showcase work for visiting entrepreneurs. Sydney's summer arts festival is more low key and noted for outdoor entertainment, particularly free opera and music in the park. In recent years it has been overshadowed by the gay and lesbian Mardi Gras, a festival of satire and theatre of which the highlight is an annual street parade which attracts an international following. Folkloric and community festivals celebrating the multicultural nature of modern Australia coexist in major centres.

The wealth of talent now touring Australia has been largely brought about by these festivals, which are supported by both state and private sponsorship. They contribute increasingly to the country's earnings from tourism. Country centres also offer a variety of festivals celebrating music with wine and food. In the 1990s several well-promoted performance events were staged requiring the audience to travel to remote parts of the continent.

Contributors to these festivals, and major rivals of the entrepreneurs, are the subsidized theatre companies. Operating since the 1960s, they now invade the commercial territory in their bid for popular support. They are structured as non-profit organizations with an honorary board of directors; they receive subsidy from the federal government through the Performing Arts Board of the Australia Council, and from their state government through their arts ministry. They are also expected to seek private sponsorship through tax-deductible donations. However, most companies still derive between 70 and 85 per cent of their income from the box office.

No theatre company has created a permanent acting ensemble. Attempts have been made from time to time under special directors but they are intermittent.

All theatre workers have a union which governs their rate of pay. Actors' Equity was founded in 1920 and in 1992 amalgamated with the Australian Journalists' Association and the Australian Theatrical and Amusement Employees' Association to become the Media, Entertainment and Arts Alliance. This union covers performers, directors, designers and technicians in all performance media. Though it has never had a reputation for being a hard-hitting union, Equity (as performers still call it) has run successful campaigns for rehearsal pay, quotas of Australian content in Australian television broadcasting, a limitation on overseas artists working in Australia, the introduction of standard contracts for all parts of the industry, the averaging of tax for those with uneven incomes, a free legal service and what is believed to be one of the world's first superannuation schemes for performers. Such superannuation support became federal law in 1993.

As in many countries, some 90 per cent of Equity members are unemployed at any given time. When employed they receive a minimum income equivalent to the average wage and on tour a living-away-from home allowance. Actors move freely between film, TV and the stage; the increased drawing power of the former has led to higher incomes for stage performance at the top end of the market. Ticket prices have increased in parallel: the cost of an average seat for a play in a major venue exceeds A$30; a commercial musical might be A$70 or A$100, a small-theatre play A$25, with discounts for students and pensioners. A cinema ticket is A$11 or less. The hourly basic wage for a clerk is A$10; for a builder's labourer A$11.60.

At the lower end survival is still difficult. For small companies union rules and those of the Australia Council disallow discounting of wages, performance rights or any other downgrading of artists' work, except in special circumstances. While this is admirable in principle it has repeatedly led to the demise of small troupes and recently the authorities have begun to relent.

The pursuit of excellence by a small population has created a dependence upon subvention to a greater extent than many countries. Besides grants to institutions, there are many grants to individual artists who receive assistance for periods of one to three years, together with state awards for literary excellence and scholarships for young talent.

Artistic Profile

Companies

Since the demise of the Trust Players in 1962, the cost of touring has continued to militate against the establishment of a national theatre company. However, funds from the Australia Council's Playing Australia scheme, instituted in 1993, have encouraged the major companies to mount cooperative productions which tour; they now approximate a permanent management supplying the outlying states with regular productions.

In 1990 a donation of A$50,000 from a Shakespeare-loving businessman initiated the Bell Shakespeare Company headed by John Bell (b. 1940), his wife Anna Volska (b. 1944) and the Australian Elizabethan Theatre Trust. Early financial troubles threatened its national touring programme; by 1996 it was receiving federal funding as a major organization, substantial private sponsorship, and flying the flag for the Globe Shakespeare organization. Its home base is Sydney.

Melbourne and Sydney have two strong rival companies, backed by state and federal funding, subscription membership and distinct agendas, and a variety of smaller companies. The Melbourne Theatre Company (MTC) is the longest established and is responsible for drama in the Victorian Arts Centre's two theatres and a studio theatre. Its repertoire follows the pattern of modern, classical and local work established by John Sumner, who retired in 1987. The Playbox Theatre Centre, established in 1976 by a pair of defectors from the Australian Performing Group and one from the MTC, has always been seen as a radical alternative to the conservative MTC; it now has a handsome two-theatre complex in a converted brewery malt house in south Melbourne and a liaison with theatre at Monash University. It performs almost exclusively new Australian work and its stable of writers is now nationally recognized.

More characteristic of Melbourne, however, is the abundance of performances in eccentric small spaces, ranging from performance art to stand-up comedy. La Mama is still a home to the experimental; the Carlton Courthouse, the larger Universal Theatre and the former homes

John Bell as Richard III, Bell Shakespeare Company 1993, directed by John Bell, costume design by Sue Field.
Photo: Branco Gaica.

of the Australian Nouveau Theatre (1981–94) – especially the Napier Street Theatre – are used by a wide variety of groups. Melbourne is also the home of comedy and satire, and its annual Melbourne Comedy Festival attracts acts nationally and internationally.

The Sydney Theatre Company (STC) was established in 1979 by the state government following the demise of the Old Tote Theatre Company. The Old Tote had risen too rapidly from its former racecourse totalizator building to the Drama Theatre of the Sydney Opera House. Withdrawal of public funding enforced liquidation in 1978.

On a new state-supported footing and playing at the Opera House Drama Theatre, the STC was quickly successful, aided in 1984 by the opening of the Wharf Theatre. The Wharf, with its harbourside restaurant and multiple spaces, doubled the audience capacity and reduced the company's costs by gathering the production department, rehearsal room and administration under one roof. The attractions of the two theatre buildings are a unique advantage in attracting subscribers and sponsorship. Its federal grant of A$400,000 now represents

only 4 per cent of its turnover. At 23,000, its subscription membership is the largest in Australia.

Architect of this success was Richard Wherrett (b. 1940), formerly of the Nimrod Theatre, and his appropriation of the Nimrod style left that theatre with a dilemma it never resolved. A campaign in support of female employment confused and alienated its old audience. In 1984 it sold the building to a syndicate of theatre workers who renamed it the Belvoir Street Theatre and established it as a non-profit cooperative with a strong social agenda. The leading figure in the takeover was Chris Westwood (b. 1946) who became founding general manager. The present artistic head is Neil Armfield (b. 1955), who has returned to the tenets of an ensemble of actors and mounted a strong challenge to the STC.

A small but significant company in Sydney is the Griffin Theatre Company which in 1980 became tenant of the Stables Theatre, created by Nimrod in 1970 in Nimrod Street, Kings Cross. They exist to perform only new Australian work and the makeshift environment is sympathetic to experiment. The Stables was bought in 1987 by a charitable trust which also provides the Griffin with low-cost space for administration.

The open barn of the Performance Space is the other major experimental venue in the city, used by performance artists, musicians, and cross-media performers like the acrobatic dancers Legs on the Wall.

On the west coast, Perth has a very different temperament. Being the most isolated capital in the world, it has a history of creating its own entertainment, some of high quality, and is rightly resentful of imported actors and shows which interrupt the pattern of employment. From the early 1950s many British theatre people were imported under the £10 post-war immigration scheme and remnants of the English rep approach still survive. The Playhouse became the acknowledged state theatre company while assistance was given also to the Hole-in-the-Wall Theatre. Separate agendas were never resolved satisfactorily, an enforced amalgamation failed, and at the time of writing both companies were defunct. Their place was being assumed by the small Swy Theatre, renamed the Perth Theatre Company; Deck Chair Theatre Company in the port of Fremantle, which works with the Italian community and local interest groups; and Black Swan Theatre Company.

The Black Swan, founded in 1991, is Australia's first actively multi-ethnic theatre company, with a brief to develop the skills of Aboriginal actors. It remounted and toured extensively *Bran Nue Dae*, Australia's most successful musical to date and now has an Aboriginal training programme headed by the choreographer Michael Leslie (b. 1956). Its chair and patron is the financier Janet Holmes à Court, whose property includes six London theatres purchased in the 1980s from Sir Lew Grade.

In Adelaide the propitious terms on which the State Theatre Company was created ensured until 1992 that it was, per seat, the most highly subsidized theatre company in the country. Despite this, the company has been plagued by controversy, beginning uncertainly without a home of its own and attempting in turn to create an ensemble, a classical company, a radical dynamo and a home for local work. The bankruptcy of the State Bank in 1993 sharply reduced local support to the point that the artistic structure was dismantled and replaced by an executive producer.

The State Theatre Company's only mainstream rival, the Stage Company, closed in 1986. Smaller groups tenuously survive. Special interest groups are doing better. In Port Adelaide Vitalstatistix, a self-reliant group founded in 1984, creates works by women and performs in jails, community centres, even on trains. Doppio Teatro (founded 1983), a bilingual company working in the Italian community, tours nationally and has won several awards. The Junction Theatre (founded 1983) creates its own small-scale productions for the inner western suburbs and fulfils an important role in facilitating the work of other smaller companies.

Brisbane theatre is currently dominated by the Queensland Theatre Company (QTC), initially housed in the dismally titled State Government Insurance Office (now Suncorp) Theatre. But it took the founding director, Alan Edwards (b. 1925), many years to gain acceptance. It was finally achieved with the opening of the Performing Arts Complex in 1985, providing the small Cremorne Theatre for the company. A multi-theatre home is now rising, adjacent to the complex in south Brisbane to be opened in 1998. The QTC's programme has been for the most part a reflection of the successes, classical and new, of the southern states.

Elsewhere in Brisbane the amateur Arts Theatre survives and thrives, as does La Boite (on a non-professional basis) featuring a programme of new Australian and overseas work.

Many short-lived companies providing social satire, comedy and classical work have also contributed.

Public funding has encouraged the establishment of many small regional theatre companies with varying success and endurance. Some are attached to universities. Some are Aboriginal or ethnic-based. All depend for survival upon subsidy and the continuing dedication of the participants. One of the most successful is the Murray River Performing Group (founded in 1979) which created the now internationally known children's troupe, Flying Fruit Fly Circus, with its own training school. New Moon Theatre Company survived spasmodically from 1982–91 touring north Queensland. A similar company based in Broome in north Western Australia was established in 1994. In 1996 an attempt by theatres in three New South Wales (NSW) country centres to set up a touring circuit failed when the Hunter Valley Theatre Company went down. Vast distances and small populations are still the major obstacles to overcome.

Money, and with it a gradually maturing public attitude towards the arts as the face of national self-expression, has given new authority to artists in the 1990s. In the theatre the standard of performance, design and direction has risen steadily. Australia now has more and better theatre than it has had since the coming of cinema. The price has been, however, that the industry has grown within a culture of dependence upon subvention; the amateur theatre, which historically created the intellectual climate and subverted orthodoxy, has been excluded from participating in the achievement.

Dramaturgy

The first half of the century in Australia was dominated by a theatre of reproduction. Aspiring playwrights worked in the amateur theatre or, from the 1930s, in radio drama and serials. *Rusty Bugles* made a rare escape onto the mainstage; and there were occasional expatriate successes like Hugh Hasting's comedy-drama of the British Navy, *Seagulls Over Sorrento*, which ran for three years in London before being mounted in Australia in 1952.

Ray Lawler's *Summer of the Seventeenth Doll* pioneered the change. Not only did the play manage to contain within the conventional three-act form the sprawling, directionless lives of its characters and their colourful vernacular, but also it gave to the working-class origins of the Australian character a new recognition and respect. It was a towering achievement by a local craftsman whose materials, to that point, had been worlds far away and long ago. Its immediate audience success was supported by the energies of the new Australian Elizabethan Theatre Trust, and the potential for professional production spawned a significant group of plays, including *The Shifting Heart* (1957) by Richard Beynon (b. 1927), *The Multi-Coloured Umbrella* (1957) by Barbara Vernon (1916–78), *A Spring Song* (1958) by Ray Mathew (b. 1929), Peter Kenna's *The Slaughter of St Teresa's Day* (1959) and Alan Seymour's *The One Day of the Year* (1960). But to the distress of many of the Trust's sponsors, the plays seemed to share with the *Doll* a preference for the seedier side of life: suburban racial prejudice, illegal betting, violence, offensive behaviour. The Trust Players were abandoned and most of the writers sought a living abroad.

In retrospect the playwrights of the 1950s can be seen as the end of the colonial period of Australian playwriting rather than the beginning of the contemporary theatre. The plays are conventionally realistic in form: their originality lies in their atmosphere, character and expression, which even at the time was seen by some as consciously seeking the more colourful aspects of Australian life. The plays survive variously but it is fair to say that *Rusty Bugles* is now a more accurate signpost to the future than the *Doll*. *Rusty Bugles* combined form and content: a sense of powerlessness and deracination with the raw language and hearty camaraderie of army comedy. It also made use of irony and a loose Chekhovian structure sympathetic to the rhythms of Australian English, which were later widely adopted by the new writers.

The plays of the period were all surrounded by controversy, none more so than Patrick White's *The Ham Funeral* (1961) which, like *The One Day of the Year*, was banned by the governors of the Adelaide Festival. The cause was a scene in which a derelict discovers a foetus in a dustbin; but historically the play's significance lies in its expressionist form, which encouraged younger writers to venture away from the safety of naturalism. White, already the author of the novels which led to his Nobel Prize for Literature in 1973, wrote three more plays in quick succession. His anti-naturalistic, intellectual style was, however, in advance of his audience and it was not until the late 1970s, through the work of the directors Jim Sharman and Neil Armfield, that his theatrical strength began to be

reassessed and he was encouraged to write four further plays.

From 1962 onwards, small experimental theatres began to offer new opportunities. By 1971 venues existed in all capital cities dedicated to creating a new drama. Most of it was satirical, ribald and iconoclastic, reflecting the climate of protest against censorship laws, parochialism, the Vietnam War, university teaching, staid government and a variety of social justice issues. Many of the plays were group-written, with the haste and topicality of a newspaper. All of them revelled in Australian language and mores, some drawing inspiration from Barry Humphries, and all eschewed realistic form. Songs were introduced, sometimes dance, and a conscious link was made with the old burlesque and vaudeville, seeing these as the only indigenous forms historically achieved. The most notable of such plays is *The Legend of King O'Malley* (1970) by Michael Boddy (b. 1934) and Bob Ellis (b. 1942), a rumbustious musical play based on the life of a Texan trickster who became a prominent Australian parliamentarian. Other satirical works dealing with Australia's past reflected a national mood of self-examination.

The second phase focused upon the individual and produced a stream of plays which dealt with the disruptions of social change. The early plays of Alex Buzo, like *The Front Room Boys* (1969) and *Rooted* (1969), deal with the persecution of characters perplexed by change and are written in a vernacular of the modish. Jack Hibberd's monologue, *A Stretch of the Imagination* (1972), is a Beckettian review of the old Australia now lost. John Romeril in *The Floating World* (1974) employs inept shipboard entertainment to examine Australia's trade relationship with Japan and creates a vivid portrait of an old prisoner-of-war facing the horrors of recovered memory.

David Williamson emerged from this same group with a more overtly political agenda. Williamson was the first of the writers to move from the back street to the main stage and he became the most bankable playwright in Australia's history. His eighteen published plays have been widely produced; many are frequently revived, some are filmed, some exported.

Williamson is a craftsman admired for his economy, his pungent, ironic humour and his understanding of his audience. It has been said that the political changes in Australia can be traced chronologically through his plays, as his characters' dilemmas mirror the public issues at stake. The abusive policemen in *The Removalists*

(1971) suggest a relationship between public protest and private repressions; the fading hopes at an election-night party in *Don's Party* (1971) parallel those of the youthquake of the 1960s; the horse-trading of suburban football players in *The Club* (1976) presages the management take-overs of the 1980s.

A need to defend the new freedoms in the 1970s moved him on to concerns of compromise and corruption in the 1980s and personal morality in the 1990s. His most recent plays deal with corruption of the media and invasion of privacy; with liberal humanism versus political correctness; and with the dangers inherent in the single-minded pursuit of truth.

Australia's most directly political playwrights are Jack Davis, who in his sixties discovered the stage was his forum and received national acclaim for a series of humorous and compassionate works about the history of Aboriginal deprivation, and the left-wing Stephen Sewell (b. 1953) whose angry, epic works on the machinations of political parties, nuclear science and international banking demonstrate how small individual betrayals can be magnified on a global scale. The theatre has been used by many Aboriginal activists like Davis for polemical work; as the theatre becomes recognized as common ground for black and white, plays of increasing quality are beginning to emerge.

In the early 1970s two older playwrights preceded Patrick White's return to the theatre: Dorothy Hewett (b. 1923) in Perth, an established poet, and Peter Kenna, who returned to Sydney from London in 1971. Hewett's work was inspired in the first instance by the imaginative world opened by Patrick White and by the Shakespearian stage of the New Fortune Theatre. Her broad, poetic canvas and voluptuous style, confronting her audience with a female metaphysics and biology, proved a challenge to the overwhelmingly male theatre hierarchy. Her first major play, *The Chapel Perilous* (1971), which interpreted the life journey of a rebellious woman poet as a heroic quest, quickly became a rallying point for women and remains a landmark in the late 1990s.

Kenna's major work is *A Hard God* (1974), the first in a trilogy of the Cassidy family: Irish Catholic, working class. The Irish influence upon the early contemporary theatre is marked, contributing humour, poetry, wry observation and a guilty conscience. Kenna's work is exemplary, creating characters which are Australian and yet deracinated from a heritage they never knew. The trilogy contributed a fresh recognition of

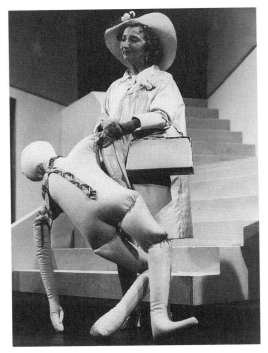

Margaret Ford and her 'husband' Matey in Raymond Omodei's 1972 Playhouse production of Dorothy Hewett's *Bon Bons and Roses for Dolly*, designed by Bill Dowd.
Photo: Simico.

that heritage, a fresh experiment in form involving two time planes, and was the first important dramatic writing to examine homosexuality.

Other work in which the Irish Catholic influence is evident, particularly its Catholic education, includes the plays of prison life in the early 1970s by Jim McNeil (1935–82); *The Christian Brothers* (1975) by Ron Blair (b. 1942), a one-man play of disappointed ideals; and the plays of Jack Hibberd and more recently Nick Enright. Enright's *St James' Infirmary* (1992) and *Good Works* (1994) are complex examinations of the influences of religious superstition and isolation upon developing minds.

One writer whose reputation overseas is growing is Louis Nowra (b. 1950), a prolific author of plays and film scripts, who writes sprawling, picaresque works of black humour, much of it real and imagined autobiography. His best known play is *Cosi*, also a film, the story of a group of mental patients attempting to rehearse Mozart's *Così Fan Tutte*. Michael Gow (b. 1955) also reached prominence in the 1980s with *Away* (1985), the most performed play for a decade. The story of three families on their summer holidays, it uses several Shakespearian plays as context to bring quarrels and tragedy to a reconciliation.

The rapid rise in new writing in the early 1970s received support in 1973 by the establishment of an annual Australian National Playwrights' Conference (ANPC), which is held in Canberra, where selected plays receive developmental work. Its history has been plagued by argument and the struggle for sponsorship, but it now has a full-time home in Sydney and conducts year-round workshops, seminars and script assessment. Many contemporary playwrights received early assistance through the conference.

In other cities there are several small writers' theatres and groups supporting new writing; and in Sydney Playworks was set up as a national resource to assist women's writing. Under the direction of the Playworks' founder, Ros Horin, the Griffin Theatre in Sydney has expanded into further development of plays. A Women's Theatre Group in Melbourne (1974–7) and a consciousness-raising exercise at the Nimrod Theatre in 1981–2 gave opportunity to women writers and directors. A decade has matured their work and altered the outlook of male writers towards the potential of the female actor.

Women playwrights now hold their own on the mainstage, notably Hannie Rayson (b. 1957), a prolific writer whose play *Hotel Sorrento* has received overseas attention and been filmed; Alma De Groen (b. 1941), one of the most formally complex of Australian playwrights; Katherine Thomson (b. 1955); Jill Shearer (b. 1936); and Joanna Murray-Smith (b. 1962). Their work is making an impact by its rigorous re-examination of Dorothy Hewett's territory and the opposing needs of freedom and dependence. Another is Tes Lyssiotis, writing about the Greek immigrant experience, particularly the story of her mother, a proxy bride. Immigrants' stories are widely exploited in community theatre, which has its own writers creating topical social and political statements.

Major and minor grants to writers, including playwrights, are made annually by the Literature Unit of the Australia Council and there are a number of private legacy awards and fellowships. Each state has annual literary awards, including drama, worth A$15,000 and more to the winners. More lavish Creative Fellowships up to five years for artists in mid-career were instituted by Treasurer Paul Keating in 1989 but were cancelled in 1996 by the coalition government of John Howard.

Directing and Acting

The loss of authority by the amateur theatre with the coming of public subsidy is particularly ironic because it was the amateur theatre that first created the cult of the director in Australia. The role of director – producer, originally – came to Australia with the new realism.

In the commercial theatre the decline of the actor-manager led to the importation of directors from London and New York to reproduce the major successes; this still continues. From 1918 the amateur theatre began to throw up personalities dedicated to experiment and the amateur nature of the talent soon placed them in a teacher–pupil relationship. The style of directing in Australia until the 1970s included a teaching process in which every aspect of a performance was devised by the director.

The first generation of NIDA graduates began to change all that. At the same time in Melbourne, Brechtian theory began to be introduced in the 1950s, then a variety of academic courses introducing drama as a medium for teaching communications skills. Both elements produced by degrees an actor-centred drama, grounded in individuality and self-reliance, which was consolidated by the Victorian College of Arts (VCA) in 1976. Two directors who emerged from this philosophic base and developed it into acting theory were Peter Oyston (b. 1938) founder of the VCA, and Lindy Davies (b. 1946), dean of drama since 1995. Their work has been widely influential. Unlike Sydney, where directors dominate, in Victoria energies have gone instead into producing distinctive, multi-talented performers, principally in comedy, like the political impersonator Max Gillies (b. 1941), the whimsical comedian Rod Quantock (b. 1947) and performance artists like Lyndal Jones and Jenny Kemp (b. 1949).

A younger individualist is the director Barrie Kosky (b. 1967) who established the Jewish company Gilgul in 1992. His productions have been uncompromising and controversial in their demands on audiences. In 1996 he consolidated his reputation as leader of the ethnically based avant-garde as director of the Adelaide Festival, introducing a spectacular programme of largely non-textual productions demonstrating the achievements of multi-skilled artists.

The success of the established theatres has related directly to the style of the talents that founded them. The Melbourne Theatre Company director, Roger Hodgman (b. 1943), has continued the path laid down by John Sumner. The driving force in the Playbox's success has been the actor and administrator Carrillo Gantner (b. 1944). An adroit politician and cultural counsellor at the Australian Embassy in Beijing (1985–8), he has drawn on many resources to assure the security of the company and made it the first to establish strong artistic links with China and Japan. Since 1994 the director has been Aubrey Mellor (b. 1947), formerly director of the Queensland Theatre Company, who has consolidated the Playbox's policy of promoting new Australian work.

Another influential *auteur* is Jean-Pierre Mignon (b. 1951), who founded the Australian Nouveau Theatre (1981–94) presenting French-based work in a style which often approached performance art.

Meanwhile Sydney from the late 1960s began to become a centre for a new breed of freelance directors. Among them were Rex Cramphorn (1941–91) from Queensland, who established

his Performance Syndicate (1965–75) as a Grotowski-style commune to reinterpret the classics, and who later had an influential period as director of the Playbox Theatre; Brian Syron (1940–93), an actor-director trained by Stella Adler in New York, who was a powerful influence in the development of Aboriginal actors; John Tasker, another actors' director who after South Australia broke into the commercial theatre with *The Boys in the Band*; and Jim Sharman (b. 1945) who at 22 directed for Harry M. Miller the Australian production of *Hair* (1969) and then *Jesus Christ Superstar* (1972). He directed *Hair* in several major centres, including Tokyo and Germany, and *Jesus Christ Superstar* in London. Sharman was the first Australian to join the international circuit of blockbuster directors. His designer, Brian Thomson (b. 1946), has achieved equally great international renown.

The Nimrod Theatre developed a stable of directors. Richard Wherrett became director of

Nimrod Theatre's 1979 production of David Williamson' *Traveling North*, designed by Ian Robinson. Photo: Peter Holderness.

the Sydney Theatre Company in 1980 and set about creating theatre that was 'grand, vulgar, intelligent, challenging and fun'. He made it a director's and designer's theatre, creating a standard of design which Sydney had not seen in local work before and promoted actors for the first time in showy productions like the musical *Chicago,* with the musical stars Nancy Hayes (b. 1944) and Geraldine Turner (b. 1950), and Rostand's *Cyrano de Bergerac,* starring John Bell. He established a firm audience base on which the company has continued to build. Wayne Harrison (b. 1953) brought a stronger dramaturgical structure to the company when he took over in 1990 and doubled the output of plays and employment of actors. He introduced sometimes confronting content, instituted several experimental arms and has actively sought to make the company entrepreneurial. The domination of the director at the STC, and the extent of the dramaturgical work undertaken, was revealed in 1996 in a public dispute between David Williamson and Harrison over stage interpretation during the première season of Williamson's play *Heretic.*

John Bell, also a founder of Nimrod Theatre and director when it closed in 1986, carried on the Nimrod style of Shakespeare into his own company: broad brushwork with an emphasis on eclectic design and an appeal to young audiences. Neil Armfield was appointed director of Belvoir Street Theatre in the mid-1990s. He received his early training with Bell at Nimrod. Armfield has an impressive record of interpreting new work by contemporary writers and established a loose ensemble at Belvoir Street with an ethnically diverse base.

The major work on mixed-race production, however, has been done by Andrew Ross (b. 1947), director of the Black Swan Theatre Company in Perth. He worked closely for a decade with the playwright Jack Davis to develop his skills and has sought out and trained Aboriginal actors to supply his casts. He directed *Bran Nue Dae,* a hugely successful musical with an Aboriginal cast, originating in the old pearling port of Broome, in the remote north of Western Australia.

A director distinctive for her understanding of actors, and who had her start at the Sydney Theatre Company where she was a leading actor, is Robyn Nevin (b. 1942). In 1994 she became associate director of the MTC and in 1996 was appointed director of the Queensland Theatre Company. Women directors are still a small minority in the Australian theatre but during the 1990s there has been active encouragement, supported by the Australia Council. The best known among them is Gale Edwards (b. 1955) who, after being associate director of the State Theatre Company of South Australia, came to prominence as Trevor Nunn's associate on *Les Misérables* in 1985. This led to a career commuting between Australia and Britain, where she directs for the Royal Shakespeare Company. Her productions are notable for their athleticism and visual impact.

Katharine Brisbane

Music Theatre
Dance Theatre

Until the end of World War II, Australian musical theatre was a mixture of British and American writing. The exigencies of war had forced J.C. Williamson's into repeated revivals. Then the new musical (*Oklahoma!, Annie Get Your Gun, Kiss Me Kate*) flooded the theatres and Australia felt part of the world again. They had US directors and US leads, and artists were proud of the skill with which they could reproduce exactly the design and choreography. More than once producers claimed that these productions were better than the original. Ironically, in 1996 when Australian producer John Frost took the Adelaide Festival Centre's production of *The King and I* to Broadway, it won four Tony awards for best production, design and performance.

Sporadic attempts were made to introduce Australian themes. In 1958 the Trust successfully mounted *Lola Montez* (music by Peter Stannard, lyrics by Peter Benjamin and book by Alan Burke) based on the scandalous adventures in the Australian gold-fields of the nineteenth-century dancer, while in 1962 J.C. Williamson's took up the Canberra production of a musical by Albert Arlen, book by Lloyd Thomson and Nancy Brown. This was *The Sentimental Bloke,* based on C.J. Dennis's classic ballads of working life in Melbourne in the 1920s. But generally until the 1970s the reproduction of US musicals was conducted systematically, the majority by the US director Fred Hebert (1912–72) who worked steadily in Australia from 1957, and ballet mistress Betty Pounder (1921–90). Meanwhile, most of the experiment was conducted in intimate revue or on an amateur or part-amateur basis through schools and studios run by retiring professionals. Employment was also provided to singers and dancers by the Music Hall restaurants which had a vogue from 1960 and the returned services and sports clubs which began to provide lavish entertainment from the 1960s after gaining poker-machine licences.

Ballet and contemporary dance were better served, emerging with greater strength and individuality than might have been the case if they had not had to endure the double bind of geographical isolation and financial hardship. Now that the reproduction industry is rarely to be found outside Cameron Mackintosh's productions, and Australia is beginning to export back to Britain and the United States, the energy, colour and audacity of the Australian imagination is much more compelling.

If there is one distinguishing feature in the varied and flourishing forms of dance in the late 1990s, it is theatricality. An Australian character is evident in the nature of the movement itself – generosity and breadth of gesture with an expansive sense of projection – as well as in the style of presentation, which places great importance on the involvement of designers, composers and live musical performance, even among the smallest groups. Australian audiences expect a strongly projected theatrical experience from dance and they usually get it.

The total theatre approach to dance has a historical basis. While Anna Pavlova's tours in 1926 and 1929 had built eager audiences for ballet, Australian dance benefited more from being the lucky recipient of a legacy from the twentieth century's golden age of ballet, the Diaghilev era. Following Diaghilev's death in 1929, Colonel de Basil brought several Ballets Russes touring companies of his former dancers to Australia in the 1930s and their vivid theatricality had a profound effect upon stage design and taste in dance. This impact was consolidated when many stayed in Australia – some by choice, others stranded by the start of World War II – sharing their expertise as performers, teachers and artistic directors.

One of them was Helene Kirsova (c. 1911–62), who founded the Kirsova Ballet in Sydney in 1941 with a repertoire of established ballets and her own work. Featuring former de Basil dancers as well as local performers, this was Australia's first professional dance company. In Perth, another de Basil dancer, Kira Bousloff (b. 1914), set up a school and a company in 1952, starting with short seasons and then establishing it on a professional basis in 1970 as the embryo West Australian Ballet.

The most important influence was that of a flamboyant Czech, Edouard Borovansky (1902–59). The Borovansky Ballet grew out of the school he established with his wife Xenia in 1939 and performances for the Melbourne Ballet Club in 1940. Backed by J.C. Williamson's from 1944, the company toured Australia's vast distances with a lively, accessible repertoire of new works and popular classics. Australian dancers and audiences were nurtured as never before.

In the contrasting style of modern expressive dance, developed in her birthplace of Vienna, Gertrud Bodenwieser (1890–1959) established a school and the Bodenwieser Ballet in Sydney in 1940. Her fluent, dramatically sculptured way of moving remains a distinctive force today through former company members who became teachers, including Margaret Chapple (1923–96), Keith Bain (b. 1926) and New Zealander Shona Dunlop.

It took incoming artists to recognize the possibilities of translating Australian themes into dance for the theatre. Borovansky's first such ballet, *Terra Australis* (1946), explored the effect of white settlement on Australia's black population and natural environment. In the 1950s, Bodenwieser choreographed the ballad 'Waltzing Matilda' for TV and, for the stage, *Aboriginal Spear Dance, Central Australian Suite* and *The Kunkarunkara Woman*.

British dancer Joyce Graeme (b. 1918) stayed in Australia after a long Ballet Rambert tour and founded the National Ballet Theatre in Melbourne in 1948. In the process of encouraging Australian performers and creative artists, this company produced the first realization of John Antill's ballet score *Corroboree* in 1950, choreographed by Rex Reid (b. 1931) and designed by William Constable. Four years later, another version was choreographed by Beth Dean, American by birth but long resident in Australia, using the same designs and involving the Bodenwieser Ballet.

Australian dancer, choreographer and director Laurel Martyn (b. 1916) performed overseas but chose to make her major career in Australia, where she became the founding director, chief choreographer and principal dancer of the Melbourne-based Victorian Ballet Guild. Growing out of a programme of four world premières by Martyn in 1946, it was renamed Ballet Victoria in 1967 and under that title hosted a tour with Natalia Makarova and Mikhail Baryshnikov as guest artists in 1975. While its repertoire included key classical works such as *Les Sylphides* and *Giselle*, this company's greatest impact came from its excitingly creative output of original works to commissioned scores. They included works with Australian themes such as Martyn's two-act ballet based on C.J. Dennis's *Sentimental Bloke* (1952) and her shorter, historical ballet about the tragic life of an Aboriginal woman, *Mathinna* (1954), to music by Esther Rofe.

All these companies had a precarious and erratic existence. Even with commercial support, the Borovansky Ballet went into recess and its dancers into musicals to survive. Borovansky's sudden death in 1959 coincided fortuitously with Australian government moves to fund a national ballet company; the Australian Ballet gave its first performance on 2 November 1962.

Peggy van Praagh (1910–90), later Dame Peggy, was brought from Britain to be the Australian Ballet's founding artistic director. Her association with the Sadler's Wells Ballet, later the Royal Ballet, was a dominant influence but it was underpinned by her broad background of international styles through the teaching of such diverse artists as Agnes de Mille, Anna Sokolova and Gertrud Bodenwieser.

Her contacts with British choreographers Frederick Ashton, Antony Tudor and John Cranko helped shape the Australian company's early years – as did the work of American choreographers John Butler and Glen Tetley, whose *Gemini* (1973) is one of the Australian Ballet's creative milestones. Van Praagh's nurturing of choreographic talent among the company's dancers produced a new generation of Australian choreographers, including Graeme Murphy (b. 1950) and Meryl Tankard (b. 1955).

The appointment of Robert Helpmann (1909–86), later Sir Robert, as co-artistic director of the Australian Ballet in 1965 reinforced the company's theatrical drive and high-profile overseas associations. In 1964 he had choreographed its first all-Australian work,

The Display, in which beer drinking at a bush picnic leads to macho displays and a symbolic rape of a girl by a lyre bird. The music was by Malcolm Williamson (b. 1931) and design by Sidney Nolan (1917–92).

The Australian Ballet has always toured extensively at home and abroad from its Melbourne base, impressing audiences in its early years more with its freshness and attack than finesse. Following van Praagh and Helpmann, Anne Woolliams (b. 1926) of the Stuttgart Ballet became artistic director, followed (after a return appearance from Dame Peggy) by one of the company's greatest former dancers, Marilyn Jones (b. 1940). From 1983 to 1996, Maina Gielgud (b. 1945) applied her English and European background to polishing the company's technique. It is now one of the world's major classical companies.

The highlight of Gielgud's final year, before a former company principal Ross Stretton (b. 1952) came from his most recent appointment as assistant director of American Ballet Theatre to take over in 1997, was a triple bill by three Australian choreographers: Meryl Tankard, Stephen Page (b. 1965) and Stanton Welch (b. 1969), who with Stephen Baynes (b. 1956) had been a resident choreographer with the Australian Ballet for the previous two years. This venture into local creativity was an exciting move by the national company.

Meryl Tankard became artistic director of the Australian Dance Theatre (ADT) in 1993, adding her name to the company's title. The Adelaide-based ADT was founded in 1965 by Elizabeth Cameron Dalman (b. 1934) as Australia's first modern dance company. It has travelled a variety of stylistic paths since then under different directors; its current approach is a wide-ranging sweep of dance theatre possibilities being developed by Tankard following her six years with Pina Bausch's Wuppertaler Tanztheater in Germany.

The West Australian Ballet, the nation's oldest, has been under the artistic direction of Barry Moreland (b. 1940) since 1983. He has followed a classically based creative path of commissioned works – often by company members or Moreland himself – with some nineteenth- and twentieth-century milestones such as *Giselle* and Balanchine's *Allegro Brillante*.

The Queensland Ballet's stylistic base is also classical but the repertoire is almost entirely contemporary, with the artistic director since 1978, Harold Collins (b. 1940), choreographing many of the company's personal versions of famous ballets for its highly accessible programmes. The Queensland Ballet's founding artistic director was the Paris-born dancer Charles Lisner (1928–88), who established the company under his own name in 1960 with the aim of fostering Australian creative talent, renaming it in 1962.

The Sydney Dance Company is a major overseas touring company, noted for its theatrical daring and diversity of original works with a contemporary edge. Founded as Ballet in a Nutshell in 1966 by Suzanne Musitz (b. 1937), it travelled under the title Athletes and Dancers and then the Dance Company (NSW) before adopting its present name in 1979. Its artistic director and chief choreographer since 1976 has been Graeme Murphy who is regarded as the outstanding Australian dance creator and communicator of his time. His output has made an influential contribution to late twentieth-century Australian theatre, involving leading composers, designers and visual artists.

Smaller regional companies include Dance North, which operates from a strong community base in North Queensland's Townsville, touring extensively in its home state with occasional forays interstate and to Southeast Asia. Established as a fully professional company in 1985 under the artistic direction of Cheryl Stock (b. 1948), Dance North grew out of the North Queensland Ballet Company, which was founded in 1970 as an amateur showcase for local dance talent.

The character and focus of small companies depends greatly on their directors. Stock's special interest is the dance of Vietnam, and she developed strong bonds between dance communities in Townsville and Hanoi. Under the direction of choreographer Graeme Watson (b. 1948) from 1997, Dance North is consolidating its associations with the people and history of its immediate surroundings.

A Malaysian-born Chinese who trained as an architect in Australia, Kai Tai Chan (b. 1944) contributed generously to the nation's multicultural arts and understanding when he turned dancer and choreographer to establish One Extra Company, a dance theatre group concerned with issues and ideas. Under Chan's leadership for fifteen years from 1976, One Extra was a unique and significant force in the performing arts. Since he left, its fortunes have varied.

Some companies have grown from styles and cultures beyond Australian shores. The Bharatam Dance Company, founded in Melbourne in 1987, is based on Indian classical dance but explores other Asian and western influences. The more recently established Padma Menon Dance Theatre in Canberra is concerned with bringing together India and Australia in themes and styles. Danza Viva has been presenting theatre performances of Spanish and flamenco dance in Perth since 1985.

But the most exciting dance developments since the 1970s have come from Australia's indigenous people, evolving from the foundation in Sydney in 1975 of a school now known as the National Aboriginal and Islander Skills Development Association (NAISDA) College. Its popular title was the Aboriginal Islander Dance Theatre (AIDT), and this was carried over to the professional company formed in 1991 to inform the general public of Australia's indigenous culture through performances at home and overseas. Under its founding director and chief choreographer, Raymond D. Blanco (b. 1961), AIDT's repertoire has mixed traditional dance with original works whose

Janet Vernon and Ross Philip in the Sydney Dance Company's *Some Rooms*, 1983. Choreography by Graeme Murphy.
Photo: Branco Gaica.

influences range world-wide, yet maintain a focus on the dancers' heritage.

While AIDT is working its way slowly to shaping its artistic character from its cultural roots, Bangarra Dance Theatre under the direction of Stephen Page since 1991 has been flying. Founded in 1989 by US-born Carole Johnson as a professional outlet for the talents of AIDT graduates, Bangarra caught the public imagination in Australia and overseas with *Ochres,* choreographed by Page with Bernadette Walong (b. 1965) in 1994, to music by David Page (b. 1961).

The earthy directness of *Ochres* draws from sources as diverse as Australia's indigenous heritage and modern dance styles. It blends traditional spirituality and present-day social attitudes, reflecting the current situation of the Aboriginal and Torres Strait islander people as a product of their ancestral culture and the multifaceted energies of their twentieth-century urban environment. Poetic and political, this could be

the future for a style of dance that is distinctly Australian.

Around the nation, there are many groups drawing on the indigenous culture for performances. Some are designed for tourist viewing, providing a reliable income for the communities that present them. Others are seen on the festival circuit in Australia and overseas. A few are exploring a blend of past and present. The Aboriginal Centre for the Performing Arts, established by AIDT graduate Michael Leslie in Perth in 1993, is targeting mainstream musical theatre by providing a bridging course that embraces songwriting as well as performance, giving confidence and theatrical understanding to would-be performers aged 17 and over.

Australia now looks outwards and exports its artistry. Perhaps the most interesting young, independent talent in the late 1990s is Gideon Obarzanek (b. 1966), who works part of the year in his home country, where he founded the group Chunky Move in 1995, and choreographs regularly for the Nederlands Dans Theater, based in The Hague.

David Atkins (b. 1955) has built on his tap-dancing skills and irrepressible showmanship to make an international impact as a dancer-manager. Starting with *Dancin' Man* in 1988, he developed his flair for combining great tunes and irresistibly silly storylines into persuasive entertainment culminating in the phenomenal success of his show *Hot Shoe Shuffle,* including an award-winning season in London's West End in 1995. His chief dancer and co-choreographer Dein Perry (b. 1962) has since set up his own all-tap show, *Tap Dogs,* with a feisty bunch of young men who nearly all went to the same teacher in Newcastle, NSW, and are now tapping their way across the world in work boots and shorts, also winning an Olivier award for choreography in their London season.

Music theatre has not matched the achievements of dance in Australia, perhaps because of the domination of commercial production and opera. A number of musicals in the American mode were attempted in the 1950s and 1960s but the more original work has been achieved through the subsidized theatre companies. A number of small avant-garde opera groups produce work intermittently. Variety and burlesque has flourished, particularly through the rumbustious one-man musical parodies of Reg Livermore (b. 1938), notably *The Betty Blokk Buster Follies* (1975) which had extended seasons. The most celebrated contribution that Australia has made to music theatre is probably

Djakapurra Munyarnyun in the Bangarra Dance Theatre's 1996 production of *Ochres* at the Festival of Perth. Choreography by Stephen Page and Bernadette Walong, music by David Page. Photo: Ashley de Prazer.

The Rocky Horror Show by the New Zealander Richard O'Brien, which opened upstairs at the Royal Court Theatre, London, in 1973 while *The Removalists* was playing downstairs. Intrinsic to the creation were the director Jim Sharman and designer Brian Thomson, who took the show around the world and later made *The Rocky Horror Picture Show*.

The commissioning of music to accompany plays began in the 1970s and is now common practice; this has led to many informal partnerships. The playwright Nick Enright (b. 1950) has proved an accomplished book and lyric writer and has collaborated notably with Terence Clarke (b. 1935) in a favourite musical parody *The Venetian Twins* (1979) based on Goldoni's *The Servant of Two Masters*, and the romantic *Summer Rain* (1983); and with the composer Max Lambert. The composer Alan John (b. 1958) has written widely for the theatre. His opera *Jonah Jones* (1985) with writer John Romeril was significant but his major work was *The Eighth Wonder*, with book by Dennis Watkins (b. 1954), a compelling work about the disputes over the building of the Sydney Opera House, presented in that house by the Australian Opera in 1996.

But by far the most successful musical to date has been *Bran Nue Dae* (1989), book and music by Jimmy Chi and the Kuckles band. This is an all-Aboriginal work, a picaresque story of a boy's expulsion from a mission school in north Western Australia, his travels to Perth and return home. Its music is an eclectic amalgam of styles from Kurt Weill to country music, reggae and revivalist hymns and its message is one of reconciliation of all the mixed-blood people of the world. Its success was followed in 1996 by the musical, *Corrugation Road*.

Jill Sykes, John West, Katharine Brisbane

Theatre for Young Audiences

Subsidy, government intervention and a few remarkable individuals have shaped young people's theatre – a movement that includes children's theatre, Theatre-in-Education and youth theatre – all developed with financial support from federal and state government arts bodies and education authorities. After a burst of energy in the late 1970s and 1980s, progress has been erratic and new directions continue to be sought. Theatre for schools is accepted, youth theatre is flourishing and while children's theatre seeks an audience, commercial productions, mainly of British shows, continue to enjoy popular success during school holidays.

In the nationalist cultural movement, young people's theatre has been significant. Up to 80 per cent of the repertoire is Australian. Other trends include the emergence of Aboriginal playwrights and themes and acknowledgment of the diverse parental cultures of young Australians. Many companies reflect the concerns of these people and are developing an Australian self-image that is multicultural.

Professional theatre for children and young people in Australia began after World War II. In 1955 there was only one organization performing programmes related to school studies, the Shakespeare in Jeans Company of the Young Elizabethan Players. Other early companies included the Arena Theatre Company and the touring Australian Children's Theatre based in Melbourne, the Australian Theatre for Young People in Sydney, and Patch Children's Theatre and the Children's Activities Time Society (CATS), both in Perth. In 1975 there were some twenty full-time companies touring schools and performing in the community. The numbers peaked at thirty or more in the 1980s but by 1996 had declined by half. To a degree this was compensated by numerous project-based groups which undertook one-off tours and seasons.

The concept of Theatre-in-Education came to Australia largely from Britain and influenced the early companies' repertoire. The first Theatre-in-Education company was the Pageant Theatre (1967–76) in Sydney which toured to schools. In the early 1970s Barbara Manning, after visiting England, adapted the model into her Salamanca Theatre Company in Hobart. Founding English persons in Theatre-in-Education directors also came to Australia: David Young to the Arena in Melbourne (1973–5) and later to Hobart; and Roger Chapman to Adelaide, first to the Magpie Theatre Company in 1977 and then as director of Carclew Youth Performing Arts Centre, 1982–8. These and similar companies began, along with other artistic movements, to shape a consciously Australian style. Scripts were usually based on the curriculum or relevant issues. Their primary function was to educate through entertainment by the provision of small, flexible touring companies which performed in schools supplemented by workshops, discussion and follow-up programmes. Federal government funding was most important in this period as was that of the states of Tasmania and South Australia.

Since the late 1980s, Theatre-in-Education companies no longer label themselves as such and many perform beyond schools. Some of the work is challenging: social issues like peace, equal opportunity, racism, sexual relationships and old age predominate. Commissioned plays are a feature. However, with the increasing need to find unearned income from government subsidy and other sponsorship, a concern has been the extent to which these sources of money dictate 'approved' subjects over original, creative themes.

Children's theatre (in-theatre productions for young audiences) also provokes debate about appropriate content. There is no repertoire of non-indigenous Australian traditional stories or fairytales. Occasional productions are well done; however, most are conservative in content and played only in school holidays. Costs are as high as adult theatre but income is much lower – factors which militate against experimentation. Repertoire has been deeply indebted to British theatre, though playwrights Jack Davis, Anne Harvey (b. 1936) and Dorothy Hewett have contributed to an Australian style; some, like Davis, have written plays not specifically intended for young people. Also noteworthy are adaptations of Australian children's literature, such as the popular *Two Weeks with the Queen* by Mary Morris (b. 1944), adapted from Morris Gleitzman's novel.

Notable influences upon young people's theatre include the playwrights Peter Charlton (1947–90), Nick Enright, David Holman (b. 1942), Richard Tulloch (b. 1949), Peta Murray (b. 1958) and John Romeril; directors Errol Bray (b. 1940), Angela Chaplin (b. 1957), Brian Joyce (b. 1951) and Andrew Ross; and pedagogues John Lonie (b. 1946) and Chris Westwood. Outstanding distinctly Australian works include Young's *Eureka* (1974) about the gold rush and its effect upon the British wool industry; Harvey's *I'll Be In on That* (1975), a history of trade unionism; *Strike at the Port* (1978) collectively created by the Magpie company; Tulloch's *Year 9 Are Animals* (1981); and Charlton's *Wolf Boy* (1982), a version of the wild-child story; *Dags* by Debra Oswald (1985) about teenage self-image; Enright's *A Property of the Clan* (1992) which dealt with the rape and murder of a schoolgirl; and *Spitting Chips* (1995) by Peta Murray, about a child coping with grief. Jack Davis's *Kullark* (1979) and *Honeyspot* (1986) along with Graham Pitts's (b. 1944) *Mesh* (1980) and *Memo* (1980) were the first successful plays dealing with ethnic issues and all found receptive audiences of young people.

Youth theatre (performed and often created by young people, usually under the guidance of professional theatre artists) is a growing cultural and social influence. Forty companies received federal subsidy in 1996 to pay professionals. Training and workshop programmes are undertaken; the best produce fine work that expresses young people's ideas and nurture young writers, directors and designers. Leaders in youth theatre are the Australian Theatre for Young People and the Shopfront Theatre for Young People in Sydney; Canberra Youth Theatre; Unley Youth Theatre, Adelaide; Contact Youth Theatre, Brisbane; Corrugated Iron Youth Theatre, Darwin; Yirra Yaakin Aboriginal Youth Theatre, Perth; St Martin's Youth Arts Centre, Melbourne; and the Flying Fruitfly Circus, Albury-Wodonga.

The biennial Australian Festival for Young People (earlier known as the Come Out Festival) in Adelaide, the Next Wave Festival in Melbourne and the Out of the Box Festival in Brisbane have an enviable record in the creation of new work and its exposure to a wider public. They have become events of national significance.

Other influences of national importance are Carclew Youth Arts Centre, which is a focal point for resources and has been seminal in the promotion and development of Australian youth arts; InterPlay, the international young playwrights' festival for writers aged 14–22; the International Association of Theatre for Children and Young People (ASSITEJ) Australia, which has a successful record in the promotion of Australian youth performing arts overseas; the Australian Script Centre in Hobart; and *Lowdown*, Australia's youth performing arts magazine (and longest surviving arts publication) published from Carclew, which has been pivotal in the promotion and recognition of young people's theatre.

Michael FitzGerald

Puppet Theatre

Australia's isolated settlements and extended touring conditions have contributed to making puppetry an integral part of community entertainment, and in recent years the imaginative use of technology has drawn it firmly into the avant-garde. There was no Aboriginal tradition in puppetry and early Australian puppetry was either the glove-puppet Punch and Judy or marionette shows. Overseas marionette companies began arriving in the 1870s with full-length programmes. By the turn of the century, marionettes, like ventriloquists, had become a popular part of variety bills. Meanwhile from the 1930s interest grew in puppetry as a craft, usually undertaken by artists or teachers of art.

In Melbourne, W.D. Nicol (1907–78), a Scots-born art teacher, was a pioneer influence upon many later artists. He was a founder of the Puppet Guild of Australia and ran the Littlest Theatre in the 1940s. In Sydney Edith Murray (1897–1988) began using puppets to teach disturbed children. Her Clovelly Puppet Theatre, established in 1949, was an amateur group which for thirty years provided children's theatre with marionettes and glove-puppets.

From 1952 interest was increased by the tours of the Hogarth Puppets from Britain and the emergence of Australia's best known puppeteer, Peter Scriven (b. 1930). As a teenager Scriven had been a member of Nicol's group, and at 18 began presenting a solo marionette act as part of a touring variety show. In 1953 he formed the Peter Scriven Puppets and presented full-length shows in major theatres. His best known work, *The Tintookies*, opened in Sydney in 1956 and was the first of a series of large-scale, full-length marionette shows. This was a musical show about Australian bush animals watched over by magical small humans called the Tintookies. It was followed by *Little Fella Bindi* (1958), the story of an Aboriginal boy and his friendship with native animals, and *The Magic Pudding* (1960), an adaptation of the children's story by Norman Lindsay (1879–1969).

Of special influence was Scriven's puppet master, Igor Hychka (b. 1914), a Polish-Russian immigrant who had worked with Podrecca's famous marionette company and brought a robust Italian tradition to Australia. His teaching improved skills in manipulation and had a nation-wide impact. Scriven gained the support of the Australian Elizabethan Theatre Trust and in 1965 formed the Marionette Theatre of Australia, which toured through Australia and Asia. In 1969 his Tintookie puppets and many others were destroyed by fire and from that time he has largely lived in Asia. He returned to the Marionette Theatre in 1974 and was succeeded 1976–84 by the shadow-puppeteer Richard Bradshaw (b. 1938). During Bradshaw's period the company moved from marionettes to rod-puppets and developed shows for adult audiences, some with sharp political intent. One of his collaborators was the cartoonist Patrick Cook. In *Smiles Away*, set in the outback, the puppeteers were actors in the drama and manipulated lifesize puppets from behind. The company acquired a home in 1980 in a converted Sailor's Home at Sydney's Circular Quay. Financial problems led to the company ceasing operation in 1988.

Initiatives for new forms of puppetry, involving visible performers, came from the Tasmanian Puppet Theatre under L. Peter Wilson (b. 1943) formed in 1969. His influences have largely been from Japan and eastern Europe; he has encouraged designers, composers and visual artists to cooperate in creating

Egrets in a mating dance from Spare Parts Puppet Theatre's 1994 production of *The Last Sanctuary*.

sophisticated theatre. One of the major successes was *Momma's Little Horror Show* (1976), which introduced the director Nigel Triffitt (b. 1949) to puppetry and the animation of objects, an area in which he has continued to be creative. The Tasmanian Puppet Theatre ceased in 1980 and in 1981 Wilson became artistic director of Spare Parts Puppet Theatre Company, of which he was a co-founder, in Fremantle, Western Australia. The company has its own theatre and also tours. It creates shows for adult audiences and children and has had resident artists and directors from Japan, China, the Czech Republic and the United States. It has collaborated with other kinds of performers and visual artists in mixed-media productions. Wilson moved to New Zealand in 1996.

Confusingly, another leading Australian puppeteer is Peter J. Wilson (b. 1953) who in 1993 became artistic director of Company Skylark, based in Canberra. He was a co-founder of the Handspan Theatre Company in 1977 and also worked with the Tasmanian Puppet Theatre and Polyglot Puppet Theatre, although he continues to be a member of Handspan. He trained as a dancer and his skills have strongly influenced his work as a director and as a puppeteer visible to the audience. He was a leading performer in Nigel Triffitt's *Secrets* for Handspan (1982) which went to several festivals in North America and Europe. He came to national attention as a performer in Handspan's *Cho Cho San* (1984), a mixed-media re-creation of the Madame Butterfly story by Daniel Keene (b. 1955) in which the role of the protagonist was shared by a lifesize puppet, operated in full view by Wilson, and an actor/singer. The play was revived by the Playbox Theatre Company in 1987 and toured to China. As co-artistic director of Handspan in 1990 he collaborated with playwright John Romeril on the children's puppet play *Reading Boy*.

Handspan Theatre Company of Melbourne began in 1977 as a traditional puppet company but quickly moved away from using puppets as imitation actors into experimental theatre aiming to provide a predominantly visual experience. It has a full-time artistic director and administrative staff, but its policy is determined by its thirty or so members, most of whom are performers or puppet-makers. It is a touring company which creates works for children and adolescents but is best known for its innovative theatre for adults. This has included the interpretation of Picasso's *Four Little Girls* (1988) by the dance director Ariette Taylor (b. 1938), *Viva*

La Vida Frida Kahlo (1993), and *Daze of Our Lives* (1995), a performance based on the drawings of the artist Mary Leunig, an amusing, wild fantasy around a housewife played by an actor. Handspan is Australia's best known avant-garde puppetry company and has often toured overseas, to Europe, Asia and the Americas.

After the Tasmanian Puppet Theatre ceased in 1980, its former resident designer, Jennifer Davidson (b. 1929), replaced it in 1981 with the Terrapin Puppet Theatre, in Hobart. In 1991 her place as artistic director was taken by dance-trained Annette Downes (b. 1963) under whom the company has made some ambitious ventures into work for adults. In Melbourne Polyglot Puppet Theatre, founded in 1978 by Naomi Tippett, creates works, mainly for children, with leading local puppeteers. The Sydney-based designer-director Kim Carpenter (b. 1950) uses puppet techniques to great advantage in children's shows for his Theatre of Image. In Adelaide Carouselle Theatre, founded by theatre-workers from Poland, celebrated its tenth anniversary in 1995 with a production of *Don Quixote* directed by the Czech director Joseph Krofta who has also directed for Spare Parts. The company played at European puppetry festivals in 1996.

Many overseas companies tour Australian festivals: the Philippe Genty Company from France is a regular visitor and in 1996 created a new show, *Stowaways*, in Adelaide with local performers. This toured Australia and played in Paris. Australian puppeteers also travel extensively. Richard Bradshaw is one internationally renowned solo performer who since 1972 has performed in Europe, Asia and North America. A protégé of Edith Murray, he designs and makes his own shadow-puppets and creates every aspect of his performance. Another international solo performer is Neville Tranter (b. 1955), a former Queenslander based in the Netherlands since 1976. He works in view with large figures with whom he interacts as a central character in powerful, confronting shows for adult audiences.

Television from 1956 provided employment for several puppeteers. Of these the most enduring is Norman Hetherington (b. 1921), who began making marionettes in 1952 when he was an occasional player with the Clovelly Puppet Theatre. His Mr Squiggle first appeared on ABC TV in 1959 and remains a favourite. Hetherington was resident designer for the Marionette Theatre, 1986–8.

Richard Bradshaw, Katharine Brisbane

Design

In the late 1970s, Bill Redmond, a newly appointed artistic director of the Old Tote Theatre Company, wasted no time in complaining of the 'tremendous lack of trained personnel in all backstage departments' of the industry. Further, he announced that 'in matters of design, lighting, scene painting and construction, creation of props and production management [Australia is] the backwoods nation of the world.' His public concerns were endemic to a fledgling profession and confirmed two continuing problems: the dearth of workshop and apprenticeship facilities and the persistence of local managements in engaging overseas designers. This debate, despite the handful of Australian designers having forged successful careers in Britain and North America, including Warwick Armstrong, Barry Kaye (b. 1932), Loudon Sainthill (1919–69) and John Truscott (1936–93), was positioned at a time in Australia's theatre history when much introspective soul searching was attempting to rationalize the nationalistic fervour of the problematic 1950s and 1960s with the internationalism that would ignite the extrovert activities of the 1980s and 1990s.

The appointment of Anne Fraser (b. 1928) as the first professional non-commercial resident designer, at the Union Theatre Repertory Company in 1955, marked a decade of readjustment and empirical learning, particularly by audiences still comfortable with the representational painted backdrop or the well-honed box set of the commercial theatre. Tours by the Shakespeare Memorial Theatre Company from Stratford-upon-Avon and the Old Vic from London after the war had emphasized the significance of stage design to the creation of a total stage unity.

Prior to this pivotal mid-century transition it was the commercial managements, dominated by J.C. Williamson's and the Garnet Carroll organization, that provided most opportunity for décor, most confined to backdrops. The purpose of the scenery was simply to place the performers in context; the emphasis of design was on the craft.

The commercial theatre declined with the economic depression of the 1930s and competition from the cinema and the repertory and Little Theatre movements began to play an important part in the cultural life of Australia. These amateur endeavours, with a diverse repertoire that tackled contemporary European and North American texts, provided the opportunity for the pioneering work of Australian designers such as Don Finley (b. 1902), Vane Lindesay (b. 1920), Florence and Kathleen Martin, Loudon Sainthill, Elaine Haxton (b. 1909) and William Constable (b. 1906). Notable among many other fine artists who contributed to the medium was Norman Lindsay (1879–1969), who designed settings and costumes for Douglas Stewart's *Ned Kelly* in 1944.

Don Finley, whose first excursion into the theatre was with Louis Esson's Pioneer Players in the 1920s, was a prolific writer on stage design and the latest trends abroad. He was one of the first theatre artists to realize the potential of lighting to express mood, championing the ideas suggested by European scenic reformers Adolph Appia and Edward Gordon Craig, concepts that would not make an impact here until the last quarter of the century.

Overwhelmed by the tour of the Colonel de Basil Russian Ballet Company in the 1930s, the young Loudon Sainthill found the Kirsova Ballet, formed in 1941, a significant training ground for his evolving aesthetic. Much influenced by Miro, Bakst and de Chirico, Sainthill was intoxicated by colour. He earned adulation in London during the 1950s and 1960s as an imaginative genius. The Borovansky Ballet, which absorbed the Kirsova after Helene Kirsova's departure and was itself absorbed into the Australian Ballet in 1962, became the company that used designers most frequently.

Specialist courses in design did not exist at this time and the representations on stage reflected the dramaturgical move into realism. Anne Fraser, who considered her work painterly, set a standard for the meticulous attention to the minutia of realistic detail. John Truscott, working with the Melbourne Little Theatre, pursued similar objectives incorporating a limited use of the new lighting technology to impart some emotional qualities to the productions. Tony Tripp (b. 1940) and Graeme McLean (b. 1944) have evolved this tradition of design and today provide an insightful alternative amid the current trend in minimalist work.

With the growth of the Australian Elizabethan Theatre Trust and satellite companies around the country (as well as the development of the Adelaide Festival of the Arts) many young designers, after studying in London, returned to participate in the new industry. Until this time the evolution of a career in stage design (albeit casually) had been dominated by visual artists like John Brack (b. 1920), Arthur Boyd (b. 1920), Sidney Nolan (1917–92) and Jeffrey Smart (b. 1921) who welcomed the larger canvasses offered by the stage. In 1959 a debate began around the influential Antipodean Exhibition of Figurative Art (and the so-called Antipodean Manifesto by Bernard Smith) which attempted to analyse the figurative trends of the previous decade: introspective, broad, tactile and relentless. A decade later in Melbourne, the Field Exhibition (1968) at the National Gallery of Victoria provided a stark alternative in the hard-edged, non-figurative presentation of work that ignored the obsession with the Australian identity. This school, represented by Frank Hinder (1906–92), John Passmore (1904–84), Clifton Pugh (1924–90) and John Percival (b. 1923) among others, was notorious for its preoccupation with a US-based imported abstraction. The prevailing playwriting trend, however, grappling with nationalist concerns, questioning identity and aware of the quality and validity of that identity, demanded a more indigenous representation of the landscape (as well, in a number of notable cases, the landscape of the Australian conscience and spirit). Along with these polarized views (still evident to some in an aesthetic distinction existing between Sydney and Melbourne) the decade also saw the continuing preoccupation with a more decorative design approach made popular by Cedric Flower (b. 1926) and refined by Kenneth Rowell (b. 1920), Kristian Fredrikson (b. 1940) and later Hugh Colman (b. 1946) who all found their niche in designing for dance and opera. A result of this cultural debate saw a widening in the vocabulary of visual expression. Later, artists like Fred Williams (1927–82) chose not to be defined by either school, preferring to explore a peculiar combination of the abstract and the figurative. The Perth-based designer, Andrew Carter (b. 1959), is making a significant contribution to contemporary dance in this way, challenging audiences by his articulate, often figurative, overlay of a unique spatial composition.

It was, however, Desmond Digby (b. 1933) with his designs for Patrick White's *The Season at Sarsaparilla* in Adelaide that heralded the move away from realism. Wendy Dickson, too, encouraged a healthy progression from pure decoration, a move away from naturalism

towards a greater truth to materiality and atmospheric creation. With Dickson, Digby activated locally a prevailing European trend of more integral collaboration with directors in the interpretation of the text, an inclination that led Robin Lovejoy (1923–83) to experiment with visual dramaturgy as designer of his own productions at the Old Tote. A greater sense of experimentation emerged in theatrical communication with new paints and plastics and the evolving specializations in illumination and projection. Yoshi Tosa (b. 1938), by the end of the decade, refined this trend with a selected minimalism focusing on lines, shape and pattern.

Stage light, tentatively, began to move beyond its function of removing darkness or providing shadow towards a true affiliation between concept and visual reality. Stan Ostoja-Kotowski (b. 1922) contributed groundbreaking work with early experiments in sound scape with illumination, while William Akers (b. 1929), having gained experience in London, pioneered with the Australian Ballet the establishment of an electrics department suitable for a major touring repertory company. At the same time Les Bowden (b. 1939), with the Trust Opera, began to perfect methodology for efficient refocusing of standard grids. Sue Nattrass (b. 1941), initially as an associate designer to imported musicals, was able to exploit American technologies while Jameson Lewis (b. 1943) provided insights into European trends. Nigel Levings (b. 1949), with a methodic persistence, further enhanced the professional standing of artists. With larger and more complex grids, John Rayment (b. 1953) made greater demands on available resources, forcing the industry actively to embrace the new technologies in an expanding range of venues. Roger Barratt (d. 1994) employed 'colour and movement' with wit and style, while Nick Schlieper (b. 1958), much influenced by David Hersey and the so-called White Light School in Britain, placed greater emphasis on 'making meaning'. He spearheads a new trend that extols more inclusive pre-production collaborations.

The 1960s saw an effective, albeit formalistic, use of platforms, flats and gauzes to provide 'spaces' for the action and this approach did much to release the new drama from the shackles of the English playhouse and proscenium arch. What remained a problem, however, was the lack of opportunity to emulate the illusory and decorative qualities of new scenic art techniques so favoured by Oliver Messel and Cecil Beaton in Britain. At this time it was only J.C. Williamson's or the Princess Theatre in Melbourne that could provide the much-sought-after vertical paint frame or experienced scenic artist, an extraordinary situation considering that a century earlier scenic artists such as Alexander Habbe (1829–96) and John Hennings (1835–96) had been regularly called before the curtain to receive applause for their scenic spectacle. This scarce resource was further exposed by the arrival of a number of European designers to prepare designs for the Trust Opera Company. Henry Bardon (b. 1923), who started an international career as an assistant painting sets for Lila de Nobili, Desmond Heeley (b. 1931) and Tom Lingwood (b. 1927) created settings that promoted the theatrical illusion and a more rigorous attention to finishing and theatre craft, especially scenic art, and were instrumental in focusing attention on a general deficiency in the subsidized company workshop and its

responsibility for skills development. Friedrich Bliem, as a designer and scenic artist, was a key contributor to the growing strength of the Trust workshop.

Significantly, by the mid-1970s the Melbourne Theatre Company could boast a marvellous art finishing department and Australian designers were at the forefront of contemporary international practice. (In the 1990s, the visual revolution continued in terms of mixed media and interdisciplinary.) The still youthful industry was vicariously stimulated by the ideas of John Cage, along with the American 'happening', the realization of Brechtian influences and the growing political potential of agitprop performance, the student theatre revolt against the prevailing realism, and the move out of the nineteenth-century playhouses into non-traditional theatre spaces. All these elements contributed to the making of a turbulent, yet highly productive 1970s decade. New writing and attitudes to directing and production focused attention towards

Melbourne Theatre Company's 1973 production of Louis Esson's *The Time Is Not Yet Ripe*, directed by Malcolm Robertson, designed by Kristian Fredrikson.

theatre space, as opposed to architecture, and the more direct symbiotic relationship between the audience and the performance. A more vulgar appreciation of the theatre experience attracted architects, designers and artists from other fields, who were fascinated by the opportunities these circumstances provided. Peter Corrigan (b. 1944) and Brian Thomson, primed by the Pop Art revolution, reasserted the primacy of the scenographer's contribution. With expertise and flair, they each provoked an energized contemporary climate that concentrated on the pure elements of design (line, shape, colour, texture and the exploitation of space in venues that ranged from converted stables, salt factories, boat sheds and wharves) to provide alternate readings to the now much more internationalist and discriminating drama.

Thomson set a standard for innovation with broad visual gesture enhanced by a critical analysis of his own work: his palette, with a tendency to rely on the iconographic, is highly selective and he applies structure and surface quality that often enlightens, occasionally subverts, the spiritual conception of the production. As with Finley, Thomson exhibits many of the philosophic qualities of Edward Gordon Craig, whose influence can also be detected in Shaun Gurton (b. 1948) and John Stoddart (b. 1936).

During the 1980s, indigenous peoples began to make a national impact upon the contemporary stage, informed by their ancient heritage in visual arts, dance and music. Bangarra Dance theatre, the Aboriginal and Islander Dance Theatre in Sydney and Kooemba Djarra Theatre Company in Queensland all promote the work of indigenous designers; progressive work in Western Australia has emerged from the designers Joe Hurst, Raymond Meeks Arone (b. 1957), Tim Neuth and the lighting designer Mark Howett (b. 1963).

More generous production budgets and the splashy demands of sponsorship in the 1980s fostered the spectacle and to some extent forced the profession to grow up: Lawrence Eastwood (b. 1948) took advantage, with larrikin, high camp and witty realizations, while Roger Kirk (b. 1948) found his domain with ostentatious cleverness in settings and, particularly, costumes. Although much theatre at the time was criticized for favouring form over content, designers were at last exploiting with relish the now extensive resources of the theatre workshops.

The growing pool of professional designers

Shaun Gurton's set design for the 1997 Sydney Theatre Company production of *The Comedy of Errors* at the Sydney Opera House.
Photo: Tracey Schramm.

(growing, in most cases, due to the establishment in 1959 of the Diploma in Theatre Design at the National Institute of Dramatic Art) were now in a position to advance their own thesis and began to use their work to address theory and practice. Vicki Feitscher (b. 1945), Jenni Tate (b. 1947), Richard Jeziorny (b. 1949) and Anna French (b. 1950) have pursued, with intuitive economy, the possibilities of texture and minimalism; Mary Moore (b. 1945), Michael Scott Mitchell (b. 1960), Stephen Curtis (b. 1957) and Robert Kemp (b. 1950) constantly innovate by vigorously responding with intelligence to the text, with designs that illuminate, surprise and delight; and the absolute preoccupation with image has elicited fascinating and highly charged visual feasts from Kim Carpenter and Nigel Triffitt.

John Senczuk, Derek Nicholson

Theatre Space and Architecture

There are currently more than seventy theatre auditoria used regularly for professional theatre in Australia. These exclude those built on campuses for educational purposes, some of which receive professional use during city arts festivals. Of those seventy, half are theatre spaces in regional centres with populations from 12,000 to 150,000 people, and are likely to be shared between touring theatre and local amateur or community theatre groups. Some amateur groups have their own performance spaces, frequently in converted buildings such as churches, courthouses, former cinemas; occasionally purpose-built, they are usually in end-stage or proscenium format. However, many groups present their performances in halls that range from well-equipped town halls and community club facilities, to austere shed-like municipal halls in country villages.

The metropolitan conurbation of Sydney gives an indication of the wealth of community groups that supplement a healthy commercial and subsidized professional theatre. There, over sixty groups spend more than A$2.5 million a year on productions, the most expensive costing up to A$150,000, and all attracting an audience of more than 200,000 a year. The city also supports some twenty full-time professional theatre spaces seating a total of 15,000 patrons, plus the Sydney Entertainment Centre, which is capable of seating 3,500 in the lyric-theatre mode, and up to 12,000 for pageant performances, sport and rock music concerts.

From the first purpose-built theatres in New South Wales, Australia was quick to copy the latest designs from Britain. The format of a raised dress circle and pit penetrating beneath was derived from London's Royal Coburg Theatre as early as 1838 in Sydney (Royal Victoria Theatre) and 1841 in Adelaide (Queen's Theatre). By 1855 Melbourne boasted the Victorian-style four-level Theatre Royal that had all its auditorium and stage dimensions either the same or greater than those of the Theatres Royal, Drury Lane and Covent Garden, and seated 3,300 people. By the 1880s to house performance by local and touring companies, the theatres constructed in the capital cities represented the rich style of, at first, late Victorian architecture and then, in the early years of the twentieth century, Edwardian style. The stages were equipped to receive the Drury Lane melodramas and US spectaculars, including *Ben Hur* with its on-stage chariot race.

These theatres contained a considerable number of cast-iron posts supporting the two or three tiers above the pit. These were mostly removed when auditoriums were rebuilt in the 1920s, with the exception of the historic Theatre Royal, Hobart (opened in 1837) with its recently restored 1911 auditorium. Almost original is the richly decorated His Majesty's Theatre, Perth (1904), but in 1980 it reopened as the city's major performing arts venue after a clever rehabilitation that drew back the auditorium posts to allow uninterrupted sightlines. The conversion also subsumed the former front-of-house hotel into sympathetic foyers and bars, and built a new backstage and fly tower.

Moving pictures and the Depression brought an end to many working theatres and following the end of World War II it was recognized that the diminished commercial theatre endangered Australia's cultural life. In 1956 an international architectural competition for an opera house in Sydney initiated the concept of the state-funded performing arts centre. Ironically, it was in the 1960s and early 1970s that most of the old theatres, by then neglected and regarded as fire-traps, were demolished or succumbed to fire. Heritage orders against demolition have been placed on the few that remain. A few of the old gold-fields theatres in country towns are still standing.

After much controversy the Sydney Opera House opened in 1973, and the same year Adelaide opened its 2,000-seat Festival Theatre within the Adelaide Festival Centre. The semi-thrust-stage Playhouse, flexible studio Space Theatre and an open-air auditorium followed. The three theatres of the Victorian Arts Centre in Melbourne opened in 1984: the State (Lyric) Theatre seats 2,000 and has the largest and most luxuriously equipped stage in the country. The Queensland Performing Arts Complex in Brisbane opened in 1985; its Lyric Theatre is adaptable for audiences from 1,000 to 2,000 on three levels. The small Cremorne Theatre (named after the demolished vaudeville house on the site) is the home of the Queensland Theatre Company; it will share with other users the Southbank Playhouse Theatre, seating 850, added to the complex in 1998.

In the early 1960s regional theatres began to replace the old Schools of Arts and Mechanics Institute halls of the nineteenth and early twentieth centuries, but many retained the flat-floored auditoriums for social events. Government intervention encouraged local councils to consider more functional theatre buildings. As a result most country and suburban theatre buildings were built in the 1970s and 1980s, with a seating capacity of from 500 to 1,000, designed with a fly-tower stage to accept touring productions; some also included a small studio theatre.

With the coming of subsidy, most capital cities developed an alternative theatre to rival the major state company; it is for this type of theatre that the most innovative modern theatre spaces have been designed. These companies, which have continued the historical trend of adapting existing buildings to theatrical specifications, can be found in converted spaces: a salt and tomato sauce packing factory (Belvoir Street Theatre, Sydney, completed 1974); an inner-city stage-coach stables (Nimrod Street, now Stables Theatre, Sydney, opened 1970); a 220-metre (715-foot) long finger wharf extending into Sydney Harbour, opened in 1984 and now containing a thrust-stage Wharf Theatre 1 and studio-style Wharf

Upper terrace of the Adelaide Festival Centre, with Herbert Hajek's sculpture in the foreground.
Photo: Tony Lewis, the *Australian*.

Theatre 2, a flexible open space used for cabaret, together with workshops and rehearsal space for the Sydney Theatre Company, Sydney Dance Theatre and Australian Theatre for Young People; a boat shed (Ensemble Theatre and restaurant, North Sydney, rebuilt in 1984); and a brewer's malt house (CUB Malthouse, opened 1990), home of the Playbox Theatre Centre, with its thrust stage Merlyn Theatre and flexible studio Beckett Theatre. Adelaide has a similar conversion under construction. It is in these theatres that the in-the-round, thrust stage, corner stage and open-end stage formats are to be found. The most individual purpose-built theatre is La Boite theatre-in-the-round (1972) in Brisbane, built to confirm the style and needs of its semi-professional company. Some of the impetus for alternative theatre design came from university campuses, the most noteworthy being that of the University of Western Australia in Perth. It initiated building of thrust stage theatres in

Australia with the opening in 1969 of the 600-seat Octagon Theatre which is regularly used for professional performances, particularly as part of the Festival of Perth. Less successful has been the larger thrust stage York Theatre, part of the three-auditoriums Seymour Theatre Centre opened at the University of Sydney in 1975.

The mixture of federally and state-supported opera, ballet and drama companies, alternative theatre companies, commercial entrepreneurs and improved facilities has, between the 1970s and 1990s, seen a marked increase in audiences, particularly in the large cities of Sydney and Melbourne. With the demise in the mid-1970s of J.C. Williamson Theatres Ltd, a partial vacuum was left in the industry until the Cameron Mackintosh organization set up in Australia. Its long-running spectacular musicals, together with the general increase in audiences, exacerbated the shortage of suitable theatres of 2,000 or more seats. Sydney, which was suffer-

The Regent Theatre in Melbourne.
Photo: courtesy of Marriner Theatres.

ing most, was the first city to resort to reusing lavishly decorated former picture palaces: the State Theatre, with its inadequate stage, and the rebuilt and restored Capitol Theatre. The latter, with a completely new stage and production facilities, built to accept the long-running musicals such as *Miss Saigon*, opened early 1995. A new 2,000-seat lyric theatre was opened in 1997 adjacent to the Sydney Casino at the Darling Harbour convention, exhibition and entertainment complex. It is contracted to the Andrew Lloyd Webber organization.

As commercial theatres in Melbourne have come on to the market they have been purchased by the developer David Marriner. His first was the high-Victorian Princess Theatre (1886), the stage of which was rebuilt (and auditorium refurbished) in 1990 to accommodate the Macintosh organization's musicals, initially *Les Misérables*. Marriner also purchased the Comedy Theatre and the former 1929 Forum picture palace 'twinned' in the mid-1960s. Another large former cinema, the Regent, closed for a quarter of a century, was, under the direction of Marriner, restored to its former French Renaissance grandeur and opened with *Sunset Boulevard* late in 1996.

Although the main areas of population are temperate in climate, weather is relatively unpredictable and open-air theatrical performances are generally reserved for arts festival events. The spaces used are usually fit-ups in parks or gardens adjacent to the city. Perth, however, with a more stable climate, does have two purpose-built venues on the campus of the University of Western Australia. The Sunken Garden, a small Greek amphitheatre opened in 1948, saw many festival productions but is now too romantically overgrown for most performances. The New Fortune Theatre, a quadrangle in the Arts Faculty Building, reproduces in modern architecture the dimensions of the original Fortune Theatre contract of Elizabethan London and is used for experiments into acting style and open-air festival productions.

Ross Thorne

Training

The changes in training for performers between the 1970s and 1990s have been enormous. Four major factors have contributed: the introduction of drama as a senior school subject in most state education systems; the growth of the university sector and the number of departments offering practical drama and theatre-related programmes at undergraduate and more recently post-graduate level; the accreditation by the Commonwealth Department of Education, Employment, Training and Youth Affairs of specialist private schools for fee-paying diplomas; and the breakdown of the hegemony of English theatre training systems.

The National Institute of Dramatic Art (NIDA) was inaugurated in 1958 and originally offered a two-year Diploma in Dramatic Arts. It was the first, and for many years recognized as the only, national provider of vocational training at any level. Since 1994, NIDA has offered a Bachelor of Dramatic Arts. The more recent institutions include the School of Drama within the Victorian College of the Arts (1976), now affiliated with Melbourne University, the Theatre Department within the Faculty of Performance, Fine Arts and Design at the University of Western Sydney, Nepean (1981) and the Academy of the Arts at the Queensland University of Technology (1991). Since 1995 the Western Australian Academy of Performing Arts, Edith Cowan University, has offered a Diploma of Performing Arts and the reputation of its musical theatre component continues to grow.

In 1996, twenty-eight universities throughout Australia were offering drama and theatre related subjects in undergraduate programmes. Various educational models have been developed with differing degrees of emphases on, and balance between, vocational training, practice and liberal education. These models range from the well-established liberal arts approach taken by the University of New South Wales, whose School of Theatre and Film Studies was, in 1960, the first in Australia; to the highly theoretical BA Honours in Performance Studies at Sydney University. The Drama Centre at Flinders University in Adelaide provides professional training for students in acting and directing within a theoretical framework. Not all twenty-eight universities claim to be training for the industry. Most maintain that they are laying foundations for a variety of career paths.

Dance is offered as a subject in schools throughout Australia. It has been moved from the health and physical education area to become one of the five art forms on the curriculum. It is generally taught at eight levels, up to the Year 12 tertiary entrance qualification.

Outside the formal education system, there is a plethora of private dance schools, even in the smallest communities. The full range of dance styles is taught, including classical ballet, modern dance, tap, jazz, contemporary, highland and national styles. Teacher training programmes and accreditation are offered by organizations such as the Royal Academy of Dancing, Cecchetti Society, British Dancing Association, British Ballet Organization, École Classique and Australian Institute of Classical Dance.

The Australian Ballet School, established in Melbourne in 1964, prepares dancers of 15 years and up for a professional performing career, awarding graduates of the three-year full-time course an advanced diploma in dance. From the average of five hundred students who apply annually, only thirty-five are offered places. The Australian Ballet School also has a one-year teacher training programme.

The Victorian College of the Arts offers a Bachelor of Dance and a variety of post-graduate courses. Also in Melbourne, the Performing Arts Department of the Box Hill College of Technical and Further Education is initiating an advanced diploma of arts in dance teaching and management; Victoria University of Technology Footscray Campus has a BA in performance studies. Deakin University Rusden Campus, which offered the first tertiary dance programme in Australia, offers four BA courses embracing specialist dance and/or drama studies.

In Adelaide, the Centre for the Performing Arts (CPA) offers a three-year full-time course with the emphasis on contemporary dance at technical, aesthetic and creative levels. In 1997, financial cutbacks at the University of Adelaide reduced its BA (Dance) programme to a third-year course for accreditation based on two years of practical training in the CPA diploma course. In Perth, the Western Australian Academy of Performing Arts has a BA (Dance). In Brisbane, the Queensland University of Technology Academy of the Arts offers a BA (Dance), associate degree in dance and a BA Honours (Dance). Other universities also have limited dance courses. Also in Sydney, the National Aboriginal and Islander Skills Development Association (NAISDA) College has one-, two- and three-year certificate and diploma courses in dance.

All these institutions have distinct philosophies in their approach to dance, enabling a diverse choice for Australian students and performers who want to pursue further studies in dance.

No formal training courses for puppeteers yet exist in Australia; practitioners are usually trained on the job. The major puppet companies have invited directors from Japan, China and the Czech Republic for periods of residence to develop Australia's skills base; grants have been made available by the Australia Council for specialist training within Australia and overseas. All the significant Australian artists in puppetry have spent long periods abroad.

There are six higher education institutions which offer stage design as a programme of study. Two course structures exist: one is studio-based, the other is a major within a liberal arts course in Theatre Studies. The first stage design course was established by NIDA in 1959 and has contributed to the acceptance within the industry of designers as a vital member of the creative team in theatre practice. There are no post-graduate or research programmes. A few stage designers have attempted to develop a debate and theoretical dialogue about the art and practice of stage design. Notable among these are Mary Moore, Eamon D'Arcy, John Senczuk and Michael R. Anderson.

Three other training opportunities can be identified: Technical and Further Education Colleges (TAFE), private schools and artist-initiated ongoing training programmes. The Centre for the Performing Arts, TAFE, South Australia, offers an Associate Diploma in Acting; TAFE in Victoria offers an Associate Diploma in Theatre Technology; in NSW the Eora Centre for Aboriginal Studies offers a Certificate of Adult Basic Education, Visual and Performing Arts, and a Certificate of General Education, Visual and Performing Arts. Private theatre schools have a long history in Australia; Ensemble Theatre School in Sydney and St Martin's Youth Performing Arts Centre in Melbourne are two of the oldest. Under new government policy these schools now offer diplomas in competition with government-funded institutions. Alongside these developments has been the growth of actors' centres offering maintenance classes, new skills and special workshops.

Actors' centres are of vital importance for ongoing training and as a base for master classes. While the traditional Anglo-Saxon training techniques still dominate some institutions, with Australia's growing multicultural population including performers from Asia and central Europe, the return of expatriate Australian performers trained in contemporary Asian and European techniques and the increase in visits from overseas master teachers, the sourcing of theatrical styles, ideas and training methods from other cultures is of increasing importance. The sites for such explorations are Sydney's annual Contemporary Performance Week, Adelaide Fringe International Theatre Workshops, the Multicultural Theatre Alliance annual festival, Asian Theatre Festival and artists-in-residence programmes with theatre companies and universities.

Gordon Beattie

Criticism, Scholarship and Publishing

Serious criticism of theatre by journalists and academics, scholarly and historical research, and publication of plays did not exist in any sustained manner until the 1990s. Artists from the 1950s onwards frequently lamented that naïve journalists were given the job of reviewing new productions – a practice that still occurs occasionally – and looked longingly for an antipodean Shaw or Kenneth Tynan who, while offering incisive and sophisticated criticism, would decisively support daring new writing and stage experimentation. A figure of that stature has yet to emerge.

As elsewhere, geography is partly at fault. The scattered capital cities each have one dominant (or only one) newspaper (the evening papers disappeared during the 1980s); reviews in this one publication have great impact within that city, and none outside it. When long-term byline critics emerged in the 1960s such as H.G. Kippax at the *Sydney Morning Herald*, Leonard Radic at the Melbourne *Age* and David Rowbotham at the Brisbane *Courier Mail*, they quickly became objects of attack for their perceived biases, intolerances and ability to make or break local productions; their uniquely powerful position was sometimes more to blame than the individual.

The one newspaper published and read nationally, the *Australian*, began in 1964 and has done much to break down this provincialism. Katharine Brisbane between 1967 and 1974 was the first genuinely national theatre critic. For the first time, as awareness of other centres of activity and a sense of comparative standards grew, it became possible to think of an 'Australian' theatre rather than a number of semi-autonomous regional dramatic movements. This national-reviewing policy was later abandoned. With the exception of Adelaide, the *Australian*'s current reviewers are university academics, although the arts editor Deborah Jones travels extensively and commissions feature articles from all the Australian states, as well as maintaining regular national bulletins.

Significant works of scholarship and critical interpretations emerged even more slowly. Leslie Rees's nationalistic *Towards an Australian Drama* (1953, revised and expanded in 1978 as *A History of Australian Drama*) and John West's *Theatre in Australia* (1978, a history of the commercial theatre) are the pre-1980 sources still consulted. Even now the only single-volume critical account in print is Dennis Carroll's *Australian Contemporary Drama* (1985, revised 1995) originally researched in the 1970s and now showing its age. Radic's *The State of Play* (1991) is a Melbourne-based view of the same dramatic renaissance; Peter Fitzpatrick's *After 'The Doll'*, long out of print, is a better analytical study of the period from 1955 to its publication in 1979.

Apart from trade publications and occasional celebratory and lavishly illustrated commemorative works, little analysis or documentation has been published of individual theatre companies (particularly alternative companies), of the performing arts industries, or (except in more general works and those from government agencies) the arts policies which have so altered the shape of those industries. An exception is Justin Macdonnell's *Arts, Minister?*, a history of federal government subvention since 1968. This is being increasingly addressed, however, by research theses at honours and post-graduate level, which are beginning to document the recent past and to analyse industrial patterns before and after subsidy.

Liz Jones's study of the Melbourne La Mama Theatre is a rare example of a well-documented theatre group, as is Steve Capelin's 1995 work on Queensland protest theatre, *Challenging the Centre: Two Decades of Political Theatre*. Peta Tait's two works on feminist theatre and Colleen Chesterman's survey-based *Playing with Time: Women Writers for Performance* have made significant inroads into that area of activity. However, the numerous monographs and edited collections of articles on individual playwrights, particularly the Editions Rodopi series on Louis Nowra, David Williamson, Jack Hibberd, Patrick White, Alma De Groen and others, and the Methuen series, taken over in 1988 by Currency Press, which includes similar studies of Buzo, Williamson, Hibberd, Hewett and Sewell, have made author-based criticism the major interpretative approach to the contemporary Australian stage. Aboriginal playwrights are still unrepresented except for sections in more general works such as Adam Shoemaker's two books.

The 1995 *Companion to Theatre in Australia* is by far the most comprehensive work of historical and biographical documentation for all periods, colonial to contemporary. It summarizes, corrects and updates nearly all research to that date as well as breaking major new ground, and will be a primary reference tool for many years. *The Australian Stage: a Documentary History* (1984) is another important research resource. The journal *Australasian Drama Studies*, ongoing twice-yearly since 1982, has been the most consistent source for critical commentaries on recent scripts and companies and for interviews with playwrights, particularly Nick Enright, Tes Lyssiotis, Janis Balodis (b. 1950) and Michael Gurr (b. 1961) who have not yet been the subject of a monograph.

Australasian Drama Studies emanates from the Australian Drama Studies Centre at the University of Queensland, which has published several database volumes listing performances of Australian plays; it also has strength in postcolonial drama. A similar centre at the University of New South Wales has produced several works of theatre history, documentation and criticism. The National Australian Studies Centre at Monash University in Melbourne has begun to make a significant contribution to both research and performance. Other university centres for specialized stage scholarship include those at Sydney (interdisciplinary performance studies), at Newcastle and Wollongong, NSW (community theatre), New England at Armidale, NSW (women playwrights) and Flinders in Adelaide (feminist performance), while La Trobe in Melbourne and Perth's Murdoch and University of Western Australia have individual scholars researching and working extensively in Asian theatre and performance.

The publication of Australian plays was only occasional until 1971 when Philip Parsons and Katharine Brisbane established the Sydney-based Currency Press. By far the major publisher in the field, it now has an extensive list of plays by most living Australian playwrights, plus a significant number of works of criticism and scholarship. Currency's history has been one of repeated risk-taking: it has aided the sales of its new writing by providing texts as programmes for initial theatre seasons and drawn new attention to forgotten works. Its success has been built in partnership with the development of Australian drama syllabuses in secondary schools and universities.

Richard Fotheringham

Further Reading

Akerholt, May-Brit. *Patrick White*. Australian Playwrights Monograph Series. Amsterdam: Rodopi, 1988.

Australasian Drama Studies. Brisbane: University of Queensland Department of English, 1982 to date.

Australian and New Zealand Theatre Record. A monthly facsimile reproduction of newspaper theatre and dance reviews. Sydney: Australian Theatre Studies Centre, University of New South Wales, 1987–96.

Brokensha, Peter and Ann Tonks. *Culture and Community: Economics and Expectations of Arts in South Australia*. Wentworth Falls, NSW: Social Science Press, 1986. 162 pp.

Capelin, Steve. *Challenging the Centre: Two Decades of Political Theatre*. Brisbane: Playlab, 1995.

Carroll, Dennis, *Australian Contemporary Drama*. Revised edn. Sydney: Currency, 1995.

Chesterman, Colleen, with Virginia Baxter. *Playing With Time: Women Writing For Performance*. Playworks, 1995.

Fitzpatrick, Peter. *After 'The Doll': Australian Drama Since 1955*. Melbourne: Edward Arnold, 1979.

——. *Williamson*. Sydney: Methuen Australian Drama Series, 1987.

Fitzsimmons, Brian Arthur. *The Place of David Williamson in the History of Australian Drama: A Provisional Perspective*. Boulder, CO: University of Colorado, 1982. 364 pp.

Fotheringham, Richard, ed. *Community Theatre in Australia*. Revised edn. Sydney: Currency, 1992.

Griffiths, Gareth. *John Romeril*. Australian Playwrights Monograph Series. Amsterdam: Rodopi, 1993.

Guthrie, Tyrone. 'Report On Australian Theatre'. *Australian Quarterly* (June 1949).

Hainsworth, J.D. *Hibberd*. Sydney: Methuen Australian Drama Series, 1987.

Holloway, Peter, ed. *Contemporary Australian Drama*. Revised edn. Sydney: Currency, 1987.

Hutton, Geoffrey. *It Won't Last a Week: The First Twenty Years of the Melbourne Theatre Company*. Melbourne: Sun Books, 1975.

Jones, Liz, with Betty Burstall and Helen Garner. *La Mama*. Melbourne: McPhee Gribble/Penguin, 1988.

Kefala, Antigone. *Multiculturalism and the Arts*. Sydney: Australia Council, 1986. 69 pp.

Kelly, Veronica. *Louis Nowra*. Australian Playwrights Monograph series. Amsterdam: Rodopi, 1987.

Kiernan, Brian. *David Williamson: A Writer's Career*. Revised edn. Sydney: Currency, 1996.

Love, Harold, ed. *The Australian Stage: A Documentary History*. Kensington, NSW: New South Wales University Press, 1984. 384 pp.

——. *The Australian Stage: A Documentary History*. Sydney: University of New South Wales, 1984.

Lowdown, Youth Performing Arts in Australia. A bi-monthly publication. Adelaide: Carclew Youth Arts Centre.

Macdonnell, Justin. *Arts, Minister? Government and the Arts in Australia*. Sydney: Currency, 1992.

——. *Fifty Years in the Bush: The Arts Council in New South Wales*. Sydney: Currency, 1997.

McCallum, John. *Buzo*. Sydney: Methuen Australian Drama Series, 1987.

McGillick, Paul. *Jack Hibberd*. Australian Playwrights Monograph Series. Amsterdam: Rodopi, 1988.

Parsons, Philip, with Victoria Chance, gen. eds. *Companion to Theatre in Australia*. Sydney: Currency, in association with Cambridge University Press, 1995.

——. with Victoria Chance, gen. eds, adapted. *Concise Companion to Theatre in Australia*. Sydney: Currency, 1997.

Pask, Edward H. *Ballet in Australia: The Second Act 1940–1980*. Melbourne: Melbourne University Press, 1962.

Perkins, Elizabeth. *The Plays of Alma De Groen*. Australian Playwrights Monograph Series. Amsterdam: Rodopi, 1994.

Radic, Leonard. *The State of Play*. Melbourne: Penguin, 1991.

Rees, Leslie. *A History of Australian Drama*. Sydney: Angus & Robertson, 1978.

Rowse, Tim. *Arguing the Arts: The Funding of Arts in Australia*. Melbourne: Penguin, 1985.

Shoemaker, Adam. *Black Words, White Page: Aboriginal Literature 1929–1988*. Brisbane: University of Queensland Press, 1989.

——. *Swimming in the Mainstream*. London: University of London, 1990.

Spinks, Kim, ed. *Australian Theatre Design*: Sydney: Australian Production Designers' Association, 1992.

Sumner, John. *Recollections At Play: A Life in Australian Theatre*. Melbourne: Melbourne University Press, 1993.

Sydney Theatre Company. *Walking On Water: Sydney Theatre Company At the Wharf*. Sydney: Currency, 1994.

Tait, Peta. *Converging Realities: Feminism in Australian Theatre*. Sydney: Currency, 1994.

——. *Original Women's Theatre: The Melbourne Women's Theatre Group 1974–77*. Melbourne: Artmoves, 1993.

Turcotte, Gerry, ed. *Jack Davis: The Maker of History*. Sydney: Angus & Robertson, 1994.

Vella, Maeve and Rickards, Helen. *Theatre of the Impossible: Puppet Theatre in Australia*. Sydney: Craftsman House, 1989.

Ward, Peter. *A Singular Act: Twenty-five Years of the State Theatre Company of South Australia*. Adelaide: State Theatre Company and Wakefield Press, 1992.

West, John. *Theatre in Australia*. Sydney: Cassell, 1978.

Whiteoak, John, and Scott-Maxwell, Aline, gen. eds. *Companion to Music and Dance in Australia*. Sydney: Currency, 1998.

Williams, Margaret. *Dorothy Hewett: The Feminine as Subversion*. Sydney: Currency, 1992.

Zuber-Skerritt, Ortrun. *David Williamson*. Australian Playwrights Monograph Series. Amsterdam: Rodop, 1988.

BALI

(see **INDONESIA**)

BANGLADESH

One of the most densely populated nations in the world – in 1995 it was estimated that over 128 million people were living in the country's 144,000 square kilometres (55,600 square miles) – the modern state of Bangladesh is historically and culturally connected to Bengal in eastern India. In 1947, when the British left India, the subcontinent was partitioned to create the Muslim state of Pakistan and it was at this time that what is now Bangladesh was separated from Bengal. Called East Pakistan and separated from what was then called West Pakistan by some 1,600 kilometres of Indian territory, it soon became clear that those who made up the population of the future Bangladesh had their own dreams of independence based on both language (Bengali) and their own socio-cultural ethos.

In the months and years following the creation of the new state, politics and culture came to be dominated by groups from West Pakistan. When West Pakistan refused to accept Bengali as one of the state languages, political battles erupted into civil confrontations. In 1971 the East Pakistan Awami League, led by Sheikh Mujibur Rahman, popularly called Bengabandhu (Friend of Bengal), gained political control and insisted on a new constitution with greater powers of self-government for East Pakistan. West Pakistan responded by sending in armies, an all-out civil war began in which millions lost their lives and millions of others fled to India. Independence was declared by East Pakistan in March 1971 though the war went on through December of that year.

Now calling itself Bangladesh (Nation of the Bengalis), the country quickly elected Mujibur Rahman as its first prime minister. Assassinated in 1975 during a military coup, Mujibur Rahman was replaced by the martial law government of General Ziaur Rahman. Civilian government was not restored until 1979. In 1982 General Hussein Muhammed Ershad came to power, made a number of radical amendments to the constitution, founded his own political party and ruled through 1990 when he was forced to step down and was imprisoned on charges of corruption. In 1991, Khaleda Zia, widow of former President Ziaur Rahman, became the new prime minister. She and her party – the Bangladesh Nationalist Party – ruled for five years. During her regime, democracy, secularism and Bengali nationalism – three basic ideals that had inspired the fight for freedom from autocratic rule in 1971 – were trampled under foot. Large-scale corruption in the government predominated, popular discontent grew and, in the national general election held in June 1996, Khaleda Zia was ousted and Sheikh Hasina, daughter of Sheikh Mujib and the leader of the Awami League, the party that gave leadership to the freedom movement, came to power.

As in many countries where social change has dominated daily life, cultural activities have tended to take a back seat. Nevertheless the arts have long been a part of Bengal tradition with the great Bengali poet and dramatist Rabindranath Tagore (1861–1941) among the best known internationally.

Among the oldest of formal Bengali traditions, spanning nearly a thousand years, is that of storytelling. But other forms have had long popularity as well: pantomime shows, verbal duels between two poets singing their lines on an open-air stage accompanied by dance-like movements and *jatras* (musical folk plays). In some areas, stories tended to be told in ballad form with the lines recited like songs. This has, however, almost completely disappeared. In one northern area of Bangladesh *gambhira* – in which two characters, a grandson and a grandfather, engage in a duel of words full of satire, jokes and lively repartee – is still a living form. Woven around such themes as illiteracy, child marriage and wedding dowries, *gambhira* is always improvised. *Jatras* and *palagans* (ballads) are also still vital, though their earlier forms and tone have undergone considerable change. In the beginning, a *jatra* took its story from some myth or legend and was performed in an open space, field or market-place after trading hours were over. Later it leaned on history and literature for plot but it has now moved closer to modern theatre. *Jatra* performances are now sometimes held on a proscenium stage with modern makeup, lighting and other devices, although the acting style continues to be stylized and voices high-pitched. *Palagans* are a blending of poetry, solo and choral songs and lively movements. Its themes are taken from legends, myths, ancient and contemporary history as well as present-day social life. *Alkaap* (literally comic caricature) is another popular form comprising song, dance and comic rhymes while *kavigan* is a duel of two groups of singers and musicians – each led by a poet-singer – who carry on extempore debates in verse.

Such dance and music forms have always been an integral part of the theatre tradition of Bangladesh and many full-length plays utilize it. Jasimuddin's (1903–76) *Nakshikanthar Math* (*The Field of the Embroidered Quilt*), for example, has been frequently performed in Bangladesh and is a very successful dance drama. Tagore made a significant contribution to the genre of dance and music theatre as well with his works *Chitrangada*, *Tasher Desh* (*The Kingdom of Cards*), *Shyama* and *Chandalika*. In these plays dance movements, songs and intense dramatic conflict are brought together to create a powerful non-realistic theatre. Such music-dance dramas, however, tend to be used experimentally more than anything else in social plays.

As for western-style spoken drama, it was the British influence in India that led, from the nineteenth century onward, to occasional performances in schools and local amateur groups. All roles were played by men as religious tradition demanded. Through the first half of the twentieth century, most of the groups involved were in the capital of Dhaka, a city of just under 4 million then. But without government, religious or institutional support, the idea of a western-style theatre had little chance to develop. With the struggle for independence growing on the subcontinent by 1947, however, attitudes began to change. Plays with a clear political tone began to be written and the seeds of a viable spoken drama began to grow.

The growth was begun in part by the return home in the late 1940s of a number of Bengali writers, many of whom had been living in Calcutta. The early plays of such writers as Nurul Momen (1906–90), Showkat Osman (b. 1919), Munier Chowdhury (1925–71) and Asker Ibn Shaikh (b. 1925) were written in a much more realistic and satirical vein than had been seen before in Dhaka. All found their subject matter in daily life, the existence of the poor, in the actions of greedy landlords, black-marketeers, religious hypocrites, corrupt bureaucrats and those who were fighting for an autonomous Bangladesh.

The Bengali Language Movement of 1952 was a watershed that had far-reaching impact on both the political and cultural life of the country. Led essentially by students and built around the battle for recognition of Bengali as the official language, it was a movement that writers such as Munier Chowdhury could not resist. A major figure in the modern history of Bangladesh theatre, Chowdhury was one of many arrested during the language movement. While in jail in 1953 he wrote one of his most important plays, *Kabar* (*Grave*), a one-act drama that effectively portrayed both the mood and atmosphere of the period including the struggle of those who died for their mother tongue. The play, first produced clandestinely inside the prison in 1953, has since been publicly performed many times across the country with great success. Even in the late 1990s it retains a unique stature in the history of Bangladesh spoken theatre.

Structure of the National Theatre Community

Government subsidy of theatre does not exist in Bangladesh, forcing companies to rely almost exclusively on the sale of tickets. In the mid-1990s, theatre tickets were generally priced at 20, 30, 50 and 100 Taka, with 44 Taka equalling about US$1. (The price of a cinema ticket at the same time ranged between 12 and 26 Taka.) A successful show might yield 12,000 Taka for an evening of which about 7,000 Taka would go to rent the hall, lights, and pay for makeup, transportation of sets and publicity. Profits, if any, would be used to capitalize the group's next production (sets, props, costumes, music recordings) or to pay deficits from past offerings. For groups not attracting full houses, donations and loans from business organizations or individuals were usually sought. Direct sponsorship by businesses was extremely rare.

For all these reasons, no one in Bangladesh is able to earn a living entirely from theatrical work and rehearsals must be held after normal working hours. The majority of theatre activity still takes place in Dhaka where some companies have earned solid reputations for both their production levels and for the plays they choose to produce each year.

Because of a lack of well-equipped playing spaces, two or three different community halls (none seating more than 350) are shared by all the producing companies. On any given evening in Dhaka throughout the year, one can usually find at least two performances to choose from.

Artistic Profile

Companies

During the early 1950s a number of semi-professional theatre troupes began to emerge, among them the Habib Productions in Dhaka. In 1951–2, Habib Productions staged three Bengali plays, all by popular Calcutta writers. Habib was also responsible for integrating women into its company. Following the Habib experience, students of both sexes were emboldened to perform together in 1952 at Dhaka University, albeit to the disapproval of university authorities.

Perhaps the most significant group to emerge in the 1950s, however, was the Drama Circle, which pioneered the idea of repertory companies, what came to be called in Bangladesh 'group' theatres. Under the leadership of Bazlul Karim (1939–77), the Drama Circle's approach to all aspects of theatre was considered not only extremely modern but also politically progressive. Between 1956 and 1959, the company produced a steady series of important Bengali-language plays including *Poetasters of Ispahan* (based on a popular West Bengal play), Tagore's symbolist play *Raktokarabi*, Arthur Miller's *All My Sons*, Bernard Shaw's *You Never Can Tell* and an original work called *Manchitra* (*Map*) by Anis Chowdhury (1929–90), no relation to Munier Chowdhury.

Small groups began to emerge in other parts of the country. In 1955, the Dhaka University Central Students' Union produced four different plays on four successive nights, introducing to the country the idea of a multi-play theatre season. Beginning in 1960 the Bangla Academy, the intellectual centre of the struggle for Bengali language and culture, introduced a prize for playwriting and sponsored seasons of new plays. The academy also brought in theatre groups from Britain and the United States. Over the next decade a number of plays of increasing quality began to appear. Among the dramatists whose work received still wider recognition during this time were Asker Ibn Shaikh, Nurul Momen, Munier Chowdhury and novelist and short-story writer Syed Waliullah (1921–71).

In the 1970s, as the liberation movement began to sense its success, theatre activities continued to grow with the creation of companies such as Parapar (established 1970), Aronyak (1971), Natya Chakra (1972), Theatre (1972), Dhaka Theatre (1973) and Nagorik (established in 1968 but not really active until 1973). In the years since 1973, the 'group' theatre movement in independent Bangladesh continued its steady growth and by the late 1990s over fifty groups were in operation in Dhaka alone.

Nagorik was the first company to introduce a formal ticket system for regular performances. The group, eclectic in its repertoire, has presented adaptations or translations into Bengali of Molière, Brecht, Albee, Shaw, Ferenc Molnar, Camus, Carl Zuckmayer, Beckett and Shakespeare. It has also successfully produced the early Bengali farce, *Buro Shaliker Ghare Ron* (*The Elderly Rogue*) by Michael Madhusudan Dutt (1824–73), three Tagore plays, *Achalayoton*, *Muktadhara* and *Bisharjon*, the Bengali historical drama *Shahjahan* by D.L. Roy (1863–1913) and *Baki Itihash* by the West Bengal writer Badal Sirkar (b. 1925).

The group known simply as Theatre has devoted itself mainly to producing original plays like *Paer Aoaja Jai* by Syed Shamsul Haq and *Akhono Kritodash* and *Meraj Fakirer Ma* by Abdullah Al-Mamun, reflecting contemporary life although it also counts among its successes a production of Shakespeare's *Othello* and adaptations of two Tagore novels, *Dui Bon* (dramatized by Momtazuddin Ahmed) and *Ghore Baire* (dramatized by Abdullah Al-Mamun and Zia Ansari) and Bankim Chandra Chatterjee's (1838–94) *Krishnakanter Will* (dramatized by Abdullah Al-Mamun).

Dhaka Theatre, composed mostly of young actors, utilizes populist folk forms as well as modern dramaturgy. Among the company's most popular performances have been *Kittonkhola* and *Keramat Mangol*, two loosely knit epic dramas by resident playwright Selim Al-Deen. Other Dhaka groups of note in the 1990s were Aronyak, Dhaka Padatik, Natya Chakra, Lokonatyadal, Natyakendra and Dhaka Little Theatre.

Outside the capital, regularly producing companies exist in the port city of Chittagong (Arindom, Nandikar, Tirjok, Kathak, Angon, Gonayon, Chattogram Theatre, Mancha Mukut, Theatre Workshop and Prativash); in the north (Rajshahi Theatre, Anusheelon, Bogra Theatre, Meghdoot, Tarun Sampradaya, Sarathi, Rangpur Padatik, Shikha Sangsad, Nabarupi and Shapla); in the south (Khulna Theatre, Bodhon, Anirban, Barisal Natok, Kheyali and Shabdaboli); in Comilla (Janantik, Jatrik and Barnachora); in Noakhali (Subochon and Sanglap); in Mymensingh (Mukul Fouj); in Faridpur (Suniyom, Baishakhi and Faridpur Theatre); in Chuadangaa (Anirban); and in Kushtia (Bodhon and Nupur).

Dramaturgy
Directing and Acting

The creation of indigenous plays lies at the artistic heart of Bangladesh's literary theatre. In the 1940s and 1950s, most utilized conventional realism as the primary style although there were certainly many exceptions. One can now find plays produced in a wide range of styles including verse dramas, documentary dramas, absurdist and epic plays, plays with socio-political content, history plays and adaptations of modern and ancient classics.

Among the most important of the early

Aly Zaker and Ataur Rahman in Nagorik's *Dewan Gagir Kissa*, an adaptation of Brecht's *Puntila*.

dramatists was Nurul Momen. Momen's long one-act play, *Nemesis*, was written against the backdrop of the Bengal famine of the early 1940s, while his *Rupantar* (1948) is a witty comedy in the well-made-play tradition. The anti-capitalist satires of Showkat Osman, on the other hand, were clearly influenced by Ben Jonson, Molière and Shaw. In *Amlar Mamla* (1949), he skilfully paints a tragi-comic portrait of a self-deluded bureaucrat, while in *Kankormoni* he exposes the machinations of black marketeers.

Munier Chowdhury's *Kabor* (1953) introduced expressionistic techniques into the theatre. Chowdhury was equally adept in exploiting tragic and comic situations as evidenced by his anti-war tragedy *Raktakto Prantor* and his university-based comedy, *Chithi*. Asker Ibn Shaikh, writing during the 1950s and 1960s, was known for his dramas of rural society – *Padakhshep, Vidrohi Padma, Duranta Dheu* and *Virodha*.

In the 1960s, novelist and short-story writer Syed Waliullah wrote two unconventional plays, *Bohipeer* (1960) and *Tarangabhanga* (*Lashing of the Waves*, 1964). *Tarangabhanga* – enriched thematically by existentialist philosophy and technically by surrealistic dramaturgy – constitutes a playwriting landmark in the contemporary theatre of the country; it is absurdist at one level, but with hidden suggestions of the grim political realities of the tumultuous 1960s under Pakistan's military regime. One must also mention here another absurdist drama, Sayeed Ahmed's (b. 1931) *Kalbela*, a story of a group of villagers trapped on a remote island, counting their last moments before an approaching hurricane.

Enamul Huq (b. 1937), who also emerged as a verse-playwright in the 1960s, is the author of three music-dance dramas, *Uttaraner Deshe, Hajar Tarer Beena* and *Rajpatha Janapatha*. The first and third plays deal with issues of socio-economic development and industrial labour while the second revolves around the life and achievements of Kazi Nazrul Islam (1899–1976), considered to be the greatest Bengali poet after Tagore.

During the 1970s, at least four dramatists emerged who, by their diverse contributions, added new vigour to the national scene – Syed Shamsul Haq (b. 1935), Abdullah Al-Mamun (b. 1942), Selim Al-Deen (b. 1948) and Mamunur Rashid (b. 1948). Haq, who had already made a name for himself as a poet, short-story writer and novelist, is the author of

five verse plays: *Payer Awaj Pawa Jai* (*You Can Hear the Footsteps*), a moving drama set against the War of Liberation; *Nural Deener Sara Jiban* (*The Entire Life of Nural Deen*), about a peasant uprising during the British Colonial period; *Ekhane Akhon* (*Here Now*), about the banality of contemporary urban life; *Irsha* (*Jealousy*) and *Juddha Ebong Juddha* (*War and War*), a docu-drama about the corruption of revolutionary ideals. Haq has successfully produced verse translations of Shakespeare's *Macbeth* and *The Tempest* as well as a very loose adaptation of *Julius Caesar* called *Gono Nayaka*, which parallels recent Bangladesh political history. His plays have been produced by both Nagorik and Theatre in Dhaka.

Abdullah Al-Mamun, a director and actor with Theatre, is also the company's resident playwright. Social commentary as well as a witty and satiric style combine in his work with a hard-hitting realism to make his plays extremely popular across the country. Among his major plays are *Subochon Nirbashane* (*Good Sayings in Exile*), *Akhon Duhshomoy*, (*Bad Times Now*), *Senapati* (*The General*), *Akhono Kritadash* (*Still a Slave*), *Kokilara* (*The Kokilas*) and *Meraj Fakirer Ma* (*Mother of Meraj Fakir*).

Selim Al-Deen, the resident playwright of Dhaka Theatre, is a bold experimenter. His *Sangbad Cartoon* and *Muntasir Fantasy* are sharp satires with strong political overtones while three of his other plays, *Kittonkhola, Keramat Mangol* and *Hat Hadai*, combine

Ferdousi Majumdar in Theatre's one-woman play *Kokilara*, written and directed by Abdullah Al-Mamun.
Photo: Rana Lodh.

elements of folk forms with modern symbolism. His plays *Chaka* (*The Wheel*) and *Jaibati Konyar Mon* (*The Mind of the Young Woman*) have been written in a narrative style.

Mamunur Rashid, an actor and director with Aronyak, is the author of a number of dramas dealing primarily with class conflict and exploitation. Among his most popular plays are *Ora Kadam Ali* (*They Are Kadam Ali*), *Iblis* (*The Devil*), *Ekhane Nongor* (*Anchor Here*), *Guinea-Pig* and *Pathor* (*Stone*).

Many classic plays from world drama have been translated into Bengali since the 1970s. Among them are plays by Aeschylus, Sophocles, Euripides, Aristophanes, Marlowe, Ibsen, Strindberg, Hauptmann, Goethe, Chekhov, Lorca, Brecht, Synge, Yeats, Williams, O'Neill, Wilder, Wilde, Pinter, Sartre, Camus, Cocteau, Anouilh, Giraudoux, Beckett, Ionesco, Wole Soyinka and Heiner Müller. Many of these plays, however, have not been presented on stage. Among successfully staged translated/adapted plays are some works of Shakespeare, Brecht, Molière, Ibsen and Beckett.

Dhaka Theatre's production of *Jaibati Konyar Mon*, written by Selim Al-Deen and directed by Nasiruddin Yousuff.

Music Theatre
Dance Theatre

For a discussion of music and dance, see the opening, historical section and **Artistic Profile**.

Theatre for Young Audiences

There was no tradition in Bangladesh's literary theatre for specifically children's plays. There were plays written for children, though, which were performed during special occasions at educational institutions. The first theatre doing work specifically for young audiences – beginning in 1979 – was the Dhaka Little Theatre. Since then it has presented a number of plays including an adaptation of Tagore's *Tasher Desh*. There are now other children's organizations and adult theatre groups that occasionally present plays for young audiences including western classics in Bengali adaptations such as Shakespeare's *The Merchant of Venice*.

Puppet Theatre

Bangladesh had a rich tradition of puppetry in a place called Brahmanbaria in the central-western part of the country. Shows were presented to unsophisticated but appreciative audiences. With the incursion of the cinema, however, puppetry soon disappeared. However, there are signs of a revival, albeit in a limited way, in Dhaka. Mustafa Monwar (b. 1935), a painter trained in Japanese puppetry, opened a Multimedia Puppet Development Centre in 1994 in Dhaka with a view to experimenting with puppets and producing new puppeteers.

Mustafa Monwar and his puppets.

Theatre's production of *Antigone* translated and directed by Khairul Alam Sabuj.

Design

Until the 1960s design was left mainly to scene painters with the emphasis mainly on creating the illusion of reality. After the 1970s dependence on painting decreased and sets began to be designed realistically or, on occasion, symbolically or surrealistically. Syed Jamil Ahmed, Mansur Ahmed and Quamruzzaman Runu are among the leading designers.

Theatre Space and Architecture

Two auditoriums are regularly used in Dhaka by all the groups on a rotating basis. One belongs to the Bangladesh Women's Association and the other to the Bangladesh Girl Guides Association. Each can accommodate 350 spectators. They have a single-tier seating arrangement and the stage is a proscenium with only modest technical facilities.

The Academy of Fine and Performing Arts of Bangladesh also has a large auditorium that can accommodate 800 spectators. It has a fairly big proscenium stage and some modest technical equipment but it is mostly used for public functions and is available to theatre companies only occasionally.

The government has indicated interest in building a national theatre with three stages and advanced facilities. Work started in 1996 and one auditorium was scheduled to be completed in 1998 and the full project by 2002.

In Dhaka, plays are also presented from time to time in the auditoriums of the British Council, the Goethe Institute and in a municipal hall in the old part of the city. In the outlying districts, local companies mostly use halls of the National Academy of Fine and Performing Arts which has branches throughout the country.

There have been some successful attempts at creating outdoor spaces for performances, especially in rural areas by the Gram Theatre (Village Theatre) and some non-governmental development agencies.

The growth of street theatres (*patha natak*) began to change the notions of many theatre professionals regarding the use of traditional space.

Training

Departments of dramatics exist in three universities in Bangladesh, the University of Chittagong, Jahangirnagar University and University of Dhaka. Students at the BA and MA levels are given both theoretical and practical training with the emphasis, however, on the academic side.

There is, in addition to these, a part-time Theatre School in Dhaka, established in 1980 and run by the Society for Education in Theatre where a one-year certificate course in acting is offered. There too, the students receive both theoretical and practical training in theatre arts – acting, improvisation, set design, lighting, voice, movement and directing. Similar training is offered on a smaller scale by Natya Shikshangon. However, most artists learn on the job or through occasional workshops sponsored by the various companies and by foreign cultural centres.

Criticism, Scholarship and Publishing

Theatre criticism appears in the pages of daily newspapers and periodicals after openings. These are, in most cases, written by journalists with no formal training in theatre criticism. A quarterly, *Theatre*, edited by Ramendu Majumdar (b. 1941) and first published in 1972, offers more serious criticism of plays as well as scholarly articles on various aspects of theatre arts and information on international theatre events. It also publishes new plays written in Bengali and foreign plays that have been translated into Bengali.

Books on theatre, including historical studies and theoretical discussions, are published from time to time by the Bengali Academy, but mostly by private publishers outside academic institutions. The Bengali Academy has also published a large number of both original and translated plays in Bengali. One private publishing house, Muktadhara, has brought out a large number of dramatic works by Bangladesh playwrights.

Kabir Chowdhury

Further Reading

Ahmed, S.J. *Hajar Bachor: Bangladesher Natok O Natyakala* [A thousand years: Drama and theatre art of Bangladesh]. Dhaka: Bangladesh Shilpakala Academy, 1995. 88 pp.
——. 'Theatre for Development and Cultural Identity'. MA thesis, University of Warwick, 1989.
Al-Deen, Selim. *Madhyajuger Bangla Natya* [Bengali drama of the Middle Ages]. Dhaka: Bangla Academy, 1996. 528 pp.
Biswas, Sukumar. *Bangladesher Natyacharcha O Nataker Dhara* [Tradition of drama and theatre of Bangladesh]. Dhaka: Bangla Academy, 1988. 544 pp.
Chowdhury, Kabir. *Prasango Natok* [Concerning theatre]. Dhaka: Bangladesh Shilpakala Academy, 1981. 290 pp.
Hyder, A.R.Z. 'A Small House Beside a Highway: A Play for Television With an Essay; Development of Drama and Theatre in East Pakistan'. MFA Thesis, University of Hawaii, 1968.
Hyder, Zia. *Natya O Natok* [Dramatics and drama]. Dhaka: Bengali Academy, 1985. 112 pp.
Ibrahim, Neelima. *Bangla Natok: Utsa O Dhara* [Bengali drama: Evolution and development]. Dhaka: Nawroze Kitabistan, 1972. 524 pp.
Majumdar, Ramendu. *Bishoy Natok* [On theatre]. Dhaka: Muktadhara, 1987. 99 pp.
Mamud, Hayat. *Gerasim Stepanovitch Lebedeff.* Dhaka: Bengali Academy, 1985. 464 pp.
——. ed. *Bangladesher Natya Charcha* [Theatre of Bangladesh]. Dhaka: Muktadhara, 1986. 293 pp.
Mamun, Muntasir. *Unish Shatake Bangladesher Theatre* [Theatre of Bangladesh in the nineteenth century]. Dhaka: Suborno, 1986.
——. *Unish Shatake Dhakar Theatre.* [Theatre of Dhaka in the nineteenth century] Dhaka: Bangladesh Shilpakala Academy, 1979. 139 pp.
Rahman, Ataur. *Natya Prabondho Bichitra* [Articles on theatre]. Dhaka: Bangla Academy, 1995. 108 pp.

BHUTAN

(Overview)

A landlocked country located in the East Himalayan mountains of central Asia, Bhutan is bounded to the north by the Tibetan region of China, and to the south, east and west by India. The country, which spans an area of roughly 47,000 square kilometres (18,100 square miles), had an estimated 1997 population of some 1.7 million people. Of these, 50 per cent are Bhote, who are believed to be the earliest inhabitants of the region. Ngalops compose about 20 per cent of the population and are of Tibetan origin while Nepalese account for 25 per cent of the population. The official language of the country is Dzongkha, a Tibetan dialogue spoken mainly by the Bhote people. Many of the educated Bhutanese are additionally fluent in Hindi and English. Bhutan is the only country in the world where the Lamaistic form of Mahayana Buddhism (Buddhism's Tantric form) is the official religion.

Bhutan has been closely linked to Tibet since about the seventh century AD; independence from Tibet dates from 1630 when a dissenting Tibetan lama made himself the first *dharma raja* (spiritual leader) of Bhutan. A subsequent *dharma raja* appointed a *deb raja* (temporal ruler) to administer the country. However, real power was ultimately wielded by provincial governors. Formal British interest, which became Indian interest after India gained its independence in 1947, began in 1774 when a treaty was agreed upon with the British East India Company. In 1865 the British agreed to support Bhutan financially and in 1910 the country agreed to be guided in foreign affairs by the British government in India.

Sir Ugyen Wangchuk, the most powerful of the provincial governors, assumed control of the government in 1907 and was elected the first hereditary *maharaja* of Bhutan. By the 1950s, the country had achieved political stability and a degree of economic prosperity. A desire to open the country to the outside world along with aid from Britain permitted the establishment of the first western-style schools and the sending of students to India for advanced training. In 1971, Bhutan joined the United Nations and, in 1985, appointed a permanent representative. In 1997, the king, who remains closely allied with India, was Jigme Singye Wangchuk, who ascended the throne in 1972, the fourth in the hereditary, familial line to lead the country.

Bhutan, or Druk Yul in the Dzougkha language (Land of the Thunder Dragon), was off limits to foreigners for centuries and continues to restrict the number of visitors to the country every year. It was only in 1974 that the government opened its borders to tourists. But from 1988, foreigners were formally disallowed to visit most of Bhutan's temples, fortresses or monasteries to prevent 'commercialization of the religion' and to protect the 'sanctity of its ceremonies'. Most Bhutanese citizens still wear traditional national dress and zealously protect and preserve their culture, traditions and way of life from western values and concepts. The capital, Thimphu, is the centre of Bhutanese culture and includes a radio station and newspaper.

Throughout the year, with the exception of the period during which summer monsoons are prevalent, people in each major town celebrate *tsechus* (masked dance festivals). These events draw thousands of participants, some of whom walk for days in order to attend. The festivals are joyous expressions of Buddhist culture, combining fine clothes and beautiful jewels. The underlying purpose of the festival is almost always spiritual as the dances are often morality plays wherein good inevitably triumphs over evil or they depict historical events, particularly those surrounding the life of the king's patron saint, Padmasambava.

The ground upon which festivals are held must always be ritually purified and consecrated by lamas. The dancers themselves, whether monks or laymen, always perform in a trance-like state, the dancers attempting to transform themselves into the deities they represent. A limited number of foreigners are allowed to observe the festivals but they must travel in groups and are confined to itineraries set by the government. Lamas also perform important subsidiary services, for example, treating illness and performing in the masked dances.

Paro Tshechu, the year's largest celebration, takes place in the spring at the Paro monastery and is the country's greatest tourist attraction. Even so, the government has been reducing the number of tourists allowed to view it since 1983.

Tantric rituals constitute another major factor during performances. For Bhutanese, the many festivals offer a special opportunity to become immersed in the meaning of their religion and to gain religious credit. They are also occasions for seeing people, social exchange, and even for flaunting success. People bring out their finest clothes and their most beautiful jewels. Men and women joke and flirt. An atmosphere of carnival – with slightly ribald humour – prevails. Jesters, wearing burlesque masks, often approach the watchers with provocative jokes and never tire of performing pranks or raising wild laughter with their witticisms.

Dance is at the centre of these festivals and is used didactically to illustrate ancient stories and legends of Buddhist mythology and history. Such dances, performed mostly by men who display grace and rhythmic strength, are the most cherished folk art of Bhutan. Some dances are specifically for women and most of them are dignified circle dances with the women marking time with small steps. It is the women, too, who sing the old songs of the mountain people, handed down from ancient times. Such songs,

Monks' Orchestra of Mongar Dzong with drums and trumpets strike up the rhythm for the masked dancers.
Photo: Ursula and Augusto Gansser.

88

like the dances, reflect a strong Tibetan influence. The instruments, which accompany both songs and dances, usually include *dungchen* (long trumpets), *gyaling* (oboes), *nga* (double-sided drums held in a frame and beaten with a curved drumstick), *rolmo* (cymbals with vertical movements) or *silnyen* (cymbals with horizontal movement), trumpets made from a femur, and conch shells. Other instruments used less regularly include the *damaru*, a small, double-faced, hand-held drum beaten with hard pallets attached by strings and *drilbu* (small bells). Such orchestration gives rhythm to the dances and ceremonies and punctuates the singing or recitation of texts.

If the northern part of the country is deeply influenced by Tibet, the southern part of the country is more culturally influenced by Nepal. These multiple influences are clearly reflected in both dance and music. In the south, dancers usually accompany themselves by singing, with musical instruments used only on official occasions. A flute, drums and more recently a harmonium and guitar make up the orchestra for southern Bhutan. In the north, the orchestra usually consists of a *lim* (flute), a *dranyen* (seven-stringed lute), *piwang* (a two-stringed violin played with a bow) and (more rarely) a trapezoidal, tabletop zither played with a wooden mallet.

Dances from the southern part of Bhutan have a more lively rhythm; in the rest of the country, a much slower rhythm is used which speeds up as the dance progresses. Though many of the songs have a religious base, there also exist mystical songs composed by saints, as well as prayers and biographies of saints sung by monks. These songs, associated with daily life, are generally in the vernacular and are much freer, even allowing for a certain amount of improvisation. For the *chams* (religious dances), dancers wear spectacular costumes made of yellow silk or rich brocade, often decorated with ornaments of carved bone. For certain dances they wear masks which may represent animals, fearsome deities, skulls, manifestation of Guru Rimpoche (a seventh-century reincarnation of Buddha) or simply human beings. The masks are so heavy that dancers protect themselves from injury by binding their heads with strips of cloth to support the masks, also enabling them to see through the mouth opening.

The dances can be grouped into three broad categories: didactic works or pieces with morals, such as *Pholey Moley* (*The Dance of the Princes and Princesses*) and the *Dance of the Judgment*

During the *Dance of the Big Drums* all evil is expelled by the sound of drums and trampled into the earth by 'thunderbolt' steps.
Photo: Ursula and Augusto Gansser.

of the Dead; dances that purify and protect from demonic spirits, like the *Dance of the Stags*, the *Dance of Fearsome Gods* and the *Dance of the Black Hats*; and dances that proclaim the victory of Buddhism and the glory of Guru Rinchope which include the *Dance of the Heroes* and the *Dance of Eight Manifestations of Guru Rimchope*. All the dances in the last category are performed with drums.

Pholey Moley is one of the Bhutanese public's best loved dances. Somewhat licentious, it is performed in two versions. In the first, the love of King Norzang for his favourite wife, Yidrogma, provokes the jealousy of the king's other wives. When the king goes off to war, the other women force Yidrogma to flee for her life. When the king returns from battle, he learns of the conspiracy and his anger and his love are in conflict. In the end, he convinces Yidrogma to come back and live with him.

In the second and more popular version of the story, two princes go off to war, leaving their wives with their servants. Without the princes, the princesses and the maidservants start living more ostentatiously than they should. When the princes return, they learn of this tasteless behaviour and, as punishment, cut off the noses of their wives. The servant too cuts off his wife's nose. But soon the princes feel guilty and call for a doctor to sew back the noses. Although the doctor gladly sews back the noses of the beautiful princesses, he is far less enthusiastic about sewing on that of the maidservant. In the end, the doctor relents and everyone is reconciled.

Another dance, *Shawa Shachhi* (*Dance of the Stag and the Hunting Dogs*) depicts the conversion to Buddhism of the hunter Gonpo Dorje. More dramatic than other dances, it is very long and usually performed in two parts, each of which lasts a whole day.

The preparation of such community dances is done under the guidance of lamas, who are trained for this purpose. Monasteries arrange for the learning of music and the recitation of mantras, which, according to Tantric beliefs, must be recited in a particular way to the accompaniment of specific instruments. As a prologue and between the dances, a *Hero Dance* takes place. The dancers wear long, dark blue, widely pleated robes, girthed with sword belts. Their heads are crowned by the Rings of Knighthood. Some wear helmets and wield buckled shields covered with rhinoceros skin.

All dances take place in the courtyards of monasteries or in front of temples before *tankas* (painted backdrops). Most *tankas* are huge scrolls made of silk and appliqué work. Created by monks, *tankas* are stitched together with golden thread.

European-style written/spoken theatre does not exist. Even television has yet to enter into Bhutan. Only radio exists, mostly for passing on information.

Returning therefore to dance and music, it cannot be overemphasized that it is anonymous, it is religious and, as a result, it has no aesthetic function by itself. A Bhutanese does not get involved in an 'artwork' but rather in a religious work, which is considered a pious act and which will earn merit. The criterion is faith. This attitude explains to some extent why Bhutan is not interested in exposing its citizens to modern trends, or even to the idea of modernity. Even the classical Indian theatre, which is widely known and practised in many forms all over south Asia, has failed to cross the borders of Bhutan.

Ravi Chaturvedi, WECT staff

(*The writers would like to acknowledge their intellectual debt in the preparation of this article to a number of earlier scholars in the field, especially to François Pommaret, C. Olschak and Pradyuman P. Karan.*)

Further Reading

Bestway To Bhutan. www.bestway.com/bhutan.html

Etiquette for Tsechu Festivals in Bhutan. www.lightlink.com/cpost/festival.html

Festivals of Bhutan. www.gorp.com/abvclds/festival.htm

Karan, Pradyuman P. *Bhutan: A Physical and Cultural Geography*. Lexington, KY: University of Kentucky Press, 1967.

Miller, Robert and Beatrice Miller. 'Bhutanese New Year's Celebrations'. *American Anthropologist*, no.158 (February 1956).

Olschak, C. *Bhutan: Land of Hidden Treasures*. New Delhi/Bombay/Calcutta: Oxford and IBN Publishing Company, 1971.

Paro Tsechu Programme. Translated and arranged by Tashi Wangmo. Thimphu: Department of Tourism, Royal Government of Bhutan, 1983. 26 pp.

Pommaret, François. *Introduction to Bhutan*. Hong Kong: Odyssey, 1991.

Rahul, Ram. *Royal Bhutan*. New Delhi, 1983.

The Royal Dancers and Musicians from the Kingdom of Bhutan [motion picture]. New York: Asia Society and S.I. New House School of Public Communications, 1979.

BRUNEI DARUSSALAM

Brunei Darussalam is a sultanate located on the northwestern coast of the island of Borneo. Covering an area of 5,800 square kilometres (2,200 square miles), the country also includes thirty-three islands. Brunei's only immediate neighbour is the eastern Malaysian state of Sarawak, which divides the country into two parts. The capital is Bandar Seri Begawan.

About 64 per cent of the Bruneian population of some 300,000 people are ethnic Malays. Of the remaining population, about 20 per cent are Chinese and 16 per cent minorities such as Dayaks, Ibans and Belaits. The official language is Malay; English and Chinese are also spoken. Islam is the state religion. The country has tremendous oil wealth and the Sultan of Brunei – the twenty-ninth in his line – is one of the wealthiest individuals in the world.

The recorded history of Brunei spans about 600 years but prior historical references to the area have been found in Chinese and Hindu documents of the sixth and seventh centuries AD referring to Brunei as 'Polo', 'Puni' and 'Poli'. Brunei rose to prominence in the fifteenth and sixteenth centuries when the country extended its power throughout the whole of Borneo and into areas of the Philippines.

Brunei's golden age centred on two rulers, Sultan Bolkiah and Sultan Hassan. Under their rule, the royal court developed a splendour and ritual on a par with anywhere in the world and the territorial and religious influence of the country reached its peak. First visited by Europeans in 1521, trade developed quickly. The Spanish captured the capital in 1580 but did not remain very long. In 1645 a Spanish expedition failed to end Malay piracy in the region and by the end of the eighteenth century, the country became noted as a haven for pirates. In 1849, the British, seeking to protect commerce between Singapore and northwest Borneo, began assaults against the pirate fleets and within five years was able to destroy them. During this period, the then Sultan of Brunei, Omar Ali Saifuddin II, had granted Sarawak to the British army officer James Brooke as a reward for helping him put down a civil war. Brooke assumed the title rajah and gradually extended his territory at the sultan's expense. Brunei's power and territory went into a marked decline at this time and the country was reduced to almost its present size. In 1888, it became a British protectorate. In 1906, the administration of the sultanate was placed in the hands of a British resident, although the sultan remained in nominal authority. In 1959, Sultan Omar Ali Saifuddin III declared the first written constitution. However, Britain remained responsible for its defence and foreign affairs.

Invited to join the Federation of Malaysia in 1963, Brunei chose to remain a British dependency. In 1979, the British government signed a new treaty with Sultan Muda Hassanal Bolkiah and five years later Brunei Darussalam became an independent, constitutional sultanate.

There are four forms of traditional performance in Brunei – dance, song, poetry and storytelling. Early dances were connected to mystical powers and were believed capable of curing illness and protecting the community from evil. This is seen in such dance styles as *anding, alai, bubu, alai mambang* and *alai sekap*. Other dances are specifically seen during the harvest such as the *temaruk*. Performed by older women who move in a circle, the dance is lightened by the sounds of traditional instruments such as the *gulingtangan* and the *sape*. Performed for the entire village, the *temaruk* gives thanks for the new harvest and prepares the community for the next harvesting season. Originally from the native Ibans, this dance has been modified for current Muslim sensibilities.

Folk songs tend towards the narrative and usually deal with legendary figures or tell local history. *Adai-adai* tells of the traditions of a fishing village. Traditional poetry in its turn takes many styles. In *diangdangan*, the performer plays a musical instrument called a *donbak* while reciting the poem. The most famous *diangdangan* is called *Bujang Si Gandan*. A variation is the *badundang*, performed by various sized groups. Still another form, *pantun*, is usually performed the night before a wedding. The *pantun* gives advice to the bride and groom while the *trituran* form (direct storytelling) requires that practitioners know how to act, sing and dance.

A written but music-based theatre began to emerge in Brunei after 1922. It was in that year that a troupe of traditional artists was sent to Singapore as part of the entourage of Sultan Muhammad Jamalul Alam II. Participating in the Malaya and Borneo Cultural Festival in honour of the visit of the Prince of Wales, these artists attracted attention for their own art and for the first time came into contact with western-style arts. It was the Indonesian and Malaysian musical theatre style known as *bangsawan* that began to become popular after the Seri Indera Zanzibar Bangsawan Group performed in Brunei in the early 1930s. This was followed by other visits from *bangsawan* groups through the mid-1940s. Among the groups that performed in Brunei during this period were Bangsawan Si Bakir from Libya, Seri Noran Bangsawan Group from Singapore, Taman Setia Bangsawan Group led by Mamat Mashar and other professional *bangsawan* groups from Rembang (Java) led by Kapitan Ali.

Just after World War II, a new form of musical theatre emerged in the country – *wayang bangsawan*, a musical theatre utilizing puppets. Many of its plots were based on Malay legends or love stories that almost always ended happily. A number of comic performances also were part of the repertoire. Among the most popular of these were *Abu Nawas*, *Musang Berjangut*, *Sang Karcil* and *Mat Jenin*.

Wayang bangsawan had episodic and didactic plots and incorporated comic, farcical, melodramatic or even serious elements. Most were unscripted and all had non-realistic settings.

Sandiwara, another traditional Indonesian and Malaysian form, also attained popularity. Performed in a proscenium style, it was presented before audiences in small venues. Teachers and students were among the first to support *sandiwara*; the performers used this form to focus theatrical art more on social issues than had been seen to this time. Many stories utilized historical characters. Pioneers in this form included Sabtu Muhammad, Hussin Yusof, Nordin Abdul Latif and Mohammad Noor Othman. Among well-known productions were *Hang Tuah*, *Hang Jebvat*, *Megat Terawis*, *Laksamana Bentan*, *Sultan Mahmud Mangkat Dijulang*, *Jong Batu*, *Kota Batu*, *Marhum Tumbang Di Rumput*, *Bendahara Saleam* and *Mahlota Berdarah*.

Some of these works focused on issues of morality, separated families, contracted marriages and conflicts between generations. In this way, the social conditions of contemporary Bruneian society were examined for the first time. *Bulean Sulah Iban Mengandung* was one of the most popular *sandiwara* scripts in the 1960s. Written by Haji Ahmad Hussein, it was adapted from the novel by Alias Jarun. Many of the productions were staged at SOAS College.

In 1962, Sasterawani Brunei (Brunei Writers' Association) staged two *sandiwara* – *Marhum Tumbang Di Rumput* and *Sultan Mahmud Manghat Dijulang*, both by Haj Ahmad Husswin and Ghaffer Jumat – reflecting a growing realism in the form. But after political rebellion that year, theatre performances declined drastically and performances ceased entirely in Brunei until the end of the 1960s because of the State of Emergency laws.

Several theatrical writer-directors returned to the form during the early 1970s, all educated in Cairo – Shukrin Zain, M.S. Yahya, H.O. Badaruddin and Adi Rumi. Basing their short scripts on Islamic concepts, they helped launch a new period of theatre in Brunei. Most of their early plays were *drama sebabak* (one-acts) and they quickly became popular (partly because they were not very demanding in terms of production costs). Needing only a simple stage, *drama sebabak* carried messages about social issues and encouraged awareness of Islamic thought. These works were often played as part of poetry recitals.

The formation of Television Brunei in July 1975 attracted the general public to this new art and many theatre practitioners turned away from live theatre. Early scripts followed the *drama sebabak* style. Shukrin Zain, Hamid

Ahmad and Wahab Mohamad later adapted *sandiwara* for the medium in such shows as *Membangun, Tunggul Batu Merah* and *Kembali Ke Pangluman Ibunda*. All these shows emphasized nation, country and religion from a Bruneian/Muslim/Malay perspective.

In 1982 the government's Language and Literature Bureau began organizing scriptwriting competitions in conjunction with Independence Day and New Year celebrations. As a result, several noted writers began to look more seriously at approaching more wide-ranging topics. Among these writers were Pg Haji bin Pg Haji Mohammed Tahir, Masri Ji Akip, Magon Ghafar and Narsiah. Many of the winning plays were later broadcast on television.

A year later the first National Stage Drama Competition was held with nearly a thousand performers divided into some twenty groups participating. The ten best scripts were published in Brunei's first drama anthology, *Warisan Sebuah Wasiat*. One of the first important modern groups, Rusila was founded in 1982 and staged a number of established plays as well as one original play of note – *Biduk Lalu Kiambag Bertaut* (1984) by Haj Abdul Rahman Yusof. This play focused on the historical development of the country. Rusila participated in all the subsequent national competitions and showed many different dramatic styles. Judges and audiences, however, seemed to prefer the old *bangsawan, sandiwar* and *drama sebabak*.

In the 1990s, there were three groups regularly performing in Brunei – Rusila, Kumpulan Putera Semi (KPS, Young Artists' Group), founded in 1980 and Kastea, founded in 1984. Kastea, the most adventurous of the groups, has staged absurdist plays and even plays for children.

In 1990, Rusila – with government sponsorship – also began doing theatre in rural communities and developing a theatre for social action. The group has staged a show about drug abuse (*Dadah*) and another about relations between local communities and the police. Kastea has performed abroad on several occasions, including once in 1990 at a festival in Kuala Lumpur.

In terms of performance style and design, when *wayang bangsawan* was first performed, it utilized a proscenium style, with curtains, backdrops and costumes. During intermissions, a singer with an orchestra played in front of the stage. For *sandiwara* productions, no backdrops were used, nor were there intermissions. Sets were more realistic – living rooms, bus stops or forests. *Sandiwara* also used everyday conversation. In *drama sebabak* no curtains were used;

either realistic sets or an empty stage were the background in order to emphasize the poetic.

During the 1990 theatre competition, several groups improvised around established texts. In the KPS production, directed by Zefri Ariff, the use of shadow plays and improvisation made particulary interesting statements about the modern and the traditional in Brunei. Rusila's production, however, utilized *bangsawan* techniques including some improvised song and dance. By the mid-1990s, the government was encouraging a blend of Malay culture and Islamic thought.

No established western-style theatre building exists in Brunei and there is no national theatre organization. The government has generally not engaged in theatre subsidies and admissions are not charged for shows. Brunei theatre is at best a growing, but still largely non-professional, activity.

Zefri Ariff

Further Reading

A. Ahmad Hussin. 'Penulisan Drama dan Kemajuannya'. *Kertaskerja Seminar Sastera anjuran Asterawani*. Bandar Seri Begawan Brunei, 1964.

Abdullah Hussain. 'Literature in Brunei Darussalam'. *Malay Literature* 1 no. 1 (July 1988).

Al-Marhum Bengiran Shahbandar Pengiran Md Salleh Ibnu Pengiran Syarmayuda. *Syair Rakis* Pusat Sejarah Brunei, 1983.

A. Rahman Yusof. *Kiambang Bertaut* [Play anthology]. Dewan Bahasa dan Bustaka Brunei, 1991.

Budaya Bangsa. Dewan Bahasa dan Pustaka Brunei, 1989.

Dato Paduka Haji Mahmud bin Haji Bakyr. 'Sumbangan Pencipta Kreatif (Termasuk Sasterawan) Terhadap Tamadun dan Pembangunan Ummah'. *Pertemuan Pengarang Brunei Darussalam-Kalimantan-Indonesia, Sabah, Sarawak, Labuan* (8–12 October 1992).

Haji Abdul Rahman Mohammed Yusof. *Drama Kemerdekaan: Warisan Sebuah Wasiat*. Jawatankuasa Decil Pementasan Drama dan Hiburan Hari Kemerdekaan, 1983.

——. 'A Perkembangan Teater di Brunei'. *Beriga* (April–June 1984): 57–62.

——. 'Aspek Sosial dan Budaya Sebagai Rujukan Kepada Penulisan Skenario di Brunei'. *Bahana* 19 (November 1984): 34–7.

Haji Ahmad Mohammed Arshad. 'Penulisan Drama dan Kemajuannya di Brunei'. *Kertaskerja*

Seminar Sastera anjuran Asterawani. Bandar Seri Begawan Brunei 1964.

Haji Magon Hajo Ghafar, ed. *Sasterawani Bangsa: Antologi Drama* [Writer's union plays: A drama anthology]. Dewan Bahasa dan Pustaka Brunei, 1993.

Haji Mohammed Hj Serudin. 'Penulisan dan Perkembangan Drama Pentas di Brunei'. *Ikhtisar Bahasa dan Sastera*, 1983.

Haji Mohammed Yussop bin Bakar. *Adat Perkahwinan Orang Melayu Brunei di Muim Saba.* Dewan Bahasa dan Pustaka Brunei, 1989.

Ikhtisar Bahasa dan Sastera. Dewan Bahasa dan Pustaka Brunei, 1983.

Intisari Debudayaan Brunei. 3rd edn. Dewan Bahasa dan Pustaka Brunei, 1986.

Kamus Bahasa Melayu Brunei. Dewan Bahasa dan Pustaka Brunei, 1991.

Mas Osman. *Biografi Penulis Brunei.* Dewan Bahasa dan Pustaka Brunei, 1987.

Muhammad Abdul Latiff. *Suatu Pengenalan Sejarah Kesusasteraan Melayu Brunei.* 2nd edn. Dewan Bahasa dan Pustaka Brunei, 1985.

Patani. *Pengiran Indera Mahkota (Antologi Drama).* Dewan Bahasa dan Pustaka Brunei, 1991.

Pehin Orang Kaya Amar Diraja Dato Seri Utama and Jaji Awang Jamil Al-Sufri. *Liku-liku Perjuangan Pencapaian Kemberdekaan.* Dewan Bahasa dan Pustaka Brunei, 1992.

Pg Haji bin Pg Haji Mohammed Tahir and Mohammed Salleh bin Abdu Latif. *Drama Kanak-kanak: Tabung Pecah.* Dewan Bahasa dan Pustaka Brunei, 1990.

S. Miradi/Suhaimi bin Haji Ladis. 'Penglipur Lara Satu Penelitian Ringkas'. *Jurnal Pendidikan.* Jabatan Perkembangan Kurikulum, Kementerian Pendidikan Brunei, 1990.

Yahya M.S. *Asas-Asas Kritik Sastera.* Dewan Bahasa dan Pustaka Brunei, 1983.

Yura Halim. *Adat Mengulum Bahasa.* Dewan Bahasa dan Pustaka Brunei, 1993.

BURMA

(see **MYANMAR**)

CAMBODIA

(Overview)

Cambodia was once the most powerful kingdom in Southeast Asia. For most of the second half of the twentieth century, however, it has been one of Asia's most war-ravaged lands. Bordered by Laos, Vietnam and Thailand and covering an area of 181,000 square kilometres (69,900 square miles), Cambodia's population was estimated in 1995 at 10.5 million with 85–90 per cent of the population ethnically Khmer and the remainder Chinese, Vietnamese and Cham. The national capital is Phnom Penh.

From the first to the fifth centuries AD, Funan, a Hindu-influenced kingdom, ruled the territory. By the sixth century, the Khmer Empire had ascended and over the next 800 years extended its control over much of Southeast Asia. This empire became the most powerful in the region between the ninth and fourteenth centuries; Khmer culture and art became highly developed, especially its court forms. Major architectural monuments at Angkor, which lies in the northwest part of present-day Cambodia, were some of Southeast Asia's most spectacular attractions. They reflected the Hindu and Buddhist influences then pervasive in Cambodia.

Between the fourteenth and nineteenth centuries, the empire declined and Cambodia lost much of its territory in ensuing wars with Siam (Thailand) to the west and Vietnam to the east. Massive population and artistic losses resulted as well with court artists (many of them women from royal families) being taken as captives. From an estimated population of 10 million in the thirteenth century, the number of those living in Cambodian territory fell to 800,000 by the mid-nineteenth century. The French established a protectorate in the area in 1863, adding Cambodia to its Indo-Chinese colonies, which included Vietnam and Laos.

In 1945, Cambodia declared its independence from France when Japan ended French power in

Indo-China. But after World War II, the French again claimed Cambodia. During this period, with Norodom Sihanouk as king, Cambodia waged a campaign for independence, which finally came in 1953. Over the next fifteen years, Sihanouk struggled to maintain Cambodia's neutrality in the war between communist and anti-communist forces.

Despite these efforts, Cambodia was unable to avoid involvement in the Vietnam War with North Vietnamese and Viet Cong forces establishing bases in the country and with the United States bombing much of Cambodia's countryside. In 1970, Sihanouk was overthrown by General Lon Nol. The Kingdom of Cambodia became the Khmer Republic, which followed a clear anti-communist policy that threw the country into a five-year civil war. In 1975, communist forces – the Khmer Rouge – defeated the Lon Nol government and the country was renamed Democratic Kampuchea.

Under the dictatorship of Pol Pot, the country attempted a total reorganization of society. The use of money was abolished, as were schools (for the most part) and temples. Families were separated. Perceived enemies of the state – many of them traditional artists – were tortured and executed. In the process, as cities were emptied to provide agricultural labour and access to food and medicine was restricted, millions of Cambodians died. Virtually all artistic activity was forbidden and the country cut off contacts with most of the outside world.

After the Pol Pot regime was removed by force following an invasion by the Vietnamese Army (along with Cambodian forces who had escaped from the Khmer Rouge) in early 1979, Cambodia went through a new civil war but at the same time tried to re-establish its earlier forms and structures. Part of this restructuring included the welcoming back into society of artists who had survived the 'killing fields'. It was estimated at this point that 80–90 per cent of the country's artistic community had perished under the Khmer Rouge. During the 1980s, both in Phnom Penh and in the countryside, the country's traditional arts began to be re-created while also welcoming more modern art forms including European-style spoken drama.

In the 1980s, provincial cultural offices and the municipality of Phnom Penh supported troupes working in a variety of styles. Most strongly supported was the country's dance and music heritage, the root of all Cambodian theatre arts, with most of the funding coming from the Ministry of Information and Culture through the National Department of Arts. Among the institutions quickly re-established was the School of Fine Arts in Phnom Penh, reopened for the 1980–1 school year. The country's University of Fine Arts, first founded as the Royal University of Fine Arts in the 1960s and which had to close its doors when the Khmer Rouge took power, reopened in 1989.

Also during the 1980s, while the country was called the People's Republic of Kampuchea and then the State of Cambodia, the rebuilt performance troupes began to tour, first in smaller cities of Cambodia and later to Vietnam, the Soviet Union and as far away as eastern Europe. By the early 1990s Cambodian artists were participating widely in the world community of artists, in a *Ramayana* festival in India and in international festivals in Japan, Britain, Hong Kong and the United States, among other places. The 1990 tour across the United States was the first official cultural contact between the United States and Cambodia in close to twenty years.

Cambodia's royal family, who had been in exile since 1970, finally returned in 1991 as part of a United Nations-brokered peace plan to end the civil war. Elections were held in 1993 and the country once again became the Kingdom of Cambodia with King Norodom Sihanouk on its throne. Under royal patronage, the country's largest traditional dance and music ensemble, the Royal Dancers of Cambodia, began to perform both at home and abroad for state occasions as well as for an enthusiastic public.

The oldest of the traditional forms and the root of the work done by the Royal Dancers is the *lakhon kbach boran*, also called *lakhon luong* (literally ancient drama or royal drama). Performed by women of the court, this graceful and beautiful type of classical dance has been associated with the country's royalty for over a thousand years. Chou Ta-kuan, a Chinese traveller who visited Cambodia in the late thirteenth century, reported the importance of such dance to the court and temple celebrations. One festival, he wrote, was simply called 'to dance'. Describing a ritual procession in a temple, he noted 'the musical instruments render a clamourous noise that charms the spirit. Then all around is the dancing of men and women.'

Recognizable for its *kbach* (elegant gestures) and spectacular costumes and headdresses, the royal dance has come to embody both historical traditions and the essential values of Khmer culture. The dancer, for example, epitomizes

Classical (court) dance of Cambodia: 'Apsara' performed in the Royal Palace, Phnom Penh, 1992.
Photo: Toni Shapiro.

Khmer ideals of beauty, grace and continuity, not only between past and present but also between the realms of gods and humankind. Certain sacred performances are seen as a communication between kings and their deities and a bridge between the natural and supernatural worlds. In one ritual dance known as *buong suong*, dancers on behalf of the royalty would seek rain and other blessings for the land and the people. The dance itself was one offering among many that included incense, fruits, flowers and other foods.

Traditionally, dancers were trained from childhood in the royal palace. They ventured outside only rarely, and then just to attend the king. It was not until 1941 and the crowning of Norodom Sihanouk that dancers were finally allowed to live outside the palace and to marry. It was also at this time, under the guidance of Sihanouk's mother, Sisowath Kossamak Nearyroth, that men were invited to join the royal troupe for the first time, but only to add athleticism and energy to the role of the monkey king. Princess Norodom Buppha Devi, daughter of King Sihanouk, later toured the world as principal dancer of the royal troupe. This 1960s tour marked the first time that Cambodian dance was seen around the globe. Under royal patronage, the dancers also performed *buong suong* ceremonies in various sites around the country, striving to bring hope and prosperity to the populace and showing the newly liberated dancers off to the people.

While most classical dance-dramas are rooted in *Ramayana* (*Reamker* in Khmer) they also include episodes from the lives of the Buddha and historical legends. Pure dances – those that do not tell a story but are meant rather to evoke certain emotions or spiritual passions – are part of the repertoire as well. Dancers specialize in one style of role: the giant, the prince or male deity, the princess or female deity, or the monkey king. Cambodian dance-dramas are also unique in that they show representations that, although based on *Ramayana*, contain episodes that do not exist in the original. All these dances are accompanied by the *pin peat* ensemble, the same type of group that plays at Buddhist ceremonies. Primarily percussive, the ensemble is made up of *roneat aik* (a high-pitched bamboo xylophone), *roneat thung* (a low bamboo xylophone), *roneat daek* (metal xylophone), *kong vong touch* and *know vong thom* (small and large sets of tuned gongs), *sampho* (a double-sided barrel drum), *skor thom* (two large drums) and *sralai* (quadruple reed instrument akin to an oboe) and *chhing* (cymbals). A choir sings story texts while dancers express the plot through movement and gesture. Such music is intended to be both ritualistic and entertaining. The former gives it the power to please the spirits while the latter sets an atmosphere and tries to enliven the listener's mind. The music also signals certain set kinds of passages in the dramas – the entrance of a prince, for example, or the preparation for battle.

Dance movements and gestures also signal specific meanings. Sometimes these are communicated abstractly, other times in a more literal manner. A combination of posture, internal expression, sung text and music propels the storyline. Dance movements are performed both standing and kneeling. Most of the dances also include tableaux.

Costumes are made of sumptuous brocade, silk and velvet. Gold sequins are embroidered into intricate patterns that glitter in the light; elaborate crowns vary according to character. Props and accessories are used only to enhance the dance. They can include large set-pieces such as a painted backdrop of ancient temple walls, as well as bows, arrows, sabres, swords and clubs. All these costumes and accessories are considered sacred and are treated with great care and respect.

Another of the many forms of court dance is the *lakhon khol* (masked dance-drama), the repertoire of which consists solely of material from the *Reamker*. It includes substantial recitatives declaimed by skilled singers and is also accompanied by a *pin peat* ensemble. All performers are men in the masked forms though only those who play demons or monkeys actually wear masks. Performances traditionally take place during ritual occasions and can continue over many nights. The country's best known *lakhon khol* troupe is now located in Kandal Province.

Lakon bassac is not a court form but rather a popular form of musical drama, named after the area, now in southern Vietnam, where the people lived who first created this genre in the early twentieth century. Cambodian and Vietnamese elements fuse in this performance style that boasts martial-arts-style moves and

Nang sbek thom (large shadow-puppets) of Cambodia: a scene from the *Reamker* performed along the riverside in Phnom Penh, 1996.
Photo: Toni Shapiro.

operatic singing. Stories are taken from local and historical legends though new stories can be staged as well. *Lakhon bassac* was especially popular during the 1980s and early 1990s, with hundreds of troupes performing for audiences throughout Cambodia.

Still another form of traditional Cambodian theatrical art is shadow puppetry and three basic styles can be identified. *Nang sbek thom* (literally large leather-puppets) is a shadow play that uses figures of up to 1 metre high to stage episodes of the *Reamker*. Each puppet is manipulated by a dancer-puppet master using long wooden sticks both from behind the screen where the puppet casts a shadow and from in front of the screen where it can be seen by the audience as a silhouette. During the performance, any number of puppeteers can participate. The smallest of these puppets represent clowns, folksy characters and monkeys. Medium-sized puppets, with figures shown in profile and set within frames with no movable parts, represent single characters. The largest and most intricately designed cut-outs show two or more characters in a specific locale. The dancer-puppeteers portray the story while a narrator recites it and the *pin peat* orchestra plays specific melodies.

Nang sbek touch or *ayang* (in contrast to the above these are small leather-puppets) is performed in a covered booth mounted on stakes with a cloth screen covering the front. A torch or petroleum lamp is used to cast the shadows. Designs can be quite intricate and the repertoire consists of legends and local lore, with comic and satirical commentary interspersed throughout.

Sbek poua (coloured-puppets) seems to be another form but one found only in the courts. Indeed, such puppets were discovered only recently in the royal palace and research has just begun in this area. Artists believe the coloured-puppets were used as daytime entertainment at court.

Other forms of performance currently to be seen in Cambodia include *yike*, a kind of folk opera with satire that combines some classical dance movement and sung drama, and *ayay*, improvised repartee singing, dotted with witty satirical commentary.

Lakhon niyey (spoken drama) was introduced to Cambodia only in the 1950s by French expatriates. First seen in French and later in Khmer adaptations, the form developed a following first among educated people and then among people in the countryside. Cambodian comedies in a Molièresque style are now written by Hang Tun Hak. Most emphasize ways to cope with societal and moral dilemmas. Beyond these, spoken drama is very much a minority art form in Cambodia.

WECT staff

Further Reading

Brandon, James R., ed. *The Cambridge Guide to Asian Theatre*. Cambridge: Cambridge University Press, 1993.

Cravath, Paul. 'Earth in Flower: An Historical and Descriptive Study of the Classical Dance of Cambodia'. PhD dissertation, University of Hawaii, Honolulu, 1986. 684 pp.

Pich Tum Kravel. *Sbek Thom: Khmer Shadow Theatre*. Phnom Penh: Unesco; Ithaca, NY: Cornell University Southeast Asia Program, 1995.

Sam, Sam-Ang. 'The Pin Peat Ensemble: Its History, Music and Context'. PhD dissertation, Wesleyan University, Fort Worth, TX, 1988.

Sam, Sam-Ang and Chan Moly Sam. *Khmer Folk Dance*. Newington, CT: Khmer Studies Institute, 1987.

Shapiro, Toni. 'Dance and the Spirit of Cambodia'. PhD dissertation, Cornell University, Ithaca, NY, 1994.

——. 'The Dancer in Angkor'. *Asian Art and Culture* (winter 1995): 9–23.

CEYLON

(see **SRI LANKA**)

CHINA

The largest country in Asia and the most populous country in the world, the People's Republic of China in 1996 had a population estimated at 1.224 billion living on a land area of 9.6 million square kilometres (3.7 million square miles). China's major cities – its capital Beijing and the national financial centre Shanghai – are located along the eastern coast and are the most economically advanced as well as being the nation's two cultural centres. China has fifty-six different ethnic groups of which the Han is the largest. Other major ethnic groupings include the Tibetan peoples, Mongolians, Hui, Wei Fu Er and Zhuang. The official language across the country and the one most widely spoken is Putonghua (Mandarin).

China is divided into twenty-three provinces (including the Republic of China, formerly Taiwan), five minority autonomous regions (including Tibet) and four municipal councils under the direct rule of the central government. Hong Kong was returned to China in 1997 and Macau returns in 1999; both will be known as Special Executive Regions. The Chinese constitution provides for religious freedom and though most Chinese are not religious there are many practising Buddhists, Taoists, Christians and Muslims. Under the constitution the People's Congress wields the greatest power, with the Chinese Communist Party the ruling political structure.

With over 5,000 years of recorded history, China is also one of the world's oldest continuing civilizations. The first united empire dates to 221 BC under Qing Shi Wang, the beginning of a feudal period which lasted some 2,000 years. The feudal period ended in 1911 with a democratic revolution led by Sun Yat-Sen that overthrew the ruling Qing dynasty and established the first Chinese Republic. When Japan invaded in 1937, it occupied large areas of eastern and central China leading to what was called the Eight Year Battle of Resistance. When World War II ended in 1945, Japan's surrender included the return of Chinese lands and its departure from China. A three-year civil war followed which ended in the creation of the People's Republic of China and the installation of the Communist Party as its head under its Chairman Mao Zedong. Non-communist forces fled to the island of Taiwan.

Positive changes in many fields followed as Mao led the country both politically and culturally but significant economic change took longer. A radical attempt to change the country's development began in 1966 and lasted for a decade. Known as the Cultural Revolution, it disastrously affected the lives of the entire Chinese population, virtually stopped the economy and not only destroyed the careers of many artists but also threatened the survival of many traditional art forms. In the late 1970s the government, led by Deng Xiaoping, began a series of initiatives which attempted to atone for the horrific consequences of the Cultural Revolution. Deng advocated reform, promised a more open policy in all aspects of political and commercial life and began a new era of rapid social and economic development. During the 1980s and into the 1990s China's GDP annually grew by nearly 10 per cent, making the country one of the fastest growing economies in the world.

Chinese theatre traces its beginnings back some 3,000 years to folk songs and dances. As early as the Han dynasty in the third century BC, records show the appearance of people acting on a stage in short sketches that had plot, dialogue and theme. What is still not known is whether those sketches were written down. Clearly, however, some of these early performances evolved into court entertainments along with singing, dancing, acrobatics and wrestling while other entertainments were given at fairs for the common people.

In the Tang dynasty (seventh to ninth centuries) such theatrical performances were already quite widespread. The earliest extant theatrical writings date to the Southern Song dynasty (1127–1279). The latter half of the thirteenth century saw the establishment of the Yuan dynasty by Mongol rulers (Kublai Khan's dynasty) and it was during this period that Chinese theatre developed its splendour. Some scholars have referred to this as a golden age of Chinese drama. Most Yuan dynasty playwrights were already well-established poets who began writing for theatre only after having already mastered poetic techniques. Many of their dramatic works are still produced and continue to exercise influence on China's traditional theatre. Among the major Yuan dynasty plays still done

are *Snow in Midsummer* by Guan Hanqing, *The Chalk Circle* (which inspired Brecht's *Caucasian Chalk Circle*) and Wang Shifu's *West Chamber*. During the eighteenth century, these early theatre forms began to be seen in various regions of the country, each utilizing the folk art of the region as well as regional dialects. In 1790, various theatre troupes from Anhui Province were invited to perform their regional art in Beijing. Copied by Beijing artists, this is the formal beginning of the art that would become known as *jing xi* or *jing ju* or outside the country simply as Beijing Opera. Quickly developing into a sophisticated art form, Beijing Opera soon became the most important of all Chinese theatre styles. Indeed, the form now boasts some 300 different regional styles, all of which can seem similar to foreign audiences but which vary widely in approach.

Over the centuries, these traditional theatre forms – colourful and spectacular – have been enriched and expanded by an astonishing range of brilliant artists including the most famous of Chinese traditional actors, Mei Lan Fang (1894–1961), a *dan* actor (a male actor specializing in women's roles) whose work impressed both Brecht and Stanislavski. But in the late twentieth century, particularly with China's rapid economic development, a gap has begun to open between the changing contemporary society and the society for which traditional theatre was created. The beginning of these changes formally dates back to 1919 and the establishment in May of that year of what was called the New Cultural Movement. This movement argued for the acceptance of western culture and criticized all of the traditional art forms, the theatre with particular virulence.

An entire generation of intellectuals was influenced by this new ideology. Chen Du Xiou (1880–1942), Wu Shi (1891–1962), Liu Ban Nong (1891–1942) and Qian Xuan Tong (1887–1939), to name but a few, all published essays in the magazine *New Youth* criticizing the feudalistic ideology that was the basis for most traditional theatre. Attacked as well was its literary quality and its 'artistically naive' performances. This movement proposed to 'reform the old theatre' first by identifying its flaws. But its criticism was extreme and biased and the attacks had negative as well as positive effects. One positive effect was that a number of important traditional artists such as Mei Lan Fang, Zhou Xin Fang (1895–1975), Xun Hui Sheng (1900–68), Cheng Nian Qiou (1904–58) and Shang Xiao Yun (1900–76) did make attempts to change the art somewhat by embodying contemporary life and ideologies of the time. Actors began to wear more contemporary clothing and plays began to be written that disseminated more modern democratic thinking.

Plays with historical themes were adapted and began to make allusions to contemporary society and politics. New plays were written to reflect the growing patriotic spirit in the wake of foreign incursions. At the same time, performances in traditional theatres became more precise and refined. A new generation of actors emerged at this time attracted to such ferment and traditional theatre companies began to be invited to perform in Japan, in Europe and as far away as the United States. The four international tours made by Mei Lan Fang during a fourteen-year period in the 1920s attracted a great deal of public and critical acclaim. On the negative side, the art form suffered from instability, plays in the traditional style stopped being created, certain outdated styles became entrenched, most traditional theatre troupes were without support and artists working in the form had little security.

After the establishment of the People's Republic of China in 1949, traditional theatre was revived and held up as a treasure for the nation by the new government. Theatre companies were reassembled, this time with subsidies given directly by the central government or by local government. Schools were established in every province to train future artists in this field. Theatre artists suddenly had financial security and some were even elected to be representatives of the People's Congress and the Political Discussion Committee and were accorded special status.

An Improvement Committee was soon established to help traditional theatre develop further. Consisting of forty-two experts in the field, its principal aim was to supervise the development of the art, and a specialized academic institution was established – the Chinese Traditional Theatre Research Institute (now part of the China Arts Research Institute). Thanks to this support, traditional theatre grew in importance during the 1950s and 1960s. More theatre companies were set up, new talent emerged (particularly in Beijing Opera) and even some previously neglected styles of this sung theatre – Hunan Huagu Opera and Yunan Huadeng – became newly respected theatre forms. Even new styles of the old art were created. By 1959, there were 368 distinct styles as compared with just 100 a decade earlier, and some 3,000 theatre companies in existence as compared to 1,000.

Rediscovered and genuinely appreciated during this period, in the mid-1950s some 50,000 traditional plays were performed nationwide, 14,000 of which were put into script form. A large number of these were later published. Certain of the modern adaptations, it was agreed, were improvements on the originals. Among these was *Fifteen Strings of Coins* from the Kun Opera, which had been adapted from an earlier version by the Zhejiang Kun Su Theatre Company in 1956. The new version received plaudits from critics and public alike and remained in the company's repertoire for years after and was even filmed. The production

Chinese traditional performers.

Zhejiang Kun Su Opera Company's production of *Fifteen Strings of Coins*.

was so successful that it may well have saved this particular style (Kun) from extinction.

Other plays such as *Harmony Between the Emperor and the Prime Minister, Tale of the White Snake* (Beijing Opera), *Liang Shan Bo and Zhu Yin Dai* (Yue Opera), *Heavenly Marriage* (Huang Mei Opera), *Autumn River* and *Trace the Snowmarks* (Chuan Opera), *Qing Xiang Lian* (Ping Opera), *Hua Mu Lan* (Yu Opera), *Ge Ma* (Chu Opera) and *Liu Hai Cut the Wood* (Hunan Huagu Opera) are some of

the adaptations of the time which achieved wide recognition. There was a surge of new plays that used the tenets of traditional theatre. Some had plots taken from history such as *Man Jiang Hong* (Beijing Opera) and *Yu Qian* (Shao Opera); some took plots from traditional folk tales and legends such as *Female Warriors of the Yang Family* and *Bore Forest* (Beijing Opera), *Dream of Red Mansions* (Yue Opera), *Zhun Zhao Breaking Into Court* (Pu Xian Opera) and *Marriage Change Among Sisters* (Lu Opera). Others utilized contemporary material: *Luo Han Qing* (Hu Opera), *Liu Qiao Er* (Ping Opera), *Beating the Gong* (Hunan Huagu Opera), *Tale of the Red Lantern* and *A Girl With White Hair* (Beijing Opera).

Traditional theatre, because of its long history, has strict rules and is both complicated and stylized, all of which presents difficulties for modern audiences. By letting the skills evolve with the times, however, and by introducing new techniques, theatre artists made considerable strides in allowing these forms to continue to reach the widest possible audiences.

In the late 1950s and early 1960s, however, a more radical leftist philosophy began filtering down to the public. The beginning of the Cultural Revolution, its effect on traditional theatre was enormous. In 1963, a propaganda

Li Shen Theatre Company's production of *Zhun Zao Breaking Into Court* (Pu Xian Opera).

slogan was introduced which stated 'Write Exclusively About the Thirteen Years', meaning that theatre, along with all other art forms, should reflect the life of the nation only since 1949. It also suggested that the traditional repertoires of most groups and the many new historical plays that had begun to be written and which contained clear contemporary relevance should be staged.

By 1966 this and criticism had also become a way to eliminate political adversaries. It was in that year that Chairman Mao's wife, Jiang Qing, Kang Sheng and two others (the Gang of Four) organized a large-scale movement which challenged political criticism generally and, more specifically, some of the new historical plays. Thus was the Cultural Revolution started. Quickly spreading all over China, the political upheaval and the unstable social order that followed virtually destroyed China's traditional theatre. During the next decade, only eight 'model' productions (five of which were in traditional theatre form) were allowed to be performed and these eight were seen everywhere over and over again. All other plays were either banned or attacked. Most theatre companies as a result were disbanded and many theatre professionals were punished for their work. Some were forced into manual labour in the provinces. Some were physically punished. Others went to prison. The nation's arts were all but destroyed.

It was October 1976 when Jiang Qing and the other members of the Gang of Four fell from power and the Cultural Revolution came to an end. At the same time, Deng Xiaoping began to implement a series of reforms, an open-door policy in the arts, and theatre in all its forms was reborn. New companies, research institutes, theatre schools and arts journals – all stamped out by the Cultural Revolution – began to be seen once more. The older generation (those who had survived) returned to the stage to take their place alongside young professionals. New plays began to be written, this time with an even stronger focus on historical subject matter. Two major works from this time – *Scholar from Ba Shan* (Chuan Opera) and *Xu Jiou Jing's Promotion* (Beijing Opera) – reflected a new interpretation of recent history. The first is a tragedy and the second a comedy but both portray courageous and righteous officials in ancient times who despise power and fight for the rights of the common people. The two plays were very typical of traditional theatre in the 1980s.

At the end of the 1980s the Shanghai Beijing Opera company produced a play called *Cao Chao and Yang Xiou* which was based on the complicated relationship between a statesman during the time of the warring states, and a scholar who served as one of his aides. The plot allowed for a penetrating exploration of the humanity of politics (or lack thereof) and reflected the new freedom of expression and experimentation after the Cultural Revolution. The *People's Daily* called it 'the pinnacle of traditional theatre since the end of the Cultural revolution' (25 December 1988).

In the 1990s productions like *Si Ma Xiang Ru* (Kun Opera) and *Jing Long and Fu You* (Hui Opera) continued to experiment with combining traditional theatre and modern ideology, and they were warmly welcomed by their audiences. During this period, good quality contemporary plays with roots firmly in traditional theatre were also performed, many of the best pieces coming from regional groups. These plays both reflected the new reforms, its effects on the agrarian community, and the changing ideas and lifestyles. These productions also reflected real life and for doing so they were enthusiastically applauded.

In the waves of economic and social reform during the 1990s and the open-door policy, a distinctly western influence started to appear even in traditional theatre, an influence that attracted even more attention. Certain playwrights started to tailor obviously western artistic approaches to traditional formats. One clear example was *Pan Jing Lian* by Wei Ming Run (b. 1941, a Chuan Opera playwright). Wei himself called the play an 'absurd Chuan Opera'. He utilized elements of Brecht's *verfremdungseffekt* bringing in a number of well-known characters from famous literary works – both western and Chinese – to comment on his heroine's character. Wei's approach was a major change from the norms of traditional theatre.

Western theatre classics were also being adapted to the Chinese stage utilizing traditional theatre forms with great success. Successful examples included *Macbeth* which became *The Tale of Bloody Hand* (Kun Opera), *Medea* (Hebei Bangzi) and *Good Person of Sichuan* (Chuan Opera). These three productions later went to theatre festivals in, respectively, Edinburgh, Greece and Germany. All three encouraged greater dialogue between east and west.

As for the history of western-style spoken theatre in China, it is much briefer when compared to the archives of material on traditional theatre. Existing in China for less than a century, it was initiated by the Spring Willow Drama Society, an organization of foreign students, including several Chinese, living in Japan. Returning to China with western-style scripts, their first performance was *Lady of the Camelias* in 1907. Popular among intellectuals and more experimental artists, in the 1920s and 1930s, a relatively large number of Chinese dramatists left the country for varying periods of time to study spoken theatre in Europe, the United States and Japan. On their return, they set up companies specializing in the new art form.

Among these companies were the Nan Guo Drama Society with Tian Han (1898–1968) as its artistic director, the Theatre Association with Hong Shen (1894–1955) as its leader, and the Shanghai Art and Drama Society headed by Xia Yan (1900–95). Yu Shang Yuan (1897–1970), Xiong Fo Xi (1900–65) and Ou Yang Yu Qian (1889–1962) were among the famous artists to set up spoken drama schools in Beijing, Guangzhou and other places in China; many outstanding playwrights and productions were seen at this time. Even more theatre groups emerged in the 1930s. One of the more interesting ones was the National Defense Theatre, formed by a group of patriotic writers as part of the anti-Japanese resistance war. The group specialized in resistance plays and staged many western classics in which resistance was a theme, plays which sought to inspire their audiences to fight the Japanese aggressors.

During the three years after World War II – and due largely to the civil war in China between the communist and Guomingdang forces – spoken theatre was at a rather low ebb. New plays, however, were being produced and the Metropolitan School of Experimental Theatre was established. The founding of the People's Republic of China in 1949 was also a huge impetus for the affirmation of spoken drama. State-subsidized theatre companies were established all across the country. Along with them, two university-level educational institutes were set up in Beijing and Shanghai to train professionals for the spoken theatre – Central Theatre Academy and Shanghai Theatre Academy – both supervised by the central government.

The First National Theatre Festival took place in 1956. Through the 1950s and 1960s a number of plays which would ultimately become modern classics in China were premièred: Lao She's (1899–1966) *Long Xu Creek* and *Tea House*, both based on daily life in

Guan Han Qing at the Beijing People's Art Theatre.

Beijing; Cao Yu's (1910–97) historical play *Courage and the Sword;* Guo Mo Ruo's (1892–1978) *Cai Wen Ji* and Tian Han's *Guan Han Qing.* The performing arts also adopted a more realistic style – Beijing People's Art Academy and Shanghai People's Art Theatre particularly – the latter introducing an adaptation of Brecht's theories and theatre practice by Huang Zhou Lin (1906–94). Both theatres contributed significantly to the overall development of spoken drama in China.

Spoken theatre was also introduced to minority nationalities in the country at this time. Shanghai Theatre Academy was asked to train the first generation of Tibetan theatre professionals while the Central Academy trained people for Wei Wu Er theatre. Graduates of both these projects became founding members of new theatres in Tibet and Xinjiang.

The leftist movement that preceded the Cultural Revolution also had an impact on the development of spoken theatre. Productions reflective of the conflicts of daily life were challenged and cultural exchanges wound up being limited to the USSR and eastern Europe. Also influential in the early 1960s was the 'Only Write About Thirteen Years' campaign which had a large limiting force on dramatists. The decade of the Cultural Revolution virtually devastated spoken drama as well; almost every theatre group in the country was forced to cease artistic activity.

Spoken theatre surged once more after the downfall of the Gang of Four and the political reforms of the late 1970s and early 1980s. Artistry and creativity were allowed to flourish once again in the theatre academies and performing institutions. A number of realistic plays were quickly produced which reflected the profound social changes at this time. *Where*

Tibetan theatre performance.

That Is Silent, Power and Justice and *Primrose* all caused palpable responses in audiences. The older generation were encouraged to let loose their imaginations and again many fine historical plays were written including *Wang Zhao Jun* by Cao Yu and *Making a Place in the World* by Wu Zhu Guang (b. 1917).

Cultural exchanges with other countries also opened. *Tea House*, a Beijing People's Art Academy production, toured France, Switzerland and Germany in 1980. This event marked the beginning of an influx of exchanges with the rest of the world and a number of major companies brought productions to China.

Tea House by Lao She at the Beijing People's Art Theatre.

Arthur Miller came to China at this time to direct *Death of a Salesman* at Beijing People's Art Theatre in 1983. In 1986, the first Shakespeare Festival in China was jointly held in Beijing and Shanghai with more than twenty productions staged. In 1989 the noted American director Richard Schechner staged a Chinese play by William Sun in Shanghai.

From the mid-1980s, spoken drama in China faced the same difficulties as elsewhere in the world largely due to the impact of television and film. Fewer productions were staged and theatre artists were forced to experiment with both form and content. Taking their cues from various schools of modern theatre from the west while at the same time utilizing elements of traditional Chinese theatre, the creative perspective began to change once more and a number of experiments began to be seen.

In the thirty years or so prior to 1980, naturalism had dominated the spoken theatre stage in China but by 1982, when Beijing People's Art Theatre produced *Absolute Signal*, things began to change. This play examined the very nature of theatre moving freely through time and space in order to present the psychology of its characters. The production attracted a great deal of attention in the theatre community. Following in this style, Gao Xin Jiang (b. 1940) wrote *Bus Stop*,

an absurdist play that leaned heavily on imagery and stream of consciousness. Huang Zhou Lin directed *Dream of China* at Shanghai People's Art Theatre, which combined western symbolist style with the tenets of traditional Chinese theatre. Beijing People's Art Theatre produced *The Nirvana of Gou Er Ye* which relied on psychological illusion. Central Academy of Drama's *Account of Events in Sang Shu Ping* blended a Brechtian storytelling technique with poetic symbolism. The success of these productions started a resurgence of spoken drama in China.

In the 1990s, China's theatre faced enormous hurdles, none larger than the move towards market economy. During this decade, the overall number of companies declined and a large number of theatre professionals left to work in television. In response, many groups turned towards alternative theatre techniques and alternative venues. Two Festivals of Experimental Theatre were held in 1989 and 1993. *Those Who Are Left Behind and Waiting* (Shanghai People's Art Theatre) compressed the distance between performer and audience both physically and psychologically and has since become part of the theatre's repertoire. *Si Fan* (Central Experimental Theatre Company) and *Dream of the Butterfly* (Shanghai Theatre Academy) were

Shanghai People's Art Theatre production of *Dream of China*.

both performed at the Japanese Experimental Theatre Festival and won acclaim from international audiences.

To meet the demands of the new market economy, the theatre community in China is now paying a great deal of attention to western-style musicals. But with limited financial resources, there has yet to be a successful production of one. Nevertheless, training for actors and directors in this specific art has begun in both Beijing and Shanghai.

Structure of the National Theatre Community

The entire Chinese theatre community – in 1996 this meant some 2,696 performing arts groups and over 200,000 theatre artists – is in large part supervised and subsidized by the central government. About 90 per cent of the theatre community is involved in traditional theatre.

Beijing boasts the largest number of groups because all the national ('China') companies are based there as well as companies sponsored by military groups and national businesses. Again, all are under the direct supervision of the Ministry of Culture. Next in number is Shanghai. Provincial capitals are home to various companies and most provinces have groups outside their capital cities.

Since the introduction of a market economy in the late 1980s, all companies are much more self-sufficient than they were and have to earn larger amounts of their income at the box office. Subsidies dropped quickly in the 1990s from almost 90 per cent of income to around 30 per cent. To make up the difference, theatres have also been encouraged to find sponsorships from business. As part of this change-over, a number of private theatre companies have also been established.

The half-dozen or so national troupes that exist in Beijing all have between 200 and 300 employees. These include the China Youth Art Theatre, Central Experimental Theatre, China Beijing Opera Company, Children's Art Theatre Company, Central Opera and Ballet Theatre, and China Opera and Dance Company. Each of these groups have seasons in Beijing and then tour widely. Provincial companies tend to be slightly smaller with between 100 and 200 people on their payrolls. Other companies tend to have fewer than 100 employees.

The small group of privately owned and operated theatres have modest numbers of actors and staff. Operated in large measure by retired actors or administrators, these theatres do many shows using actors on a contractual or show-by-show basis. On occasion stars from the state companies have appeared in private theatre productions. One of the most active and most typical of these new private theatres is Shanghai Modern Theatre Society, which has produced several popular productions. One of its most successful productions was an adaptation of Albert Camus's *The Plague* (1996) in which a single actor played all ten roles. The company received a grant from the French Embassy to help with production costs.

Another dynamic element in the Chinese theatre community is the work of amateur groups, who often do things that are far more difficult for professionals to attempt. Existing all over China, some of these groups have been in operation for decades and their influence has been important. Such groups at Beijing Normal University and Fudan University in Shanghai have produced not only Chinese plays but also plays by foreign writers and have even done plays in other languages. During the First Shakespeare Festival in China, university groups staged productions of *Much Ado About Nothing* and *Timon of Athens*. Workers' groups and local governments also have their own companies which stage shows at the various people's cultural centres across the country. The government awards prizes for the best amateur productions and performances.

There is no specific rehearsal period for professional groups. Some work for weeks, others work for months to prepare their productions. New plays usually rehearse at least six to eight weeks. Because of a lack of budgets for publicity and also by tradition, most shows are sold by theatre salespeople to businesses, companies, unions and schools. Up to the early 1980s, there was a government cap on ticket prices all across China keeping them to about five times the price of a film. Since market economy was introduced, however, ticket prices have risen and now vary widely. In major cities, ballet tickets might sell for between 200 and 300 RMB (between US$25 and US$40), about ten times

A one table, two chair set in traditional theatre.

the price of a film ticket. Tickets for traditional theatre productions are usually kept to between 60 and 80 RMB (about US$10).

The All China Theatre Workers' Society was established in 1949. In 1953 it changed its name to the Chinese Theatre Society. A voluntary association, it represents the interests of all theatre professionals and holds a national congress every five years for its members. With headquarters in Beijing, the society has branches in all provinces and autonomous regions except Taiwan.

The country's highest theatre prize is the annual Wenhua Award given by the Ministry of Culture. In Shanghai, the White Magnolia Prize is given annually by the Shanghai Culture and Arts Union.

The China Arts Festival (formerly known as the China Theatre Festival) takes place every two years, the country's most important theatrical event. The festival is hosted in a different provincial capital on a rotating basis. Annual festivals also take place in the various provincial capitals.

A Chinese Centre of the International Theatre Institute and national centres for other specialty areas such as design and technology (affiliated to the International Organization of Scenographers, Theatre Architects and Technicians, OISTAT) also exist but have tended to be mostly limited to Beijing theatre people.

Artistic Profile

Every province and autonomous region in China has a Beijing Opera Company. A traditional form popular all across the country, Beijing Opera dates back to the late eighteenth century. It was in 1790 that four southern Hui Theatre troupes – Shanqing, Sixi, Chuntai and Chunsi – visited Beijing. Collaborating with the Han Singing School (originally from Hubei Province), the groups mixed together story forms and folk music with music and performance methods from the elegant Kun (the oldest opera style in the country dating back to ' : mid-sixteenth century) and Qin Operas. The result was a form that came to be known as Beijing Opera. Based to a very great degree on historical tales, Beijing Opera now has a

The Drunken Courtesan, with Mei Lan Fang as the courtesan.

repertory of some 1,300 plays of which about 300 are regularly done. The best known are *The Drunken Courtesan, The Forked Road, Picking Up the Jade Bracelet* and *Fisherman.*

A stylized form, Beijing Opera has four main roles, Man, Woman, Painted Faces and the Clown, each with its own subdivisions. Patterns, colours and costumes reveal age, rank and identity. Each painted face role denotes a different set of physical and psychological qualities. A very physical form, Beijing Opera requires training in its unique speech and voice patterns, acting and stunt fighting. Sets are always simple – two chairs and a table – so changes in time or space must be shown through gesture and dialogue with emotions mainly shown through song and dance. Though the audiences for Beijing Opera are still relatively large, audiences in the 1980s and 1990s have tended to be middle aged or older, suggesting that the form is no longer connecting to young people, especially young girls. Conscious efforts are being made to change this situation in the 1990s through tours and school productions.

Given the mixed roots of Beijing Opera, it is not surprising to see hundreds of subtly different regional forms of the art. Each is distinct to the trained eye and ear in terms of music, dialect and/or folk style. The most important of these forms are the Yue Opera, which originated in Zhejiang Province and is particularly popular in Shanghai; the Huangmei Opera from Anhui; the Chuan Opera from Sichuan; the Ping Opera from Hebei; the Banzi Opera from the north of China; the Yu Opera from Hunan; and the Yue Opera from Guangdong (Canton), Guangxi, Hong Kong, Macau and Southeast Asia. The latter is different from the Shanghai Yue Opera and, although it has the same name,

it is written with a different character in Mandarin.

The Shanghai-style Yue Opera originated at the beginning of the twentieth century. Beginning its life as a folk form consisting simply of song and storytelling, it gradually developed into a more serious theatrical art form and in the 1920s it was introduced in Shanghai. Initially all the Yue performers were male but during the 1930s only women were allowed to perform it and beauty in costume and song became the main attractions. Yue Opera borrows Kun Opera techniques and by the 1950s Yue Opera companies could be found in some twenty provinces. Less popular in the north in recent decades, Yue has never lost its following in the southeast and coastal regions of China.

Huangmei and Ping Opera have similar histories and have developed a popularity in both the north and south due to their beautiful lyrics and scores. The other styles mentioned have histories of over 150 years. Yu (also known as Hunan Bangzi) and Hebei Bangzi both utilize a relatively uninhibited music and are heavily reliant on regional folk art. The second and more southern form of Yue borrows widely from spoken drama, western opera and film and is the most popular opera form with overseas Chinese.

As Beijing Opera is performed country-wide, spoken drama is limited to large and middle-sized cities; it has a large following among intellectuals and students. Chinese plays – both contemporary and historical – are regularly performed alongside the western classics. Shakespeare, Molière, Ibsen and Chekhov, to name just a few, are all well known in China. Plays ranging from experimental productions of Goethe's *Faust* to theatre school productions of George Ryga's Canadian classic *The Ecstasy of Rita Joe* have been performed in major cities to keenly interested audiences. However, productions of contemporary western plays have been the exception rather than the rule and examples of alternative production styles are quite rare.

Stanislavski was a major influence in acting technique starting from the early 1950s with Brecht's acting methods appearing later in the decade. Huang Zhou Ling, former artistic director of the Shanghai People's Art Theatre, was the most prominent promoter of the Stanislavski method. Since the late 1980s, there has been an influx of writings on new styles and methods from overseas.

Dramaturgically speaking, short plays have become quite popular – fifteen to twenty minutes in length. Plays reflecting issues from contemporary life are also popular and have helped to develop a wider audience for spoken theatre.

Western-style opera (also known as High Opera) exists alongside the many Beijing Opera groups. The Central Opera Company was established in 1953 and has performed classics ranging from *Madame Butterfly* to *The Marriage of Figaro*. Shanghai Opera and Dance Company has collaborated with opera professionals from the United States, Russia and Germany and has had particular success with *Romeo and Juliet*, *Die Fledermaus* and *Carmen*. Operas of note by Chinese composers include *A Girl With White Hair* written in the 1940s, *Red Squad in Hong Hu* and *Jiang Jie*.

A blended form of Chinese folk music and western opera developed through the New Culture Movement of 1919. Known as New Opera, it is a combination of folk song and dialogue and enjoys a wider audience than western opera in China.

Like opera, there are two types of dance theatre in China. The first is ballet, brought to China by expatriates in the 1920s. It was not until 1954 that a formal ballet school was established by the government leading to the founding of the Professional Ballet School in 1959. Other schools have since opened in Beijing, Shanghai and Guangzhou. The repertoires of companies from these schools include western classics such as *Swan Lake*, *Giselle* and *Don Quixote* along with Chinese ballets such as *A Girl With White Hair*, *Red Female Battalion* and *Liang Shan Bo and Zhu Yin Dai*.

A second dance form of note is that performed by the National Dance Theatre – a combination of Chinese traditional dance and folk dance. In 1956, the Dance Troupe of the Chinese Opera and Dance Company premièred a major production, *Treasure Lotus Lamp*, based on a tale from ancient mythology. Other representative company works include *Little Knife Society*, *Ribbon Road and Flower Rain*, *Princess Wen Chen* and *Phoenix Singing in Qi Shan*. The National Dance Theatre has incorporated certain elements of modern dance in order to reinvigorate expressive interpretation. There are similar types of ballet and national companies now in existence in virtually all the provinces and autonomous regions of China.

The western-style musical is still a very new art form in China. In 1987, the Central Opera Company, with the support of the Eugene O'Neill Theater Center in the United States, pro-

duced two American musicals – *The Music Man* and *The Fantasticks*. In 1996, the Shanghai Stage Arts and Crafts Centre produced its own version of *Phantom of the Opera*, calling it *Floating Ghosts at Midnight*. Also in 1996, the Central Academy of Drama produced a Japanese musical, *A Cat That Wants to Be a Man*. The show had a run of thirty-two performances.

Companies

The best known theatre company in China is the People's Art Theatre in Beijing. Established in 1950, it stages four or five new plays per year while working in repertory. The company has the country's top actors, directors and designers and has generally produced realistic plays – both Chinese and foreign – since its inception. Among its most important productions have been *Tea House* (played in several foreign countries), *Camel Man Xiang Zi*, *Lao She*, *Chai Wen Ji*, *Guo Mo Lo*, *Guang Han Qing* and *Thunderstorm*. Since the 1980s, the company has been successful at bringing together the best elements of Chinese and western production styles.

Outside of Beijing, the most important company is the People's Art Theatre in Shanghai which, along with Beijing's Central Experimental Theatre and Beijing's China Youth Art Theatre, was among the first Chinese groups to try Brechtian narrative approaches in their work.

In the area of traditional theatre, the leading Beijing Opera troupes in the capital are China Beijing Opera Company and Beijing Opera Company. Shanghai Beijing Opera Company is probably the foremost traditional group outside of the capital. All of these groups were founded in the mid-1950s and have been home to some of the greatest theatrical talents in the country. The Beijing companies tend to be more conservative in their approaches than the Shanghai group, which tends to focus more on experiment and reform within the strict structures of the art.

Shanghai Kun Opera Company and Northern Kun Opera Company in Beijing are next in importance in the traditional theatre community. Shanghai Kun Opera Company was founded in 1978 and its artists are highly talented and versatile in many areas of the art. Its best known productions include *The Peony Pavilion*, *The Palace of Longevity*, *Romance Over the Wall*, *Coming Down the Mountain*,

Chuan Opera performer.

Dramaturgy

In traditional theatre, scripts must leave great room for actors to be creative. Props are kept to a minimum and this too has an effect on the type of script that has emerged in these forms which utilize spectacular costumes, acrobatics, makeup, song and dance as their primary elements. Even the development of storylines is much more basic and therefore far more flexible than western dramaturgy. The structure of most traditional plays is simple and straightforward usually centring on a single character and a single event. It was the playwright Li Yu (1610–80) who first advocated the dramaturgical theory still followed at the present time: 'establish the main character and storyline; keep the subplots to a minimum.'

But there are plays still being written in these traditional styles and modern playwrights have added in new elements which purists attack and modernists applaud. The most distinguished of the early modern dramatists in both traditional and spoken theatre was Tian Han, who studied in Japan for six years. The author, adapter or translator of more than 120 plays, Tian's work includes 32 traditional theatre scripts. The chairperson of the China Dramatist's Society from 1949 to 1968, he was also director of the Traditional Theatre Reform Bureau of the Ministry of Culture and director of the Arts Administration Bureau. An expert in traditional theatre, he initiated the inclusion of more modern styles in the art. His best loved plays were *Tale of White Smoke* (1952), *Romance in the West Room* (1958) and *Xie Yao Huan* (1961).

Fan Jun Hong (1916–89) was another of the important early modern writers of Beijing Opera. The head of the literary section of China Beijing Opera Company, he adapted the Chinese classic, *Tales of Liang Shan*, into an opera called *Hunting for Tiger*; the play was a huge success, winning a Ministry of Culture prize. He later co-authored a series of other plays that would become among the favourites of modern Beijing Operas: *The Woman Warrior of the Yang Family*, *Man Jiang Hong*, *A Girl With White Hair* and *Eliminating Three Evils*.

Wei Ming Run, a Chuan Opera playwright, is known for his imaginative and innovative stylings of the form. Prolific during the 1980s, he wrote a new play every year, each one in a different style and with a different feel. *Yi Dan Da* (1980) is a tragedy about a Chuan Opera star while *Scholar From Ba Shan* (1983)

Stopping the Horse and *Fifteen Strings of Money*. Northern Kun Company was formed in 1957 and its repertoire includes major productions such as *Escape at Night, Marrying Off the Sister, Going Abroad, Qin Wen* and *Hong Xia* (the last two being modern operas).

Shanghai Yue Opera Company, Anhui Huangmei Opera Company of Sichuan, Chuan Opera Company, Hunan Yu Opera Company, Qin Opera Company in Xian and Guongdong (Canton) Yue Opera Company are other important regional groups. All were founded in the 1950s drawing the leading theatre professionals of their time and all reshaped their particular forms of the art. Shanghai Yue Company has leaned towards the romantic in its best known works such as *Liang Shan Bo and Zhu Yin Dai, Dream of the Red Mansions, Jade Ornament, Chasing Fish* and *Testing Her Love*. All these productions have been made into films and all have toured widely.

Most of the Huangmei productions have their roots in folk song and folk dance but have been blended with historical and contemporary references. Among their successful productions have been *Heavenly Marriage, The Lantern Festival* and *Gathering Grass for Livestock*.

describes the psychological journey of an honest writer who experiences the destruction of illusion. *Pan Jing Lian* (1985) uses a more modernist western approach to investigate the life of a woman in ancient China while his *Sunset on Qi Shan* debates greatness and weakness in politicians utilizing a historical framework.

Guo Qi Hong (b. 1940) is a writer known for his work with a range of opera companies – China Ping Opera Company, Beijing Opera Company in Beijing and Northern Kun Opera Company – and the Beijing People's Art Theatre. Like Wei, he has been averaging a play a year since the late 1970s. Many of his works deal with the lives of well-known writers and scholars of earlier periods, reflecting them through a range of rich and complex emotions. Among his major works are *Si Man Qian* (1978), about a writer in the Han dynasty; *Chen Zao Cai* (1981) and *Queen of Ping Opera* (1983), about different stars of Ping Opera; *Tales of Nan Tang* (1986), about the life of poet Li Yi; and *Si Ma Xiang Ru* (1995), about one of the great writers of the Han dynasty.

In the field of spoken drama, several generations of writers have emerged each with their characteristic styles. In the 1920s and 1930s the most important were Cao Yu, Guo Mo Ruo, Lao She and the aforementioned Tian Han.

Cao Yu, born Wan Jia Bao, is most often spoken of as the father of spoken drama in China. His work not only is realistic in a middle Ibsenian style but also has elements of O'Neill-style expressionism. Melodramatic, his plays attracted real attention to western realistic genres throughout his life. Among his most produced plays are classics such as *Thunderstorm* (1933), *Sunrise* (1935), *The Wilderness* (1937), *People of Beijing* (1941) and *Family* (1942). Among his later works of note are *Clear Sky* (1954), *On Courage and Sword* (1961) and *Wang Zhao Jun*, the last two based on historical characters. Late in his career, Cao Yu was chair of the Chinese Association of Writers and Artists, chair of the China Theatre Society, artistic director of the Beijing People's Art Theatre and honorary president of the Central Academy of Drama. His death in 1997 was mourned by many.

Guo Mo Run wrote several dozen plays from the 1920s on. His early works were all epic in style. By the 1940s he had turned to historical subject matter in such works as *Flower of Kerria* (1941), *Qu Yuan* (1942) and *Symbol of the Tiger* (1942), all lauding patriotism and stirring up anti-Japanese feelings. One of his most

popular and personal plays is *Cai Wen Ji*, a play about a powerful woman who was poet, politician and eventually the only Empress of China. Produced by Beijing People's Art Theatre with enormous success, the play mirrored Guo's own career.

Lao She wrote more than twenty plays between 1949 and 1966, his best known being *Tea House* (1957). *Tea House*, like his 1950 drama *Long Xu Creek*, is a story that powerfully reflects the changing lives of Beijingers. A three-act drama covering a period of fifty years, *Tea House* introduces a dozen characters each coming from different walks of life. A powerful realistic play – among the best produced by a Chinese dramatist in this style – the play was hailed for its vivid imagery.

One of the early masters of the spoken form too was Tian Han, author of more than seventy spoken dramas from the 1920s to the 1940s. Among his early works, the best known are *The Night To Catch a Tiger* (1924), *Death of a Star* (1927) and *The Broken Clock* (1932). His *Journey of Beauties* (1947) tells of three women during the War of Resistance. Containing twenty-one scenes, the play structurally utilizes both theatre and cinematic techniques. Perhaps his most famous later work is *Guang Han Qing* (1958), a play about a Yuan dynasty playwright. His 1960 drama *Princess Wen Chen* is about historical events involving the friendship between the Chinese Han people and Tibetans.

A second generation of playwrights emerged in the 1970s and 1980s, among them Sha Ye Xing, Zong Fu Xian, Gao Xing Jian and Yang Li Ming. All born around World War II, each revealed skills in working with essentially realistic material in very different styles. Sha Ye Xing (b. 1939), for example, is the author of a number of satirical works such as *Mayor Chen Yi* (1980) about a charismatic mayor of Shanghai and was based on historical fact. His controversial 1988 play *Confucius, Jesus Christ and John Lennon* is an absurdist comedy dealing with philosophy, heaven and the modern world. A graduate of Shanghai Theatre Academy, Sha later became artistic director of the Shanghai People's Art Theatre. His *Confucius, Jesus Christ and John Lennon* was produced in English in Toronto, Canada, in the early 1990s.

One of the more controversial plays of this period was *In the Depths of Silence* (1978) written by Zong Fu Xian (b. 1947). A four-act drama, the play was about a rally organized in Tiananmen Square against the Gang of Four. The play reflected the feelings of many Chinese and was produced widely. Written in a realistic style, the play encouraged many others to work this way.

Two younger writers of note are Gao Xing Jian and Yang Li Ming (b. 1947). Gao is the country's best known experimentalist. An absurdist for a time and then a symbolist, his most important plays are written in a stream-of-consciousness style: *Absolute Signal* (1982), *Bus Stop* (1983) and *Savage* (1984). Yang, from Heilongjiang province, is a graduate of the Central Academy of Drama and his works reveal regional tones (particularly of northeastern China). His best known work is *Black Stone* (1987).

Directing and Acting

Until the 1950s, actors rather than directors were the controlling forces in traditional theatre. Since that period directors have been accorded professional status by government agencies and began to be assigned to traditional theatre companies.

Perhaps the most distinguished director to emerge from this changeover in status was Ah Jia (1907–95). Trained in calligraphy as well as Beijing Opera, his work as artistic director of the China Beijing Opera Company in the 1950s and 1960s was known for its lyrical qualities as well as for his concern with historical and theoretical aspects of the art. Among his most important and most debated productions were *A Girl With White Hair* (1958) and *Tale of the Red Lantern* (1964), the latter a portrayal of contemporary Beijing life.

The greatest traditional actor of the modern period is generally agreed to be Mei Lan Fang, whose life was devoted to reforming and developing Beijing Opera as an art form. It was Mei who broke down stylistic barriers and modernized the handling of female roles (the young female, the traditional female and even the woman warrior, allowing a breath of fresh air into their interpretation. Inventive musically, his

Tale of the Red Lantern, a modern Beijing Opera produced during the Cultural Revolution.

gentle and elegant singing style, later known as the Mei Style, attracted huge audiences. Mei also helped to introduce Beijing Opera to other countries with his numerous foreign tours.

In the area of spoken theatre, two of the country's most influential directors have been Jiao Ju Yin (1905–75), the long-time director of Beijing People's Art Theatre, and Huang Zhou Ling, an artistic director of Shanghai People's Art Theatre. Jiao, who had a doctorate from the University of Paris, joined Beijing People's Art Theatre in the early 1950s, introducing Stanislavski's ideas to the Chinese theatre while retaining important aspects of traditional performance (particularly in areas of pace and emotional release). His best known production was *Tea House*. Huang studied in England and was also influenced by French director Jacques Copeau's ideas on populist theatre. Huang was the first director in China to introduce Brechtian performance concepts. One of his major productions in this style was Brecht's *Mother Courage*.

Theatre for Young Audiences
Puppet Theatre

Chinese theatre for young audiences dates to the 1920s when a group of artists headed by the musician Li Jing Huei (1892–1967) produced a number of productions specifically for children. It was not until 1937, however, that the first formal children's theatre company was estab-

Qin Bei Chun's *The White Horse Fei Fei,* produced by the Shanghai Children's Art Theatre of the China Welfare Institute.

lished in Shanghai. Sixty years later, twenty-two such companies were in operation all across the country.

The two largest and oldest groups are Beijing's China Children's Art Theatre Company (founded in 1961) and Shanghai's Children's Art Theatre of the China Welfare Institute (founded by Soong Qing Ling in 1958). In the years since the revolution and the establishment of the People's Republic of China, children's theatre has been widely supported. In the mid-1990s, in fact, policies were formulated by the Ministry of Culture, which even saw regular tours by children's companies to rural farming communities.

Among the most important names in the history of Chinese children's theatre are Ren De Yao (b. 1918), Ou Yang Yi Bin and Qing Bei Chun (b. 1945).

The origins of Chinese puppets are not clear. The might have been imported from India or they might have developed independently from funeral statuary or even from *fang xiang-shi* (ritual dance). Whatever their origins they were known as early as the Han dynasty, reached their greatest popularity during the Song dynasty (960–1279) and were still widely popular as late as the Tang dynasty. Throughout all these periods, puppet-like figures were widely used in funeral celebrations as links between the world of the living and the world of the dead, for religious purposes (supplicatory performances) and for magic (purification of houses from demons).

Such puppets came in a wide variety of forms: shadow-figures, rod-puppets, string-puppets, water-puppets, *yaokui* ('powder' puppets) and 'on the body' puppets, the latter actually being children moving like puppets while being carried on the shoulders of adults.

From the time of the Ming dynasty, puppets began to appear in local opera productions and took up the repertory and styles on their own following the approaches of actors and design. During the Cultural Revolution, classical themes were replaced by contemporary themes with clear political underpinnings. At the same time, a professional puppet theatre for children began to develop.

From the late 1970s, the classical puppet styles have been revived. In all its forms, puppetry still replicates local live opera styles using the same stories, forms and even the same types of musical instruments – dulcimers, lutes and gongs that control the rhythm of the movements. Costuming, sculpting of puppet heads

China Puppet Theatre Company's production of *The Eight Gods Crossing the Sea*, puppet theatre in string form.

and makeup all accord with the live opera traditions including the use of only four principal groups of characters: men, women, 'painted faces' (traitors and other aggressive individuals) and clowns. These four groups are further divided into fourteen subgroupings connected to sex, age, profession and social position.

Shadow theatre grew from the art of the storyteller, who would utilize illustrated scrolls which over the centuries began to 'move'. The shadow figures themselves consisted of silhouettes cut from parchment made from donkey, sheep or buffalo hide. Transparent and colourful, they are projected on to a white screen with light from an olive oil lamp (now with electricity) and manipulated with three rods held perpendicular to the screen. According to the tradition of Chinese painting, each figure may include several perspectives – profile, full face or three-quarter view. Most figures are presented only in profile but clowns, painted faces and demons present three-quarter views while holy figures and gods are shown full face. Each figure has nearly a dozen separate parts linked at the joints. About 20 to 30 cm high (8 to 12 inches), the figures, taken from the classical repertory, tend to be quite stylized while more contempo-

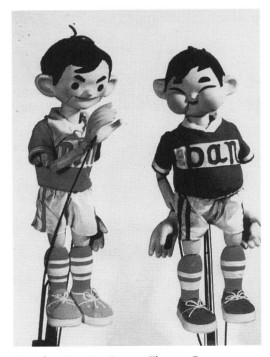

Saturday, Wu Han Puppet Theatre Company.

rary figures have been extremely influenced by cartoon designs.

The screen itself for shadow theatre normally measures about 120 cm (about 4 feet) wide by 75 cm (2.5 feet) high and is made of heavy paper or thick gauze facing the audience on a slightly inclined angle. The principal figures are operated by a single manipulator who is helped in some instances by an assistant. The performance is accompanied by a singer-narrator and a small group of musicians. Such shadow theatre performances are known throughout most of China's provinces with the most ancient traditions coming from Shenxi. Connected to this form is what can be called the Glass Covered Relief shadow theatre found in the Chaozhou region of Fujian province. In fact, it is a puppet theatre with three-dimensional puppets manipulated by three rods from behind – as shadow figures – but separated from the audience not by a screen but by a pane of glass that replaces the traditional screen. Performances are again taken from the local opera tradition.

In other provinces, one finds rod-puppets of different sizes. Sometimes they are as small as glove-puppets; sometimes they are as large as 90 cm (3 feet) tall with large heads and mechanized faces (movable eyes, lips and, in the case of clowns, even movable tongues and noses). They are again made up following local opera traditions.

String-marionettes were known as far back as the Tang dynasty. With sophisticated construction, the wooden bodies allow many unusual movements (including fingers). They are manipulated by as few as five strings or by as many as twenty-five strings. One of the best of these marionette theatres is in Xuanzhou, a theatre that follows the repertoire, design and musical styles of Beijing Opera.

Glove-puppets seem to have been first seen during the Ming dynasty. Used at that time by solo performers who carried small stages in the form of little houses over their heads, the performers' bodies were covered with tunics tied at the ankles. Glove-puppet troupes of two or three players developed particularly in Fujian and Taiwan. Their stages have beautifully painted prosceniums following local tradition. About 30–35 cm (a foot or so) high, they are still composed of wooden, sculpted heads with beautifully painted faces and costumes in the form of colourfully ornamented square sacks with small wooden hands and feet. Hands often include holes into which weapons or other props can be placed. The puppets are made by special craft workers and artists who also make religious figurines. The most famous of the craftsmen was Jiang Jiazou (1871–1954). Chinese glove puppeteers are masters of manipulation. Even with such small puppets they are still able to present all the dances and symbolic gestures of the classic operas.

The repertoire of classic puppet theatre consists of popular episodes from historical novels such as *The Story of Three Kingdoms*, episodes from historical romances such as *Travel Towards the West* and *The Legend of the White Serpent* as well as love and adventure stories. For religious and magic performance, the most popular were *Xuantan Tames the Tiger* (a play used regularly for purifying houses from demons) and *Eight Immortals Come To Wish Long Life* (a supplicatory play).

The social status and influence of puppet theatre artists has greatly improved since the establishment of the People's Republic with puppet theatre festivals now regularly organized by the cultural departments of various levels of government. A China Puppet and Shadow Play Association was established in 1980 to help promote these arts. Also from the 1980s on, puppet shows have been regularly broadcast for children on state television.

A system of apprenticeship exists for the art (in the main, sons apprenticed to their fathers) though systematic schooling did begin in the 1970s when a three-year course was begun at the Shanghai Theatre Academy. Other schools have now followed this example.

Design
Theatre Space and Architecture

Design is not a major factor in traditional Chinese theatre with actors relied upon as the primary focus and means of telling stories and expressing emotions. Specific gestures and movements have been created to describe the actions (rowing a boat, climbing stairs, etc.).

Simple props are added to help create different environments. In general, the stage itself is kept empty save for a table and two chairs.

One of the design elements most used, however, is the painted face to identify different characters and states of emotion. Other elements used include wigs and stylized beards. No attempt is made at verisimilitude. Costuming is also used to reveal character or for beauty (for example, long flowing sleeves and huge peacock feathers).

Since the 1950s, stage design has gradually become an increasingly important element in spoken drama, particularly in plays which require realistic or naturalistic elements. From the 1970s onward, design has become less and less realistic even in plays that apparently call for realism.

The country's two most respected designers in this area of spoken theatre have been Zhang Zheng Yu (1904–76) and Su Shi Feng (b. 1920), both of whom helped increase awareness across all areas of Chinese theatre for the role of the designer and the visual impact design could have in the overall theatrical creation. Design has now become a widely taught skill and large design departments can be found at the Central Academy in Beijing and at Shanghai Theatre Academy.

China's first theatre spaces date to the Han dynasty (third century BC) – raised wooden stages with curtains covered over by a tent-like structure. Audiences watched the performances from outside the tent. In the Song and Yuan dynasties the tent was expanded to protect the audience as well and a raised area was created to give audiences seating.

Near the end of the nineteenth century, European-style proscenium theatres began to be introduced and in the decades since this has become the norm in theatre architecture although in the 1960s some companies preferred to work in thrust configurations. The country's largest indoor theatre space is the Grand National Theatre in Beijing. Built in 1983, it covers an area of some 11,300 square metres and seats 1,750. Similar large spaces also exist in Hong Kong.

In the 1990s, some groups were seeking alternative venues to play in. Even the prestigious Shanghai People's Art Theatre in 1996 staged a production of Shakespeare's *Much Ado About Nothing* in Huang Pu Park.

Brecht's *Galileo* at the Central Experimental Theatre.

Goodbye, Paris at the Shanghai Youth Theatre Company.

Training
Criticism, Scholarship and Publishing

Traditional theatre artists are trained from childhood often in family-run companies. After the People's Republic came into being, patronage moved to the state and training became part of the responsibility of state troupes. The first separate institution for traditional training was established in 1950 – the Chinese Music Drama Institute, which now has five departments including Beijing Opera, music, directing, dramaturgy and stagecraft.

Formal training for spoken drama goes back to 1907 when the private Tong Tian School was established in Shanghai. In 1950, the new People's Republic established two national training academies – Central Academy of Drama in Beijing and Shanghai Theatre Academy (the latter originally being an autonomous wing of Shanghai Experimental Theatre School). Both academies are under the direct supervision of the Ministry of Culture.

The Central Academy (home of the state theatre archives) and Shanghai Theatre Academy both teach directing, acting, design and dramatic literature. Though students learn about traditional forms, the actual training and skills taught relate to spoken theatre. Students

Auditorium of the Experimental Theatre at the Shanghai Theatre Academy.

The first theatre museum in China.

live on the campus with their faculty for the entire four years of their training. Shanghai Academy also has a department of television arts. All courses at both institutions are part of university-level degree programmes (BA, MA or PhDs). Both academies also accept foreign students who must pass a language training course. Both academies also have research institutes which publish magazines and journals such as *Theatre* and *Theatre Arts*.

Graduates of the academies were for many years guaranteed jobs by the government and were assigned to companies all over the country. Since the Reform Policy of the 1980s, this is no longer true.

The most important research institute for Chinese theatre – Chinese Arts Research Institute – was established in 1980. It has two divisions, one for traditional theatre and three for spoken drama, and offers studies in history, theory and performance research. The institute issues its own studies and research papers.

Under the Ministry of Culture are a number of state publishing houses, some of which deal with books in the arts including theatre. The most specialized publisher is the China Theatre Publishing House, which has issued hundreds of important titles relating to theatre. Among its

major publications have been a twelve-volume series, *Collected Regional Drama* (published between 1950 and 1963); a ten-volume series, *Collected Essays on Chinese Traditional Theatre* (1959); a nine-volume series, *Collected Theatre Theory in Translation* (1957); a *General History of Chinese Traditional Theatre* (1980–1); and *Historical Documents on Chinese Modern Theatre* (1989).

More than thirty theatre journals and magazines exist; among the most important are *Theatre Monthly* (with a circulation of 200,000), *Theatre in China*, *Play*, *Theatre Research*, *Theatre* and *Theatre Arts*.

Theatre criticism itself takes two forms – written and oral. Written criticism appears in many publications ranging from those mentioned earlier to daily newspapers. Oral criticism is usually organized by theatre associations or theatre companies who invite audiences to discuss the productions they have seen with the artists involved.

On the scholarly side, leading critics include Zhang Geng (b. 1911) and Yu Qiou Yu (b. 1946). Zhang Geng, connected with both the Central Academy and China Arts Research Institute, edited numerous volumes of theatre history and aesthetics including *The General*

History of Chinese Traditional Theatre (three volumes published in 1980–1) and Theories of Chinese Traditional Theatre (1989). Yu Qiou Yu, connected to Shanghai Theatre Academy, has written three of the more important works on modern theatre theory and aesthetics – History of Theatre Theories (1983), Psychological Aesthetics of Theatre (1985) and An Historical Survey of Chinese Theatrical Culture (1985).

Rong Guangrun
Translated by Zhang Fang
Additional material provided by Henryk Jurkowski

Further Reading

Bin, Ru, ed. Theatre Section, Collection of Chinese Children's Literature. Chong Qing Publishing House, 1994. 347 pp.

Brecht and China. Bejing: Chinese Centre of the International Theatre Institute, n.d. (c.1985). 26 pp.

Chen, Bai Chen and Dong Jian. History of Modern Chinese Theatre. Beijing: China Theatre Publishing House, 1989. 732 pp.

Chen, Jack. The Chinese Theatre. London: D. Dobson, 1949. 63 pp.

Ch'en, Kuo-fu. T'ien fu chih hua: Ch'uan chu i shu ch'ien t'an [Chinese play: Overview of the arts]. Sichuan: Ch'ung-h'ing, 1983. 248 pp.

The Chinese Puppet Theatre, trans. J.T. MacDermott. London: Faber & Faber, 1961. 55 pp.

Chinese Research Institute of Children's Theatre, eds. Collection of Essays on Research of Children's Theatre. Beijing: China Theatre Publishing House, 1987. 398 pp.

Chinese Research Institute (Theatre Division). Collection on Stage Design. Beijing: China Theatre Publishing House, 1982. 458 pp.

Chinese Theatre Association. A Brief Introduction of Chinese Theatre. Beijing: Chinese Centre of the International Theatre Institute, n.d. (c. 1983). 32 pp.

Darrobers, Roger. Le Théâtre chinois. [The Chinese theatre]. Paris: Presses Universitaires de France, 1995. 127 pp.

Gong, He De. Research on Stage Design. Beijing: China Theatre Publishing House, 1987. 412 pp.

Guang, Yu Zhe, ed. The Art of Puppet Theatre. Shanghai: Shanghai Cultural Publishing House, 1959. 99 pp.

Historical Documents on Fifty Years of Spoken Drama. 3 vols. Beijing: China Theatre Publishing House, 1958. 910 pp.

Howard, Roger. Le Théâtre chinois contemporain [The contemporary Chinese theatre]. Brussels: La Renaissance du Livre, 1978. 106 pp.

Hsu, Tao-Ching. The Chinese Conception of the Theatre. Seattle, WA/London: University of Washington Press, 1985. 685 pp.

Huei, Li. Biographies of Modern Theatre and Film Artists in China. Jiang Xi People's Publishing House, 1981–4. 981 pp.

Jia, Ah. Further Studies on the Principles of Traditional Theatre. Beijing: China Theatre Publishing House, 1991. 347 pp.

Jiag, Xinhuei. Zhongguo Eiju Shi Tanwei [Looking for details in history of Chinese drama]. Jinan: Qilu Publishing House, 1985. 363 pp.

Jiong, Zhang. General Survey of Dramatic Literature in the People's Republic of China. Beijing: China Theatre Publishing House, 1990. 390 pp.

Kalvodová, Sís, Vanis. Chinese Theatre, trans. Iris Urwin. London: Spring Books, 1959. 38 pp.

Ling, Huang Huei, ed. Selective History of Modern Chinese Dramatic Literature. An Heui Publishing House, 1990. 373 pp.

Ling, Huang Zhuo. Words of a Director. Shanghai: Shanghai Arts and Literature Publishing House, 1979. 294 pp.

Ma, Wei. Xiju Yuyian [Language in drama]. Shanghai: Shanghai Publisher of Art and Literature, 1985. 263 pp.

Mackerras, Colin, ed. Chinese Drama: An Historical Survey. Beijing: New World Press, 1990. 274 pp.

——. Chinese Theatre: From Its Origins to the Present Day. Honolulu: University of Hawaii Press, 1983. 220 pp.

——. The Chinese Theatre in Modern Times: From 1840 to the Present Day. Amherst, MA: University of Massachusetts Press, 1975. 216 pp.

Mackerras, Colin and Constantine Tung, eds. Drama in the People's Republic of China. Albany, NY: State University of New York Press, 1987. 353 pp.

Ming, Yu Ren, ed. Management of Theatre Companies. Shanghai: East China Normal University Press, 1988, 123 pp.

Organizing Office, All-China Stage Design Exhibition, eds. Art on Chinese Stages. Beijing: China Theatre Publishing House, 1986. 216 pp.

Poupeye, Camille. Le Théâtre Chinois [The Chinese theatre]. Preface by Georges Sion. Brussels: Labor, 1984. 239 pp.

Ran, Li Mo. Li Mo Ran on the Art of Acting. Beijing: China Theatre Publishing House, 1989. 350 pp.

Riley, Jo. Chinese Theatre and the Actor in Performance. New York: Cambridge University Press, 1997. 348 pp.

Ru, Cheng Shi. *On Children's Theatre*. Beijing: China Theatre Publishing House, 1994. 422 pp.

Scott, A.C. *Actors Are Madmen: Notebook of a Theatregoer in China*. Madison, WI: University of Wisconsin Press, 1982. 225 pp.

——. *Literature and the Arts in Twentieth Century China*. New York: Doubleday Anchor, 1963. 212 pp.

Sheng, Gao Wen, ed. *History of Chinese Contemporary Dramatic Literature*. Nan Ning: Guang Xi People's Publishing House, 1990. 442 pp.

Sheng, Hu Miao. *Theatre Space Filled with Signs*. Beijing: China Theatre Publishing House, 1987. 412 pp.

Snow, Lois Wheeler. *China on Stage*. New York: Random House, 1972. 330 pp.

Stalberg, Roberta. *China's Puppets*. San Francisco, CA: China Books, 1984. 124 pp.

Sung, Xin. *Xiqu Wugong Jiacheng* [Textbook of physical training in Chinese theatrical performance]. Beijing: Chinese Drama Publishing House, 1983. 443 pp.

Tan, Dasien. *Jengo min-jien si-jiu ien-jiou* [Study of Chinese folk theatre]. Taipei: Gu, dziun, 1984. 158 pp.

Tan, Wenbia. *Zhongguo Gudai Xiju Shi Chugao* [First draft of history of Chinese ancient play]. Taipei: Lianjung Publishing, 1984. 275 pp.

Tang, Wen Pjau. *Dzen-go gu-dai si-dziu-cui gau* [Study of the origin and evolution of Chinese theatre]. Taipei: Lein-chin, 1984. 278 pp.

Wu, Yan Zhe, ed. *History of Education of Modern Spoken Drama in China*. Shanghai: East China Normal University Publishing House, 1986. 373 pp.

Xu, Wang. *Introduction to the Management of Performing Arts*. Shen Yang: Liao Ning Educational Publishing House, 1990. 361 pp.

Ying, Jiao Ju. *Collection of Jiao Ju Yin's Theatrical Essays*. Shanghai: Shanghai Arts and Literature Publishing House, 1979. 452 pp.

——. *Evolution of a Director*. Beijing: China Theatre Publishing House, 1988. 365 pp.

——. *Theatre in the People's Republic of China*. Beijing: China Theatre Publishing House, 1990. 316 pp.

Ying, Zhang Fa. *History of Chinese Traditional Theatre Troupes*. Shen Yang: Shen Yang Publishing House, 1991. 479 pp.

Yu, Qiou Yu. *Aesthetic Psychology of Theatre*. Si-chuan People's Publishing House, 1985. 401 pp.

——. *History of Theatre Theories*. Shanghai: Shanghai Arts and Literature Publishing House, 1983. 666 pp.

Yun-tong, Luk, ed. *Studies in Chinese–Western Comparative Drama*. Hong Kong: Chinese University Press, 1990. 224 pp.

Zhang, Geng. *On the Art of Theatre*. Beijing: China Theatre Publishing House, 1980. 234 pp.

Zhang, Geng and Guo Han Cheng. *General History of Chinese Traditional Theatre*. Beijing: China Theatre Publishing House, 1980. 1,193 pp.

Zhou, Ding Yan. *History of Chinese Puppet Theatre*. Shanghai: Xue Ling Publishing House, 1991. 159 pp.

Zhou, Xun and Chunming Gao. *5,000 Years of Chinese Costumes*. Shanghai: Chinese Costumes Research Group of the Shanghai School of Traditional Opera, 1987. 256 pp.

Zung, Cecilia S.L. *Secrets of the Chinese Drama: A Complete Explanatory Guide to Actions and Symbols as Seen in the Performance of Chinese Dramas*. New York: B. Bloom, 1964. 299 pp.

COOK ISLANDS

(see **SOUTH PACIFIC**)

FIJI

(see **SOUTH PACIFIC**)

FRENCH POLYNESIA

(see **SOUTH PACIFIC**)

GILBERT ISLANDS

(see **SOUTH PACIFIC**)

HONG KONG

(see **CHINA**)

INDIA

The second most populous country in the world – estimated in 1997 at 970 million inhabitants – India covers a vast land area of more than 3.1 million square kilometres (1.2 million square miles) in southern Asia extending from the Himalayas in the north through to the Indian Ocean in the south. A subcontinent on its own, India has seventeen official languages with Hindu and English the most widely spoken, and over 1,650 dialects in regular use. Some 83 per cent of the population are Hindus with the remainder made up of 12 per cent Muslims, 2.5 per cent Christians and 2 per cent Sikhs. The literacy rate was estimated in 1995 at 62 per cent for men but only 34 per cent for women.

Among the world's oldest civilizations, the people of the Indian subcontinent have helped to bring into being four major religions – Buddhism, Hinduism, Sikhism and Jainism. Indian Vedas are among the oldest manuscripts in the world and for thousands of years have articulated society's social and religious codes.

Among the most ancient of epics are the Indian *Ramayana* and *Mahabharata* whose stories – dating to between the tenth and fifteenth centuries BC – are still told, sung and danced in many parts of Asia. In philosophy, the Bhāgavad Gitā, the Purānas and the Upanishads continue to attract the world's thinkers while cultural anthropologists have long studied India's ancient theatrical traditions, most far older than those of classical Greece.

In the sixth century BC, Buddhism and Jainism originated in eastern India; over the next thousand years Buddhism spread over most of Asia, making India a holy land to be visited by pilgrims. During this same period, part of western India was conquered by Persia, which brought India into contact with the Greek world. Following an invasion by Alexander the Great in 326 BC, the King of Magadha (modern Bihar), Chandragupta Maurya (325–290 BC), created his own empire in the north by conquering several smaller kingdoms. In turn, Dravidian kingdoms in southern India spread Indian influence to parts of Southeast Asia; Hindu empires were established in Cambodia, Thailand and Indonesia. It was another Maurya dynasty king, Ashoka the Great (c.280 BC), who came closest to uniting the vast country when he brought under his control territories from Hindukush (present-day Afghanistan) in the north to Sri Lanka in the south. It was also under Ashoka that Buddhism was declared the state religion and non-violence was made state policy. After Ashoka's death, however, the empire began to disintegrate once again.

Under Kanishka (c.70 BC), the country was ruled from Purushpur (now Peshawar near the Pakistani–Afghani border). Kanishka also organized the first Buddhist Congress where Buddhist theosophy and the role of Buddhism in daily life were debated. By the first century AD – due in part to the weakness of later Buddhist rulers – Brahmanism became a new force under the leadership of Pushyamitra of the Shung dynasty. This change was clearly reflected in all the art forms of the time, including theatre.

By the fourth century AD the Guptās, a new dynasty, came to power in the north. A golden age for Indian culture, poets and artists flourished, several universities were established and new mathematical concepts developed, including the principle of zero. This was also the great age of classical Indian drama. Northern India was conquered by Muslim invaders from central Asia in the eleventh century resulting in the founding of the Sultanate of Delhi, which dominated the region for two centuries. In 1398, the Mongol conqueror Tamerlane (Tamburlaine) invaded and India was again split into a number of kingdoms. A Mogul descendant of Tamerlane and Genghis Khan – Baber – conquered northern India in 1526 and proclaimed himself the first Mogul Emperor. Mogul architecture reached its highest development during the reign of Emperor Shah Jahan (1627–58), who built the Taj Mahal at Agra as a tomb for his wife.

Vasco da Gama is credited as being the first European to discover the sea route to India in 1498. Soon after, European traders – Portuguese, Dutch, French and English – began trading cotton, silk, spices and rare woods. In 1739, Nadir Shah of Persia defeated the Mogul armies and the political chaos that followed paved the way for the spread of British power in India. In 1858, the British government took over control of the East India Company and in 1877 Queen Victoria was proclaimed Empress of India.

A nationalist movement soon emerged which won some political gains for India but constitutional reforms were not carried out until after World War I. The movement also supported non-violence, the development of native arts and crafts, and changes to the Hindu caste system. Eventually the movement urged a boycott of British goods and the rejection of taxation without representation.

In 1935, Britain initiated a new constitution for India but the country's large Muslim minority complained that their religion and culture was being weakened, and by 1942 the Muslims were demanding a separate state. On 15 August 1947 the Indian subcontinent achieved its independence from Britain but at the same time was partitioned into two separate nations – mostly Hindu India and Muslim-based Pakistan. In 1950, India formally became a republic under a new constitution. Hostilities broke out between India and Pakistan in 1965 and again in 1971. Later that year, East Pakistan separated from West Pakistan and the East became the new nation of Bangladesh. In 1975, the former independent kingdom of Sikkim became India's twenty-second state.

India's theatrical history and culture is equally complex. Panini, the earliest known Sanskrit grammarian and scholar, writing in his *Ashtadhyāyi* approximately around the sixth century BC, refers to the *Natyasutra*, a textbook for *nata* (a Sanskrit word with several meanings – actor, dancer, acrobat), attributing it to Silālin (thought to be an actor community) and Krisasva. In the epic *Mahabharata*, there are references to *natas*, and the later *Ramayana* speaks of *nartaka* (dancer) and *nātaka* (drama). Patanjali, in his *Mahābhāshya*, composed around 150 BC, mentions three modes of presenting the Krishna story – narration, showing the pictures depicting the story, and enactment of the episodes with the help of actors. The oldest existing fragments of Sanskrit plays reveal a complex and highly developed dramatic structure. Yet, exactly when theatre came into being in India or when the first drama was written, what the title was or who the dramatist, has not been ascertained. The nature and scope of the *Natyashastra,* the ancient Indian text of dramaturgy, and its comprehensive treatment of drama, indicate that it contains the analysis and codification of a rich theatrical tradition already in existence.

The *Natyashastra* (literally, *A Treatise on Theatre*) is an encyclopedic work on dramaturgy that is essential to an understanding of Indian theatre. Ascribed to Bharatmuni (Bharata the sage), the date of its composition is not certain. One school of thought is that the *Natyashastra* is not the work of a single author, but rather a compilation of material containing the knowledge and wisdom acquired by several generations of actors. This view is supported by the fact that Bharata in Sanskrit is also a generic term, meaning actor. Now generally believed to have been written between the second century BC and the second century AD, the manuscript of the *Natyashastra* was discovered, reconstructed and translated during the past century. Consisting of thirty-six chapters, it is a comprehensive treatise on the theory and practice of drama.

In its first chapter, the *Natyashastra* records the legend of the origin of drama. The legend is important to an understanding of Indian drama. The gods, led by Indra, their king, went to Brahmā, the god of creation, and requested him to create an art form which would give pleasure to the eyes and ears alike. They also asked Brahmā to create another Veda in the form of this art, which would be accessible to people of all castes, unlike the existing four Vedas which could be recited and sung only by the Brahmins and were denied to the Shudras, the low-caste people. Brahmā went into deep meditation and created the art of drama, taking elements from all four Vedas – *kathya* (verbal recitation) from the *Rig Veda* (the oldest book of hymns in India), *gita* (song) from the *Sama Veda*, *abhinaya* (acting or mimetic art) from the *Yajur Veda*, and *rasa* (sentiment or emotion) from the *Atharva Veda*. Drama was called the *Natya Veda*, and was given the status of the fifth Veda. The first performance was held at the occasion of Indra's flag staff festival, and the first performers were Bharata and his 100 sons. The gods were the audience. Because of disruption by the demons, Brahmā requested Vishwakarmā, the divine architect, to construct a structure where the performance could go on without hindrance. Vishwakarmā then built the first theatre. Shiva, the god of destruction, and his wife Pārvati, added dance to this art form. Vishnu, the god of preservation, evolved the four modes of presentation. All three gods of the Indian trinity were thus involved in the creation of drama. The last chapter of the *Natyashastra* describes the art being brought down from heaven to earth by King Nahusha.

Interpreted variously, the legend is significant in defining the Indian concept of theatre. Being connected to religion almost since its origin, traditional Indian drama has since been associated with the gods, performed as an act of worship, watched as an act of devotion. It is connected to the temples, to rituals, and draws material extensively from the two Indian epics, *Ramayana* and *Mahabharata*, the *Puranas* and other religious texts. The purpose of drama, as articulated by Brahmā, was instruction. In the Indian aesthetic tradition, drama is known as *drishya-kavya* (visual poetry); in performance it is *prekshā* (spectacle). Drama and dance are so inseparable in Indian aesthetics that it is at times impossible to distinguish them as two separate art forms.

The *Natyashastra* gives a detailed description of all aspects of the art of acting, especially hand gestures and bodily movements. Four elements of acting are described – *angikā* (bodily movements), *vāchikā* (speech), *ahārya* (costume and makeup) and *sāttvika* (the psychological energy of the actor). Various combinations of these result in different theatrical forms though all are present in each form in some degree or another; 108 *kāranas* (postures) are discussed, and there is a detailed description of the steps, movements and postures for the actor-dancer. In addition, Bharata discusses the construction of the theatre and stage, including rituals for its purification and consecration, the preliminaries of a performance, stage conventions, poetic compositions, grammar, audience, costumes, music and dance. Bharata also describes *angarachnā* (makeup), *rangpatti* (curtains and scenery), *rangabhoomi* (theatrical space) and *dhwani prabhāva* (sound effects). According to Bharata, it was the interaction of these elements which created sensory experiences, as well as varying levels of meaning, for the audience. Different theatrical forms of India emphasize different elements – *kuttiyāttam* and *yakshagāna*, using elaborate makeup, fantastic costumes and complex hand gestures, are spectacular in appeal, while the appeal of *ankia nat* and *pandvani* is essentially lyrical. Forms like *chhau*, without words, emphasize the visual aspects of theatre.

The *Natyashastra* also includes important discussions on performance theory and the aesthetics of performance. The *Natyashastra* has had tremendous influence over the development of traditional Indian performing art forms – dance, drama and music. It is, in fact, the *Natyashastra* more than anything else that has guided Indian theatre throughout its long history, even into modern times when the theatre of the country began to be deeply influenced by theatre aesthetics from other parts of the world.

The classical Sanskrit theatre is considered to have enjoyed a position of prestige from the time of the composition of the *Natyashastra* through the golden age of the Guptas (fourth and fifth century AD), until it started to decline with the coming of the Moguls. It enjoyed royal and religious patronage, with one great king, Harsha (seventh century AD) being not only a connoisseur, but also a playwright. Of the two great periods of classical drama in the history of the world, the era of Sanskrit drama is one. More Sanskrit plays have survived than Greek, and a greater number of Sanskrit playwrights. It is a fascinating body of dramatic texts from which Indian theatre has drawn repeatedly over the centuries and continues to do so. Ashwaghosha, who is thought to belong to the court of Kanishka, is the earliest known playwright. Fragments of three plays discovered in Russia and published in 1911 are thought to be Ashwaghosha's work. (It may be noted here that the dates of composition of Sanskrit dramatic texts and of the dramatists themselves have not been determined with any degree of certainty.) Bhāsa (fourth century AD) is considered to be the author of the earliest complete plays in Sanskrit. Thirteen plays, collected and published in 1912, are ascribed to him. *Swapnavāsavdattā* (*The Vision of Vasavdatta*) is undoubtedly his best work; his *Urubhanga* (*Broken Thighs*) and *Karnabhara* (*Karna's Burden*), two one-act plays, are the only tragedies in the entire body of classical Sanskrit literature. His works are the most theatrical in Sanskrit drama, which is essentially poetic in nature.

Sudraka (between third and eighth centuries AD) composed the *Mrichhakatika* (*The Little Clay Cart*), which is a long and structurally complex play that has been staged repeatedly over the centuries. It is unique in that it is the one great comedy in the Indian repertory.

Kālidasa (fifth century AD) is universally considered to be one of the greatest poets and playwrights of India. *Abhijnānashakuntalā* (*Shakuntala*) is his masterpiece, the greatest piece of poetic drama in India and famous the world over. His other plays are *Mālvikāgnimitra* and *Vikramorvasiya* (named after their protagonists). Bhavbhuti (seventh or eighth century AD) also belongs to this distinguished group of playwrights. He is the author of two mythological plays – *Mahāvircharita* (*Mahāvir's History*) and *Uttararāmcharita* (*Rama's Later History*), and a social drama, *Māltimādhav* (*Mālti and Mādhava*). Other important Sanskrit playwrights were Vishakhadatta, whose *Mudrārākshasa* (*The Minister's Seal*) is a political play of intrigue; Harsha (author of *Ratnāvali*, *Nagananda* and *Priyadarshika*); Banabhatta (seventh century AD), who supposedly wrote *Parvatiparinaya*; and Bhattnarayana (seventh to eighth centuries AD), who composed *Venisamhāra*.

Classical Sanskrit theatre was literary and poetic. Often the plays were written as sheer vehicles for poetry. In classical literature, drama falls under the category of poetry, translated by performance into visual poetry. It was called *rupaka* (literally, that which has a form). The term itself emphasizes the visual aspect of drama, the spectacle of it. The visualization was achieved by stylized hand gestures and postures. Of the ten major types of drama identified in the *Natyashastra*, the *nātaka* was the highest, most complete, structured and grand. Its subjects were drawn from the epics and the *puranas* and dealt with ancient romantic or mythological themes. This was the form chosen by Kālidasa, Bhāsa and Bhavbhuti. Another type of drama was known as *prakarana*, the theme and plot of which may be totally invented by the writer. Sudraka's *The Little Clay Cart* is the best example we have of a *prakarana*.

Most Sanskrit plays were idealistic tales of love, based on stories from mythology or religion. Most have a happy ending. The plays began with a prologue, the *nandi*, which was a benediction, an invocation singing the praises of a god or gods and asking for blessings for the performance. It praised the audience, announced the title of the play and its author, and introduced the subject matter. Most plays end with a prayer as well, called *bharatvākyam*. Part of the play and yet separate from it, the prologue and epilogue link the world of the performance to the real world. The person delivering the benediction was the *sutradhāra*, a very important figure in Indian theatre. The term *sutradhār* literally means holder of the thread or string, and could refer to the stage manager, director or leader of the theatrical troupe. Often one person combined all three functions. Traditional Indian performances – both classical and folk – still follow the convention, although the *sutradhāra* has different names in different forms.

The Sanskrit theatre acknowledged the presence of the audience. In soliloquies, monologues and asides, the actor addressed the audience directly. The *vidushaka* (jester), another conventional character in classical drama, had an important function in maintaining a link between the performers and spectators. The *rasa* theory, so integral to Indian performance aesthetics, necessitates a shared creation and enjoyment of the performance experience in which both the actors and the spectators are crucial and essential participants.

The works of the classical Indian drama have remained important to generations of theatre practitioners in India; they have been adapted in regional languages and performed regularly. They continue to influence not only Indian theatre, but also classical Indian dance forms. A rich and sophisticated theatrical tradition flourished in India almost uninterrupted for 1,200 years, when it went into decline around the tenth century AD. The Sanskrit language split into vernaculars and developed into the various regional languages. From the time of the Persian invasion, theatrical activities began to be marginalized. By the arrival of the Muslims between the seventh and eleventh centuries AD, theatre was restricted still further, eventually disappearing almost entirely from public life in courts and cities. About this time, Sanskrit drama was replaced by the growing folk theatre. Its stories, ancient mythology, legends, epics and Puranic tales, religious stories and popular lore formed the subject matter of the various emerging theatrical forms. The traditions and conventions flowed from the classical to the folk where they have continued uninterrupted. Theatrical performances continued in communities where they can still be found during festivals and fairs, weddings and religious celebrations, in a variety of forms involving music, dance and spectacle that continue to connect them to the *Natyashastra*.

Contemporary Indian theatre is as diverse, as complex and as multifaceted as the country itself. India is a country of dramatic contrasts and stunning paradoxes. Its 970 million people, as earlier indicated, speak seventeen official languages and several hundred dialects, live in twenty-two states, adhere to one of six major religions, and celebrate numerous festivals. The states and territories are almost cultural entities in themselves; within their boundaries and flowing around them, exist individual and very distinctive cultures, revealed in language, styles of dress, festive and cultural celebrations, arts and crafts, and ritualistic and performative traditions. Within this multicultural, multilingual India, where abject, unimaginable poverty and lavishly opulent lifestyles coexist, such polarities serve as a paradigm for the coexistence of widely different genres and modes. One can attempt to classify Indian theatrical expressions in terms of

their polarities: Indian theatre is classical theatre and folk theatre and modern theatre; it is street theatre performed on corners, and 'elite' theatre, performed in air-conditioned auditoriums on proscenium stages; it is rural theatre and urban theatre, religious theatre and secular theatre; it is Bengali theatre, Punjabi theatre and Marathi theatre; it is political theatre with a clear and direct message, and it is pure entertainment, performed for the sheer joy of it; it is performed during religious and cultural festivals, and it is performed as ticketed shows for a specific period of time. And yet even these categories are not clear-cut and definitive; the boundaries are blurred and they feed constantly into each other.

Literally hundreds of theatrical forms simultaneously coexist within the country. Each has its own theatrical history, performance traditions and distinguishing characteristics, and yet they contain within themselves infinite space for innovation, creation, and exploration. In order to give form to such a vast subject, we shall look at the traditional theatre of India – religious, folk and classical (and these are not air-tight categories – they constantly merge, overlap and form interesting configurations) and the modern theatre of India. Brief descriptions of most forms are provided. Limitations of space make it impossible to include each and every one of them; the omissions or the brevity of description in no way reflect on their importance.

Traditional forms, as embodying performance texts, dramatic texts, techniques, movement patterns and codified gestures that have been handed down from generation to generation, are an integral part of the Indian way of life. Most Indians have grown up watching the traditional theatre of their region, or are familiar with it. In most regions, it is still alive – something they and their children can see. Traditions have an important and positive role in Indian culture. The thematic content of traditional forms is derived from a common source – Hindu religion and mythology, particularly the two epics and the *puranas*. Traditional Indian theatre is sung and danced and mimed. Theatre in India is an art into which all other arts feed: dance, song, music, drama, mime, acrobatics, martial arts and puppetry. Most traditional Indian art forms are a composite of all these elements, and sometimes invite a multiplicity of classification; *kathakali*, for example, is dance, classical theatre, music theatre, mask theatre and religious theatre.

For a clearer understanding of how these forms evolved and became part of India's contemporary theatre, it is useful to divide the country into five cultural regions: the north (composed of the states Jammu and Kashmir, the Punjab, Himachal Pradesh, Hariyana, Delhi, all but the southern part of Uttar Pradesh and all but the western and southern parts of Rajasthan); the west (composed of western Rajasthan, Gujrat, Maharashtra, Goa and part of Madhya Pradesh); the central area (composed of the southern parts of Rajasthan and Uttar Pradesh, the eastern part of Maharahtra and the northern part of Andhra Pradesh); the east (composed of several northeastern states along with Orissa, Bengal, Bihar and Assam); and the south (composed of Andra Pradesh, Tamilnadu, Karnataka and Kerala).

The most famous traditional theatre forms of the north are the *Ramlila* and the *Raslila*, cycle plays dealing with the two *avataras* (incarnations) of Vishnu Rāma and Krishna – two of the most important gods of the Hindu religion. This is theatre deeply and inseparably linked to religion. The Lila plays commemorate and re-enact events in the life of Rāma and Krishna. *Ramlila* has a tradition of more than 400 years, and the dramatic text is the great epic in Hindi, *Rāmacharitmānasa* by Tulsidās (sixteenth century). Performed once a year during September to October on the occasion of the Hindu festival of Dashahara, it celebrates Rāma's victory over the demon king Rāvana. It is performed all over north India, in virtually every city and village of Uttar Pradesh (and by several groups in the same city simultaneously) and in other regions as well, hence there is a wide variety in the styles and modes of presentation. The famous *Ramlila* of Rāmnagar (near Varanasi) performs the entire epic in thirty-one days; at other places it may select important episodes and present them as a cycle drama in seven, ten or twenty-one days. Often processionally performed, it incorporates pageants and tableaux as elements of the performance. The poetic text is recited by a group of singers, while the actors on the stage silently enact the events or sit quietly during the descriptive passages. The audience participates in many rituals that take place during the performance; for them the actors represent actual gods and goddesses and devotion is expressed by touching their feet, shouting their glory and taking part in *aarti* (a ritual of worship) at the end of each performance. *Ramlila* is pure community theatre, staged on platforms in the open. Professional *Ramlila* troupes have been formed that perform on proscenium stages in towns.

The *Raslila* (*rās* means dance, *lila* means play) is an operatic play with Krishna's life as its theme, and is enacted at Mathura and Vrindavan (130 kilometres or 80 miles southeast of Delhi) every year during August and September as part of the celebrations of the birth of Krishna. Songs about Krishna and Radha, his consort, composed by Surdas (sixteenth-century Hindi poet) are sung and danced and are an integral part of *Raslila*, as are various religious rituals and ceremonies which frame the performance. Having grown out of the bhakti movement and evolved in the temples in the sixteenth century, the *Raslila* is religious, devotional performance and is never presented on city stages as pure entertainment. There are several *lila* plays, most dealing with Krishna's childhood and youth, his romantic interludes with Radha and depicting his enormous power. The scripts are loose and flexible and constantly improvised. *Raslila* is sometimes just sung by the performers (*rāsdhāris*), without an accompanying dramatic enactment, thus highlighting the predominantly poetic and musical nature of the form. This is an example of India's music theatre, if *Raslila* may be described thus. The dance content is visually charming, though not highly stylized. It is a devotional theatrical expression of the community celebration of Krishna's birthday.

Apart from these two theatrical forms, based on religion, the north is also home to several forms in the folk tradition. Folk theatre may be religious or secular. Folk performances are essentially non-classical, regional, mainly rural, and deal with social themes. They are vigorous and unpretentious and are a composite of various things – comic sketches, scenes from historical plays, legends or satire. They break into song and dance and music at various junctures. They may be performed year-round or on special festive occasions by professional troupes or by amateurs who come together, especially for the performance. They are mostly free to the public.

The main theatrical tradition of folk entertainment in north India is the *swāng*. Essentially a musical folk drama dating from the eighteenth century with stories in verse sung in various modes (classical, semi-classical and popular folk), it has assumed different forms in different regions. The *nautanki* of Uttar Pradesh, *khyal* of Rajasthan and *bhagat* of Agra are all forms that belong to the *swāng* tradition. The actors may use appropriate costumes and makeup or appear in their ordinary clothes. The companies move from place to place and perform at fairs, festivals, social occasions and religious celebration for the crowds that gather to watch them. During the performance, one actor goes around collecting money (pay-what-you-can) from the audience. The cast used to be all male, but lately women have been playing female roles. *Swāng* basically means impersonation.

In the *swāng* tradition is the *naqal* of Punjab: farcical in nature, it relies heavily on improvisation by the *naqalchi*. *Naqal* literally translates as imitation or mimicry, and the *naqalchi* is a mimic. (The actor may also be called *bhand*, the village buffoon. The *bhands* are itinerant clowns.) It is a centuries-old tradition in the villages, and very popular at marriages. It may be a solo performance, or a troupe may have two or three people. Dressed in rustic clothes and holding a leather binder to slap each other with, the actors perform a series of small skits in a small space on the ground, in an open field or compound. Each lasts about ten minutes, and is made up of quick, witty repartee, earthy humour and gentle satire. The subject matter is purely social – hilarious situations from everyday life. This is a totally secular form.

The *nautanki*, performed in Uttar Pradesh, Punjab and Rajasthan, is an operatic drama which also belongs to the *swāng* tradition. It has a limited dance content, and combines it with elements of singing, recitation, storytelling, mime and clowning. Evolving out of the recitation of ballads, epics and narrative poems, the emotional dramatization and dances were added later. It enacts stories of legendary heroes and heroines, kings, saints and robbers. The orchestra sits in a semicircle on the stage and the important musical instruments are *nagara* (kettledrum), harmonium, *sarangi* (wooden stringed instrument) and clarinet. Originally using classical and semi-classical melodies, the music has become increasingly influenced by film music. In the language, music, costumes, themes and characters of this folk form can be seen a blend of two cultures – Hindu and Muslim. The language, devoid of literary pretensions, is simple, and a mixture of Hindi, Urdu, Persian, Rajasthani, Braj and several local dialects. In the course of its history, the *nautanki* played an important role in the freedom movement of India, by incorporating themes of patriotism and nationalism. The female parts were originally acted by men using gaudy makeup and costumes. Later, *nautanki* companies owned solely by women were formed and were suspect as being common bawdy houses. There is an element of eroticism in *nautanki* that can easily cross the line into vulgarity and crassness. For this reason, it was considered undignified for an educated, sophisticated patron to enjoy, or even see, the *nautanki*. The 'nautanki' style' of acting became a derogatory term, meaning melodramatic and crude.

The *bhagat* of Agra (a city in Uttar Pradesh, known for the Taj Mahal), considered to be the parent form of *nautanki*, is 400 years old. *Bhagat* means 'devotee', and in its earlier stages was dramatized devotional singing performed by the devotees of the Vaishnava cult. Tales of valour, romance and legendary kings were later additions, but the form, basically operatic, retains its religious character. Religious rituals at the beginning and end serve as a frame for the performance which consists of singing praises of gods and goddesses, to the accompaniment of musical instruments similar to those used in *nautanki*. At the beginning of the performance, an actor playing Ganesh (the elephant-headed god), dances on the stage wearing an elephant mask. He is later worshipped by other actors. The language of the *bhagat* is a mix of Hindi, Braj and Urdu. Other cities famous for *bhagat* are Mathura and Vrindavan.

Another traditional folk form of north India is the *bhand pathar* of Kashmir, also called *bhand jashna* (festival of *bhands*). It evolved three or four hundred years ago in the courts of Muslim rulers. It consists of a blend of music, dance, clowning and satire, and focuses on contemporary social issues. Performed in the open in the village square, liveliness, humour, caricatural representation of characters and, above all, biting satire characterize the form.

The western region of India is the centre of some of the country's most widely spoken and influential languages, such as Marathi, Gujarati, Hindi, Konkani, Malwi, Marwari, Mewari and Shekhawati. It has an equal variety of folk forms including *khyal* and *bheel gouri* in Rajasthan, *bhavai* in Gujarat, *tamasha* in Maharashtra and Goa, and *maanch* in western Madhya Pradesh.

Tamasha (literally, spectacle; the term also connotes fun, play, entertainment), the traditional theatre form of Maharashtra, originated and flourished in the court of the Peshwas in the eighteenth and nineteenth centuries. Combining elements of music, dance, speech and song, the *tamasha* is a unique form, characterized by its erotic tone. The drummers and the women dancers form the essential part of this performance, along with the reciter-singer and *sangodaya* (buffoon). Two drummers, the *dholakiwala* (*dholaki* is a long, horizontal drum slung from the neck) and the *halgiwala* (*halgi* is a small drum kept at chin level), initiate the performance and are present throughout. Other instruments unique to the form are the *tuntuna* (one-stringed instrument) and *manjeera* (a pair of small metal cymbals). Harmonium and clarinet are also used. The instrumentalists stand behind the lead singer, the leader of the troupe, who links up various dramatic episodes, some depicting Krishna's romantic escapades with the *gopis* (milkmaids). Various types of songs are sung, the main one being the *lavani*, a narrative poetic song expressing love and sung with vigour and passion. A *tamasha* performance may contain up to thirty *lavanis* and take up more than half of the performance time of six hours. The *lavanis* are enacted by the dancing girls in bright costumes, lavish jewellery and makeup, and form the core of the *tamasha*. Some shows present *lavanis* only as a full programme; known as *sangeet bari*, they belong to the genre of music and dance theatre. Because of the eroticism of *tamasha*, which sometimes degenerated into open lewdness, it was generally rejected by the upper classes. *Tamasha* was performed originally by the Mahars and the Mangs, two of the lower caste communities, who were sweepers (janitors) by ancestral profession. It catered to the lower sections of society. Originally performed in the open, the *tamasha* is now performed all over Maharashtra in modern auditoriums with proscenium stages. Theatre troupes now cater to middle- and upper-class tastes. The *tamasha* has become a respectable form of entertainment, attracting the attention of theatre critics and literary scholars.

Bhavai is the folk theatrical form of Gujarat, traditionally performed during *Navratri* (nine days and nights of fasting and prayers, just before the festival of *Dushera*), in front of the shrine of Amba Mata, the presiding deity of *bhavai*, or before a lamp which is a symbol of the goddess. Thus, it is as much a form of entertainment as an offering to the goddess. Also performed in the Malwa region of Madhya Pradesh and some parts of Rajasthan, *bhavai* was created in the late fourteenth century by Asaita Thakar, a Gujarati Brahmin who, according to legend, was later cast out of the community. *Bhavai* performers came to belong to Trigala, which became a caste in itself. Asaita was also a poet and a singer. He wrote 360 *veshas* or playlets (the term *vesha* means masking or dressing up, or a scene), out of which 60 are still performed, with additions of characters and scenes from local and contemporary life. Most *veshas*

are character-sketches or social plays full of humour, and each may last from thirty minutes to a few hours. In one night, several *veshas* on unrelated themes may be performed, with the *naik* (director or chief of the troupe, *natyashastra*'s *sutradhar*), providing the link by introducing them and commenting on them. A *bhavai* performance may go on all night. The dialogue delivery is stylized, the makeup exaggerated with the eyebrows and moustache bushy, the clown's face painted, and the costumes colourful and distinct to the region. Songs and dances are an integral part of the performance. Performed within a circle drawn on the ground, called *paudh* or *chechar*, with the audience sitting all around, *bhavai* uses instruments called *pakhawaj* (drums hanging from the neck), *narghan* (small drums tied around the waist), *sarangi* (stringed instrument with a haunting melody), cymbals, and the dramatic *bhungal* – a 1.5 metres (5 feet) long copper pipe tapered at one end and bell-shaped at the other. The *bhungal* is unique to the *bhavai*, and is used for entries and exits, dramatic moments and climaxes. Female roles were traditionally played by men. The *ranglo*, the jovial and boisterous clown making playful and ribald comments, is a stock character, who along with the *naik* always remains on the stage, and sometimes acts a role in a vesha, effortlessly slipping in and out of character. Another unique feature of *bhavai* is the use of burning torches called *kakras* (tightly rolled cloth soaked in oil and burning at one end); actors make dramatic entries and dance holding them, bringing it closer to their faces to illuminate strong emotions. The dances are performed solo or in a group, and, with the colourful swirling skirts made of 24 metres (26 yards) of material and the *odhni* (headscarf), create a spectacular effect. In rural west Gujarat, the *bhavai* is touring theatre: the troupes perform in various places. Since independence, the form has been adapted and elements incorporated into modern Gujarati theatre.

Khyal is the folk operatic form of Rajasthan, combining music, singing, dancing and enacting medieval legends, historical accounts, love tales, stories from mythology, and popular tales of brave local heroes and their chivalry. Originally a style of composing poems and singing them, the *khyal* as a theatrical form came into being in the seventeenth century. *Khyal* itself means imagination or thought, and on a bare stage devoid of any settings, the form directly appeals to audience imagination. Lyrical in nature, *khyal* also belongs to the genre of theatre of entertainment, with no religious affiliations, and is in the *swāng* tradition. *Khyal* has a variety of styles which evolved from different regions and composers – *kuchamani* style, *shekhawati* style, *alibakshi* style and *turra kalangi ke khyal*, with dancing, singing and music being the essential elements. Different styles of *khyal* use different types of stage. Prompters with a copy of the dramatic text remain on the stage at all times, a convention *khyal* shares with neighbouring *maanch* of Madhya Pradesh, where they are known as *pustakji* (*pustak* is a book). Rajasthan is well known for its tradition of heroism, and Prithviraj Chauhan, Amar Singh Rathore and Dhola Maru are famous *khyal*s that sing the legends.

Very similar in form and nature is *maanch* of the Malwa region in Madhya Pradesh. The term literally means stage. As a theatrical form, it originated in the second half of the eighteenth century. The plays draw upon the same material as in the *khyal* for their content, but make use of Malwa folk music, and the language is Malwi, mixed with Hindi. The plays are in verse, and are meant to be sung, the chief musical instruments used being the *dholak* (drum), harmonium and *sarangi*. The singers and musicians sit on the stage, which is set up with ritualistic ceremonies of worship performed by the guru, usually the playwright-director. Open on all sides, it is decorated with flowers and leaves. Each performance is preceded by rituals of sprinkling the stage with water, and spreading it with a (make-believe) carpet. The actors sing while performing these activities. At the beginning, all the actors stand on the stage in full costume and makeup and sing the invocation with their hands folded and their eyes shut. The performers are introduced; sometimes the characters of the play about to be enacted are announced, and then the play begins. Elaborate makeup, colourful costumes and beautiful jewellery is used. The dancing is vigorous and graceful; as in many Indian traditional theatrical forms, the actors have to be experts in singing, dancing and acting.

The central region is also the centre of tribal culture and ritualistic theatre. The main folk and tribal forms here include the music- and dance-based *nachya* and *pandwani*. *Nachya* belongs to the Chhatisgarh region of Madhya Pradesh and is influenced by its *ganda* musicians and the entertainment form of *gammat*, popular in Vidarbha (also in Madhya Pradesh). Selecting a situation from the real life of agricultural communities, *nachya* performers improvise dialogues while rehearsing. It is a totally improvised performance in the sense that no written text is followed or prepared. The treatment is essentially humorous and satirical. The play begins with an invocation to the god Ganesh and then to goddess Saraswati. In one form of *nachya*, the *Jokkad Pari*, the performers also make use of burning oil torches and entertain the audience by singing and dancing. In some *nachya* troupes men act all the parts, male and female, while others use women performers. *Pandvani*, evolved by the tribals of Chhattisgarh, is essentially storytelling accompanied by music. There is no dancing, no costumes and no makeup. It tells the story, in verse, of the five *Pandavas*, heroes from the epic *Mahabharata*. The troupe has one narrator-singer, who sits and sings holding a *tambura* (a long, stringed musical instrument) and a pair of cymbals, with one or two co-singers who sit around him playing the harmonium and *tabla*. During the course of narration, he slips in and out of the characters he is singing about, sometimes playing several characters simultaneously. Dialogue with the co-singers is also used. Since the 1950s both of these theatre forms have begun to be seen in city theatres. Crossing tribal boundaries, they have attracted the attention of contemporary directors and actors who have used these forms in modern crossover experiments.

India's eastern region includes such major cities as Calcutta and Patna as well as mixed tribal populations along the borders with Bangladesh, Mynamar, Bhutan and China. Among the many colourful traditional theatre and dance forms seen here are the popular *jatra* in Bengal (a form also widely popular in Orissa, Bihar and Assam, as well as in Bangladesh), *chhau* and *bidesia* in Bihar and *ankiya nat* in Assam. *Jatra* (also known as *yatra*) translates as a pilgrimage or voyage. It is performed on a bare stage open on all sides with the audience sitting all around. The form has its origin in the devotional singing and dancing by the followers of the Krishna Bhakti movement of the fifteenth century. Over the course of centuries, *jatra* became secular and started dealing with contemporary social and political themes. In the nineteenth century the themes became patriotic and it reflected the dissatisfaction of the people with British rule. Many *jatra* plays were banned by the British. *Jatra* traditionally draws upon historical and romantic tales, and using them as a framework, effortlessly weaves in issues of public interest. Performed in rural and urban areas with equal fervour, it is a vigorous spectacle performed with an intense frenzy that fills the audience with emotions of equal intensity. Music is the main element in the *jatra*. Musicians sit in two groups, facing each other. *Dholak* (drum), *pakhawaj*, trumpets, flute, clarinet, *behala* (violin) and cymbals are used with dramatic effect. *Jatra* stands apart from many other folk forms in that the singing is done by the actors. The songs are in classical, semi-classical, and folk styles. The generic character called *Vivek* (conscience) is unique to *jatra*, and in its dramatic function is akin to the chorus in a Greek tragedy. He comments on the action, expresses the feelings of the characters, and philosophizes; he does all this through singing. He may appear in any scene suddenly. *Jatra* actors come from all classes of society. Traditionally, all roles were played by men, but women have now joined the *jatra* companies. Sometimes the cast is mixed, with some female parts played by men and some by women. Prose dialogues, sword fighting, stunts, acrobatics and dancing are also used in *jatra*. The play begins with a climax. *Jatra* is performed all year. There are professional troupes that travel and perform in neighbouring states of Assam, Orissa and Bihar. They are invited to perform at weddings, festivals and other celebrations. There are also amateur companies. During the Durga Pooja, the main festival in Bengal, *jatra* competitions are held, sometimes with several troupes performing in one night. During this time, there is a *jatra* being performed in every street of Bengal. It is undoubtedly one of the most popular and dynamic folk theatre forms of India. During the 1960s, there was a revival of interest in the *jatra* form. Utpal Dutt and Shambhu Mitra, two prominent Bengali directors, used *jatra* techniques in their productions and their work inspired several other practitioners of modern theatre.

Ankia nat (literally, one-act play), the traditional operatic drama of Assam, is performed to celebrate the birth and death anniversaries of Sankardeva (fifteenth and sixteenth centuries AD), a great religious and social reformer, and founder of the order of the Vaishnava monastery. The plays called *ankia nat* were written by Sankardeva and his main disciple, Madhavdeva. Subsequently, many other writers have written new plays. The plays are in Assamese, mixed with Vrajboli. Based on the legends of Rama and Krishna, they primarily depict episodes from the life of Krishna. The plays, lyrical in tone, glorify bhakti, the cult of

devotion; they are in the form of devotional singing, with actors coming on stage to speak the dialogues and sing their songs. Krishna himself appears on stage as a character. The actors' faces are made up with black, red or blue. Masks are also used. The dialogue is delivered in a lyrical manner. The *sutradhāra* is very important in *ankia nat*. He initiates the performance by singing and dancing, announces the entrances of other characters, narrates off-stage action, and comments on the action being performed. The group of musicians sitting on the stage are called *gayana-bayana mandali*, and use drums called *khol*. The singing and dancing are more important than dialogue. The plays are staged in the *namghar*, the prayer halls of Vaishnava monasteries.

Chhau is the name of the traditional dance-drama of the eastern regions of India. There are three styles of *chhau* – *Seraikella chhau*, *Mayurbhanj chhau* and *Purulia chhau*, named after the three districts in the states of Bihar, Orissa and West Bengal respectively, where this unique form is performed. The areas, located geographically in three separate states, are contiguous, and form a kind of *chhau* belt. *Chhau* is a generic term for a form with three distinct styles, similar, but each with its unique characteristics.

Seraikella and *Purulia chhau* performers wear masks, though of very different kinds, whereas the *Mayurbhanj* style is performed without masks. *Chhau* dances have a strong ritualistic content. In essence, *chhau* may be described as ritualized body movements. The movement techniques in *chhau* are derived from the martial arts of the region, especially the *parikhanda* exercises (*pari* means shield, *khanda* means sword). The themes are taken from nature (birds and animals), everyday life (chores of cleaning the floor, working in fields) and from Hindu mythology. There is an absence of dialogue between characters. Body movements, not songs or dialogue or narration, delineate the themes. The body is also the instrument for expressing the characters' inner emotions. The *chhau* may be said to be a dramatic dance, with theatrical characteristics. All three styles have very different patterns of movement, musical accompaniment, and costumes. Only men perform in *chhau*.

Seraikella chhau is a unique form of masked dance drama, patronized and performed by the princes of the erstwhile royal family. The princes have also been teachers and mask-makers. The other performers are the tribals of the region,

A *seraikella chhau* performance, 1993.
Photo: courtesy of SNA.

the labourers and farmers. It is performed annually in the month of April, on the occasion of
Chaitra Parva (a twenty-six-day spring festival),
in the courtyard of the royal palace, in front of
the Raghunath temple dedicated to Rama.
Elaborate rituals, in which the whole community participates, are an inseparable part of
Seraikella chhau, and vital to an understanding
of the performance. *Chhau* dances are held only
on the last three days of the celebration. They
are made up of short compositions, each lasting
seven to ten minutes. The dancer impersonates
an animal, bird, person, god, tree, storm, etc.,
and acts out a complex set of movements using
mainly the lower limbs of the body, the whole
leg or only the calf, rather than the face and
hands, which are usually used extensively in
other dance styles. The treatment is suggestive
and interpretative, rather than realistic. *Chhau*
dance movements are highly stylized and
demand concentration and a focusing of the
whole body in depicting a state of being.
Seraikella chhau movements are slow and have a
lyrical charm. A definite pattern of walking

(gaits), body stances, poses and dance movements give the style its unique vocabulary.
Masks are an essential element of *Seraikella
chhau*. Made of red clay found at the Kharkai
river banks, the masks are abstract, simple in
their austerity, stylized and suggestive. They do
not realistically identify the character being portrayed. The masks reflect the lyrical grace of the
form. A full-sleeved upper garment with rich
adornments is worn. The lower body is draped
in a *dhoti* (yards of material draped around the
hips and thighs).

Four types of drums are used to provide the
rhythm to which the movements are set – *dhol*,
dhumsa (a little drum shaped like a bowl), *tikra*
and *nagara*. The *mahuri* (a wind instrument) is
used, and sometimes a harmonium. Vocal
accompaniment is minimal. The music is purely
instrumental, and only the instrumental
melodies accompany the dance. The *chhau*
dancer is totally silent. The abstraction and stylization give *Seraikella chhau* a high degree of
sophistication.

Mayurbhanj chhau is performed in the south-
eastern part of Orissa. It is performed at the
Chaitra Parva and also at Dashahara, which is a
recent practice, and is associated with rituals
and fertility rites. The group of people who
perform the dances belong to what is known in
India as the backward or depressed classes, the
lower sections of society – the peddlers, rickshaw-pullers and others. In Mayurbhanj and the
area adjacent, there is a large variety of tribal
population. There is a strong influence of tribal
dances on the form; in fact, some of its elements
are purely tribal. In *Mayurbhanj chhau*, the
movements are much more vigorous and rustic
than *Seraikella chhau*. The body is once again
the instrument of expression. There is a lot of
jerking, wriggling of hips and knees, and acrobatics. Ropes, pots and poles are used for a
display of acrobatics. Some dances depict only
martial drills. Themes related to the Shiva and
Krishna legends are enacted, and content and
characters drawn from the two epics. Some
dances revolve around themes from everyday
life, like the hunter dance. The actors do not
wear masks, but their faces resemble a mask by
their immobility and stiffness. In the absence of
the mask, the stances and gaits are used to establish the character.

The main instruments accompanying the
dance-drama are the *mahuri* and *teula* (a string
instrument) and sometimes a bamboo flute.
There is a variety of percussion instruments –
the *dhol* (two-headed drum, shaped like a

barrel), which leads the performance, *caditiadi* (short cylindrical drum played with two thin sticks), *nagara* (drum) and *dhumsa* (kettle-drum). There is a great complexity in the playing of the instruments. There is some vocal accompaniment.

Despite being a folk dance, *Mayurbhanj chhau* has acquired a distinctive stylization. In its stances, it has a strong affinity with the Odissi dance style.

Purulia chhau is a masked dance-drama, also performed by the classes underprivileged in socio-economic terms – labourers, farmers, rickshaw-pullers, and so on. Mostly they belong to the supposedly lower castes and tribes. Although the dance style belongs to a group of 'backward' classes, as a dance form it is highly sophisticated. The thematic content is drawn from the epics and *Puranas*. The *Ramayana* and the *Mahabharata* are enacted, sometimes in one night (using selective episodes), or in three to four successive nights. The dance technique is highly structured and rigorous. The stances and gaits are emphasized; all parts of the body are used. Jumps and leaps of extraordinary complexity are the most outstanding feature of the style. There are some leaps in which the actor lands on the ground on his knees. They are a unique feature of *Purulia chhau*. The masks are realistic, not abstractions like the masks of *Seraikella chhau*. The actors also wear large crowns and headgear. The upper body costumes are ornate. Only tights are worn on the lower body, with multi-coloured ribbons forming stripes on them.

The *dhol* player stands and leads the performance. The *dhumsa* player sits on the ground. The *shehnai* provides the melody. The rhythmic structure of the percussion instruments is complex. In this style of *chhau*, the vocalist sings the invocation at the beginning, introduces each character before its entry, narrates the scene and links the episodes. Instrumental music accompanies the dramatic action throughout.

Chhau dances are open-air performances. The acting area on the ground is a 6 metre (20 feet) square, with a narrow passage 4.5–6 metres (15–20 feet) long. The dancing enclosure is circular. The musicians sit near the performers. The audience sits on the ground on three sides of the acting area. The performance goes on all night.

In the southern region, Kerala remains the centre of a variety of classical theatre and dance forms, including *kathakali* and *kuttiyāttam*, along with several forms of spectacular folk theatre. Other theatre forms seen in this area are *bhagvat* and *therukoothu* in Tamilnadu, *yakshagana* in Karnataka and *burrakatha* in Andhra Pradesh. Also found in this region are many classical dance forms – *bharatnatyam*, *kuchipudi* and *oddissi* – that are performed in beautiful arena settings within some of the region's most spectacular temples, many dating back more than a thousand years. One also finds in this region the *karnataka* style of singing, a form quite different from other classical Indian music. Almost all performance forms in this region are rooted in the two classical epics – *Mahabharata* and *Ramayana* – or in related mythology.

Kathakali (literally, story play), the classical dance-drama of Kerala, India's southernmost state, is a form characterized by artistic splendour. Though it is dated from the end of the sixteenth century, it has its roots in much older forms. In its high degree of stylization, techniques of performance and its conventions, *kathakali*, along with *kuttiyāttam*, its parent form, is the most representative of the *natyashastra* tradition. Its movements, makeup, costumes and dances are codified and stylized.

Like most traditional performance forms in India, *kathakali* plays perform stories from the epics and the *puranas*, especially the *Bhāgavata Purana*, which tells the story of the life of Lord Krishna. The form has about 500 plays in its repertoire, composed by playwrights in Malyalm, the native language of Kerala. Storytelling is the essence of the performance and is done at three levels – recitation-narration, singing and movement-gesture. Three groups of performers are involved in the creation of a *kathakali* performance, with their roles clearly differentiated – the actor-dancers who, through hand gestures, facial expressions and body movements, enact the story; the reciter-singers who sing and narrate the text; and the percussionist-musicians who keep the rhythm. All three groups are simultaneously present on the stage.

Kathakali companies are traditionally all male. The performance style is highly physicalized and the actors go through years of rigorous training. There are no rehearsals for a performance, only intense actor training, which is a way of life for the performers. Over years they literally absorb the performance score in their bodies, which is then unravelled in the performance. The choreography is highly developed. The actors perform vigorous scenes of dramatic confrontations between gods and demons.

Kathakali performance of *Duryohana Vadham* by Vyasakora Masood, Kerala, 1993.
Photo: courtesy of SNA.

Intricate and complex hand gestures and heightened facial expressions play a very important role in *kathakali* and are used in a visual interpretation of the text. Eye movements are very significant in expressing the inner states of the characters. Most of a *kathakali* actor's acting is done through his eyes and hand gestures (*mudrās*). The performer literally speaks the character's dialogue through hand movements. There are twenty-four basic hand gestures and their arrangements, uses and combinations total seven hundred. They convey ideas, objects, feelings and actions. Each gesture or configuration of the fingers can convey up to fifty different things: the knowledgeable spectator follows the meaning from the context and familiarity with the text.

Kathakali has units of pure dance (*nritta*) called *kalasam*. The dancers assume a basic rectangular posture and throughout the performance return to it intermittently. The actor-dancer wears a large, multilayered skirt, brightly coloured scarves, heavy headgear carved out of wood, a decorated breastplate and a full-sleeved coloured jacket. The makeup is highly stylized, colourful and very elaborate, making the actor's face look like a painted mask. Intricately designed and symbolic, it

focuses attention on the performer's eyes. It is an important aspect of the production. The costume and makeup can take up to four hours to put on. The creation of a role or character is achieved by the codified makeup, costume, a repertoire of dance steps, hand gestures, patterns of stage movement and the use of the face and eyes.

Three types of drums are used – *centa*, *maddalam* and *itekka* – each with its own individual sound and function in the performance. Brass cymbals are also used. The two singers sing the entire text – narration and dialogue in a vocal style characterized by elaboration and repetition. Rulers of the princely states in Kerala before independence were great patrons of *kathakali*, maintaining troupes, writing plays and occasionally participating as performers. The Kerala Kalamandalam, the state academy for the performing arts of Kerala, provides full-time training for *kathakali*.

The only surviving performance tradition of the classical Sanskrit drama *kuttiyāttam* (*kuti* means combined, *attam* means play) has preserved for over a thousand years the ancient styles of performances as discussed and codified in the *Nātyashāstra*. It is the most complex and rigidly textured form of temple drama. The form evolved in the temples of Kerala and has been performed in temple theatres called *Kuttampalams* during temple festivals by a few artist-Brahmin families. Only since the 1960s has it been performed outside the region in city theatres. The government of India sent a troupe on a performing tour to France and Poland in 1981.

Storytelling in complex patterns is the essence of *kuttiyāttam*. It selects only one act of a Sanskrit play for performance and may take three to seven days to enact it. Speech (*vackika*) is overplayed in *kuttiyāttam* just as bodily acting (*angika*) is in *kathakali*. There are repetitions and great elaborations of the dramatic text, which may or may not be accompanied by gestures. The text is recited first with gestures and then enacted only through gesture. Speech is changed in a stylized sing-song pattern and is in the manner of vedic chanting. Much of the elaboration is brought about by the *vidushaka* (court jester) who is present throughout the performance to translate the dramatic text (which is in Sanskrit) into the native Malyalam. He also summarizes events and comments on the action. Often improvising, he brings humour and satire into a solemn performance and helps to loosen its rigidly structured form.

Kuttiyāttam has many intricate preliminaries and preludes which are an important part of the performance. The performance techniques are codified and the makeup and costumes are stylized. The musical instruments are the two *mizhāvus* (drums), *kuzhittāla* (small pair of cymbals) used by the *Nāngyar*, the woman musician who is also the singer and vocalist, *itekka* (or *idakka,* the instrument played with a small stick, also used in *kathakali*) and two wind instruments – *kompa* (trumpet) and *kurun-kuzhal* (pipe). Sometimes a *sankha* (conch shell) is used. The performance text of the selected acts from Sanskrit plays has survived in stage manuals for centuries. No new scripts or performance techniques have been added. The highly developed and stylized techniques of *kuttiyāttam* place it in a class of its own; it is total theatre, using work, movement, costume, makeup and design to create an integrated experience.

Another form of temple drama from Kerala is the *krishnattam*, which presents the life story of Krishna in eight cycle plays. From his birth to his departure to heaven, it enacts the story in song and dance. A form of devotional dance-drama, the text for the form was created in the seventeenth century in Sanskrit by King Manadeva, a member of the Calicut ruling family. Since then it has been performed by only one troupe attached to the Guruvayur temple as an offering. The dancer-actors perform using symbolic hand gestures, while the text is sung by the reciter-singer. There is an emphasis on pure dance movements. The makeup, costume and jewellery is similar to that used in *kathakali* but the necessity of facial expressions is minimized because of the use of wooden masks, painted in various colours.

Yakshagana (*Song of the Yakshas* – divine beings in the service of Kubera, the Hindu god of wealth) is a traditional rural form of operatic dance-drama dating to the late sixteenth century. The earliest play, *Virāta Parva* (*Grand Festival*), an episode from *Mahabharata* by Vishnu Varanballi, is said to date to 1564. Subsequently, plays have been written over the centuries by poets and devotees. Some of the song dramas are of high literary and dramatic merit. The themes are drawn from *Ramayana* and *Mahabharata* as well as the *Puranas*; the characters are mythological heroes, gods and demons. All plays invariably have battle scenes. It is a form characterized by masculinity and vigour in its basic temperament. All roles, including female, are performed by men.

The main preference of the form is storytelling and the *bhāgavata* (reciter-singer of the dramatic text) sits upstage, alternately narrating the events, singing on behalf of the actors (in first person) revealing their inner thoughts and feelings, commenting on their actions as a detached observer, speaking to the actors and linking events. The songs are literary compositions set to distinct music, which falls between folk and classical, and the singing is high-pitched. The *bhāgavata* keeps the beat with tiny cymbals. The success of a *yakshagna* performance is as dependent on the art of the *bhāgavata* as it is on the actors. Also on stage is an assistant singer, the *sangeetkar* and three instrumentalists playing the *maddale* (drum), a pipe and a *chande* (a barrel-like drum with a sharp clattering sound, extremely effective in battle scenes). The *bhāgavata* also pronounces the rhythmic syllables of the drum to accompany the actors' footwork. Dialogues are improvised and the style of speech stylized and elaborated upon by the actors.

The towering headgear of the *yakshagana* is its most striking costume feature. Called *mundasu*, it is a giant turban with golden threads: the effect is opulent and dramatic. The actors wear a coloured jacket, a *dhoti* (draped

Yakshagana production by K.S. Hegde, 1992.
Photo: courtesy of SNA.

lower garment), silk scarf and elaborate ornaments made of gilded wood. Vivid colours are
used in the makeup to create a dazzling effect.
Despite the massive headgear, heavy costumes
and jewellery, the dancing is fast and expert,
with intricate footwork at times and energetic
and vigorous movements at others. There are
acrobatic hops, kicks, leaps and jumps in the air.
Very effective use is made of the half curtain,
held by two stagehands.

The open-air *yakshagana* performances are
held in village squares, fields or on beaches. The
stage is a square at ground level, with four poles
fixed in the four corners to mark the area. The
audience sits on three sides. The performances
last all night.

In the 1980s, the *yakshagana* became a very
popular traditional form and has been presented
in cities on proscenium stages where it loses much
of its vigour and intensity in the confined setting.

The *tala maddale* is a variation of *yakshagana*, an indoor performance without costume,
makeup or dance held during the monsoon
season. The *bhāgavata* sits on the floor along
with the drummers and the artists sit in two
rows opposite each other. A play rich in argument, philosophy and narration is chosen and
sung or recited.

The *bhāgavata mela* is the traditional dance-
drama of Tamilnadu, performed once a year in
Melattur village at the religious festival of
Narsimha Jayanti in the first week of May. This
is a form steeped in religion; the play is their way
of paying homage to the deity. The performance
of the plays in its repertoire takes place in the
temple on a platform in front of the deity and
goes on all night.

In *bhāgavata mela*, which evolved in the seventeenth century, the focus is on the body. The
gestures are classical, the dancing vigorous.
Most dancing is descriptive and illustrates the
sung/recited text. The units of pure dance interrupt the storyline and temporarily halt the
action. The hand gestures are elaborate. The

accompanying music is in the *karnatāka* style. Most of the singing is done by the actors themselves. While dancing they recite, sing and speak in prose. This puts a tremendous demand on the performers and makes for a fascinating theatrical performance.

The actors inherit the art and preserve the tradition. The costumes and props of the temple drama are treated as sacred objects. The mask of the god Narsimha in the play *Prahlad Charitram* composed by Venkatarama Sastri (1759–1847) is preserved in the Narsimha temple in a special case fixed on the wall and is worshipped daily. It is a great honour to act as the god Narsimha and the actor, having fasted all day, goes into a trance at the climactic moment. Standing between religion and theatre, the *bhāgavata mela* performance is a commemorative event that retains its ritualistic context.

Kuchipudi is a dance-drama that originated in the seventeenth century in the village of the same name in the sate of Andra Pradesh. The performance starts with elaborate rituals of purification to sanctify the stage. The *sutradhāra*, the singer-narrator Bhāgavalā, sings an introduction of the characters after each one has done a brief dance. Bhāgavalā also explains their background, purpose and role. All roles are played by men. There is a lyrical quality in the performance and the acting is expressive. *Bhama Kalpam* (the story of Satyabhama, the wife of Lord Krishna) is the most popular and famous play in the repertoire of *kuchipudi*. Both *bhāgavata mela* and *kuchipudi* perform episodes from Hindu mythology and traditional legends. In both, speech is limited. The dialogues are short and link the songs to the narrative sequences. Both present a unique blend of recitation, singing and performance.

The *burrakatha* of Andhra Pradesh, the most popular of all folk forms of the state, is a dramatic ballad sung by three people. *Burra* is a hollow pumpkin instrument with four strings; *katha* means story. The *burra* player is the main singer and his two companions are the chorus, providing humour, questioning the leader and drawing out the story. They play the long drum of Andhra Pradesh, which is hung from their neck. The performers sing and recite the prose narrative while standing. Sometimes they take a few steps forward or circle to the rhythm of the drum. The main singer wears anklets and performs acrobatic movements. A famous tale in the 1940s was the *Ballad of Venkatarmani* about a boy who ate his mother's ears. Predominantly musical and narrative, the form is a perfect vehicle for the narration of heroic stories.

The *harikatha* of Andhra Pradesh is a form of religious discourse incorporating recitation, singing, storytelling and narration. Traditionally used for narrating stories from the epics and *Puranas*, the form interweaves poetry, dance and prose. The artists were called *haridas* (the servants of Krishna). They were in the tradition of itinerant singers prevalent in virtually every region of India.

The *veethi natakam* (street play) is the main form of traditional folk theatre in Andhra Pradesh. The performance takes place in the open, generally on the street. The form has a loose structure. The acting is crude and the language used is the common vernacular. The *sutradhāra* is the link between the drama and the audience, cracking jokes with them as well as with the characters. The *sutradhāra* sings and narrates the events. The actors have to engage in vigorous dancing and so they are not the singers. Rather, there is a chorus to accompany them. The costumes and makeup are loud and bright colours are used.

Most southern Indian traditional theatrical forms are a living illustration of Bharata's concept of theatre as visual poetry. *Kuttiyāttam*, *kathakali* and *yakshagana* especially are forms that please the eye; with their elaborate costumes, colourful makeup, fantastic headgear, complex body movement and symbolic hand gestures. They are theatrical spectacles.

Among the most exciting things about the contemporary Indian theatrical scene is that thousand-year-old forms can and do coexist with new and experimental work reflecting both contemporary sensitivities and new indigenous idioms. The traditional and the modern are both integral and relevant to the Indian way of life and to Indian theatre today.

By 'modern' Indian theatre is generally meant an urban theatre created primarily by people from the middle or upper-middle class, who are also the audience for this theatre. It places more emphasis on the dramatic text, in contrast to traditional theatre, where the performance text dominates. Modern theatre in India evolved in the latter half of the nineteenth century, under the influence of the British who had proclaimed India their colony by then. As such, it was a product of colonial culture and was deeply influenced by western theatre. It emerged in three cities that were established by the British as commercial ports and had no previous history – Calcutta in the east, Bombay in the west and

Madras in the south. They soon grew to be large urban centres. To propagate western thought and education in the country, universities were established in these cities in 1857 modelled on western institutions. British drama was introduced in the curriculum, with an emphasis on Shakespeare and the eighteenth-century dramatists, whose plays – in English – began to be seen in various parts of India. With the spread of English language and literature, the first plays were performed by Englishmen on proscenium arch stages and attracted an urban, middle-class audience whose values and tastes had been influenced by the British-style education they received, and by the interaction with the British necessitated by working with them in administrative and trade situations.

Urban Indian theatres imitated the touring British theatre groups and inevitably inherited the conventions of the British stage – elaborate stage settings, a drop curtain, wings, footlights, machinery for special effects, the clear separation of the audience and the performers, and the sale of tickets. The last two factors had the deepest and longest lasting impact on the very concept of theatre in India. Until then, Indian theatre had depended on patronage – royal, religious and official. Now, suddenly, theatre was a commodity and a means of making a profit for the producers, available to a select group who could afford it. Indian theatrical tradition had also allowed a variety of spaces for performance – temple precincts, streets, fields and market-squares. The proscenium stage shattered the traditional intimate audience–performer relationship and totally altered the traditional concept and character of theatrical space. Theatre was no longer an inseparable part of the daily life of people; it was a separate 'thing', visibly and consciously removed from them.

Drama written in Indian languages and performed by Indian actors did not emerge until the late nineteenth century. As early as 1843, Wajid Ali Shah (1822–87), the ruler of Awadh, had written a musical dance-drama called *Radha Kanhaiya Ka Qissa* (*The Tale of Radha and Krishna*), which was staged privately at the court. In 1851, he staged another play based on the love story of Princess Ghazala and Afsana-e-Ishka (*The Tale of Love*, 1853). In 1854, Agha Hasan Amanat, an Urdu poet from Lucknow, wrote a musical drama, *Indra Sabha* (*The Court of Lord Indra*), with songs in Urdu and Hindi. It was performed by almost every theatrical company during the latter half of the nineteenth century. Standing between literary drama and

folk play, it subsequently became a part of the repertoire of several Nautanki companies. In Maharashtra, *Sita Swayamvar* (*The Wedding of Sita*) written in 1843 by Vishnudas Bhave, was the first Marathi play. In Bengal, Dinbandhu Mitra's *Neel Darpan* (*The Blue Mirror*, or *The Mirror of Indigo Planters*) was staged in 1872 in Calcutta. But in general, this period was characterized by the performances of western dramatists in English and in several regional languages. English drawing room comedies were staged in some of the remotest parts of India.

The phenomenon of theatre as a vehicle for profit began to attract the attention of Parsi businesspeople (Parsis are followers of the Zoroastrian religion, traditionally merchants and businesspeople by profession), resulting in the establishment of several theatre companies on a commercial basis. Because of ownership, funding and administration by the Parsis, they came to be known simply as Parsi Theatres and dominated the urban Indian theatrical scene almost until the late 1930s. It is interesting to note that virtually all the actors, playwrights, directors, designers and staff of the Parsi Theatre were in fact Hindu and Muslim.

The plays, usually mythological in content and performed on proscenium stages, were seen by a wide range of communities all over India. Some of the greatest successes of this 'professional theatre' of the late nineteenth century were the spectacular productions of stories from *Ramayana* and *Mahabharata*. Employing European stage conventions and indigenous material, these shows were usually a crude potpourri of song, dance, farce and mime. The Parsi theatre companies had for their model the many Victorian commercial theatres in operation in Britain. The first two of these new Indian groups were the Victoria Theatre and Alfred Theatre, both established in 1871 and both of which toured widely. Other groups grew from these two including the New Alfred Theatre and the Original Theatre. As audiences increased, Victorian-style theatre buildings soon went up in many of India's larger cities, most of them copies of Covent Garden and Drury Lane in London.

Original plays were created for these groups in both Hindi and Urdu, all with the primary goal of making a profit. Perhaps the most famous of those writing for the Parsi Theatre was Agha Hashra Kashmiri (1879–1935) who did several Shakespearian adaptations including *Safed Khoon* (*White Blood*, 1906) based on *King Lear*, and *Saide Hawas* (1907) based on

King John, as well as several popular original plays including *Khoobsoorat Bala* (*Beautiful Maiden*, 1909), *Yahudi Ki Ladki* (*The Jew's Daughter*, 1913), *Bilwa Mangal* (1915) and *Sita Banwaas* (*The Exile of Sita*, 1927).

Another writer of note at this time was Narayan Prasad Betab (1872–1945), author of *Mahabharat* (1913), *Ramayan* (1915), adaptions of the great Indian epics, adaptation of Shakespeare's *Comedy of Errors* called *Gorakh-Dhandha* (*The Confusion*, *c.*1924), and *Zahari Saanp* (*Poisonous Snake*), an attack on British rule; and *Kumari Kinnar* (*Miss Kinnara*, 1928), – an attack on the British book *Mother India* by Miss Mayo.

Still another popular dramatist of the period was Radhey Shyam Kathawachak (1890–1963), whose plays often brought in religious issues. Among his important works were *Veer Abhimanyu* (*Brave Abhimanyu*, 1916), *Bharat Mata* (*Mother India*, 1918), *Prahalad* (1920), *Krishna Avtar* (*Incarnation of Lord Krishna*, 1926), *Draupadi Swayambar* (*The Wedding of Draupadi*, 1929) and *Ishwar Bhakti* (*Worship of God*, 1929).

The Parsi contribution lies not so much in the field of theatre, but in music and in the creation of unforgettable melodies. In Marathi, the music for touring productions like *Sharda* (1899) by G.B. Deval, an attack on child marriages, *Manapaman* (*Self-Respect and Insult*, 1911) written by K.P. Khadilkar and set to music by Govind Rao Tembe, perhaps the most successful musical in Marathi theatre, and *Panditraj Jagannath* (1960, with music by Vasant Desai), is still popular all over Maharashtra. This style of musical theatre – *sangeet natak* – was quite perfected in Maharashtra. Parsi (Natak Mandali) performances were staged in semi-permanent structures on proscenium stages, with wings and drop curtains. Elaborate in spectacle and focusing on special effects, this theatre was far removed from people and their daily lives. Even when they spoke Hindi or a regional language, they used a language no one used. They evolved an idiom that did not have even a remote connection with issues of contemporary times and made no attempts to handle them.

This kind of urban theatre met its end in the 1930s with the coming of talking films simply

A 1990 Parsi-style production of *Shah Jahan* by D.L. Roy.
Photo: courtesy of S. Tyagasajan.

because movies could provide the same kind of spectacle in a much better way. Many theatre halls were converted into cinemas. The actors and actresses, musicians, singers and playwrights turned to a burgeoning film industry which quickly came to dominate popular culture in India.

Not all of the dramatists working in the new literary style were writing commercially. One of the earliest to work against this style was Bharatendu Harishchandra (1850–85). Determined to build a more serious Hindi language theatre, Harishchandra began what came to be called the 'parallel' theatre movement, a political style of populist theatre that sought to arouse social awareness and national feeling. Consciously non-commercial, he gathered around him a small group of young people to perform his plays – *Bharat Durdasha* (*The Sorry State of Bharat*, 1880) *Andher Nagri* (*Corrupt State,* 1881), and his most famous play *Satyavadi Harishchandra* (*The Truthful King,* 1875). Unfortunately, his death at the age of 35 ended his tremendous promise; the literary Hindi theatre quickly lost its centre and what impetus it had. The movement would not re-emerge until the late 1940s.

Such work was not totally new. As far back as the late nineteenth century, theatre was employed as a forum for propagating social and political ideals, and it soon became a medium of protest. With the growing resentment towards British rule and the rise of nationalism, intellectuals and leaders soon realized the potential of theatre as a political weapon and decided its purpose should be to influence public opinion and raise social awareness, to delight and educate. In Maharashtra and Bengal, two politically aware states that played a key role in the Indian independence movement, theatre moved away from its concerns with mythological heroes and historical romances and began to focus on social issues like widow remarriage, divorce and the plight of the labouring poor. Thus, the Hindi theatre was not the only one to develop its own forms and styles between the late nineteenth century and the early years of independence.

The Bengali language theatre too evolved during this same time period. Initially influenced by the Parsi movement, it began to acquire professional characteristics as early as 1872. Bengali theatre also found its own socially rooted writers, among them Dinbandhu Mitra (1831–73), author of *Neel Darpan* (*Indigo Mirror*, 1860) which focused on the dismal living conditions of indigo planters; it was staged in 1872 by a nationalistic group of actors, directors and writers calling themselves the National Theatre Company of Calcutta. Anti-British in its outlook, this group began to tour widely, eventually splitting into two groups; one worked in Hindi and called itself the Hindi National Company (its first production was Micheal Madhusudan Dutt's (1824–73) *Sarmishtha* on 5 April 1876) while the other became the Bengali National Company, which staged a new production of *Neel Darpan* as its first production under director Girish Chandra Ghosh (1844–1912). The British realized the power of Indian theatre during its production in Lucknow in northern India in 1875. The play called for agricultural labourers to revolt against their landlords and, what was more unforgivable, depicted the rape of an Indian peasant woman by a white planter. The theatre was stormed by an angry crowd of Britishers and the performance was halted. The actors were packed off to Calcutta.

It was this specific production, as well as political developments elsewhere in the country, that eventually led British authorities to impose strict censorship rules through the passage of the Dramatic Performances Control Act in 1876. The Act stipulated that every play had to go through a censorship procedure before being licensed for performance. The British government subsequently used the Act to suppress any artistic activity which it felt could be interpreted as being anti-government. Even local police officials had magisterial powers under this Act and were able to ban performances, arrest actors and even confiscate a group's property. The Act was still in force in 1997 although it was rarely used. One of the few times it was used was in the 1975–7 period when a State of Emergency was declared across the country. During this period, innumerable theatre people were jailed and many groups banned. Subsequent protests led the government to cease such use of the Act but the fact remains that no government has withdrawn the Act entirely.

As a direct consequence of the Dramatic Performance Control Act, national and political protest became underground and concealed, surfacing cautiously, in allegorical and symbolic forms, in productions of a historical or mythological nature. Frustrated dramatists focused their attention on Hindu society, exposing its evils and corruptions – child marriages, the *sati* system, dowries and so on.

It was the writings of Rabindranath Tagore (1861–1941), the winner of the Nobel Prize for Literature in 1913, which gave an entirely new dimension to Bengali art and changed the direction of the nation's theatre once again. Tagore chose not to associate himself with the professional Parsi Theatre. Rather he chose as his model more classical Sanskrit forms. Working symbolically, Tagore's plays found their greatest admirers in the post-independence period.

By the 1930s, both the Hindi and Bengali-language theatres had become caught up in the national independence movement led by Gandhi and Jawaharlal Nehru (1889–1964). Although the Dramatic Performance Act was still operative and the production of clearly political plays remained difficult, playwrights throughout the country continued to write such plays and virtually all the new professional theatres in the country – the so-called regional theatres – strived to stage them. Establishing a totally different aesthetic base from the commercial Parsi groups, most members of the regional theatres tried to connect their activities to community issues. As such, they enjoyed wide support and patronage not only from their own specific communities but also in some cases from their entire regions. Most such groups were built around specific linguistic or cultural concerns and could be found in various parts of the country from Bengal and Maharashtra to Karnataka and Kerala. Their work was particularly important in the independence struggle and, when independence was achieved, most were granted significant subsidies by local and national governments.

The Bengal famine of 1943 was a good example of how such groups fanned the independence movement and helped to evolve a tradition of socially rooted protest plays in the country. Not only did they work from regional stages to make important statements, but also Bengali intellectuals, poets, actors and artists took to the streets to perform, sing and generally share in the miseries of the millions who perished at this time. Some Bengali groups toured across India to raise public awareness. The public response showed the cultural community that theatre could take a role in national life but perhaps only when it left the security of a formal theatre building.

Out of such ferment grew the Indian People's Theatre Association (IPTA) in 1943, a national movement with units in every Indian state. Operating until 1950 when it splintered, the IPTA provided regular visits of well-known companies including Parsi Theatre productions.

IPTA's activities led to improved standards of production (and theatre management) across the country and to the inclusion of women on the professional stages. Though women had been seen as early as 1933 in *Andhalayachi Shala* (*School for the Blind*), a production in the Marathi language, it was not until IPTA led the way that women began to take a more regular role in theatre activities.

The wounds of independence in 1947 were so deep and painful that intellectual and artistic life right across the country went into shock during the late 1940s and 1950s. It was not unusual during this time to see actors and other theatre workers on the streets not doing theatre but rather collecting food, clothing and money. The assassination of Gandhi in 1948 was yet a further blow to national stability. All these issues were subsequently reflected in stage performances though most from this period revealed exceptionally low artistic standards.

But eventually Indian theatre began a self-conscious quest for identity, an attempt to define its 'Indianness', to reconnect to the past from which it had been cut off by colonial intrusions. This is one of the primary impulses that has shaped Indian theatre in the post-independence period, and it led playwrights and directors to turn to folk and traditional theatrical forms for structure and style.

One of the first of the new productions to reflect the country's changing realities was Dharam Vir Bharati's (b. 1925) play *Andha Yug* (*The Blind Age*, 1954), set on the last day of the great war, a well-known tale from *Mahabharata*. The play, heard on All India Radio, created a sensation and allowed the author to make a variety of comments on such subjects as war, the miseries of partition, loss of faith and national identity. It also quickly attracted many directors wanting to put it on stage. In 1963, it was staged before Prime Minister Nehru.

But because the models and conventions of western realistic theatre were borrowed and always remained alien to Indian theatre, such initiatives always had problems. Tagore had tried to resolve the inherent conflict between the two styles in his lyric plays, but he failed to find compatible production styles. In the 1950s, therefore, there seemed a perceptible need to forge a theatre that did not model itself on the British example, but was, in its own unique way, Indian. Thus was born what has been termed the 'theatre of roots'. In retrospect, it is seen as part of the decolonization process, Indian theatre's studied attempt at liberating and distancing itself from the influence of the western realistic theatre.

Director Habib Tanvir was one of the first at this time to break away from realistic theatre. He formed his Hindustani Theatre in Delhi in 1954; his productions of *Agra Bazar* (*Agra Market*, 1954), a play he wrote on the life of the famous Urdu poet Nazir of Agra, and of *Mitti Ki Gadi* (1959), an operatic version, in the *nautanki* style, of the Sanskrit classic *Mrichhkatikam* (*The Little Clay Cart*), used music, dance and poetry. The latter production was performed, with six tribal artists in the cast, without curtains, props or sets, and called *nai* (new) *nautanki* by Tanvir. He subsequently continued his experimental work with the tribal communities in his home state of Madhya Pradesh, synthesizing folk and modern theatrical traditions. His theatre is characterized by a sense of gaiety and celebration. He used *maanch*, the rural drama form of Chhattisgarh,

for presentations in a modern sophisticated form. He called his group Naya Theatre (New Theatre) and was still producing new work – *Charandas Chor* (*Charandas the Thief*) – in 1975. His productions were skilful and innovative, and he proved that rural theatre could be used as a basis for a modern and truly Indian theatre, firmly rooted to the soil.

This was the impetus for similar theatrical activity in Bombay, Delhi, Calcutta and other centres. Director B.V. Karanth's production of playwright Girish Karnad's famous play *Hayavadana*, inspired by the *yakshagana* of Karnataka – a form Karanth was familiar with since childhood – is another good example. Using music, mime and movement from the earlier form, his productions were landmarks in India's contemporary theatre's encounters with tradition. Karanth later successfully adapted stylized conventions, gestures, vocal patterns and rhythmic movements for his production of Kalidasa's *Malvikagnimitram*. His works are

Ratan Thiyam's 1985 production of *Antogni* in Manipuri style.
Photo: courtesy of SNA.

clearly stylized with exaggerated theatricality. His actors perform conveying a full consciousness of the audience, a sense of playfulness. In his 1979 production of *Andher Nagri* (*Unjust Town*), a nineteenth-century Hindi farce by Bharatendu Harishchandra, the actors played at playing the script, thus creating multiple layers of reality. He used similar devices to distort reality. He also used music to underline and sustain the theatricality of his performances.

Of all contemporary directors in India, K.N. Panikkar of Kerala has made the most consistent and meaningful use of folk forms and performance styles for urban theatre, incorporating the stories, music, dance movements, conventions and rhythms from *kathakali*, *kuttiyāttam* and *teyyam*. For subject matter he has turned to classical Sanskrit plays, directing the plays of Bhasa – *Madhyama Vyagogam* (*The Play of the Middle One*), *Urubhangam* (*Broken Thighs*), *Karnabharam* (*Karna's Burden*) and *Kalidasa* (*Shakuntala and Vikramorvasiyam*). In some of his productions he used *kalaripayattu*, the martial art form of Kerala, which he also utilized in training the actors of his company, Sopanam.

Ratan Thiyam, a well-known director from Manipur, used traditional Manipuri martial art Thang-Ta movement techniques in his production of *Urubhangam*, which, along with *Chakravyuha* (*Army Formation*), his best known production, was a stylized performance in Manipuri. The overall impact of Thiyam's theatre was spectacular and original.

Other, younger directors followed who carried on the experimentation with tradition. In 1973, Jabbar Patel, a leading Marathi director, produced Vijay Tendulkar's *Ghasiram Kotwal* (*Ghasiram the Police Chief*), inspired by the Dashavatar folk form of *konkan*. This is considered to be another milestone in the history of modern Indian theatre. He used a human curtain of ten singers who alternately concealed and revealed the action. Patel's other successful production was playwright P.L. Deshpande's *Teen Paisacha Tamasha* (1978), an adaptation of Brecht's *Threepenny Opera*.

During this period in Gujarat, Dina Gandhi used the traditional *bhāvai* form in her production of *Mena Gurjari*. Shivram Karanth wrote new operas in Kannada based on the

Shakuntala directed and designed by Ebotombi, 1987.
Photo: courtesy of S. Tyagasajan.

yakshagana tradition. Sheila Bhatia, a Punjabi writer-composer, produced *Heer Ranjha*, an opera inspired by folk melodies and the folklore of the love story of Heer and Ranjha. Bengali theatre director and radical playwright Utpal Dutt started making use of *jatra* in 1969, making it a vehicle for his left-wing ideology. Younger directors like M. Ramaswamy, Kartick Awasthi and Bansi Kaul carried on in a similar vein.

In the entire body of the 'theatre of roots', music and dance movements – essential to Indian performances over the centuries – were used in the realization of the performance text. Music functioned almost as an autonomous theatrical language, an independent text along with verbal acting and bodily movements. A variety of musical instruments were used, especially drums of several types. Music became integral to the actors' movements, acting, gaits, entrances and exits.

Making a conscious break from the realistic mode, this new theatre turned to stylization – the essence of traditional Indian theatre for centuries. It employed ritualistic and martial arts elements, and oral techniques like recitation, narration, chants and rhythmic repetition of *bols* (syllables) to transform the dramatic text into the performance text. These were also utilized, along with acrobatics and warm-up exercises, in the development of acting styles.

This theatre's use of tradition was reflected in the design and structure of performances, and in the emphasis placed on the body in the art of the actor. Tanvir, Karanth and Thiyam rejected the proscenium theatre and sought to discover or create new performance spaces that enabled a closer actor–spectator relationship. Thus the dramatic text was freed to create its own environment. Post-independence Indian theatre has consistently rejected the proscenium stage and constantly engaged in the search for and use of unusual performance spaces. This is clearly evident in the street theatre of India. The proscenium, a foreign element in India's theatrical universe, has never found real acceptance, particularly with avant-garde theatre.

Instead of conventional rehearsals, actor training and acting workshops became the focus. The performances were characterized by an intense physicality, rather than by the spoken word. Recognizing a shortage of quality scripts, some directors chose Sanskrit plays, some adapted or re-created existing realistic plays and others evolved their own scripts to suit a particular theatrical form.

Soon came institutional support. The Sangeet Natak Akademi launched a programme in 1984 sponsoring traditional performances, festivals and exhibitions in Delhi and in other cities in India. This resulted in the exposure of urban theatre artists to the richness, variety and vigour of traditional theatre. The main objective was to encourage younger directors, and initiate an interaction of folk forms with urban theatre work. Competitions were held and cash grants provided to directors who created productions using elements from traditional theatre. Director Waman Kendre of Bombay dramatized Uttam Bandhu Tulpe's novel *Zulva* in Marathi for a festival sponsored by the Akademi. C.K. Jambe, the head of the repertory company of Ninasam, a theatre group in a village in Karnataka, regularly made use of elements of traditional theatre for his productions, which toured in the villages of Karnataka. Neelam Mansingh Choudhary of Chandigarh directed *Heer Ranjha* and *Raja Bharthari* (*King Bharthari*) in the *naqal* form, using narrative, storytelling, music, dance, mime and *naqqals* (traditional performers of the form) as actors. Several directors, using regional performance conventions, local legends and folk tales as thematic material, also used regional dialects.

Paradoxically, this theatre was considered to be avant-garde, because it broke away from the conventional realistic theatre, and yet in reality, it connected to the 2,000-year-old *Natyashastra* tradition. Ultimately, it came in for criticism on the grounds that 'form' was imitated at the expense of 'content' and that decontextualization of tradition failed to establish any links to contemporary life and its issues and problems. Traditional performances were seen to be transported from their own environment to proscenium-bound, air-conditioned theatres in cities or foreign countries. This alteration of context, it was argued, reduced Indian theatre to mere exotica, devoid of soul. It was also criticized because inevitably, the directors became more important, the focal point of attention, rather than the performance itself, or the actors.

What was seen to be a movement gradually petered out. Currently, Ninasam is one of the few theatre groups using traditional theatrical forms and styles, and K.N. Panikkar continues his work at his Sopanam Company in Trivandrum. In the summer of 1996, he wrote *Arambachakkan*, his adaptation of the myth of Orpheus and Eurydice. The play in Malayalam was directed by US director Erin B. Mee, using *mohiniyattam* movements, among other traditional elements. His company also produced two Sanskrit plays during the same time Kalidasa's *Vikramorvasiyam* and Bhasa's *Duta Vakyam* (*The Word of the Messenger*). As for other urban directors, it was as if they had had their encounter with tradition, experienced it, experimented with it, but ultimately did not know, or could not decide, what to do with it. This continuing failure to resolve the rural–urban dichotomy is viewed by critics like Rustom Bharucha to be one of the greatest failures of modern Indian theatre. There is no sustained theatrical interaction between people in the cities and villages.

Dissatisfied with theatre being a benign form of pure entertainment playing to a middle-class audience, some theatre groups have taken to the streets, performing in front of factory workers, groups of students, labourers, farmers and slum-dwellers. Badal Sircar of Calcutta was one of the first to practise and popularize the idea of taking performances to the people. In 1976, he started having Saturday afternoon open-air and free performances of his group, Satabdi, in a corner of Curzon Park (now Surendranath Park), with passers-by as audiences. On occasional weekends, he would take his actors to nearby villages for performances. Using improvised dialogue, minimal props and encouraging active audience participation, he called his theatre 'Angan-Manch' or open-air theatre. Totally rejecting the idea of funding, publicity and the sale of tickets, he believed that theatre can be free only when it is amateur.

Safdar Hashmi of Delhi was another important early practitioner of street theatre in India. A reputed columnist for the *Economic Times*, he had been engaged since the mid-1970s in developing a kind of political theatre that would reflect the concerns and problems of India's working class and peasantry. Picking up where IPTA had left off, Hashmi rejected the use of traditional forms, feeling that it necessarily involved the accompaniment of traditional content, with its superstitions, backwardness and emphasis on feudal structures. In 1973, he started his group, Janam (Birth), which was also an acronym for Jana Natya Manch, meaning People's Theatre Platform, a name reflecting his left-wing political ideology. By 1989, the year of Hashmi's murder, it had performed over four thousand times and had produced more than twenty plays, most of them written by Hashmi. A number of the plays were translated into almost every major Indian language. Each play dealt with a specific social or political issue.

His group performed in open spaces on the ground, in colleges, parks, outside factories, in a stadium, and on the lawns of the Boat Club in central New Delhi. The most famous and successful production was *Machine* (1978), the first play written by Hashmi, dealing with the exploitation of workers. It became legendary because it was performed all over India, playing to working-class audiences in their thousands. Other plays include *Gaon Se Shahar Tak* (*From the Village to the City*, 1978), a play about the displacement of migrant rural workers; *Hatyare* (*Killers*, 1979), dealing with the problem of communalism; *DTC ki Dhandhli* (*The Corruption of the Delhi Transport Corporation*, 1979), protesting about 100 per cent fare hikes; *Aurat* (*Woman*, 1979), depicting women's issues like dowry, wife-beating and bride-burning; *Teen Crore* (*30 Million*, 1979), focusing on the growing unemployment in India; and *Apharan Bhaichare Ka* (*Abduction of Brotherhood*, 1986), about the separatist movement in Punjab.

Hashmi was killed in 1989 during a performance of his play, *Hulla Bol!* (*Attack!*), dealing with the government repression of the labour movement. It was being performed outside a factory in east Delhi to support the local election campaign of the Communist Party of India (Marxist), when Hashmi was attacked and beaten to death by a rival candidate from the Congress (I) Party along with nearly a hundred hired thugs. Another performer was also shot dead.

Hashmi's death shocked the nation and united the entire Indian artistic community in a massive upsurge of protest. Shows were cancelled and rallies held all over the country. Film, television and theatre personalities in Bombay, Calcutta and Delhi attended gatherings.

The work of Safdar Hashmi and Badal Sircar has deeply influenced several theatre artists in the years following. Prominent among these is the Delhi-based director Tripurari Sharma, who also teaches acting at the National School of Drama (NSD). After graduating from the NSD, she formed her company Alarippu, which performs, in the streets, market-places, villages and urban enclaves, plays that have been developed in workshops and rehearsals, and that deal with social and political themes, local concerns and women's issues. She also does mainstream theatre in commercial halls, and directs TV serials. She has conducted street theatre workshops across India, and works with women's groups, college students, factory workers, villagers, paramedics and doctors. Her play *Kaath Ki Gaadi* (*The Wooden Cart*) was commissioned by Unicef, and addresses the problems of lepers – their ostracization by society, and the stigmas and taboos associated with the disease. An unconventional play, it is episodic in structure and held together by a narrator. It was a very successful production. She also evolved performance scripts on subjects like the coming of multinational companies to India, religious fundamentalism, communalism, corruption in public life, the working conditions of factory workers, and the effect of the dollar on the Indian economy. She also focuses on women's issues – especially in *Daughter-in-Law*, her first play – depicting their search for identity and changing roles in Indian society. Her production of Mohan Rakesh's *Adhe Adhure* (*The Half People*) is notable for its empathetic portrayal of the central character, a woman, her directorial vision overruling the conception of the same character by the playwright.

Sharma is one of the most original and creative theatre artists currently working in India. She has represented India at the first women playwright's conference in the United States in 1988, been the coordinator of a one-year project on women and theatre for the women's conference in Beijing, and has won several national awards.

Another community theatre group based in Delhi is Aloke Roy's Jagran (Awakening), working in community education and development through the use of pantomime. Active since 1968, the group has performed in the resettlement colonies of Delhi, incorporating elements from the western and Indian traditions to create performances relevant to slum-dwellers and their lives. *Harijan*, *Alcoholism*, *The Monster of Malnutrition*, *Dowry*, *Blackmarketeer* and *Drugs* are the names of some of their performances also reflecting the nature of their themes. The performances are held in open spaces, fields and parks, on the bare ground. They make use of a narrator, usually Roy, who comments on the action and engages in dialogue with the spectators. Audience participation is encouraged. Exaggerated gestures and movements are used as part of the acting technique, and very effective use is made of mime. White makeup is used by actors, with the mouth and eyes painted, to give the effect of a mask. The actors portray caricatures, and the group has travelled widely within the country and performed abroad, including Britain, France, Denmark, Finland, Jamaica, Canada and the USA.

Perhaps the biggest problem now facing theatre artists in India, as it has been for the decades since independence, is that theatre in India has, by and large, failed to be a means of earning a living for playwrights, directors, actors, critics and technicians. This is the most fundamental and inescapable fact about modern Indian theatre, and one that is sadly and universally lamented by almost everyone working in it. The viability of theatre as a profession, a means of earning a living and making a profit, are minimal. Most groups barely cover their costs through ticket sales and advertisements in brochures; producers and directors have to rely on grants and subsidies from the government, from western agencies (like Unicef and the Ford Foundation), from corporate sponsorship (also minimal), as well as engage in other professions to fund their projects and productions. This phenomenon is a function of several complicated social, historical, economic and geographical factors, perhaps the most important being the fundamental notion, propagated in the *Natyashastra,* and carried on over the millennia, that theatre has an elevated status, almost comparable to religion, and you cannot, or should not, buy or sell religion, live off it or make a profit out of it. The Indian psyche is perhaps subconsciously uncomfortable with the idea of paid theatre; consequently, even the most talented actors, excellent directors and brilliant playwrights have had, out of necessity, to turn to other professions to earn a living – office jobs, teaching in colleges and universities, businesses, government positions or in television and film – which provide a steady income to support themselves and their style of life.

In the 1960s and 1970s it was film that graduates from the National School of Drama inevitably gravitated towards. Many playwrights (Girish Karnad being the most prominent), directors and actors (Utpal Dutt, Om Shivpuri, Sulabha Deshpande, Dina Pathak) worked in films to sustain their theatrical activity. For some of the greatest practitioners of Indian theatre, who are technically amateur, being 'professional' means being serious about their work, not earning their bread through it. Most people do theatre out of sheer love for the art form. It is viewed almost as a leisure activity, despite the existence of a body of dedicated and thoroughly professional (in their work ethics) theatre artists who have produced performances of exceptional quality and bold innovation.

Another major challenge that live Indian theatre now faces is from the television and home video industry. The spread of cable television, since the late 1980s, with its profusion of soap operas, and film-based programming and the easy access to home video, is having a tremendous impact on theatre audiences, which continue to dwindle in numbers. Television is encouraging people to stay at home, particularly on weekends, where they can watch made-for-television dramas and serials in the comfort of their own home, without having to spend money on public transportation and the purchase of tickets.

Jasmine Jaywant, Ranbir Singh,
Ravi Chaturvedi

Structure of the National Theatre Community

Although modern theatre activity is spread throughout the country, Bombay, Calcutta and Delhi are the most active centres with regular performances taking place throughout the year. Each of these cities has an active commercial theatre. Important smaller centres include Jaipur, Lucknow, Bhopal, Chandigarh and Simla. Beyond these, most state capitals have at least one or two regularly producing theatre groups.

From the 1950s, the government had begun to establish cultural policies for the country including the establishment of three new academies for the arts: Sangeet Natak Akademi (Central Academy of Performing Arts), Lalit Kala Akademi (Central Academy of Fine Arts) and the Academy of Literature. Autonomous organizations were also established within each state to promote the arts and such government support added greatly to the growing amount of theatre activity.

In 1959, a National School of Drama was established in New Delhi under the auspices of the Central Academy of Performing Arts. Its first director was Sathu Sen. Replacing Sen two years later was Ebrahim Alkazi (b. 1925). Trained at the Royal Academy of Dramatic Art (RADA) in London, Alkazi's vision for a new kind of Indian theatre quickly began to inspire many young theatre people right across the country. Beginning with western classics, Alkazi insisted the school explore Indian classical forms as well. By 1962, the activities of the school had attracted wide national attention and performances of western plays such as Ibsen's *A Doll's House* and Molière's *Scapin* began to be seen along with original Hindi plays such as Mohan Rakesh's (d. 1972) *Ashadh Ka Ek Din* (*A Day of Rain*).

Alkazi's production of Kalidasa's Sanskrit classic *Abhijnana Shakuntalam* (written about AD 6) was staged during the 1964 International Congress of Orientalists in New Delhi and opened the way for many other Sanskrit classics to find their places on India's stages. The school went on to produce works in other Indian languages, including *Jyotsana Ani Jyoti* (*Jyotsana and Light*) by Gangadhar Gadgil (b. 1923) in 1967, a play in the Marathi language. In 1964, a professional repertory company was started at the school. Its success with audiences inspired similar groups, some with support from the state and others with support from corporations such as the Shri Ram Centre for Art and Culture sponsored by the DCM group of Industries. Other groups began to work in Calcutta, Delhi and Bombay as students from the National School of Drama spread their skills across the country.

Still another exemplary development was the establishment in 1981 of Bharat Bhawan, a multidisciplinary arts centre funded directly by the Madhaya Pradesh government in Bhopal. Working mostly in Hindi, the centre's theatre company has since performed in other languages and has hosted the visits of many international touring groups, usually in association with foreign cultural agencies including the British Council and the American Centre. The Indian Council for Cultural Relations, part of the External Affairs Ministry, has also worked extensively in this growing area ensuring not only that groups from abroad come to India but also that Indian groups travel to other countries.

The state academies of drama, dance and music play a major role in national theatre life as sponsors of festivals and hosts of workshops. The Central Academy, for example, annually organizes a series of regional dramatic festivals focused on the work of young writers and directors. The series culminates in a national festival in Delhi.

Government cultural departments at state levels offer modest subsidy to theatre groups. The central government gives small annual grants to both groups and individual artists. The

NSD Repertory Company's 1992 production of *Julius Caesar* directed by Ebrahim Alkazi.
Photo: courtesy of S. Tyagasajan.

Ravindra Manch Society, a governmental agency in the city of Jaipur, follows a different model and primarily funds an annual festival for groups in the region. As a third model, cultural centres in Bhopal (Bharat Bhawan) and Jaipur (Jawahar Kala Kendra) subsidize their own in-house productions at the same time as they support and organize national festivals.

Regional cultural centres exist in several smaller locales such as Patiala, Udaipur, Allahabad and Nagpur, which have regularly organized festivals, set up exchange programmes and sponsored local tours. The Prithvi Theatre in Bombay organizes an international festival every two years with support from both the private and corporate sector. All groups supplement their incomes with appeals to the private sector.

It is rare when shows are sold out. Only when productions include well-known film and television stars is there any chance of playing to full houses even with modest ticket prices of from 5 to 50 rupees (from 25 US cents to about US $2.50). Even then, it is rare for a serious production to make back its original investment. Audiences in the 1990s still prefer films and television and most good actors and directors are inevitably drawn into these areas if they wish to make commercially viable careers. Only in major cities are ticket prices higher but never more than 200 rupees for a commercial production with a major star. Film prices are consistently higher than theatre prices in most cities (Bombay and Delhi being the exceptions).

Theatre workers are not organized and as a result the interests of actors and theatre technicians are only minimally protected.

A study in 1984 tried to identify the role of government subsidy and the function of existing government-funded cultural institutions but the report was never officially presented to parliament by its government sponsors and no actions were taken.

Ravi Chaturvedi

Artistic Profile

Companies

In India, the word 'company' is used only to refer to registered corporate entities whose goal is to make a profit. Moreover, a company must be registered with the government under the National Companies Act and must fulfil certain legal requirements with significant tax implications. Companies, for example, are not allowed to receive public monies in the form of grants, but may be eligible for business loans. Those who work for a company also fall under the rules of the National Factory Act. Though some theatre groups do choose to work in this way, it is very much the exception rather than the rule.

Rather than companies therefore, most theatre activity in India takes place under other rubrics with not-for-profit goals. Many choose to call themselves 'groups' while others prefer to be known as associations, societies or even simply as voluntary organizations. In 1957, the government tried to link these not-for-profit terms under the Registration of Societies Act. All groups registered under this Act were to be not-for-profit in their goals, were allowed to receive public funds and private donations to acquire immovable property and were generally tax exempt. Most important, they were allowed to set their own levels of remuneration and, when a profit was made, it had to be returned to the organization itself.

Only purely commercial theatre groups now operate as 'companies', with almost every other type of theatre activity, including the operations of traditional theatre groups, working under the Registration of Societies Act. Most of these traditional groups, in fact, are family-oriented operations with training beginning for chosen family members as children.

Virtually all traditional groups are known by the name of their leading actors or by the name of the best known member of the family and, given the fluid nature of the groups, their names change over time. The best known *kuttiyāttam* group in Kerala, for example, is the Chakyar group, called so in recognition of its star and director Madhav Chakyar (b. 1922). Groups like the Chakyar play primarily in their own areas of the country although occasional tours are undertaken. In some areas there are as many as ten different groups in operation doing traditional performances, usually during festival and holiday times. Most of the traditional groups perform between fifty and a hundred times a year.

On the spoken theatre side, the most regularly producing group is the Repertory Company at the National School of Drama in New Delhi. This group has a core of twenty actors and technicians and receives a regular subsidy from the government.

Other such groups include the theatre of the DCM Group of Companies which, like the National School of Drama group, employs actors on a yearly contract. The Bharat Bhawan Cultural Centre in Bhopal also has a repertory group of twenty and functions on the same pattern as the NSD Repertory.

Other prominent groups operate in Maharashtra and include Natya Sampada (founded in 1964) which has produced more than forty shows, the Goa Hindu Association (formed in 1950) which has also produced over forty shows, and Avishkar (founded in 1970), which has produced some thirty plays.

There were many early professional troupes of note which deserve recognition. Among them are the Vishnu Das Troupe founded by the popular actor Vishnu Das (1819–1901) in the mid-nineteenth century; Narharbuwa and Aryoddharak troupes in Maharashtra; Shahhunagarwasi Theatre in Shahhunagar, which mostly staged the plays of Shakespeare; and Kirloskar Natak Mandali, which staged *sangeet natakas* (musicals). Playwrights such as Anasaheb Kirloskar (1843–85), G.B. Deval (1854–1916) and Sripad Krishan Kolhatkar (1871–1934) were associated with the last company from its beginnings.

Another important group was the Gubbi Theatre of Karnataka, founded in 1884 by Gubbi Chudanna, Abdul Aziz Saheb and Sahukar Neelakanthappa. The group's first production was an adaptation of a *yakshagana* play. In 1924, the company built a theatre in Bangalore, the Channa Basaveshwara Natak Shale. It was expanded twice, in 1930 and in 1946. In 1925, the company began the country's first touring children's theatre.

Also of early note was the Ratnavali, founded in 1906 in the city of Bangalore. Under the direction of A.V. Varadachar, the Ratnavali company continued in operation for more than two decades when the death of its founder in 1926 led to the group's closing. Music was a significant part of the company's working style, in this case music based on classical ragas.

An early cooperative theatre was begun in the town of Halgeri. The company the Sri Halasiddheswar Prasadita Sangeet Nataka Sabha – was directed by Linganagowda Patil but became nationally known under the leadership of the comic actor Dodda Jettappa.

In 1905, another group, Maharashtra Natak Mandali, was formed; it raised production standards still higher. Run by Ganpatrao Bhagwat, this group successfully produced the plays of K.P. Khadilkar (1892–1948) and helped to establish his reputation as a dramatist of the first rank.

In the 1920s, the professional Marathi theatre began to emerge with several star actors starting their own groups. Keshavrao Bhonsale, a long-time member of the Kirloskar Natak Mandali, began his Lalit Kaladarsha, a group which staged many plays by Mama Warerkar (1883–1964). In 1922, Lalit Kaladarsha produced Warerkar's *Satteche Gulam (Slaves of Power)* in which realistic settings and lighting were used for the first time. In 1931 Keshavrao Date staged for Samarth Natak Mandali the first modern play written in Marathi, *Sarala Devi* by Waman Bhole (b.1893).

In 1933 in Bombay, the playwriting career of Prahalad Keshav Atre (b. 1898) began with a production of the comedy *Sashtang Namaskar (The Warmest Welcome)* at the Balmohan Natak Mandali in Bombay. Among his other plays of note were *Gharabaher (Inside and Outside)*, *Udyacha Sansaar (Udaya's World)*, *Lagnachibedi (Marriage Ties)*, *Vande Bharatam (Salute to India)*, *Mee Ubha Ahe (I Am Standing)* and *Jag Kay Mhanel (Whatever the World Means)*.

In 1942 actor-writer-director M.G. Rangnekar (b. 1907) founded Natya Niketan, gathering around him popular stage and film actors. His first production was his own play *Ashirwad (Blessings)*, a play dealing with the life of a middle-class family. Other Rangnekar plays by Natya Niketan have been *Kulvadhu (Bride of the Clan)*, *Vahini (Sister)*, *Ek Hota Mhatara (There Was an Old Man)*, *Rambha* and *Bhatala Dili Osri (Shelter to the Brahmin)*, the latter a satire dealing with the problem of housing in Bombay.

In the city of Bombay, an important Marathi-language theatre was operated by Bal Gangadhar Tilak, Veer Savarkar (1883–1966), N.C. Kelkar (1872–1947) and playwright K.P. Khadilkar. The theatre was an active part of the independence movement and its plays called for numerous social reforms. To get around the Dramatic Performance Act, Marathi playwrights used mythological themes to interpret allegorically excesses of British rule. Khadilkar's most important plays included *Keechak Vadh (The Death of Keechak)*, a drama challenging the partition of Bengal and *Bhau Bandki (Fight Between Brothers)*. Other plays of note produced by the theatre were Vishnu Hari Aundhkar's (1894–1942) *Beband Shahi (Chaotic Rule)*, R.B. Gadhari's *Raja Sanyasa (The Ascetic King)*, Vaman Rao Gopal Joshi's (1881–1954) *Rakshasi-Mahatvakansha (Monstrous Ambition)* and *Rana Dundubhi (Trumpets of War)*, and Mama Warerkar's *Satteche Gulam (Slaves of Power)*.

As for theatrical styles, it is no surprise to find that in the modern theatre, music and dance remain important factors, a testimony to the continuing significance of traditional performance forms within the Indian arts community. The inclusion of music in Brecht's plays was no doubt one of the major reasons for his success in India from the 1950s onward. Of particular interest have been his *Threepenny Opera* and *Herr Puntila and His Man Matti*. Another very popular success in this style was a 1978 musical adaptation of Gogol's *Revizor (The Inspector General)* directed by Bansi Kaul (b. 1949) in the city of Lucknow.

In 1952, the Little Ballet Troupe was formed by Shanti Vardhana. The group's first production was a dance-drama called *Ramayana*, built around a classical tale done by three dancers, a drummer and puppets. The production later played in Paris. After Shanti Vardhana's death in 1954, the group continued operations under the leadership of his dancer wife Gul Vardhana (b. 1928) but in 1964 it moved to Gwalior where it re-emerged as the Rangshree Little Ballet Troupe. One of its most successful later works was a musical fantasy called *The Scarecrow* based on a piece of writing by Nehru.

Also proving modern connections with classical music and dance forms is the work of Uday Shankar whose 1944 production of *Bhooka Ha Bengal (Bengal Is Hungry)*, about the great Bengal famine, integrated the arts of music and dance with film. Of note here too is the work of Mrinalini Sarabhai at the Darpan Academy in Ahemdabad, the capital of Gujarat; Kathak Kendra of Delhi and Jaipur and Shriram Bhartiya Kala Kendra of Delhi, which have both done many works on mythological themes; and the one-time *kathakali* dancer Astad Deboo from Bombay who has blended Indian classical training with western-style modern dance to

Thanatamorphia: Many Faces of Death, a work by Astad Deboo, Bombay 1990.

create a number of innovative crossover works. Deboo, who often dances solo, has performed regularly in both Europe and the United States and has done some innovative choreography with deaf dancers.

Dramaturgy

One of the first things that needs to be said of Indian dramaturgy is that in modern Indian theatre, the categories of playwright, director and actor often overlap. Some directors write plays, act in them, design scenery, lighting and costumes; others choose existing plays and employ technicians to do sets and lighting. The former mode perhaps comes instinctively to Indian practitioners of theatre; the practice is as old as the *natyashastra*, where the *sutradhar* was a necessary figure in performances, embodying a multiplicity of roles – he could be the writer, director, actor, stage manager, singer and/or leader of a troupe. What follows is a description of playwrights who gained national eminence, whose works, in their native languages and

translations were widely read, performed and seen.

Indian dramatists of the late nineteenth century were strongly influenced by the well-made-play tradition of the European theatre. Ibsen, Chekhov and Shaw as well as early Strindberg all became popular with educated middle-class audiences. By the turn of the century, a similar Indian theatre emerged. One of the earliest of these plays – and one still popular in India – was G.B. Deval's *Sharda*, a drama about the sale of young girls into marriages. Another that continues to draw packed houses is Ram Ganesh Gadkari's (1885–1919) *Ekach Pyala* (*Only One Peg*), a powerful tragedy depicting the evils of alcohol.

The first really important play written in the twentieth century was *Andha Yug* (*The Blind Epoch*, 1955), a five-act verse play in Hindi written by Dharam Vir Bharati, an important Hindi novelist and literary figure. Based on *Mahabharata*, it is a shattering tragedy of the Kaurava family, a tragedy which develops into global war. Beginning with a blind king, the events ultimately corrupt and corrode every rung of society. Using a storyteller to present this mythical material, Bharati utilizes structures reminiscent of not only classical western forms but also early Indian forms. The play became a model for almost every contemporary director, and several productions of it were seen across the country. When written, it was intended to be a radio play. This was the only play written by Bharati.

The other significant Hindi playwright – who was also a fiction writer of the post-independence Indian theatre – was Mohan Rakesh (1925–73). His major plays, *Ashadh Ka Ek Din* (*A Rainy Day*, 1958), *Lahron Ke Rajhans* (*Swans of the Waves*, 1963) and *Adhe Adhure* (*The Half People*, 1969) are classics of Indian theatre that not only have been performed consistently by almost every major theatre director in India, but also are used as texts in a large number of universities in Hindi-speaking areas. His plays are an example of literary drama at its best that has also lent itself to theatrical performances.

Following independence, Theatre of the Absurd became a major influence in urban centres with plays by Jean Genet, Eugène Ionesco and Samuel Beckett being regularly performed. It was these works which significantly influenced Indian playwrights in the 1960s such as Mohan Rakesh (1925–72), Badal Sirkar, Adya Rangacharya (1904–85), Tendulkar and Girish Karnad (b. 1938).

India's leading contemporary playwright is Girish Karnad, who writes in his native Kannada, the language spoken in the state of Karnataka (formerly known as Mysore). Also an actor and director in films and television, he was one of the leading forces in the resurgence of Indian theatre in the 1960s, in its search to find its roots and define its identity. He has drawn the thematic content of his plays from Indian myths, legends, tales, historical figures and from social and cultural traditions. *Yayati* (1961), his first play, is based on the story, found in *Mahabharata*, of King Yayati and his tragic efforts to prolong his youth. *Tughlaq* (1964) has for its protagonist the Moghul King Mohammad-bin-Tughlaq of the fourteenth century, who was a radical visionary far ahead of his times, a fact that ultimately leads to his tragedy.

Karnad's *Hayavadana* (1971) is an adaptation of Thomas Mann's *Transposed Heads*, which was itself based on an Indian folk tale of the twelfth century found in *Kathasaritasagara*. *Naga-Mandala* (1988) was based on two

Kannada folk tales, fascinatingly interwoven, one framing the other. A production of *Naga-Mandala* was staged at the Guthrie Theatre in Minneapolis in 1993. This was the first time a contemporary play in an Indian language was produced by a major regional theatre in the United States. It premièred in Toronto in 1997. *Tale-Danda* (1990) is the story of the twelfth-century poet-saint Basavanna.

Karnad's plays have been translated into other Indian languages and various European languages. *Hayavadana* won a national award as the best play in 1972 and Karnad the best playwright in the same year. Karnad's significance in theatre lies in his having made a successful use of traditional Indian styles of performance to fashion a distinctly modern Indian theatre. Where other playwrights and directors of the 1960s and 1970s applied folk techniques to an otherwise realistic story, Karnad's *Hayavadana* and *Naga-Mandala* used folk tales for their subject matter. The content was non-realistic, and so the folk styles were especially suited to translating them into performances. Karnad's thoughts on modern Indian theatre, as articulated in his articles and interviews, are some of the most insightful on the subject.

Some of the most significant dramaturgy in post-independence Indian theatre has come from Maharashtra and Bengal, two of the country's states with rich literary and theatrical traditions. Maharashtra has produced theatre personalities of lasting and national endurance and appeal. P.L. Deshpande (b. 1919), a brilliant comic writer and satirist, as well as an actor and singer, has written a number of plays, and several comic revues. He also adapted western classics for the Marathi musical stage – *Oedipus Rex*, *Pygmalion* and *Threepenny Opera*. He is the author of *Tuze Aahe Tujapashi* (*Whatever Is Yours Belongs to You*), which focuses on topical problems, *Batatyachi Chal* (*Low Cost Housing*) and *Asa Me Asa Me* (*Thus I Am*).

The most creative and innovative Marathi playwright of modern times is Vijay Tendulkar (b. 1928). He has indulged in bold experimentations in dramatic form and in his use of sparse and understated language. His early one-act plays were written as radio plays and were broadcast before being staged. *Shreemant* (*Gentleman*), *Mee Jinklo Mee Harlo* (*I Have Won I Have Lost*) and *Maadi* were among his early successful plays. His most famous play *Ghasiram Kotwal* (*Ghasiram the Police Chief*, 1972) employs the traditional musical *dashavatara* form, revitalizing it to depict present reality. The play exposes corruption in contemporary political life and the evils of the caste system. His plays are characterized by a subdued emotionality and a unique idiom. His style is spare, his writing unforced, revealing an ironic, unsentimental view of life. *Shantata Cour Chaalu Aahe* (*Silence! The Court Is in Session*), *Sakharam Binder* and *Gidhade* (*Vulture*) are other important plays by him. Instrumental in revitalizing post-independence Marathi theatre, his plays have been staged commercially as well as experimentally in Marathi and in other major languages of India.

Maharashtra is the only state in India that has had a continuity of professional theatre for the past 150 years and where the present-day commercial theatre is thriving, the centres being Bombay and Pune. Bombay has the largest variety of theatre productions available in the country – ranging from family dramas, comedies, serious dramas, musicals and experimental plays – and is perhaps the only city in India that has successfully withstood the coming of films and television, largely due to an audience loyal to commercial theatre.

Vasant Kanetkar (b. 1923), a contemporary Marathi playwright, has written several significant plays for the commercial stage – *Vedyache Ghar Unhat* (1957), *Matsyagandha* (1962) and *Phakat Ekach Karan* (*Just One Reason*). His best known play is *Raigadala Jevha Jaag Yete* (1962). Many of his plays include music and his *Lekure Uddand Zhali* (1966) was modelled on western-style musicals. An instant hit due to its wittiness and clever structure, it was revived in the late 1980s and was again successful. Jayawant Dalvi (b. 1925), a barrister and playwright in Bombay, wrote successfully for the commercial stage. His play *Nati Goti* is the story of a mentally challenged boy and his sexuality. Other notable dramatists writing for the commercial stage are Ratnakar Matkari (*Ghar Tighancha Hava*), P.L. Mayekar (*Ayi Retire Hote*), Suresh Khare, Shekhar Tamhane and Prashant Dalvi, whose *Char Chaughi* and *Dhyani Mani* were particularly successful.

The early one-act plays of Tendulkar and Matkari, written in the mid-1950s, attempted to break away from the commercial Marathi theatre, where melodrama, sentimentality and an exaggerated acting style were the order of the day. Some were more descriptive and verbal than dramatic, but through the modernity of their themes, their originality and their language, they infused a new vitality in Marathi

theatre. Matkari composed a number of one-act plays that formed a vital part of the new and experimental theatre of Maharashtra. His *Lok Katha '78* (*Folk Tale '78*) was one of the most powerful experimental plays of the 1970s. Later he turned to the commercial stage. His *Ghar Tighancha Hava* is one of the most interesting plays on the commercial stage and is based on the life of a famous social worker whose separation from her alcoholic husband and quest for her own identity lead to her daughter's suicide. Tendulkar and Matkari actually made a successful transition from being considered avant-garde to being considered commercial and, in the freshness of their approach, gave new life to the commercial theatre in Bombay.

Tendulkar influenced an entire generation of playwrights, chief among them Mahesh Elkunchvar and Satish Alekar, two major playwrights of the 1970s. Elkunchvar's best play *Wada Chirebandi* displays a maturity and restrained emotion contrasted with the rawness of his earlier work. His characters display an emotional strength without being melodramatic.

G.P. Deshpaned and Achyut Vaze were other important playwrights writing in the 1970s. Deshpande is best known for his political play, *Uddhvasta Dharmashala* (*The Ruined Inn*).

Satish Alekar (b. 1941), the best known contemporary Marathi playwright, uses elements of earlier forms in his own work. With an innate ease, he makes use of traditional Maharashtrian musical styles such as *keertan*, *powda* and *lavani* as well as film songs and tunes from the theatre of Bal Gandharva (an immensely popular actor-singer from the early decades of the twentieth century) in plays like *Mahanirvana* (*The Great Redemption*), *The Terrorist* and *Begum Barve* (*Madame Barve*) to create a dramatic and ironic effect. The influence of Tendulkar is perceptible in his style of dialogue. *Begun Barve* is one of the modern classics of Marathi. The fantasy of an aged actor who played female roles all his life, the play starts with his marriage to a clerk followed by his 'pregnancy'. Sadly, his most cherished dream is ruined at the end by the owner of the theatre company. It is a poignant study intermingling the conscious and the subconscious desires of the human mind while successfully portraying the varying strains of the new Marathi stage.

The new generation of Marathi playwrights continue to extend and transform the rich tradition of Marathi theatre, writing plays that reveal the social, political and aesthetic concerns of the present. Rajeer Nik and Chetan Datar from

Bombay and Makarand Sathe, Sanjay Pawar and Chandrashekhar Phansalkar in Pune have created a large and interesting body of work in the 'parallel' or experimental theatre. Naik heads a theatre group in Bombay called Antarnatya (Inner Drama). His plays include *Mitli Papni* (*The Closed Eyelid*) and *The Last Book*, in which the characters from *Mahabharata* engage in debate with the author of the epic, Vyasa. In doing so, this witty and poignant play questions societal norms and relationships. Phansalkar's best known play is *Tax Free*, written as part of a writer's workshop conducted by the Theatre Academy in Pune. A dark comedy with shocking and brutal humour, it was immediately successful in performance.

Another playwright of importance is Datta Bhagat whose play *Wata Palwata* (*Routes and Escape Routes*) is one of the first Dalit plays, examining the dilemmas and problems faced by the Dalit movement at this juncture of its history. (The word *dalit* means downtrodden or oppressed and the term is used to refer to the communities belonging to the 'lower' castes of Hindu society who have traditionally been discriminated against.) Playwright Tushar Bhadre has been doing street theatre in Satar, a district in Maharashtra, since the early 1980s.

The dramaturgy of Bengal is equally rich and varied. Perhaps the name most familiar outside India is that of Rabindranath Tagore. He made an important contribution to the world's dramatic literature but his many plays are not now frequently produced outside Bengal. Tagore's early work did not attract many directors, although everyone recognized his powerful themes as well as his ability to reveal human relationships. Rejecting the commercial Bengali theatre as it existed, Tagore fashioned many of his plays after the classical, literary Sanskrit drama. Many of his plays, some performed as early as 1886, were dramatized versions of his short stories and novels. The poet himself dramatized *Jogajog* (1936, originally a novel), *Chirakumar Sabha* (1925, also originally a novel), *Grihaprabesh* (1925) based on his short story *Sesher Ratri*, and *Sodhbodh* (1926) based on his short story *Karmaphal*. Others were dramatized by Bengali actors, directors and playwrights. Tagore's original dramas include *Raja O Rani* (1890), *Godaye Galad* (a comedy, 1910) and *Basikaran* (1926)

Avoiding naturalism entirely, Tagore's work much in verse – stresses the suggestive. His most important plays are *Rakta Karabi* (*Red Oleanders*, 1924), *Dak Ghar* (*The Post Office*,

1913), *Kabuliwala* (*Man From Kabul*, 1961), a dramatization of his short story by the same name by Debnarayana Gupta, and *Mukta Dhara* (*Open Stream*). A painter as well, his work bears the unmistakable imprint of Fauvisman in his attempt to reveal the secrets of nature through symbolic imagery. His play *Mukta Dhara*, for example, deals with human desire to control nature and is set against the construction of a dam.

Tagore's work brought a new vision to Indian dramaturgy as he consciously turned away from the professional and commercial theatre of the nineteenth century as well as from the well-made-play tradition. In general, his work is symbolic and lyrical. On the public stage however, his plays were not very popular or commercially successful, due to the simple fact that his genius was essentially poetic. Widely travelled, Tagore late in his career began to attract the attention of film directors.

The modern theatre of the 1990s reflects this continuing quest for new subject matter while acknowledging and absorbing the essential lessons of not only the Indian tradition but also of even wider pan-Asian theatrical traditions. It is perhaps Mohan Maharishi's (b. 1940) work that best sums this up. A Rajasthani playwright and director working in Punjab, he has brought many of these varied elements together in his work. In 1994, he utilized the historical figure of Albert Einstein in a quasi-biographical play, *Einstein*, to juxtapose scientific achievements with the contradictions of everyday reality. The play was produced by the repertory company of the National School of Drama at Delhi and it utilized music. In this sense, his plays are a real meeting point for west and east and clearly offer new perspective on the future of the contemporary Indian theatre.

Director Shambhu Mitra's (1915–97) stagings of Tagore, Sophocles and Ibsen, P.L. Deshpande's one-man shows *Asa Me–A sa Me* (*I Am Like This*), Utpal Dutt's (1929–93) *Angaar* (*The Fire*, 1961) and *Teetash Ek Nadir Naam* (*A River Called Teetash*, 1963) along with Ebrahim Alkazi's groundbreaking productions of *Oedipus Rex*, *Yerma* and *Waiting For Godot* were remarkable in articulating this new Indian theatrical style.

Jasmine Jaywant, Anjala Maharishi

Directing and Acting

In the traditional theatre, directing has always been done by the leading actor, an approach

Mohan Maharishi's 1994 production of *Einstein* at the NSD.
Photo: courtesy of S. Tyagasajan.

that was suggested as far back as the *Natyashastra* of Bharat some 2,000 years ago. The concept of an autonomous director was not introduced into India until the Parsi Theatre in the late nineteenth century, following the British actor-manager tradition. In many cases the director was also the playwright.

The country's most important director of written and spoken scripts in the post-independence period was RADA-trained Ebrahim Alkazi. His spectacular productions of both Sanskrit and western classics gave new energy to the post-independence theatre and his productions quickly found receptive audiences in Bombay and later in Delhi. An innovative designer as well as a director, Alkazi often chose unusual venues for his productions and he was particularly adept at utilizing historical monuments as he did in productions of *Andha Yug* (*Blind Epoch*) by Dharam Vir Bharati (b. 1925) and *Tughlaq* by Girish Karnad. His realistic interpretation of *Ashadh Ka Ek Din* (*A Day of Ashadh*) by Mohan Rakesh effectively explored the conflicting attitudes of emotion and daily reality.

After making his reputation with these productions, Alkazi was named head of the National School of Drama in New Delhi. His outstanding productions there of both western plays and classics such as *Oedipus Rex* along with his interest in developing modern Indian dramatists made his work important as well as popular. As well, he introduced a more systematic method of teaching performance skills than had been seen in India to that time and regularly invited innovative directors from abroad to work with his students. Without doubt, Alkazi inspired an entire generation of actors, directors and designers.

Other directors of note have included Mohan Maharishi, whose productions favour a rich theatricality; B.V. Karanth, who has regularly experimented with ritual and folk forms seeking to integrate both into a more vibrant contemporary theatre; Vijaya Mehta (b. 1934), one of India's few female directors, who has infused classical plays with an energetic choreography and who has found new energy sources in her work with actors; and Habib Tanvir, another RADA-trained director who has done significant experimental work with tribal communities.

During the late 1980s and early 1990s, a number of directors began to work imagistically creating their own play texts and, in many cases, simply 'borrowing' existing texts and significantly adapting them, sometimes without the playwright's consent. Among those working in this way have been Rajinder Nath (b. 1935) with his Abhiyan group in Delhi, the Bombay director Satyadev Dube (b. 1936), Om Shivpuri (d. 1989) and Bhanu Bharti (b. 1947).

A number of directors have chosen to work outside traditional venues, bringing theatre to remote communities, prisons, factories and even red light districts. Leading practitioners in this field have been M.K. Raina (b. 1948), Bansi Kaul and Prasanna (b. 1951)

A completely different theatre style with completely different directorial aesthetics was introduced to India in the 1940s. It was at this time that the country's street theatre movement began with its political and social agenda. Effectively used to protest against the presence of the British Raj, the form has been used widely ever since and has attracted many well-known actors and directors. Early on, the form was associated with the Communist Party of India and the Party has always been a strong advocate of such positions and its theatrical approaches. Street theatre groups have even had political impact from time to time: with street theatre support, the first election to the Provincial Assembly of West Bengal in 1952 put fifty-two Party members into office. Perhaps the most important director to work in this way was Utpal Dutt.

Throughout its history, street theatre performances have also attracted large audiences since shows are free. During the 1970s and 1980s, it was reinvigorated by a large number of artists including playwright Badal Sirkar who wrote his *Juloos* (*The Procession*) and *Bhoma* for such groups. The show played to large audiences in Calcutta, Bombay and Delhi. M.K. Raina is another director of street theatre who did a notable production of Gorki's *The Mother* in front of various factories, a production that led other writers and directors to take productions to such communities.

The IPTA and Jan Natya Manch (People's Theatre Platform) were also left-wing in their orientation and both regularly utilized street theatre to get their messages across. Their work was particularly effective during periods of social upheaval and both groups suffered political attacks and police repression. In the 1980s, a Lucknow group's members were arrested, jailed and many of the actors badly abused. As late as 1989, serious attacks on these groups continued when the young director and actor Safdar Hashmi of Jan Natya Manch was killed by factory musclemen during a performance of his production of *Hulla Bol* (*Attack*) done in front of a factory in Sahibabad (near Delhi).

Street theatre was perhaps used most effectively to protest against the poison gas leakage that killed 2,500 people at the Union Carbide factory in Bhopal in 1984. Groups involved collected money for the victims and led attacks on what they argued were unchecked environmental conditions among multinational corporations working in the country. Even mainstream directors staged sympathetic protest productions on the streets of virtually every major city. One notable production from this period was a play called *Muavaje* (*Compensation*) by Bhishma Sahni (b. 1915) written in 1990 and staged by M.K. Raina. Another director, Sharan Singh, a left-wing activist from Punjab, was particularly active with his street theatre troupe and significantly aided in increasing political awareness in the region between 1981 and 1993.

A festival of street theatre groups is now held annually in Delhi under the sponsorship of the Safdar Hashmi Memorial Trust (SAHMAT). The festival includes poster and painting exhibitions, performances, seminars and conferences.

Sunita Dhir, Prakash Syal, Ravi Chaturvedi

Music Theatre
Dance Theatre

For a discussion of music and dance, see the opening, historical section and **Artistic Profile**.

Theatre for Young Audiences

Children's theatre in India is a post-independence phenomenon. Traditionally, puppet theatres offered specific entertainment to young people in the community but as the traditional arts became more and more limited to non-urban areas, the need for a more active children's theatre became clear. It was under the administration of Prime Minister Nehru that in 1950 a series of *bal-bhavan* (houses for children) were established in ten major cities. Included in these buildings were children's libraries and spaces for theatrical presentations. Later, additional youth centres were established ensuring that every capital city in India was able to promote children's interests in various fields including theatre.

In 1988 in Delhi, the National School of Drama (NSD) established a programme geared exclusively to training teachers in theatrical techniques. Ever since, during summer vacations, production-oriented workshops in this field have been done by the NSD as well as by the Ministry of Culture.

One of the earliest specific efforts in the area of theatre for young audiences came in Bombay in 1959 when Sudha Karmarkar, a professional actress, employed a full adult cast for the first time in a play for children. Until that moment, what children's productions there were focused on simply providing children with performance opportunities in western fairytales and Indian folk stories. These were staged with fantastic sets, costumes, special effects and music. Karmarkar's company, Bal Rangbhoomi (Children's Theatre Space), became an instant success with children as well as with parents. Among the group's early hits were productions of *Aladdin and His Magic Lamp*, *Madhumanjiri* and *Kal-Lavya Kandyachi Kahani* (*Tale of the Trouble-Shooting Onion*), the latter by Ratnakar Matkari, who would go on to found his own group, Bal-Natya (Children's Theatre). Among his later plays were *Nimma Shimma Rakshas* (*The Half-Made Demon*) in 1963, *Shubham Karoti Kalyanam* (*Good Deeds Bring*

Hindi version of *Mahashanti* (*Great Peace*) performed by the NSD Repertory Company, 1990.
Photo: courtesy of S. Tyagasajan.

Well Being, 1964), and *Rajakanyechi Savali Harvali* (*The Princess Without a Shadow*) in 1964. Both groups include young people in their casts. Matkari's work has incorporated various traditional theatre forms.

During the 1960s, All India Radio Bombay produced a large number of children's plays which motivated many professional Marathi playwrights – among them Vijay Tendulkar, P.L. Deshpande and Gangadhar Gadgil – to write for the form. Many of these plays were later published and used in various school curricula. During this same period, the Marathi actress Sulabha Deshpande (b. 1937) established a children's wing of her experimental theatre group Avishkar, which was run by her director/actor husband Arvind Deshpande. The children's wing was called Chandrashala (The Moon School) and it included regular training for young people. Perhaps the most outstanding production by this group was *Durga Zali Gauri* (*Durga Became Gauri*, 1982), a full-length ballet with a cast of seventy children.

One other group of note here is the Delhi-based Umang (Enthusiasm), established in 1979 by Rekha Jain. Each summer, the group stages a new play adding impressively to the growing repertoire of children's theatrical literature in Hindi. Among the group's major productions have been *Natkhat Krishna* (*Mischieveous Krishna*) in 1992 and *Sa Re Ga Ma* (*Do Re Me Fa*) in 1994.

Puppet and Mask Theatre

It is difficult to find the exact origin of the rich art of Indian puppetry though Sutradhara (Stringholder) appears as a character in several ancient plays. There is a clear reference in the *Natyashastra* to mechanically operated animals (*sanjeeva*) which adds to the historic record that inanimate figures were operated by ancient puppeteers. It is also said that King Vikramaditya in the seventh century AD possessed thirty-two puppets and was an early patron of the art.

However and wherever the art began, in present-day India one can find three basic types of puppet figures: wooden string-puppets, leather shadow-puppets and rod-puppets manipulated from above. A fourth variety – the glove-puppet or hand-puppet – also exists but is now rarely found, being used mostly by itinerant showmen and mendicants in rural areas.

Rajasthani string-puppets are the oldest type. The *kathputali nat* (manipulator, literally wooden doll actor) works with strings but without a wooden control. One end of the string is tied to the head or waist of the puppet while the other end is wrapped around the fingers of the puppeteer. About 60 cm (2 feet) in height, the puppet's head is made of wood and the limbs of stuffed cloth. All are painted a basic grey colour with the nose and eyes crafted in a stylized manner to throw the features into relief. Rather than legs, they have long skirts which can be manipulated to suggest movement.

The traditional stage for these string-puppets is created by simply turning a handmade cot woven with coarse string on its side. A black cloth provides the background with the puppeteer standing behind the cloth and bending forward to manipulate the figures. Most troupes consist of the puppeteer, a drummer and a female singer. Most belong to a single family. Kerosene lamps light the stage from both sides. Some Rajasthani puppets have specific characters. These include dancing girls, a combined horse and rider puppet, a juggler and a snake-charmer with his snake. Stories come from medieval legends, and performances include folk dances, war scenes and danced scenes of romance.

A second type of string-puppet, known as *sakhi-nata* or *kandhai-nata*, is found in the eastern state of Orissa. This form utilizes the Gopa-lila (stories based on the Krishna legends), with the figures – between 9 inches and 2 feet (22–60 cm) made of paper rather than wood. Most of the figures are also without defined legs.

In the southern state of Tamilnadu, *bommalattam* (string puppet shows) have been used in villages as part of magical rites to bring rain and to prevent the spread of disease. The rulers of Tanjore in the eighteenth and nineteenth centuries became patrons of the art, which was linked to classical music and the dance form known as *bharata natyam*.

Stories are invariably drawn from religious lore since the performances are supposed to inculcate faith in God and encourage righteous behaviour. The musicians working with the puppeteers are themselves classical singers. They are accompanied by the *mridangam* (classical percussion), *talam* (small cymbals), flute and *ndaswaram* (a type of clarinet). Some of the best exponents of classical music have been associated with these performances.

The *bommalattam* puppet is unique, being manipulated from above by a string or rod, the latter fixed to the puppet's hands and the turban on the puppet's head. It is the head movements as well as the hand movements (controlled by rods) that give the puppet its special style. The puppets are decorated with rich jewellery and special silks from the region and perform classical dances.

In Mysore (in Karnataka) one also finds round marionettes called *sutrada-gombe* or *sutrada-bombe*. Unusual in shape, these string puppets are connected to the characters of *yakshagana* and are, as usual, seen on virtually every festive occasion. Stories are taken from either *Ramayana* or *Mahabharata*.

Shadow puppetry is widely found in the southern rural regions of Andhra Pradesh, Karnataka and Kerala. The Karanataka shadow play – called the *tagalu gombe-atta* – utilizes brightly coloured and highly decorated puppet cut-outs. Some represent individual figures while others represent groups such as Rama and Hanuman's army of monkeys or Kaushalya and her son. *Killeketa* is the name of both the central character in this style and the name of the early nomadic purveyors of this art. Killeketa appears with his wife Bangarakka. Both are comic figures, ugly and repulsive, with enormous visible sexes. Cut from goat skin, deer skin or buffalo hide and fixed with wires, the figures are used to relate epic stories. Performances last through the night ending at dawn.

In Andhra Pradesh, the shadow theatre known as *tolu bommalatta* utilizes flat leather puppets called *keelu bomma* which are joined with strings. Ornately coloured and more or less lifesized they are perforated to let light shine through. Faces are drawn in profile and thin bamboo rods are used to move the limbs while a long, single wooden rod is tied vertically to the puppet to keep it erect. Manipulation requires great skill as the puppeteers working from behind need to avoid having their own shadows appear on the curtain. An elaborate religious ceremony using music and dance – as mentioned in *Natyashastra* – is done before each performance and clearly shows the continuity with theatrical traditions of the past. A stage for *tulu bommalatta* is always erected in the open air, while the repertoire is full of extreme dramatic activity – the burning of Lanka, the marriage of Seeta, the Ram-Ravan battle, and the Pandava-Kaurava battle to give just a few examples. In the *pavikuttu* puppet show from Malabar, the shadow-puppets are kept quite still with reciters furnishing songs and dialogue from behind the screen. A simpler variety from the same region is called *pacubu*.

The *putul nach* (rod-puppets) of West Bengal are large (about 1.4 metres or 4.5 feet) and are built over a bamboo base. The body and limbs are also made of bamboo. A belt is used to manipulate the figures with both hands holding strings going up to the neck. The arms are manipulated by a single string with a rod projecting from the shoulder to act as a lever. Drums and cymbals accompany the dialogue as well as the singing.

Orissa, Kerala and Tamilandu also have a history of glove-puppets with the puppets in Kerala based on *kathakali* dancers. Like *kathakali*, stories are taken from the *Mahabharata*. Performances are accompanied by *chenda* (a type of drum) and *talam* (cymbals). Orissa glove-puppets, made of wood and paper, are rarely now seen and the art is almost extinct in the region.

The Bharatiya Natya Sangh – a cultural organization in New Delhi – has undertaken several noteworthy projects for the rehabilitation of puppetry. Their workshop and museum employs craftworkers who have been trained by masters in the art. Bharatiya Kala Kendra, another Delhi organization, has employed and trained puppeteers in an effort to keep this ancient art alive. Bhartiya Lok Kala Mandal in Udaipur also trains puppeteers and provides them with performance opportunities. The Shreyas School of Puppetry in Ahamadabad trains puppeteers for work in schools.

One of the few modern puppet groups is Contemporary Puppet Theatre in Calcutta, which has been experimenting with glove-puppets and rod-puppets with some success.

Anjala Maharidhi

Design

Most traditional theatre forms take place in virtually any given space since little or no scenery is employed in their staging. Time and place are either narrated or represented through time-honoured theatrical conventions. Acting is stylized, consisting of codified gestures, postures and facial expressions, the use of specific stage properties, elaborate and spectacular costumes, music and the overall magic that permeates such performances.

Painted scenery was introduced to the Indian stage in the eighteenth century by the British, who established proscenium theatres and began staging plays in English in Calcutta, then the capital of the British Empire in India. The use of such painted scenery was soon emulated by other groups. The Parsi commercial theatre followed this tradition and invented new techniques and devices for quick scenic changes and stunning visual effects. The use of such astonishing devices can still be found in commercial theatre productions at Manohar's National Theatre, at the Madras and Kalanilayam Theatre in Kerala and in several other commercial theatres across the country.

It was the Bengali actor and director Sisir Kumar Bhaduri (1889–1959) who strove to bring about change by making stage scenery more interpretative. In collaboration with designers such as Mani Gangopadhyay, Charu Roy and Anath Maitra, he produced a number of plays including Tagore's *Visarjan* which are remembered for being among the first designs to work on an evocative and interpretative level.

In the 1930s, the revolving stage was introduced at the Rangmahal Theatre by Sathu Sen, who also introduced box sets which would work as part of such technology. A number of older spaces in Calcutta soon began converting their stages to turntable as well. Calcutta's theatre was, in fact, revolutionized by Sen whose influence continued into the 1960s.

In Bengal, Rabindranath Tagore had earlier repudiated the kind of realistic settings which had dominated the professional theatre of his time. It was Tagore who linked stage and auditorium in his visual design, making them into a single unit. Other Bengali theatres, the Bahorupee group for example, also began to reject the two-dimensional, pictorial tradition, replacing it with plastic, three-dimensional and more evocative settings. Khaled Chaudhury's designs for Tagore's *Rakta Karabi* (1954) and

Ibsen's *Putulkhela* (*A Doll's House*, 1958), both directed by Shambhu Mitra for Bahorupee, reflected the new trend.

Chaudhury's design for the Tagore play established the harsh society of the play with the poor dwelling on low ground and the privileged occupying higher ground. The harsh rigidity of stone was symbolic of the harshness and rigidity of the society. In *A Doll's House* too, he eliminated walls but kept those windows and doors which had a significant bearing on the action of the play. By a careful arrangement of the furniture and other mundane objects of a middle-class household he created a clear line that pointed to the door from which Nora would leave in the final scene.

The later designs of Surya Roy and Anil Banerji clearly show how effective line, colour and texture could be in creating mood and atmosphere especially in Roy's design for Tagore's *Muktadhara* and Banerji's design for Tagore's *Visarjan*.

With the establishment of the National School of Drama in 1959, the concept of scenic design in India underwent a sea-change. Under the directorship of Ebrahim Alkazi who, besides being a director, was also an able designer, the school established new aesthetic principles for the Indian theatre and its students carried these ideas to every corner of the country. Alkazi's interests were wide, ranging from classical Greek to Sanskrit plays, from Shakespeare to contemporary western and new Indian writing. As a result, his designs were not confined simply to the proscenium but extended into other spaces as well: ancient monuments, open courtyards, terraces. Ingeniously interpreting each space to the mood and atmosphere of the play, Alkazi managed to design widely varying sets even for the same play (as in his three different productions of *Tughlaq*). These included a proscenium theatre, an open-air theatre with a banyan tree in the centre, and a third using the Old Fort of Delhi. Each design was completely different yet each projected the essential ideas of the play, which focused on a person far ahead of his time impatiently putting together his vision of a brighter world but left very alone in his dreams.

Alkazi's designs always managed to take into consideration the shape, size and nature of the space itself with his colours, lines and textures summing up the conflicts that each character lives through. His design for *King Lear*, for example, showed that even a small space like the Studio Theatre at the National School of Drama could be transformed to capture the poetic depths and primitive atmosphere of the play. The walls in this case were made of rusted iron sheets with two large primitive masks at the rear fixed on a revolving flat which shifted with each scene. Stools were covered with steel plates further contributing to the evocation of the barbaric period that Shakespeare created.

The epic dimensions of Dharam Vir Bharati's *Andhayug* came to life in Alkazi's production, when the inner conflicts of its archetypal characters were depicted against time-worn ruins. The addition of a huge broken wheel against the walls further suggested the mood of the play and clearly represented the destiny of the characters living inside. Well-proportioned platforms and steps leading to them made the set functional as well. In contrast, Alkazi's depiction of the delicateness of Mohan Rakesh's *Ashadh Ka Ek Din* in the open air was established through minute details of a well-to-do household and later by showing the same details worn by time. In all his work, Alkazi encouraged designers to interpret and integrate rather than to simply imitate. The lesson was an important one.

Through the millennia, Indian theatre has found varied methods of arranging theatrical space and establishing modes of actor–audience relationship. For most traditional forms, space is fluid. As such, the proscenium theatre – a modern addition in India – is quite unsuitable. Even for the production of classical Sanskrit plays, the proscenium is not a comfortable fit because it curbs the essential freedom of movement as locales change even in the same scene and characters are often shown moving from one locale to another. Design solutions in such plays often need to be quite ingenious. At Punjab University, for example, the Department of Indian Theatre presented two Sanskrit plays Mahendra Vikrama's *Mattavilasam* and Bhasa's *Urubhangam* in which director Kumar Varma

and his designer Mahendra Kumar interpreted the plays in terms of space. In the first play, they used platforms at each end of the auditorium and an elevated ramp with the audience on either side. This arrangement – apart from creating the feeling of a city street – also helped in establishing an exceedingly intimate audience–actor relationship. In *Urubhangam*, the set resembled a large wheel with the audience seated inside the spokes and the actors surrounding the audience on the circumference.

Other designers noted for their innovative work include Bansi Kaul, Nissar Allana and Robin Das. Kaul has done several plays in remote provincial towns and villages where proper theatres and even material for the construction of sets are not easily available. He has found innovative methods often using only locally available materials.

In traditional theatre forms, costumes are highly stylized symbolically representing the nature and qualities of the various characters. In *yakshagana*, *kathakali* and *kutiyāttam* audiences easily identify characters by costumes and makeup. Such stylization also lends these characters an ethereal quality, another hallmark of traditional theatre. This is also in contrast to the commercial Parsi theatre that emerged in the nineteenth century and which employed fanciful and colourful costumes and painted backdrops.

Again, it was the influence of the National School of Drama in this area which broke the tendency toward realism in the modern Indian theatre. The works of costume designers Roshan Alkazi and Kokila Mawani were of particular significance in this regard. Their designs blended and suggested the style of the overall production and integrated completely, an interpretation more than a representation.

In terms of lighting design, a number of enterprising Indian firms have started designing and manufacturing their lighting equipment and designers have begun installing them all over the country.

G. Kumar Verma

Theatre Space and Architecture

Performance spaces in India are almost as varied as the theatrical forms themselves, the difference in their nature, character and structure reflecting the variety and diversity of theatrical forms. Basically, theatre spaces in India may be looked at under two general and broad categories – existing or devised spaces used for traditional performances, and those used for the staging of modern plays, with some very interesting mixes and overlaps.

Highly structured traditional performances of an inherently religious nature – *kutiyāttam*, *krishnattam*, *therukuttu* and *yakshagana* – use special sacred places, like the various areas in a temple complex. Here, a variety of spaces, the main one being the courtyard surrounding the temple, become the performance ground. Sometimes there are adjoining halls, either walled, or simply overhead structures without walls supported by pillars. These are called *mandapas* (porch halls). In the temples of north and south central Kerala, there are large rectangular wooden structures in front of the deity, to the right of it.

Called *kuttampalams*, these were the spaces used for the enactment of *kuttiyāttam* – Kerala's classical Sanskrit drama. They are unique in that they are the only surviving examples of ancient, permanent theatre architecture in India. At least nine have survived, of which three are still in use, the others being in ruins. The largest and the most regularly used is the impressive *kuttampalam* of the Shiva temple in Trichur. The interior measures 22 × 15 metres (72 × 50 feet) and the stage is a square measuring 6.5 × 6.5 metres (21 × 21 feet). Dating to *c.* AD 800, it seats about 500 spectators. The theatre of the Irinjalagada Temple is smaller, the interior being 20 × 16 metres (67 × 54 feet) and the stage is 4.3 metres (4 feet) square. The famous Krishna temple of Guruvayur has the smallest structure measuring 10 × 7 metres (32 × 24 feet), the stage being 3 metres (9.5 feet) square. The stages of the *kuttampalams* have four pillars supporting a roof above the stage, except for the one at Trichur, which has twelve pillars. In most theatres, the underside of the roof has ornate wood carvings or paintings as decorations. All of the stages are slightly elevated, about 30 cm (1 foot) above where the audience sit on the floor on three sides of the stage. While performing, the actors face the shrine and the temple deity. The performance is an act of devotion, an offering to the gods who are also the audience, and the act of watching the performance is an act of worship.

There are two doors that connect the performance area to a dressing room at the back, the left door being used for entrances and the right one for exits. Performances are punctuated by the rhythmic beat of two *mizhavu* (copper drums) that are placed on stands near the back wall between the two doors. This reduces the acting area. An oil lamp, situated centre-stage down, provides the only lighting. There is no scenery or props used in *kuttiyāttam* performances, or in

Kuttampalam: traditional performance space for *kutiyāttam*.
Photo: courtesy of SNA.

most other traditional performances for that matter.

The annual performance in May of *Bhāgavata Mela* in Tamilnadu takes place on a platform created before the presiding deity at the Narasimha temple in Mellattur village. *Krishnattam*, the devotional dance-drama of Kerala, is performed by only one troupe associated with the great Krishna temple at Guruvayur, and only at the temple. Devotees may commission or 'sponsor' a performance (i.e. bear its financial cost) in order to have a wish fulfilled.

In instances when such traditional temple-based performances are taken elsewhere, the performance space (an ordinary stage) is made sacred by performing specific rituals and sometimes installing the presiding deity on the stage. With the growth of an awareness of Indian theatrical traditions, performance troupes of *yakshagana* or *kuttiāttam* have toured within India and abroad. The stage remains for the Indian performance artist a sacred and holy place; before entering the performance area, for rehearsals or performance, even the actors of modern theatre touch the floor of the stage with their right hand and then touch the same hand to their eyes and forehead, a gesture affirming the sanctity both of the space they are about to enter and of the act (of performing) they are about to engage in. This is also an invocation to the gods and a seeking of their blessings.

Performances also take place in front of the temple in villages all over India, when the temple entrance is directly on to the street or alley and the temple is not part of a larger complex. The temple thus is an imposing backdrop: pre-existing architecture is used, rather than creating elaborately designed scenery. The ritualistic *rasa* dances based on the Krishna legend, the *lai haroba* processional ritual in Manipur, and the *teyyam* ritual dances of Kerala are examples of this type of performance.

Most traditional performances are open-air community events, and take place in a lively, relaxed and festive atmosphere of general gaiety and bustling activity. They are also free of charge. In the *Lilā* plays, the performance area (a temporary, makeshift stage constructed on a raised platform for the purpose, covered by a coloured canopy called the *shamiana*), is part of an environment characterized by temporary shops selling tea, food, toys, statues of gods, popular religious literature, souvenirs, and accessories for worship. The performance takes place in the middle of this intense activity,

which, though not a part of the staged event, vitally determines its character, essentially by framing it. The spectators move freely from one area to another, affirming the coexistence of the performance and non-performance events. Out-of-frame activity enables the performers to step out of their personae especially during the rituals in religious plays and musical/comical interludes in social and secular plays. Conversely, spectators freely participate in religious rituals like *arati* (worshipping the deity by waving a lit oil lamp placed in a large saucer in a circular motion, while singing a devotional song) and shouting *Krishna Bhagavan ki Jai* (Glory be to Lord Krishna) or *Ramchandraji ji ki Jai* (Glory be to Lord Rama).

Most traditional performances take place on a stage remarkable for its bareness and the total absence of props or scenery. It is a neutral space transformed by the performer. The actors create the place and time of the action through their movements, hands and facial gestures and recitation of a text that describes the place. In the *natyashastra*, Bharatmuni has not only discussed the construction of a *natyamandapa* (theatre hall) and prescribed elaborate rituals and procedures for the consecration of the stage, but also talked of dividing the stage into *kakshya-vibhaga* (zones), a symbolic, imaginary division by means of which a single stage could represent several different locales simultaneously, such as a house, garden, palace, street or an ascetic's cottage. This enabled the actor already present on the stage to change locales without ever actually exiting the stage. Artists in the traditional forms usually walk in a conventional, usually circular movement and 'arrive' at the new destination. The audience, thoroughly familiar with the convention, adjust mentally to the change of scene without anything changing visually or physically. The accompanying dramatic text usually vividly describes the new locale. In a joint exercise of the imagination to which the actors and spectators are both party, the theatrical space is transformed dramatically.

In *kathakali* performances, the performance space is at ground level, not elevated. The stage is created by clearing a rectangular area about 6 × 9 metres (20 × 30 feet). Four wooden poles are inserted in the four corners with bright pieces of cloth covering them to define the acting area. The audience sits on all three sides as in the *kutampalams*. A brass lamp, about 1 metre (3 feet) high and kept at downstage centre is the focal point and the entire performance is created in relation to it. It separates the audience from the actors and is the only source of light. The lamp has two wicks – one faces the audience and the other faces the actors. Constantly fed by oil, it burns brightly and remains a point of reference, the actor comes close to the lamp to demonstrate a strong facial expression. The audience sits in darkness while the performers move in the semi-darkness. For some scenes, especially those of violent physical combat, actors leave the performance area and perform in the midst of the audience.

Originally a temple drama, *kathakali* has become very popular due to a revived interest in the form and its context has changed. Performances are held in many places – village temples, a compound in a school or in a family residence, even a proscenium arch stage in a city, with electric lights. The theatre at Kerala Kalamandalam, Kerala State Arts School, with an architectural blend of the principles of stage construction as detailed in the *natyashastra* and the regional style unique to Kerala, is another impressive structure in which *kathakali* is performed.

Also used is a half-curtain in multiple colours. Usually 3 metres (10 feet) long and 2 metres (6.5 feet) wide, it plays an important role in dramatizing the actors' entrances and exits. It is held by two stagehands who stand on the stage in full view of the audience. The curtain conceals the actors' body; their faces and feet are visible to the spectators. The half-curtain also enables the actors to appear and disappear in action; as soon as the curtain is removed, we see them already riding a chariot, meditating, or playing a musical instrument, thus eliminating the necessity of entering and then setting out to perform these actions. Actors also 'disappear' (by holding up the curtain) while engaged in combat or in ritualized acts of killing or dying.

Another use of theatrical space is the *namaghar* or *bhavnaghar* (congregational prayer hall) used for Ankia Nat in Assam. Rectangular in shape, it is part of a larger complex of a Vaishnava monastery. Used daily for prayer, it is also used for theatrical performances on special occasions. The hall is usually divided into separate areas by using collapsible bamboo and reed walls, which are removed for a performance. The space is decorated with colourful paper streamers, flags and banners. At one end of the hall sits the group of singers and accompanists, and at the other end the *bhāgavata purāna* is placed on a pedestal. The performers enter and exit from the side of the musicians, with the dressing room to their rear. A ground-level passageway connecting the two ends, 37×5.5 metres (about 40×6 yards), is the performing space. The audience sit on the floor on both sides of this passageway. The centre of the passageway is used for the main action of the play and is demarcated by a small canopy hung from the ceiling. Other platforms with their own separate canopies along the passageway represent different locales such as a palace or a temple. The sacred book is the focal point and the action is presented facing it, with dimly lit earthen lamps illuminating the performance area.

Like *kathakali*, *yakshagana* is performed on an unadorned, neutral space. Sometimes two or three *yakshagana* troupes are sponsored to perform in a common open area. A specific 4.5–6 metre (15–20 feet) square performing arena is assigned to each. The audience watches the two or three presentations simultaneously. Competitive in nature, it resembles a sporting event with cheering and applause from the audience.

The design of space for an annual northern Indian performance of *Rāmlilā* – a cycle of plays based on Rama's life – deserves special mention. Part of the festival of *Dushehra*, which is celebrated generally in the month of October to commemorate the victory of Lord Rama over the demon king Ravana and symbolically the victory of good over evil, the *Rāmlilā* is performed in virtually every city, town and village of Hindi-speaking India over a period of ten days, though the duration can vary between fifteen and thirty-one days, and re-enacts episodes from the *Rāmcharitmānasa*, the epic poem on Rama's life, a Hindi version of Sanskrit Ramayana, written in the seventeenth century by Tulsidas. It is an outdoor performance, open to everyone in the city. The performance is made up of a series of tableaux, song-dramas, pageants and arena plays, including floats and processions.

The performance space of the *Rāmlilā* varies depending on the place: it can be a narrow street, a market-square in a village or an open space in a city. Most big cities have special grounds called *Rāmlilā maidan* (ground) with permanent stone or brick platforms about 1 metre (3–4 feet) high. Covered with a canopy, they serve as stages. In smaller towns, temporary wooden platforms may be erected for holding the performances. At Ramnagar which is famous for its elaborately staged *Rāmlilā*, and also at Mathura, different episodes are enacted at different sites. The locales are spread across the city, within a 4-mile radius, and the action of

Rāmlilā shifts from one locale to another. Each site represents a particular place mentioned in the *Ramcharitamanasa*, and has permanently built modest structures forming an integral part of the town's architecture. They are reserved solely for the enactment of the *Rāmlilā* and are guarded all year. A day's action is generally confined to one locality, except when a procession is inherently a part of an episode, in which case the audience moves from one locale to another in procession. The whole town is thus used as a performance area.

The *Rāslilā* is traditionally performed on the *rasamandala*, a circular stage at floor level in the temple courtyard, with a small platform at one end. The action takes place at two levels: the platform stage presents Krishna and Radha in *jhankis* (tableaux or stage pictures) and the ground-level stage is used for their dances with the *gopis* (milkmaids).

For the staging of folk and popular performance events, ordinary, pre-existing spaces and open-air venues, decorated temporarily, are utilized, the most common being the street. In addition, market-places, city or village squares, gardens, parks, open fields, courtyards, schools and colleges, and open grounds outside the city are frequently used. The concept of a dramatic performance as an open-air street show is inherent in the Indian cultural consciousness. The names of some of the performances demonstrates this, for example *therukuttu* (street play) and *veethi natakam* (street play).

The *jatra* of Bengal is an open-air drama. It is performed on a platform raised 0.75 metres (2.5 feet) and 5 metres (16 feet) square. It is cordoned off by ropes and short bamboo poles. The orchestra sits on two ramps, 15 cm (6 inches) lower than the stage, running parallel on opposite sides. The spectators sit on all four sides. A narrow pathway connects the stage to the dressing room 18 metres (60 feet) away. Similar to the *hanamichi* of the Kabuki theatre of Japan, it goes through the audience. Apart from being used for entrances and exits, at various junctures of the performance, it also becomes part of the acting area.

The *khyal* of Rajasthan uses structures called *mahal* (palaces) or *jharokha* (windows) of various heights. These may be as high as 6 metres (20 feet) and are used to show the descent of the heroine, frequently a queen, to the main platform, 1.5 metres (5 feet) high. The musicians sit on a smaller adjacent platform. The open-air stage for *maanch* may be as high as 3.7 metres (12 feet). The *bhāvai* acting area is

circular, with a diameter of about 3 metres (10 feet), drawn on the ground using the point of the Naik's sword and sanctified before the performance. The audience sit all around the space. All entries to the acting circle are through a gangway that runs through the audience.

The *tamasha* of Maharashtra is performed on a low platform surrounded on three sides by the audience. In the *naqal* of Punjab, the actors perform in the midst of the audience in an open space, moving about freely and forging passages as new performance areas. *Nautanki* is performed on platforms about 1 metre (3–4 feet) high, surrounded by the audience. There is rarely a rigid demarcation between audience and performers in most Indian folk performances.

It is thus paradoxical that the modern theatre that emerged in India during the mid-nineteenth century chose the proscenium arch stage for its theatrical expressions. This primarily western convention, with all its attendant paraphernalia – elaborate stage settings, the curtain, the footlights, the clear separation of the audience – was, for most part, accepted by the Indian theatre. This virtually changed centuries-old theatre practice. The first proscenium theatres were built in Bombay and Calcutta in the 1860s, and inevitably led to a total change in the traditional concept and nature of theatrical space. The actor–audience separation deeply affected their traditional intimate relationship, forcing audiences to view performances from a fixed point. Since then, virtually all the country's theatres have been built with proscenium arch stages.

New Delhi's numerous theatre halls are concentrated near Sangeet Natak Academy and the National School of Drama. Among them is the impressive building of Sapru House, used mainly for commercial theatre, especially the production of comedies in Punjabi. The Sri Ram Centre, a popular venue for performances of both theatre and dance, also has a small basement theatre used for experimental productions. The National School of Drama has the intimate, 200-seat studio theatre designed by Ebrahim Alkazi, who in the 1950s was staging productions by his Bombay-based Theatre Group in an improvised theatre on the terrace of his own house overlooking the Arabian Sea. The design of the studio theatre exemplifies how such small areas can be effectively converted into theatrical space. Alkazi also designed the open-air Meghdoot theatre for the school on a plot of land meant for a large permanent theatre. The open-air space – with a banyan tree at the centre

Auditorium of the B.M. Birla Science and Technology Centre, Jaipur.

– has been imaginatively used for plays like *Godan* (an adaptation of a novel by Premchand, dealing with Indian village life), *Tughlaq*, *Caucasian Chalk Circle* and *Othello*. He also mounted a magnificent production of *Tughlaq* among the ruins of an ancient Muslim fort in New Delhi.

In Bombay, theatre buildings are more scattered. As home of the National Centre for the Performing Arts, there is a complex of theatres in the Fort area, Bombay's financial and commercial hub. There are several theatre buildings for the commercial production of Marathi plays, the major one being the prestigious Shivaji Mandir, Dinanath Mangeshkar Hall, Gadkari Rangayotan (in the suburb of Thane), Sahitya Sangh, the Ravindra Natya Mandir and the Mumbai Marathi Sahitya Sangha are popular theatre halls owned and operated by the State government of Maharashtra. For experimental productions, there is the Chhabildas School Hall, a large performance space in the Chhabildas Boys' High School. During the day the hall is used by school children, and in the evenings is converted into temporary theatre. The 'set', if any, must be dismantled at the end of each day. Unconventional theatrical productions play to full houses here. Prithvi Theatre, a small, well-equipped, three-quarter round

theatre was constructed in 1979 at Juhu Beach. It is one of the best small theatres in the country and home to productions of various small and experimental theatre groups in Marathi, English and Hindi. Another popular venue for staging of unconventional productions is the Experimental Theatre, which opened in 1985 as part of the National Centre for the Performing Arts.

The commercial theatre houses of Calcutta are situated in the north within a few city blocks. The Star, established in 1888, is the most prestigious and famous. It is also the most expensive to stage a production in. Some of the others are Minerva, Bijon, Rangmahal, Muktangan, Tapan and Biswaroopa. In the mid-1980s the Circarena was built, which is the only arena theatre in the country.

Most amateur and experimental theatre groups are located in South Calcutta, which has many modern theatre buildings. The Academy of Fine Arts, part of a larger complex including a museum and a library, is an important theatre building where productions are regularly held. Calcutta is the centre of experimental theatre in India, and the artists have consciously attempted to move away from using rented proscenium stages. Instead they have sought to use ground and available performance spaces, such as public parks, school halls, city streets, open fields, and open halls of buildings under construction.

Bengali playwright and director Badal Sirkar has been a pioneer and a leading practitioner of experimental theatre in Calcutta, and has openly expressed his disdain for commercial theatre. He has also experimented with manipulating existing performance space. Within the given performance context, Sircar creates various spatial relationships between audience and performers, encouraging an interaction reminiscent of the active role of the audience in traditional Indian theatre. The nature of the interaction is itself open to change as the performance progresses. He has inspired newer directors to experiment in a similar vein.

In the south, Madras is the home to the Museum Theatre, a majestic nineteenth-century building with a proscenium stage. The Music Academy Hall is a modern building. These and other theatre buildings in Madras have conventional proscenium arch stages, conducive to the production of spectacular historical mythological plays such as the ones performed by Manohar's National Theatre. Theatre groups in the south are usually touring companies. The National Theatre and Kerala's Kalanilaya Vistavision Dramascope Company (based in Trivandrum) when performing in other places build temporary theatres to mount their productions. K.N. Pannikar, the leading experimental theatre personality of Kerala, staged some of the performances of his Sopanam group in the courtyard of the Maharajah of Tritavillinar's palace.

The Studio Theatre at Punjab University is also worth mentioning in this context. Its long, irregular, covered stage has been used in various ways, at times as an arena, at other times as a thrust.

Virtually every city in India has at least one theatre building that is used for the performance of modern plays. Most of these buildings, while providing space for productions, are also regularly used for conferences and fashion shows. Touring groups, in contrast, often play anywhere – schools, playgrounds or factories – and such unconventional spaces have been utilized effectively by street theatre groups which often deal with political themes.

Jasmine Jaywant

Training

Traditional theatre training has long been done in India by members of the groups themselves. These included master–apprentice training – often between parents and children – in such forms as *nautanki*, *jatra*, *tamasha*, *kathakali*, *yakshagana*, *swāng*, *bhavai*, and *Rāslilā*.

The first university drama department in the country was set up at the University of Baroda in 1941 with courses offered up to the PhD level along with a diploma course in dramatics. Baroda later helped other universities and state academies to formulate courses and teaching programmes in this field. It has also provided an opportunity for the training of teachers and amateur artists through various drama camps which it has organized from time to time.

Professional training for the modern theatre emerged in 1959 when the National School of Drama was set up in New Delhi. National and international in outlook, under Ebrahim Alkazi the school's productions spanned the whole dramatic tradition. The National School of Drama set as its initial aims, first, to maintain and develop the school for studies and training in dramatics, second, to develop suitable patterns of teaching and to establish high standards of theatre education, third, to ensure a flow of trained personnel and teachers for the future needs in the field, and fourth, to promote research in drama and to collect suitable material of archival value. In its early years, the school followed these goals under Alkazi's strict discipline. When he left in 1977, however, the school was hit with strikes, a lack of qualified teachers, and the diversion of its faculty towards television and films.

Other schools emerged within various universities. Among the best of these has been the Department of Indian Theatre at Punjab University, the University of Baroda and, from 1978, the Institute of Dramatic Arts at the University of Rajasthan in Jaipur. The latter is the country's only autonomous university centre for training in theatre arts.

In 1984, on the initiative of Prime Minister Indira Gandhi, a conference of education ministers and education Secretaries was called in New Delhi to study the role of drama in education.

The conclusion was that drama had been a neglected subject at both the elementary and university levels. The conference recommended strengthening existing drama departments and opening new centres of theatre teaching at both the undergraduate and graduate levels and to introduce the subject at the school levels. This resulted in the opening of several new departments of theatre.

There are now thirty-two such departments offering various degree and diploma courses, virtually all at graduate level. Only the department of dramatics at the University of Rajasthan in Jaipur offers 3A courses in dramatics, while Rabindra Bharati University trains technicians.

Similar initiatives have yet to be taken at a less advanced level. In all universities, theatre departments have financial problems because they are treated like other academic departments rather than as unique programmes with special requirements. Unlike students at the National School of Drama, university students are rarely given scholarships or fellowships.

Local and state academies are rare in the performing arts though a few do exist on a very marginalized basis. Among them are the Bhartendu Natya Academy in Lucknow and the Drama School of the Goa Art Academy.

Ravi Chaturvedi, Sunita Dhir, Prakash Syal

Criticism, Scholarship and Publishing

Serious criticism and the analytical study of performances and playwriting did not exist in any sustained manner during India's pre-independence period. But after 1950, with the fall of colonial rule, more serious criticism and scholarly work emerged in the field. Virtually all the major newspapers and magazines engaged the services of academics and journalists to review theatre performances which provided a new and friendly environment for serious criticism to emerge on the national scene.

Academic critics such as Frank Thakurdas, Ramesh Chander and Nemi Chand Jain (b. 1918) were engaged by the *Times of India, Hindustan Times, The Statesman* and *Indian Express*, all leading newspapers with a wide readership. By 1970, a second generation of critics had emerged led by Kavita Nagpal, Jaidev Teneja, Nikhat Quazmi, Gayatri Sinha and Deepa Gaholt among others. Similar developments were seen outside of Delhi in centres such as Bombay, Calcutta and Bangalore.

In the 1960s, the first theatre journals were started with the publication of *Natrang* (in Hindi), edited by N.C. Jain and later on *Enact* (in English), edited by Rajinder Paul. Both were effective in reflecting theatre activities throughout the country and both reached a national and an international audience. *Enact* also regularly published English translations of Indian plays, a practice which brought many playwrights to national attention and led to productions of their scripts. *Enact*'s team of contributors included people from across the country and enabled it to reach a large part of the theatre

community. Natrang was equally popular in the Hindi community.

During this same period, provincial academies also started regular publications, including *Sangit Natak* at Delhi's Central Academy, *Rangyog* at the Rajasthan Academy at Jodhpur and *Chhayanat* by the Uttar Pradesh Academy at Lucknow. In addition to these journals several literary journals began sections of theatre reviews. More specifically, the left-wing Hindi magazine *Uttarardh* published an exclusive issue on the subject of 'people's theatre' on 1 May 1983. The issue included thirty-three short plays, a veritable anthology of street theatre scripts.

In the 1980s, a new journal of literary criticism appeared in Delhi under the general editorship of G.P. Deshpande (b. 1938), himself a playwright. Entitled the *Journal of Arts and Ideas*, it appeared irregularly but gave serious attention to theatre from an interdisciplinary standpoint. This journal attracted many eminent scholars whose literary background and scholarly approach to theatre established new directions for theatre criticism.

A number of scholars – among them R.C. Mehta, Sujatha Vijayraghavan, Anuradha Kapoor (b. 1951), G.H. Tarlekar, K.S. Upadhyay and Ashok Ranadey – have documented specific aspects of Indian theatre. Perhaps the most significant scholarship in the field to this point has been done by Kapila Vatsyayan (b. 1928) whose book *Traditional Indian Theatre: Multiple Streams* analyses both the philosophical and performative aspects of traditional Indian forms. Another book of note is Mahendra Bhanawat's analysis of various folk theatre forms in relation to social customs, *Lok Rangmanch* (*Folk Theatre*). Lakshmi Narayan Lal (b. 1927), himself a playwright, has written a useful history and structural analysis called *Parsi–Hindi Rangmanch* (*Parsi-Hindi Theatre*) while N.C. Jain has created a valuable perspective on the modern Indian theatre in his books *Adhunik Hindi Natak Aur Rangmanch* (*Modern Hindi Drama and Theatre*) and *Rang Darshan* (*Theatre View*), both published in Hindi.

In the 1990s, two new journals of criticism appeared in Calcutta: *The Seagull Theatre Quarterly*, which publishes mainly reports and reviews, and *Theatre International* which, under the editorship of Amitava Roy (an actor and academician), focuses more on academic criticism and analysis.

Ravi Chaturvedi

Further Reading

Ambras, Tewia. 'Tamasha: People's Theatre of Maharashtra State'. PhD dissertation, Michigan State University, 1974.

Anand, Mulkraj. *The Indian Theatre*. New York: Roy Publications, 1951.

Barba, Eugenio. 'The Steps on the Riverbank'. *TDR* 38 (winter 1994): 107–19.

Bhanawat, Mahendra. *Lok Rangmanch* [Folk theatre]. Jaipur: Bhartiya Lok Kala Mandal, 1971.

Bharucha, Rustom. *Chandralekha: Woman/Dance/Resistance*. New Delhi: HarperCollins, 1993.

——. *Rehearsals of Revolution: Political Theatre of Bengal*. Honolulu: University of Hawaii Press, 1983. 276 pp.

——. *Theatre and the World: Performance and the Politics of Culture*. London/New York: Routledge, 1993.

——. *The Theatre of Kanhaiyalal: Pebet and Memoirs of Africa*. Calcutta: Seagull Books, 1992.

——. 'Under the Sign of the Onion: Intra-cultural Negotiations in Theatre'. *New Theatre Quarterly* 12 (May 1996): 116–29.

Bhat, G.K. *Theatrical Aspects of Sanskrit Drama*. Pune: Bhandarkar Oriental Research Institute, 1983.

Chaterjee, Sunit Kumar. *Indian Drama*. Delhi: Publication Division, Ministry of Information and Broadcasting, Government of India, 1981.

Chopra, P.N., ed. *Folk Entertainment in India*. Delhi: Ministry of Education and Culture, 1981.

Dasgupta, H.N. *Indian Stage Vols I–IV*. Calcutta: Metropolitan Publishing House, 1944.

——. *The Indian Theatre*. Delhi: Gian Publishing House, 1988.

Daugherty, Diane. 'Facial Decoration in Kathakali Dance-Drama'. PhD dissertation, New York University, 1985. 214 pp.

Devi, Ragini. *Dance Dialects of India*. Delhi: Vikas, 1972.

Dharwadkar, Aparna. 'Performance, Meaning and the Materials of Modern Indian Theatre: Interview with Girish Karnad'. *New Theatre Quarterly* 11 (November 1995): 335–70.

Frasca, Richard Armand. 'Pāncāli Capalām (The Vow of Draupadi): Images of Ritual and Political Liberation in Tamil Theatre'. *TDR* 38 (summer 1994): 89–105.

——. 'The Terukkuttu: Ritual Theatre of Tamilnadu'. PhD dissertation, University of California at Berkeley, 1984. 430 pp.

——. *The Theatre of the Mahabharata: Terukuttu Performance in South India*. Honolulu: Hawaii Press, 1990.

Frost, Christine-Mangala. 'Thirty Rupees for Shakespeare: A Consideration for Imperial Theatre in India'. *Modern Drama* 35 (March 1992): 90–100.

Gargi, Balwant. *Folk Theatre of India*. Calcutta: Rupa, 1991. 217 pp.

——. *Theatre In India*. New York: Theatre Arts, 1962.

Ghosh, Manmohan. *The Natyashastra Ascribed to Bharat Muni*. Calcutta: Granthalaya Pvt, 1967.

Gokhale, Shanta. 'Marathi Rangabhoomi'. *Yatra* 3 (1994) 3–36.

Gupta, Somnath. *Hindi Natak Sahitya Ka Itihas* [A history of Hindi dramatic literature]. Allahabad: Hindi Bhawan, 1958.

——. *Parsi Theatre: Udhabhau Aur Vikas* [Parsi theatre: Origin and development]. Allahabad: Lokbharati Prakashan, 1981.

Hawkes, S.J. 'Forms of Chhau: An Investigation of an Indian Theatre'. PhD Dissertation, University of Exeter, UK, 1983.

Jain, N.C., ed. *Adhunik Hindi Natak Aur Rangmanch* [Modern Hindi drama and theatre]. Delhi: Macmillan Company of India, 1978.

——. *Indian Theatre: Tradition, Continuity and Change*. New Delhi: Vikas, 1992. 98 pp.

——. *Rang Darsham* [Theatre view]. Delhi: Macmillan Company of India.

Kabshu, Parminder Kaur. 'Jagram: Theatre for Education and Development'. *New Theatre Quarterly* 5 (May 1989): 124–39.

Kale, Pramod. *The Theatric Universe*. Delhi: Popular Publications, 1974.

Karnard, Girish. 'Theatre in India'. *Daedalus* 118 (fall 1989): 331–52.

Kotovskaja, M.P. *Sintez iskusstv: Zreliscnyje iskusstva Indil* [Synthesis of the arts: Performing arts of India]. Moscow: Nauka, 1982. 255 pp.

Lal, Lakshmi Narayan. *Parsi-Hindi Rangmach* [Parsi-Hindi theatre]. Delhi: Rajpal & Sons, 1973.

Madhur, Shivkumar. *Bharat Ke Loknatya* [Indian folk theatre]. Delhi: Vani Prakashan, 1980.

Mathur, J.C. *Drama In Rural India.* Delhi: ICCR Publications, 1967.

Mee, Erin B. 'Contemporary Indian Theatre: Three Voices'. *Performing Arts Journal* 19 (January 1997): 1–26.

Mukherjee, Sushil Kumar. *The Story of the Calcutta Theatres: 1753–1980.* Calcutta: K.P. Bagchi, Company, 1982.

Mukhopadhyay, Das Gupta, ed. *Lesser Known Forms of Performing Arts in India.* Delhi: Sterling Publishers, 1978.

Naidu, V. 'Ramayana and Mahabharata: Contemporary Theatrical Experiments in English With Indic Oral Traditions of Story-telling'. PhD dissertation, University of Leeds, 1994.

Nair, Parmeshwar. *History of Malayalam Literature.* New Delhi: Sahitya Academy, 1967.

Narayan, Birendra. *Hindi Drama and Stage.* Delhi: Bansal, 1981.

Nayak, Bapu Rao. *Origin of the Marathi Theatres.* Maharashtra Information Centre, 1967.

Ojha, Dashrath. *Hindi Natak Udhbhau Aur Vikas* [Hindi drama: Its origin and development]. Delhi: Rajpal & Sons, 1954.

Parmar, Shaym. *Traditional Folk Media.* Delhi: Communication Publishers, 1977.

Piretti Santangelo, Laura. *It teatro indiano antico. Aspetti e problemi* [Ancient Indian theatre: Aspects and problems]. Bologna: Clueb, 1982. 133 pp.

Rabindranath Tagore: A Centennial Volume (1861–1961). Sahitya Akadmi. 1961.

Rahu, Kironmoy. *Bengali Theatre.* New Delhi: National Book Trust, 1978. Rangacharya, Adya. *The Indian Theatre.* Delhi: National Book Trust, 1980.

Rangnath, H.K. *The Karnataka Theatre.* Dharvad: Karnataka University, 1960.

Richmond, Farley P., Darius L. Swann and Phillip Zarilli, eds. *Indian Theatre: Traditions of Performance.* Honolulu: University of Hawaii Press, 1990.

Schechner, Richard. *Performative Circumstances from the Avant Garde to the Rāmlilā.* Calcutta: Seagull Books, 1983.

Shah, Anuparna and Uma Joshi. *Puppetry and Folk Dramas: For Non-Formal Education.* New Delhi: Sterling, 1992. 174 pp.

Sirkar, Badal. *The Third Theatre.* Calcutta: Badal Sirkar, 1978.

Solomon, Rakesh H. 'Culture, Imperialism and Nationalist Resistance: Performance in Colonial India'. *Theatre Journal* 4 (October 1994): 323–47.

Srampickal, J.J. 'Popular Theatre as a Medium For Conscientization and Development in India'. PhD dissertation, University of Leeds, 1989.

Thompson, Edward. *Rabindranath Tagore: Poet and Dramatist.* Delhi/New York: Oxford University Press, 1991.

Tourlet, Christiane and Jacques Scherer. *Quand le Dieu Rama joue à Benarês* [When the god Rama plays in Benares]. Cahiers Théâtre Louvain 689. Cahiers Théâtre Louvain, 1990. 203 pp.

Varadpande, M.L. *Krishna Theatre in India.* Atlantic Highlands, NJ: Humanities Press, 1982. 145 pp.

——. *Traditions of Indian Theatre.* New Delhi: Abhinau Prakashan, 1978.

Varadpende, M.L. and Sunil Subhedar, eds. *The Critic of Indian Theatre.* Atlantic Highlands, NJ: Humanities Press, 1982. 203 pp.

Vatsyayan, Kapila. *Traditional Indian Theatre: Multiple Streams.* Delhi: National Book Trust, 1980.

Venu, G. and Nirmala Paniker. *Mohiniyattam: Attaprakaram With Notation of Mudras and Postures.* Trivandrum: Author, n.d. 204 pp.

Wade, Bonnie C. *Performing Arts in India: Essays on Music, Dance and Drama.* University of California Centre for South and Southeast Asia Studies Monograph Series 21. Berkeley, 1983. 270 pp.

Yajnik, Y.K. *The Indian Theatre.* London: Allen & Unwin, 1933.

Zarrilli, Phillip B. *The Kathakali Complex: Actor, Performance and Structure.* New Delhi: Abhinav, 1984. 406 pp.

Journals

Chhaya Nat (in Hindi), Lucknow: Uttar Pradesh Academy.

Enact, Delhi (in English; began 1967, ceased publication 1987).

Journal of Arts and Ideas, Delhi.

Journal of Asiatic Society of Bengal, Calcutta.

National Centre for the Performing Arts Journal, Bombay (began 1972).

Natrang (in Hindi), Delhi.

Sangeet Natak (in English), New Delhi: Publication of Central Academy of Drama (began 1965).

Sangit Natak Akadmi Bulletin (in English) New Delhi: Publication of Natrang Trust.

Seagull Theatre Quarterly, Calcutta: Seagull Books.

Theatre International, Calcutta: Avant Garde Publishers.

INDONESIA

An archipelago consisting of some 13,670 islands – only 6,000 of which are inhabited – Indonesia covers 1,924,600 square kilometres (744,300 square miles) stretched across a vast area of the Indian and Pacific Oceans between Australia and the Asian mainland. Among the largest of its 300 ethnic groups are Javanese (45 per cent), Sundanese (14 per cent), Madurese (8 per cent) and coastal Malay (8 per cent). About 5 million Chinese also live in Indonesia. Nearly half of the population of 170 million lives on the central island of Java. Each group has its own languages, customs, rituals and arts and most are descended from Asian regions around the Saluen and Mekong rivers.

During the Napoleonic Wars, Java was occupied for a time by the British. Eventually the Dutch took political control over the area, calling it the Netherlands East Indies. By the beginning of the twentieth century, with liberal elements growing among the colonizing Europeans themselves and with the victory of Japan over Russia in 1905 as a model, an awareness of the possibility of independence was born. In 1908, a group of educated Javanese created an organization aimed at the progress of indigenous people through improvements to an extension of the education system. The birth of this organization, Budi Utomo, was followed by others, some based on ethnic solidarity, some on religious orientation, some on national ideals, while still others – such as the communists – on economic and political ideology. In 1928, several youth organizations began a unification process with a Sumpah Pemuda (Pledge of Youth) expressing their loyalty to one nation, one motherland and one language – Bahasa Indonesia – which is widely spoken. It is this period (1908–28) in which one finds the clear conception and birth of the modern spirit of Indonesia.

The events and moods of World War II accelerated the struggle. Taking advantage of a vacuum in Asian and European power just after Japan's surrender in 1945, Indonesia proclaimed its independence. Not recognized as independent until 1949, Indonesia during the 1950s experimented with political liberalism but the experiment ended in civil war and a presidential decree returned the country to its 1945 constitution. From 1959 to 1965, President Sukarno (1901–70) began another political experiment, this time with what was called 'guided democracy'. Authoritarian in style, guided democracy ended in an aborted communist *coup d'état* in 1965. A new regime led by General Suharto (b. 1921) took power in 1966, brought Indonesia back into the United Nations, and was still in power in the mid-1990s. At the same time, another political experiment was being carried out, the establishment of what was called Pancasila Democracy, an attempt at creating a unified Indonesia, a belief in one god, humanistic values, democracy and social justice.

As a developing nation, Indonesia's per capita income was US$80 in 1968, $110 in 1972, $240 in 1979, $350 in 1980 and $650 in 1993. In numbers, the progress has been positive, but in reality the gap between the rich and the poor was widening. Between 1969 and 1970, for example, 58 per cent of Indonesians lived in poverty while between 1970 and 1976 the number had grown to 68 per cent. In 1994, however, only 30 per cent of Indonesians were officially living in poverty.

Jakarta, founded as a city in 1619, is the capital and lies near the northwestern coast of Java. Other major cities including Bandung, Surabaya and Yogyakarta, the latter being one of the major centres of Javanese culture. Banjarmasin is the largest city on Indonesian

Borneo (Kalimantan) while Batam and Padang are two important ports in Sumatra. Macassar (Ujung Pandang) is the largest city in Celebes. The largest cities on Timor are Dili and Kupang. Ambon, on Ambon Island, is the chief city of the Moluccas. Though the country's major religion is Islam, on the island of Bali most of the inhabitants are Hindu.

Indonesian theatre, in its growth and development, cannot be easily separated from the growth and development of the nation itself. Early forms – the kind found in Bali which influenced the French theorist Antonin Artaud – were based on folk traditions, popular music and dance forms, and court styles. More modern forms of theatre tend to focus on 'national' rather than community issues. Another distinguishing feature of the modern Indonesian theatre is its use of Bahasa Indonesia, the Indonesian language, as opposed to local languages. In the early years of the Indonesian struggle towards independence, the use of Bahasa Indonesia was seen as a challenge to both colonialism and narrow ethnic tribalism.

Between the many early folk and traditional forms and the birth of the modern Indonesian theatre, however, *bangsawan*, or as it was known in Indonesia (particularly Sumatra), *stambul,* became widely popular. Performed in the Malay language (a language understood in most major cities because of its imposition by the Dutch), *stambul* was a mixture of music, dance and storytelling with clear Indian and Middle Eastern roots. The word itself is a short form of Istanbul and became attached to *bangsawan* due to its association with Jaafar Turki, who popularized Middle Eastern stories and themes in his *bangsawan* performances.

By the first half of the nineteenth century *bangsawan/stambul* had become a mixture of many performative elements, some indigenous and some not. Transitional forms, stories taken from Middle Eastern, Indian and local Malay sources, closely resembled that of modern musical plays but there was also a strong melodramatic strain, lavish costumes, much dancing, singing and standardized character types. The older forms were ultimately rejected in favour of forms introduced by the many Europeans and Euro-Asians living in cities such as Jakarta, Bandung and Surabaya. By the first decades of the twentieth century, playwrights and directors were experimenting with western realism and naturalism, not only dispensing with the dances and songs of the *bangsawan* and *stambul* but also rejecting their long, didactic speeches. The

well-made play dominated through the 1940s, with melodramas the most popular.

The oldest of the Indonesian theatre forms – *wayang kulit*, for example – are still close to their ritual origins and their dramatic patterns are still greatly determined by them. *Wayang kulit* is often based on rites of passage. A similar root is apparent in *pantun*, the Sundanese minstrelsy, such as in the story of *Mundinglaya* – a call, a test and heavenly intervention or blessing. One finds this in *babad* (literary works with historical elements). The *babad* is also found in many folk theatres including *ketoprak* and *ludruk* in middle and eastern Java and *sandiwara* and *masres* in western Java. The dominant pattern is also seen in *vishnu-avatar*. When the world is disturbed by some evil king or demon, heaven sends a god to re-establish peace and order. Many later dramatic works were based more directly on stories from the classical epics *Mahabharata* and *Ramayana*.

In many of these forms, the tale is built around a search for identity, usually featuring a young knight who has gone to a hermitage seeking spiritual instruction. In one of the most popular versions the knight learns he is the son of Arjuna, the third of the Pandava brothers. Arjuna has given the boy-knight a certain ring or *kris* (traditional dagger). This begins his search for his father, a search that leads him on many perilous journeys, through proofs of his nobility and into various philosophical discourses. Though on the surface a romantic story, symbolically the tale goes very deep with the search for parentage really a search for human or communal identity. The knight in turn is trying to find his own place in the human community as well as his more spiritual place in the cosmos. Such a pattern is very strong in the Sundanese story *Ciung Wanara*.

Later modern 'Indonesian' plays followed a more western style with writers clearly rejecting indigenous forms. Many of the plays were quite awkward and inarticulate – such as *Bebasari* (1931) by Rustam Effendie, the first play with a clearly nationalistic theme – but by the mid-1930s realism was mastered by the Pane brothers, Sanusi and Armijn. Among their important works from this period are *Kertajaya* (*King*, 1932), *Sandhyakala ning Majapahit* (*The Twilight of the Kingdom of Majapahit*, 1933) and *Manusia Baru* (*The New Man*, 1934).

The growth and development of western-style dramatic form and theatrical practice was accelerated and heightened by the nationalistic struggle itself. The occupation of Indonesia by

Teater Payang Hitam's (Black Umbrella) production of *Ciung Wanara* by Saini K.M. directed by Rahman Sabur.
Photo: Herman Effendie.

Japanese military forces during World War II had a paradoxical effect on theatre. Because there was a requirement for performance permits, playwrights were required to prepare meticulously detailed scripts, a practice not common before the occupation since indigenous theatrical practice relied most heavily on improvisation. The three and a half years of occupation were therefore one of the most productive in terms of western-style playwriting. Though many of the plays were still of little literary merit, some became literary treasures.

Among those was *Citra* (*The Image*, 1944), written by Usmar Ismail, a play about an irresponsible playboy who slowly learns the importance of fighting for the motherland. Though the spirit of nationalism in the play is mixed with elements of Japanese propaganda – necessary in those times – the commitment to independence was clear.

During the actual fight for independence between 1945 and 1950, theatrical activities were in great demand. Plays kept the fighting spirit of the people high and helped them not to lose sight of the ideals for which they were fighting. Many performances were performed on the front lines on makeshift stages in open fields. The country never knew such a time when life and the stage had so vital and strong a connection. Even the commercial modern theatre – used for escapist work – was staging plays about revolutionary heroes while folk performances also saw kings, queens, princes and demons giving way to long bearded revolutionaries, faithful girlfriends and wicked Dutch soldiers.

But lively and vital as it was, the war years did not produce many memorable performances or particulary good plays. It was in the decades just after the war that artists had a real opportunity to go beyond the local, to contemplate the war for independence and, for many, to become disillusioned. The war, its sufferings, the many tests of courage and human values it engendered, questions of treason, hypocrisy, heroism, cowardice, self-interest and sacrifice took centre stage in such plays as *Fajar Sidik* (*The Dawn*, 1955) by Emillia Sanosa; *Captain Syaf* (1951) by Aoh Kartahadimaja; *Pertahanan Terakhir* (*The Last Defence*, 1954) by Sitor Situmorang; *Titik-titik Hitam* (*Black Dots*, 1956) and *Sekelumit Nyanyian Sunda* (*Sundanese Song*, 1959), both by Nasyah Jamin.

Others dealt with corruption, political opportunism, the erosion of national ideals, the yet unchanged condition of the poor and the emerging clash of nationalism, Islam and communism. All these themes were to be found in *Awal dan Mira* (*Awal and Mira*, 1951) and *Sayang Ada Orang Lain* (*It's a Pity There Are Other People*, 1953) by Utuy T. Sontani. Even adaptations, such as *Pakaian dan Kepalsuan* (*The Dress and the Hypocrisy*, 1956) by Akhdiat Kartamiharja, based on *The Man in the Grey Suit* by Averchenko, and *Hanya Satu Kali* (*Only Once*, 1956), based on John Galsworthy's *Justice*, expressed similar concerns.

The western-style theatre was further rooted with the establishment of the National Academy of Theatre in 1955 under the direction of playwright and film-maker Usmar Ismail and his associate Asrul Sani, a poet and screenwriter. Many graduates of the Academy went on to become outstanding actors and directors, among them Teguh Karya (b. 1934), Wahyu Sihombing, Tatiek Malyati, Pramana Padmadarmaya, Galib Hussein and A. Kasim Ahmad. Perceived to be the theatre of the revolution as well as the theatre of the future, it was attended by a small, well-educated minority. The feeling was that to return to folk forms, such as *stambul* and *dardanella*, would mean a betrayal of an artistic ideal that was as cherished and jealously defended as the national ideal itself.

It was in an effort to resolve this dilemma that Jim Lim (Jim Adhilimas, b. 1936) turned back to the rich traditions of the ethnic theatre in the country in an effort to find ways of linking the two forms. Backed by the Bandung Theatre Study Club, an organization he initiated, Lim – one of Indonesia's best realistic actors and directors and known for his productions of *Awal dan Mira* and Chekhov's *Uncle Vanya* – launched his new crossover style in 1960 with a

Bandung Theatre Study Club's 1991 production of *King Lear* directed by Suyatna Anirun.
Photo: Herman Effendie.

production of *Bung Besar* (*The Big Boss*) by Misbah Yusa Biran. He directed the play in the style of *longser*, a Sundanese folk theatre. Widely criticized for his experiment, he persevered. By 1962 he was adding in elements of *wayang kulit* as well as Sundanese music, the latter in his direction of *Pangeran Geusan Ulun* (*Prince Geusan Ulun*, 1961) by Saini K.M. (b. 1938), utilizing shadow-puppets. In his direction of an adaptation of *Hamlet* (1963) by Jaka Tumbal, he continued his experiments by integrating *gamelan* music, *chirebon*-style masked dance and *longser*-style clowning. As well, he followed new western trends, introducing to Indonesian audiences absurdist elements in productions of *Caligula* by Albert Camus and *Rhinoceros* and *The Bald Soprano* by Eugène Ionesco. In 1967, he left Bandung for Paris where he worked for many years as an actor. Continuing Jim Lim's work was Suyatna Anirun (b. 1936). Like Jim Lim, Anirun also mixed elements of western and ethnic theatre to communicate with a culturally mixed audience.

Experiments continued in the work of Rendra (W.S. Rendra, b. 1936) who, after studying in the United States, established the Bengkel Teater Yogya (Yogya Theatre Workshop), a company working in what they called 'teater mini-kata' (minimal word theatre). He experimented with rhythmic movement, sounds, words and mime. His productions of *Bibop* (1967) and *Rambate-rate Rata* (a working chant used by labourers, 1968) opened still greater possibilities for a blended theatre.

The 1970s saw the production of still more new plays and many more groups. The establishment of an arts centre in Jakarta – Pusat Kesenian Taman Ismail Marzuki (Ismail Marzuki Park Art Centre) – helped launch new theatrical activities not only in Jakarta but also in other major cities such as Bandung, Surabaya, Yogyakarta, Medan, Padang, Palembang and Ujung Pandang. Over the next few years, sixty-seven plays were written by seventeen playwrights and performances of new works were seen regularly in festivals and during theatrical seasons. Seminars and formal discussions were held about theatre in general and about particular aesthetic problems, while names such as Stanislavski, Brecht, Artaud and Grotowski began to be heard. During the 1970s, departments of theatre were established at the Jakarta Institute and the Academy of Performing Arts in Bandung. Many universities began to organize student troupes to meet the new interest on their own campuses.

In the 1980s and 1990s, Indonesian theatre continued as a mixture of western and ethnic elements. Taking from the west a structural solidity, direct thematic articulation, realism and sequences, it took from the country's ethnic heritage a sense of specific imagery and symbolism. As for Brechtian and Artaudian idioms and styles, Indonesian artists have now recognized them as their own. Sundanese *longser* and Javanese *ketoprak*, for example, are perceived as the roots of Brecht, while various Balinese styles are the source of Artaudian ideas and practices.

In the late 1990s, new theatrical idioms were still being developed by major artists such as Teguh Karya. A film director as well as an accomplished actor and director for the stage, Karya's most memorable productions have included Strindberg's *The Father* (1960), Robles's *Montserat* (1964) and Jeff Last's *Jayaprana* (1964).

Though indigenous theatre forms are quickly vanishing, their influence on the modern Indonesian theatre remains very strong. A generation of modern pioneers all have either had personal experience with these traditions or they remember seeing them as young people. All testify that these early theatre forms left deep impressions on them and significantly shaped their imagination and creativity.

Structure of the National Theatre Community

Indonesia's rich theatre spectrum expresses the sensibility of a nation that is culturally influenced by both east and west. Supported by people of all ethnic groups, the traditional theatre expresses a national sensibility while the audience for the modern Indonesian theatre, in contrast, is probably the most 'Indonesianized'.

Intellectuals – for the most part high school and university students living in urban areas – see the modern Indonesian theatre as an outlet for the national language, the national system of education and mass media. Urban areas are its centre with each major city having between one and ten independent troupes; university cities

Ajip Rosidi's *Masyitoh* directed by Rahman Sabur and produced by Teater Payung Hitam (Black Umbrella).
Photo: Herman Effendie.

generally have more. Since the 1970s, universities have been an important base for this movement.

The audience for the modern theatre is an urban one since those who attend need a level of education and culture to match that of the artists. Nevertheless, the intellectual content and artistic style of the modern theatre is foreign to most inhabitants of the country's many small towns and villages. As such, in these locales, entertainment is provided more by traditional performance forms, dance or music.

There are many festivals sponsored by the government or done with the cooperation of private enterprise. But for reasons of funding and the lack of an established infrastructure, festivals are not held regularly. When they are held, awards are given to playwrights, directors and performers.

A national award, which is of greater prestige, is given yearly, usually around Independence Day, to those who have shown dedication and achievement in the general arts field. Among theatre artists who have won the award are Jim Lim, Teguh Karya, W.S. Rendra, Arifin C. Noor, Suyatna Anirun, Rujito and Riantiarno.

Artistic Profile

Three styles of theatre exist side-by-side in Indonesia – the indigenous traditional forms, the national (also called the 'Indonesian' theatre) and a purely western theatre style.

The indigenous theatre is based in traditional storytelling in a wide variety of forms and is rooted in the cultural heritage of the various ethnic groups. Though influenced by outside theatrical factors and practices, some important features still distinguish these from both the national and western styles as well as from one another. Although sometimes difficult for foreigners to distinguish, there are major differences. For example, though Sundanese and Javanese music might seem similar, they differ greatly in their characters and in their use of tone scales. Sundanese music is also more lively, while Javanese music is more contemplative. Sometimes the Sundanese and the Javanese use tone scales with the same name, but even here the resulting sounds are different. The same is true in movement.

Most indigenous theatre forms are in decline artistically and socially all across the country. Nevertheless, some are important to mention. *Mak yong*, for one, is a music and movement theatre of the Malay ethnic group of eastern Sumatra and the Riau Islands. An ancient dance-theatre form incorporating elements of ritual, stylized dance and acting, vocal and instrumental music, song, story and formal as well as improvised spoken text, *mak yong* is believed by many to have divine origins.

Randai, originally developed from storytelling, incorporates dance, song and music and serves as a method of handing down folklore and tradition. It expresses the theatrical imagination of the Minangkabau people of western Sumatra. The term *randai* implies a circle or circular formation around a particular location. *Legong*, a women's dance in Bali, another traditional form, is derived from the *Panji* or *Malat* cycle of legends.

Topeng, literally meaning mask, is the masked dance theatre of the Chirebonese people of western Java. It has an aesthetic fascination for many and is the oldest of the many forms of dance and acting. *Ketoprak*, a form of theatre found in middle and eastern Java, involves the use of spoken text, improvisation, somewhat stylized acting, archetypal characters, dance and music. The *ludruk* and the *wayang wong* are theatrical forms in which dance, stylized acting, dialogue, singing and the recitation come together in performance. These two theatre forms are still very close to the life of those living in middle and eastern Java.

The Balinese have their own varied theatrical heritage, one rooted in qualities of beauty. The *arja*, for one, is a form of musical comedy still seen in the region. Performances incorporate elements of song, dance and pantomime and are accompanied by a *gamelan* orchestra, an ensemble made up mainly of bronze percussion instruments, suspended gongs, bronze and wooden xylophones, drums and a spiked fiddle. *Cak*

Department of Theatre, Advanced School of Performing Arts of Bandung's production of *Ubu Roi* directed by Joko Kurnain in the style of *randai*.
Photo: Herman Effendie.

(*kechak*) is a Balinese dance probably left over from pre-Hindu times that has developed into an art form which uses stories from the *Ramayana* while the *barong* is the physical manifestation of a confrontation between forces – usually man and the supernatural. All have strong dramatic elements.

In Java and Bali, puppet theatre is among the oldest of the forms and the most respected. In western Java the Sundanese *wayang golek* (a wooden-puppet theatre) is most popular, while in middle Java, eastern Java and Bali, the leather-puppet shadow theatre is most important. There are also *amak abir* theatres in the Lombok Islands, a form only moderately known even among other ethnic groups.

The audiences for these forms are mostly composed of the communities themselves though more and more foreigners – both as tourists and scholars – have become attracted to them for their beauty, their dramatic power and their connections to religion and healing.

In major cities such as Medan and Padang in Sumatra; Jakarta, Bandung, Yogyakarta and Surabaya in Java; Denpasar in Bali; and Ujung Pandang in Sulawesi, a more literary theatre – known to most as the Indonesian theatre – has developed. This theatre is a mixture of both ethnic and western elements. Focused on the post-independence period, this theatre tends to attract those who are well educated and have mastered the Indonesian language, have studied the same national curriculum in school, have had the same compulsory subjects in universities, listen to and watch the same programmes on radio and television, and read the same national newspapers. This 'Indonesian' theatre deals almost exclusively with problems particular to Indonesia as a nation.

Western theatre, in contrast, generally includes performances of established plays from Europe and the United States, classical works and ballet. Performed by students of departments of foreign languages at the various universities, western theatre attracts students, foreigners and those who want to test their mastery of English. Ballet school companies in Jakarta and Bandung regularly perform classics such as *Swan Lake*, *Cinderella* and *Sleeping Beauty*.

All companies in the country – whatever style they work in – have constant financial problems and are confronted regularly by suspicion from both the civil and military authorities. As a result, few organizations operate either on a predictable or profitable basis. The many modern groups

vary greatly in size from five to as many as fifty. One theatre group – Bandung Theatre Study Club – officially has no members, but has a chairperson, secretary and treasurer, who are jointly responsible for planning, executing and evaluating workshops and performances. Conversely, in a single national ceremony thousands of artists might be recruited for a historical pageant.

Besides box-office receipts, theatre groups occasionally finance performances by cooperating with private business which are given credit on posters, in programmes and in other promotional media. As well, groups work with local newspapers and broadcasting enterprises. Sometimes a sympathetic government office may also give a small amount of money or a letter of recommendation to be used in lobbying with private enterprises.

Some theatre groups also tour both locally and nationally. But such tours depend on many factors and usually only the best known have any chance to get funded. Among the few groups who have toured internationally are the Rendra Theatre Workshop, Small Theatre, Independent Theatre, Comma Theatre, Bandung Theatre Study Club and Gandrik Theatre. Tour funding is often a mix of monies from the central government, the provincial government and private enterprise.

The price of entrance tickets varies greatly across the country but is generally relatively low, ranging from Rp 500 (25 US Cents) to no more than Rp 50,000 (US$25). The difference is due to the prestige and achievement of the group or the presence of a great actor in the performance. Another factor is the economic status of the province in which the group performs. The cost of goods and services in Bandung, for example, is about twice those in Yogyakarta. Jakarta is considered the most expensive city.

Another factor determining price is the familiarity of the audience with modern theatrical art. In small towns in which such theatre is still new, groups must keep prices low. Despite this, some local theatre groups are compelled to sell expensively because, for reasons of prestige, the audience will not buy cheap tickets. These groups sell their tickets from Rp 5,000 (US $2.50) to Rp 15,000 (US $7.50).

Companies

There are about a dozen active theatre groups in the major cities in addition to the innumerable ethnic theatre performances in smaller towns and villages. Most urban companies operate on a non-professional basis. Among the best known are Bumi Teater (Earth Theatre) led by Wisran Hadi in Padang in western Sumatra, in Jakarta the Teater Populer (Popular Theatre) led by Teguh Karya, Teater Kecil led by Arifin C. Noor, Teater Mandiri (Independent Theatre) led by Putu Wijaya, and Teater Koma (Comma Theatre) led by N. Riantiarno. W.S. Rendra's famous Bengkel Teater Rendra (Rendra Theatre Workshop) performs mostly in Jakarta.

In Bandung, Studiklub Teater Bandung (Bandung Theatre Study Club) was founded in 1959 making it one of the oldest modern theatre organizations in Indonesia. In the mid-1990s, it was being run by Sutardjo A. Wiramihardja (b. 1939) with Suyatna Anirun as its leading director. Other Bandung-based groups are the Bell Theatre led by the director Widodo; Sanggar Kita (Our Studio) led by Yoyo C. Durachman; and Kelompok Payung Hitam (Black Umbrella Group) led by the actor Rachman Sabur. Other well-known companies include Teater Gandrik (Gandrik Theatre) founded in the 1980s in Yogyakarta, and led by director Kertarajasa and

Kesowo Murti; and Bengkel Teater Surabaya (Surabaya Theatre Workshop) led by the playwright Akhudiat in Surabaya. Almost every university has its own theatre group.

There is one group, Teater Keliling (Travelling Theatre), which moves from one place to another to perform. Led by Rudolf Puspa, it is funded by local organizations, government and private enterprise.

Dramaturgy
Directing and Acting

Western dramaturgy emerged in the second half of the nineteenth century. Indonesian adherents focused on European realism and the style remained dominant until the ideas of Brecht and later the absurdists emerged in the 1960s and 1970s. Experiments in the 1980s saw numerous attempts to introduce traditional theatre, both in structure and style, into dramaturgy and direction. Rendra, for example, the country's most important writer-director, has utilized elements of Javanese traditional *ketoprak* and *wayang wong*. The theatre of Putu Wijaya

A scene typical of Gandrick Theatre of Yogyakarta, which mixes elements of modern and traditional theatre.

reflects his Balinese heritage while Wisran Hadi, a Minangkabaunese, bases his theatre on the folk theatre of *randai*. Suyatna Anirun, a Sundanese, has also shown influences from folk theatres such as the *longser*, though he is also strongly rooted in western realism.

Rendra – poet, playwright, actor and director – is one of the best examples of these developments in national dramaturgy. Starting his career in conventional realism, his early works – *Orang-orang di Tikungan Jalan* (*Men on Road Turnings*), *Guncangan Pertama* (*The First Shock*) and *Bunga Semerah Darah* (*The Flower, Red as Blood*) – were all effective well-made plays. His work began with his staging of van Logem's realistic *Dead Voices* in 1963 and later he both wrote and directed his own plays. Among these were *Perjuangan Suku Naga* (*The Struggle of the Naga Tribe*), *Sekda* (*The Governor's Secretary*) and *Mastodon and Condor* as well as translations of Aristophanes' *Lysistrata*, Sophocles' *Antigone* and *Oedipus Rex*. During the 1980s he wrote and directed *Panembahan Reso* (*His Majesty, Reso*) and *Selamatan Anak-anak* (*The Exorcism of Sulaeman's Children*).

Arifin C. Noor is another actor and director turned playwright. Like Rendra, he is concerned about how powerless ordinary people become victims. Arifin works in a much more surrealistic mixture of Brecht and Artaud. Combined with specially composed music, his best plays have the power of lyric poetry.

The Balinese dramatist Putu Wijaya (b. 1943) began his career as a short-story writer and novelist. As a playwright, his images and symbols show a dehumanized world and a nation moving very fast in uncertain directions. His Balinese background is evident in the musicality of his theatre which fuses words, sound effects and music into a powerful artistic whole. Among his most important works are *Edan* (*Crazy*), *Aduh* (*Ouch*), *Awas* (*Watch Out*), *Aib* (*Shame*) and *Dor*.

Still another dramatist of note is Riantiarno whose early plays – *Pelangi* (*Rainbow*) and *Cermin* (*Mirror*) – deal with domestic problems. His later works are about social discrepancies and reveal a Brechtian style. Among his adaptations are *Opera Ikan Asin* (an adaptation of *Threepenny Opera*), *Opera Kecoa* (*Cockroach Opera*), *Wanita-wanita Parlemen* (an adaptation of *Lysistrata*) and *Bom Waktu* (*Time Bomb*). His combination of humour and social

Ben Jonson's *Volpone* directed by Suyatna Anirun and produced by the Bandung Theatre Study Club.
Photo: Herman Effendie.

protest are particularly attractive to the public of metropolitan Jakarta.

Suyatna Anirun is one of Indonesia's most accomplished actors and directors. Among his major productions have been Chekhov's *The Seagull* (1993) and *The Proposal* (1961); Shakespeare's *A Midsummer Night's Dream* (1990), *Romeo and Juliet* (1992) and *King Lear* (1991); Ionesco's *Rhinoceros* (1990); von Kleist's *The Broken Jug* (1989); Molière's *L'Avare*; Saini K.M.'s *Pangeran Geusan Ulun* (*Prince Geusan Ulun*) and *Panji Koming* (1988); and Utuy T. Sontani's *Sangkuriang* (1960).

In the traditional theatre, directing *per se* is not as important as in the western-style theatre. Stories performed are based on spoken literature already known to, both actors and audience. The characters in such traditional stories are mostly stereotypical. As a result, the success of performances depends not on the skill of a director but rather on the improvisory abilities of the performers. It could be said, in fact, that in most indigenous theatre, there really is no director in the western sense. Instead, there is the eldest and most respected actor who usually leads the troupe and who briefs performers about the arrangement of scenes just before the performance, leaving details to each artist.

It was not until the 1950s that western styles of directing were formally studied and names such as Stanislavski and Craig became known. From the 1960s to the 1990s, other names were added including Brecht, Artaud, Grotowski, Barba and Boal. As a generalization, directors such as Teguh Karya and Suyatna Anirun are conventional realists, Rendra and Riantiarno more Brechtian in approach while Arifin C. Noor and Putu Wijaya are more surreal and Artaudian.

Music Theatre
Dance Theatre

For a discussion of music and dance, see the opening, historical section and **Artistic Profile**.

Theatre for Young Audiences

The company Teater Ananda (Children's Theatre) led by the actress Renny Jayusman was the first regularly producing children's group. It was founded in the 1980s in Jakarta. In the 1990s other groups emerged including Teater Bobo led by Ade Puspa and Isdaryanto. In Bandung, the leading children's group is Teater Lituhayu (Happiness Theatre), founded in 1983. Its predecessor was Teater Anak Bawang (Children's Theatre, founded 1979), led by Ery Anwar and his wife, Susi Rinaldi.

Throughout the 1980s and 1990s, there were irregular efforts from the government to boost activities of theatre for young audiences. Competitions were conducted and winning plays by such playwrights as Putu Wijaya, Saini K.M., Arswendo Atmowilopo and Arthur S. Nalan were produced.

Puppet Theatre

At the root of Indonesia's many theatre forms are the rituals connected to life cycles, such as birth, marriage and death, or to agriculture, especially the planting and harvesting, or to exorcism. Many things are exorcized for their welfare; a boy who has two sisters is exorcized for being the only boy. A new house or even a new village is exorcized, to drive away evil spirits.

Puppet theatre is closely related to these rituals and is still performed for the exorcism of evil spirits to guarantee either the health of a person or the welfare of a village. The *dalang* (puppeteer) is revered as healer, magician and artist. One of the most important aspects of *wayang* (puppet theatre) in Indonesia is the position and function of the *dalang*. A *dalang* is not only an artist, but also a spiritual leader and is respected as such. Even after Islam came to Indonesia, though somewhat weakened, a *dalang* has usually still retained the aura.

This special position and function is based on the fact not only that *wayang* performance is still strongly related to religious rituals or solemn occasions, but also that the performance itself is full of religious symbolism. A good example of this is the existence and the use of the *kayon* or *gunungan* as one of the properties in the puppet theatre. *Kayon* (tree) is a symbol of *axis mundi* or ladder of the worlds. At the beginning of the performance the *dalang* will move the *kayon* or *gunungan* in such a way as if telling the audience that he is going to climb up the *axis mundi* to the upper world to meet the gods or to climb down to the lower world and meet the demons for the interest of the audience. In this respect, the *dalang* acts both as a shaman and a *hungan*. When the *dalang* goes to the other worlds to represent humanity or the community, it is as a shaman. When the *dalang* represents the gods and the demons or ancestors through the story of the performance, it is as a *hungan*. The community depends on the *dalang* to maintain communication with the other worlds and their inhabitants, which are symbolized by the puppets. This communication is considered very important for the welfare of the community.

Wayang wong literally means human-puppet. It is a kind of ethnic-traditional theatre in which the stories and characters that are usually performed by puppets are performed by humans. Limitations suffered by both leather and wooden puppets are overcome by the human actors but much of the charms and magic of the original are lost. One of the losses is in the visual aspect of the characters. In puppet theatre, the sculptural features of the leather or wooden puppets strongly express the spiritual states of the characters. Even the best makeup on people cannot achieve the kind of effect given by the puppets.

Wayang topeng is similar to *wayang wong* except that the actors wear masks. Since it is difficult for the actors to speak or sing, the *dalang* takes the burden of speaking the dialogue, recitation, chanting and narration; in *wayang wong* the actors dance and sing as well as acting and speaking their parts. Refined characters of *Mahabharata* such as Arjuna and Abimanyu or *Ramayana* such as Rama and Lasmana are usually performed by women. Whereas in puppet theatre, the *dalang* as the main actor may become the superstar, in *wayang wong* it is the individual actor within the group who becomes the idol of the audience. They come not to see the already familiar story, but to see their favourite actor.

Wayang beber literally means screen puppet theatre. Whereas other puppet theatres use leather or wooden puppets, *wayang beber* has several screens or *kelir* as its main properties. Each screen contains several scenes painted on to it. The *dalang* opens the folded screens one by one and recites and sings accompanied by the *gamelan* orchestra. The story is finished when the final screen is opened and the *dalang* recites the last parts of the story related to the last scene on the screen.

The stories are taken from *Mahabharata*, *Ramayana* or the Panji Cycles and the story of Damar Wulan.

A source of wisdom and inspiration sought by many for guidance in life, theatre using *wayang kulit* (leather-puppets) can be divided into two kinds – those pieces based on *Mahabharata* and *Ramayana*, the great Hindu epics, and those that are more secular in nature. Those based on the epics are known as *wayang purwa*. Those not based on the epics cover many subdivisions, the most important of which are *wayang klithik*, *wayang krucil* and *wayang menak* (called *wayang papak* in the Cirebon area and *wayang cepak* in the Priangan area of western Java).

The stories of *wayang klithik* are based on the *babad* (a mixture of literature and elements of history). The *babad* stories are mostly made up of events at the end of or after the age of the Majapahit Kingdom of eastern Java, namely after the fifteenth century; the *pantun* stories are built around the adventures of the princes of the Galuh and Pajajaran kingdoms of western Java, from the eighth to the fifteenth centuries. *Wayang menak* stories are based on the struggles and evolutions of Islam, especially around the character of Hamzah, the heroic uncle of the Prophet Mohammed, and his companions, especially Omar and his son-in-law Ali.

There are at least another dozen types of *wayang kulit*, but with less significance from the point of view of historical purity, literary style or quality. The best *wayang purwa* stories deal with basic spiritual problems, dramatized in passionate conflicts between good and evil, love and hatred, compassion and wickedness, vengeance and forgiveness. Characters are not intended to depict real human beings but rather are symbols of various spiritual states. As a result, they are both larger than life and closer to reality and there is much room for audiences to interpret meaning for themselves. In most of these works the spiritual problems are never completely solved and the mystery of life never loses its attraction.

The stories of the *wayang krucil* consist of *babad* whose themes are closer to those of modern literature in which the lust for power and wealth, the search for romantic love and intrigue, treason and murder all feature. Filled with archetypes, most of the plots of the *wayang pantun* are built around rites of passage (not boy-meets-girl as some western scholars have argued). Many plots deal with a young prince, usually the son of the king or of a great nobleman who responds to a mysterious call from the other world, the abode of the gods. There he is confronted with a test or a series of tests that sometimes actually cause his death. In the end, however, he is either saved or resurrected by some compassionate god or goddess and then given a heavenly reward, sometimes a magic weapon or amulet by which he can save his kingdom from enemies. Connected to *Mahabharata* and *Ramayana*, the characters are larger than life and not to be mistaken for average individuals. In the hands of masters, the form takes on an extraordinary beauty and dignity.

The original arrangement of scenes and the overall dramaturgical patterns are essential to the uniqueness of all *wayang* performances. The scenes are arranged to reveal symbolic meanings, from palace scenes to outdoor scenes and then back to palace scenes. One of the best known stories can serve as an example for many *wayang* scripts. Starting indoors, a king is being honoured by all his princes, his ministers and his knights. All testify that peace and prosperity abound. The king expresses his satisfaction and asks dancers to entertain the assembly. During the dance, a soldier enters to report that a demon has kidnapped the king's daughter. A knight volunteers to find the princess. It is here that the outdoor scenes begin. The knight in his search must first fight robbers, then demons. In his adventures he is usually accompanied by clowns (representing villagers, wise in their humorous comments and advice). At last he confronts the arch-demon, one with great magical powers. First defeated by the demon, he seeks help and advice from a hermit, perhaps his own grandfather. Prior to this deep spiritual

scene, the stage is given to the clowns to tickle the audience to laughter and ensure they are wide awake. The dialogue between the knight and the hermit covers questions of the nature of humanity and what destiny it is to fulfil life as intended by the creator. The knight is taught new magic formulae to conquer the demon. Refreshed spiritually and with a new confidence, he renews his effort to save the princess. After more trials in which he fulfils requirements demanded by the hermit – for example helping people in distress and/or overcoming sensual or worldly temptations – the knight then confronts the arch-demon for the second time and after a terrible battle vanquishes the enemy. It is here that the scenes return to the palace. The king acknowledges his gratitude to the knight in front of the assembly. He also announces his intention to retire giving both the crown and the princess to the knight.

Behind the drama lies the symbolic structure. Palace scenes are symbolic of peace, order and prosperity; outdoor scenes represent uncertainty and danger. Thus, a pattern is established of cosmos–chaos–cosmos. It is the knight's task to restore the 'cosmos' after an evil power brings in 'chaos'. And since the knight represents all humanity, the structure urges the viewer to maintain peace, order and prosperity and to protect it against evil, both from outside forces and from uncontrolled passions hiding inside ourselves.

Music is an important supporting part of the dramaturgy, but it can also be considered as a separate and complete creation, expressing the same theme as the story. The choreographic or kinetic aspects, especially the dances and movements of the main characters are also expressive of the deeper spiritual meaning of the work.

The same importance is connected to the visual aspects of *wayang*. The puppets themselves, namely the sculptural forms and their colours all reflect their respective characters and spiritual states. Those with an evil nature are usually monstrous in form while refined forms symbolize higher spiritual states.

Even the lit screen behind which the leather puppets are placed, the special lamp that creates the shadow figures and the banana wood trunk on which the puppets stand are all symbolic of the same deep meanings. Even approaching the twenty-first century, many Javanese, Sundanese and Balinese still turn to the *wayang* for inspiration and find their spiritual life strengthened by its revelations.

Because of its social role, *wayang* was a community event that took eight or nine hours, usually from sunset to dawn. All-night performances, however, are now rare and the modern performances are usually less than three hours.

This shortening of performance time seems to go with the social changes in the function of this form. In former times, *wayang* was not only a part of a ritual, but also a complete ritual in itself, an occasion for the audience, the village and the community to reaffirm its values and its spiritual well being. Even in the 1990s, although less frequent, *wayang* is still performed on occasion to exorcize evil spirits or to protect loved ones from them.

Aside from *wayang*, a more secular form of puppetry has also emerged in the years since independence, aimed at children. Among the first such troupes was Si Unyil (Unyil being a childish nickname for a Sundanese boy). The troupe was founded in the early 1970s by

Kurnaen Suhardiman and Suyadi and performs mostly on television. The style and content are based on European *guignol*. Unfortunately, this troupe, financed by the government, could only reflect approved government policy.

In the 1980s another puppet theatre, this one led by psychologist Kak Seto (Seto Mulyadi) popularized a character named Si Komo, an acronym for Si Komodo, the prehistoric dragon of the Commodo Islands of eastern Indonesia. With Si Komo came other characters beloved by children, such as Ulil the caterpillar, Cici the rabbit, and so on. The theme and the moral of the stories are of clear educational value. The forms, however, and the manipulation are not very sophisticated, since the theatre is intended for very young children. The many songs used in the theatre also show the influence of Jim Henson's Muppet figures.

Design
Theatre Space and Architecture

Those theatre styles originally staged for royal production, such as *wayang kulit, wayang wong* and *langendriyan*, are still performed in formal assembly halls or in the *pendopo*, a hall open on three sides. The stage is usually lit by a luxurious crystal chandelier hanging above the centre of the playing arena. In the non-puppet styles, performers are costumed to look like characters in puppet theatre, specifically *wayang purwa, wayang krucil* and *wayang menak*, or as historical characters from the *babad*.

The folk theatres – the *ketoprak* and *ludruk* in eastern and middle Java, the *masres, longser* and *reog* in western Java, and the *lenong* around Jakarta – are much more loose in matters of stage space and design. They can be performed anywhere, both inside or out, in courtyards or dry paddy fields, or even on a large veranda. When performed outdoors, the stage is usually arena-style with the musicians occupying an area to the side of the playing space. One important feature of such performances is the use of a torch which, in addition to helping with lighting, is also symbolic of the *axis mundi* (ladder to the other world). In Bali, it should be noted the most traditional forms of theatre are usually performed in the courtyards of shrines or temples.

The proscenium stage was not introduced to Indonesia until the nineteenth century and was quickly adopted. The *wayang wong, ketoprak* and *ludruk* in eastern and middle Java, the *sandiwara, masres, lenong* and even the *reog* and *longser* with their rural agricultural origin in western Java, are now also performed on proscenium stages utilizing modern lighting as well.

The coming of electricity at the beginning of the twentieth century inspired many theatrical artists to create spectacles that were not possible until then. In the *sandiwara* and *masres* theatre of western Java and in the *wayang wong, ketoprak* and *ludruk* of middle and eastern Java, spectacle became very important at this time, thrilling audiences with vanishing characters, flying figures, artificial waterfalls, dragons breathing fire with their red or green eyes glaring in semi-darkness, or with waves heaving in great storms. Matched and strengthened by sound effects, these spectacles still can hypnotize audiences.

As for designers, two modern masters need be mentioned – Gigo Budisatiaraksa (1935–86), a founder of the Bandung Theatre Study Club, and Rudjito, an alumnus of Rendra's Yogya Theatre Workshop. Gigo, a former student of the Department of Fine Arts at Bandung Institute of Technology, has suggested the precision of the visual arts was at the foundation of his artistic achievement. In contrast to Gigo's analytical art, Rudjito is more intuitive and less realistic. Sometimes he simply puts a single plant on an almost empty stage. Its evocative power of place, time and atmosphere is immediately com-municated. Gigo designed mostly for the Bandung Theatre Study Club while Rudjito designed for a range of directors, including Rendra, Arifin C. Noor, Putu Wijaya and Riantiarno. For his long career as a designer, Rudjito was awarded the Anugrah Seni (National Prize for Art) by the government in 1994.

Training

During the 1950s training was mostly done by the groups themselves, by visiting professionals and, for a very few, through study abroad. Exceptional artists such as Asrul Sani studied in the Netherlands; Teguh Karya went to the East–West Center at the University of Hawaii; Syuman Jaya and Ami Priyono went to the Soviet Union.

At the same time, libraries established by foreign institutes such as the British Council, the United States Information Service and the Alliance Française were also helpful in cultural areas and many new ideas were discussed in the clubs and applied in performances.

At the universities, faculties of Arts and Letters began to support student theatre clubs. Jim Lim, one of the pioneers, first became involved in theatre in the Faculty of Fine Arts at the Bandung Institute of Technology as did Suyatna Anirun and Gigo Budisatiaraksa. Rendra, too, was an alumnus of such a club in the Faculty of Letters of the University of Gajah Mada in Yogyakarta.

The 1950s also saw the first creation of specific educational institutions for theatre. In Yogyakarta a group of artists established the Academy of Drama and Film in 1952. In Jakarta, Usmar Ismail, Jayakusumah and Asrul Sani established a National Academy of Theatre in 1955. In Bandung Jim Lim and Saini K. M. participated in establishing the Academy of Theatre and Film in 1963. During the second half of the 1960s, in the political turbulence caused by an aborted *coup d'état* by the Communist Party of Indonesia, the academies faced problems and only the Film Institute survived. But in the 1970s, with the establishment of the Ismail Marzuki Art Centre in Jakarta and the Bandung Academy of Performing Arts, formal training and education in theatrical arts was given a new start. By the first half of the 1980s, the Institute of Arts of Yogyakarta had also established a department of theatre.

In addition to these, advanced workshops are regularly given by a number of companies including Rendra Theatre Workshop in Depok, by the Popular Theatre of Teguh Karya in Jakarta and Bandung Theatre Study Club. Most of the theatrical artists of the 1990s are alumni of these later institutions.

Criticism, Scholarship and Publishing

State publishing houses – Balai Pustaka and the culturally motivated Pustaka Jaya – have helped serious criticism and scholarship in the 1980s and 1990s by publishing plays by Rendra, Arifin C. Noor, Putu Wijaya and Riantiarno.

Nur Cahaya has published a number of useful studies including Saini K. M.'s *Beberapa Gagasan Teater* (*Some Ideas on Theatre*, 1981) while Angkasa published his *Dramawan dan Karyanya* (*Dramatists and Their Works*, 1983) and Binacipta his *Teater Indonesia dan Beberapa Masalahnya* (*Indonesian Theatre and Its Problems*, 1988). In 1995 Saini K.M. published another collection of essays titled *Peristiwa Teater* (*Theatrical Events*). Jakob Sumardjo's *Perkembangan Teater Modern dan Sastra Drama Indonesia* (*The Development of Modern Indonesian Theatre and Dramatic Literature*) was published by Citra Aditya Bhakti in 1992.

More in the realm of theatrical aesthetics are the personal writings of poet-playwright Rendra as well as those by other major artists such as Teguh Karya, Suyatna Anirun, Arifin C. Noor, Rutu Wijaya and Riantiarno.

In Jakarta, Radar Panca Dahana, a graduate student of socio-political sciences at the University of Indonesia, has written a number of significant critical essays on theatre. Jakob Sumardjo is a theatre historian of some note. A significant bibliography on Indonesian theatre is also now being undertaken.

Most of the leading newspapers in Indonesia, such as *Kompas*, *Republika* and *Suara Pembaharuan* in Jakarta, *Pikiran Rakyat* in Bandung and *Bernas* in Yogyakarta and the *Surabaya Post* in Surabaya have arts columns which, although they have an impact on artists and audience, are considered far from satisfactory by theatre artists themselves. This dissatisfaction and the accusation that theatre criticism really does not yet exist in Indonesia, though somewhat exaggerated, is based on the fact that most writers with critical pretensions have little theatrical background. As a result, critics follow their own personal tastes or base their judgements on generally irrelevant criteria or on purely literary criteria. Those few critics with theatrical backgrounds, many of them members or former members of theatrical groups, do not fare much better since most are limited by the style of the groups they were in.

Yet some critics of note have begun to emerge. Such critics as Bakdi Sumanto in *Kompas*, have a thorough knowledge of Euro-American dramatic literature and even some theatrical experience. Ary Batubara and Edy Purnawady are two other critics with formal theatrical education in their background. Graduates of the Bandung Academy of Performing Arts, both write regularly in national and local newspapers as well as magazines. Agus Sardjono, with a Master's degree in education, specializes in Indonesian language and literature. A lecturer at Bandung Academy of Performing Arts, he writes mostly in local newspapers in Bandung.

Saini K.M.

Further Reading

Anderson, B. Sutton. *Mythology and Tolerance of the Javanese*. Ithaca, NY: Cornell University Press, 1965.

Asmara, Cobina Gillet. 'Tradisi baru: A New Tradition of Indonesian Theatre'. *Asian Theatre Journal* 12 (spring 1995).

Aveling, Harry. *Moths*. Kuala Lumpur: Dewan Bahasa dan Pustaka, 1974.

Aznan, Suhaeni. 'Profile: Nano Riantiarno; an Indonesian Playwright Sees Life as Theatre (teater koma)'. *Far East Economic Review* 156 (n.d.): 78.

Beng, Tan Sooi. *Bangsawan: A Social and Stylistic History of Popular Malay Opera*. Singapore: Oxford University Press, 1993.

Buurman, Peter. *Wayang Golek: The Entrancing World of Classical Javanese Puppet Theatre*. Oxford: Oxford University Press, 1991. 152 pp.

Cazzola, Gabriele. *L' attore di Dio: Conversazioni balinesi* [God's actor: Conversation in Bali]. Biblioteca di cultura 56. Rome: Bulzoni, 1990. 127 pp.

Coudrin, Gildas-Louis. *Wayang Golek: tradition vivant* [Wayang golek: A living tradition]. La Gaubretiere: CEPMA, 1986. 155 pp.

Dunn, Deborah Gail. 'Topeng Pajegan: The Mask Dance of Bali'. PhD dissertation, Union for Experimenting Colleges and Universities, Cincinnati, OH, 1983. 230 pp.

Giava-Bali rito e spettacolo [Java-Bali, rite and performance]. Biblioteca Teatrale, 46. Rome: Bulzoni, 1985. 348 pp.

Hartley, Barbara. 'Wayang, ludruk and ketoprak: Popular Theatre and Society in Java'. *Review of Indonesian and Malaysian Affairs* 7 no. 1 (n.d.): 38–56.

Keeler, Ward. *Javanese Shadow Plays, Javanese Selves*. Princeton, NJ: Princeton University Press, 1987. 282 pp.

Lindsay, Jennifer. 'Klasik Kitsch or Contemporary: A Study of the Javanese Performing Arts'. PhD dissertation, University of Sydney.

Long, Roger. *Javanese Shadow Theatre: Movement and Characterization in Ngayogyakarta Wayang Kulit*. Ann Arbor, MI: UMO Research Press, 1982. 195 pp.

Mohammad, Goenawan. 'Teater Indonesia Mutakhir: Sebuah Catatan'. *Budaya Jawa* (June 1974).

Nalan, Arthur S., ed. *Aspek Manusia Dalam Seni Pertunjukan*. Bandung: STSI Press, 1996.

Peacock, James L. *Rites of Modernization: Symbolic and Social Aspects of Indonesian Proletarian Drama*. Chicago: University of Chicago Press, 1968.

Saini K.M. *Beberapa Gagasan Teater* [Some ideas on theatre]. Jakarta: Nur Cahaya, 1981.

——. *Dramawan dan Karyanya* [Dramatists and their works]. Jakarta: Angkasa, 1983.

——. *Peristiwa Teater* [The theatrical event]. Bandung: ITB Press, 1995.

———. *Teater Indonesia dan Beberapa Masalatinya* [Indonesian theatre and its problems]. Jakarta: Binacipta, 1988.

Soedarsono. *Wayang Wong. The State Ritual Dance of the Court of Yogjakarta*. Gajah Mada University Press, 1984.

Sri Muljono. 'Performance of Wayang Purwa Kulit'. *Traditional Drama Music of South East Asia*. Kuala Lumpur: Dewan Bahasa dan Pustaka, 1974.

Studiklub Teater Bandung (a collection of critical essays on theatre), 1993

Sumardjo, Jakob. *Perkembangan Teater Modern dan Sastra Drama Indonesia* [The development of modern Indonesian theatre and dramatic literature]. Jakarta: Citra Aditya Bhakti, 1992.

Zurbechen, Mary Sabina. *The Language of Balinese Shadow Theatre*. Princeton, NJ: Princeton University Press, 1987. 291 pp.

IRAN

Situated in western Asia and often considered part of the Middle East, Iran, known for most of its long history as Persia, shares borders to the north with Armenia, Azerbaijan and Turkmenistan, to the east with Afghanistan and Pakistan, and to the west with Iraq and Turkey. To the south lies the Oman Sea and the Persian Gulf (and beyond that the countries of the Arabian Peninsula). The third largest oil producer in the world, it has a land area of 1,650,000 square kilometres (637,100 square miles) and a population of some 60 million, 10 million of whom live in the capital Tehran. The official language is Persian and the official religion is the Shiite form of Islam. Other religions exist officially (Zoroastrianism, Judaism and Christianity) and unofficially (Bahaism).

Ancient Persian territories (from the sixth century BC to the seventh century AD) extended from Libya to the Chinese borders and from the Mediterranean to the Indus river. For 3,000 years it was ruled by shahs. In 1979, a revolution deposed the shah and Iran transformed itself into an Islamic Republic.

Invaded many times (Alexander in the fourth century BC, the Arabs in the seventh century AD and the Mongols in the thirteenth century), on each occasion Iran, due to its strong cultural heritage, revived and re-established its national identity. Unlike other countries which lost all ties to its ancient past, Iran always retained the memory of its ancient civilization and continued its cultural influence and exchange with Turkey, the Caucasus and the peoples of central Asia and India.

Among the great Iranians of history who created masterpieces were men of science: Razes (ninth century), Avicenna (tenth century) and Biruni (eleventh century); poets such as Ferdowsi (tenth century), Omar Khayyam (eleventh century), Gorgani (eleventh century), Attar (twelfth century), Nezami (twelfth century), Mowlavi (thirteenth century), Saadi (thirteenth century) and Hafez (fourteenth century); and painters such as Behzad (fifteenth century) and Abbasi (seventeenth century).

Since the fifteenth century, Persia, like many other Asian countries, stagnated in comparison with the European nations which entered the Renaissance. The eighteenth and nineteenth centuries were, in fact, periods of decadence for Iran. In the mid-nineteenth century Iranian travellers to the west were clearly fascinated by its technological progress and the order of law and justice. Western ideas infiltrated Iranian thinking and culminated in the Revolution for the Constitution in 1906. But not before 1925, with the advent of the Pahlavi dynasty, Reza Shah and Mohamad Reza Shah, did a real modernization begin, including the establishment of public security throughout the country, the unveiling and emancipation of women, the establishment of western-style higher education and universities, the industrialization of agriculture, road, rail and air transport, and the beginning of radio and eventually television.

In 1935, one symbol of this renewal was the decision to change the name officially from Persia (a name used only by occidentals) to Iran, the name used by Iranians themselves for millennia. The Pahlavis achieved all these reforms but ultimately did not have faith in democracy itself. This was one of the causes of the 1979 February Revolution which banished the monarchy and established an Islamic Republic, ruled entirely by the clergy, which began to censor, among other things, cultural creations, including theatre. The revolution also provoked a migration that sent nearly 2 million Iranians abroad, the largest number to the United States.

Archaeologists believe that certain figurines (some in the Brooklyn Museum in New York and some in the Albright Art Gallery in Buffalo) along with seals and stamps from western Iran dating to late 4000 BC (depicting men with ibex-horned heads, hairy bodies, wearing shoes with turned-up toes and carrying wide collars which recede down their backs into birds' tails) could represent gods or 'masters and protectors of game' or 'mythical sorcerers playing the part of animals or humanized animals'. It is also possible, however, that they were masked actors, half sacred, half profane, who served as Iran's earliest entertainers.

In October 522 BC, a *magus* who had usurped the Iranian throne was killed by Darius of the Achaemenian dynasty, thus beginning a general massacre of the *magi*. One hundred years later Herodotus says, 'This day was celebrated each year as the feast of Magophonia or the day of the slaughter of the *magi* ... the Persians observe this day with one accord, and keep it more strictly than any other in the whole year ... this day is the greatest holy day that all Persians alike keep ...'.

Certain scholars believe that this feast probably continued in the form of other celebrations like *Mir-e nowruzi*, *day be mehr*, and *'Omar koshan*. Indeed from the time of Alexander and later under the Parthians, Greek theatre was performed in the original language in Iran for Alexander's army in temporary tent theatres. More indigenous is the *gosan*, a mistral poet who sung accompanied by a musical instrument during the Parthian period (third century BC to third century AD).

> Present at the graveside and at the feast; eulogist, satirist, story-teller, musician, recorder of past achievements and commentator of his own times ... some were the laureates of their age, performing alone before kings; others provided together chair or orchestra at court or a great man's table, and yet others, it is plain, won a humble livelihood and local fame among peasants and in public places.

Parthian *gosans* were also in Armenia (*gusan*) and Georgia (*magosanni*). Objects from the same era also prove that animal masks were used, such as those of monkeys.

The Mithra god cult (from the fourteenth century BC to the fifth century AD) spread from India and Iran into Europe (as far as England) and Asia (China) adapting to the various locales. Access to the different hierarchies of Mithraism required rituals or 'mysteries' in which the believers would wear the guise and masks (perhaps due to Greek or Roman influence) of various animals (lions, crows, etc.) imitating their roars, cries and movements. Nevertheless there are no iconographical vestiges of Mithraic mysteries in Iran.

It is known that since the Sassanian period (third to seventh centuries AD) buffoons, jugglers, tightrope walkers, tumblers, musicians and dancers all played an important part in public entertainment. During the same dynasty there existed the merry and grotesque procession of the *Barneshastan-e kuseh* (The Ride of the Beardless Man), discussed at length by Iranian historians of the tenth and eleven centuries. On a cold day just before spring, a half-naked beardless ugly man, accompanied by his guards, would mount an ass, his body covered with ointment, a crow in one hand and would fan himself with the other. The crowds trailing behind would throw snow and ice at him and at the same time bestow him with gifts. The unfortunates who gave no donations were themselves splashed with ink and mud by the guards of the beardless man. This symbolic right of passage (celebrating winter's end and spring's beginning) survived for more than seventeen hundred years and was still seen up to the Islamic Revolution in 1979, performed by shepherds disguised almost like the ibex man of the fourth millennium BC. The *kuseh* character, it should be noted, is well known in Turkey as the *kose* or *kosa*.

The ritual of *Day beh mehr*, otherwise referred to in the tenth and eleventh centuries as *Botikan* (Day of Idols) must also date back to pre-Islamic Iran (prior to the seventh century). Dummies made of mud or dough were left to harden against doorways in the streets, the passing crowds bowed to these as if to kings and brought the ritual to a close by burning effigies. With the advent of Islam in Iran (seventh century AD) this custom was deemed 'idolatrous' and banned.

The *Mir-e Nowrouzi* (The Prince of the New Year) ritual also originates from ancient Iran. In this carnival-like ceremony a farcical king was elected for a reign of just a few days. This rite, which survived until 1946 in Bojnurd (northeast of Iran), was very similar to the *Fête des Vigneron* or *Fête des Fous* of the western European Middle Ages with its *Pape des Fous* (Pope of Fools). The rites of *kuseh* and *Mir-e Nowrouzi* seem to have been practised by Egyptian Copts until the end of the sixteenth century.

According to the historian *Narshakhi* (tenth century), a mourning ritual with songs called

Kin-e Siyavosh (Revenge of Siyavosh) had been taking place in Bokhara (now in Uzbekistan) for 'millennia'. *Siyavosh* was a pre-Islamic legendary prince, innocently killed by his father-in-law. This ritual is also referred to as *Geristan-e-Moghan* (The Weeping of the Magi). Up to the mid-nineteenth century, the ritual of *Siyavoshun* existed in the southern Iranian province of Fars. There are strong similarities between the mourning of *Siyavosh*, a sinless hero killed unjustly, and the heroes of the *ta'ziyeh* ritual drama which appeared some thousand years later.

The art of storytelling, *naqqali*, dates back at least to the Parthian *gosan*. In royal courts, public squares or tea houses the *naqqal* recounted, as he still does at the present time, tales of epic legends or popular picaresque romances by means of mire, hand gestures and varied vocal pitches. In the seventeenth century, *Taraz-al-akbar*, a manual, was devoted to the art of *naqqal*. An attempt to revitalize this genre was made in Mashhad (in the northeast) during the four Festivals of Tus between 1975 and 1978.

The Safavids came to power in the early sixteenth century and declared that Shiism (a division of Islam) was to be the official religion of Iran. The Shiis believe that Ali, the cousin and son-in-law of the prophet Muhammad, should have succeeded the prophet. This not taking place, the Shiis broke away, claiming the legitimate succession for Ali and his sons Hassan and Hosseyn. The latter strongly opposed the Umayyad Caliph of Damascus and left Arabia for Mesopotamia (and later perhaps Iran), where he had a following. In the desert region of Karbela he was beseiged by Umayyad troops, cut off without water, and eventually was slain along with many of his supporters in 680 AD. The commander of the Umayyads was 'Omar ibn Sa'd. From the early sixteenth century, Iranians began to celebrate the feast of *'Omar koshan* (the killing of 'Omar), a popular rejoicing in which a giant effigy of 'Omar (stuffed with wood, straw, cloth, turds and fire crackers) was burned. These feasts, when they took place in Sunni-inhabited areas, were acts of provocation. Gradually 'Omar ibn Sa'd was confused in the public mind with 'Omar ibn Khatab, the second caliph of Islam who symbolized for Iranians both the Arab invader and the Sunni enemy. The *'Omar koshan* is still occasionally and secretly performed in Azerbaijan by women, in a satirical and erotic form.

The *Shamayel Gardani* (Holding of the Icon) probably evolved in the sixteenth century. This event, in which a man, *Shamayel Gardan*, would exhibit holy pictures painted on canvas or on glass, narrating the fate of the martyrs of Shiism – *Shamayel Gardani* or *Pard-e dari* – is still practised in Iran.

Since the murder of Imam Hosseyn, the Shiis have mourned him officially on the anniversary of his martyrdom. In the eleventh century, preaching on the tragic end of the Prophet's grandson was instituted. In 1501 Hosseyn Va'ez Kashefi wrote his *Rozat al Shohada* (Garden of the Martyrs) on the sufferings and death of the Imam. Thereafter, orators recited extracts of this book, drawing from the believers tears and lamentations on the calamities of the Prophet's family. These dramatic events are now known as *Rowz-e khani* (recitation of the threnody).

The Safavid dynasty (sixteenth to eighteenth centuries) encouraged all of these above-mentioned rites and, in addition, patronized *dasteh* (elaborate religious processions). Beginning in the fifteenth century, European travellers remarked on and later described these processions which often took place on the first ten days of the Muslim month of Moharram, culminating on the tenth day with the martyrdom in Karbela. These *dastehs* beat their breasts, flagellated themselves with chains, attached locks to their flesh, and struck their heads with daggers (like the acts practised by Filipinos during Holy Week).

At times, these *dastehs* fought with each other as well since they came from different neighbourhoods. Considered pious exercises and mortifications, they symbolize remorse for not being present to help Hosseyn. Some carry *'alam* (big heavy metallic standards) decorated with tall flexible steel blades, lanterns and long ostrich feathers. Some personify events from the life of the Imam and his companions, such as their journey and tragic end. Camels might bear the bridal chamber of the unfortunate Qasem, nephew of Hosseyn, while decorated horses might carry *nakhl*, huge wooden structures, symbolizing the Imam's coffin. The biggest *nakhl*, in the city of Yazd, usually had to be carried by several hundred men. The entire procession was accompanied by dirge singers beating themselves.

Since the seventeenth century, these processions were transformed into mobile tableaux vivants. Jean Calmard has published a letter in which a French traveller in 1641, de Montheron, describes 'a kind of dramatic performance given in the Royal Square of Isfahan'. He speaks of a *tamasha* or *Spectacle de douleur*, and uses the word 'players' for the participants in these lively scenes.

In 1722 and 1735, two travellers, Salamons and Van Goch, saw these tableaux carried on wheeled chariots, showing *shabih*, personified silent characters representing the protagonists of the Karbela tragedy. This is clearly the last stage of the lengthy evolution of a ritual before it becomes verbal and takes dramatic form. In early 1770 Gmelin, a Russian traveller used the word theatre for the first time for these religious celebrations. But, in fact, it was in 1787 that an Englishman, William Franklin, saw in Shiraz and described what may be considered one of the earliest performances of *ta'ziyeh*. The word *ta'ziyeh* which originally referred to condolences and mourning, eventually came to mean tragic play, *ta'ziyeh khani*. In fact, the more correct term would be *shabih khani* (play of impersonation).

Ta'ziyeh progressed and flourished under the patronage of the Qajar shahs, particularly Naser al-din Shah (1848–96) and was equally well received and actively supported by the general public. The same shah constructed *takiyeh dowlat* in which the official and elaborate *ta'ziyehs* were performed. This ritual theatre genre became so renowned that an English Iranologist, Sir Lewis Pelly, wrote:

> If the success of a drama is to be measured by the effects which it produces upon the people for whom it is composed or upon the audience before it is represented, no play has ever surpassed the tragedy known in the Musulman world as that of Hassan and Hosseyn.

Other Englishmen, like Edward Gibbons, T.B. Macaulay and Matthew Arnold and Frenchmen such as Arthur Gobineau and Ernest Renan paid similar tributes to this Persian religious drama.

The contents of these plays narrate the journey of the Imam and his people from Medina to Mesopotamia, his battles and his martyrdom. There are also plays concerning the Prophet Muhammad and his family, the Shii saints and holy men, Quranic and biblical stories. The most prominent character in all is Hosseyn, who personifies innocence and is the intercessor of the believers. His purity and unjust death (compared with the character of Siyavosh and his funeral ritual, mentioned earlier) and submission to fate causes him to be loved and worshipped. He is also (like Jesus) the intercessor for humanity on the day of judgement; for the redemption of all Muslims he sacrifices himself. To create effects and make people cry, it should be pointed out that authors of *ta'ziyeh* not only take liberties in changing historical facts but also transform characters.

Hosseyn, for one, is regularly transformed in the *ta'ziyeh* into a man who accepts his destiny woefully. His moaning and attempts to elicit sympathy might even be irritating to some present-day audiences. By weeping, he proclaims his innocence and provokes cries and howls among the audience who in this ritual performance, also lament also their own miseries sins and oppressed conditions. The oppressed *mazlum* and martyr *shahid* are the characters best known for arousing pity among Iranians. Such a psycho-sociological phenomenon has been visible throughout Iranian history and played an essential part in the 1979 Islamic Revolution. Three large-scale *ta'ziyeh* performances, for example, were used to commemorate the first anniversary of the death of the Islamic Revolution's leader, Ayotollah Khomeni (d. 1989). The performances were presented at his mausoleum, at a *takyeh* and at Teatr-e Shahr (City Theatre).

Performers (more correctly termed 'Readers') playing the holy men and their followers in the *ta'ziyeh* are dressed in green or white, their adversaries (the villains) in red. The plays are always written in Persian and in verse, mostly by anonymous authors. The performers representing good characters sing the verse while those playing villains only recite it. The performers, not generally professional actors, come from all walks of life and play only on sacred occasions. Some masks, especially of the demon, are also used.

Thanks to the *rowze khani* and especially to the *ta'ziyeh*, Iranian classical music also survived under religious cover. Instruments used in performances include various sizes of kettledrums, several types of different trumpets, *karna* (an elongated horn heralding sorrow) and cymbals.

Since 1808 foreign travellers compared *ta'ziyeh* to the mystery and passion plays of the European Middle Ages. To make the comparison clearer, it should be said that there are two kinds of *ta'ziyeh* performances: the stationary ones and the mobile ones. In the latter, the executants roar around the streets playing consecutive episodes as they move through standing crowds. Such processions have not only medieval European resemblances but also an affinity with the Passion Week Celebrations in Guatemala, the Corpus Domini in Sicily and the Easter Procession at Sezze Romano, near Rome.

A performance of *ta'ziyeh* has special rules: circling around the *sakku* on foot or horseback means going from one place to another; a race around the *sakku* by armed horsemen symbolizes a battle; a person turning around himself means a change of place or character; a large basin of water represents the river Euphrates; and straw plays the role of the Mesopotamian desert sand. The parts of women are always played by veiled men who are not supposed to act in an effeminate manner.

The director of the performance is called *mo'in-al-boka* (the one who helps to bring tears) or *ta'ziyeh gardan* (*ta'ziyeh* director). He is constantly on the platform distributing written texts among the performers, who do not necessarily know them by heart. He also orders the protagonists around, sometimes even by prodding them with his club. He brings and removes the stage properties (for example, by clipping a piece of cotton wool in sheep blood and throwing it across the stage, he represents bloody flesh). The *ta'ziyeh* is remarkable in that the allusion to the tragedy of Karbela is sometimes shown in 'flashback' in the *Majles-e Amir-Teymur* (*T'amerlane Play*) and other times as an event to come or a 'flash forth' as in *Musa va darvish-e biabani* (*Moses and the Wandering Dervish*) where the Jewish prophet foresees the martyrdom of Hosseyn.

The unintentional modernity of such drama is also apparent: the absence of a backstage, leaving the players to wait their turn on the sides; permanent contact between stage and audience, the latter, participating constantly by weeping and breast-beating in sign of sorrow, or laughing loudly and even molesting the villains (on rare occasions the executants playing the part of Shemr, the killer of Hosseyn, have been lynched). To be realized as well in *ta'ziyeh* is the fact that for those involved (both executants and audience) the religious ritual is primary: men acting villains feel guilty in their roles and, before killing their victims, weep in sorrowful apology. This double consciousness by the actors, who are deeply religious, can be compared to Bertolt Brecht's *Verfremdungseffekt*. Even if such a comparison is made with reservations, it is an interesting phenomenon to note. A *ta'ziyeh* performance in this sense bridges the gap between time and space. Its power is such that the audience, despite the fact that it knows the story by rate, participates in it emotionally and, every time it is presented, connects in every new production with the essence of the events. This profoundly communicative power of

ta'ziyeh performances has attracted the attention of many contemporary stage directors and researchers including the English director Peter Brook and the Polish researcher Jerzy Grotowski.

From the beginning, the Shii clergy did not have a clear attitude towards such stagings. Though authorized and patronized by some, they have been rejected and condemned by others for different reasons (portraying holy men and ridiculing their personalities, the use of music, etc.). Right from the beginning there were also comic plays included in the performances called *Gusheh* or, as known much later, *Shabih-e mozhek*. The best known are *Shast bastan-e Div* (*The Tying of the Demon's Thumb*) or *Maliyat gereftan-e Jenab-e Mo'in al Boka'* (*The Impositions of Mo'tin al Boka*) or *Sargozacht-e Shirafkan* (*The Adventures of Shirafkan*). These plays, however, never broke away from religious drama to become an authentic secular national theatre. Instead, western entertainments arrived, and the *ta'ziyeh* entered an age of decay, eventually not attracting audiences at all.

In the early 1930s, during the rule of Reza Shah Pahlavi (1925–41) and a growing attraction towards western life, under the pretext of avoiding 'barbaric acts of mass exaltation' and in deference to the Turkish Sunni state, *ta'ziyeh* was banned. It survived but in a decayed and clandestine form in remote villages and resurfaced only with the revival of religious sentiment after the abdication of the shah in 1941. It remained in a poor state until the beginning of the 1960s, when intellectuals began scholarly research and gave encouragement to it by having the ban lifted and presenting fragments of *ta'ziyeh*, as compiled by Parviz Sayyad (b. 1937) in the *Teatr-e Bistopanj-e Sahrivar*. A complete *ta'ziyeh* performance, *Ta'zieh-e Hor*, was finally presented during Shiraz Festival of Arts (1967) directed by Khojasteh Kia (b. 1935) and Parviz Sayyad. The same festival in 1976 initiated an international seminar on the art organized by P.J. Chelkowski. In Shiraz and a nearby village *Kaftarak*, fourteen performances of seven passion plays were organized by Mohammad Bagher Ghaffari (b. 1946). This was presented free of charge and was attended by 100,000 spectators, including the Empress Farah.

Such theatrical activities in Iran go far back in time. Iranian shahs always had *dalqaks* or *maskhareh* (jesters and buffoons). Shah 'Abbas (1588–1629) had a celebrated entertainer, *Kal 'Enayat* ('Enayat the Bald), who was apparently an extremely talented clown. According to Bahram Beyza'i (b. 1938), in the seventeenth century troupes of *motreb* (musicians and dancers) visited rich houses, their costumes and paraphernalia in *sandoq* (trunks), performing amorous and comic musical sketches culminating in a staged brawl and an escape. Dialogued buffoonery called *taqlid* (imitations) came next. Jean Chardin, the French merchant and traveller (in Persia 1664–77), admiring the ability of Iranian acrobats and conjurers, mentions actors wearing masks performing three-hour farces and dances full of 'insolence' and 'lewdness'. In the beginning of the eighteenth century, when the Shii clergy forbade the appearance of women as dancers and players, young boys with unbroken voices replaced them *en travesti*, creating much ambiguity.

Other shows are known from this earlier period, including *kachalak bazi* (*The Play of the Bald*), *Baqqal bazi* (*The Play of the Grocer*) and *Ruband bazi* (*The Play of the Mask*). In the latter, actors walk on stilts wearing long robes. These comedies were performed in teahouses as well as in private houses on occasions of marriages, births and circumcisions. Masks were used in such popular comedies which were known generally as *ruhozi*.

Utilizing a central area in public places or courtyards of houses, the traditional pools of water were covered by wooden planks and carpets. This kind of arrangement, known as *takhte-hozi* (planks over the pool), was apparently first seen in Shiraz in the presence of King Karim Khan Zand (1750–79). So the term *ruhozi* (over the pool) or *takht-e hozi* (planks over the pool) became generic names for these improvised Persian traditional comedies, both in cities and rural areas.

The principal character of *ruhozi* is the *siyah* (a man in black face) whose date of appearance is unknown. The actor playing him blackens his face and hands with soot and grease, talks with the accent of former Iranian black slaves using crude and obscene vocabulary (like his counterparts in traditional Arabian comedies, Turkish *karagöz* and *ortaoyunu* and similar to Harlequin in *commedia dell'arte*). He freely criticizes dignitaries, rich men and social defects, and personally humiliates himself with the phrase: 'irresponsible, stupid simpleton Negro' (as the 'wise fools' in the tradition of Iranian mystics). He also manages to be very daring. Other characters in *ruhozi* are the rich and aged *haji*, his wife, son, daughter and her suitor. Similar to the *commedia dell'arte*, *ruhozi* has no written text and each player improvises on a given plot. In the beginning of the nineteenth century, Chodzko mentions that these plays mocked the mullahs including their acts of ablution and leeching.

Naser al-din Shah (1848–96), a man interested in both Iranian traditional performances and western-style theatre, had famous court jesters. The best known of his buffoons was Karim Shire'i (Karim the Sweet) who specialized in *Baqqal bazi* and to whom was attributed a certain text erroneously called *Baqqal bazi dar Hozur* (*Baqqal Bazi in the Presence of the Shah*). The text contains interesting information on comic acting. The other well-known entertainer of the same Shah was Esma'il Bazzaz (Esmail the Draper) who in his plays (unsuccessfully imitating Molière) changed the classical *baqqal* (grocer) into other characters such as a court physician, a colonel, and even the chief of the Tehran police who in 1883 reacted and had him beaten. But the comedian complained to the shah and received justice.

In the twentieth century, in order to avoid any clash with the authorities, these plays were filled with mainly pseudo-historical subject matter but included elements of contemporary criticism by the *siyah*, who double-deals his master, favours the lovers, plays dumb and at the end shows the audience the moral. A subgrouping of the *ruhozi* is the pantomime genre, *lal bazi* (play of the mute), which emerged more from dance. In about 1917, popular comedies of this type began to appear in Tehran and survived a precarious period of closings and openings due to official prudishness.

Famous purveyors of *ruhozi* in the 1920s were Akbar Sarshar, Ahmad Mo'ayed, Babraz Soltani, and two admirable *siyahs*: Zabiollah Mahari and Mehdi Mesri. During this period, a new character emerged who mocked westernized Iranians, the *fokoli* (from the French *faux col*, detachable collar).

Because of the often bawdy or political nature of improvised performances, in 1930, Reza Shah Pahlavi's censorship officers began demanding to see texts for *ruhozi* plays in advance. Against the spirit of improvisation, it severely restricted their critical aspects. In response, entertainers, actors, musicians and puppeteers would often call their performances 'private parties' and shows would take place in shop-fronts on Cyrus Avenue in Tehran. In the religious uprising of 1963, some of these shops (mainly managed by Jewish Iranians) were targets of looting and fire. In 1977 at the Shiraz Festival a tribute was rendered to the improvised popular comedies by an international symposium and performances of *ruhozi* by groups from all over Iran.

Women also had their own improvised comic performances with entirely female casts (acting even the male parts). Privately performed in houses and traditionally viewed only by women, the most appropriate term for this type of play was coined by S.A. 'Enjavi-Shirazi, an Iranian folklorist and literary scholar who called it *bazi-ha-ye namayeshi* (theatre games). Like the *ruhozi*, it is usually satirical and criticizes those with power. The women's version relies more heavily on dance and patter songs; like *ruhozi*, the basic story situations and stock characters are known to everyone in advance.

These games are designed so that most, if not all, members may participate. For this reason, the stories, plots, verses, dances and movements may appear to be simple, formulaic and repetitive. These games are further distinguished from play-party games in other areas of the world by their initiatory functions, eroticism and transgressive quality in both content and form.

The subject matter of these games indicate the types of issues that interest traditional Iranian women: keeping a husband's interest, infidelity, children born out of wedlock, being forced to marry a man one does not like or know and who has been chosen by one's parents, problems with female in-laws (with whom a young bride traditionally lives), proper and circumspect behaviour.

The most elaborate of the games is the one called *Khaleh-Ro-ro* (*Auntie Ro-ro*), an enactment by a young woman who comes to her maternal aunt (*khaleh*, also a term of endearment for any older woman) to tell her she is 'one month married and two months gone'. She is also unsure who the father is: 'the butcher, the baker or the candlestick maker'. During the course of the game, the woman stuffs her clothes with rags and with extreme verisimilitude she emulates pregnancy and eventually childbirth. The birth scene includes a midwife who enters riding a donkey (played by one of the other women), yelling, screaming and cursing. The midwife is unhappy at participating in such a dubious birth. The young mother dances round the circle of women speculating on who the father might be. Finally she unfurls the blanket showing it to be empty and chanting '*hamash bad bud*' ('it was empty').

Some of these games are performed for the sheer transgressive enjoyment that they provide the participants who would never be permitted

to act in such a manner outside of this group of confidantes. For example, one such *bazi*, *Murcheh Dareh* (*There Are Ants*) is virtually a striptease. During this dance-game, the protagonist points to various parts of her body saying '*murche dareh*' ('*there are ants here*'), meaning that it itches. 'What shall I do?' To which the chorus responds 'Take it off and throw it away' referring to her various items of clothing until the performer is nude. In another game, the participant paints a face on her abdomen, places a simple headpiece over her head and wraps a jacket below the painted face while she dances around manipulating its face and her belly.

Traditionally, the most common setting for these women's performances has been women's quarters or courtyard gardens off limits to men (except infants or very young boys). During these events, female friends, family members and female servants are invited and allowed to participate. The women sit in a circle leaving space for the performers. A rhythmic accompaniment is played on a variety of percussion instruments including the *daireh*, a framed drum. Trays, pots or pans might also be employed. The women not performing the principle roles participate as a response chorus to the patter songs sung by the principles. At intervals, everyone is encouraged to dance.

Almost every Iranian traveller to Europe between 1799 and 1870 reports in his diaries with much admiration a number of western-style theatrical performances, but as most of their travelogues remained unpublished, the public in Iran had no knowledge of these forms. Mirza Fath 'Ali Akhundzadehm (1812–78) was probably the first Iranian to write plays in the western style. He later became a Russian subject and took the name of Akhundov. A critically minded progressive writer, his pamphlets were very influential in eastern liberal circles. Fluent in Persian, Arabic, Turkish and Russian, he became an interpreter for the Russian Viceroy of the Caucasus, and wrote six comedies in Turkish Azari (1850–5). Later he translated some of them into Russian to be performed in Tiflis (Tblisi) and Baku. Among his comedies are *'Molla Ebrahim Khalil kimiyagar* (*Molla Ebrahim Khalil the Alchemist*), an attack on a charlatan who swindles ignorant people; *Monsieur Jordan*, Hakim-e nabatat (*Monsieur Jordan the Botanist*), who advocates the cause of science against superstition; *Sargozasht-e Vazir-e Khan Lankaran* (*The Story of the Vizar of Lankaran*), criticizing corrupt governors; *Khers-e Qoldorbasan* (*The Thief Catching

Bear), an amorous intrigue among peasants; *Sargozasht-e Mard-e Khasis* (*The Miser*), portraying a greedy merchant; and one on the Russian occupation of the southern Caucasus, *Vokalay-e morafe'e* (*The Barristers*), which takes place in Tabriz and is about unscrupulous lawyers who try to swindle an orphan girl. In these amusing works he gives a pre-eminent place to women and denounces abuse of power, the evils of banditry and the hypocrisy of the clergy, against whom he wrote a pamphlet called *Maktubat* (*Letters*). In it, he complains that Muslim law has forbidden theatre – a 'beautiful gift'.

Akhundzadehm, who showed the importance of European-style theatre, has been justly called the Molière and the Gogol of the east. The text of his *Tamsilat* (*Plays*) was published in Turkish Azari in 1859, read in Iran and translated into Persian by Mirza Mohammad Qarajedaghi and, with the author's approval, published in Tehran in 1874. The translator claimed it to be the first example of theatre in Persian. Both the Turkish and Persian texts are written in a colloquial language rather than the usual high-flown literary style common at the time.

The first plays written directly in Persian are by Mirza Aqa Tabrizi. He had visited Constantinople on a government mission, knew a little Russian, and was fluent in Turkish Azari and French to the extent that for more than seven years he was local chief secretary of the French legation in Tehran. He read Akhundzadehm's plays in Turkish Azari, and the author requested him to translate them into Persian, but Mirza Aqa replied (letter of June 1871) that he preferred to write dramatic pieces himself in Persian and give his compatriots a chance to see 'examples in this new manner'. Nevertheless, his plays were much influenced by Akhundzadehm, who gave him advice to be restrained, which fortunately he did not heed.

Mirza Aqa shocked conformists and believers in classical conventions of theatre (starting with Akhundzadehm and many others) who criticized his free language and disregard for the three traditional unities. Precisely these 'mistakes' give his work, despite himself, an unintended boldness and modernity. His plays denounce, in a controlled way, moral simperings, corruption of absolute rulers, and the sheepishness of people generally. Among his highly amusing comedies are *Ashraf Khan*, about forced gifts and bribes; *Hokumat-e Zaman Khan* (*The Government of Zaman Khan*), about extortion of money from simple people; *Karbala raftan-e Shah Qoli Mirza* (*The Pilgrimage of Shah Qoli Mirza*), a tale of tricks and pranks; and *'Ashaq shodan-e Aqa Hashem* (*Aqa Hashem's Love Affair*). For more than half a century, the first three plays, published in Berlin in 1921, were attributed to Mirza Malkom Khan (1837–1908). A liberal Iranian politician of Armenian origin, exiled in Europe, Malkom Khan had frequently written sketches in his political pamphlets. In 1908, the first two acts of *Ashraf Khan* were published under his name in *Ettehad* (*Union*), a constitutional journal. In 1956, two Soviet Azerbaijani scholars, by referring to Akhundzadehm's archives, said that Malkom was not the author of the plays and that Mirza Agha Tabrizi was. Despite this, when the three plays were performed in Tehran in 1967 for the first time, Malkom Khan continued to be credited as the author. In 1975, however, the plays were included in a collection of plays by Mirza Agha Tabrizi, thus creating a question for future scholarship. Bricteux believes that the comical situations and everyday dialogue make these plays masterpieces of humour, comparable to Gogol's *Revizor* (*The Government Inspector*) and Jules Romain's *Knock*.

Still another liberal writer of such works was Mirza Aqa Khan Kermani (1853–96), whose best work is *Se Maktub* (*Three Letters*), which includes the dialogue called *Susmar al dowleh* (*The Lizard of the State*), a tale of a nineteenth-century governors' tyranny.

Naser al-din Shah on his journeys of 1873, 1878 and 1889 to Europe was particularly impressed by performances of circuses, operas and theatres and later published diaries of the trips. In 1882, on the command of the shah, a European-style auditorium (*à l'Italienne*) was constructed near the Golestan Palace in Tehran, the first in the country. Mirza All Akbar Khan, Mozayen al Dowleh (1843–1932), who had studied painting in France and a Monsieur Lemaire, a French music professor were among its first directors. The first translation of Molière's *Misanthrope* (*Sargozasht-e Mardomgoriz*) was done by Mirza Habib Esfahani (printed in Constantinople, 1869), and some of Molière's other plays were performed in this theatre. This first performance had a cast of non-professional Europeans who recited the Persian lines like parrots. The shah in his diary (March 1889) noted that the attempted improvisations of his buffoon in a western play was not very successful, but 'compared to law-abiding and disciplined performances by Armenians', he preferred it.

Imitating a mode current in Turkey, French characters in translated plays and novels were given Iranian names and their manners were Persianized. It should also be said that at this point in time female roles were always performed by men. The first known performance of an actress on the Iranian stage took place in Tabriz (1879) when Aghavni Papazian, an Armenian, performed in a show before the Christian community. Muslims in Tabriz saw Christian actresses on stage for the first time in 1888. The first actresses seen in Tehran were named in the programme as Mme Golofian and Mme Babian. In 1897 they acted in plays directed by Hovaness Khan Massehian Mosaed al-saltaneh (1864–1931), a well-known diplomat and noted translator of Shakespeare.

After the Revolution for the Constitution (1906–12), and during the reign of the last Qajar, Ahmad Shah, western-style theatre began to be seen more regularly. An on-again off-again affair for decades, it has always been relatively successful for a certain public. In 1907, however, even the word 'theatre', which was among the newly proposed cultural necessities, had been suppressed as being 'obscene' during the first session of Parliament. Ironically, more than half a century later, in 1968, on the occasion of 'Abbas Nalbandian's play *Pazhuheshi* (*Research*), the theatre again was being discussed in the Parliament as an 'indecent' activity.

The subject matter of plays during the first two decades of the twentieth century tended to be either social criticism of old-fashioned customs and praise of modern western ways or patriotic fairytale musical pieces. Most typical of this period are *'Arusi-ye Jenab Mirza* (*The Marriage of His Excellency Mirza*, 1904) by Prince Mohammad Taher Mirza (1825–98); *Hokkam-e qadim va hokkam-e jadid* (*Old and New Governors*, 1916) by Morteza Qoli Fekri (1869–1916); *Haji Riya'i Khan ya Tartuffe sharqi* (*Haji Riya'i Khan, the Oriental Tartuffe*, 1918) and *Ostad Nowruz-e Pinedouz* (*Ostad Nowruz the Cobbler*, 1919) by Ahmad Mahmudi Kamal al Vezareh (1875–1930). Mahmudi, who wrote seven plays, was the first Iranian author to utilize the colourful speech of Tehran's lower classes.

During the 1920s, more and more such plays were seen by playwrights such as Abolhassan Foroughi, a philosopher (1883–1959), who wrote a play in verse *Shidush va Nahid* (1921–2); Hassan Moqadam (1896–1925), whose play *Ja'far Khan az Farang Amadeh* (*Ja'far Khan Returns from Europe*, 1923), became a popular phrase to mock westernized Iranians; Zabih Behruz (1891–1971), a scholar, in *Jijak Ali Shah* (1923) satirized the Qajar court, and much later wrote a rhymed prose play *Dar Rah-e Mehr* (*On the Road of Mitralove*, 1944), about an initiatory journey with the poet Hafez; Ali Nasr (1893–1965), who via popular idioms and dialogue wrote a didactic and moralistic work called *'Arusi-ye Hosseyn Aqa* (*The Marriage of Hosseyn Aqa*, 1939).

To avoid censorship during the reign of Reza Shah Pahlavi (1925–41), himself a strong reformer who looked with contempt towards retrograde aspects of Islamic establishments and had sympathy for pre-Islamic Iran, authors mostly escaped into historical subject matter. Political activist, journalist, playwright and director Grigor Yeghikian (1880–1951), who worked in Gillan (south of the Caspian Sea), wrote a number of well-structured plays on history including *Jang-e mashregh va magreb ya Dariush-e sevvom* (*The Battle of East and West, or Darius III*, 1924) and *Mazdak* (1930); Sadeq Hedayat (1903–51), known for the surrealistic novel *Bouf-e kur* (*The Blind Owl*) wrote two feeble plays: *Parvin, dokhtar-e Sassan* (*Parvin, the Daughter of Sassan*, 1928) and *Mazyar* (1933), both about Iranian resistance to the Arab invasion. It was during Reza Shah's rule that women (mainly Armenians and Jews) regularly started to appear on stage; for the first time Muslim men and women were permitted to attend performances together, albeit sitting in separate sections of the theatre.

After the abdication of Reza Shah (1941) and the entry of Anglo-Soviet and later US troops into Iran, political rights were re-established. 'Abdol-Hosseyn Nushin (1901–71), a member of the communist Tudeh Party, translated and staged a number of well-known western plays at this time. Anti-democratic repression (in 1949 and 1953), however, again restrained liberties.

During the reign of Mohammad Reza Shah (1941–79) a paradoxical situation was created: on the one hand greed was growing culminating in corruption and undigested westernization, while on the other hand, there were attempts, officially encouraged, to emphasize national cultural identity and revive the traditional heritage.

In 1958, a General Office of Fine Arts was established which soon included an Office of Dramatic Arts, headed by Mehdi Forough. Until the mid-1960s, almost all non-commercial theatrical activities were sponsored by this department. In 1964, the General Office of Fine Arts was integrated within the larger Ministry of Culture and Arts, an affiliation which created a stagnant bureaucracy and which negatively affected national theatre life.

Another governmental sector, the National Iranian Radio and Television (NIRT), founded in 1966, also dealt with cultural life and promoted both traditional and contemporary theatre. The NIRT, for example, founded the *Jashn-e honar-e Shiraz* (Shiraz Festival of Arts, 1967–78) with the objective of promoting all the arts, seeking appreciation for traditional Iranian art forms, and elevating the standards of culture in the country. Among other aims of the festival was the celebration of works by Iranian artists and recognizing the most modern artistic developments in the world.

Concentrating mainly on theatre and music, the Shiraz Festival brought together authentic traditional performances from Asia, Africa and Latin America (*kathakali*, *Noh*, Balinese *gamelan*, the Masked Dancers of Bhutan) and the most significant trends of contemporary theatre innovation: Peter Brook, Robert Wilson, Jerzy Grotowski, Victor Garcia, Peter Schumann, Joseph Chaikin, Terayama Shuji and Tadeusz Kantor, to name just a few. During the festival period, Iranian artists also enjoyed full freedom for their works, place of performance, hours of performance (such as sunset for Arby Ovanessian's *Vis o Ramin*, 1970; sunset and sunrise for Brook's *Orghast I and II*, 1971) and unlimited duration (seven days and nights of uninterrupted playing time for Robert Wilson's *Ka Mountain*, 1972). All these factors made the festival arguably the most important international stage of its kind during this decade.

As an example of its scope, in 1977 the Shiraz Festival of Arts had a budget of US$550,000, mostly coming from the Iranian government and from NIRT. A modest portion was raised from ticket sales. Attendance was estimated at 50,000. (The figure was even larger in 1976 when performances of *ta'ziyeh* were held free of charge in a village near Shiraz. The festival estimated that 80 per cent of its audience was comprised of people under the age of 20.)

After the Islamic Revolution of February 1979, there was a short-lived period of theatrical fervor including the staging of *'Abbas Aqa kargar-e Iran Nasional* (*'Abbas Aqua Worker of Iran Nacional*) by Sa'id Soltanpour (b. 1940), a

leftist writer who was executed by the authorities in 1981. For celebrating the anniversary of the Islamic Revolution, in 1983 the *Fadjr* (*Sunrise*) Festival was created, during which the government's Ministry of Culture and Islamic Guidance through the Centre of Dramatic Arts (CDA) organizes a certain number of theatre performances. An International Puppet Theatre Festival was held in 1989 and a Festival of Traditional Performances later that same year. In 1990, for the first time outside Iran, several *ta'ziyehs* and traditional puppet theatre performances were presented under the auspices of the internationally famous Avignon Festival in France.

The religious and political revolution of 1979 clearly affected all cultural activities in the country. Artists, for their own survival, were obliged to use anti-imperialist and moralistic slogans in their work. Later all theatre activities were centralized with every theatre's policy, programmes and new productions put under the supervision of the CDA. The CDA's first step was the creation of a *Nezarat bar namayesh* (Performance Supervision Office), a body entitled to verify everyone's cultural and political activities, past and present and approve all choices of play and styles of production. This system is still in practice.

Such a situation divided Iranian artists into two groups: one dedicated to Islam, with an objective to create an Islamic Theatre, the other, which included most of the artists from the pre-revolution period, such as director Roknedin Khosravi (b. 1932), trying to maintain a theatre based on national and international ideals. Neither group's efforts flourished.

Between 1987 and 1991, the CDA was directed by Ali Montazeri, a Muslim dedicated to the revolution as well as to theatre as an international art. He briefly managed to improve conditions: groups came out of stagnation, started to work, and a considerable number of Iranian and foreign plays were staged. Some groups were even sent to perform outside the country. These activities, however, stopped in 1991 when Montazeri was removed from his position. Each year since, fewer and fewer theatrical activities take place in Iran. Theatre performances now are sponsored only for state-organized festivals.

Structure of the National Theatre Community

Attempts to create an Iranian Actors' Union in the years 1943, 1945 and 1951, because of complicated political situations in the country, failed. Later initiatives (1967 and 1977) for establishing a Union of Theatre Artists, did not get official support. As a result, there are no unions of theatre artists of any kind in Iran.

Before the revolution there were five regularly producing theatres in Tehran. After the revolution, when it seemed that new possibilities for art were coming into being, the number rose to eleven. By the 1990s, however, the number was restricted to four.

Ticket prices are very cheap by western standards: between 200 and 500 toman (480 toman equal US$1) with film tickets at 100 toman, a packet of Iranian cigarettes 75 toman and imported ones 250 toman.

A considerable number of Iranian theatre community members now live outside the country, among them such veterans as actress Loreta Hairapetian (1911–98) and actor-director Jafar Vali (b. 1933). A few of them produce for the Diaspora, such as Parviz Sayyad, whose activities in the United States are noteworthy – *Khar* (*Ass*, 1983), *Samad be jang miravad* (*Samad Goes To War*, 1984), *Samad as jang barmigardad* (*Samad Returns From War*, 1989) and *Dadgah-e Cinema Rex* (The Rex Cinema Trial, 1989) are among his best known productions. The events described in the last play are based on the actual burning of the Rex Cinema in Abadan (coast of the Persian Gulf, 1978) where some 300 people perished in a fire, deliberately started in the cinema to advance the Islamic Revolution. *The Rex Cinema Trial*, said one critic, 'is a massive orchestration of disgust, of anger, of bitter disappointment, a self-condemnation for merely being human'.

Moses and the Wandering Dervish, adapted from a traditional *ta'ziyeh* by Mohammad Bagher Ghaffari and performed by a group of non-Iranians, has been presented in the United States (1989). Massoud Saidpour (b. 1964) collaborated with Jerzy Grotowski at the University of California (Irvine) during his Objective Drama Research sessions between 1989 and 1992 and developed a series of Sufi teaching stories which explored the adaptation of traditional Iranian materials and performance idioms for presentation by a culturally diverse ensemble. Saidpour's work on Avicenna's *Recital of Birds*, Suhrawardi's *Tale of Occidental Exile* and Jami's *The Romance of Salaman and Absal* (all done between 1992 and 1993) were later performed at the Cleveland Playhouse. There have been other professional theatre activities in European cities (Bonn, Frankfurt, Cologne, London, Paris and Rome). Among them, Shahrou Kheradmand's (b. 1939) Teatro Trastevere in Rome, for instance, has done a number of productions based on Iranian dramaturgy, while Sadreddin Zahed's (b. 1946) Le Theatre D-Nue produced an adaptation of Sadeq Hedayat's *Ce qatreh khoun* (*Three Drops of Blood*) in Paris in 1990. A small company also exists in Toronto run by Soheil Parsa (b. 1947).

Artistic Profile

Since the 1970s, thanks to various studies by theatre researchers, the traditional forms of Iranian performance, *ta'ziyeh*, *ruhozi and kheymeh shabbazi*, stopped being considered retrograde art forms and began to be recognized by theatre artists. Iraj Saghiri's successful *Qalandra Khuneh* (1975), created in Buhehr and performed in the Shiraz Festival of Arts, was part of this movement. During the years following the Islamic Revolution, these styles were widely appreciated and many authors and directors, using their dramatic potentials, attempted to create a synthesis of the traditional forms with European ones. Three productions are in this tradition: *Soug-e Siyavosh* (*Mourning Siyavosh*, 1988) written and directed by Siyavosh Tahmoures (b. 1946), *Haft khan-e Rostam* (*The Seven Barriers of Rostan* 1990) written and directed by Attila Pessiani (b. 1957), and *Raz-e arousak* (*The Secret of a Doll*, 1997) written and directed by Davoud Fathali-beygi (b. 1950).

Iran, not being a member of International Copyright Convention, has not been able to protect its own authors, nor foreign authors whose works are translated freely. This is one

Iraj Saghiri's 1975 production of *Qalandra Khuneh*.
Photo: courtesy of Shiraz Festival of Arts.

of the reasons why almost every international contemporary dramatist of note has been translated, performed or published – without royalties paid – in Iran. European authors, such as Germany's Peter Handke and Franz Xavier Kroetz, Japan's Mishima Yukio and Britain's Edward Bond and Peter Gill, have all been performed in Tehran much earlier than in some other theatre capitals. Undoubtedly the presence of these foreign plays has played a great part in the development of Iranian dramaturgy.

Music theatre in its early days was based on Azerbaijani musical comedies with Aziz Hajibekov's (1885–1948) *Mashdi Ebad* (1910) among the most popular. It is in opposition to this that Mirzadeh Eshqi (1893–1925), a patriotic-minded poet, wrote his six plays. The most famous is *Rastakhiz-e Salatin-e Iran* (*Resurrection of Iranian Kings*, 1916), in which ghosts of famous ancient kings like Cyrus, Darius, Chosroes I and even Zoroaster appear. Reza Kamal Shahrzad (1898–1937), who adapted dramas from Victor Hugo and Oscar

Wilde and composed musical fairytales such as *Parichehr va Parizad* (1921), is the second author of note in this tradition. In the 1940s, musical plays went out of fashion and almost disappeared.

Through great efforts, western-style opera started in the 1960s. The first Iranian opera was *Zal o Rudabeh* by Samin Baghchehban, presented in 1967. In the 1970s, Lotfi Mansouri directed Bizet's *Carmen* (1971), Bartok's *Bluebeard's Castle* and Ravel's *L'Heure espagnole* (1975) in Tehran. From 1979, neither musical nor opera performances have taken place in Iran.

As for dance, the horned head and hairy body of a goat existed as a head-to-foot costume for dancers in popular celebratory events frequently depicted in miniatures and drawing of the sixteenth and seventeenth centuries. Some scholars consider these dancers as *qalandar* wandering dervishes or extremist mystics. In fact, the proto-historic ibex horned man is a sort of shaman whose trances are essentially mystic. It should be noted that some Sufis in Islamic Iran were *malamati* (people of blame) who performed shameless deeds in order to elicit scorn and derision taking on the role of scapegoat for society. Rejection by the 'right-minded' populace made their devotion more sincere and truthful. This Sufi school existed between the ninth and fourteenth centuries. In the later part of the tenth century, another Sufi order, the *qalandaris*, sometimes wore lion or leopard skins and shaved their heads, beards and even eyebrows. Similarly disguised are the musicians playing and shouting that are presented in a magnificent miniature from the famous *Hafez* diwan manuscript by Soltan Mohammad 'Eraqi (*c.* 1527) where 'low comedy and religion meet. Slapstick comedians achieve sainthood; crazy laughter becomes prayer' (S. Carry Welsh). Some other drawings (sixteenth and seventeenth centuries) depict dancers and musicians in the guise of goats playing castanets. These are clearly buffoons, jesters, masqueraders and comic entertainers and by no means dervishes and *qalandars*.

In this tradition of zoomorphic masks, there existed until the 1940s in the forests of Gilan a dance-pantomime, the story of a bride abandoning her groom to elope with her lover. The performers wore masks and apparel made of goat skin. Because of its 'amoral' content, this dance is presumed to be pre-Islamic and is known as *Arus Guley*.

Dance as a form of staged performance has not generally, however, developed in Iran. European style dance productions represent isolated efforts. Despite this, Iran has had a number of remarkable dance teachers. Madame Cornelli, Madame Yelena (b. 1907) and Sarkis Janbazian (1902–67) are the best known. These ballet masters trained a future director, and a number of stars for the Iranian National Ballot Company, such as Nejad Ahmadzadeh and Hayedeh Changizian. The National, however, was short-lived (1967–79).

There have been no public dance or ballet performances in Iran since the Islamic Revolution.

Companies

For an Iran that was reformed and modernizing, Reza Shah attempted to create a National State Theatre Company in 1933 by inviting into the country the well-known Soviet Shakespearian actor Vahram Papazian (1888–1968). Papazian staged a number of productions (benefits for the Iranian Red Cross) for a season with a company that had some well-known artists such as actresses Loreta Hairapetian and Helene Nouri, and actors Nosratollah Mohtasham and Moez-Divan Fekri. Among the plays produced by the group were *Othello*, *Hamlet*, Molière's *Don Juan*, Lermontov's *Masquerade* and Pushkin's *The Stone Guest*. After these early performances, however, the group disbanded, a common occurrence since, even before this event, most groups formed only to support a star.

The post-World War II period was more favourable for such ventures and some permanent private companies were formed. Among them the most important were Ferdowsi (1947–9) and Saadi (1951–3), both directed by Abdol-Hosseyn Noushin, Loreta and Hosseyn Kheyr-Khah (1901–61). These companies performed translated plays, the first being J.B. Priestley's *Mostanteq* (*An Inspector Calls*). In this period neither the theatres nor the companies had any state support. In 1953, after the burning of the Saadi company's theatre and due to the presence of a tense political situation (with strong McCarthyite overtones), few public social gatherings were permitted. Therefore groups started to form in a clandestine manner.

Gorouh-e honar-e melli (National Art Company), animated by Shahin Sarkissian (1911–66), was the result of a series of private workshops held in his home. This company's first public appearance was in 1956, with scenes from Chekhov's *Morgh-e daryai* (*The Seagull*) and two good adaptations from Sadeq Hedayat's stories: *Mohallel* (*The Provisional Husband*) and *Mordeh-khorha* (*The Necropolis*). In 1959 the company worked on Ali Nassirian's *Bolbol-e sargashteh* (*The Wandering Nightingale*), which a year later was the first Iranian production presented at the Théâtre des Nations in Paris. The company, now being sponsored by the General Office of Fine Arts, continued its work under the direction of an actor and writer, 'Abbas Javanmard (b. 1929) and for the second time participated in the Théâtre des Nations in 1965 with Bahram Beyza'i's two one-act puppet plays, *Ghorub dar diyari gharib* (*Evening in a Strange Land*) and *Qesse-ye mah-e penhan* (*The Story of Hidden Moon*) as well as Kouros Salashuhr's (b. 1935) naturalistic *Alounak* (*The Hut*). Though subsidized by the Ministry of Culture and Arts, Gorouh-e honar-e melli dissolved in 1979.

Gorouh-e Anahita (1958–63), headed by Mostafa Oskoui (b. 1924), focused on foreign classics such as Shakespeare's *Othello* and *Much Ado about Nothing* and Ibsen's *A Doll's House*.

The company, which had its own playhouse, ultimately failed due to bad financial management. This theatre too had a subsidy from the General Office of Fine Arts.

Among the many companies formed in the 1960s Gorouh-e Pazargad, headed by Pari Saberi (b. 1932) and Hamid Samandarian (b. 1932), was the most long-lived (1964–79). Composed of well-known freelance and state-subsidized actors as well as theatre students, it was entirely devoted to contemporary western drama. Among the major playwrights it produced were Dürrenmatt, Ionesco, Sartre, Pirandello and Williams. Max Frisch's *Andorra* (directed by H. Samandarian in 1968) was one of its most noteworthy achievements. This company, which performed in various buildings including the Iran America Cultural Centre, Ararat Club and Teatr-e Mowlavi, was feebly subsidized by the Ministry of Culture and Arts.

Actor, playwright, director and film-maker Parviz Sayyad (b. 1937) in 1966 formed the Gorouh-e azad-e namayesh (Independent Group of Performing Arts). Its most noteworthy production was Manuchehr Yekta'i's long poem *Falgush* (*Eavesdroppers*), directed by Sayyad in a teahouse at the Shiraz Festival of Arts (1970). Its productions were based on both Iranian and international plays. Among the group's other successful productions, *Waiting for Godot* must also be mentioned. The group financed its work in part by selling its productions to national radio. In 1980, Sayyad and a number of his actors emigrated to the United States where, without using the original name of the company, they continued to work into the 1990s.

Anjomaneh Theatre Iran (Iranian Theatre Association, 1968–80), directed by Nasser Rahmani Nejad (b. 1939) and Sa'id Soltanpour (1940–81), was an actors' association that staged a number of politically oriented plays, among them *Amouzeyaran* (*Teachers*, 1969) by Mohsen Yalfani and Brecht's *Visions of Simone Machard* (1971). The group was supported by private donations.

Kargah-e nemayesh (Theatre Workshop, 1969–79) was founded with a policy 'to help writers, actors, directors and designers to exercise and experiment independent of commonly accepted professional restrictions'. The

Bijan Mofid's 1972 production of *Jean nessar* (*Devoted Servant*) designed by Bijan Saffari.
Photo: courtesy of Jalali.

company formed five subgroups: Tajrobi (The Experimental Group, 1969–74) directed by Shahrou Kheradmand and Iraj Anvar (b. 1943) Koucheh (The Street Theatre Group, 1970–9) directed by Esmail Khalaj (b. 1945), Bazigaran-e Shahr (The City Players, 1970–6) directed by Arby Ovanessian (b. 1942) and Bijan Mofid (1938–84), Morvarid (The Pearl Group, 1971–3) directed by Maryam Khalvati (b. 1945), and Ahriman (1973–9) directed by Ashurbanipal Babella (b. 1945).

Each group had a distinctively different repertoire, composed of national as well as international contemporary and classic plays. All the groups experimented freely with space, production techniques, actors and dramaturgy. For three years the companies were completely subsidized by NIRT, after which the subsidy was cut by 50 per cent. Some of the groups balanced their budgets by creating productions with NIRT or the Shiraz Festival of Arts.

In 1970 Gorouh-e Zaman (The Time Group) started its activities with a production of Ostrovski's Saeqeh (The Storm). This company, formed by Mahin Abbas-Taghani (b. 1929), had concentrated its work on Russian classics. Until the establishment of the Islamic Republic the group continued to work in various theatres and specialized in plays by Chekhov and Gorky. It was partially subsidized by the Ministry of Culture and Arts.

Gorouh-e Piadeh (The Pawn Group, 1971) headed by Dariush Farhang (b. 1947) and Mehdi Hashemi (b. 1946) was the only company entirely composed of ex-theatre students. In the 1970s it presented a number of important productions of plays such as Thornton Wilder's Shahr-e ma (Our Town, 1971) and Mirza Aqa Khan Kermani's Susmar al-dowleh (The Lizard of the State). The latter was presented at the Festival of Popular Traditions in Isfahan (1977). The group did not have any official financial support and its members often worked on a voluntary basis.

The last theatre to present traditional improvised comedies – the Tamashakhan-e Iran (Iran Theatre) – closed down in 1963. Thereafter, such fare was presented only at the Hafez-e no

Arby Ovanessian's 1978–9 production of Chekov's *The Lady With a Little Dog* designed by the director.
Photo: G. Nubar.

(New Hafiz) Theatre in the red light district of Tehran with Sa'di Afshar as the last important *siyah*. At the beginning of the Islamic Revolution, the Hafez-e no Theatre itself was burned down. Since then the group has occasionally performed on Islamic television.

Among non-Persian-language theatre companies, the Armenian community's theatre groups were the earliest to become active in the country (1881). The most important post-World War II companies to have an influence on the Persian language theatre were the Ararat Club Theatre Group (1950–85) directed by Aramais Aqamalian and the Armen Theatre Group (1960–9) directed by Shahin Sarkissian (1960–6) and Arby Ovanessian (1966–9). The second group was affiliated to Ararat Club for three years. These groups had private sponsors and were presenting Armenian classics and international plays, such as Derenik Demirjian's *Kaj Nazar* (*Nazar the Brave*, 1923), Levon Shant's *Jampoun vrah* (*On the Way*, 1903), *Ourishin hamar* (*For the Sake of Other*, 1901) and an adaptation of Anion Chekhov's *Shnikov dikin-e* (*The Lady With a Dog*, 1978). In 1967–9, the Armen Theatre Group performed at the Iran America Cultural Centre.

The International Theatre of Tehran, originally the Little Theatre of Tehran, was an English language dramatic group which worked between the years 1947 and 1979. A not-for-profit organization, it had over a hundred members of many nationalities and presented plays such as Shakespeare's *Taming of the Shrew* (directed by George Quinby), Ibsen's *Hedda Gabler* (directed by Arby Ovanessian, 1969), Edward Albee's *Who's Afraid of Virginia Woolf?* (1969) and T.S. Eliot's *Murder in the Cathedral* (1971), the latter two directed by the theatre's artistic director, Don Laffoon (b. 1944).

Most companies working outside Tehran have been short-lived ventures. Troop-e Sepahan, headed by Reza Arham Sadr (b. 1923) and Morteza Momayezan, established in Isfahan in 1945, is the major exception. Partially subsidized by the Ministry of Culture and Arts, its work, based on the popular comedy tradition, is highly commercial and still appreciated. Despite the changes that it had to go through, the company continues to operate.

Dramaturgy

Besides *ta'ziyeh* plays, generally by anonymous authors and mostly written in the nineteenth century, Iranian western-style play writing until the late 1970s, did not have a significant base to really develop a repertoire. It was only with the emergence of a new generation of writers in the late 1950s that such a development was seen.

Strict censorship and the Cold War (both of which had direct repercussions in Iran) created an enigmatic style of playwriting. Ali Nasirian (b. 1934), who wrote and played *Af'i-ye tala'i* (*The Golden Serpent*) in 1957, is the first of the new dramatists worthy of attention. Nasirian based his work on patterns of popular speech and the gestures of traditional public animators (*ma'rekegir*). His *Bolbol-e sargashteh* (*The Wandering Nightingale*, 1959) is based on a folk tale. In six scenes, it tells the story of a dead boy, killed by his stepmother, whose mutilated body, through the love and care of his sister, is transformed into a nightingale. The play won first prize in a contest sponsored by the General Office of Fine Arts and is among the rare titles in Iranian drama that has been restaged a number of times. With a deep interest in both the folklore and characters of traditional theatre, his later plays, *Siyah* (*Blackface*, 1960) and *Bongah-e teatral* (*The Theatre Shop*, 1974), both use the *siyah*, in dramatic situations.

The most prolific playwright of this period, Gholam Hosseyn Se'edi (1935–85), is generally known under his pseudonym, Gowhar Morad. A physician, amateur anthropologist, writer and opponent to the shah's regime in the 1960s, his first public success was with *Chub be dasthay-e Varazil* (*Club-Wielders of Varazil*, 1965). A cautionary tale of villagers who first befriend but then are threatened by hunters (representing foreigners), they are forced to take refuge in a Muslim shrine. Se'edi's other well-known plays include *Panj namayeshname az engelab-e Mashrutiyat* (*Five Plays of the Revolution for the Constitution*, 1966), *Ay bi kolah, Ay ba kolah* (*O Fool, O Fooled*, 1967), *Dikteh* (*Dictation*, 1968) and *Zaviyeh* (*The Angle*, 1968). In total, he has written well over forty plays. Uneven in quality, his most impressive works are *Vai Bar Maghlub* (*Woe to the Vanquished*, 1970) and *Dah lal bazi* (*Ten Pantomimes*, 1963). The first uses dialogue recorded in a psychiatric clinic and the second, via ten short independent acts, pictures individuals who are impotent to save themselves. In the 1980s, Se'edi fled Islamic authorities and took refuge in France. His last two plays, *Othello dar sarzamin-e ajayeb* (*Othello in a Strange Land*, 1986) and *Pardehdaran-e a'inehafruz* (*Mirror-Polishing Chamberlains*, 1986), were both written in exile.

Theatre historian and film-maker Bahram Beyza'i is also a playwright of interest with more than twenty plays to his credit. His best known is *Seh nemayesname-ye 'arusaki* (*Three Puppet Plays*, 1963). Inspired by traditional puppet shows and by works such as Maurice Maeterlink's marionette plays, they are allegorical and meant to be performed by actors as well. Beyza'i's later writings are deeply symbolic, connecting to Iranian mythology and history. His characters are trapped between mythic, historic and social issues. *Pahlavan Akbar mimirad* (*Pahlavan Akbar Dies*, 1963) portrays a wrestler who for chivalrous reasons allows himself to be defeated. *Hashtomin safar-e Sandbad* (*Sinbad's Eighth Journey*, 1964) is a poetic allegory inspired by *The Thousand and One Nights*. *Soltan Mar* (*King Snake*, 1966) is a Pirandellian exercise reflecting on the duality of existence. *Miras* (*Heritage*, 1967) and *Ziafat* (*The Feast*, 1967), two one-act plays, are allegories of responsibility. Beyza'i's *Chahar sanduqh* (*Four Boxes*, 1967) uses four characters, each dressed in a colour representing different factions of society and a scarecrow, who comes to life and, for his own safety, puts the four in separate boxes. *Nodbeh* (*Lamentation*, 1977), set in a brothel and inspired by formal aspects of *ta'ziyeh* and puppet shows, focuses on the relations of women to various classes of men during the Revolution for the Constitution. *Marg-e Yazdgerd* (*Death of Yazdgerd*, 1979) reflects on the assassination of the last Sassanian king when Muslim Arabs invade the country. *Siyavosh-khani* (*The Passion of Siyavosh*, 1993) is an experiment based on the ancient rite of *Siyavoshun*.

Since 1971, Beyza'i has been a prolific screenwriter as well (over forty screenplays). For his first directing venture in theatre, Beyza'i in 1966 chose his puppet play *Arusak-ha* (*The Puppets*). His successive directorial works in theatre have all been productions of his own writings.

Actor, singer, director and writer Bijan Mofid has written for theatre since 1957. He created a very successful improvised musical play, *Shahr-e qesseh* (*City of Tales*, 1968); its characters, aside from the narrator, are all animals representing various social types. His dialogue, based on popular speech patterns, follows traditional poetic rhythms. Under the guise of children's tales and animal masks, Mofid mocked the society of his time. His *Jan nessar* (*Devoted Servant*, 1972) was based on the *ruhozi* tradition.

'Abbas Na'lbandian (1947–89), undoubtedly the most original Iranian playwright, first

Bijan Mofid's 1968 production of *Shahr-e qesse* (*City of Tales*). Masks designed by Mohtasham.
Photo: courtesy of NIRT.

Arby Ovanessian's 1968 production of Abbas Na'lbandian's *Pazhuheshi zharf va sotorg va now dar sangvareha-ye dowre-ye bist-o-panjom-e zamin shenasi* (*A Modern, Profound and Important Research into the Fossils of the 25th Geological Era*) designed by the director.
Photo: courtesy of NIRT.

came to note during a television drama contest. *Pazhuheshi zharf va sotorg va now dar sangvareha-ye dowre-ye bist-o-panjom-e zamin shenasi* (*A Modern, Profound and Important Research into the Fossils of the 25th Geological Era*, 1968) was his first produced play. Na'lbandian, who had never before seen a play, wrote one which worked purely through its theatrical logic. In *Research ...* eight characters search, get acquainted, travel, exchange ideas, make a show of their lives, die, get resurrected, and keep going without getting anywhere. 'There is no one to help!' The eight characters include a satyr in search of a nymph, an assassinated politician in search of his young assassin, and a soldier looking for a 'conductor'. The three women include a young beauty looking for a thief, a prostitute in search of an unfaithful lover and a spinster looking for her lost dog. A philanderer in search of women and a prophet in search of 'grace' complete the list. Na'lbandian's main model is Attar's thirteenth-century allegory *Manteg al-teyr* (*Conference of the Birds*). The 'life force' of the play is a Pirandellian device, a 'director' with twelve assistants. They all have an ironic and destructive presence. Technically speaking, the play looks as if it is a college of famous sayings, ideas and styles but when acted, reveals a magical power. Its contemplative surrealistic process ends with an ecstatic awakening.

Na'lbandian's second play, *Nagahan 'haza habib-Allah ...'* (*All At Once 'Beloved of God ...'*, 1970) concerns a young school master, Fereydoun, who is suspected by his poverty-stricken neighbours of harbouring a box of jewels; on the day of Ashura rituals (which commemorates the martyrdom of Imam Hosseyn), they break in and kill him, only to discover that the box contains merely books. This play which, without imitating any formal aspect, imaginatively connects contemporary Iran with the essence of Islamic *ta'ziyeh*, had a shocking impact on religious fanatics when produced in 1972. In the 1980s Na'lbandian was imprisoned three times by Islamic authorities. He eventually committed suicide in 1989. His plays are eight in number, all bold and audacious in style. The last one, *Dastanha-i as baresh-e mehr o marg* (*Stories from the Rains of*

Love and Death, 1977) is a quintet of inter-related one-act plays. Besides his own original writings, Na'lbandian did several remarkable translations in the 1970s, from Aeschylus (*Prometheus*) to Peter Handke (*Self Accusation, Calling For Help, My Foot My Tutor*).

Other significant playwrights include Bahman Forsi (b. 1932), Akbar Radi (b. 1940) and Esmail Khalaj (b. 1945). Forsi's three experimental plays – *Goldan* (*The Vase*, 1961), *Chub zir-e baghal* (*Crutches*, 1962) and *Bahar va arusak* (*The Spring and the Doll*, 1965) all had an influence on young Iranian writers. Radi's first play *Rozaneye abi* (*The Blue Outlet*, 1962), a gentle autobiographic family drama, changed the mood of realistic writing for the stage. His style in *Az posht-e shisheh'ha* (*From Behind the Window Panes*, 1977) is more experimental. Khalaj's writing is an interesting synthesis of experimental drama and poetic realism. In his plays naturalism, private fantasy and religious fervour coexist easily. *Halet chetoreh Mash Rahim?* (*How Do You Do, Mash Rahim?*, 1971), *Goldooneh Khanom* (*Lady Flowerpot*, 1971), *Ghamar dar aghrab* (*The Moon in Scorpio*, 1974) and *Shabat* (1976) are good examples. Esmail Khalaj's works include an extremely successful Persian translation of Edward Bond's *Saved* (in collaboration with Maryam Khalvati, 1972).

Among female playwrights, Khojasteh Kia and Mahin Jahanbegloo-Tajadod (b. 1927) should be mentioned for their contributions to Iranian drama. Khojasteh Kia's most important and impressive work *Shahadatii bar mosibat-e Hallaj* (*A Testimony on the Martyrdom of Hallaj*, 1969) is an incantation using sacred material and traditional verbal formulae. Directed by the author herself, this experimental play was a significant event in contemporary Iranian theatre. Tajadod's work is based on classic literature. Her plays are contemporary poetic reflections on the meaning of ancient history. *Kheshthaiy-e rangin* (*The Coloured Bricks*, 1968) is based on Nezami's *Haft gonbad* (*Seven Domes*), while *Vis o Ramin* (*Vis and Ramin*, 1970) uses Gorgani's romantic epic poem. *Savari dar amad …* (*There Appeared a Knight …*, 1976) is a free-form rendering of Iranian mystical writings for three actors and a child. Tajadod also devised the root Avesta texts for *Orghast* (1971), a work by British poet Ted Hughes directed by Peter Brook.

Since the Islamic Revolution, no significant new dramatists have emerged.

Directing and Acting

It was through the productions of 'Abdol-Hosseyn Nushin in the 1930s that the Iranian public in general became acquainted with the role of the director in theatre. Nushin had studied in France (Conservatoire do Toulouse) and for his first venture in directing Iranian drama (1935), he chose Ferdowsi's epic, *Shahnameh* (*The Book of Kings*) adapting three episodes from it. Later invited to the Soviet Union (1936), he met the famous Jewish actor and director Solomon Mikhoels and saw at the State Jewish Theatre of Moscow his legendary production of *King Lear*. Undoubtedly *Lear*, and Louis Jouvet's productions in Paris, were the main source of Nushin's directorial inspiration. His next two attempts in producing Iranian drama came in 1938 and 1947: Akhundzadehm's *Sargozasht-e Vazir-e Lankaran* (*The Story of Vizir of Lankaran*) and his own *Khorouseh sahar* (*The Morning Cock*), were neither politically nor artistically successful. Between 1938 and 1951, Nushin produced many European plays: Sartre's *Rouspi-e bozorgvar* (*The Respectful Prostitute*), Ben Jonson's *Volpone* (in Stefan Zweig's version), Marcel Pagnol's *Mardom* (*Topaz*), Shakespeare's *Tajereh Venizi* (*The Merchant of Venice*) and Maurice Maeterlinck's *Parandeh abi* (*The Blue Bird*). Although Nushin's direction was not original, his productions, because of their technical mastery, left an indelible remarkable mark on later generations of directors.

With Shahin Sarkissian a new attitude developed in Iranian theatre. Directing for him was a meditation on the author. Through his conscientious preparations, actors started to become aware of the hidden spirit of the plays. Almost single-handedly, Sarkissian created what in the 1960s and 1970s became the essential creative impulse of Iranian theatre. His work on Hedayat's short stories, as well as on Chekhov and Stanislavski, created what was a poetic directorial approach. Sarkissian's best remembered productions include Arthur Schnitzler's *Zvarjalick* (*Liebelei*, 1960), Chekhov's *Uncle Vanya* (1963) and Akbar Radi's *Rozaneyeh abi* (*The Blue Outlet*, 1966).

'Abbas Javanmard's directing style was an attempt to bring together traditional performance and contemporary writing. His work always had a certain polish and was technically well worked out. Lighting, design and performance in his productions for Gorouh-e honar-e melli, between 1960 and 1976, are well remembered for these reasons. Jean Jacques Gauthier, the French critic, writing about *Evening in a Strange Land*, said 'these puppets, that resemble human beings with made up eyes and red cheeks appear on stage attached to strings with jerky movements and accompanied by unknown sounds, are truly wonderful' (*Figaro*, 1965). Javanmard's most successful productions were *Pahlavan Akbar Dies* (1967) and *Sagi dar kharmanjah* (*A Dog In Harvest*, 1975) by Nosratollah Navidi (b. 1937).

Film director and designer Arby Ovanessian's directing début in theatre (1967) was with August Strindberg's *Miss Julie*. But it was in 1968 with his first direction of an Iranian play, 'Abbas Na'lbandian's *Pazhuheshi ...* (*Research ...*) that he helped to revolutionize Iranian theatre. Through a bold *mise-en-scène*, in successive arrivals each character spoke and acted his or her needs. This self-conscious act gradually transformed itself into a theatrical ritual. The originality of the direction became apparent when the last character, a prophet, entered and a crucifixion was enacted completely. Here the theatrical ritual dissolved into a religious one and Na'lbandian's play gained mystic significance. The technique of this production was a meeting point of old and new theatrical techniques. The Greek and oriental theatre, character and method acting and alienation effects were used continuously for conveying a 'theatrical logic'. Peter Brook, on the occasion of the production's presentation in London (Royal Court Theatre, 1970), wrote: 'Arby Ovanessian is an international director in the sense that his beautiful work makes sense, whatever one's nationality. ... There is a lot of theatre research in the air ... Persian *Research* is a fascinating achievement.'

For his second production of an Iranian play, *Vis o Ramin* (1970), Ovanessian incorporated real time by using the sunset in Persepolis and by lighting a fire turned the performance into a ritual and a theatrical event. His productions, by simple means, have always been such evocations. The British theatre critic, Irving Wardle, wrote:

the image of mass guilt he produces in *All at Once* is one I shall not forget ... striking was its effect on the audience. In contrast with the reverently hushed opening, where tongues clicked in disapproval if anyone's foot touched the taboo acting area, the ending released a mood of desecration. Jostling each other, raising their voices, the audience, almost trampling on the buried man in their haste to get out. It was an extension of the play into the outside world; a direct continuation of the hidden crime and the scattering killers. (*The Times*, September 1972)

Besides Iranian authors, Ovanessian has produced international classics, such as Chekhov, Ibsen and Pirandello as well as more contemporary writers such as Adamov, Beckett and Handke. Here too, his work has been remarkable. For example, Albert Camus's *Caligula* was a thoughtful and intelligent production (1974–5) played without intermission and uncut, in the confining and beautifully preserved private bath-house of Darius. The director had two actors playing the role of Caligula simultaneously, creating a schizophrenic situation for the other characters. The final depravity was memorably depicted as the stone-faced, reflective Caligula stood to one side and watched his other self, a rampaging lunatic, smothering the fair Caesonia in a torment of orgasmic frenzy. In the final scene when he is killed by Cherea, it was his other self who spoke the play's final lines, 'I'm still alive!'

Ovanessian, who has directed some forty productions in four languages, has represented Iran at the Theatre of Nations Festival in Caracas (1978). Since 1979, he stopped directing in Persian and now works as both director and scholar in France. Among his productions there are *How My Mother's Embroidered Apron Unfolds in My Life* (1983) and *Shghtaivatz-e* (*The Chained One*, 1988) by Levon Shant, performed in Chapelle Saint-Louis Salpetrière.

Davoud Rashidi (b. 1932) and Ashurbanipal Babella are two other directors of note. Both have directed Iranian and foreign plays. Rashidi's work, being more conventional, was always better received. Sophocles' *Antigone* (1968) and Saadi's *Woe to the Vanquished* (1970), both starring Fahimeh Rastgar (b. 1933), were among his major productions. Babella, more adventurous, did his own *ruhozi*-inspired satire, *Emshab shab-e mahtab-e* (*Tonight There's Moonlight*, 1975) as well as *Charkh-e falak* (*La Ronde*, 1975) by Arthur Schnitzler and *Baziyeh ghatleh am* (*Jeux de massacre*, 1975) by Eugène Ionesco. Since the early 1980s Babilla has lived and worked in New York.

Iranian theatre since the early 1950s has also had a number of important female directors. One must mention in this regard Loreta Hairapetian, Mahin Oskoui, Khojaste Kia, Pari

Pari Saberi's 1995 production of *Haft sahr-e eshgh* (*Seven Abodes of Love*) based on the *Conference of the Birds*.

Saberi, Shahrou Kheradmand and Maryam Khalvati. Contrary to a great number of male directors, who do not have or did not have a distinctive working style, these women were and are working in completely different styles of production. In the 1990s, only Pari Saberi still directs in Iran. Her work which in the 1960s and the 1970s was oriented to production of such authors as Sartre, Lorca and Ionesco, has changed. For the first time in her career, in 1995 she directed a production based on Iranian literature: *Haft sahr-e eshgh* (*Seven Abodes of Love*).

Iranian theatre since World War II has had a number of unique and talented performers. Among them the actresses Loreta, Fakhri Khorvash (b. 1928), Fahimeh Rastkar (b. 1933), Shohreh Aghdashlou-Vazirtabar (b. 1948) and Susan Taslimi (b. 1948); and actors Ali-asqhar Garmsiri (1911–72), Mohammad-Ali Jafari (1924–86), Ezatolah Entezarmi (b. 1924), Mohammad-Ali Keshavarz (b. 1929), Jafar Vali (b. 1933), Ali Nasirian (b. 1934) and Parviz Pour Hosseyni (b. 1942), all of whom must be noted for the wide range of their repertoire.

Music Theatre
Dance Theatre

For a discussion of music and dance, see the opening, historical action and **Artistic Profile**.

Theatre for Young Audiences
Puppet Theatre

The Institute for the Development of Children and Young Adults (IDCYA), after some isolated theatre activities in 1971 under the direction of Don Laffoon, set up the first regular children's theatre group in Iran. Its first production, *Torob* (*The Radish*) by Bijan Mofid, was performed on a round red carpet. The company later toured and did improvised work in libraries and schools. The same centre in 1972 formed a puppet theatre company.

Behrouz Gharibpour, who had gained some experience as an actor in children's puppet theatre, in cooperation with Hunter Wolf, a professor at the University of Southern California – according to an approved official state educational previewed programme for gifted students – in 1977 directed classes for young people in acting, directing, playwriting and criticism.

Since the Islamic Revolution, puppet theatre productions have been the main concern of the IDCYA. Those working as directors in children's theatre include Marzieh Boroumand, Reza Babek, Bahram Shah-Mohammadlou and Behrouz Gharibpour. In an effort to support the puppeteers, the Islamic government sponsored the First International Puppet Theatre Festival in Tehran in 1989.

Shadow puppetry, *khiyal bazi* and *fanus-e khiyal*, rooted in east Asia, has existed in Iran for many centuries. The twelfth-century poet Omar Khayyam, in a symbolic quatrain, draws a parallel between the world as a lantern and men as whirling shadows in it. The *Fanus-e khiyal* form completely disappeared in Iran by 1910. In the early twentieth century, a shadow entertainment called *Shahr-e Farang* (European City) arrived from the west, a replica of what was known as the peep show or *la vue d'optique* of eighteenth-century Europe. Adopted also in India and the Arab world (*Sundugg al dunya*), it consisted of a large brass-bound box standing on legs with three viewers of thick lenses through which western pictures were seen, flavoured with amusing and colourful commentary. It disappeared with the advent of cinema in Iran.

Kheyme shabbaizi (The Tent of Nocturnal Play) was a puppet theatre that utilized glove-puppets for daytime performances and string-puppets for evening performances over the course of several centuries. Attesting to the historical importance of the form, Khayyam allegorically suggests: 'We are all puppets (*lo'bat*) and our destiny is in the hands of the puppeteer (*lo'bat baz*). We play on the spread of life and then go again into the trunk of death.' *Oshtornameh* (*Book of the Camel*), attributed to poet 'Attar (d. 1221), also mentions the puppet theatre, personifying the puppet master as God.

In the first half of the seventeenth century, the German traveller Adam Olearius witnessed in Iran a strolling puppeteer carrying 'a large curtain held up by a stretcher, hanging down to the puppeteer's knees concealing him and serving as a backcloth for the puppets … the lower part of the curtain has a wide and deep pocket like a kangaroo pouch'.

The main figure in the Iranian puppet theatre is *Pahlavan kachal* (Bald Hero) or *Pahlavan Panbe* (Cotton-Wool Hero), a cowardly and boastful character with an unfaithful wife. In some of the plays, the mullah is shown as falsely devout, more attached to earthly pleasures, such as wine and dance, than to other worldly rewards. Officialdom in earlier centuries seemed more tolerant towards the liberalities and obscenities of puppet theatre. In the late 1990s this entertainment continues though in a much altered form. The manipulator still hides behind the curtain but he now has his companion sitting on the side of the stage playing an instrument and talking to and for the puppets, sometimes using a *safir*, a small wind instrument placed between his lips making a strident, squeaky sound. Ahmad Khamsei (*c.*1910–97) was the last living puppet master in this tradition.

One of the first puppeteers to receive state support was Amin Quzanlar (b. 1935) who in 1957 formed a small marionette theatre company and for seven years travelled around the country, presenting plays and training teachers. His activities were sponsored by the General Department of Fine Arts.

Markaz-e teatr-e arousaki (Centre for Puppet Theatre) was created in 1972. Under the supervision and direction of a Czech puppeteer, Oscar Batek, Markaz-e teatr-e arousaki's production centre in 1976 organized the First Iranian Puppet Theatre Festival. It was for this centre, that Nosrat Karimi, who in the late 1950s had studied puppet film-making in Czechoslovakia, directed a puppet play, *Mehman-e Nakhandeh* (*Unwanted Guest*, 1985) which was also filmed.

A highly popular puppet-like game, performed largely in domestic settings, is *arusak* (doll or puppet) in which the player paints a face on a cloth placed over the feet or legs and then makes the features move. Another version occurs in performances in which a woman or man paints a face on the abdomen, places a see-through cloth over his or her head and puts a skirt or jacket over the tips below the painted face. As the performer dances about, through stomach contractions, he or she makes the facial features move to great comic effect. An example of this can be seen in the opening sequence of the Iranian film *Shab-e quzi* (*Night of the Hunchback*, 1963) directed by Farrokh Gaffary.

Among well-known Iranian writers who have written 'puppet plays' are Sadeq Hedayat and Bahram Beyza'i. *Afsaneyeh afarinesh* (*The Legend of Creation*, 1930) by Hedayat satirizes heaven, while *Arusak-ha* (*The Puppets*), *Ghorub dar diyari gharib* (*Evening in a Strange Land*) and *Qesse-ye mah-e penhan* (*The Story of the Hidden Moon*, 1963) by Beyza'i, representing the puppet master in the later play as Demon or God tearing up those puppets who wish to choose their own destinies.

With the advent of modern forms of entertainment such as cinema, radio and television, the popularity of puppet shows waned, although they could still be seen in some Tehran coffee houses.

Design

Until the mid-1950s, stage design in Iran was related to the creation of beautiful stage pictures. There was no attempt to interpret a play through theatre design. Scenography itself was almost an unknown art. A number of well-known earlier designers were really set decorators, such as Mir-Seyfedin Kermansahi, (d. 1932), Napoleon Sarvarian (1908–70) and Valiolah Khakdan (b. 1923), all appreciated only for their painted backdrops and well-built box sets.

With Aramais Aqamalian (1910–85), the stage space started to be interpreted. Through a number of constructivist sets, built on a revolving stage, he proved that the designer's task could go beyond simply decorating performance space. His constructions were extensions of each play's essential actions and the scene changes were dramatically expressive. Aqamalian's designs were not only strong statements but also beautiful and functional. No other Iranian designer has surpassed the standards he set in his most successful constructivist sets, built in the Ararat Club: *Gevorg Marzbedoouni* (1954), *Samvel* (1957) and Saroyan's *My Heart's in the Highlands* (1974).

A real change in stage design began to appear in the early 1960s when architect and painter Bijan Saffari (b. 1933), painter and sculptor Bahman Mohassess (b. 1931), director Arby Ovanessian and painter Fereydoun Ave (b. 1945) began to introduce a number of new concepts. Among Saffari's early works, *Havij*

farangi (*Poil de carotte*, 1962) by Jules Renard, is well remembered for its stark beauty and subtly coloured houses set against a light blue sky. *Obeyd* (1977), based on Obeyd Zakani's writings (fourteenth century), with its decorative colourful stage and costumes parodying the grim world of the clergy, was another successful work by the same designer.

For Ionesco's *Sandaliha* (*The Chairs*, 1966), Bahman Mohassess created a number of decorative and expressive chairs, that when put together suggested an abstract forest. One other important design, Pirandello's centenary production of *Hanri-e charom* (*Henry IV*, 1967), had stylized metallic sculptural forms, set against plain burlap screens.

Ovanessian since 1961 has designed over seventy productions and an exhibition of his work was held in the Iran America Cultural Centre in 1963. A number of his designs have been for non-conventional performance spaces. His approach is minimal, simple and void of decorative elements. As an example, one can mention *Pazhuheshi...* (*Research ...*, 1968). There he used a huge, brightly lit silver disc in a dark void, over which a metallic cloud was suspended. The bright surface of the disc, with its reflective light served to illuminate the actors, as well as doubling their images. The movement of performers on the disc created all necessary lighting changes. The costumes, mostly in tones of black, grey and white were in strong contrast to the long green dresses of the twelve 'assistant

Bahman Mohassess's 1966 production of Ionesco's *The Chairs* designed by the director.

directors'. Another Ovanessian design was for *Bazi bi harf shomareyeh yek* (*Act Without Words One*, 1970) by Samuel Beckett. Here, by using the interrelation of objects proposed by the author, the designer with cubes and scissors created a Calder-type 'mobile' image, that was both playful and laconic.

Fereydoun Ave for T.S. Eliot's *Murder in the Cathedral* (1971) designed a chrome steel altar which, towering up, opened and formed the cathedral, while the patchwork-costumed knights were stained-glass images. His other impressive work, Chekhov's *Bagh-e albalou* (*Cherry Orchard*, 1972), had meticulously designed period costumes which through their colours marked the four seasons and gave each act its appropriate tone and hue.

Among Iranian stage designers two women, Farideh Gohari (b. 1938) and Malak Khazai (b. 1943) should be noted for their distinguished work. Gohari studied scenography in Belgium. Her designs for theatre, opera and television represent a special blend of classic and modern ideas. Lorca's *Blood Wedding* (1966), Gluck's *Orfeo et Euridice* (1967) and Sophocles' *Antigone* (1968) are the most appreciated of her designs.

Khazai studied stage designing at London's Slade School of Fine Art. Her set for *Rahebe-ha* (*The Nuns*, 1972) by Eduardo Manet was stylized and architecturally impressive. Khazai's later works were more naturalistic in concept. *Sagi dar kharmanjah* (*A Dog In Harvest*, 1975) by Navidi with its hay-covered stage and blue cyclorama was her most important design in this style. In her later works, she used a large number of decorative folk elements.

Khosrow Khorshidi (b. 1937) started his work in Talar-e Rudaki, by assisting the German designer Theo Lau. After the Islamic Revolution, he worked for several years in Europe. In 1996, Khorshidi, for the Farhangsaray-e Bahman in Tehran, designed a production of the musical *Les Misérables*. Performed without music, however, it impressed audiences mostly for its ingenious scenic changes.

Theatre Space and Architecture

There are no surviving examples of ancient theatre buildings in contemporary Iran although the remains of an apparently circular space, situated in the northeast of Tehran and known as *Apame* do exist. This is generally believed to be the remains of a Greek-type theatre although even that is not confirmed by archaeologists.

Traditionally, performances of *shabih khani* take place in the open air, under a roof or in a tent. Public squares, courts or caravansaries (caravan stops) are also used. Sacred trees, which have specially constructed brick or stone platforms around, have served as a central axis for some performances.

The special buildings for *ta'ziyeh* are called *takyeh* or *hoseyniyeh*. Takyeh-e Now-rouz Khan (1798), in Tehran, is the oldest known construction. The remarkable Takyeh-e Niavaran (1856), in northeast Tehran, is the oldest surviving building. It is still in good condition, and used for performances. A number of *takyeh* buildings have galleries which during performances were richly decorated with carpets, and crystal chandeliers sometimes lent by the shah, dignitaries or members of the public. French writer and diplomat A. de Gobineau, in his monumental *Religions et philosophies dans l'Asie Central* (Paris, 1865), has vivid descriptions.

The huge round arena-like Takiyeh-e Dowlat (*c.*1873) constructed by Naser al-din Shah in Tehran, was situated southeast of the Golestan Palace. It was used for the most elaborate *ta'ziyeh* performances and its round, central stage had an 18 metre (58 feet) diameter with an additional 6 metre (20 feet) slightly raised platform around it, on which sat 4,000 female spectators. This area was surrounded by four steps, serving as seats for the males. A three-storey 24 metre (78 feet) high building with open-grilled galleries housed the princes, aristocrats and well-to-do families. The whole had a vellum mobile roof, supported by a wooden dome structure. Takiyeh-e Dowlat was knocked down in 1947 in favour of a bank building. A similar but smaller space was constructed in 1877 in Isfahan. This building was also later razed.

The first *à l'Italienne* theatre in Tehran was built in 1882 at the Armenian School in Darvazeh Ghazvin. The result of theatrical activities developed by two Armenians, Manas Aber and Hovsep Tadevosian Khayatbashi

Takiyeh-e Dowlat, 1887.
Photo: Henry Binder.

(the court tailor), the theatre, despite the fact that it was serving a non-Islamic community, offered performances for men and women on separate days. In the same year (1882), on the command of Naser al-din Shah, at the northeast of Golestan Palace, a 300-seat European-style theatre space was constructed in the Higher School of Dar al Fonun. *Gozaresh-e Mardomgoriz* (*The Misanthrope*), translated by Mirza Habib Esfahani (printed in Constantinople, 1869), and some of Molière's other plays were performed there. Due to pressure by the mullahs, this theatre was restricted to the royal family and its guests. Performances were held until 1891 when it was closed, probably because the shah saw it as a threat. The space was later transformed into a lecture hall.

A 400-seat commercial public theatre in Tehran, the Cyrus, was built by a Zoroastrian, Arbab Aflatoun Shahrokh in 1927. Reza Shah's attempt in 1939 to build an opera house failed and until 1965 the capital did not have a state theatre building. Most theatres were converted lecture halls or cinemas. Among such spaces are Jamey-e Barbod (which operated from 1926 to 1979), Ferdowsi (1943–9), Tehran (1944–50), Nasr (1963 and continues to work), Ararat Club with a revolving stage (1944 and continues to work), Saadi (1945–53), Now (1949–53), Anahita (1958–65), which worked as the first commercially run repertory theatre, and Kasra (1961–90).

Specially designed theatre buildings all date from the 1960s and later.

In 1963 the newly built Iran America Cultural Centre opened with a bilingual (Persian and English) production of O'Neill's *Long Day's Journey Into Night* directed by Professor George Quinby. The centre, situated in north Tehran, has a single stage which can serve as either a covered (400-seat) auditorium or an open-air (600-seat) auditorium. Designed in the United States by consultant architects from Frank Lloyd Wright's offices, this theatre has good sightlines and remarkable acoustics. Until 1979, a considerable number of important Persian, British and Armenian productions were performed in this space. For rehearsals and set construction, a warehouse annex was built by the same organization in 1968. This space, now called Downstage, was been used for experimental productions as well. Downstage's seating capacity was 150. Since 1979, the Institute for the Development of Children and Young Adults has been housed in these buildings.

The first Iranian state theatre, the 250-seat Teatr-e Bistopanj-e Sahrivar (1965), was built on public grounds as a gift to the Ministry of Culture by architect Aftandilian. This theatre, which opened with *Amir Arsalan* by Parviz Kardan, had a policy to present only Iranian Persian-language playwrights. Since 1979, it has been called Teatr-e Sangalaj.

The construction of a State Rudaki Opera House (designed by architect Aftandilian), was completed in 1967. Its stage and auditorium is a replica of Vienna Opera House. Until 1979, this building was called the Talar-e Rudaki and presented operas, ballets and music. After the Islamic Revolution, the opera house has been known as the Talar-e Vahdat (Unity Hall) and presents non-musical performances.

Tehran's first experimental theatre space, Kargah-e nemayesh (Theatre Workshop), was a ballet school rehearsal hall, transformed into a flexible 150–200-seat performance space by architect Bijan Saffari. It opened in 1969 with two productions, Sophocles' *Oedipus* and Samuel Beckett's *Five Dramaticules*. Five groups, presenting completely different styles of plays and productions, were regularly programmed into this space. Kargah-e namayesh was the first theatre to have its entrance bricked over by Islamic authorities in 1979.

Tehran University provided a working space for its theatre students in 1969 by transforming one of its low ceiling halls into the 300-seat Teatr-e Mowlavi. This space continues to be used at the university.

The major theatre in the capital, the 600-seat Teatr-e Shahr (City Theatre), was built under the auspices of Empress Farah Pahlavi, not far from the university, in a beautiful park. The building, under construction since the early 1960s (architect Ali Sardar Afkhami), was planned to become a national theatre with a national and international repertoire. Inaugurated in 1972 with a production of Chekhov's *The Cherry Orchard*, this imposing circular building, beautifully decorated with tiles, has a large proscenium opening, good sightlines, but a shallow stage with no backstage space. Because of its acoustic defects and an impractical underground car park, the theatre was closed for renovations in 1975. After a year's work, it reopened with partially improved acoustics, the car park transformed into a 250–300-seat performance space, with flexible staging, cinema seating and film projection facilities. Designed by consultants from Britain's National Theatre and Arby Ovanessian, the new space, Teatr-e Charsou (Four Directions),

Arby Ovanessian's 1977 production of Peter Gill's *Khalvat-e khoftegan* (*Sleeper's Den*) with Loreta Hairapetian and Susan Taslimi, designed by the director.
Photo: courtesy of Teatr-e Charsou.

opened in 1977 with *Khalvat-e khoftegan* (*Sleepers' Den*), a play by Peter Gill. Until 1979, this space operated as a repertory theatre, with a policy of producing neglected plays from both the national and international repertoire. After the Islamic Revolution, Teatr-e Shahr and Teatr Charsou, without any change of names, were put under the supervision of CDA, a department of the Ministry of Culture and Islamic Guidance.

A multipurpose cultural centre, Farhangsaray-e Bahman (Bahman Cultural House), was constructed in south Tehran to replace the old slaughterhouse buildings in 1991. The two public squares in front of it were called Khamsei (the name of the last great puppet master) and Mobarak (a popular puppet character). The centre has an impractical narrow stage and its seats have a very odd rake. The theatre was inaugurated with a puppet play, *Baba Bozorg va torob* (*The Grand Father and the Turnip*). The building houses as well the Mousey-e honarhay-e namayeshi (Museum of Performing Arts) where the Shiraz Festival of Arts collection on Asian theatre (including Oriental puppets) is exhibited.

Because of a lack of suitable European-style theatre spaces, Shiraz Festival of Arts (1967–77) often programmed the theatre performances in non-conventional spaces. This move was widely embraced by stage directors and became a source of inspiration for a considerable number of them. Among the most significant spaces used were the stairways of Apadana Hall in Persepolis (*Vis o Ramin*, 1970, directed by Arby Ovanessian); Bagh-e Delgosha Pavillion (*Constant Prince*, 1970, directed by Jerzy Grotowski); the Tomb of Artaxerxes in Persepolis and Nagshe Rostam-Vally of the Kings (*Orghast I and II*, 1971, directed by Peter Brook); a teahouse (*Falgush [Eavesdroppers]*, 1971, directed by Parviz Sayad); a fruit warehouse (*Alice in Wonderland*, 1971, André Gregory); women's quarters in Ghavam's nineteenth-century house (*Overture to KA Mountain*, 1972, Robert Wilson); a Sufi shrine and the mountainside looking down on to it (*Ka Mountain and GUARDenia Terrace*, 1972, Robert Wilson); the Royal Palace (Tachareh) in Persepolis (*Caligula*, 1974, Arby Ovanessian); Sara-ye Moshir caravansaries (*The Ship of Folly*, 1976, Terayama Shuji); and Delgosa Gardens

(*As You Like It*, 1977, Andrei Serban). Such free, improvised choices for performance space were easily accepted by Iranian audiences. They were almost a natural extension of traditionally viewed performance places. In such non-restrictive environments, Iranian contemporary theatre, in cooperation with international theatre artists, at last found a solution for its performance spaces.

Training

A school for actor training, Honarestan-e Honarpishegi, directed by Ali Nasr, was founded in 1938. It was modelled on the French Conservatoire d'Art Dramatique but it issued only a high school diploma. This was the only official theatre school in the country till 1956 when Tehran University in its Faculty of Literature began an extracurricular activity (six-month and one-year course programme) in theatre. Three American Fulbright professors, Frank Davidson, Arthur Bletcher and George Quinby, successively directed the courses. These courses in 1961 were integrated within Tehran University's Daneshkadeh-e honaray-e ziba (Faculty of Fine Arts), forming a Theatre Department offering MA degrees.

In 1964 the Ministry of Culture and Arts founded its Daneshkadeh-e honarhayeh dramatic (School of Dramatic Arts), directed by Mehdi Forough. This school was more cosmopolitan in its programme and offered BA degrees. Due to the Islamic Revolution, both these institutions were closed in 1980 although they reopened later under the supervision of the Ministry of Culture and Islamic Guidance.

Among non-official training schools or studios that have had an important impact on Iranian theatre since 1945 are the Actor Training Classes (1944–9 and 1951–2, directed by Abdol-Hosseyn Noushin); Initiation to Theater (1954–66, directed by Shahin Sarkissian); Honarkadeh-e azad-e honarpishegi-e Anahita (Anahita Independent School of Acting, 1958–63, directed by Mahin and Mostafa Oskoui) and based heavily on Soviet models of the Stanislavski System; and Kargah-e nemayesh work sessions (1969–79, directed by Iraj Anvar, Shahrou Kheradmand, Arby Ovanessian and Ashurbanipal Babella).

In 1997, besides the aforementioned two universities, for theatre studies Tehran has Daneshkadeh-e teatr-e daneshgah-e azad-e Tehran (Theatre School of the Independent University of Tehran), Daneshkadeh-e teatr va cinema (Theatre and Cinema School) and Daneshkadeh-e teatr-e Soureh (Soureh School of Theatre) which is affiliated to the Sazman-e tablighat-e Eslami (Islamic Propaganda Organization). There are theatre schools also in Arak (central Iran), Bushehr (coast of Persian Gulf) and Babol (south of the Caspian Sea).

Criticism, Scholarship and Publishing

Theatre criticism developed in Iran during the post-war years. At first Persian language reviews on theatre were mostly journalistic reports rarely touching a serious creative level. Among the most influential theatre reviewers, Shahin Sarkissian should be mentioned for his regular theatre reviews, which were appearing in the French language *Journal de Tehran* in the late 1940s. Basically, it was 'Abdol-Hosseyn Nushin's productions which were the centre of his serious attention.

Some years later, in 1952, Nushin published his *Honareh teatre*, a book that attempted to discuss performance techniques and must be considered the first of its kind in the Persian language. Since the late 1950s, other intellectuals started to write on theatre. By the end of the 1960s, theatre criticism by a new generation of critics who were trained in Europe, entered a new phase. Parviz Mamnoun (b. 1935), Iraj Zohari (b. 1940) and Amir Taheri (Parisa Parsi, b. 1937) are particularly noteworthy critics of this period. Their writings were usually published in newspapers or periodicals such as *Ayandegan*, *Negin* and *Keyhan International*.

A group of theatre reviewers, mostly

graduates from Tehran theatre schools or the university, in the 1970s popularized theatre reviewing in the Iranian press. Houshang Hesami (b. 1938), Laleh Taghian (b. 1947), Jamshid Chalangi (b. 1944) and Behnam Nateghi (b. 1945) are the most representative of this period.

In the 1980s and 1990s, only Laleh Taghian continued to write on theatre. She eventually developed a scholarly approach and her remarkable *Ketabshenasi-e teatr* (*Bibliography of Theatre*, 1992) was published by the CDA. She was also the general editor of *Faslnameh teatr* (*Theatre Quarterly*) from 1988 to 1992, and edited a number of important works, published by the CDA.

Scholarship – except for some individual efforts such as Jannati A'tai's *Bonyadeh namayesh dar Iran* (*Foundation of Theatre in Iran*, 1955), Majid Rezvani's *Le théâtre et la dance en Iran* (*The Theatre and Dance in Iran*, 1962) and Bahram Beyza'i's *Namayesh dar Iran* (*Theatre in Iran*, 1965) – also developed only after the mid-1960s. Its growth was strongly related to the advent of theatre studies in the universities in Tehran and particularly the research work of Farrokh Gaffary, Bahram Beyza'i and Parviz Mamnoun. For years, Gaffary's and Beyza'i's writings were the only reliable sources for the study of Iranian traditional theatre. After the Islamic Revolution a number of new researchers, Davoud Fathalibeygi, Faramarz Talebi and Enayat-ollah Shahidi, have added to the research and studies in this domain. There are no important published studies on Iranian European-style theatre productions or Iranian contemporary theatre movements.

Between 1950 and 1955, the Italian ambassador to Iran, Enrico Cerulli, collected over a thousand *ta'ziyeh* manuscripts in Iran and later donated them to the Vatican Library. A descriptive catalogue, prepared by Ettore Rossi and completed after his death by Alessio Bombaci, was published in 1961. This unique collection is the most important source for the future studies of *ta'ziyeh* plays. Internationally speaking, French and North American universities are among the first institutions that have encouraged basic studies on Iranian theatre. Scholars such as Ehsan Yarshater (Columbia University), Peter J. Chelkovski (New York University) and William O. Beeman (Brown University) have since the late 1970s encouraged Iranian theatre scholarship. In the United States Gisele Kapuscinski and Iraj Anvar (b. 1943) have done a number of scholarly translations from Iranian

contemporary drama and traditional *ta'ziyeh* plays. In French universities the number of dissertations presented on Iranian theatre is now considerable. Ghotbedin Sadeghi (b. 1947) and Mohammad Reza Khaki (b. 1946) have written on important aspects of Iranian traditional theatre.

In the post-World War II period, none of the theatre journals or magazines that were started survived more than a few issues. The first state-subsidized theatre magazine *Namayesh* was published in 1955 and continued till 1959 (eleven issues). Other important ones were *Anahita* (eleven issues) published by Anahita Theatre in 1960–3 and *Faslnameh teatr* (*Theatre Quarterly*, five issues) published by the Ministry of Culture and Arts in 1977–8. After the Islamic Revolution *Faslnameh teatr* continued to appear (sixteen issues between 1988 and 1992 under general editor Laleh Taghian). Since 1987 a theatre monthly, *Namayesh*, has been published by the CDA, which also publishes collected research works on theatre. Of special note in this regard is *Qaremanan-e badpa dar qesse ha va namayesh-ha ye Irani* (*The Whirlwind Heroes in Iranian Stories and Plays*) by Khojasteh Kia, published by the CDA in 1996. The other state-owned publishing centre, Soroush (affiliated with Islamic Television), in 1990 published Stanislavski's *Kar-e honarpisheh rouyeh khod* (*An Actor's Work on Himself*, 560 pp.), translated by Mahin Abbas-Taghani, formerly of the Oskoui group.

Non-state-owned publishing houses usually publish contemporary Iranian playwrights or translated international plays and other general books on theatre. Jamshid Malakpour's important research on Iranian drama, 'Adabiyat-e namayeshi dam Iran', was published in two volumes by Toos in 1983. There are now three additional volumes in the series which because of censorship problems remain unpublished. Most of the privately owned publishing houses suffer from censorship and can rarely afford to take risks.

Farrokh Gaffary, Arby Ovanessian,
Laleh Taghian
Additional material on women's domestic
performances by Anthony Shay

Further Reading

And, Matin. *Karagöz*. Ankara: Editions Dost, 1977. 125 pp.

Anvar, Iraj. 'A Study of Peripheral Ta'ziyeh in Iran'. PhD dissertation, New York University, 1991.

Beeman, William O. *Culture, Performance and Communication in Iran*. Tokyo: ILCAA, 1982. 223 pp.

Beyza'i, Bahram. *Namayesh dar Iran* [Theatre in Iran]. Tehran: Kavian, 1965. 242 pp.

BITEF 70, *beogradski internacionalni teatarski festival*. Belgrade, 1970: 52–7.

Bolukbashi, Ali (with Sadegh Kia). *Namayesh-haye Shadi-avar-e Zananeh-ye Tehran* [Women's comic performances in Tehran]. *Honar o Mardom* no. 27 (1964).

Calmard, Jean. 'Le me'c'nat des Repre'sentations de Ta'ziye'e' [The sponsorship of Ta'ziyeh performances]. *Le Monde iranien et l'Islam*, Vol. II. Geneva: Librairie Droz, 1974: 73–126. Vol. IV, 1976–7: 133–62.

Chelkowski, Peter J. 'Shia Muslim Processional Performances'. *TDR* 29 no. 3 (1985): 18–30.

——. ed. *Ta'ziyeh and Ritual and Drama in Iran*. New York: New York University Press and Soroush, 1979. 288 pp.

Chodko, Alexandre. *Jong-i Shadat, An Anthology of Martyrdom*. 4 vols. Tehran: Soroush, 1977–9.

——. *Théâtre persan: choix de téazies ou drames* [Persian theatre: choice of ta'ziyehs or dramas]. Paris, 1878.

Elwell-Sutton, L.P., ed. *Bibliographical Guide to Iran*. Brighton, Sussex: Harvester Press; Totowa, NJ: Barnes & Noble, 1983: 341–7.

Emami, Karim, ed. *Shiraz Festival of Arts: The First Ten Years (1967–76), An Illustrated Album*. Tehran: Soroush, 1976. 145 pp.

'Enjavi-Shirazi and Said Abolqasem. *Bazi-ha-ye Namayeshi* [Theatrical games]. Tehran: Amir Kabir, 1973.

Gaffary, Farrokh. 'Déguisement et cortèges en Iran' [Disguising and masquerade in Iran]. In *Carnavals et mascarades* [Carnivals and masquerades], ed. Giovanni Pier d'Ayala and Martin Boiteux. Paris: Bordas/Spectacle, 1988.

Gauthier, Ed, ed. 'Le théâtre persan' [The Persian theatre]. *La Revue théâtrale* 37 (July 1905): 865–88.

Ghanoonparvar, M.R. and John Green. *Iranian Drama: An Anthology*. Costa Mesa, CA: Mazda, 1989. 302 pp.

Gobineau. *Religions et philosophies dans l'Asie centrale*. Paris: Gallimard, 1957. 484 pp.

Hochman, Stanley, ed. *Encyclopedia of World Drama*, Vol. 3, 'Iranian Secular Theatre', by Farrokh Gaffary. London/New York: McGraw-Hill, 1984.

Jennati, A'tai Abolqasem. *Bonyadeh namayesh dar Iran* [The foundation of theatre in Iran]. Tehran: Saffi Ali Shah, 1955.

Kapuscinski, Gisele. *Modern Persian Drama: An Anthology*. New York/London: University Press of America, 1987. 227 pp.

——. 'Persian Theatre in the 1960's'. PhD dissertation, Columbia University, 1982. New York: UMI Dissertation Services, 1994. 434 pp.

Khaki, Mohammad Reza. 'L'Evolution du Ta'ziyeh vers le terrain seculaire' [The evolution of ta'ziyeh towards the secular theatre]. Thesis, Paris III, Université de la Sorbonne Nouvelle, 1991. Vol. I, 459 pp. Vol. II, 138 pp.

Khodayar, Naser and Johari Mansour, eds. *Anahita*. Tehran: Anahita Theatre Publications, 1960–3.

Khojasteh Kia. *Qaremanan-e badpa dar qesse-ha va namayesh-ha ye Irani* [The whirlwind heroes in Iranian stories and plays]. Tehran: Nashr-e Markaz, 1996. 207 pp.

——. *Shahnameh-e Ferdowsi va trajedi-e Atheni* [Shahnameh Ferdowsi and Athenian tragedy]. Tehran: Sherkateh entesharat-e elmi va farhangi [Scientific and Cultural Publications Company], 1990. 111 pp.

Krymski, Agatangel. *Perskij teatr* [Persian theatre]. Kiev, 1925.

Malekpour, Jamshid. '*Adabiyat-e namayeshi dar Iran* [Drama in Iran]. 2 vols. Tehran: Toos, 1983. Vol. 1, 532 pp. Vol. 2, 524 pp.

——. *Seyr-e tahavol-e mazamin dar shabih khani ta'ziyeh* [Persian passion plays]. Tehran: Jahaddaneshgahi, 1987. 280 pp.

Malkom Khan, Mirza. *Les Comédies de Malkom Khan* [Three plays of Malkom Khan translated by A. Bricteux]. Paris: Les Belles Lettres, 1933. 129 pp.

Mamian, Arsen, ed. *Iranahai verjin 50-amiya tatroni vastakavorner* [The past fifty years of Armenian theatre in Iran]. Tehran: Alik, 1985. 190 pp.

Mamnoun, Parviz. *Seyri dar tatr-e mardomi-e Isfahan* [A reflection on popular theatre in Isfahan]. Tehran, 1977.

Marouffi, Abbas, ed. *The First International Puppet Theatre Festival*. Tehran: The Centre of Dramatic Arts (CDA), 1989. 206 pp.

Massoudieh, Mohammad. *Taghi Mucighi-e mazhabi-e Iran: musighi-e ta'ziyah* [The religious music of Iran: music of Ta'ziyeh]. Tehran: Soroush, 1989. 242 pp.

Nasirian, Ali, ed. *Faslnameh teatr* [Theatre quarterly] nos. 1–5. Tehran: Ministry of Culture and Arts, 1977–8.

Nushin 'Abdol-Hosseyn. *Honar-e teatr* [The art of theatre]. Tehran, 1952.

Ovanessian, Arby. *Un Teatro con tradición viva* [A theatre based on living traditions]. Caracas: IVe Saison mondial du Théâtre des Nations, 1978. 82 pp.

Papazian, Vahram. *Hetadartz haiatzk* [A reflection on the past]. 2 vols. Yerevan, 1956–7. Vol. II, 382–492.

Papazian, Vrtanes. *Parskakan tatron* [The Persian theatre]. Tatron no. 1 (July). Tiflis: Mn. Martirosiantz, 1899.

Pelly, L.S. *Miracle Plays of Hasan and Hussein* (contains a translation of thirty-seven plays). London, 1879.

Rezvani Medjid. *Le Théâtre et la danse en Iran.* Paris: G.-P. Maisonneuve et Larose, 1962. 299 pp.

Rossi, Ettore and Bombaci, Alessio. *Elenco di drammi religiosi persani* [A descriptive catalogue of Enrico Cerulli's collection of 1,055 *ta'ziyeh* manuscripts]. Vatican, 1961.

Sadeghi Ghotbedin. 'L'Analyse du genre comique dans le théâtre iranien: Rou' Hozi' [An analysis of comedy in Iranian theatre: Ruhozi]. Thesis, Paris III, Université de la Sorbonne Nouvelle, 1985. Vols I, II and III, 471 pp. Vols IV and V, 284 pp.

Sayyad Parviz. *Theater of Diaspora.* Costa Mesa, CA: Mazda, 1992. 187 pp.

Shay, Anthony. 'Bazi-ha-ye namayeshi: Iranian Women's Theatrical Plays'. *Dance Research Journal* 2 no. 27 (fall 1995): 16–24.

Shirvani Hassan, ed. *Namayesh*, monthly, eleven issues. Tehran: General Office of Fine Arts, 1955–9.

Smith, A.C.H. *Orghast at Persepolis: An International Experiment in Theatre.* London: Eyre Methuen, New York: Viking Press, 1972. 246 pp.

Taghian Laleh. *Dar bareyeh Ta'ziyeh va tatr dar Iran* [On Ta'ziyeh and Theatre]. Tehran: Nashr-e Markaz, 1995. 240 pp.

——— . ed. *Faslnameh teatr* [Theatre Quarterly] nos. 1–16. Tehran: CDA, 1988–92.

——— . *Ketabshenassi-e teatr* [Bibliography of Theatre]. Tehran: Namayesh, 1992. 315 pp.

Wardle, Irving. *Rituals in the Desert.* Gambit nos 18 and 19. London: Calder & Boyars, 1971: 144–59.

Wolford, Lisa. 'Ta'wil of Action: The New World Performances Laboratory's Persian Cycle'. *New Theatre Quarterly*, no. 46 (1996): 156–76.

Yarshater, Ehsan. 'Persia'. In *The Reader's Encyclopedia of World Drama*, ed. John Gassner and Edward Quinn, 647–52. London: Methuen, 1970–5.

——— . ed. *Encyclopaedia Iranica*, Vol. III, 'Baqqal-bazi' [The play of grocer] by Farrokh Gaffary. London/New York: Routledge & Kegan Paul, 1988.

——— . *Encyclopaedia Iranica*, Vol. VI, 'Dalqak' [Jester] by Farrokh Gaffary. Cosa Mesa, CA: Mazda, 1993.

Zahed 'Ataolah and Amini Mehdi, eds. *Teatr*, six

JAPAN

Among the world's most highly industrialized nations and boasting one of the world's highest standards of literacy (over 99 per cent), Japan, approaching the third millennium, is without doubt one of the economic leaders of the new Asia as well as one of the continent's most culturally rich nations. Composed of four large islands (Hokkaido in the north, the mainland of Honshu, Shikoku and Kyushu in the south, thousands of smaller islands and the Ryoku Island chain), Japan has also been home to some of the world's most avant-garde artists whose work has taken them into a variety of multidisciplinary experiments focused on bringing this ancient country's feudal and isolated past into an effective conjunction with its capitalistic and exceedingly international present.

With an overall population estimated in 1995 at 125.5 million living in a land area of just 377,700 square kilometres (145,800 square miles), Japan is also one of the world's most densely populated nations. Tokyo, with a population of some 12 million people, is the nation's capital and largest city as well as the centre of Japan's modern performing arts and cultural communities and its major educational and communications centres.

All this is a far cry from Japan in 1945, when the end of World War II was signalled by the dropping of two atomic bombs by the United States on Hiroshima and Nagasaki, nearly obliterating the two cities, killing 340,000 people, leaving millions wounded, the country in ruins and under US military occupation. Devastated economically as well, a rebuilding plan for the country was set up by the surviving Japanese bureaucracy in conjunction with the occupation administration. The combination of massive financial aid and Japan's own strong work ethic quickly revived the nation.

It was the beginning of September when the documents of surrender were signed. By the end of September, new policies were already coming down from the Allied Powers General Headquarters (GHQ) concerning film and theatre production in the new Japan. In these first orders were clear statements that Japanese film and theatre companies were to avoid anything that would encourage rearmament, armed struggle or militant nationalism. Pacifism was to be supported in all ways. Certain of Japan's traditional art forms (*kabuki* for one) were criticized as being in potential contravention of the new policies.

Japan's traditional arts had an enormously long history and disallowing certain performances would have clear cultural ramifications. Dating back to the seventh century were various blendings of *gigaku* (music and masked dance) forms introduced to Japan from southern China and Korea. *Bugaku*, a more solemn form, added in stories and legends and took on a ritualistic quality. Shinto religious practice added in other elements over the next centuries including acrobatic entertainment. By the fourteenth century, these forms had evolved into *noh*, a formalized yet spectacular style of theatre written in a high poetic language reflecting each character's deepest emotions in a series of codified and controlled movements. Programmes of *noh* normally included *kyogen* (lighter comedies) as *entre'acte* pieces. The two great fourteenth-century dramatists of *noh* – Kanami Kiyotsugu and his son Zeami Motokiyo (still considered the ultimate authority on the form) – helped refine this essentially aristocratic art. *Noh* was designated as a ceremonial art at the beginning of the seventeenth century under the Tokugawa Shogunate and the third Tokugawa Shogun, Iemitsu (1604–51) codified the art and forbade deviation. The public was also forbidden from attending *noh* performances and by the nineteenth century the art form – with its many subtle masks – had become locked in now centuries-old traditions including the use of only men in all roles. *Noh* acting had also become a hereditary profession with techniques and titles passed down from father to son.

Kabuki emerged in the late fifteenth century and the puppet art of *bunraku* about a century later. Both these arts utilize singers and musicians. *Kabuki* uses live actors and is far livelier and, historically, far more sensual, sexual and contemporary than the more formal *noh*, while *bunraku* uses giant puppets manipulated by three puppet masters (the three-person manipulation scheme dates to the eighteenth century) wearing black costumes and who, by custom, are deemed to be unseen. The greatest of Japanese playwrights, Chikamatsu Monzaemon (1653–1725) wrote primarily for *bunraku*, one of the world's most spectacular forms of puppet theatre. *Kabuki*, now perhaps Japan's most popular traditional art form, is performed in very large theatres; the privately operated Kabuki-za and the National Kabuki Theatre, both in Tokyo, are the largest such spaces. The chief architectural feature of the *kabuki* stage is

Tokyo Globe Company's *kabuki* version of *Hamlet*.

the *hanamichi*, a raised platform jutting into the orchestra from the stage and connecting reality (the audience) with the artists (the otherworldly).

When western warships forced Japan to open to foreign trade in the middle of the nineteenth century, Japan and its cultural traditions went through a series of major changes. The Meiji court (1868–1912) saw the end of feudal power and the end of the privileged position that *noh* actors had long enjoyed. Actors began to offer public performances of *noh* at this time and within a decade *noh* theatres were being built in Tokyo. Eventually, *noh* came to occupy an important position in Japanese society. There are now over a thousand professional *noh* and *kyogen* actors, most of whom survive by teaching *noh* and *kyogen* techniques to interested amateurs. New plays are not part of the *noh* repertoire.

In 1886, interest in western (generally European) dramatic forms had become so strong that a Society for Theatre Reform was created to modernize (westernize) Japan's theatre and particularly to eliminate the sexual elements of *kabuki*. Arguments were made to eliminate the *hanamichi*, traditional music, the *onnagata* (the use of men in women's roles) and on-stage assistants dressed in black. One result of this movement was *shinpa* theatre, a transitional form which represented a blending of Japanese theatre traditions with western-style scripts. Plays by Shakespeare, Maeterlinck and even Sardou were played by turn-of-the-century *shinpa* troupes, the most famous one being the troupe of Kawakami Otojiro (1864–1911) who with his actress wife Sada Yakko (1871–1946) were immensely popular. The company toured widely and Sada's great skills led to a repeal of the 1629 law banning women from the stage.

Even more focused on western-style drama were the new *shingeki* troupes emerging in Tokyo at this time. *Shingeki* (literally new theatre) dates back to 1906 and the founding of Bungei Kyokai (Literary Arts Society); Jiyu Gekijo (Free Theatre) was founded in 1909 and modelled after André Antoine's Théâtre Libre. Bungei Kyokai closed down in 1913; Jiyu Gekijo in 1919. Following in their footsteps was Tsukiji Sho-gekijo (Tsukiji Little Theatre) which opened its 500-seat theatre in Tokyo in 1924. The company's first two seasons saw productions of plays only by western dramatists including Pirandello, Kaiser, Ibsen and Chekhov. In 1928, the company closed down but the idea of *shingeki* had been established.

By the 1930s, several new *shingeki* groups began to appear in Japan and their plays often raised issues which Japanese authorities preferred to be ignored. By 1940 and Japan's involvement in World War II, such groups were proving more and more difficult to control and major *shingeki* companies – Shinkyo Gekidan (New Cooperative Drama Group) and Shin Tsukiji Gekidan (New Tsujiki Theatre) – began to be closed down. Those not closed down were monitored closely.

The end of the war, however, also meant the reopening of the *shingeki* theatres whose style was more easily recognized by the Allied occupation authorities. It also meant the release from prison of a number of artists who had been held under the Maintenance of the Public Order Act which had sent many to jail during the early 1940s. Among these was director Hijikata Yoshi, founder in 1924 of Tsukiji Sho-gekijo. Forced to leave Japan because of his theatrical activities in 1933, Hijikata had first tried to seek political asylum in Russia. Stalin, however, was not enthusiastic to have him in Russia either and after a number of years in different locations, Hijikata finally returned to Japan in 1941 where he was almost immediately arrested. His release at the end of the war meant that changes were coming, though no one in the arts could be sure what kinds of changes.

Clearly, critical artists would no longer automatically wind up in jail for their art and police would no longer be allowed to stop or control public entertainment whenever they wished. Even censorship of scripts was disallowed under the rules announced in October 1945. On the other hand, many of the traditional forms were now to be under surveillance. *Shingeki* had become the art of choice; *noh*, *kyogen*, *kabuki* and *bunraku* were not to be trusted.

It did not take entrepreneurs very long to realize the economic potential of *shingeki* and entertainment companies such as Shochiku and Toho became early supporters and most active producers. By December 1945, with the support of Toho, the Tokyo Geijutsu Gekijo (Tokyo Art Theatre) was established. In association with the Mainichi Newspaper Publishing company, the new theatre staged a joint performance with two other important *shingeki* theatres – Bungaku-za (Literary Theatre) and Haiyu-za (Actor's Theatre) – of Chekhov's *The Cherry Orchard*. It was this performance which marked the official recommencement of *shingeki* in Japan after the war.

A new government agency was soon established to help restore the performing arts, the Geijutsu-ka, part of the newly established Department of Social Education in the Ministry of Education. Theatre was again playing a role in the mainstream of cultural life. The long-closed Shinkyo Gekidan was reopened by Murayama Tomoyoshi and playwright-director Inoue Masao. Its first public performance was Ibsen's *A Doll's House* in March 1946 directed by Hijikata Yoshi. That same month, the Haiyu-za opened its first production, Gogol's *Revizor* (*The Inspector General*). Both these productions played to packed houses in extremely large venues, partly because of the power of the productions and partly because of the underground reputation that the banned *shingeki* theatre had achieved during the war years.

Also encouraged by GHQ after the war was the establishment of labour unions such as Nihon Eiga Engeki Rodokumiai (Japanese Cinema and Theatre Labour Union) which was founded in 1946 to help the emerging film and theatre industries. Many of the country's artists quickly joined the union, a large number of them (including Hijikata and Murayama) also joining the growing Communist Party of Japan. (The connections between *shingeki* and the Communist Party at this time is an area of Japanese contemporary theatre history that still needs exploration.)

By September 1946, the first post-war arts festival was organized in Tokyo and performances began to be seen from across the country. The festival was perhaps most important for bringing the shortage of playing spaces to the government's attention. Many had been destroyed during the war and others were still being used by the military. Over the next few years, new and older spaces were made available to *shingeki* companies as they formed, merged, closed down and re-emerged in new guises.

During this same period, the Communist Party of Japan was gaining power; in 1949 it won thirty-five seats in the House of Representatives encouraging leftist artists as well as an emerging group of independent theatre companies without ties to business, the so-called Jiritsu Engeki groups. Several such theatres established themselves in factories and at other workplaces. The number soon became large enough for the establishment in Osaka of an association of workers's theatres to be formed, the Kinrosha Engeki Kyokai.

Partly in an effort to counter this move to the left, GHQ initiated the Piccadilly Theatre of Shochiku which tried, among other things, to introduce more populist western theatre styles to Japan along with commercial theatre techniques. From May to July 1950, for example, the Haiyu-za presented in this space Beaumarchais's *The Marriage of Figaro*. This was followed by seven other productions including *Hedda Gabler*. The Haiyu-za had earlier begun Japan's first post-war and first western-style theatre school in late 1949, the Haiyu-za Yoseijo (Actor's Theatre Training Academy). The academy quickly began to send out well-trained and talented actors who were well prepared for careers in *shingeki*.

During this same period, with the Cold War growing, known communists and communist sympathizers throughout the public service began to lose their jobs in what became known as the Red Purge. Private businesses quickly followed the trend and soon newspapers, publishing houses, media companies and educational institutions were firing 'Reds's left and right. It was only a short time until the outbreak of the Korean War and the beginning of a new determination by the United States to keep Asia out of the communist camp.

The Red Purge was felt strongly in the arts. Major actors and directors lost their jobs. Funding for tours by certain groups was cancelled and theatre spaces that had been long booked were suddenly made unavailable to politically suspect groups; the Mingei Theatre's production of Chekhov's *The Seagull* was one such victim both in Tokyo where its performances had to be cancelled and on tour where performances in all but one city were called off. The Purge also caused financial problems and even changes in career paths for individuals like Mori Masayuki. When Mori was forced off the stage, he became a full-time screen actor and a well-known star in the process. Ultimately, he abandoned the live theatre.

The fact is that *shingeki* was politicized and it was just such politicization in the 1940s and 1950s that attracted many artists to it. Nevertheless, some of the new theatres consciously tried to keep out of the political realm. This was true of Bungaku-za which aimed at exploring a broad range of the modern theatre's repertoire and which preferred to move in more theatrically experimental directions. It soon opened a second stage, the Atelier, and began a training centre for actors, directors and administrators. By the early 1950s, Bungaku-za had become one of Japan's three most important companies, the others being Mingei and Haiyu-za. Mingei's major success was a play about Vincent van Gogh entitled *The Man of Flame*,

which drew more than 60,000 people while the Haiyu-za was introducing writers such as Mishima Yukio to the public.

Japan regained its independence in 1952 but suspicion of communist activities continued. When the Mitsukoshi Theatre (owned by the Mitsukoshi Company) was suddenly made 'not available' to Kinoshita Junji's play *Ascension of a Frog*, a play based on an incident involving the USSR two years earlier, it was immediately assumed that this was a political act. *Shingeki* artists and groups were quickly up-in-arms. Mitsokoshi Theatre had already been booked for four productions each by the Haiyu-za and Bungaku-za companies and Mingei was scheduled to offer three of its productions there. None of the groups appreciated such problems and eventually Bungaku-za and Haiyu-za both decided to build their own theatres. Bungaku-za sought funding by approaching outside supporters while Haiyu-za closed for a year, encouraging all its actors to work in the more lucrative cinema industry for that period and asking them each to contribute a percentage to the building of the new theatre.

By 1954, Haiyu-za Gekijo (Actor's Company Theatre) was opened having been built almost entirely by the contributions of its company. Its first production was the Greek pacifist comedy, *Lysistrata*, directed by Aoyama Sugisaku. Plays by US dramatists continued to be popular at this time including Tennessee Williams's *A Streetcar Named Desire* directed by Kawaguchi Ichiro and Arthur Miller's *Death of a Salesman* staged by Sugawara Takahashi for Mingei with Takizawa Osamu in the role of Willy Loman.

Haiyu-za was the most prestigious company of the period thanks in large measure to the steady stream of outstanding actors graduating from its school. In 1953, under Haiyu-za's patronage, several new groups came into being: Shinjin Kai (Young Artists), Nakama (Friends) and Dojin Kai (The Chosen), the last group ultimately separating itself from Haiyu-za and forming Tokyo Engeki Ensemble (Tokyo Theatre Ensemble). Also growing out of these sub-groups came Seinen-za (Youth Theatre) which began to stage original plays for young people by Japanese dramatists.

A number of new groups emerged on their own including Gekidan Shiki (Four Seasons Company, founded in 1953) and Gekidan Seihai (Young Actors Company, 1954). Among the dramatists they chose to present early on were Jean Anouilh, Jean Giraudoux, William Saroyan, Jean-Paul Sartre and others from

Europe and the United States. Shiki quickly gained a reputation as a house for French drama, a reputation that sometimes held it back but which ultimately allowed *shingeki* to break away from realism as its dominant style. By 1955, the plays of Japanese dramatist Abe Kobo began to attract attention; it was clear that modern Japanese drama had finally assured itself a place on the stages of the modern world.

Politics took on a more significant dimension among the younger generation of Japanese artists. Brecht's name began to be heard more and more through the *shingeki* groups and Mishima's intense crossover dramas attracted a following at Bungaku-za where Mishima also worked as an actor. The first Brecht done in Japan was Sanki-kai's production of *Fear and Misery in the Third Reich* in 1957. But it was Haiyu-za which made Brecht's name well known in Japan with its productions during the 1960s and 1970s of *Threepenny Opera*, *Good Person of Setzuan* and *Caucasian Chalk Circle* among others. Brecht's theories began to attract attention, particularly his use of music and his ideas on theatrical alienation.

In 1957, Bungaku-za tried the most radical experiment in *shingeki* history to that point: a crossover production involving a modern spoken drama called *Akechi Mitsuhide* by Fukuda Tsuneari played by one of the major *kabuki* actors in the country, the eighth Koshiro Matsumoto. It was the beginning of many such meetings between traditional and western forms and it caused a sensation. Equally sensational was the visit to Tokyo in 1958 of the Moscow Art Theatre. The company played to packed houses and over the next decade many other internationally known troupes played in Japan with equal success.

French absurdist drama took centre stage in the early 1960s, sharply changing the direction seen just a year earlier in John Osborne's *Look Back in Anger* performed by Bungaku-za in 1959. Beckett's *Waiting for Godot* especially influenced young actors, directors and playwrights during this decade. Its first production seemed to be an angry comment on the signing of the 1960 Japan–US Security Treaty. Other developments of note included the first production to be done by the *enfant terrible* of the radical fringe of *shingeki*, Terayama Shuji, who staged his powerful *Chi wa Tattamama Nemutteira* (*Blood Sleeps Standing Up*) under the auspices of the Shiki Company, and a *shingeki* tour to China of several plays produced jointly by Haiyu-za, Bungaku-za, Mingei and Budo no Kai – *Onna no Isho* (*A Woman's Life*) and *Yuzuru* among them.

The existential works of Jean-Paul Sartre became a particular favourite in the early 1960s with young people reading his works and student theatre groups regularly producing his plays. Also staged at this time were plays by other dramatists with clear leftist leanings such as British playwright Arnold Wesker, whose kitchen sink drama, *Chicken Soup With Barley*, attracted enthusiastic young audiences when it was presented at Bungaku-za's Atelier space. Another success from the early 1960s was Russian dramatist Alexei Arbuzov's *Irkutsk Story*. Presented by the Mingei Company, it was the first contemporary Russian play to be seen in Japan.

During the 1960s and 1970s, the established companies rose and fell with several closing down entirely or re-emerging with new names and new directors. But during these same years, a new wave of energy began to be felt in the *shingeki* community as alternative-minded producing groups began to appear with clear differences to those that had come before. One of the first important alternative groups was Jokyo Gekijo (Situation Theatre) founded by playwright Kara Juro (the company was later known as Kara-gumi – the Kara Group). In 1966 came Suzuki Tadashi's experimental Waseda Sho Gekijo (Waseda Little Theatre, now known as SCOT and working outside Tokyo) and Jiyu Gekijo (Freedom Theatre and now called Black Tent) founded by Sato Shin and Saito Ren. In 1967 Terayama Shuji formed his own alternative group Tenjo Sajiki (Upper Balcony) and in 1968 Ota Shogo and others began Tenkei Gekijo (Transformation Theatre).

All of these new-wave groups began with the express intent of reforming *shingeki* but as the years passed and the daring experiments of these groups began to be seen (ranging from nudity and interdisciplinary work to stopping traffic in central Tokyo as part of a street theatre happening) it became clear that they were, in fact, seeking a totally new kind of theatre, one which moved quite far from Aristotelian norms. Their actors would often wear very stylized and colourful makeup (like classical Japanese actors working in *kabuki* or *noh*) and their productions would include traditional Japanese musical instruments but now playing rock music. Soon known as Small Theatres and as Underground Theatres, their productions were widely discussed and widely attacked. But clearly, new attention was being paid to their work all across Japan and, through their appearance at international theatre festivals, even from abroad.

All these groups shared a number of common goals: to challenge the traditional theatres of both west and east and to destroy the commercial systems that controlled theatre practice and production. Wanting groups to operate more democratically, they set up collective administrative structures and began to create productions collectively. They also sought to break away from realism in all its manifestations and to have theatrical art focus far more on the unconscious than ever before.

By the 1980s, not only was the majority of theatre activity in Tokyo and across the country *shingeki* but also experiments continued to abound. Traditional theatre forms, thanks to tourism and an ageing audience of both Japanese traditionalists and experts from around the world, were managing to maintain a loyal though diminishing following. From the 1970s on, new interest in these earlier traditions by scholars, many of them foreign, assured that their importance would not be forgotten but

neither were they any longer the centre of Japanese theatre life.

Thanks in great measure to the strengthening of the yen during the 1980s, commercial promoters began organizing tours by foreign theatre groups to Japan and many international hit shows began to include Tokyo on their itineraries. Especially popular were large-scale musicals, and by the late 1980s and into the 1990s, it had become quite common to see Japanese productions of current hits such as *Les Misérables* from Broadway or the West End of London.

The 1990s saw Japan's economic bubble burst to some extent but it was clear that Japan was continuing to be one of the main engines driving Asia's economy. The opening in 1997 of the New National Theatre in Tokyo – the country's fifth national theatre and the first to be devoted only to modern forms such as *shingeki* – symbolized in many ways both the distance that Japanese theatre had covered since World War II and how complex a creation it had become at this point in its development both to manage and understand.

Structure of the National Theatre Community

Theatre in Japan tends to be a significantly centralized activity. Tokyo was and continues to remain the hub of Japanese theatre. The majority of the country's theatre companies and theatre buildings are located in Tokyo. Other centres exist, however, especially in the areas around Osaka, Kyoto and Kobe and Nagoya.

To understand Japanese theatre activity as a whole, it is important to say that there are four different types of theatre that one can find at virtually any given moment in time: the traditional theatres doing *noh, kyogen, kabuki, bunraku* and classical Japanese dance; the commercial theatres performing Japanese versions of the latest hits from around the world; *shingeki* (modern drama) groups presenting a range of western-style comedies and dramas from both the past and present; and experimental or alternative theatres known in Japan as Small Theatres.

Traditional theatre forms can be found in Tokyo at either the national theatres or at some of the privately operated theatres such as Kabuki-za (or Minami-za in Kyoto). *Noh* and *kyogen* can still be seen in various cities while

bunraku is generally limited to performances in Kyoto at the National Bunraku Theatre or during shorter seasons at the National Theatre in Tokyo.

The commercial theatres are generally run by major producing companies such as Toho (which operates several theatres in Tokyo) and Shochiku (which operates the Kabuki-za and the Shimbashi Enbujo). Many Japanese productions of West End or Broadway hits have played in Tokyo under the auspices of these managements. In the 1980s, even organizations that were not normally known as commercial enterprises began to produce shows as well. Among them was the Saison Group which began operating the Ginza Saison Theatre in Tokyo on a more or less commercial basis. These are all private ventures without public money.

Shingeki, which most of this national article focuses on, dates to the beginning of the twentieth century and was an attempt by Japanese theatre artists to create a European-style theatre, a modern drama that would be distinct from *kabuki* and other classical forms. Bungei-Kyokai, founded in 1906 by playwright and

Tokyo Globe-Mansaku Company's *kyogen* version of *Falstaff*.

teacher Tsubouchi Shoyo (1859–1935), and Jiyu-Gekijo, begun by actor Ichikawa Sadanji (1880–1940) and director Osanai Kaoru (1881–1928), mark the official beginnings for this type of modern theatre. Further discussion of *shingeki's* history is included in **Artistic Profile**.

The Small Theatre movement of the 1960s was a reaction against *shingeki* and against society as a whole. Groups experimented with new styles and new work methods without any guaranteed funding and often without even proper venues to work in. The movement lost much of its energy by the 1980s but its influence was still being felt even into the 1990s.

Taken as a whole, in Tokyo alone each year some 3,000 different performances in these various styles can be seen.

Few theatre companies in Japan have their own spaces so administrative structures are usually quite minimal compared to Euro-American models. Companies generally operate on a commercial basis – some doing work in large rented spaces which cost huge amounts of money under the control of a business-oriented producer – and others operating regular seasons but quite often with companies engaged on a show-by-show basis.

The New National Theatre in Tokyo, a multi-space facility being used for mostly *shingeki* theatre, opera, ballet and modern dance, has an artistic director for each of its four artistic areas. Each is responsible for overall operations and programming in their particular fields and together constitute a team of producers for the venue as a whole. The New National does not have any resident companies and ensembles have to be put together for each particular production.

Traditionally, government has not been involved in funding the arts but after World War II studies were done of western funding systems – particularly European systems – and the government began to create cultural affairs departments. Early on, funding went only to groups producing traditional performances (*noh*, *kabuki* and *bunraku*) but later support was extended to other styles of work by Nihon Geijutsu Bunka Shinkokai (Agency for the Promotion of Cultural Affairs). The agency has direct involvement in the operations of the five national theatres contributing both to their funding and their overall operations. Other public agencies exist on the municipal level and a number of private organizations operate theatrical activities in various ways. The agency is also responsible for funding a variety of arts organizations, tours by companies, festivals, special events and studies of Japanese arts by foreigners and foreign arts by Japanese students and scholars.

The Japan Foundation is the government's primary agency for work on the international level. The foundation receives a large annual grant from the Japanese government to promote Japanese culture world-wide and to introduce foreign cultures to Japan. Engaged in numerous bilateral exchanges, the foundation's Asia Centre, created in 1995, is specifically focused on developing multilateral ties in the cultural and educational fields with other Asian countries.

There are a number of private foundations now in existence which promote the arts of Japan in similar ways. These range from the well-endowed and not-for-profit Saison Foundation based in Tokyo to national committees formed as liaisons between, for example, interested parents and arts groups concerned with cultural activities for children (see **Theatre for Young Audiences**). This group has financial support from both the Ministry of Education and some 400,000 parents who compose its membership. Many theatre companies, it should be noted, generate a significant portion of their annual revenue from work with this and other similar organizations. Over 100,000 people belong to Roen (Workers' Theatre Council), an organization which serves as a liaison between factory and other workers in the country and the theatre community. The organization has sponsored over 1,000 performances in given years.

Businesses regularly support performances which they feel will promote their own objectives. Performances for young people are one way that businesses regularly use to reach parents and to establish goodwill.

Municipalities are now following the government's lead and regularly support cultural activities within their areas. Tokyo Metropolitan Government, for one, has regularly supported artistic activities and has even established prizes for such things as the best children's play of the year.

A number of festivals take place regularly across the country with children's theatre festivals and puppet theatre festivals among the liveliest and most popular.

Professional theatre associations include actor and playwright's unions, critics and marionette associations and more specialized groups such as Nihon Jido Seishonen Engeki Gekidan Kyogikai (National Conference of Theatres for Young Audiences) which includes all the country's children's theatre groups (in 1997 they numbered seventy-nine). Overall membership in the organization is over two hundred, counting individuals with particular interests. This group, typical of many, is involved in issues of production as well as training and holds regular conferences to discuss and debate issues ranging from government funding to supporting new festivals. At present, virtually every children's theatre festival held in the country is sponsored in one way or another by this organization.

Various national awards exist in Japan aimed at recognising distinguished contributions in the arts. Artists may be recognized for particular performances at one level while at another they can be recognized as living national treasures. Several organizations have their own 'best' of the year awards. The most prestigious award for drama, for example, is the Kishida Gikyoku-sho (Kishida Drama Prize) given annually by the Hakusui-sha Publishing Company.

Artistic Profile

Companies
Dramaturgy
Directing and Acting

Non-Japanese have begun to change the way they look at Japanese theatre. In the past, their interest was primarily on traditional forms such as *noh*, *kyogen*, *kabuki* and *bunraku* but in the period since 1945 this has changed significantly.

Awareness of modern Japanese theatre (*shingeki*) has now grown to the point that the traditional forms, while still important from an historical and cultural standpoint, are now less significant in any study of Japanese theatre as a whole.

Shingeki dates to the turn of the twentieth century and the growing influence of western art styles. While *shingeki* flourished through the years, it was neither formally discussed nor much known about outside Japan until the 1950s. Begun during the Meiji era and heavily influenced by European theatre, *shingeki* was an attempt to establish a modern drama in Japan that would be completely different from *kabuki* and other traditional forms. Bungei-Kyokai, founded in 1906 by Tsubouchi Shoyo, and Jiyu-Gekijo, founded by Ichikawa Sadanji and Osanai Kaoru, were the movement's beginning.

Important momentum for *shingeki* was provided in 1924 when Hijikata Yoshi joined Osanai in creating the Tsukiji Sho-gekijo. Many of those connected with the new venture were in their twenties, and it was instrumental in introducing modern European drama to Japan, as well as providing training for many of the most distinguished directors and actors in the *shingeki* movement, such as Senda Koreya (director and actor, b. 1904) of the Haiyu-za, a company recognized as the leader of the *shingeki* movement in the post-war period; Yamamoto Yasue (actress, 1906–93) of Budo-no-Kai which operated from 1947 to 1964; Takizawa Osamu (actor, b. 1906) of Mingei, and Sugimura Haruko (actress, b. 1909) of Bungei-za.

The Proletariat Arts Movement was a vital force in pre-war Japan and many of the young people who worked in *shingeki* were strongly influenced by its left-wing ideology. Because of this, they were often persecuted by the government and their activities were carried out under the constant threat of arrest and imprisonment. Some of the distinguished playwrights from this time were Kishida Kunio (1890–1954), Kubo Sakae (1890–1958), Murayama Tomoyoshi (1901–77), Miyoshi Juro (1902–58) and Morimoto Kaoru (1912–46).

After the war, major companies such as Haiyu-za, Bungaku-za and Mingei became important focal points for *shingeki* activity. Many new post-war groups were formed, including Gekidan Shiki, led by director Asari Keita (b. 1933) and Seinen-za, which concentrated on original plays written by Japanese authors. Playwrights who began to produce important work at this time were Tanaka Chikao (b. 1905), Iizawa Tadasu (b. 1909), Kinoshita Junji (b. 1914), Kato Michio (1918–53), Akimoto Matsuyo (b. 1911), Abe Kobo (1924–93), Mishima Yukio (1925–70), Yashiro Seiichi (b. 1927), Miyamoto Ken (1926–88), Fukuda Yoshiyuki (b. 1931) and Yamazaki Masakazu (b. 1934).

Even in the 1950s, however, *shingeki* was still very much under the sway of European standards as was evident by the heavy emphasis on productions of translated western plays. Left-wing ideology continued to be of overwhelming importance. The Stanislavski system proved to be a major influence on the style of acting in *shingeki* circles while Senda Koreya and others were active in promoting Brecht's theories.

The 1960s brought about momentous changes. A new generation arose, developing an avant-garde movement that fiercely challenged *shingeki* as well as all established forms of theatre. Thus was the Small Theatre movement born.

For the Japanese, as for westerners, the 1960s was a time when movements demanding social change initiated a 'new wave' in various spheres of the arts. Universities and high schools across the country saw student activists challenge authority to the point where they created a social phenomenon. Japan had finally managed to work its way out of the poverty that had been brought about by its defeat in the war and this was the beginning of the boom years. In 1968 Japan's GNP passed that of West Germany and had become second in the world only behind the United States.

New anti-establishment troupes were also born at this time, groups which would ultimately change the direction of contemporary theatre in Japan. They issued no joint declarations or manifestos, they had no sponsors, no funding organization and no support from local authorities. Yet despite this, there was a spontaneous and simultaneous emergence of a momentum that was driven by a desire to challenge the established theatre system and to create something entirely new based on their talents and sensibilities.

One of the early groups, Engeki Centre 68/71 (later known as Black Tent), issued the following statement in 1969:

> Drama for us has now become like a set menu, cooked and served in the same old mechanical way, totally without flavour and utterly predictable. How much longer is this battered boat called *shingeki* going to carry us and how much further will we be able to go?

The conditions under which these groups worked were not so much chosen as thrust upon them due to financial difficulties that often meant that venues of under 200 seats were the most that the groups could afford. The first generation – founders of the Small Theatre movement – included many individuals of great talent and charisma. Among them was playwright-director Kara Juro (b. 1940), leader of Jokyo Gekijo (founded 1963). Kara has continued to use a red tent for all his open-air performances as author, director or actor. Noted for his exotic and lyrical visions and his raw vitality, in many ways he became the symbol of this movement in the 1960s. Although the group dissolved in 1987, Kara continued to work in his now symbolic tent as leader of the Kara-gumi group.

Waseda Shogekijo, founded in 1966 by director and theorist Suzuki Tadashi (b. 1939), and playwright Betsuyaku Minoru (b. 1937), is another important group in the evolution of this movement. Betsuyaku's work was at the root of the company's repertoire in the early years but after he left at the end of the 1960s, Suzuki became the sole director and the work thereafter was not connected to any particular author. Rather he came to develop what became known as the Suzuki method of physical training, a method which emphasized the lower half of the actor's body. This evolving style was used effectively in deconstructing and reconstructing both Japanese and European texts. Suzuki's theatre is austere and stylized and it seems increasingly accurate to describe his work as modern-day *noh*. Among his major productions have been *Geki-teki naru Mono o Megutte II* (*On the Dramatic Passions Part II*, 1970), *The Trojan Women* (1974) and *The Bacchae* (1978), all starring the actress Shiraishi Kayoko (b. 1941). Since 1982, Suzuki has sponsored an international theatre festival in the village of Toga (Toyama prefecture) each summer and in 1984 he renamed his group the Suzuki Company of Toga (SCOT). Between 1990 and 1994, Suzuki also worked as artistic director of the ACM theatre of Art Tower Mito.

As for Betsuyaku, he has continued to write. His early work, deeply influenced by Beckett's *Waiting for Godot* and the absurdists, evolved into a style utilizing a very precise dialogue which lays bare the hollowness of the psyche of the Japanese middle class with a bitter sense of humour. His major works include *Match-uri no shojo* (*The Little Match Girl*, 1966), *Aabuku-tatta, Nii-tatta* (*Bubble Bubble*, 1976), *Nishi Muki Samurai* (*The Samurai Facing West*, 1977) and *Shokoku o Henrekisuru Futari no Kishi no Monogatari* (*The Tale of the Two Knights Errant*, 1987).

Ota Shogo (b. 1939), the resident playwright and director of Tenkei Gekijo (founded 1968) was similar to Suzuki in his emphasis on the body of the actor but in his style of theatre inner silence held sway. Ota made his actors move in slow motion and in his successful tetralogy *Plays of Silence* there was virtually no dialogue. The first play in the tetralogy, *Komachi Fuden* (*Legend of Komachi*), had its première at a *noh* theatre in Tokyo in 1977 and was later played in the west. Proceeding at an almost surrealistically slow pace, the play features an old woman who at one point takes almost five minutes to walk 2 metres and fifteen minutes to get to centre stage. By slowing down the action to such an excruciating degree, Ota said he was trying to show those 'things that cannot be seen in a world moving at high speed' and 'things that can only be seen when one pays full attention'.

The other plays in the tetralogy include *Mizu no Eki* (*The Water Station*, 1981), *Chi no Eki* (*The Earth Station*, 1985) and *Kaze no Eki* (*The Wind Station*, 1986). *The Water Station* toured Europe, the United States, Australia, Canada and South Korea to high acclaim. In 1988 Ota dissolved Tenkei Gekijo. Two years later he was named artistic director of the Citizen's Theatre in the Shonan-dai Cultural in Fujisawa City near Tokyo where he continued to work through the 1990s producing such plays as *Sara-chi* (*The Plot of Land*, 1992).

Terayama Shuji (1935–83) was a playwright and poet, an essayist, a film director and the leader of the experimental theatre laboratory Tenjo Sajiki, which operated from 1967 until his death in 1983. The company was adventurous, bold, unique and known both in Japan and abroad. Terayama's goal was to bring about a 'revolution of principles and reality that would not depend on politics'. He did not try to develop a single methodology but is perhaps most

Terayama Shuji.

Terayama Shuji's production of *Nuhi-Kun* (*Servant's Orders*).

distinctive for the way in which he toyed with diverse styles of experimental theatre, led by his endless supply of exotic and curious ideas.

His *Aomori-ken no Semushi Otoko* (*The Hunchback of Aomori*, 1967) was one of his earliest examples of a freakshow done in a folk art style. *Galigari Hakase no Hanzai* (*Dr Knock*, 1975) was a street play lasting thirty hours which dragged in ordinary passers-by. This dramatic happening started at the same time in different parts of Tokyo and ultimately created an uproar. *Kankyaku-seki* (*Please Don't Be Seated*, 1978) attacked theatrical norms forcing the audience out of its seats and into the middle of the play. *Nuhi-Kun* (*Servant's Orders*, 1978) was a tightly balanced experiment filled with both spiritual and visual beauty.

Terayama called his work 'meta-theatre'. Questioning the very nature of art itself, he used the most theatrical elements to break the confines of theatre in his work. Erasing the essence of the 'theatrical', his work ultimately embraced elements that were traditionally beyond the borders of theatrical art. He once described his work thus:

Theatre without actors where everyone is the actor. Theatre without a theatre where every-where is a theatre. Theatre without an audience where everyone is the audience. Street theatre. House theatre. Theatre by letter. Theatre in a room. Theatre on a phone.

Terayama was eternally avant-garde; he continued to look for new ways to do theatre and to view theatre and he continued to change. Committed to experiment, to change, he never stopped questioning the nature of art. His untimely death at the age of 47 in 1983 truly marked the end of an era in Japanese theatre. It also elevated Terayama into the realms of myth. Indeed, posthumous publications of his writings continued into the 1990s and studies of his work are still being undertaken.

The Tokyo Kid Brothers is in a way a Terayama-inspired group for it was begun only a year after Tenjo Sajiki by an original member of Terayama's group, director and playwright Higashi Yutaka (b. 1945). The group's shows included rock-style music; among their early successes were *Tokyo Kid* (1969) and *Ogon Bat* (*Golden Bat*, 1970) shows about love and friendship among disaffected young people. The latter ultimately had a six-month run under the banner of New York's La MaMa Experimental Theater Club. In 1972, the company attempted to establish a commune called Utopia of Cherries in Tottori prefecture but the plans collapsed. The experience was reflected in the group's 1972 play, *Kiiroi Ribbon* (*Yellow Ribbon*).

Unlike Terayama's goal of finding an apolitical theatre, playwright and director Sato Makoto (b. 1943) and his Kuro Tent (Black Tent Group) intended from the beginning (1968) to be very political. Indeed, Sato sought to create a politicized theatre movement. The Black Tent company travelled across Japan from 1970 and attracted attention wherever it played.

Sato's most important dramatic works are *Nezumi Kozo* (*The Rat*), a series of connected plays created between 1969 and 1971 that traced the history of Japan, and *Kigeki Showa no Sekai* (*The Funny World of Showa*), a trilogy created between 1972 and 1979. The company has shown real interest in making connections with other Asian groups and has had particularly strong connections with groups in the Philippines.

Director Kushida Kazuyoshi (b. 1942) and actress Yoshida Hideko (b. 1944) were associates of Sato and the Kuro Tent. They left the group to found their own theatre, On Theatre Jiyu Gekijo in 1975, a company known for its apolitical and very urbane entertainment. The group's *Shanghai Bansuking* (*Shanghai Dance King*, 1979) by Saito Ren (b. 1940) with Kushida as director takes place in Shanghai during the 1930s and 1940s and follows a group of Japanese jazz musicians. The show has been revived several times and has been very successful in smaller venues. On Theatre has continued to use music in its work, usually with the cast doubling as musicians. In 1989, Kushida became artistic director of Theatre Tycoon in Tokyo, a theatre built by the Tokyu Group.

Another important artist who started out in the small theatres and then moved into commercial theatre to present highly visual, flamboyant and adventurous productions is the director Ninagawa Yukio (b. 1935). Ninagawa started his career as an actor and later helped to found Gendai Jin Gekijo (Modern Man's Theatre, later changed to Sakura-sha) in 1968. He became known there for his stagings of plays by Shimizu Kunio (b. 1936) reflecting the struggle of young left-wing Japanese fighting against a repressive social system. When the company disbanded in 1974, he joined the Toho company as a resident director. His bold and energetic stagings brought a breath of fresh air into the conservative world of commercial theatre. Among his major successes for Toho were productions of

Romeo and Juliet (1974), *Oedipus Rex* (1976), *Medea* (1978) and *Chikamatsu shinju Monogatari* (*The Chikamatsu Love Suicides*, 1979). All were praised for their crowd scenes and magnificent settings but also for taking into consideration a populist viewpoint, throwing ordinary people onto the same stage as heroes.

Ninagawa also utilized Japanese costumes and historical detail in his productions of European classics; this juxtaposition of west and east was theatrically stimulating. Ninagawa's production of *Macbeth* (1980), which transported the play into sixteenth-century Japan and which later toured to Europe and the United States, came to be regarded as one of his key works. He saw the stage of this production as a huge Butsu-dan, a Buddhist family altar, and directed the production as an elegy for those who died in battle. The three witches were played as *kabuki onnagata* and the entire set was enveloped in cherry blossoms. The sound effects used at Macbeth's death were the sound of tear gas canisters of the type launched at students by riot police in 1969 to quell riots at Tokyo University. Ninagawa's *Macbeth* was a requiem for the dead of his generation who had struggled against the system and failed.

His 1987 production of *The Tempest* was set as a *noh* play rehearsal on the island of Sado (the same island where Zeami, the perfecter of *noh* concepts, had been banished). Prospero became the director of the whole and the dream sequences were done in a style reminiscent of *noh* and *kyogen*. In 1991, Ninagawa, using British actors, directed a production in London's West End of Shimizu Kunio's play, *Tango At the End of Winter*.

Another popular and prolific playwright is Inoue Hisashi (b. 1934), one of the masters of Japan's contemporary drama as well as Japan's most famous novelist. Inoue's background is closer to *shingeki* than to Small Theatre. After writing a number of radio plays, he turned to the stage with a curious comedy, *Nihonjin no Heso* (*The Navel of Japan*) in 1969. Written in the well-made-play tradition, this play – like most of his work – was intelligent, clever, warm and liberal in spirit and social criticism. Since 1984, his works have been most consistently premièred by the Komatsu-za.

Inoue's most important work is a series of plays about the lives of famous Japanese writers, religious leaders and military figures, all depicted in unusual ways. These include *Omote Ura Gennai Kaeru Kassen* (*The Official and Hidden Story of Gennai and the Battle of the*

Frogs, 1970), *Dogen no Boken* (*The Adventures of Dogen*, 1972), *Shimijimi Nippon, Nogi Taisho* (*Hearty Japan, General Nogi*, 1979), *Kobayashi Issa* (a Haiku poet, 1979), *Ihatobo no Geki-ressha* (*Theatre Train from Ihatobo*, 1980), *Zutsu Katakori Higuchi Ichiyo* (*Headache, Stiff Neck, Higuchi Ichiyo*, 1984) and *Ningen Shikkaku* (*Fit to Be Human*, 1989). Other of his highly acclaimed works include *Yabuhara Kengyo* (*The Great Doctor Yabuhara*, 1973), about a blind man who chooses a life of crime in the Edo period, and *Ame* (*Rain*, 1976), something of a suspense play set in the same period.

One of Inoue's most popular plays is a monologue for an actress called *Kesho* (*Makeup*, 1982). Set in the dressing room of an actress, the play has been toured successfully by actress Watanabe Misako both in Japan and abroad. Most of these plays have been staged by Inoue's longtime collaborator, the distinguished director of the Chijinkai Company, Kimura Koichi (b. 1931).

The Small Theatre movement of the 1960s did not emerge from thin air. It co-incided with the emergence of the Off-Off-Broadway movement in New York and the work of the Living Theatre, Robert Wilson and Richard Schechner among others, all of whose productions were written about in Japan. Also influential at this time were the ideas of the Polish director Jerzy Grotowski, who emphasized the importance of the body and whose writings were translated into Japanese at this time. There were also regular reports on the work of Ariane Mnouchkine's Théâtre du Soleil from Paris. All these experiments had real influence in Japan.

However, it would be wrong to conclude that it was foreign work which led to the creation of the Small Theatre movement in Japan. This movement was very much a Japanese development which grew from Japanese soil though it was also one which received much stimulation from the so-called international avant-garde. What is perhaps more interesting is that a similar search for new theatre methodologies was occurring at the same time in many Asian countries including the Philippines, Thailand and Indonesia. Perhaps it is most accurate simply to note this strange phenomenon of the 1960s: the almost simultaneous appearance around the globe (particularly in North America, Europe and Asia) of a connected series of innovative developments in the arts.

In Japan, this movement accomplished several important things. First, it created a genuine and original Japanese contemporary theatre, one rooted in the Japanese character rather than being a pale imitation of the west. Second, these groups created their own plays instead of relying on translated work. Most often the director of the company – usually a resident playwright – would write and then stage a play on a particular subject. Third, the structure of dramatic literature changed drastically. In place of linear, realistic plays one suddenly had complex, multi-layered structures where time sequences were distorted and where the walls that separated the ordinary from the extraordinary and reality from illusion faded away. Suzuki created collage plays where fragments from world literature would be deconstructed and reinterpreted while Ota Shogo explored an abstract silence.

Fourth, there was a new emphasis on the body of the actor, a movement away from text and declamation. The physical became a means of highlighting the essentially dramatic. Kara Juro's 'privileged body' theory and Suzuki's physical method emerged from precisely this area of work. One might also say that it was an attempt to absorb into the contemporary theatre elements of traditional Japanese theatre where the actor rather than the text was primary.

Fifth, theatre space was transformed. No longer were formal theatres the only venue for performances. Open spaces, small theatres, tents, open-air spaces and even streets were now able to be used for performances. One might even mention here the Yokohama Boat Theatre (founded in 1981). Led by playwright Endo Takuro (b. 1928), the company mounted its shows on a wooden boat moored on a canal in Yokohama. It is important to note that such utilization of non-traditional venues led to clashes between artists and civic authorities from time to time. Members of Kara Juro's troupe were arrested after mounting a tent performance in defiance of established regulations in 1969. Terayama Shuji and his Tenjo Sajiki group were stopped by police after their Tokyo-wide street play in 1975. Even the tent performances of Kaze no Ryodan (founded 1982), a group known for its anti-monarchist sentiments, were often forcibly cancelled.

Finally, there were numerous attempts to bridge the gap between traditional and contemporary theatre. Reinterpreting the practices and aesthetics of centuries of traditional theatre with a critical eye was also part of the effort to create a rooted theatre. In the 1970s, Suzuki and Ninagawa, among others, presented *kabuki* plays in experimental ways. Renniku Kobo, a company founded in 1971 by Okamoto Akira (b. 1949) tried to blend *noh* with experimental techniques. The group used words utilized in traditional *noh* but not its format, combining the text with computer-generated music. Indeed, in the next generation, companies such as Hanagumi Shibai (founded in 1984) and led by Kano Yukikazu (b. 1960) called its performances a blend of pop music and *kabuki*, neo-*kabuki*.

What is particularly intriguing is that this search for cultural identity from the late 1950s to the early 1970s paralleled Japan's economic boom years. The economic achievements were obviously crucial in restoring Japan's confidence in itself following the confusion and poverty that followed the country's defeat in the war. The economic process was a monumental and well-organized official attempt to regain national pride. Compared to that, it might be appropriate to see the Small Theatre movement as a more modest but equally important attempt by the Japanese theatre community also to help the nation recapture a sense of cultural identity.

The 1970s saw a second generation of artists emerge. Influenced by the previous generation, however, they were determined to create something very different. Many of them, to begin, had direct experience of the student unrest that had erupted on university campuses in the late 1960s across Japan. The playwright Yamazaki Tetsu (b. 1947), a part of this generation, has identified one characteristic of his contemporaries as a need for theatre to be lifesized as opposed to the larger-than-life work of those who preceded them. This is an important point.

Yamazaki argues that the theatre people of the 1960s with their burning desire for change saw theatre on a scale that was bigger than life. They attempted to use the art as a way of releasing human beings into a realm of changes that would also be larger-than-life. Audiences too, he says, wanted to go beyond life, to touch larger areas, to transcend everyday reality. The second generation, though, no longer saw any meaning in such a separation and felt that audiences were no longer interested in it either. This detached analysis seems accurate as a statement of a generation that had experienced defeat on the campuses and had witnessed the horrific violence of disciplinary actions and factional in-fighting among the newer left-wing groups. Much of the theatre work of this generation therefore does depict human beings as they are – lifesize with a dash of bitter, critical sense of humour thrown in.

A typical example is the work of playwright and director Tsuka Kohei (b. 1948), a second generation Korean resident and leader of Tsuka Kohei Jimusho (founded 1974). His plays were quite popular with their ironic and bitter-sweet depictions of people who struggled desperately – with somewhat excessive passion – in order to live dramatically in a world cut adrift from ideals and ideology. These were plays that coolly mocked the predicament of a Japanese people who were better off materially but who were feeling spiritually empty. Tsuka made a noteworthy contribution as director and teacher of talented actors who were able to avoid excessively mannered acting.

Among Tsuka's major works are *Senso de Shinenakatta Otosan no Tame ni* (*For Father Who Couldn't Die in the War*, 1972), *Atami Satsujin Jiken* (*The Atami Murder Case*, 1973), *Kakumei Shoku Koza Hiryu-den* (*Revolution for Beginners – Legend of the Flying Dragon*, 1973), *Stripper Monogatari* (*The Stripper's Story*, 1975), and *Kamata Koshinkyoku* (*The Kamata March*, 1980). Tsuka's plays and productions brought laughter into Japanese contemporary theatre. Many plays that followed began to emphasize comic elements.

Yamazaki Tetsu, mentioned earlier as an actor with Kara Juro's Jokyo Gekijo, has been director of the Ten-i-21 company since 1980. He wrote a series of plays known collectively as *Field Notes for Crime*, plays about real-life crimes that occurred in Japan. The crimes become starting points for grotesquely distorted explorations of the angst-ridden Japanese psyche. Director Ryuzanji Sho (b. 1947), another second generation artist, has been the head of the Engeki-dan group and since 1984 the Ryuzanji Jimusho. His best work was on the *Ryuzanji Macbeth* (1988), which brought Shakespeare into a contemporary Asian setting, and the *Ryuzanji Hamlet* (1990), which was built around the violent 1989 events of Tiananmen Square.

Takeuchi Juichiro (b. 1947) writes plays that show ordinary people struggling to survive in a violent world. Intelligently written and with a mordant sense of humour, the plays show the absurdity of a world that traps individuals while emphasizing the friendship that helps to free them. The leader of the group HI-HO2 since 1990, his major works include *Lemon* (1978), *Hisan na Senso* (*The Pathetic War*, 1979), *Z* (1979); *Table Manners, Tokeru Uo* (*Table Manners, Melting Fish*, 1981) and *Himawari* (*Sunflowers*, 1988).

Okabe Kodai (b. 1945), playwright and leader of the Ku-kan-Engi, founded in 1970, writes in the dialect of his native city of Matsuura (Nagasaki prefecture). As he was growing up, the city was prosperous thanks to its coal-mine but as oil became the country's main source of energy the town went into an economic decline. Okabe's plays show the fate of small cities unable to share in the country's economic miracle while depicting the lives of the city's people with warmth and humour. Among his best plays are *Wajin Den* (*Tale of the Original Japanese*, 1975), *Hizen Matsuura Kyodai Shinju* (*The Suicide Pact of a Brother and Sister in Matsuura, Hizen Province*, 1978), *Nichirin* (*The Sun*, 1978), *Shoro-Nagashi* (*The Lantern Festival of the Dead*, 1980) and *Ayako* (1988).

A former member of Tenjo Sajiki and co-author of several plays with Terayama Shuji is Kishida Rio (b. 1950), a writer who focuses on themes of the darkly sensuous emotions and desires of women, and the struggle between the sexes. After Terayama's death, she founded the Kishida Jimusho which later merged with director Wada Yoshio and his Rakuten-dan. Together, the two groups perform as Kishida Jimusho + Rakuten-dan. Her plays are characterized by an ingenious structure and a strong storyline. Her most important works are the visually stunning *Ito Jigoku* (*The Woven Hell*, 1984), *Kiken naKankei* (*Dangerous Liaisons*, 1985) and *Wasurena-gusa* (*Forget-Me-Not*, 1986).

Ikuta Yorozu (b. 1949) was the first Japanese playwright to bring science fiction and theatre together. The strong influence of Philip K. Dick is evident in his play *Nancy Tomato no Mittsu no Seikon* (*The Three Stigmatas of Nancy Tomato*, 1984). His work is characterized by a nostalgic lyricism and a complex structure in which time and space are layered. His work is best characterized by a speech by one of his own heroines: 'The past is always new, and the future strangely familiar.' *Yoru no Kodomo* (*Children of the Night*, 1986) was a haunting meta-play about a woman cartoonist overpowered by the characters she creates.

In a country as highly centralized as Japan, the success of the Nagoya-based playwright Kitamura So (b. 1951) is unusual. The leader of Project Navi since 1986, his play *Hogi-uta* (*Song of Praise and Rejoicing*, 1979) explores a post-nuclear world in which almost everyone has died. Among the survivors in this comedy are a troupe of entertainers who become latter-day

Adams and Eves and who connect to those around them with the patter of stand-up comedians. His other important plays include *The Shelter* (1982), *Juichinin no Shonen* (*The Eleven Boys*, 1983) and *Duck Soap* (1987).

A third generation emerged in the late 1970s and the face of Japanese theatre changed once again. Many of those who belonged to the second generation had contact with the first generation and were often influenced by them. The succeeding generations, however, the children of Japan's economic boom years who had known Japan only as a country that was becoming affluent, had come to regard the first generation as part of the establishment. Unlike the two previous generations, it was rare for them to take any critical interest in politics or society. Their rise made theatre in Japan more carefree.

Most representative of this generation is the playwright and director Noda Hideki (b. 1955), leader of the Yume no Yuhmin-sha which operated from 1976 to 1992. Noda's talents and wide-ranging activities made this former student theatre group from the University of Tokyo the most popular company among young Japanese by the mid-1980s. The company was also very good at getting corporate sponsorship for their work, something relatively rare among the Small Theatres until this time. Noda not only directs his plays but also writes and stars in them. His work is marked by a light-hearted wordplay, ingeniously derived structures and a speed of delivery that is sometimes too fast for the audience to keep up with. He shows a strong desire to recapture childhood and other lost roots; this nostalgic lyricism combines with the intellectual appeal of his work to give it a real attraction. In 1987 and 1989 productions of Noda's works played at the Edinburgh Festival and later at the Brooklyn Academy of Music in New York. Among his well-known works are *Hanshin* (*The Demi-God*, 1986) and *Gansaku Sakura no Morino Mankai no Shita* (*An Imitative Version of Under the Flowering Forest of Cherry Blossoms*, 1989). In 1993, Noda founded a new producing organization, Noda Map, and dissolved his earlier company at the height of its popularity.

The increase in groups led by women is another phenomenon of the 1980s and 1990s. Kisaragi Koharu (b. 1956) founded the Noise Troupe in 1983. Her work tends to be socially critical and is set against modern technology and driven cityscapes. Her work has a clear feminist approach and stylistically, she often utilizes video equipment. Among her major works are

Romeo to Freesia no aru Shokutaku (*Romeo and a Dining Table With Freesia*, 1979), depicting a Tokyo where everyone is the same; *Doll* (1983), a story of a group of girls who commit group suicide; and *Moral* (1984). In 1993, the Noise Troupe disbanded.

Another important figure in the women's movement is Watanabe Eriko (b. 1955), a playwright and actress who is the leader of the Gekidan 3 Sanjumaru (Three Circles Theatre) established in 1978. Her play *Yoru no Kage* (*Night Shadows*, 1981) deals with feelings and the considerations given or not given to one's familiars. A complex and multilayered drama, it deals with the distant dreams and memories of a brother who mourns the untimely passing of his older sister. Her style is like a Chinese box, one level inside another, rarely realistic. Other important works of hers include *Ge-Ge-Ge no Ge* (1982), *Old Refrain* (1987) and *1 no 1no 6* (1990).

Aoi Tori is one of the few women's groups belonging to a slightly older generation. Established in 1974 by six actresses – including Kino Hana (b. 1948) and Serikawa Ai – the group's productions are all collectively created. The plays reflect the concerns and longings of the group members and very often are realistic in tone. In 1985, the group produced their first non-collectively written play, Caryl Churchill's *Cloud Nine*.

Other women's groups of note include Nitosha, established in 1981, a two-person troupe consisting of Nagai Ai (b. 1951), and Oishi Shizuka (b. 1951); and Jitensha Kinkurito, a group formed by seven women from Nihon Women's University in 1982 including playwright Iijima Sanae (b. 1963) and director Suzuki Yumi (b. 1963).

Through the 1980s, many new playhouses were built by businesses and the evolution of a fourth generation could be seen juxtaposed against this element of the continuing bubble economy. One of the fourth generation groups created at this time was Daisan Butai, founded in 1981 by playwright-director Kokami Shoji (b. 1958). Attracting a wide following among young people, his *Asahi no yo no Yu-hi o Tsurete* (*A Sunset Like Dawn*, 1981) cleverly transported Beckett's *Waiting for Godot* to the world of a toy company constantly being pushed to create newer and better software for computer games. Kokami shows a fondness for modern and futuristic settings where there is no longer any ideology or thought, a world that has been emptied of feeling and where people strug-

gle to put a brave face on their oppressive loneliness. His work is witty and filled with sight gags and laughter. The actors must connect to the audience by the sheer force of their personalities because the stage is usually quite bare. Apparently blithe entertainment, deep-down there is an inconsolable sense of isolation and loneliness. His important works include *Uchu de Nemuru Tame no Hoho ni Tsuite* (*How To Sleep in Outer Space*, 1981), *Modern Horror* (1984), *Hushabye* (1986) and *Tensi wa Hitomi o Tojite* (*Angels With Closed Eyes*, 1987).

In direct contrast to Kokami's hip taste, the playwright Kawamura Takeshi (b. 1959) and the Daisan Erotica (established 1980) are known for their brutal, violent energy and the dramatic scope of their very imaginative works. Kawamura's *Nippon Wars* (1984) is about combat androids who have been given the ability to love. They finally attempt rebellion only to find that this too had been programmed, for this was 'the final lesson that had to be learned'.

Clearly this fourth generation is one for whom the 'myths have crumbled'. Previous generations at least had the illusion of revolution and self and the protection of narrative to sustain themselves. All of these have now been lost. Kawamura's plays – *Radical Party* (1983), *Genocide* (1984), *Shinjuku Hakken-den* (*The Shinjuku Version of the Tale of Eight Dogs*, 1985) and *Body Wars* (1988) – clearly reflect these new circumstances.

Two other factors are common to the work of these new and highly motivated playwrights of the 1980s and 1990s. First, many of their works are set in the near future rather than in the present day, works featuring robots or a world destroyed by nuclear holocaust. Second, there are more meta-plays with a complex box-within-a-box structure, plays that underscore the fictionality of theatre.

Takahashi Isao (b. 1961) is another fourth generation playwright looking at the present through the near future. The leader of the Showma group (established 1982), Takahashi compared Japan in the not-too-distant future to a benign prison in his play *Gokuraku Tombo no Owaranai Ashita* (*The Never Ending Tomorrow of the Eternal Optimist*, 1986). This post-modern prison encourages its inmates to engage in artistic pursuits and those who show particular talent have their sentences shortened. Escape from this apparently lenient facility, however, is impossible. The protagonist begins with a six-month sentence which is lengthened to twenty years after numerous failed attempts at escape. Eventually he is shot dead.

Because of the large number of interesting new groups that have begun to work in the 1980s and 1990s, it is possible to mention only some of the most important briefly here: Tokyo Kandenchi (established 1977), founded by Emoto Akira (b. 1948) and formerly known as the On Theatre Jiyu Gekijo; Kato Kenichi Jimusho (established 1980), a production organization under the leadership of actor Kato Kenicho which has focused on British and North American light comedies; Tobiraza (1982), led by playwright Yokouchi Kensuke (b. 1961), a company which produces fairly orthodox plays; Riburesen (1983) which has produced much of the work of playwrights Ito Yumiko and Ohashi Yasuhiko (b. 1956); and Yu Kikai/Zenjido (1983), a group built around actress Takaizumi Atsuko and actor Shirai Akira, which has dealt with plays on family issues and modern city life.

In addition there is Engeki Shudan Caramel Box (1985), focusing on young people's issues and particularly the plays of Narui Yutaka (b. 1961); Tokyo Ichi-kumi (1985), a group built around actor Otani Ryosuke and playwright Harada Munenori (b. 1959); Mode (1987) founded by director Matsumoto Osamu (b. 1955), formerly of Bungaka-za and noted for its high performance level; Rinko-gun (1983), a group which has staged many socially aware plays especially by its house author Sakate Yoji (b. 1962); Seinen-dan (1982), known for its hyper-realistic productions especially of plays by resident playwright Hirata Oriza (b. 1962); and Tokyo Sunshine Boys (1983) specializing in the ingenious situation comedies of playwright Mitani Koki (b. 1961).

In Osaka, major new groups include Minami Kawachi Banzai Ichi-za (1980) led by playwright Naito Hironori (b. 1959) and Gekidan Sinkansen (1980) led by director Inoue Hidenori (b. 1960), the latter known for his combination of gags and rock concert atmosphere. There has been a remarkable increase in the number of troupes begun by Korean nationals who perform in Japanese. Tsuka Kohei, the most popular figure of the 1970s, was the first to begin such a group, followed by Shinjuku Ryozanpaku (1987) led by Kim Suzin (b. 1954) and Chong Wishin (b. 1957), a playwright. The company's work overflows with an energy reminiscent of theatre of the 1960s; it has performed

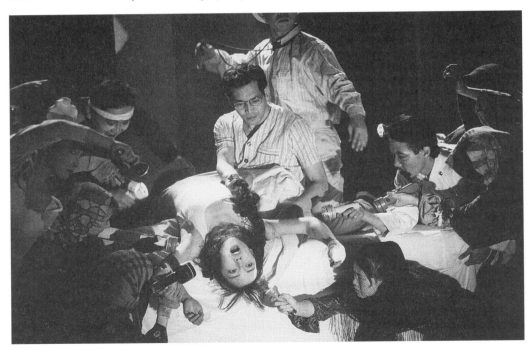

Shinjuku Ryozanpaku Company's 1993 production of *A Cry from the City of Virgins* by Kara Juro, directed by Kim Suzin.
Photo: Katsu Miyauchi.

in Germany, South Korea and China. Also of note here is the South Korean writer Yu Miri (b. 1968), leader of Seishun Gogatsu-to. Much of her work is autobiographical and her *Sakana no matsuri* (*Festival of Fish*, 1992) brims with the desire to reunite a dysfunctional family.

There are an increasing number of performance groups whose work defies easy categorization. The most interesting are Osaka's Ishin-ha (1970) led by Matsumoto Yukichi (b. 1946) with its large-scale settings; Kyoto's Dumb Type (1984), made up of multimedia artists and scenographers which won high praise for its *pH* (1990) and which utilized a large high-tech set; and Tokyo's Pappa Tarahumara (1982) led by director Koike Hiroshi (b. 1956) which uses stillness and music.

Compared to the radical struggles of the 1960s, the theatres of the 1980s and 1990s are without doubt quieter and more sophisticated. Avant-garde is no longer their goal; the emphasis now is on entertaining an audience and artistic maturity. Theatrical experiment is no longer a major issue. At the same time, as Takahashi Isao's work indicates, contemporary theatre in Japan is trying to break through what Kokami Shoji has called 'the soft invisible wall' that still exists between the many companies that are each working quite separately. The activity being seen in the work of the many Korean nationals in Japan shows the cultural power that can be generated by working together. It is also a good indication of the pluralism that is becoming more and more evident in the Japanese theatre and further proof that there is still great vitality and diversity worth looking for in contemporary Japanese theatre.

Senda Akihiko

(Parts of the above come from a lecture given by Senda Akihiko for the Japan Foundation and subsequently issued in booklet form in 1994. WECT would like to acknowledge its debt to both Mr Senda and the Japan Foundation for their support in the preparation of this section.)

Music Theatre
Dance Theatre

Paralleling the development of *shingeki* in Japan has been western-style classical ballet which first appeared in Japan around 1912 when the Italian dance master G.V. Rosi began to introduce its techniques. Almost on its heels came the introduction of modern dance techniques under the influence of Mary Wigman and the German *neue Tanz*. This expressionist tendency is clear even in the late 1990s in the work of many Japanese modern dancers. In the 1950s, the major influence was Martha Graham. Small companies sprang up over these decades but modern dance did not find a Japanese form until the 1960s when *butoh* emerged from the avant-garde art movements of the period.

The founder of *butoh*, very much a post-modern evolution, was Hijikata Tatsumi who formulated the physical radicalism of this new style as a kind of neo-dadaism. His ideas have had a significant effect ever since on other contemporary Japanese theatrical forms. Determined to break away from the pre-existing concepts of dance and dance theatre, Hijikata showed that the body had its own physical structure capable of expressing a much wider range of emotions than had been heretofore utilized. Under his choreographic eye, the *butoh* dancer was at once grotesque, absurd, erotic or torn with terror.

Determined to express elements that cannot be expressed in words, Hijikata argued against earlier forms of dance for their attempts to explain and objectify what was essentially literary or obvious (elements like delight or distress). Compared with the symmetrical beauty of conventional dancers, *butoh* dancers with their stooped legs and oversized facial caricatures are the picture of deformity in motion. Hijikata's goal was the rescue of the body from responsibilities of logical signification. The body of the *butoh* dancer is therefore removed from points of normal balance and the idealized beauty of the traditional dancer.

Without any need to take pride in its powerful musculature or physical strength, the *butoh* body simply exists in space in a new kind of irreducible beauty without equivalent anywhere else. In this way *butoh* accomplishes a reversal in aesthetic consciousness. Its fundamental structure lies in the contradiction between the impulse towards self-destruction and the impulse to resist total dissolution.

Sanki Juku's 1981 production of *VII MSTO*.

Metamorphosis becomes the next evolution – the desire to transform the body from its usual state into a state of spirituality. The dancer seeks to degrade the ideal body into the human body full of emotion on a deeper, more powerful level. The human body is transformed into the non-human (spirits, animals, inanimate objects) or the rejected (the diseased, the criminal, the old). Such metamorphosis requires the rejecting of the ego by the dancer.

Another school of Japanese modern dance stresses transformation as well but a transformation rooted in sexuality. The company, H Art Chaos, was founded by Oshimah Sakiko who, rejecting the extremism of *butoh*, creates her works by blending more traditional modernism with pop elements transforming and metamorphosing them one into the other.

Other artists have attempted to cross the borders between the art forms, particularly those between dance and visual art, dance and music, dance and traditional theatre. During the 1970s, performance art became the art of choice for the avant-garde who wished to experiment with multidisciplinarity. From this point on, the artistic vision of the body was significantly changed and it led to the invasion of borders by artists from various fields.

From the dance world, the major assault came from Teshigawara Saburo, one of the most active and fascinating artists working at the time. Through the 1980s and 1990s, his work could be described only as post-*butoh*. Where *butoh* is turned inward and is self-consciously mysterious, his work is a series of simple, smart and repetitive visual images. He seeks to excite his audience with direct physical representations that do not depend on previously existing techniques. His work has drawn powerful and enthusiastic responses from young audiences wherever his company (the Kyoto-based Dumb Type) has played, both in large cities and small. His pieces often deal with gay themes and have even dealt with AIDS (indeed, the producer of the group, Furuhashi Teiji, died of AIDS in 1995) and have been greeted enthusiastically.

Other groups working in multidisciplinary ways include Nomado, Pappa Tarahumara, Strange Kinoko, Kaital-sha, Nest, Leni Basso and Agua Gala. Most of these groups use the latest technology including computer-generated music, laser lighting and electronic sound manipulation in their work. In general, their choreography is violent, fast and loud with the dancers' bodies convulsed and cramped. Indeed, if one can take anything from these experiments it is their apparent warning of imminent crises in the human ability to receive any additional flooding from the world of technology.

One cannot ignore in this evolution of modern dance in Japan the influence of post-modern groups during the 1960s. Such experiments arrived in Japan via New York and included a range of extremely fine dancers and talented choreographers committed to pushing the mainstream of modern dance in less rigid directions. Many moved toward a kind of minimalism which eventually became self-defeating.

Subsequent work by many of these dancers has moved into areas where sheer physical power is utilized for high-tension movements to create an extremely clean and simple theatrical enchantment. Among leading dancers who worked or are still working in the post-modern field are Yonei Sumi, Takeuchi Toshiko, Matsuyama Yoshihiro and the Resonance company, Kitamura Mami, and Yamazaki Kohta. Some of these dancers have also experimented with North American 'contact improvisation'.

Among more mainstream modern dancers, one must note the work of Kisanuki Kuniko, Takemoto Kazuko, Ehara Tomoko, Nohmi Kenshi, Takeya Keiko and Mochizui Tatsuro.

Kuniyoshi Kazuko

Theatre for Young Audiences
Puppet Theatre

The rebirth of theatre for young audiences in Japan after World War II is quite precise: a production (the sixty-fourth in its long history) by Theatre Todo of Maurice Maeterlinck's play *The Blue Bird* directed by Miyatsu Hiroshi in Tokyo. The production opened on 24 December 1945. The Todo, in operation since 1928, had operated almost continuously even during the war but had ceased operation in early 1945. Its reopening was a signal to other groups that they too could start performing once again. Composed of both adult and child performers – as most youth companies were before the war – the Todo was Tokyo's best known such group and among its most popular.

But there were many other groups as well at the time. Of the more established groups, Zenshin-za (Going Forward), founded in 1939, was of particular interest because it was created by a group of *kabuki* actors determined to break away from traditional concerns. Started up once again in 1946, the company performed a range of plays for young people including original Japanese scripts such as *Shitakiri Suzume* (*The Sparrow Who Lost its Tongue*) to Shakespeare (*Merchant of Venice*). The company found its largest audiences in elementary and high schools across the country. Zenshin-za was awarded a special prize in 1948 (Asahi Bunka-sho – Asahi Prize for Cultural Merit) for its contributions in this field. Other long-established groups which restarted at this time were Kodomo Gekijo (Children's Theatre), Shonen Gekijo (Kids' Theatre) and Seinen Gekijo (Young People's Theatre).

During the 1950s a number of newer groups emerged both in Tokyo and in the provinces. Among the latter were Gekidan Tanpopo (Dandelion Theatre) in Hamamatsu, a group which was still operating in 1997. As well, many of Tokyo's new *shingeki* groups decided at this time to set up children's theatres partly hoping that they would be able to develop new audiences for the future and partly to develop paid tours.

The growing Japanese economy caused even more rapid growth in the field during the 1960s. Perhaps the most interesting of the groups was Mokuba-za (Rocking Horse). Originally a children's puppet theatre, the group slowly evolved towards a kind of shadow theatre utilizing both forms with nearly lifesize figures and productions of traditional western children's fare such as *The Little Match Girl*. Other groups formed at this time include Gekidan Hikosen (Airship Theatre) and Gekidan Gingatetsudo (Galaxy Train).

Nissei Children's Theatre was founded in 1964 and increased audiences significantly. Sponsored by the Japan Life Insurance Company (Nihon Seimei Hoken Gaisha), Nissei managed to reach over 100,000 children with its 1964 musical, *Hadaka no Osama* (*The Emperor's New Clothes*). Because of the business sponsorship, the company did not have to charge for tickets and audiences were consistently large. The show has been performed annually every year since and continues to

Zenshin-za's (Going Forward) production of *Santa Maria in the Moonlight*.
Photo: courtesy of ASSITEJ Japan.

attract audiences and a positive image for its sponsor. As a result, other corporations have turned to sponsorship in the field with equal success.

Another innovation in the field was the creation in 1966 of an association of children's theatre supporters which attracted large numbers of parents and children. Starting in Fukuoka it spread through western Japan and by 1974 had become the National Association for Children's Theatre. In 1997, some 400,000 people were members of the association, which organized performances nation-wide.

Many theatre groups staged productions specifically for this organization and soon found that work for children could well help them support their work for adults as well. Particularly active were Kansai Geijutsu-za (Kansai Art Theatre) in Osaka and, in Tokyo, Mingei, Geiijutsu-za (Art Theatre), Engeki Ensemble (Theatre Ensemble), Gekidan Nakama (Theatre Company) and Teatoru Ekol (Echo Theatre).

A number of new companies also began at this time exclusively doing work for children including one of the country's most innovative groups, Kaze-noko (Free As the Wind). Kaze-noko, which has since toured to many parts of the world, turned to elements that had not traditionally been used in this form – improvisation and work with objects that metamorphosed into other things. Its 1960 production of *Caledonia-go no Shuppan* (*The Sailing of the Caledonia*) and its 1961 production of *Bottako March* established Kaze-noko as Japan's foremost children's theatre and as one of the world's innovators in this form. Kaze-noko later began its own school – Jido Engeki Kenkyu Jo (Research Institute for Youth Theatre).

Thanks to support from the government's Department for the Promotion of Art and Culture as well as the pioneering National Association for Children's Theatre, companies now regularly tour even to outlying areas with productions for young audiences. In 1995, for example, twenty-nine companies toured the country bringing shows to twenty different prefectures and drawing over 110,000 people in total.

In terms of puppet theatre, at the end of World War II it was exceedingly difficult to bring together companies of actors but it was not quite so difficult for puppeteers to bring puppets to perform anywhere that people would gather, indoors or out, with or without proper

Theatre Urinko's production of When I Met Myself.
Photo: courtesy of ASSITEJ Japan.

stages. Puppeteers in fact were among the first artists to reach out to war-weary communities and in February 1946, less than a year after the war ended, twenty-five puppet troupes sent representatives to a national conference on puppetry. Organizer of this meeting was the puppeteer Kawajiri Taiji (b. 1914), director of the Puk Puppet Theatre, a group dissolved by the government before the war for its social criticism. The company continued to be a leader in post-war puppetry in Japan until Kawajiri's death in 1994. Kawajiri's best known production during his long career was a powerful puppet production of *Faust*.

Two other groups of importance which began operations as a result of Puk's theatrical inspiration were Ningyo Gekidan Kyogeki (Kyogeki Puppet Theatre) in Kyoto and Hitomi-za (Hitomi Theatre) in Kamakura. These two companies, along with Puk, dominated modern puppetry in Japan right into the 1990s. All toured regularly and worked in a more or less realistic mode. Their early repertoires were geared to both adults and families and they performed regularly in factories and university communities.

During the 1950s, these and all other modern puppet groups in the country suffered from a perceived lack of political connection to national democratic movements. Most groups had turned away from realistic subject matter and had found audiences in elementary schools. Younger puppeteers sought innovation rather than politics. One such was Fujishiro Seiji whose troupe Junu Pantoru (Young Painter) began with glove-puppets but soon turned to shadow-puppets and attracted wide attention. Later changing the name of the troupe to Nigyo To Kagee Gekidan Mokuba-za (Rocking Horse

Hitomi-za's production of *Chikara Taro* (*Stray Man Taro*).

Shadow and Puppet Theatre), the company's productions literally became larger and larger. By the mid-1960s, the group was using a shadow screen 12 metres (39 feet) wide and 6 metres (20 feet) high with masks and costumes covering the now live actor's body from head to toe. Performing for more than 1,000 people at a time, it was not unusual for Mokuba-za to reach over 150,000 people in a single season. But expansion also caused the company to over-reach itself and in the early 1970s, the group went bankrupt. Fujishiro, however, did not give up and returned to the group's original name, performing mostly for children.

By 1953, despite the long tradition of *bunraku*, puppetry in Japan was considered to be almost purely an art for children and the intro-duction of modern puppets to Japanese televi-sion simply underscored the notion. Most televised puppet shows still cling to this notion. Indeed, the National Association of Children's Theatre with its 700 branches represents huge potential audiences. One of the most successful groups at working with the organization through the years has been Musubi-za which, since its creation in the mid-1960s, has staged hundreds of successful shows across the country, some didactic and some simply entertainment.

Perhaps the most unusual puppet group in Japan is Hitomi-za's Puppet Theatre for the Deaf. Utilizing puppeteers with hearing disabili-ties as well as those with normal hearing, the group works primarily for deaf audiences but has found popularity as well with hearing audi-ences. The company utilizes masks, pantomime and body language in its shows which have been successfully played all over Japan and on occasion abroad.

Another unusual company is Hyakki-yako Dondoro (The Hundred Demon Night Train) in Iijima (Nagora Prefecture) which is a one-person puppet theatre working exclusively for adults. This company too has had success performing in Europe.

In 1997, fifteen permanent puppet theatre stages existed across the country, the oldest being Puk Puppet Theatre in Tokyo built in 1971. All have between 100 and 300 seats. Playing in schools and other community halls, some 140 puppet troupes reach an audience of over 6 million people annually, the great major-ity of them children. The largest troupes are Puk and Hitomi-za which each have over ninety people involved in the work. The repertoire of most is a combination of traditional Japanese fairytales and a strong mix of western fairytales

by writers such as the Brothers Grimm and Hans Christian Andersen. Original pieces are the exception rather than the rule.

Puppet styles also vary widely from tradi-tional *bunraku* with its manipulators on the stage (some of the newer groups are also utiliz-ing manipulators on the stage) to puppets manipulated with wooden rods or more tradi-tional marionettes and glove-puppets.

One of the few companies also interested in research in the field is Takeda Ningyo-za (Takeda Marionette Theatre) which offers regular workshops in its rehearsal space and research centre in Iida. One of several mari-onette troupes in the country, others of note are Yuki-za in Tokyo and Minomushi (Inchworm) in Amagasaki City (Hyogo prefecture).

Shadow-puppet troupes continue to emerge with Fujishio still providing leadership and inspiration. Among other troupes working in this style are Minwa-za (Folktale Theatre) in Tokyo which has returned to the old Utsushi-e shadowgraph style (a style that virtually disap-peared a hundred years ago) and Gekidan Yuyake (Sunset Theatre), a one-person chamber shadow theatre located in Hikisa in Shizuoka prefecture.

Mask-style performances have all but disap-peared being replaced by full body costumes representing animals or even Disney-style char-acters. These shows are particularly popular with families having been seen first and popular-ized by television.

Twenty-five puppet theatre groups are part of Nihon Jido Seishonen Engekidan Kyogikai (Conference of Japanese Theatre for Young Audience Companies) while Nihon Ningyogekijin Kyokai (Association for Japanese Puppetry) has 350 members, both groups and individuals. Still another association of note in this field is the Japanese section of the International Puppeteers' Union (UNIMA) founded in 1967 and which in 1997 had 330 members. The membership of UNIMA includes a number of researchers in the field. Its first Japanese president was Kawajiri Taiji (d. 1994) from Puk Puppet Theatre.

There are also some two thousand amateur puppet groups in Japan, many connected to the national family arts association. Both profes-sional groups and amateurs work together and there is much cooperation in this field. One example is the annual Ningyo Geki Carnival Iida (Iida Puppet Theatre Carnival) held every August and attracting some two thousand puppet aficionados (groups and individuals).

Puppet shows are played over a period of four days in eighty venues both indoors and out. Normally around thirty workshops and lectures are held during the event. The carnival began in 1979 with sixty groups performing and has expanded every year. In 1996, the carnival drew two hundred different puppet companies.

Ogawa Nobuo, Koshiro Uno

Design

Japanese stage design clearly breaks down into two basic areas: the traditional arts which were dominated by stage painting (*noh, kabuki, bunraku* and various dance forms) and modern design imported from Europe and utilized primarily for *shingeki* from the end of the nineteenth century.

The unique style of the *kabuki* stage, developed during the Edo period (1603–1867), was designed to reach a large public. When European-style buildings began to be constructed at the turn of the twentieth century, the *kabuki* stage continued virtually unchanged within them. Painters and carpenters were still to be the main creators on these stages, the autonomous designer not yet having emerged.

As interest in *shingeki* began to grow, however, the designer system began to play a larger role. New materials were added into traditional visual patterns and eventually visual questions were left more and more to experts in the field. A new generation of traditional visual designers emerged led by Komura Settai, Torii Kiyotada, Nagase Chokuryo, Matsuoka Eikyu, Yasuda Yukihiko, Ezaki Kohei and Maeda Seison. Others have come from the visual arts and are more closely linked to Japanese traditional painting – Tanaka Ryo, Kugimachi Kumaji, Nakajima Hachiro and Oda Otoya – while still others have come to specialize in one particular form of the traditional performing arts such as Kawakami Kiyoshi, who has focused on *bunraku,* and Kimura Sohachi, Ito Seiu and Hamada Yujiro, who focused on *shinpa* (new-wave theatre experiments at the turn of the century which attempted to

Michael Nyman's opera *Tempest* directed by Robert Lepage, 1994.

modernize *kabuki* but which ultimately had very little effect on either *kabuki* or *shingeki)*. Taking the traditional arts as their source, their goal was to help create more populist art.

As the new western-style contemporary play emerged along with operas and variety revues, Japanese designers were called upon to adapt existing stages for these forms. Their models were European theatres from the nineteenth century and designs in this style quickly followed. Over the twentieth century, design styles changed; in the first half design was imitative and generally uninteresting. In the post-war period, however, as national colour and tone was added, a much more Japanese design style began to be seen.

The end of the war brought a new influx of North American design trends. Many of the major new post-war companies hired designers as part of their new commitment to *shingeki,* and post-war technological innovation brought rapid mechanical advancements. The new freedom of the 1960s led away from North American styles and helped to create more national images and systems of design.

Added in was a new interest by many of the 1960s anti-establishment experimental groups in working in alternative venues (with the attendant design challenges this called for) and still another generation of visual design artists came to the fore working with companies such as Terayama's Tenjo Sajiki and Suzuki's Waseda Shogekijo as well as groups like Jokyo Gekijo and Kuro Tent. Working with these groups were many contemporary visual artists such as Komai Tetsuro, Takamatsu Jiro, Yoshida Yoshi and Miki Tomio. The stage was at long last being recognized as one of the visual arts and designs were no longer something simply to be attached to plays.

Another manifestation of this new energy was the establishment at this time of the Japanese Association of Stage and Television Artists (JASTA), a group aimed at improving design generally as well as ameliorating the general conditions of designers themselves. The organization has also been involved in developing contacts with designers in other countries.

Odagiri Yoko

Theatre Space and Architecture

In 1997, Japan opened its fifth national theatre. Primarily used for *shingeki* theatre, opera, ballet and concerts, the new building, Shin Kokuritsu Gekijo (New National Theatre) was located in one of the prestigious central areas, Shinjuku. The four earlier national theatres include the Kokuritsu Gekijo (National Theatre) in Tokyo, built in 1966 and used almost exclusively for *kabuki* performances; Kokuritsu Engei Jo (National Variety Theatre), also in Tokyo, opened in 1979 and used for musical and variety performances; Kokuritsu Nogaku Do (National Noh Theatre) in Tokyo, opened in 1983 and used almost exclusively for *noh* and *kyogen* performances; and Kokuritsu Bunraku Gekijo (National Bunraku Theatre), located in Osaka and built in 1984 for *bunraku* performances. It is these five structures which are at the heart of Japanese performance space although, as national spaces, they are neither as opulent as some of the country's commercial theatres nor as alternative as many of the country's experimental underground venues.

The concept of national theatres in Japan goes back to the nineteenth century when many theatre artists called for the construction of spaces for traditional performances. In the 1920s the idea was revived but it was not until 1955 that the government responded in concrete terms and made available significant sums of money to allow the first national theatre to be built. Opened eleven years later, the theatre was by that time one of about 140 spaces in the country being used for theatrical performances (mostly *shingeki* productions). The importance of having a space for traditional theatrical art had begun to be understood.

In the decades since the opening of the first national theatre, performance spaces have mushroomed across the country and in the mid-1990s there were some 1,200 venues in use in Japan ranging from opulent spaces built into shopping centres or as part of department stores (some holding over 3,000) to functional (used by small *shingeki* groups) to spaces that were never conceived of for theatre (used by various Small Theatre groups). The majority of these theatre spaces are privately owned.

The New National contains three different halls: a 1,800-seat opera house, a 1,000-seat playhouse and a 440-seat 'pit's theatre in which seating can be moved to accommodate the needs of the production. Constructed on five levels (with four additional underground levels) the whole covers an area of some 28,000 square metres. Near the New National is another theatre, the Tokyo City Opera, a privately owned and operated space holding 1,600 seats. Together, the two theatre buildings create a lovely ambiance.

The opera house in the New National is computerized and the sliding stage can be moved into four different configurations. The theatre's 30 metre (98 feet) high ceiling allows even the largest of stage settings to be moved in and out easily. The acoustics are also near perfect with the audience seated on four levels. No seat is more than 30 metres from the stage.

Nineteen separate rehearsal spaces have been included, each matching the dimensions of at least one of the three halls.

The Kabuki National Theatre has two halls – a 1,600-seat mainspace and a 600-seat smaller hall. Used almost exclusively for *kabuki* performances, the space is also utilized on occasion by other traditional performance groups doing music, dance or even *bunraku* puppet theatre.

The private Kabuki-za also has its own large theatre in central Tokyo.

The National Noh Theatre, opened in 1983, holds 591 seats and also has display areas, a library, rehearsal and training spaces, while the National Bunraku Theatre has 700 seats. Traditionally, *noh* was performed under a roofed stage with the audiences seated on two or three sides. The stage floor in the National Noh Theatre is made of 400-year-old Japanese cypress from Aichi prefecture while the pillars and stage structure are from 2,000-year-old cypresses from Taiwan.

As for other theatres, many exist inside public or private buildings. This tradition goes back to the end of World War II when many theatre spaces in Tokyo and other cities were destroyed because of Allied bombings. As new office buildings went up, theatre groups were given permission to play in large open spaces within them. Popular with audiences, and clearly attracting people to these buildings, the theatres were allowed to continue operating within them; eventually the idea of having permanent theatres in these spaces caught on with big business. Unlike audiences in the West End of London or on Broadway, which filter out on to streets, most

Japanese theatres are found on the upper floors of buildings and audiences have become used to taking lifts and stairs to get to theatres. Playhouses are now an accepted part of business areas.

In the mid-1950s, the Haiyu-za opened one of the country's first independent theatres – that is, a theatre not attached to something else. Built in the central area of Rappongi, the theatre had entrances at street level and had a larger stage than usual. Although quite typical of theatres in most other ways, the theatre became a model for others and independent theatres began to appear in other parts of the city. Independent theatres now exist all across the country, the best known being Suzuki Tadashi's SCOT in the village of Toga which has become an international centre for theatre experiment and performance.

Perhaps the best known theatre architect in the country is now Isozaki Arata, designer of the Globe Theatre in Tokyo (specializing in Shakespearian performances), the Geijutsukan (Art Hall) in Mito City (Ibaraki prefecture) and two spaces in Shizuoka City (one indoor and one outdoor). Isomura was also the architect for Suzuki's Greek-style amphitheatre in Toga.

The 1960s underground groups opened the field even wider with their interest in working in non-traditional venues. Tents, shrines, vacant lots and even warehouses began to be used. Terayama Shuji worked regularly with his Tenjo Sajiki company in found spaces on streets as well as in his own workshops. Even in the 1990s, many who early in their careers worked with such groups still prefer non-traditional to traditional venues; for example Kara Juro (formerly of the Red Tent Theatre) is still working in tent-like spaces.

Imamura Osamu, Tanokura Minoru

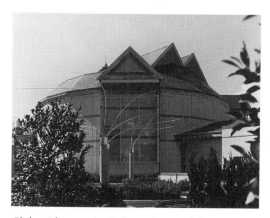

Globe Theatre in Tokyo designed by Isomura Shin.

Training
Criticism, Scholarship and Publishing

Training for Japanese traditional theatres begins at a young age and continues over decades. Reformed and improved in recent times, such approaches to the traditional arts function as both a spiritual and a technical standard for actors to follow earlier generations into the art. In fact, traditional theatrical genres such as *noh*, *kabuki* and *bunraku* all operate their own training programmes within their respective national theatre structures.

Such traditional methods, however, do not necessarily work for *shingeki* or for other aspects of the contemporary theatre. In the years just after World War II, therefore, new training methods were tried. Teachers came to Japan expert in the Russian Stanislavski system and the American Method system. Others learned and imitated the declamatory style of the Comédie-française while still others took the British outside-in approach. Eventually, Japanese actors learned that no matter how useful the actual method, none could be applied intact to another culture, particularly a culture so different in language and body expression as Japan.

It was the director and theorist Suzuki Tadashi who most effectively evolved a training method for Japanese actors, one based on Japanese physicality, language and cultural traditions. Once trained in this way, actors seem to be better able to express themselves both physically and emotionally in Japanese plays. Suzuki has long used these methods in working with his own actors first in Tokyo and later in the village of Toga. Connected to centring the actor in the lower half of his or her body, the Suzuki Method has produced outstanding results for some but has been rejected by many others as being unsuitable for their work.

In this sense, there is no common training method in contemporary Japan. Each group works in whichever way is most effective. Many of the companies formed since the 1980s have adopted non-realistic styles while those founded in the 1950s through the 1970s tend to have a much more realistic base to their work. To this end, a rather large number of companies have established their own conservatories. Most include physical training, voice work and singing.

A number of private training institutions also exist as do *ad-hoc* workshops which have provided an injection of new methodologies and ideas in the 1990s.

There is much outstanding scholarly writing on traditional forms of theatre – by both Japanese and foreign writers – but relatively little of real scholarly interest has been done on modern Japanese theatre by either national or international writers. Among national critics on *shingeki*, the most important writing has come from Senda Akihiko, drama critic of the country's largest newspaper, *Asahi Shimbun*. His study of Japanese theatre since World War II, *The Voyage of Contemporary Japanese Theatre* (1995) is perhaps the best book yet done on this period. Among foreign scholars, David G. Goodman did some very fine issues as editor of a journal published in the 1970s called *Concerned Theatre Japan*.

Probably the best theoretical works *from* the modern period are those by the director Suzuki Tadashi, who has outlined his ideas on theatre and theatre training in several volumes including *The Sum of Interior Angles*, his best known work and one that has been translated widely.

A number of useful theatre journals regularly publish serious discussions on aspects of the modern theatre. One of the first to publish in the post-war period was *Shingeki*, which published regularly from the 1960s through the 1980s when it evolved away from its original title and came to be known as *Spec*; however, *Spec* survived only two years.

The most provocative of the existing journals has been *Teatoro* (*Theatre*) which opens its pages to actors, directors and designers as well as critics, very often giving them an opportunity to debate with one another on statements already published in newspapers. If there is one clear editorial position in the journal it is a wide-open, anti-establishment approach.

Another journal of note is *Higeki Kigeki* (*Tragedy Comedy*) which, despite its generally high level of debate (or perhaps because of it) has little impact on the contemporary theatre world. The journal deals with general issues of theatre theory and has published many useful round-table debates.

The newest of the contemporary theatre journals is *Theatre Arts*, published by the Japanese

Centre of the International Association of Theatre Critics (AICT). Begun in 1994, the journal appears twice a year with each issue devoted to a different subject such as 'Sexuality and Theatre' or 'Theatre and War'. The journal, funded by the Sezon Bunka Zaidan (Saison Cultural Foundation), is open both to working theatre critics connected to newspapers as well as to scholars in the field.

Theatre publishing has never been thought of as commercial. It is relatively rare when a theatre title is issued by a commercial publisher. Two theatrical photo magazines also exist and both have significant circulations: *Engeki Book* (*Theatre Book*) and from Osaka, *JAMCI* which publishes interviews with theatre personalities.

The most important collection of theatre memorabilia in the country is at Waseda University Theatre Museum while important collections of traditional theatrical arts exist within the various national theatres.

Tanokura Minoru
Translated by Yatsuko Katsura

Further Reading

Arnott, Peter D. *The Theatres of Japan*. London: Macmillan, 1969. 319 pp.

Betsuyaku, Minoru. *Serifu no aru Fukei* [The speaking landscape]. Tokyo: Hakusui-sha, 1964.

Bowers, Faubion. *The Japanese Theatre*. Rutland, VT, 1974.

Goodman, David G., ed. and transl. *After Apocalypse: Four Japanese Plays of Hiroshima and Nagasaki*. New York: Columbia University Press, 1986. 325 pp.

—— . ed. and transl. *Japanese Drama and Culture in the 1960s: The Return of the Gods*. Armonk, NY: M.E. Sharpe, 1988. 363 pp.

Hijikata, Tatsumi. *Yameru Maihime* [The wounded art]. Hakusui-sha, 1983.

Hirata, Oriza. *Toshi ni Shukusai wa Iranai* [City festivals and their uses]. Bansei-sha, 1997.

Kan, Takayuki. *Kaitai suru Engeki* [The breakdown of the theatre]. Renga Shobō Shinsha, n.d.

—— . *Zoku Kaitaisuru Engeki* [The breakdown of the theatre II]. Renga Shobō Shinsha, n.d.

Kara, Juro. *Tokkenteki Nikutai Ron* [On the privileged flesh]. Hakusui-sha, 1997.

Kazama, Ken. *Chichioya no iru Fukei* [Landscape with a past]. Tokyo: Seikyū-sha, 1990.

—— . *Engeki no Arano kara* [From the wilderness of drama]. Tokyo: Seikyū-sha, 1984.

Kisaragi, Koharu. *Toshi Minzoku no Shibaigoya* [Playhouses for city people]. Chikuma Shobō, 1980.

Kishida, Rio. *Genso Yugi* [The play of fantasy]. Jiritsu Shobō, 1987.

Kitagawa, Toen. *Syumaku no Shiso* [Thoughts of the end]. Hakusui-sha, 1995.

Kobayashi, Nobuhiko. *Kigeki Jin ni Hanataba o.* [Flowers for the comic actors]. Shinchō-sha, 1996.

—— . *Nihon no Kigeki Jin* [Japanese comic actors]. Shinchō-sha, 1982.

Kurabayashi, Seiichiro. *Gekidan wa Ikiteiru* [Living theatre]. Gekidan Kyo, 1996.

Miyazawa, Akio. *Kangaeru Mizu, Kono Hoka no Ishi* [The thinking water, the other stones]. Dōbun Shoin, 1995.

Nishido, Kojin. *Shogekijo wa Shimetsu Shitaka* [Has the Little Theatre movement passed?]. Renga Shobō Shinsha, 1996.

Nomura, Takashi. *Gikyoku to Butai* [Dramas and stages]. Liburo, 1996.

Ortolani, Benito. *The Japanese Theatre from Shamanistic Ritual to Contemporary Pluralism*. Revised edn. Princeton, NJ: Princeton University Press, 1995. 375 pp.

Ōta, Shōgo. *Hisho to Kensui* [Soaring and suspension]. Jiritsu Shobō, 1975.

—— . *Rakei no Gekijo* [Uncovered theatre]. Jiritsu Shobō, 1980.

Ōzasa, Yoshio. *Dojidai Engeki to Gekisakka Tachi* [Contemporary theatre and its playwrights]. Geki Shobō, 1980.

—— . *Dorama no Seishin-shi* [The spiritual history of drama]. Shinsui-sha, 1983.

—— . *Gendai Engeki no Mori* [The forest of contemporary theatre]. Kodan-sha, 1994.

Saeki, Ryuko. *Ika suru Jikan* [Alienated time]. Shōbun-sha, 1973.

Senda, Akihiko. *Hirakareta Gekijo* [The open theatre]. Shōbun-sha, 1976.

—— . *Theatrical Renaissance*. Shōbun-sha. 1983.

—— . *The Voyage of Contemporary Japanese Theatre*. Honolulu: University of Hawaii Press, 1995.

Shichiji, Eisuke. *Ekkyo suru Engeki* [Theatre crossing the border]. San-ichi Shobō, 1997.

Shinido, Kojin. *Mirukoto no Boken* [The adventure of seeing]. Renga Shobō Shinsha, 1991.

Suzuki, Tadashi. *Media no Genzai* [The present media]. Perkian-sha, 1991.

—— . *Naikaku no Wa* [The sum of interior angles]. Jiritsu Shobō, 1973.

—— . *The Way of Acting: The Theatre Writings of Tadashi Suzuki*. New York: Theatre Communications Group, 1986.

Terayama, Shuji. *Meiro to Shikai* [Labyrinths and the Dead Sea]. Hakusui-sha, 1993.

Tomita, Hiroyuki. *The History of Theatre for Young Audiences in Japan*. Tokyo: Shoseki, 1976.

Periodicals

Asian Theatre Journal. 1984–present.

Canadian Theatre Review (CTR 20). Special issue on contemporary Japanese theatre including the full text in English of Sato Makoto's play, *My Beatles* (fall 1978): 46–79.

Concerned Theatre Japan. Edited by David G. Goodman.

Engeki Book [The Drama Book]. Engeki Bukku-sha (Drama Book Co.).

Higeki Kigeki [Tragedy Comedy]. Hayakawa Shobo.

JAMCI. Matsumoto Kobo.

Teatero [Theatre]. Teatoron-sha (Theatron Co.).

Theatre Arts. Published by Kokusai Engeki Hyoronka Kyokai (International Association of Theatre Critics). Bansei Shobo.

KAMPUCHEA

(see **CAMBODIA**)

KAZAKHSTAN

(Overview)

Formerly known as the Kazakh Soviet Socialist Republic when it was part of the Soviet Union, Kazakhstan is roughly five times the size of France with a land area of 2,717,300 square kilometres (1,049,200 square miles). The second largest republic in the Commonwealth of Independent States, Kazakhstan extends from China on the east to European Russia on the west. To the south it is bordered by Kyrgyzstan, Uzbekistan and Turkmenistan. Almaty, formerly Alma-Ata, is the capital and largest city with 1,147,000 inhabitants.

With an estimated population of 17,267,600 in 1994, Kazakhstan is unique among the republics of the former USSR in terms of ethnic composition. Kazakhs constitute a minority – less than half the total population – in their own country. They are still, however, the single largest ethnic group, with 43.2 per cent of the total population. Russians, the next largest group, constitute 36.5 per cent.

Beginning in the nineteenth century, large-scale immigration boosted the number of Russians and other peoples, while the number of Kazakhs declined as a result of attacks by Russian settlers and forced collectivization. Large numbers of Germans (4.1 per cent of the total) and Ukrainians (5.2 per cent) also reside in the republic. Some Kazakhs are followers of Islam. The official state language is Kazakh, but only about 40 per cent of the population speaks this Turkic language. Russian is the most widely spoken language in the country.

Almost 60 per cent of Kazakhstan is urbanized, the highest level of urbanization among the republics in central Asia. Slavs are concentrated in the north and in large urban areas, especially Almaty, where they constitute a majority. Formerly an agrarian society, the Kazakh economy underwent rapid industrialization during the Soviet period. As a result, nomadic lifestyles have almost completely disappeared from modern Kazakhstan. In 1993 the country adopted its own constitution and a year later a free-trade zone was established between Uzbekistan and Kazakhstan, which was soon joined by Kyrgyzstan.

The region that is now Kazakhstan was originally settled by Turkic tribes in about the eighth century and it was incorporated into the Mongol Empire of Genghis Khan in the thirteenth century. The Kazakhs, a mixture of Mongol and Turkic peoples, emerged in about the fifteenth century. Russian intrusions into what is now Kazakhstan began in the sixteenth century; by the end of the seventeenth century, a formal relationship had developed between the czarist government in Russia and the Cossacks, who protected the Russian frontier in exchange for title to land and local autonomy. In the eighteenth century a line of Cossack settlements and fortifications was established across the northern boundary of the steppe region in Kazakhstan in order to defend the Russian frontier against incursions of Kazakhs and other nomads. By 1866 all of present-day Kazakhstan was under their control. Cossack outposts grew into peasant settlements when a large number of Russian and other Slavic immigrants coming to the steppe increased.

After the socialist revolution of 1917, an autonomous republic was established in eastern Kazakhstan but was quickly absorbed by Bolshevik forces. In 1920 the area of present-day Kazakhstan was organized as an autonomous republic. In 1936 it was admitted to the USSR as a constituent republic.

In the late 1920s Soviet authorities under Joseph Stalin instituted a policy of forced settlement and collectivization of the nomadic Kazakh population. As a result of the policy, Kazakh culture and lifestyle were destroyed. Hundreds of thousands of Kazakhs were killed and many others emigrated to China. In 1954 the Soviet government launched the Virgin and Idle Lands Programme and a new wave of Slavic immigrants flooded into the republic. As a result, Slavs for a time became the largest ethnic group, a position they relinquished to the Kazakhs some years later.

In the Kazakh Constitution of 1924, Russian and Kazakh had both been proclaimed official state languages, but over the next decades Russification prevailed. There were also two changes of script, from Arabic to Latin in 1929, then from Latin to Cyrillic in 1940. In 1990 Nursultan Nazarbayev became president of the Kazakh Soviet Socialist Republic and re-established a close economic, military and political relationship with Russia.

Kazakh folk art has itself been shaped during the course of many centuries by the country's feudal patriarchy and traditional nomadic life. Although the country had no written literature, it did have a rich poetic and musical folklore. Songs, stories and legends expressed the bitter lot of the people suffering under twofold oppression – that of the feudal rich and the czar's tyranny. Such stories and legends spoke of populist dreams of freedom and a better life.

Communal games, wedding rituals, public events and *kyz-oinaks* (dramatic sketches) also contain clearly theatrical elements. Also developed was *ku*, an often improvised solo comic art. Similar to the art of *skomorokhs* (buffoons) in old Russia, a *ku* performer needed a good, richly modulated voice, a well-trained body and a flair for pantomime and improvisation. Part storyteller, part historian, the *ku* actor knew the history of the people and had a keen eye for human vice and weakness that he would both speak about and ridicule.

Various types of competitions were extremely popular including *aityses* (contests of poets), *akyns* (contests by folk poet-singers) and contests among musicians. All artists were at the same time authors, improvisors and performers and were known as *sal* or *sari*. Invited as guests of honour to feasts and celebrations, they wore bright clothing and performed to the accompaniment of string instruments called *dombra* and *kobyz*. The *aitys* itself is both a contest in speaking skills as well as a dispute, a kind of discussion of current community issues. The songs and aphorisms for the *akyns* were very theatrical in nature and often passed down through generations, becoming part of the indigenous cultural heritage. An occasional *aityses* could still be seen even in the 1980s.

The intensive process of cultural colonization in the nineteenth century led to the total Europeanization and Russification of Kazakh life in many spheres of activity, especially in literature and the performing arts. After 1917, Sovietization was added as well to these dual systems of impact. Theatrically the manifestation of this was the development of written plays without music. By the early twentieth century, local amateur groups began to emerge in the larger cities and attracted young intellectuals.

It was after the October Socialist Revolution in 1917 that many newly organized, mobile, semi-professional companies began to emerge, each playing a propagandistic role among the indigenous population. January 1926 marked the birth of the first Kazakh State Theatre in the old capital of Kzyl-Orda. When the capital was transferred to Alma-Ata in 1928, the theatre moved as well. Though the first Kazakh-written drama, *Maldybai* by I. Mendykhanov, appeared in 1912, the real father of written national drama is considered to be Mukhtar Auezov (b. 1897). His *Karakoz, Enlik-Kebek* and *Abai* (1940) are rich in folkloric elements and all later became Kazakh classics. In the 1930s and 1940s, the most popular dramatist was Gabit Musrepov whose major works based on legends were *Kyz-Zhibek* (1934) and *Kozy-Korpesh and Bayan-Slu* (1940), both romantic tragedies directed by M. Nasonov. In 1937, the theatre received the title of the Kazakh Academic Drama Theatre and became a genuine centre of national theatrical art.

During this same period, traditional art forms were discouraged, officially regarded as 'primitive' and gradually replaced with modern – that is, European/Russian/Soviet – art forms. Kazakh Soviet art at this time reflected political priorities including plays about the rise of Soviet power, the subsequent industrialization of the country and collectivization of agriculture, the advantages of socialism and the wisdom of communist leaders. This was similar in all the Soviet republics. The only national features to be found in these works were the specific locales of the plays and some folkloric touches in costumes or historic details. 'Idealization of the past' had to be carefully avoided by theatres and playwrights since it was considered 'anti-Soviet', a label which could ruin any career. During the Great Patriotic War (1941–5) historical plays made up a considerable part of the Kazakh theatre repertoire. In this genre, *Akhan-Sere and Aktokty* (1942) by Musrepov and the folk-comedy *Aldar-Kose* by Shakhmet Khusainov and *Kara Kipchak Koblandy* by Mukhtar Auerzov are worth mentioning.

The anti-fascist play *Professor Mamlock* by Friedrich Wolf became the first foreign play to be seen on a Kazakh stage. Another significant play, *Guard of Honor* (1942) by Auezov and Alzhapar Abishev, was a study in the selfless heroism of Kazakh soldiers on the battlefield.

As in all the Soviet Asian republics during this war period, Kazakhstan was a temporary home for theatre groups from the Ukraine, Russia and Belarus. Staged near the end of the war was a memorable production of Shakespeare's *Much Ado About Nothing* (1945) by two Russian directors – Olga Pyzhova and Boris Bibikov – with two Kazakh stars, Khadisha Bukeyeva (Kate) and Shaken Aimanov (Petruchio).

The post-war years showed the need for skilful directors. Though the State Theatre expanded its range of genres and subjects, it was still constrained by socialist-realism, the state policy from 1946. Performances on current events were prevalent and popular subjects included the reconstruction of the countryside and collective farming as seen in *Spring Wind* (1953) and *Yesterday and Today* (1955) by Khusainov and *Single Family* (1949) by Abishev. These and many other works like them fulfilled an ideological function rather than a creative one; they were similar to hundreds of conflictless performances seen all across the USSR. The only modest achievement in the field during these years was the general improvement in standards of production of Russian and foreign classics by writers such as Ostrovsky and Molière.

Perhaps the most popular comedy of the 1950s was Abishev's *Envy* (1955) staged by M. Goldblat at the Academic Theatre and subsequently restaged all across the republic. Later Goldblat was severely criticized for his work and ultimately fired.

The mid-1950s – the years of the Khrushchev thaw – also saw a relaxation in official strictures and censorship and the Kazakh theatre tried to overcome its outdated repertoire and its dramatic weaknesses. Although the themes generally remained the same, liberalization allowed authors to examine reality with a new critical and even humorous attitude.

The 1960s saw the emergence of a greater number of plays by young dramatists. The production of the first play by Kaltai Mukhamedzhanov, *A Wolf-Cub Under a Hat* (1959), a comedy about the life of Kazakh city youth, was staged by a young director, Azerbaizhan Mambetov, a graduate of GITIS (State Institute of Theatre Arts in Moscow) directing department in 1957. A second successful comedy by Mukhamedzhanov, *The Match-Maker Has Arrived* (also directed by Mambetov) followed. Soon after came the first Kazakh musical comedy, *Oh, Those Girls!* by K. Shangitbayev and K. Baiseitov. Popular throughout the Soviet Asian republics, it helped develop a new taste for the rich traditions of Kazakh comedy.

The many changes in the country at this time found their dramatic expression in *Saule*, where the conflict between the two styles of Communist Party leadership appeared for the first time on a stage. Less a criticism of the system than a response to new party policy and changes in the country's moral atmosphere, this play by Takhari Akhtanov, along with *Buddies* by A. Tazhibaev, showed selfless fighters for social justice and continued to support utopian communist ideals.

Stage adaptations of important literary works began to be introduced to the repertoires of all Soviet theatres in the 1960s. Among Kazakh adaptations, a popular favourite was the original stories of Chengiz Aitmatov. Two plays based on his works, *Poplar in a Red Kerchief* and *The First Teacher*, were successfully staged by the newly formed Kazakh Young Audiences Theatre. Aitmatov's story, *Mother's Field*, was produced by the Academic Theatre in 1964 and proved a major event in the theatre season. A tale of the fate of Soviet women and mothers, the production, directed by Mambetov, turned it into an epic populist tragedy. Mambetov's later productions were also powerful and his work dominated the Kazakh Academic Theatre from the early 1960s until the end of the 1970s, when he left for work at the Kazakh Film Studio. Mambetov was replaced as director of the Academic Theatre by Baiten

Omarov, and manager-director-actor Raimbek Seitmetov, who favoured both national works and modern plays. The large-scale drama *Morning Echo*, an epic adaptation of Auezov's novel, was Omarov's début. He then staged *Apkee* (*Elder Sister*) by Dulat Isabekov. It was during this period that the Kazakh theatre saw its first productions of Pirandello, García Lorca and plays by several eastern European playwrights, all staged by Seitmetov. In 1982 Mambetov staged a powerful *Uncle Vanya* with Vanya played as a lonely idealist by A. Moldabekov. In 1988 Mambetov returned as director of the Academic Theatre.

Also operating in the capital at this time was the Lermontov Russian Drama Theatre whose repertoire was even more tightly connected to the propagandistic tasks of the USSR. In the 1970s, the theatre staged plays for major socialist anniversaries and about the struggle for Soviet power in Kazakhstan. However, playful performances, directed by M. Mamilov – *Til Ulenspiegel* by Grigory Gorin, *Amadeus* by

Til Ulenspiegel by Gigory Gorin, directed by M. Mamilov and performed at Lermontov Russian Drama Theatre.
Photo: courtesy of *Teatr*.

The Mysteries of Mukams at the Uighur Music and Drama Theatre.
Photo: courtesy of *Teatr*.

Peter Shaffer and Russian fairytales for children – were more popular with audiences.

By the end of the 1980s, a new openness had finally emerged, one in which theatre professionals discussed the lack of gifted directors and objective theatre criticism and called for playwrights of significance. Good plays, it was argued, appeared too rarely and the republic's theatres felt a genuine lack of interesting material. Among the new dramatists of note to appear were Takhari Akhtanov, Kaltai Mukhamedzhanov, Sakenu Zhunusov and Akim Tarazi but too often their plays featured stereotypical subjects, characters and conflicts.

By the 1990s as well, the ideas of Mambetov were too strong to let other talents emerge. What new energy there was seemed to come from the theatre work of the minority ethnic theatres, particularly the Uighur Music and Drama theatre. Founded in 1934 in Almaty, the company maintained a genuine consciousness of its national heritage and developed traditions within Kazakhstan's multinational makeup. Through its history, it developed a number of significant folk epics and realized its own traditions, as in the musical drama *Anarkhan* (1976) staged by Mambetov as a people's tragedy, or in spectacular musical performances such as *The Mysteries of Mukams* (1981). Its repertoire too was varied and included plays by Kazakh authors along with Russian and internationally known writers.

In the years since independence, the Kazakh theatre – like all theatre communities in the former Soviet Union – has suffered economically. State support has all but disappeared. Yet the few groups that have survived seem determined to revivify theatre in all its manifestations and make theatre once again an art that responds effectively to a wide and varied community.

Natasha Rapoport

Further Reading

Akiner, Shirin. *The Formation of Kazakh Identity*. London: Royal Institute of International Affairs, 1995. 83 pp.

Ikov, A. *Gastroli Uigurskogo respublikanskogo muzykalno-dramaticheskogo teatra* [Tour of Uighur Republican Musical-Drama Theatre]. *Teatr* 11 (1981).

Istoria sovetskogo dramaticheskogo teatra [History of Soviet dramatic theatre]. 6 vols. Moscow: Nauka, 1966–71.

Kabdiyeva, Sania. *Farida Sharipova. Teatr* 1 (1981).

Kaidalova, O. *Traditsii i sovremennost. Teatralnoye iskusstvo Srednei Azii i Kazakhstana* [Traditions and contemporaneity. Theatrical art of Middle Asia and Kazakhstan]. Moscow: Iskusstvo, 1977. 296 pp.

Kaskabasov, S.A. *Rodniki iskusstva: Folkloristskie etjudy* [Wellsprings of art: Folklore sketches]. Almaty: Oner, 1986. 123 pp.

Kholodova, Galina. *Tragedia Voinitskogo* [Tragedy of Voinitsky]. *Teatr* 3 (1983).

Lvov, N. *Kazakhski teatr* [Kazakh theatre]. Moscow: Iskustvo, 1961. 190 pp.

Turovsky, Valerii. *Uroki masterstva i masterstvo urokov* [Lessons of skills and skills of lessons]. *Teatr* 10 (1979).

KHMER REPUBLIC

(see **CAMBODIA**)

KIRGHIZIA

(see **KYRGYZSTAN**)

KIRIBATI

(see **SOUTH PACIFIC**)

KOREA

Divided into two republics since 1948, Korea is located on a peninsula in northeast Asia roughly 1,000 kilometres (600 miles) long and 215 kilometres (135 miles) wide at its narrowest point. North and South Korea together cover a land area of 219,000 square kilometres (84,500 square miles). The two Koreas had a combined 1995 population of approximately 69 million (of which almost 49 million lived in the south) and all of whom speak a single language, Korean. One of the most ethnically homogenous countries in the world, Korea also has one of Asia's highest literacy rates, nearly 100 per cent. The Korean alphabet, Han-gul, consists of ten vowels and fourteen consonants and was created by a group of scholars under the patronage of King Sejon in 1443.

Mountains cover some 70 per cent of Korea's land area with the peninsula divided into north and south slightly north of the thirty-eighth parallel. In the south lies the Republic of Korea, also known as South Korea, while in the north is the People's Republic of Korea, also known as

North Korea. South Korea consists of nine provinces, one special city (the capital, Seoul) and five major cities, Pusan, Taegu, Inch'on, Kwangju and Taejon.

The ethnic roots of the Korean people lie in Mongolia and other parts of northeastern Asia. The earliest Korean state was Old Chosun in the northwestern part of the country. Conquered by the Chinese in 108 BC, colonies were established that served as outposts of Chinese civilization. Until AD 313, the Chinese colonists lived peacefully alongside the people of Korguryo, a Korean kingdom located in the same area. When Chinese influence in the area weakened in the third and fourth centuries, the kingdoms of Paekche and Silla emerged and, on the southern coast, Kaya. In the mid-sixth century, Kaya was conquered by Silla and Korguryo and Paekche suffered territorial losses. All these kingdoms had individual strengths: Korguryo was a military power, Silla had a strong and stable socio-political structure, and Paekche, with extensive relations with China and Japan, had a high social standard but was militarily weak. Ultimately, Silla, with the help of China's Tang dynasty, absorbed the other two states and established the first unified Korean state.

Buddhism was a powerful influence in shaping Silla's intellectual and artistic sensibilities and it was Silla's indigenous culture which was the principal impetus for Korean cultural and social evolution. A distinctive Korean state developed by the tenth century. In 1904, Korea was conquered by the Japanese; in 1910 it became a Japanese colony and Japanese political and cultural influence became strong.

In August 1945 Japan surrendered to the Allies and ultimately withdrew from the Korean Peninsula, leaving the Soviet Union to control the north and the United States to control the south. In 1948, South Korea established an independent government. North Korea invaded the south in June 1950, setting off the Korean War. When the war came to an end (or rather was suspended by truce talks) two Koreas – and one of the world's most heavily armed borders – came into being, a situation which continued to exist in the late 1990s with Seoul the capital of the Republic of Korea and P'yongyang the capital of the People's Republic of Korea.

In the south, a military dictatorship came to power in 1960 and gradually imposed censorship and regulations against various social activities including journalism and the arts. It pushed its policies towards clear dictatorship through the so-called Yushin Constitution. Military governments ruled until 1993 when Kim Young-Sam was elected president, the nation's first genuinely civilian government in thirty-two years.

Performative elements have existed in Korean culture for some 5,000 years with *kugak* (music) and dance evolving into recognizable and separate performing arts over the centuries. The court forms tend to be slow and complicated while the folk forms are faster and more lively. Also utilized in many of these forms are masks. The *kkoktu kaksi* (puppet forms) emerged between the seventh and fourteenth centuries, probably via itinerant players from other parts of Asia. Part hand-puppet, part rod-puppet and part string-puppet, the *kkoktu* is essentially a satirical art utilizing standard character types. During the Choson period (1392–1910) regular performances of both masked and unmasked dance-dramas began to be seen, the masked dances (rooted in court performances) called *sandae-guk* and the non-masked song plays called *chaphui*.

Masks are utilized in many Korean performance forms.
Photo: courtesy of Korea National Tourism Corporation.

Nineteenth-century Korean theatre was based primarily on these traditional forms as well as on the aforementioned *p'ansori* (itself a traditional solo chant utilizing what sounds to be hoarse voices) and other arts such as acrobatics. Actor improvisations added new elements. Over the early decades of the twentieth century traditional forms began to merge with newer forms influenced by events taking place primarily in Japan and in the west. By the 1920s, several new styles were being seen, among them a western-style, text-based theatre known historically as the New Theatre and represented most effectively by the Towol Hoe group; the *shin-pa*, a popular musical and comedy theatre linked to several earlier traditions; and a politically oriented Leftist theatre represented by groups such as the Yumkoon (founded in 1923) and the Poolkaemi (founded in 1927).

In 1902 Korea's first indoor theatre was built, the Hyup-yul-sa, a space subsidized and supported by the royal family and whose repertoire consisted heavily of *pan-sori*. Attacked by traditionalists and Confucians for misleading and corrupting young people and the national spirit, the theatre was closed in 1906 as much for mismanagement as anything else. Another early attempt at creating a new-style theatre was seen in 1908 with the opening of the Wongaksa Theatre. Text-based but with traditional links, the theatre attracted attention with its production of *Eunsegye* (*The Snow-Covered World*) by Lee In Jik (1862–1916). Unfortunately, the theatre was closed down following Japan's annexation of the country. With the annexation,

Japanese authorities attacked virtually all Korean traditions including the various music dance and theatre forms, attempting to wipe them out in the process. Indeed, between 1930 and 1945, masked dance performances and puppet performances were banned by the Japanese colonial administration.

Shin-pa theatre, however, a form connected to Japanese contemporary culture, was encouraged. A Japanese word meaning new-style (the comparison in Japan being with the old style of *noh* and *kabuki*), *shin-pa*, though concerned initially with political enlightenment and elements of propaganda, eventually popularized itself, becoming melded with everything from war stories, mysteries and melodramas to sentimental love stories. Such shows – involving music – had their greatest popularity between 1904 and 1921 with the most important group being the Hyukshin Dan founded in 1911 and run by Lim Sung Ku (b. 1887) until his death in 1921. Most of the group's plays were basic confrontations between good and evil, or about the importance of social fidelity and the political enlightenment of the illiterate. Lim's death led to the break-up of the group. Though other groups survived into the late 1920s (Chuisungjwa, for example, a group started by Kim So Rang, was still touring as late as 1929), the popularity of the style faded quickly.

It was in 1920 that Hyun Chul (1891–1965) returned to Korea from Japan where he had studied with Shimamura Hogetsu, head of Tokyo's Geijutsu-za. Hyun soon established his own acting school, the Yesool Hakwon, which introduced a more literary theatre to the country, the *shin-guk* or what came to be called the New Theatre. Among the school's early productions were Ibsen's *A Doll's House*, two Chekhov one-acts (*The Bear* and *The Marriage Proposal*) and *Hamlet*, translated by Hyun Chul based on an earlier Japanese translation. Western plays began to be studied by several literary groups including Keukyesool Hyuphoe (Theatre Arts Association). The group in 1923 began its own amateur touring company – calling it Tongwu Hoe (Earth and Moon Society) – and spread the New Theatre style even further. The first Korean play in the New Theatre style was staged by Tongwu Hoe, *The Death of Kim Yong II* by Cho Myung Hi, and was toured to some twenty-five cities under the direction of Park Seung Hee. It was this group more than any other that established the New Theatre in Korea, staging countless original, translated and adapted plays from the international repertoire. The group also produced a number of major artists who would influence the national style for many years to come, including actress Pok Hye Sook, actors Suk Kim Sung and Su Wul Yung and designer Wun Woo Chun, among others. Park himself contributed over 200 pieces to the repertoire and was responsible for the establishment of playwrights such as Lee Suk Woo and Park Chin. The company introduced realism into the Korean theatre through acting style, costume and setting, the use of the vernacular on stage and through a directing style based on fidelity to the text.

By the 1930s, interest in the New Theatre had grown considerably, triggering the creation of a theatre arts research association in 1931 called Keukyesool Yungoohoe. Organized by a group of university people majoring in western literature, this group of intellectuals aimed to broaden the popular base for New Theatre, to improve the methods and skills of the existing New Theatre groups and to offer workshops and lectures in the field. In 1932, the group staged its first experimental production, Gogol's *Revizor* (*The Government Inspector*), directed by Hong Hae Sung. According to contemporary reviews, it was the best new theatre production seen in Korea since the days of the Towol Hoe ten years earlier.

Hong remained director of the Keukyesool Yungoohoe (its official name until 1938) through 1934. Trained in Tokyo at the Tsukiji Shogekijo, his repertoire consisted of mainly translated foreign plays. The influence of Tsukiji was clearly perceptible, however. Among his major productions were Chekhov's *Cherry Orchard* and a German expressionist play from 1918, Reinhard Goering's *Seeschlacht*. Focusing for the most part on western realism, only two of his eleven productions were original scripts by Korean writers. Yet the fact that there were two indicates his interest in helping to develop Korean dramatists interested in working in this form. For the record, the most successful of the two was Yoo Chi Jin's *Tomak* (*The Mud Hut*).

Yoo himself took over as co-director of the group when Hong left to pursue more commercial interests. Working with Suh Hang Suk as his co-director, Yoo tended to support the production and development of Korean plays though he still produced an interesting selection of the European and North American repertoire including Schnitzler's *Blind Brother*, Heyward's *Porgy*, Galsworthy's *The Winner and the Loser* and Tolstoy's *Resurrection* (adapted from the novel). Among the Korean plays staged were Lee Moo Yung's *Daydreamers*, his own *Chesa* (*The Memorial Service*), Lee Kwang Rae's *Master Park* and Lee Soo Hyang's *Omoni* (*Mother*).

By 1938, a new generation of young Koreans moved into the theatre, most having been trained at the Korean Student Arts Theatre in Tokyo. The group changed its name at this point to Keukyunjwa and produced many western plays including Maxwell Anderson's *Winterset* and Clifford Odets's *Awake and Sing*. But despite the connections with Japan, Japanese occupation authorities became distrustful of the group and forced it to disband in 1939 through censorship, arrests and the suppression of one of Yoo's best plays, *So* (*The Cow*, 1934). The play was not seen again until 1942 when it was rewritten and retitled with some of the harsher criticisms taken out. His later work showed a retreat from realism to a new romanticism and eventually into historical subject matter. Though criticized by some for his caution, the fact is that Japanese colonial policies were extremely strict and Yoo had little choice in the matter.

Looking back, it is difficult to offer a decisive judgement on this important early group. On the one hand, it is clear that Keukyesool Yungoohoe was ideologically neutral, politically and artistically extremely conservative and an extension of Japanese student influences. It was too heavily dependent on foreign scripts, essentially an amateur activity, too occasional in terms of frequency of productions and showed a tendency towards commercialization towards the end of its existence. On the other hand, it introduced both foreign and original plays in a new style to Korean audiences in a serious way, introduced new styles of realism as well as expressionism and western satire to the stage, legitimized the study of theatre and dramatic theory and upgraded the quality of stage performance from folk-oriented to professional levels. Whatever the final opinion might be, it is clear that this group was the primary agent for extending the impulses of the New Theatre movement during the 1930s and that it was the most important group of its type to emerge in Korea since the Tongwu Hoe experiments of the early 1920s.

Parallel to the New Theatre movement during the 1920s and 1930s was the rapid development of the Leftist Theatre in such cities as Seoul, Taegu, Kaesan, Haeju, Hamheung and Pyungyang. Mostly limited to less formal outdoor spaces because of constant monitoring by Japanese authorities, productions took place widely but sporadically. Other theatre activities included a growth in commercial productions in both the major cities and on tour and the appearance of several student theatre groups, some tending towards political work and others tending towards the more literary New Theatre.

Of the commercial initiatives, the most representative was Tongyang Keukchang in Seoul. In 1935, its management built the country's first commercial playhouse and supported regular seasons by two groups under its sponsorship – Chungchoonjwa and Howhasun. When one played in Seoul, the other toured. Their popular repertoires – *Deceived in Love and Defrauded in Money*, *Choon Hyang Jun* and *Mother's Love* – attracted large and responsive audiences. Tongyang Keukchang remained the only commercial management in the country until 1945.

It was in December 1940 that the Japanese authorities decided to impose further controls on the Korean theatre through the organization of a new state-supported theatre association, the Chosun Yunkeuk Hyuphoe. Two years later they also began the Chosun Moonwha Hyuphoe (Korean Theatre Culture Association). Both groups attempted to eliminate Korean language and culture from the stage and to undercut indigenous cultural values. These early years of the 1940s were a dark period indeed for Korean theatre and for Koreans themselves.

By 1945, the Leftist Theatre which had been almost extinct in the last years of the war, began to re-emerge with new force. Its advocates quickly took over the Japanese-founded Chosun Moonwha Hyuphoe and reorganized it under the name Yunkeuk Konsul Ponbo (Theatre Rehabilitation Headquarters). Also redirecting the Korean Theatre union under the banner of progressive theatre, Theatre Rehabilitation Headquarters absorbed a number of commercial groups as well as many newly formed groups with leftist tendencies. Through early 1947, these groups dominated Korean theatre life. Their productions consisted mainly of political or historical plays but generally lacked depth and rarely went beyond sentimentality and propaganda.

The re-establishment of Keukyesool Yungoohoe in 1946 was the beginning of the new anti-leftist movement and it was soon followed by Keukyesool Hyuphoe (Theatre Arts Association) in 1947. Yoo Chi Jin, still a leading dramatist, wrote a series of nationalistic plays arguing against left-wing policies. Even more decisive was a US Military Government policy which banned left-wing theatre people from performing. Only the commercial *shin-pa* groups managed to survive this difficult period virtually untouched.

Perhaps the most important event in Korean theatre between World War II and the outbreak of the Korean War was the establishment of a national theatre. Discussed by leading theatre people as early as 1946, plans for such a theatre were brought up in the new National Assembly just after independence in 1948. Just two months before the Korean War, plans were formally approved with Yoo Chi Jin to be its first director and two companies to be attached to it, Shinhyup and Keukhyup. In April 1950, the theatre staged its first production and in June its second production (the latter attracting the largest audience in Korean history). But the war frustrated the National Theatre's success. During the war period, the National Theatre moved its base of operations to Taegu but offered little in the way of theatrical initiative.

By the time the war ended, many performers and directors had left Seoul for other countries and other cities, a number of them moving to the north for political reasons. The National Theatre – indeed the theatre generally – was virtually without resources by this time. The theatre faced a lack of financial support, a lack of public interest and a lack of government policy in the artistic field. Returning to Seoul, the National had to rent Shikongkwan (Citizen's Hall) out of its very modest government subsidy.

Among the few bright lights during this time was the work of Shinhyup. Separating itself from the National, the company toured widely in the Pusan and Taegu areas and almost as soon as the war ended the group returned to Seoul and began to offer performances there. It had already staged *Hamlet* in 1951 and had followed its success with productions of *Othello* and *Macbeth*. Before the war ended it had staged a number of plays by Yoo Chi Jin and after the war ended included in its repertoire plays by Tennessee Williams and Arthur Miller. By the end of the 1950s, the group had staged more than fifty productions, about half of them Korean works. Directed by Lee Hae Rang with Yoo Chi Jin as its resident playwright, the company established 50 per cent as a norm for the balance between national and foreign plays. It also established Kim Tong Won as one of the country's leading actors.

Among the first of the new post-war groups to emerge was Chejak Keukhoe (Production Theatre Group), founded in 1956. Defining

itself as a 'truly modern' theatre group, it constantly compared its work to Shinhyup which it called apathetic and establishment. Chejak Keukhoe staged plays by younger Korean writers and tried to absorb new trends from abroad. One of its major successes came in 1960 when it staged a production of John Osborne's *Look Back in Anger*. But the freedom of the early 1960s – including its many student protests – was short-lived; by 1962 the military coup by Park Chung Hee deposed the civilian government. Nevertheless, changes had been made: many new voices, both as writers and on the stage, had emerged and a new, non-commercial movement had been initiated. Akin to 'off' and 'alternative' movements in other countries, these new experimental groups – known as Little Theatres – funded their own activities from the pockets of their members. One of the early successes of the movement was a production of Eugène Ionesco's *The Lesson* which clearly reflected the new temperament and attitudes of the period. By the end of the decade, nearly a dozen such groups existed in Seoul, each working to present seasons with unprecedented openness. Heavily influenced by European and North American experimental theatre, they also staged the occasional production of a western classic by Shakespeare, Molière and Goldoni. New plays by young writers on themes of immediate significance, however, were the real stock and trade of these new groups.

It was television more than anything else that sapped the vitality of the Korean theatre in the late 1960s and 1970s. The popularity of the electronic media had become enormous and almost everyone who would support the theatre had a television by this time. Actors, directors and writers all found that television paid considerably more than the stage and many artists simply left for its greener fields. Those who remained in theatre were the idealists, isolated but unyielding. Further exacerbating the situation was a lack of suitable playhouses and the shrinking audiences (made up mostly of university students) made commercial exploitation of any successful production almost impossible.

The National Theatre was restructured in 1961 with the military government transferring its administrative functions from the Ministry of Education to the Office of Public Information (later to become the Ministry of Culture and Public Information). The theatre was given Citizen's Hall as its exclusive performance space and was encouraged to include opera and ballet in its mandate. Over the next eleven years, the company produced forty-one plays, thirty-three of them by Korean dramatists (a sharp contrast to the experimental groups whose repertoires were heavily foreign). At the same time, though, the new support for the National Theatre had a number of negative effects. The government who chose the theatre's new director and the choice at the time was not a good one – the person appointed knew little about theatre. The budget, too, allowed little scope for anything the least bit out of the ordinary.

On the positive side, the extraordinary career of dramatist Yoo Chi Jin continued during this decade with his personal determination to establish a new playhouse. Already the founder of the Korean Centre of the International Theatre Institute (1958), an organization he chaired until his death in 1974, Yoo convinced the US Rockefeller Foundation to grant US$65,000 (the largest commitment ever made to a cultural initiative from abroad) towards the building of his new theatre centre. Adding these funds to money raised within the country, he built a theatre halfway up Namsam Mountain near the centre of Seoul. Completed in 1962, the Drama Centre's opening production was *Hamlet*. His original plans were to have the theatre operating year-round, to run shows for as long as possible, to produce an ensemble capable of staging both classical and new works, to establish a theatre school, and to set up a research institute housing a theatre museum. Only a few of his aims were met during his lifetime. The theatre's biggest problem was simply filling its 450 seats. Artistically, the work was less than hoped for since government subsidy continued to be meagre.

Another initiative of the 1960s was the celebration of the 400th anniversary of Shakespeare's birth in 1964. In honouring this occasion, a Shakespeare Quatercentenary Festival was held which sponsored eight major productions by seven different groups. The largest cultural event in Korean history, the festival lasted two months and attracted over 40,000 people. Whether this event succeeded in enlivening the theatre community of the country continues to be a moot point but there is no denying that the event had the immediate effect of injecting new energy into the theatre community of the time.

During the 1970s those writers who had started careers with the small theatres began to move on to larger ones. The decade seemed to be a continuing search for a redefinition of theatre.

New initiatives abounded such as experiments with Antonin Artaud's Theatre of Cruelty and in the expansion of collectively created works. The theatre community as a whole was becoming conscious of its needed national identity and of issues such as cultural independence. A number of directors began to utilize traditional theatre forms again involving dance, music and masks. Many such experiments were less than satisfying but the best of these made clear statements that something essential in the national psyche could still be touched. Students at Seoul National University, for example, utilized traditional satirical theatrical styles to protest government authoritarianism.

In 1973, the National Theatre moved to its own a new building but despite this improvement in space and technical resources the company continued to be hobbled by budgets that remained far below what the troupe needed to stage plays, ballets, operas and – as the government required – traditional forms. As a result, play selection remained far behind public taste.

Real state subsidy finally emerged as a force in 1974 with the establishment of the Korean Culture and Arts Foundation. Made possible by the country's growing economic strength and a renewed interest in the arts by a more affluent population, the new foundation supported activities in the fields of literature, fine arts, theatre, dance and music. It also supported major national ventures such as the Korean Theatre Festival (now called the Seoul Theatre Festival) which began in 1977 and which annually funds eight productions of new plays. The most successful productions are also encouraged to continue their runs at the Munye Theatre (opened in 1981). Funding of the foundation has generally increased each year.

The existence of state support also led to the creation of a number of new theatrical companies outside of Seoul. These regional troupes, many of them originally amateur groups, have since 1983 held their own national Regional Theatre Festival.

But even public funding has not really managed to improve the basic structure of the Korean theatre since the 1960s. Though the theatre now enjoys an unprecedented freedom of expression, it still has not made theatre a living part of the national culture honestly reflecting social realities and change. Nor has there been any improvement in methods of distribution of state support to allow new groups to emerge. And, of course, the continuing

Korean dance.
Photo: courtesy of Korea National Tourism Corporation.

growth of mass technology has continued to send younger generations in other directions.

In the late 1980s and into the 1990s, directors and writers have continued to experiment with a blending of modern and traditional forms, bringing together masked dances with political argument, *pan-sori* with the Brechtian epic, puppet plays with professional acting. Known as *madang keuk*, this crossover style of the 1980s and 1990s has utilized shamanistic rites and ancient-style masks, issues of political immorality and foreign dependency. Unfortunately, most of the actors working in this way do not have the skills needed to realize such experiments. Yet this movement seems to hold important promise for the future.

Structure of the National Theatre Community

Theatre in Korea is still not a professional affair if one uses the word professional in the western sense. There are some commercial endeavours and artists in these situations can earn significant sums of money. But there are also many small theatres in which the artists work for minimal amounts or sometimes even for nothing.

Government subsidy remains minimal and businesses rarely find any motivation to fund theatrical work. Nevertheless, a range of approaches exists including everything from commercial enterprises at one end of the spectrum to school performances at the other, from those engaged in the practice of traditional forms to those working in small experimental groups. In between, one finds typical spoken theatre groups in the capital (the National Theatre, for instance) and regional theatre groups in smaller cities.

The Korean National Theatre Association (KNTA), a nation-wide organization representing virtually all theatre people, numbers some 3,000 individuals and groups including various city representatives. Approximately 105 theatre groups are included in this number and 107 theatre facilities. There are probably at any given moment another 50 or so groups in operation who do not belong to the association. From a geographical standpoint, about 40 per cent of the membership in all categories of the association is based in Seoul. In the late 1980s, the association noted that there were approximately 1 million people who attended the theatre annually, a figure that was rising steadily. The KNTA acts as coordinator and peacemaker between the various theatre groups and theatrical interests. It is also the primary sponsor of the Seoul Theatre Festival in association with the Korean Arts and Culture Foundation.

Individual organizations also exist representing the interests of playwrights, directors, actors and critics. The Korean Centre of the International Theatre Institute is the oldest such centre in the eastern Asia. There are Korean

Sebbaram (*The East Wind*).
Photo: courtesy of ASSITEJ Japan.

sections of the International Association of Theatre Critics (AICT), the International Federation for Theatre Research (FIRT), the International Puppeteers' Union (UNIMA) and the International Association of Theatre for Children and Young People (ASSITEJ).

With the exception of the single National Theatre and three municipal theatres, all groups in Korea are organized as private ventures. Financial aid from the Korean Culture and Arts Foundation and other government sources is given only to groups who are invited to participate in the Seoul Theatre Festival (started in 1977) or in the Regional Theatre Festival (started in 1983). The only other official support given is the Aid Project for New Korean Plays begun in 1986. The Seoul Festival has regularly sent some of its winning writers, directors, designers and actors abroad for short periods to observe foreign trends.

About one-third of the country's actors earned over 2 million won in 1987, the last year for which figures are available. Just under half the country's actors earned less than 500,000 won. About 50 per cent of those who listed acting as their profession participated in four or more productions annually.

Groups in the capital stage on average some 140 productions per year, new plays accounting for some 42 per cent of the total.

Artistic Profile

Companies

Since World War II, some 200 different modern theatre groups have been formed in Korea. Some, of course, quickly disappeared but many have remained. On the one hand, this shows a remarkable interest in modern theatre; on the other, it shows a remarkable instability among these groups, considering that spoken theatre is still very much a minority art form.

The most important of the post-World War II groups is without doubt Shinyup, organized in 1950 as a subsidiary of the National Theatre. Its company was mainly recruited from the anti-left group Keukyesool Hyuphoe which was active until just after the war. Shinyup's opening production was Yoo Chi Jin's *Wonsoollang*, a historical play. When the Korean War began, the company continued its activities outside Seoul. Its repertoire was a mix of Korean and foreign plays, classics and Broadway hits. After 1960, the company lost much of its focus and became less and less important nationally. Yet its importance in continuing the heritage of the New Theatre and establishing realistic genres on the Korean stage cannot be overestimated. During its history it produced well over a hundred plays.

Chejak Keukhoe was formed in 1956 by a group of young actors concerned about what they felt to be Shinyup's commercialism. This group launched the Little Theatre movement in Korea and its alternative production styles attracted a wide range of university students as both members and as audience. Its motto was 'experiment and search'. Often staging one-act pieces by its company members, its production in 1960 of John Osborne's *Look Back in Anger* was a milestone in introducing new-style drama on the Korean stage. Eventually moving away from experimental work, the company became increasingly professional but at the same time lost much of its energy.

The first absurdist play performed in Korea was Eugène Ionesco's *The Lesson* by the Shilhum Keukchang (Experimental Theatre) of Seoul National University, a company founded on the Seoul University campus in 1960. Aimed at both the academic study of drama and at professional performance, the group quickly found itself in financial trouble. Its core members were eventually lured away by television but the group continued introducing new work to Korean audiences by dramatists such as Friedrich Dürrenmatt and Max Frisch. Eventually securing a 100-seat theatre of its own, it has staged over one hundred productions and continues in the 1990s as a force in the country's theatre community.

The Drama Centre was both a theatre space and a company created by Yoo Chi Jin in 1962 with support from the Rockefeller Foundation. Attracting leading artists from many of the established theatres, the company set as its goal 'the rehabilitation of the Korean theatre'. Within a year, however, financial problems slowed the company considerably, the size of the troupe was reduced and the number of productions cut back considerably. In the early 1970s, the company received a new influx of energy when Yoo's son, Yoo Duk Hyung, following his return from theatre studies at the University of Texas and Yale University, began doing experimental work with the troupe. Following Yoo Chi Jin's death in 1974, the company changed its name to the Tongrang Repertory Company, Tongrang being Yoo Chi Jin's *nom de plume*.

Kuklip Keukdan, founded in 1962, is committed to 'reviving national theatre through the production of original plays appropriate for national interests'. The company early on concentrated on discovering and producing original Korean plays. Part of the National Theatre after it moved into the new National Theatre building in 1973, it began to offer a safe blend of original and foreign works. There were times when the company seemed to represent official state policy too closely in its work but on the whole its commitment to Korean work remains unchallenged. From the 1980s, the company also began to experiment with traditional forms in a more modern context. Conservative in all areas, its foreign productions have included Greek tragedies and works by Shakespeare, Molière, Ibsen, Hauptmann and Chekhov among others.

A unique group emerging in the 1960s was Minjoong Keukchang. Attempting to be a 'theatre for the people', it was founded in 1963 by a group of university students and professors. Its early seasons consisted of satirical plays, most often by dramatist Lee Keun Sam. Still active, the company in the late 1980s began turning towards US drama ranging from David Mamet and Sam Shepard to popular musicals such as *Guys and Dolls*.

Sanha was founded in 1963 by a number of artists who had made their reputations on radio. Determined to popularize theatre, the group staged plays mostly by Cha Bum Suk. Also offering the occasional foreign play, the group tried to create a theatre 'attuned to the public but with high artistic values'. Sanha disbanded in 1983.

Kagyo (Bridge) was founded in the mid-1960s by graduates of several university drama departments. The company, whose members were mostly in their twenties, drew its repertoire from the plays of Edward Albee, Eugène Ionesco and Lee Keun Sam, a satirist. It later did tours to schools, churches and prisons.

Another company of note during the late 1960s and through the 1970s was Kwangjang.

Founded in 1966, it sought to reach a wide public by producing old and new plays from the European repertoire: Shakespeare, Chekhov, Wedekind and Dürrenmatt. Composed of established actors in their thirties and forties, the group occasionally tried its hand at new plays but had greater success with foreign works. By the late 1970s, it had started to move in a more commercial direction.

Also founded in 1966 was Chayoo Keukchang. Run by designer Lee Byung Bok and director Kim Chung Ok, the company operated in a financially innovative way, offering members shares of profits. Beginning with light comedies, Chayoo Keukchang staged an immensely successful production of Rolf Hochhuuth's *The Deputy* and also ran a café theatre where it staged new short pieces. By the late 1970s, the group changed its focus and began experimenting with improvisational work and later added traditional folk elements. Among the styles and ideas it has worked with have been Zen Buddhism, shamanism, *pan-sori*, puppets and mask dances. Its many experiments have drawn attention at festivals as far away as Spain, France and Japan.

One of the country's first women's groups was Yoin Keukchang, also founded in 1966. Early on, the company produced many plays by Tennessee Williams and García Lorca, plays that focused on women's issues. Later it added plays by Korean writers. Composed entirely of women, it would bring in male actors from other groups as needed. Since the 1980s, the company's repertoire has not differed significantly from other groups.

Other companies of note include Sungjwa, begun in 1969 with an emphasis on stage diction and which has had its major successes with Williams and O'Neill; Sanwoollim, founded in 1970, which has had particular success with the French avant-garde including Simone de Beauvoir's *La Femme rompue*; Minye Keukchang, another group whose work has focused on bridging traditional and modern theatre; and Yunwoo, founded in the 1980s and one of the few groups with a theatrically active social consciousness.

From the mid-1980s, many companies have experimented with the staging of western-style musicals. The more daring have attempted to blend these western musicals with traditional Korean styles of music and dance. The *madang keuk* style, for example, is generally performed outdoors (indeed the name means outdoor play) and includes improvised song and dance against a backdrop of social satire. Many of the groups active in the 1980s and 1990s have taken up the general style adding into it more scripted political, economic and social references easily understood by their public. This new form of *madang keuk,* from the 1980s onward, has become particularly popular with younger audiences.

After its beginnings as part of the work and everyday life of common people, dance in Korea became a matter of religious expression. Then, during the Yi dynasty (1392–1910) dance became identified with professional entertainment, first as performed at the court and now to be seen at the Korean Traditional Performing Arts Centre. Its characteristic style remains graceful, elegant and refined. The movements are gentle and flowing.

Modern dance began in Korea in 1922 when Ishii Baku of Japan first performed in Seoul. Studying with him, young Koreans were encouraged to develop their own style, combining their native lyricism with new techniques borrowed from Japan and the west. In 1937, Ch'oi Seunghee toured the western world with great success, while Yuk Wan-sun successfully introduced the technique of Martha Graham. In the 1970s Hong Sin-cha, though based in New York, organized her own company, which had great success in Seoul. With the emergence of musical theatre experiments, the number of dance groups in the country has also increased. The Korean Dance Festival, initiated in 1979, has annually staged some twenty new dance pieces resulting in new stimulation for Korean choreography.

Dramaturgy

Writers of traditional drama are unknown since traditional texts grew from religion and folklore elements. But with the emergence of the New Theatre movement in the 1920s and the influence of more western traditions, writers began to take their rightful place in the theatrical hierarchy. During the 1920s and 1930s, under Japanese occupation, the ideological confrontation between the right and left political wings within the country divided writers. Leftists tended to write propagandistic plays strongly coloured by Marxist thought while writers of the right tended to write nationalistic plays dealing with issues related to independence.

Yoo Chi Jin, the first dramatist of real impor-

tance in the modern period, dealt with the struggles of an independence fighter in his early play *Chogook* (*Mother Country*) and later wrote a series of plays with plots borrowed from early Korean history but with themes strongly relevant to the contemporary political situation. Among his representative works are *Pyul* (*Stars*, 1948), *Chamyung-go* (1949) and *Wonsullang* (1950). He also wrote a number of anti-communist plays including *Tong-gok* (1950), *Na To Ingani Toeryunda* (*I Want to Be a Human Being*, 1953) and *Purun Sung-in* (*A Blue Saint*, 1955), the latter growing from the Korean War. One of his late plays, *Hangang-un Hurunda* (*The Han River Flows*, 1958) shows signs of change in his dramaturgical style but basically his realistic vision of the war-torn Korea and its people never changed. Consistently realistic, his plays at root show a strong patriotic sentiment and a belief in some greater enlightenment. One might refer to his style – and many who followed him – as Historical Enlightenment plays. A prolific writer with thirty-five plays to his credit, Yoo moved away from playwriting in 1960 when he began to focus all of his energy on the creation of the Drama Centre, a theatre and study centre.

Another writer of note is Oh Young Jin (1916–74) who moved against the political trends of his time. Utilizing traditional values and local customs, his work was a conscious attempt to break away from western themes and subject matter. Transplanting folk subjects into a European dramatic style, his characters reveal a comic vision of life with a strong satirical edge. One can also note his strong anti-Japanese and anti-communist feelings in representative works such as *Maeng Chinsa Taek Kyungsa* (*The Wedding Day*, first written as a film scenario in 1943), *Sarait Lee Choong Saeng Kakha* (*The Honourable Lee Choong Saeng Is Alive*, 1949), *Poong-un* (1957), *Hae-nyo Mutte Oruda* (*A Diver on Land*, 1967) and *Huh Saeng Jon* (1970). Unfortunately he had no immediate followers with most writers of the period inclined towards a more realistic portrayal of the changing society.

Cha Bum Suk had horrific experiences during the war and his early works focus on issues of brutality and dehumanization. A realist with an inclination towards sentimental lyricism, Cha draws his materials from folk customs, village and urban life and socio-political problems. His best known work is *Sanpool* (*Mountain Fire*, 1963). Based on a true story, the play depicts the victimization of villagers during the war. Other works of note by Cha include *Pulmoji* (*Sterile Land*, 1957), a portrait of tradition replaced by the new culture, *Chung Kiwa Chip* (*The Blue Tiled House*, 1964), *Yoltae-o* (*Tropical Fish*, 1966), a contemporary love story, and *Hakiyo* (*Oh Love, My Crane*, 1981), a strongly lyrical play.

The last of the important post-war playwrights was Lee Keun Sam, a witty satirist. While the aforementioned Oh Young Jin utilized a traditional form of satire, Lee's works have much more of a post-war type of irony. His plays have a fast tempo, witty dialogue and deal with extremely contemporary situations. He openly criticizes society, politics and culture. Though the criticism is superficial at times, the satire is powerful and often hilarious. Many of his best works also have an allegorical quality and exist on several levels at once. Among his best plays are *Taewangun Chukkirul Kobuhanda* (*The Great King Refused to Die*, 1960), *Widaehan Shilchong* (1963), *Shippal Kongwhakuk* (*The Eighteenth Republic*, 1965), *Kukmul Issaomnida* (1966) and *Abelmaneui Chaepan* (*The Trial of Abelman*, 1977).

By the 1960s, a new generation of writers was emerging. Though their themes still centred on the tragic division of the country, separation of families or wartime experiences of starvation and depravity which they had gone through as youngsters, what most characterized their work was their attempt to capture these experiences at an inner level with a nihilistic world-view. Different from their predecessors, they no longer kept to the rules of mimetic writing, but began to introduce elements of the existential, absurd and Brechtian epic drama into their works. The changing outlook of society also generally affected their work and many formal experiments took place at this time. Sensing that nothing was secure in an age of uncertainty, they turned inward to capture the psychological landscape. The result was a series of complex works portraying anxiety and non-feeling in a world essentially bereft of morality.

Two writers particularly came to be representative of this generation – Yoon Dae Sung and Oh Tae Suk. Yoon is particularly known for his analytical approaches to issues. He was among the first of the new writers to introduce traditional mask plays onto the modern stage projecting social themes in epic frameworks. His *Nobi Moonsu* (1973) projects contemporary meaning on to an historical situation while his 1974 play *Choolseki*, based on a true story,

effectively dramatizes the dehumanization of a mass-media society.

Oh Tae Suk's non-realistic style, also aimed at anatomizing modern consciousness, quickly made him Korea's foremost absurdist. Transcending normal logic and utilizing dialogue that breaks through linear sequencing, his style is imbued with traditional usage but at the same time is laden with modern implications. It is Oh's emotive language, however, which most clearly sets him apart from other dramatists in the country. Among his major plays are *Choboon* (*Grass Tomb*, 1973), *Tae* (*The Umbilical Cord*, 1974) and *Choon-poong's Wife* (1975). Oh also directs his own work with notable success.

Among the generation of writers emerging since the 1970s, one of the more notable is Lee Jae Hyun, a political refugee from North Korea. His early lyrical writing in such plays as *Pakkoji* (1965) and *Tsul Mool* (*Ebbing Tide*, 1974) focused on the divided Korea and was filled with nostalgia for his lost home. In works such as *Porodul* (*Prisoners of War*), set in a prisoner-of-war camp, he dramatizes the loss of one's humanity, a subject he returns to in his 1983 drama, *Chok kwa Paek* (*The Red and the White*).

Noh Kyung Shik is a local colourist who utilizes varying dialects in portraying the poverty-stricken life of the peasantry. His drama *Talchip* (1971) is about a village woman on one level; on another, it is a tale of national tragedy. *Sojakchi* (1979) deals with a similar issue.

Another lyrical writer working in this way is Yoon Cho Byung, who writes of the helplessness of rural villages in the face of exploitative industry and who portrays the life of miners unable to escape from the hold of the past. His plays *Nongto* (*The Farmland*, 1981) and *Punggumsori* (*The Sound of the Organ*, 1985) clearly reflect these concerns.

One of the country's few novelists to turn to dramatic writing is Choi In Hoon, who tends to draw his subject matter from folk legends. His first play, *Odisu Muosi Toeo Mannari* (*We Shall Meet Again Transformed*, 1970), deals with the tragic meeting of a general and a princess. A poetic dramatist, he is convinced of the persuasive power of archetypal fables that are expressed in an economized language. One of his major works is *Yennal Yetchoge, Who I, Who I* (*Once Upon A Time, Who I, Who I*, 1974), a tragic tale about a baby destined to be a hero.

Kim Eui Kyung was an early leader of the

Little Theatre movement of the 1960s working as both a director and an administrator. He began writing plays in the 1970s with several focusing on historical subject matter. His most representative work, *Namhan Sansung* (1974), redefines the invasion of Korea by China in the seventeenth century, imbuing it with contemporary meaning. Another of his plays, *Shikminchieso On Anarchist* (*The Anarchist from the Colony*, 1984), analyses the consciousness of an anarchist/nationalist under Japanese occupation through court procedures.

Two writers making their reputations in the 1980s and 1990s are Lee Kang Paek and Lee Hyun Wha. Lee Kang Paek is an allegorist with superb dramatic sensitivity. His subject matter derives from both past and present. His major works include *Kyulhon* (*Getting Married*, 1974) and *Pomnal* (*A Spring Day*, 1984), a folk tale in a Brechtian style. Lee Hyun Wha, on the other hand, is a much more urban dramatist. Though not overtly political, in plays such as *Pulga-pulga* (1987) he looks at the condition of existence in modern Korea and has the ability to mirror the past in the present and the political in the cultural.

Directing and Acting

Since the mid-1930s, a number of important directors have made major contributions to the Korean theatre. The first was Lee Hae Rang (b. 1916) who studied acting in Japan in the mid-1930s. Committed to Stanislavski's ideas on acting and staging, Lee went on to direct more than 200 productions in his long and varied career including *Hamlet*, O'Neill's *Long Day's Journey into Night*, Chekhov's *Three Sisters* and Goethe's *Faust*. Equally at home with original plays, his long career took him into the 1990s.

Another Japanese-trained director was Lee Chin Soon (1916–84) who directed his first professional production at the age of 31. Another realist in the Stanislavski tradition, he had great success with Chekhov's works and directed a number of original Korean plays including the

Korean classical opera *Chun Hyang Jun*. Much of his late work was in this genre.

Lim Young Ung began his professional directing in the mid-1960s and quickly established a reputation for experimental work. His production of Beckett's *Waiting for Godot* was a landmark in the modern Korean theatre and his production of Simone de Beauvoir's *La Femme rompue* enjoyed a record run.

The US-trained director Yoo Duk Hyung studied at the University of Texas and later at Yale. After his return to Korea in 1969, he began staging a number of new North American experimental works which courageously challenged the well-established realism of the time. In Oh Tae Suk's play *Choboon*, he brilliantly incorporated Korean drama with western techniques. He later became head of the Drama Centre's theatre school, a post he took over on the death of his father, the playwright Yoo Chi Jin.

The first director to introduce Brechtian theory into Korean stage practice was Huh Kyu. His early experiments were with Korean folk plays; this innovative work was later taken up by Minye Keukchang. Huh has also staged a number of traditional operas (*Chung-guk*) and has served as director of the National Theatre.

Kim Chung Ok trained in France where he studied both French and cinema. During the 1960s he showed an outstanding talent for directing comedies in the French style but from the 1970s on he began to experiment with both collective creation and with blending traditional Korean forms with modern western styles. He later served as head of the Korean Centre of the International Theatre Institute.

One of the country's more innovative directors in the 1980s and 1990s has been Ahn Min Soo, whose later work has been focused on the presentation of image theatre utilizing Oriental movement and chanting. A director with a keen interest in English and US drama is Chung Chin Soo. As translator-director, he has been responsible for productions of plays by Harold Pinter, Tom Stoppard, Sam Shepard and David Mamet.

Music Theatre
Dance Theatre

For a discussion of music and dance, see the opening, historical section and **Artistic Profile**.

Theatre for Young Audiences
Puppet Theatre

The earliest attempts at developing a theatre specifically for children date to the 1920s when the country was still ruled by Japan. In 1923, Bang Jung Hwan, an author of fairytales, wrote his first play for children, *A Bagful of Song*. This play and a number of others were later published. In 1925, Yun Suk Jung won a prize from the newspaper *Dong Ah* – the country's first competition for children's scripts – for his play *An Owl's Eye*. That same year, a group of university students produced the play and shortly thereafter the country's first children's drama club was formed. By 1930, a children's theatre, Baik Yang, was begun by Hong Yun Pyo, a playwright and director. Over the next decade the group presented many of Hong's plays including *The Stone Bridge* and *The Lost Doll*.

Still another children's theatre group was begun after the liberation from Japan in 1945, Ho-Dong at the newly created Institute of Children's Art. In 1946, a children's play was heard on national radio – Yo Ho's *An Adventure* – and a collection of plays was published called *Hand in Hand*. Children's plays eventually began to be included in the elementary school curriculum. In 1956 a Children's Drama Festival was begun by *Junnan*, a newspaper, with some thirty groups participating. Five years later, the Korean Children's Drama Association was organized as was the Institute of Korean Children's Play. Joo Pyung, a major figure in the field, wrote a number of new plays for children including *Birds* which later toured Japan.

By the mid-1990s, more than a dozen children's theatre groups were in existence, many of them coming into being in the 1970s and 1980s on a more or less professional basis. Among the major groups starting at this time were Hyundai and Min Jung, both focusing on productions for teenagers and Myungjak, Family Drama Troupe, and Dong-Rang Theatre for Young People. Dong-Rang later staged a play by Young Dai Sung called *Wandering Star* seen by over 100,000 people in Korea. The play later toured to Australia. Also formed during this period was a Korean section of ASSITEJ. In 1995, it had a membership of more than 150 individuals.

Dungge Dungge Tale.
Photo: courtesy of ASSITEJ Japan.

Since the early 1960s, several attempts have been made to establish a modern puppet theatre tradition in Korea. Among those who have set up such theatres have been Ko Kyu Hwan, Huh Kyu, Cho Yong Soo and Kong Ho Suk. During this same period, Choi Chang Bong began giving regular puppet performances on Korean television. But such efforts were relatively isolated.

In 1979, a marionette theatre called Orit Kwang-dae was established by Lee Kyung-Hee, who produced a regular series of puppet performances at the Kongkan Theatre. The group's most successful production was *Yang-ju byul-sandae*, which included a traditional Korean mask dance done by marionettes. The production was later shown in Germany (Dresden, 1984) and in former Yugoslavia (Ljubljana, 1988). That same year Lee helped to establish the Korean Centre of UNIMA and began a quarterly puppet magazine *Kkoktu-geuk*.

Other puppet groups began to emerge in the 1980s including Cholani (later changing its name to Seoul Inhyung Geuk-hoe), the shadow group Theatre Yung (founded in 1984 by Kang Sung Kyun) and Rang-Rang (founded in 1985 by Kim Ok Rang). During this decade, puppeteers were brought to Korea from all over Asia and other parts of the world to give workshops under the auspices of UNIMA Korea.

In 1984 the Seoul International Puppet Festival was held for the first time, a festival which has been held annually ever since. In 1988 and 1991 a second international festival was held – the Seoul Marionette World. A national festival has been held annually since 1989, the Choon-chun Festival in Choon-chun City.

In 1997, Korea boasted some thirty puppet groups throughout the country.

Design
Theatre Space and Architecture

In the Korean theatre, the technical fields that are least developed are those of stage design, costuming and lighting. Though the old realistic picture frame stage has all but disappeared from the Korean theatre and new design styles have become rather common, the fact is that the presence of independent designers is still the exception rather than the rule.

Among the few designers whose work has stood out has been Kim Chung Whan (1912–73), Chang Chong Sun (1924–87) and, of the younger generation, Choi Yun Ho. Kim was trained in Japan in the 1930s and his early designs were quite realistic for productions such as *Revizor* (*The Government Inspector*). Later working at the Wongaksa Theatre and at the Drama Centre, during his career he designed – or rather assisted directors in designing – several hundred productions. A naturalist, he was also the first to utilize a revolving stage in the country. Chang succeeded Kim as the most important stage designer and during his long career he worked on some 500

live theatre productions and thousands of television shows.

Choi also began working in a realistic style but by the end of the 1970s his work was taking a much more non-realistic direction. By the 1980s his abstract and fantastic designs were attracting much attention for themselves but had not yet succeeded in establishing any sort of influence.

In terms of theatre spaces, there are 106 regularly used spaces in South Korea. Numbers are unavailable for theatres in North Korea. Of the 106 in the south, 40 have 500 or more seats and 17 have over 1,000. About half of the largest theatres are in Seoul with the other half spread across the rest of the country. Most of the over 1,000-seat theatres are inadequate technically for live productions. As a result, it is the 500 to 1,000-seat theatres that are most often used.

The few groups that have their own spaces tend to work in small theatres, those holding about 150 seats. Few productions at these theatres have extended runs.

Training
Criticism, Scholarship and Publishing

There is very little theatre training available in Korea and those most interested in professional careers must go abroad. Indeed, the first university Drama Department (at Chungang University) was not begun until 1958 and though several other universities followed its lead, few members of the professional theatre community have graduated from such schools. Rather, most theatre people have come from such diverse fields as law or agriculture, while many of the drama school graduates have wound up in the more commercial field of television production.

In the area of scholarly research, Professor Lee Du Hyun's *Hankuk Sinkeuksa Yongu* (*A Study of Modern Korean Theatre*, published in 1966) was the first important historical survey in this field. A number of other works followed dealing with the development of traditional theatre or pre-1945 dramatic literature.

A specialized theatre journal was launched into 1970, *Yunkeuk Pyungron* (*Review of Drama*) under the editorship of Yoh Suk Kee, carrying commentary on current productions along with theoretical essays and reviews of current events. The journal lasted until 1980. A second journal was begun by the Korean National Theatre Association in 1976, *Hanguk Yunkeuk* (*National Theatre Review*) and was still publishing in the 1990s.

Among critics of note are Oh Hwa Sup who has introduced British and American plays in translation; Lee Keun Sam, also known as a playwright; and Lee Tae Ju, Lee Sang Il, Yoo Min Young and Hang Sang Chul.

Yoh Suk Kee
With Lee Du Hyun, Yoo Min Young, Kim Eui Kyung

Further Reading

Chang Han-Gi. *Hanguk Yonkuksa* [History of Korean theatre]. Seoul: Dongguk University, 1986. 360 pp.

Cho Dong-Il. *Talchumui-youksawa-wonli* [History and theory of mask theatre]. Seoul: Hongik-SA, 1987. 406 pp.

Cho Jong-Gi. *Hanguk Mudae Design ui Pyoenhwa ae Kwanhan Yeongu* [History of Korean stage setting: From 1945 to present]. Seoul: Kim Im-Ode, 1986. 281 pp.

Cho Oh-Kon, transl. *Traditional Korean Theatre.* Studies in Korean Religions and Culture 2. Berkeley, CA: Asian Humanities Program, 1988. 364 pp.

ITI Korean Centre. *The Korean Theatre.* Seoul: 1981. 90 pp.

Jang Han-Ki. *Minsock Gug Gua Dongyang Yungug* [Korean traditional theatre and oriental theatre]. Seoul: Kim Young-Guy, 1983. 272 pp.

Jo Hung-Yun. *Hangu-gui Mu* [Korean ritual performance]. Seoul: Dong Sick Choi, 1983. 151 pp.

Kaehwagi Yunkeuk Sahwesa. *A Social History of Theatre in the Enlightenment Period.* Seoul: Saemun-sa, 1987. 271 pp.

Kardoss, John. *An Outline History of Korean Drama.* New York: Long Island University Press, 1966. 33 pp.

Kim Jae-Chel, ed. *Kuokkutaksi-Norum* [Puppet theatre: Kkotugaksi]. Seoul: Korean Traditional Drama Institute, 1986. 165 pp.

Kim Woo-Taek. *Hankuk Juntongyo-nkukkukwa ken goyumoodae* [Korean traditional theatre and its performing place]. Seoul: Sungkyunkuan University Press, 1986. 209 pp.

Korean Culture and Arts Foundation. *Moonye Yungam* [Annual survey of culture and arts]. Seoul, published since 1976.

Korean National Commission for Unesco. *Korean Dance, Theatre and Cinema.* Seoul: Si-sa-vong-o-sa, 1983.

——. *Wedding Day and Other Korean Plays.* Seoul: Si-sa-vong-o-sa. 1983. 211 pp.

Lee Du-Hyun. *Hankuk Sinkeuksa Yongu* [A study of modern Korean theatre]. Seoul: Seoul National University Press, 1966. 331 pp.

——. *Hanguk yonkuksa* [History of Korean theatre]. 2nd edn. Seoul: Hakyonsa, 1987. 374 pp.

——. *et al. Kuklip Keukchang Samsipnyon* [Thirty years of Korean national theatre]. Seoul: Korean National Theatre, 1980. 914 pp.

Lee Sang Il. *Chukjae wa Madang-keuk* [Festival and madang-keuk]. Seoul: Chosun-Ilbo-sa, 1986. 311 pp.

——. *Hankuk Yunkeuk-sa* [A history of Korean theatre]. Seoul: Minjung-sugwan, 1973. 310 pp.

Park Jin Tae. *Hanguk kamyunkuk yongu* [Study of Korean mask theatre]. Seoul: Saemoon-sa, 1985. 220 pp.

Park Kwang. *Pansori-sosa* [Short history of Korean musical theatre]. 2nd edn. Seoul: Singumoonhwa-sa, 1983. 225 pp.

Seoul Drama Critics Circle. *Hankuk Yunkeuk-kwa Cholmun Uisik* [Korean theatre and young consciousness]. Seoul: Minum-sa, 1979.

Shin Chung-Ok. 'Yungmikeuke Yiipkwa Hankuk Sinkeuk-ea Kichin Yunghyang' [A study on the reception and influence of British and American plays in Korean theatre]. PhD dissertation, Hankuk University of Foreign Studies, 1987.

Suh Yun-Ho. *Hankuk Kundai Hikoksa Yungu* [A study of modern Korean drama]. Seoul: Korean Cultural Research Center, 1982. 368 pp.

——. *Hankuk Yunkeuk-ron* [A treatise on Korean theatre]. Seoul: Samil-gak, 1975. 254 pp.

Suh Hang-Suk *et al.* 'Yunkeuk' [Theatre]. *Moonye Chonggam* [General review of arts and literature] (1976): 387–468.

Sung Kyung-Lin. *Hanguk-ui mooyong* [Korean traditional dance]. Seoul: Kyoyang Guksa, 1976. 217 pp.

Swortzell, Lowell (ed.) *International Guide to Children's Theatre and Educational Theatre*. New York and Westport, CT: Greenwood Press, 1990.

Um, H.K. 'Making P'ansori: Korean Musical Drama'. PhD dissertation, Queen's University, Belfast, 1992.

Yoh Suk Kee. *Hankuk Yunkeuke Hyonsil* [Present state of Korean theatre]. Seoul: Tonghwa-chulpan-kongsa, 1974. 360 pp.

——. 'Hankuk Yunkeuk' [Korean theatre]. *Hankuk Hyundai Munhwasa Daege* [History of contemporary Korean culture] 1 (1975): 459–93.

——. *Tongseo Yunkeuk-ui Pigyo Yungu* [A comparative study of theatre east and west]. Seoul: Seoul University Press, 295 pp.

Yoo Min Young. *Hankuk Hyundai Higoksa* [A history of modern Korean drama]. Seoul: Hongsung-sa, 1982. 616 pp.

——. *Hankuk Yunkeuk Sango* [Miscellanies on Korean theatre]. Seoul: Moonye-pipyung-sa, 1978. 391 pp.

——. *Kaehwagi Yunkeuk Sahwesa* [A social history of theatre in the enlightenment period]. Seoul: Saemun-sa, 1987. 271 pp.

KYRGYZSTAN

(Overview)

An independent republic geographically part of central Asia and formerly known as the Kirghiz Soviet Socialist Republic of the Union of Soviet Socialist Republics (USSR), the country is more commonly known as Kirghizia; it is bordered on the north by Kazakhstan, on the east by China, on the south by China and Tajikistan and on the west by Uzbekistan. Bishkek (with a population of about 625,000 in 1990), formerly called Frunze, is the capital and largest city. The second largest city is Osh (218,000) in the Fergana Valley. Less than 40 per cent of its population (estimated in 1994 at 4.69 million) live in urban areas. The country has a total land area of 198,500 square kilometres (76,600 square miles).

The majority of the Kyrgyz population are followers of Islam and speak a Turkic language. Russians, who live principally in Bishkek and other industrial centres, are the largest minority with 22 per cent of the population. Other significant minorities include Uzbeks who live primarily in the Fergana Valley and constitute 13 per cent of the population, Ukrainians, Germans and Tatars. In 1990 there was a series of violent clashes between Uzbeks and the Kyrgyz population in the Osh area; relations between the two sides remained tense through the decade.

The economy of the republic was formerly based almost exclusively on agriculture but underwent extensive industrialization during the Soviet period. Agriculture, however, remains a predominant part of the economy. After independence from the USSR, Kyrgyzstan experienced extended economic stagnation. In 1994, it joined with Kazakhstan and Uzbekistan to establish a free-trade zone.

Although Kyrgyzstan follows principles of democracy and the Communist Party has been outlawed since independence, its governmental system retains several aspects of the old Soviet-era system. President Askar Akayev, however, is the only head of state who never served in the Communist Party's state apparatus.

Earliest settlements of the Kyrgyz tribes on the modern territory of Kyrgyzstan can be traced to the first century BC, when Kazakh–Kyrgyz communities migrated south from Siberia. Genghis Khan conquered the region in the thirteenth century; in the nineteenth century it was under the control of the Kokand Khanate. In 1860–70, Russian czarist forces defeated the Khanate and incorporated present-day Kyrgyzstan into the Russian Empire. In 1916 many Kyrgyz and other central Asian peoples revolted against Russian rule. The czarist regime responded severely and thousands of Kyrgyz had to seek refuge in China to survive.

After the October Socialist Revolution in 1917, the Kyrgyz resisted but were defeated by Bolshevik forces. In 1921 the area became part of the Turkestan Autonomous Soviet Socialist Republic – which also included portions of present-day Kazakhstan, Tajikistan, Turkmenistan and Uzbekistan. In 1924 the area became the Kara-Kirghiz Autonomous Oblast. In 1926 it was upgraded to an autonomous republic and became a full-fledged constituent republic of the USSR in 1936.

Beginning in the late 1920s, the republic experienced extreme cultural and political repression, saw the influx of Russians and other peoples in large numbers and underwent large-scale industrialization. The dissolution of the

USSR in 1991 led to the republic's independence. It joined the United Nations a year later.

Until the beginning of the twentieth century, Kyrgyzstan had no professional theatre or permanent companies. Some original artists were *akyns* (singer-improvisers and storytellers of national epic). *Aitysh* – a competition of *akyns* – was among the most popular of early theatrical forms. There were also comedians called *kuuduldar* in Kyrgyzstan.

A more literary theatre began to appear after the October Revolution in 1917 under the cultural influence of Russian theatre; early performances in Kyrgyzstan were given in Russian. These included Ostrovsky's *On the Profitable Position* and one of the first revolutionary plays, Volny's *Two Worlds*, both staged by an early amateur group in Pishpek in 1918 called Svoboda (Freedom). This same group – deeply committed to revolutionary principles – was later involved in the founding of the Kyrgyz National Theatre.

By 1921, professional performances began to be seen, along with the first newspapers and magazines in the country. In 1926 a studio for training theatrical workers was established, many of whose students later became leading actors on the national stage. The first Kyrgyz plays, *Kaiguloo Kakay* (*Unhappy Kakay*, 1926) by M. Tokobaev and *Karachach* by Ksymaly Jantoshev focused on the hard life of Asian women before the revolution. A Russian-language drama theatre was established in Frunze in 1927 and by the end of the decade, the Studio, under the direction of N. Yelenin, was staging not only Kyrgyz plays, but Russian classics as well. Both had an impact in terms of developing theatrical sophistication and an awareness of social issues. The Studio also toured widely, presenting its productions even in remote villages.

In 1930 the Studio became Kyrgyzstan's first State Theatre, opening its inaugural season with Jantoshev's *Alym and Maria*. Support for collectivization and particularly for the development of *kolkhozes* (collective farms) became a recurrent theme in the dramaturgy of the new company over the next decades.

In July 1941, just after the beginning of the USSR's involvement in World War II – or, as it was called, the Great Patriotic War (1941–5) – the Kyrgyz State Drama Theatre was established. Its company included graduates of the Kyrgyz Studio at GITIS (State Institute of Theatre Arts, Moscow). This theatre, along with hundreds of others across the Soviet Union, staged plays with themes of war. Also staged were plays about the historical past of the Kyrgyz people and their struggle against foreign invaders that sought to support the fighting spirit of the people. *Kurmanbeck* by Jantoshev and *Janyl* by Kubanychbek Malikov and Amankul Kuttubayev played to large and enthusiastic houses and ran in nearly all Kyrgyz theatres. Other plays of note were *Avenger* by Raikan Shukurbekov and *Oath* by A. Tokombaev, both about the patriotism and heroism of the Soviet people in their ongoing fight against fascist invaders.

Reconstruction of the war-ravaged country and plays focusing on peace became regular post-war subjects. *Kurman* by Tiktobolot Abdumamunov, *In One House* by Jantoshev and many others were professionally smooth but conflictless plays – realistic fairytales for adults. In August 1946, the Communist Party issued a new law regulating theatres and their repertoires, specifically requiring plays to 'reflect the ideals of socialist realism'. This became the 'official' style in the arts until the mid-1980s. Like many other theatres in the Soviet republics, the Kyrgyz theatre looked to Russian Soviet drama, adapting it to local national traditions. Beginning in 1947, translations of Russian Soviet plays appeared in the Kyrgyz national repertoire. Among them were *The Russian Question* by Konstantin Simonov, *Liubov Yarovaya* by Konstantin Trenev and a play about Lenin called *A Man With a Rifle* (1952) by Nikolai Pogodin.

After the war, other theatres emerged in Przhevalsk that also toured remote areas with special easy-to-set-up performances that sometimes reflected the repertoire of the home theatre. The production of *Without a Dowry* (1948) by Ostrovsky at the Issyk-Kul theatre is one of the production highlights from this period.

Productions of western classics, especially those of Shakespeare who was extremely popular in central Asia, were even more significant. During the war years, the Kyrgyz State Drama Theatre successfully staged *Twelfth Night* in a playful production by director O. Sarbagyshev with the actor Muratbeck Ryskulov as Sir Toby. In 1950 another production of note was *Othello* with Ryskulov in the title role. The opportunity to interpret such classical characters was an important training experience for actors and also a way to overcome dogmatic strictures. Ryskulov also starred in Gorky's *Yegor Bulychov and Others* (1953).

National playwriting, however, was the

weakest link in the development of the Kyrgyz theatre despite the occasional success of plays such as *We Are Not Those We Are Supposed to Be* by Malikov and Kuttubayev, a play that revealed the reality of *kolkhoz* life.

Stylistic and production restrictions began to be lifted in the mid-1950s, after the death of Stalin. However, although the powerful state mechanism was relaxed, it nevertheless remained in operation. One of the first signs of positive change was the appearance of satirical comedies such as *The Narrow Ravine* (1953) by Tiktobolot Abdumamunov and *The Lasso for the Shrew* (1955) by Jantoshev. Though audiences were now allowed to laugh at slapstick, more serious issues were rarely explored. Utilizing the literary dramatic style called the grotesque (situational absurdity), the new style was quickly attacked by engaged critics for being a 'perversion of reality'. Such labels could close every theatre's door for playwrights.

Another problem of the indigenous Kyrgyz theatre during these years was the wide gap between companies of skilful and experienced actors and the very weak national repertoire with which they were expected to work. The new plays were uninteresting and conflictless. As a result, companies turned to other Asian writers or remained outside of the major cities, often as touring companies. Such nomadic structures, on the other hand, served the farther regions of the republic quite well.

By the late 1950s, Kyrgyz writers were turning to folklore for thematic material and upgraded versions of folk tales were played regularly. Among the best were *Saryngi* by K. Eshmambetov and *Kurmanbeck* by Jantoshev about the mythical folk hero called Batyr. Other playwrights wrote about the 1917 Revolution and the evolution of the Soviet state. Among these were *Kanybeck* by Jantoshev, and *Ashyrbai* by Tiktobolot Abdumamunov.

In 1952 a group of gifted young performers were sent to study at GITIS in Moscow. By 1957 these GITIS graduates joined the Kyrgyz Drama Theatre and significantly raised the performance level in both Soviet and world classics such as *The Imaginary Invalid* by Molière, *Cunning and Love* by Schiller and *Guilty Without Guilt* by Ostrovsky. It was a distinct change for a conservative theatre whose repertoire had badly stagnated.

In November 1957 the first festival of the republic's drama and musical theatres took place in Frunze, a preview to a festival of Kyrgyz art held shortly after in Moscow. Such festivals (showcasing a decade of art) were a very popular form of official examination of the Soviet republics' art and culture. The Ministry of Culture got an opportunity to criticize the smaller remote republics, to test their ideological loyalty, to award medals, titles, prizes and benefits to companies and artists.

The Third Congress of Kyrgyz writers in 1959 slightly re-energized the national dramaturgy. *Flowers in the Mountains* (1960) by Sh. Beishenaliev (directed by M.Nazaraliev) and *The Inquiry Continues* (1961) by Tokombaev (directed by J. Abdykadyrov), focused on the social and ethical problems of careerism, slander and baseness. The humanistic drama *The Destiny of Father* (1960) by B. Jakiev, starring Ryskulov, is worth mentioning. Fatal mistakes and sufferings of conscience were shown in *The Conscience Doesn't Forgive* (1963) by Abdumamunov. Despite these exceptions, plays, production styles and stage designs – limited by dogmatic criteria – remained archaic for years. Regional companies fared still worse in terms of funding with comedies and musicals their most preferred genres.

During the 1960s the most important place in the Kyrgyz repertoire belonged to *Face to Face* (1961), Chingiz Aitmatov's novel adapted for the stage. Directed by J. Abdykadyrov, it revealed the betrayal and heroism in post-war Kyrgyz. The deserter Ismail in this production was only one of many starring roles for the actor Asanbeck Umuraliyev as the role of his wife Seide was for Baken Kydykeyeva.

Aitmatov, Kyrgyzstan's best known national writer and humanist, was later translated into many Soviet languages and subsequently into many foreign languages. His prose works gave the stage some of its best and most original dramatic material including *The Mother's Field* (1964) directed by Nazaraliev.

The 1960s saw the first productions in Kyrgyzstan of Chekhov's psychological dramaturgy. *Uncle Vanya* (1960) was directed by V. Molchanov with S. Jumadylov as Vanya and N. Kitaev as Astrov. Following the style and principles of the Moscow Art Theatre's productions, Molchanov also directed *Anna Karenina* by Tolstoy with three different interpretations of the title role by Kydykeyeva, S. Balkybakova and Z. Moldobayeva. The Russian classic *Woe From Wit* (1966) by A. Griboyedov, directed by V. Tsygankov, with A. Umuraliyev as Chatsky was another important success for the Drama theatre.

Performances devoted to special anniversaries were common under the Soviet theatre system and such performances were often at official request. In 1967 on the fiftieth anniversary of the October Revolution, the play *Family*, about Lenin's family, by I. Popov was staged. Such official prescriptions and obedience to ideological necessity by state-supported art institutions led to the same type of controls as seen earlier under socialist-realism.

Nevertheless, Kyrgyz theatre worked to make its repertoire more significant. Theatres brought to the stage many world classics, such as Shakespeare's *King Lear*, *Othello* and *Romeo and Juliet* during the 1960s and 1970s. A brightly emotional yet sincere and lyrical production of *Taming of the Shrew* directed by M. Rubinstein was another highlight. B. Shaltayer and A. Seibakmatova succeeded in combining the comic and the romantic in their interpretations of Petruchio and Katharine.

The 1970s brought more innovations, particularly in the work of director Iskender Ryskulov, the son of the actor Muratbeck Ryskulov. After graduating from GITIS in 1972, Ryskulov worked as chief director and manager of the popular Youth Theatre in Osh. Established as the third Kyrgyz Studio within the acting department at GITIS under I.

Rayevsky, the group's graduation productions – *The Last Ones* by Gorky, *The Seagull* by Chekhov, *Le bourgeois gentilhomme* by Molière, *A Fellow From Our Town* by Simonov, *The Green Bird* by Carlo Gozzi and *Life-Giving Water* by A. Dyikanbaev – not only were good training for young actors but later became important parts of the company's early repertoire. Joining the repertoire later were plays by Shakespeare, Gogol, Gorky and Pushkin along with translated Russian and Kyrgyz authors. Works based on Aitmatov – especially *The White Steamer* – occupied a prominent place in the repertoire. Among the Osh theatre's important national productions were *The Sunrise* by A. Tokombayev, *Don't Tell Anyone* and *The Narrow Ravine* by Abdumamunov, *Thousand Dreams* and *The Ancient Tale* by M. Baidzhiyev, *Echo* and *Still* by B. Omuraliev and *The Sunny Island* by M. Gaparov. Under Ryskulov, the company remained the most advanced and interesting theatre in the republic for more than a decade.

The tour of this company to Moscow in 1978, and its participation in the first All Union Festival of Youth Theatres in Tbilisi (Georgia) in 1982 brought the group to national attention, as did its 1984 production of *Mongrel Mutt*

Farewell, Gulsary! by Ch. Aitmatov.
Photo: courtesy of *Teatr*.

Running by the Edge of the Sea, based on a story by Aitmatov. In 1984 Ryskulov became the artistic director of the Academic Theatre in Frunze. His first production there was based on Aitmatov's *Farewell, Gulsary!*, which was highly criticized, especially for its visual designs, although it was a strongly metaphoric performance with a sincere and daring tone. Actor Asanbeck Umuraliyev played the leading role of Tanabai as a very typical Kyrgyz character.

Ryskulov's next production was Shakespeare's *Richard III* done with two quite different casts. One, with the young M. Alyshpaev in the title role, was done as a very dynamic and cruel tragedy; the other, with a more mature cast led by Jumadylov as Richard, was much more introspective with a weak and perplexed protagonist.

The quasi-fairytale *The Moan of the Bowstring* (1986) by B. Jakiev was a modern and poetic rendering of a folk parable and much more significant than some of the plays recommended by state authorities. This epic play – at once humorous and lyrical – told the story of the Death Devil and two brothers who killed their younger brother for his inheritance. Clearly, the warning was that little quarrels can lead to hell. It was this production that allowed the director finally to join the various acting studio generations within the Kyrgyz State Drama Theatre. In 1986, the Moscow director Leonid Kheifetz staged a well-received production of *The Cherry Orchard* at the Kyrgyz Drama Theatre.

The Russian Drama Theatre also occupied an important place in the Kyrgyz theatre because of the country's large Russian diaspora. In the 1980s, this theatre had its own stars, among them Emmanuel Prag and Leonid Yasinovsky. Unfortunately, for years no artistic director stayed longer than two seasons. As well, a number of its productions were criticized and forbidden by authorities. A more fruitful period began with the appearance of director Vladislav Pazi in the mid-1980s. Pazi managed to develop a more varied repertoire of some Soviet plays – the

philosophical *Scaffold* by Aitmatov, *Kolyma* by Ignaty Dvoretsky, *Look Whose Coming!* by Vladimir Arro, *Old House* by A. Kazantsev, *The Last Voyage* by M. Baijiev, and *Dictatorship of Conscience* by Mikhail Shatrov – and some foreign ones – *The Decameron* after Boccacio, *Friends*, a black comedy by the Japanese playwright Abe Kōbō, *Brave Soldier Shweik* after *Hasek* (directed by Jan Novak) and *The Dresser* by Ronald Harwood.

In 1988 – with *glasnost* and *perestroika* in the wind – the Russian Theatre group from Kyrgyzstan toured to Moscow. The theatre's attempts to reflect political events, however, were criticized as naive. Interestingly, in the early 1990s, despite economic and market crises, it was Kyrgyzstan's Russian Theatre that was one of the nation's most stable companies, proving not only artistry but its own point of view towards indigenous problems.

Theatre training continues to take place at the Kyrgyz State Arts Institute in Frunze (now Bishkek) under the direction of the Ministry of Culture. In the 1980s, choreographic and applied arts high schools had also been established in Frunze along with the Przhevalsk musical school and fine arts schools in Osh and Frunze. Such schools – including music, ballet, drama, opera, sculpture and painting – had about 1,500 students graduating annually.

Natasha Rapoport

Further Reading

Istoriya sovetskogo dramaticheskogo teatra [History of Soviet dramatic theatre]. 6 vols. Moscow: Nauka, 1966–71.

Kazmina, N. *Smotrite, kto k nam prishel!* [Look who is coming to us!]. *Teatr* 3 (1989).

Levikova, E. *Chetviortyi tour* [The fourth tour]. *Teatr* 3 (1987).

LAOS

A landlocked country on the Southeast Asian mainland, Laos is bordered by China to the north and Vietnam to the east. With a land area of 236,800 square kilometres (91,400 square miles) the population was estimated in 1995 at 4.8 million people, virtually all ethnically Laotian. There are nevertheless minorities of Vietnamese, Chinese, Indians and Pakistanis. Lao is the official language with French widely spoken. Some 85 per cent of the population are Theraveda Buddhists with another 15 per cent following animist beliefs. The capital is Vientiane.

The Lao people arrived in present-day Laos from southern China between the thirteenth and fourteenth centuries, conquering the indigenous population in the process. In 1353, they founded a kingdom called Lan Chang (kingdom of a million elephants). Buddhism was established at this time as the state religion. Lasting until the eighteenth century, the kingdom eventually broke up into three separate states. Ruled by Siam (Thailand) for most of the nineteenth century, Laos came under French control in 1893. Along with Vietnam and later Cambodia, the area was known collectively as Indo-China.

During World War II, Laos was occupied by the Japanese and after the war an independence movement emerged. In 1949, Laos won self-government and virtual independence within the French Union. The Geneva Agreements of 1954, agreements that ended the Indo-China War, recognized Laotian independence. Conflicts soon began between forces loyal to the royal Laotian government and forces loyal to the Communist Pathet Lao guerrillas, who were supporting the

North Vietnamese in the Vietnam War. A new Geneva Agreement in 1962 offered Laos neutrality with power divided among three different groups. Despite this, the struggle between communist and non-communist forces went on. In 1975, the Pathet Lao took control of the country.

Culturally, Laos is rooted in its many varied music and dance forms. Primarily influenced by its Buddhist roots, other stimuli have come from its various neighbours including India from the west, China from the north and Indonesia from the south. The storytelling tradition in the country is a rich one and there have long been professional dance and music troupes that perform on many social and religious occasions.

In the sung storytelling forms, it is always men who are the solo singer-actors.

Dance forms have grown from the royal court dances of the fourteenth and fifteenth centuries. Tradition says that the dances were introduced to Laos following Khmer (see **CAMBODIA**) tradition as Khmer monarchs had troupes of female dancers, many of them part of the monarch's own family. This same tradition, later adopted by the Thai people, meant not only that court women were allowed to dance publicly but also that such entertainments – including their court orchestras – were officially approved. Masked dances and shadow puppetry were added to this tradition somewhat later. Here as well, solo dances were the favoured model although a number of small group dances were also in the repertoire. Since 1959, training in both classical and folk dance has been offered by the Natasin School of Music and Drama in Vientiane. A professional company, attached to the school, has a quite inventive and Thai-influenced repertory, unlike the palace group in Luang Prabang, which seeks to preserve the classical Lao style.

Modern spoken drama did not appear in Laos until the 1920s when Thai spoken drama troupes began to tour in Laos. Lao groups began adapting the spoken drama forms to Laotian tastes, adding in group singing, dancing and *jataka* stories. From about 1975, these forms have increasingly taken on western characteristics including the use in some of pop music.

Characterization tends to be focused on types rather than individuals and stories tend to be based on legends and other known tales.

The shadow-puppet tradition deals most often with stories from legend and/or the *Ramayana*. Puppets are made of leather and are manipulated by several puppeteers. The shadow-puppet theatre in Laos, unlike its Malaysian and Indonesian counterpart, has no ritual significance.

WECT staff

Further Reading

Bowers, Faubion. *Theatre in the East: A Survey of Asian Dance and Drama*. New York: Thomas Nelson & Sons, 1956. 374 pp.

Brandon, James. *The Cambridge Guide to Asian Theatre*. Cambridge: Cambridge University Press, 1993. 253 pp.

Catlin, Amy. 'Laos'. *International Encyclopedia of Dance*, 1988.

Ratnam, Perala, ed. *Laos and Its Culture*. New Delhi: Tulsi, 1982.

Visages du Laos [Faces of Laos, sound recording]. Le Chant du Monde, 1960s.

MACAU (MACAO)

(see **CHINA**)

MALAYA

(see **MALAYSIA**)

MALAYSIA

One of the most prosperous nations in Southeast Asia, Malaysia consists of two parts, separated by some 650 kilometres (400 miles) of the South China Sea. West Malaysia occupies most of the Malay Peninsula. East Malaysia occupies most of the northern section of the island of Borneo. The two parts of the country have a total land area of some 329,800 square kilometres (127,300 sq. miles). The nation's capital, Kuala Lumpur, is located in West Malaysia.

Of Malaysia's 19.3 million people (estimated 1994), Malays comprise approximately 59 per cent of the population with Chinese comprising another 32 per cent. About 9 per cent of the population are Indian. Such a multicultural mix is reflected as well in the religions practised in the country, which include Islam (the official state religion), Buddhism, Confucianism, Taosim, Hinduism, Christianity and Sikhism.

The official national language is Malay or, to give its complete designation, Bahasa Malaysia. English is also widely used. Among the Chinese population, Mandarin is taught in schools; several other Chinese dialects are found. Among Indians, there are many Tamil speakers, while other Indian languages are also known. In East Malaysia, Kadazan and Iban are widely spoken.

Until the late nineteenth century, rivers represented the country's main trade and travel routes. Networks of modern roads and highways now link the country's cities, towns and villages. In the late 1990s, Malaysia was an active member of the Association of Southeast Asian Nations (ASEAN) and had trade and political links across the region. A constitutional monarchy, Malaysia has a series of state sultans who, every five years, take turns as Supreme Head of the Nation. Political power is held by a prime minister, who is head of a parliamentary democracy.

In prehistoric times, the Malay Peninsula was inhabited by waves of migrations from the north. About five thousand years ago, Malays settled in the lowland and riverine areas where they engaged in agriculture and fishing, while the aboriginal peoples shifted to the interior and highland areas.

Hindu civilization extended into the Malay Peninsula from the first to the tenth centuries. During this period a number of prominent Southeast Asian kingdoms came into being, including the Malaccan Sultanate which – supplanting Sumatra – became the region's power base at the beginning of the fifteenth century. The early rulers of Malacca converted to Islam through contact with Indian and Persian traders and Islam eventually became the dominant faith. The Malaccan Sultanate later established contact with China to obtain political recognition. In turn, a Chinese princess, accompanied by special envoys, journeyed to Malacca to wed one of the sultans. This historical event was recorded in the *Sejarah Melayu* (*The Malay Annals*), a seventeenth-century quasi-historical chronicle; eventually, it made its way into Malaysian theatre performances.

Throughout its history, the Malay peninsula was colonized by various powers. In 1511, Malacca fell to the Portuguese. From 1537 to 1620, Acheh, a state in North Sumatra, colonized parts of the peninsula. Although Acheh never defeated the Portuguese, it proclaimed sovereignty over the Malay states of Johor, Pahang, Kedah and Perak. In 1641, the Portuguese were defeated and Malacca fell to the Dutch. But it was British colonization and colonial policy which had the greatest impact on then-Malaya.

The Anglo-Dutch Treaty of 1824 divided Malaya and Indonesia into two spheres of influence: the British had sovereignty over the Straits Settlements of Penang, Malacca and Singapore and the Dutch had sovereignty in Indonesia. In 1874, the Pangkor Treaty established the British Residency system in Perak. By 1896, the British Residency system was extended to cover the newly created Federated Malay States which comprised Selangor, Perak, Negeri Sembilan and Pahang. By 1914, all eleven peninsular Malay States were under British colonial rule. Britain ruled Malaya (and the Straits Settlement of Singapore) in all aspects of political and economic life, refraining only where Malay religion and customs were concerned. The latter remained the prerogative of the respective sultans.

During this period of British colonial rule, Malay society remained divided into two main classes: the ruler (which included the sultan, his heir and other aristocrats) and the ruled (which included the majority of Malays). The ruler and the ruling class were educated in English while the masses received enough education to perpetuate their lives as farmers and small-scale fishermen. In addition, the British brought workers from India and China. Indians worked as labourers on rubber estates, as railway employees and in the government bureaucracy. The Chinese immigrants came to work in the tin mines, in other industries and as merchants. This racial composition and division of society along ethnic lines established during British colonial times set a longstanding multicultural pattern in the country.

During 1942–5, Malaya was occupied by the Japanese. After World War II, with Japan defeated, the British returned once again to Malaya and sought to introduce a plan to nullify the sovereign powers of the sultans and give citizenship to all immigrants in the country. Malays were united in opposing the proposal which was ultimately abandoned by the British. This opposition also set the stage for a concerted effort to achieve independence. The year 1946 saw the formation of the United Malay National Organization (UMNO) and, in 1948, the Federation of Malaya was established. From 1946 to 1960, a State of Emergency was declared in an effort to quell a communist insurgency. In 1957, Malaya became an independent country. In 1963, after the people of Singapore, Sabah and Sarawak voted through a popular referendum to gain independence from Britain by joining the Federation of Malaya, the modern nation of Malaysia was established. In 1965, Singapore separated from Malaysia and became an independent republic.

The immediate post-independence period – from 1957 until mid-1969 – was filled with developmental activities in many fields, including culture. Nevertheless, the population was still economically divided along ethnic lines. This disparity led to riots in May 1969 and caused the government to re-evaluate its policies and the goals of the new nation. During the 1970s the government attempted to restructure society to ensure greater economic parity among the people as well as stronger national unity. While the special rights of the Malays were retained, the citizenship rights of other groups were upheld. In the arts attempts were made to define national culture as essentially Malay culture with Islam as its base. Other communities were expected to contribute from their own cultural heritages. Through the decade, however, an international Islamic revival affected the balance and students became particularly militant. Muslims sought to reinvestigate their religious roots and religious values began to be emphasized in daily life and work.

As well, the country was challenged at this time by an economic recession, a split in UMNO (which has continued to be the ruling party since independence) and a constitutional crisis. At the end of the 1980s, the prime minister announced *Wawasan 2020* (*Vision 2020*), a goal meant to inspire Malaysians to help their country become a fully developed nation – socially, culturally, economically and politically – by the year 2020. Through the 1990s, Malaysia has continued to enjoy a new political stability and economic progress, as well as a renewed sense of cultural and artistic awareness.

Theatre in many forms exists in all four of the country's major languages: Bahasa Malaysia, Mandarin, Tamil and English. The Malay-language theatre, which has the longest and most continuous history in the country, is usually divided into three categories: traditional, transitional (popular) and modern.

Traditional theatre forms, which have roots in the Malay community, include *wayang kulit* (shadow-puppet theatre), *menora* (a Thai-influenced dance-drama traditionally performed with an all-male cast), *mak yong* (a Malay dance-drama in which women usually perform all roles except the clown), *kuda kepang* (an Indonesian hobby-horse trance dance), *dikir barat* (a call-response performance using verse and poetry sung to music), *boria* (a comic sketch followed by a call-response form of sung processional), *randai* (a martial arts-derived dance-drama from Sumatra), *main puteri* (a traditional Malay healing ceremony that involves trance and dramatic elements), *mek mulong* (a dance-drama performed in Kedah) and the storytelling tradition of the *penglipur lara*. Some of these forms exhibit foreign influence (Thai, Javanese, Sumatran, Indian and Arab) and were introduced into the country by foreign settlers and traders. The origins of many forms remain largely conjectural, but *wayang kulit*, for instance, has been nurtured for at least five hundred years in Malaysia.

Bangsawan constitutes the transitional popular category and bridges the gap between traditional and modern Malay theatre. Containing elements of both according to scholar Cantius Leo Camoens (1980–1: 192), it is also transitional because it was created during a period of change in Malayan society when the British colonial presence meant increased urbanization and western influence in the country (Mohammed Safian Hussain *et al.* 1974: 168).

Malaysian theatre scholars also tend to agree with James Brandon who, in *Theatre in Southeast Asia*, identifies *bangsawan* as popular theatre since it is commercial, professional and urban-based.

The origins of *bangsawan* date back to the 1870s when a drama troupe from India called Wayang Parsi (Parsi Theatre), comprised of Parsis who performed in Hindi, introduced a novel style of theatre to Penang audiences. *Wayang parsi* stories were adapted from Indian and Arabian tales as well as from western drama. Ornately costumed performers depicted the fantasy world of gods and goddesses. Songs and dances were interspersed throughout the productions. Local troupes created an imitation *wayang parsi* style which was popular until 1884 in Penang and, to a lesser extent, in Singapore.

Bangsawan, a distinctly Malay theatre form, evolved as an offshoot of *wayang parsi*. In 1885, the first professional *bangsawan* group was organized in Penang. In the early 1900s, *bangsawan* troupes carried on the professional character of the *wayang parsi*, particularly in Penang, Perak and Selangor. Like *wayang parsi*,

A *bangsawan* performance.

the *bangsawan* repertoire was adapted from Indian, Arabian and western tales, but it also included Chinese and Malay stories. The Malay language replaced Hindi and the original characters in the foreign tales became Malay.

The period 1902–35 constitutes the golden era of *bangsawan* theatre, when many *bangsawan* groups – both large and small – were formed in Malaya. The groups were enthusiastically received wherever they played, including Indonesia. Due to competition among troupes and financial instability, many groups rose quickly only to fall and be replaced in popularity by others. *Bangsawan* was at its peak of success from 1920 to 1935.

Between 1935 and 1945, *bangsawan* declined due to World War II and the Japanese occupation (1942–5). Audiences diminished, little profit could be made and performers were in danger during the war. Under these conditions, many troupes folded. The Japanese used *bangsawan* for pro-Japanese, anti-British propaganda purposes and placed restrictions on performances.

At the end of the war, only five groups remained (Rahmah Bujang 1987: 36) and only a few more started up again. Troupes had difficulty replenishing their supply of costumes and properties lost during the war; also, many performers had died. The fifteen years following the war (1945–60) witnessed the further decline of the art.

Economic conditions in the country in the reconstruction period were poor. In addition, the public was preoccupied with political issues arising from Britain's Malayan Union proposals until the Federation of Malaya was formed in 1948 (Camoens 1980–1: 169). Some *bangsawan* troupes did, however, respond to the political situation by giving performances in support of the struggle against the Malayan Union.

Then, from 1946 to 1960, *bangsawan* was affected by the State of Emergency in Malaysia aimed at curbing the communist insurrection. *Bangsawan* performance schedules were constrained by curfews imposed during the emergency. Troupes continued to fold during the 1950s, and by the 1960s and 1970s, there were apparently no professional troupes like those of the earlier era remaining (Camoens 1980–1: 177–8).

By the time stability in the country returned after the Emergency, modern commercial media like film, radio and television, as well as new dramatic forms (*sandiwara* and *drama moden*) were attracting audience attention. Film was the earliest competitor. Star *bangsawan* performers left their theatre troupes to make films which offered higher salaries and more glamour and status. *Bangsawan*'s role as popular entertainment was thus usurped by film and radio during the 1940s and 1950s and by television after its introduction into Malaysia in 1963.

In 1972, the government sponsored the formation of a *bangsawan* troupe to perform in Federal Land Development Authority (FELDA) settlements. The mobile troupe entertained and at the same time educated the settlers about government policies and modern ways to improve their life.

Simultaneous with the development of *bangsawan* was the development of *sandiwara* theatre, the first phase of the modern drama movement in Malaysia. Soom after *bangsawan* gained popularity in the Malay States and the Straits Settlements, various troupes began touring Indonesia. Not only was the *bangsawan* style warmly received there, but also it was adapted and significantly altered, soon becoming known as *stambul*. The Indonesian *stambul* theatre in turn toured Malaya. Between 1891 and 1906 the *stambul* was similar to the *bangsawan*; however, between 1906 and 1926, the *stambul* began to develop along more realistic lines depicting modern stories based on contemporary life. These and succeeding changes resulted in part from western influences on Indonesian drama.

After 1926, the trend towards realism in Indonesian theatre continued, and the *stambul* came to be called *sandiwara* (drama). During the 1920s and 1930s, Indonesian troupes introduced *sandiwara* into Malaya. These productions influenced the development of local Malay drama, particularly in the use of scripts for performances and the growing importance of the director in organizing the performance from start to finish (Camoens 1980–1: 184–7).

At the same time Indonesian troupes were generating interest in new styles of drama in Malaya, significant drama activity among Malays was occurring at the Sultan Idris Training College at Tanjung Malim, Perak (established 1922). Although drama activity occurred in other schools, what was done at Tanjung Malim was of the most consequence, particularly because of its Malay Translation Bureau (established 1924) which produced translations of plays such as *Macbeth*, *Julius Caesar*, *Faustus* and *Black Mask*. These plays were performed by teacher trainees through the dramatic society of the college. An original play was written at the college in 1938 and a graduate of the college wrote and directed four plays during 1944–5 (Camoens 1980–1: 219).

Za'ba (Zainal Abidin bin Ahmad, 1895–1973), an esteemed linguist and language teacher and the head translator at the Translation Bureau, is considered a pioneer in helping to establish modern Malay drama through his translations of several plays and theoretical works about drama by Arab writers, such as Tawfiq al-Hakīm. Between 1929 and 1930, Za'ba translated some of Charles and Mary Lamb's *Tales from Shakespeare*.

The adaptation and translation of foreign plays thus preceded the writing of modern drama. Although plays by Malay authors were published in magazines and newspapers prior to World War II, insufficient documentation exists to determine with certainty what constitutes the first written or performed modern Malay play. Shaharom Husain (b. 1919), a major *sandiwara* playwright, states that he staged his first play in 1930, although it was not fully scripted. During the 1930s he staged two other plays that he had written in full.

Sandiwara drama continued to be written and staged during the Japanese occupation. Under Japanese censorship, *sandiwara* performances conveyed anti-British propaganda. Shaharom Husain maintained his interest in theatre during the occupation, directing his play *Lawyer Dahlan* in 1943.

It was after World War II that productions of *sandiwara* plays became a common community and group activity and that the style assumed maturity as a dramatic art. It was also after the war, as *sandiwara* managed to fill the cultural gap created by the decline of *bangsawan*, that the term *sandiwara* came into general use in Malaya (Camoens 1980–1: 223).

During the nationalist period following the war and immediately after independence in 1957, *sandiwara* playwrights wrote plays that supported the nationalist cause. Inspired by Indonesian, western and, to a lesser extent, Arab dramatic models, Malay theatre enthusiasts undertook the task of creating a modern drama in Bahasa Malaysia. This language, it was felt, was vital to developing a nationalist spirit, a view strongly advocated in the early 1950s by the influential Singapore-based writers' association, Angkatan Sasterawan 50 (The Writers' Generation of the 1950s) or ASAS 50. During the 1950s and early 1960s, Singapore was a centre of Malay theatrical activity, even more so than peninsular Malaysia. The fact that Singapore was already a centre for modern Malay literature facilitated the growth of theatre generally in the city-state.

The significance of the Sultan Idris Training college in terms of drama continued after the war. There, and at other colleges as well, teachers and students held performances which included their own written sketches and plays. Better education for Malays after the war meant a higher rate of literacy and greater receptivity to modern drama. The publishing of scripts in magazines, newspapers and finally in book form in 1951 also helped promote the new drama. Shaharom Husain became a prominent teacher/playwright of the period, fostering *sandiwara* drama among his colleagues and students at the Malay Teachers' Training College in Johor.

Sandiwara was mainly an amateur activity which various sectors of the community pursued with serious commitment. During the *sandiwara* period, theatre festivals and competitions began to be held as a means of encouraging the new drama. Dewan Bahasa dan Pustaka (the Language and Literature Agency, established in 1956 as a quasi-government publishing house) organized playwriting contests as a means of fulfilling its mandate to promote Malay language and literature. The then-Ministry of Culture, Youth and Sports (now the Ministry of Culture, Arts and Tourism) also began to sponsor drama festivals and competitions during this period.

In surveying factors that contributed to the growth of the new drama, radio plays should not be overlooked. Radio dramas, also called *sandiwara*, were promoted immediately after the war as a type of social drama which would help build national consciousness, educate the public and provide moral guidance, as well as for entertainment. Usman Awang (b. 1929), a founding member of ASAS 50 and an important playwright of *sandiwara* stage drama (and later styles), first wrote radio plays.

In addition to initiating the advent of the playwright in Malay drama, *sandiwara* also entailed the involvement of a modern-style director, one who would oversee all aspects of production and train the actors as well. In contrast to *bangsawan*, an improvised form, *sandiwara* required that actors memorize their dialogue. *Sandiwara* dramatists relied upon western or western-influenced Indonesian plays as models of serious, straight drama, that is, plays that were uninterrupted by extraneous forms of entertainment, such as the interludes of *bangsawan*. Through plays depicting historical themes, *sandiwara* drama began to question the status quo of Malay society. *Sandiwara* playwrights also depicted contemporary life, presenting moral lessons related to negative aspects of modernity.

The realistic drama of the 1960s, commonly called *drama moden* (modern drama), constitutes the second major phase in the development of modern Malay theatre. Furthering the realist trends introduced in *sandiwara* and strongly influenced by Indonesian and western realistic plays, the 1960s playwrights firmly allied modern Malay drama with international (western-derived) modern theatre, while maintaining the local identity of their works. Thus, recognizing that realism offered a direct, understandable medium for communicating ideas relevant to their new society, these writers adapted a clearly realistic mode which became the dominant style in Malay theatre from 1963 until the end of the decade.

With the responsibilities of independence at hand, *drama moden* playwrights thought it essential to portray social issues realistically. Whereas *sandiwara* plays portrayed both historical and contemporary times, *drama moden* playwrights were committed solely to creating on stage the image of contemporary society. Through their plays, *drama moden* playwrights endorsed the idea of national development and the philosophy of progress but expressed concern that the development occur in accordance with traditional values and attitudes.

Generally speaking, the 1960s was a period of increased public interest in modern theatre. Theatre education was promoted through seminars, talks, workshops and contests (Camoens 1980–1: 301–3). The amateur status of actors, playwrights and other theatre practitioners continued to characterize dramatic activity during the *drama moden* period.

The experimental theatre of the 1970s, also called *teater kontemporari* (contemporary theatre), constitutes the third identifiable phase of the Malay modern drama movement. This experimental style of theatre began when Noordin Hassan (b. 1929) staged his anti-realistic music drama *Bukan Lalang Ditiup Angin* (*It Is Not the Tall Grass Blown by the Wind*, 1970). Within a few years, avant-garde drama, which was in many cases a deliberate and radical departure from realism, became accepted as the creative style of the day. Contemporary playwrights viewed realism as a western form of theatre that was inappropriate in an era of intensified efforts to promote Malay culture. These artists gave priority to sources of inspiration from their own imagination and background and from the indigenous traditional theatres of the country in order to provide the modern stage with a distinct Malay identity.

At the same time that experimental theatre became the dominant style in the Malay-theatre world, it also established Malay drama as *the* modern drama in the country. In a large measure, Malay theatre became increasingly important as a cultural activity in the 1970s as a result of the government's efforts to foster Malay culture in the aftermath of the riots of 13 May 1969. Some important theatre artists who had been working in English-language theatre at this time decided to reconnect with the country's indigenous roots, such as dramatist Syed Alwi (b. 1930), performers Faridah Merican (b. 1939) and Rahim Razali (b. 1949), and critic/director Krishen Jit (b. 1939). Thus, the new energies emanating from Malay theatre in the first half of the 1970s drew attention away from English-language theatre and were very likely a cause of the decline in the number of English plays written and produced by Malaysians as the decade of the 1970s progressed.

The success of experimental theatre during the first half of the 1970s in terms of audience response caused artists to ponder why audiences declined during the latter half of the decade. Some concluded that theatrical experimentation had become too abstract and remote from mainstream audiences who wanted entertainment and escape from the pressures of daily life.

The post-1969 era not only witnessed attempts by the government to restructure society so as to eradicate poverty (especially in the Malay community), but also was a period of Islamic revivalism. At the start of the 1980s, Noordin Hassan's plays, *1400* and *Jangan Bunuh Rama-Rama* (*Don't Kill the Butterflies*) evidence a new approach to what he termed *teater fitrah* (theatre of faith).

As the 1980s progressed, Malaysia surmounted economic setbacks, coped with a split in the country's major political party (UMNO), confronted a judicial crisis and challenged monarchical prerogatives. Meanwhile, the Islamic revival became a mainstream phenomenon, one in which divergent groups and extremism were closely monitored by the government. In the cultural sphere, there was a visible reduction of government support for the arts and for theatre in particular, in response to Islamic sentiment. There was, for instance, no longer support for national theatre festivals.

Thus, the latter half of the 1980s saw a diminished Malay theatre world, as potential artists turned to religion and/or economic concerns.

Fortuitously, at this point in time, there was a mini-renaissance of English-language drama, compensating, in effect, for the temporary slowdown in Malay-language theatre activity. Historically, English-language theatre in Malaysia developed as an outgrowth of British colonialism which had brought English-language education, western literature and drama, and amateur theatricals to the Malayan urban population. Prior to the mid-1960s, Malaysians who participated in English-language expatriate-led productions did so mainly as actors. However, in the mid-1960s, the Malaysian Arts Theatre Group (MATG) began to promote Malaysian drama. In 1965, MATG became a Malaysian-run organization and the Malaysian members began to involve themselves fully as writers, directors, producers and technical designers. Among the new breed of English-language dramatists, some of whose works were compiled by Lloyd Fernando (b. 1926) in *New Drama One* and *New Drama Two*, are Edward Dorrall (b. 1936), Syed Alwi (b. 1930), Lee Joo For and Patrick Yeoh; only Syed Alwi has remained theatrically active until the present day.

These first playwrights from the English-language education/work milieu sought to give expression to Malaysian life and concerns in the post-independence period. No doubt envisioning themselves as part of an artistic vanguard, they sought to Malaysianize modern theatre through the use of plots, characters, themes and settings drawn from the realities of life in the new nation. Although they shared with their Malay-language counterparts a sense of pride in what Malaysian artists could accomplish, in fact Malay and English-language theatre practitioners during the 1960s were rarely aware of each other's efforts. At the start of the 1970s, however, certain drama festivals were held that brought Malay and English-language artists together to encourage an interchange of ideas and mutual recognition. This effort was an attempt to create a positive multi-cultural experience in the aftermath of the May riots.

As a result of new government measures implemented to ease racial tensions after 13 May and to create greater economic parity among the ethnic communities, the language of education in public schools and universities was progressively converted from English to Bahasa Malaysia, with English taught as a second language. Also, in light of a new national cultural policy that emphasized the role of Malay culture in the formation of a national culture (although the role of other communities in contributing to national culture was acknowledged), the government gave substantial support to Malay-language theatre through the sponsorship of festivals, competitions, seminars and workshops. Under these socio-cultural conditions, Malay drama rose in terms of national recognition and, as mentioned, the 1970s saw a rich flowering of theatrical experimentation among Malay playwrights/directors. At the same time, however, there was a noticeable decline in English-language theatre activities.

However, English-language theatre did not die out completely. Indeed, during the 1980s, there were signs of a renewed confidence in English-language theatre and a more flexible approach to the issue of language and drama in Malaysia. New English-language theatre groups emerged (e.g. Five Arts Centre, Kamikasih (We Love), Actor's Studio and Instant Cafe Theatre), featuring works by a new wave of Malaysian playwrights (e.g. K.S. Maniam (b. 1942), Leow Puay Tin (b. 1957) , Kee Thuan Chye (b. 1954) and Chin San Sooi) as well as by contemporary international playwrights. Maniam wrote of the conflicts and complexities of Indian Malaysian life. Leow Puay Tin reflected upon childhood memories in Malacca. Kee Thuan Chye spoke for a more integrated Malaysian society. Chin San Sooi staged musicals based on Chinese-Malaysian history as well as Chinese legendary tales. By 1995, English-language theatre had firmly re-established itself as a vital part of Malaysian cultural life.

In addition, since the beginning of the 1990s, modern Chinese drama (in Mandarin) has also demonstrated a comeback. In the post-World War II era through the 1960s, most of the Chinese plays performed in Malaysia were written and staged in a conventional, realistic mode. Thematically, the plays drew upon life in China or in the Chinese-Malaysian community. This trend continued into the 1970s, although there were fewer active playwrights and productions. Chen Zhen Yen, from Klang, was noted for his realistic social dramas about Chinese family relationships. Yau Tuo, originally from mainland China, also gained recognition in the 1960s and 1970s for his realistic portrayals of contemporary Chinese life, as well as his historical plays about China. In *Monk*, a play based on a modern Taiwanese novel, Yao Tuo depicts the story of a woman who falls in love with a Buddhist monk.

Since the mid-1960s, the Dramatic Arts Society has been the major organizing agency for modern Chinese plays. The society organized theatre festivals during 1977–9, but due to a lack of funds and sponsorship, the festivals were discontinued during the 1980s. In 1991, this special event was resumed as a week-long National Day Drama Festival, with sponsorship from the Ministry of Culture, Arts and Tourism. After a decade of reduced drama activity, new experimental trends appeared in contemporary Chinese theatre. For instance, for the 1991 festival, Soon Chua Mae (b. 1963) directed an experimental version of Yau Tuo's *Monk*, using only the two principal characters. The National Day Drama Festival has continued to be held annually in the Malaysian Tourist Information Centre (MATIC), a popular Kuala Lumpur venue. Malay drama groups as well as Mandarin groups have been invited to perform for this occasion.

In 1988, the Malaysian Institute of Arts (MIA), primarily a Mandarin-medium institution, began to train students in its performing arts programme. Since 1991, MIA graduates have been trying to break from the realistic mould of modern Chinese theatre and create along more innovative, experimental lines. Particularly in small-scale directing projects, they have now devised more personal improvisational styles. For major graduation projects, they tend to select established international works, such as Shakespeare's *A Midsummer Night's Dream*, *Rashomon* and Pirandello's *Six Characters in Search of an Author* which are also beyond the conventional selections and style of the Dramatic Arts Society. Some MIA graduates formed the Theatre Education Committee, which organizes drama workshops for secondary school students on a volunteer basis.

The Malaysian Institute of Art tries to work cooperatively with the Dramatic Arts Society, in spite of their different theatrical expectations. For example, both participate in the National Day Drama Festivals. MIA graduates also write and direct new plays for the society. The 1994 production of *Naja*, for instance, based on a popular Taiwanese movie, was innovatively staged by playwright/director Ho Shih Pin, a recent MIA graduate. Scenes in the play alternated between Chinese legendary time and the youth culture of contemporary Malaysia.

Both MIA and the Dramatic Arts Society participated in the ambitious 1994 production of *The Legend of Yue Fei*, which was sponsored by the Malaysian Chinese Cultural Society and other Chinese asociations. In this poetic, epic work, guest director Ma Huei Tien from the Central Academy of Drama in Beijing speaks through the long monologues of general Yue Fei to explain and thereby reinterpret the latter's legendary cowardice in retreating from battle. With a post-modern touch, Ma includes a modern-day history student who wanders throughout the piece trying to comprehend the reasons behind Yue Fei's actions. Performed originally in Singapore, the Malaysian production included four principles from the Singapore cast. The China-Singapore-Malaysian Mandarin-language event may herald a new era in cooperative theatre ventures. In general, it should be noted that most Chinese Malaysians do not understand Mandarin. Therefore, the audience for many plays comprises mainly students who may be studying at Chinese vernacular schools. However, *The Legend of Yue Fei* drew a wide spectrum of audience members since the legend is well known.

The first half of the 1990s witnessed a new vitality in Malay-language theatre. The government resumed and increased support for cultural activities in general and for theatre in particular, demonstrated by the establishment of the country's first National Arts Academy, which offers a diploma in theatre arts. New theatre spaces were opened and the government planned to develop a comprehensive national theatre facility. Government sponsorship of productions continued on a regular basis.

There was a new move by the government to support theatre in English, as well as in Malay, to encourage tourists and other foreigners in the country to appreciate Malaysia's multicultural heritage and artistic expertise. In the mid-1990s, some well-known Malay plays have been translated and performed in English. This fresh encouragement for culture and theatre in particular, indicates the government's awareness that Malaysians need to develop culturally and artistically, as well as industrially and technologically. As the country positions itself more squarely on the international stage, there is an awareness that cultural sophistication is integral to successful international relations.

Structure of the National Theatre Community

Since 1970, the Ministry of Culture, Arts and Tourism (known previously as the Ministry of Culture, Youth and Sports), through its creative branch, Kompleks Budaya Negara (National Cultural Complex), commonly referred to as KBN, has sponsored theatre seminars, workshops, training programmes, festivals and competitions which have aided in the development of contemporary Malay-language theatre. Each state in Malaysia has its own theatre groups, many of which have proliferated through the encouragement of this ministry as it implements its various theatre programmes.

In 1990, Majlis Teater Kebangsaan Malaysia (National Theatre Council of Malaysia), better known as TEMA, was established. TEMA is the realization of the dream and vision of a national theatre council first voiced in the 1970s. Under TEMA's encouragement, most states have organized their own theatre councils, appropriately named after the respective states (e.g. Majlis Teater Negeri Kedah or the Theatre Council of Kedah). Most states have now joined TEMA through their respective theatre councils which select representatives to serve on TEMA's executive board. Representatives from various colleges and universities that have drama activities/departments also serve on this board.

The main objectives of TEMA are to unify the many theatre activists and groups throughout Malaysia; to oversee, advise and create an atmosphere that is conducive for nurturing, developing and encouraging theatre in Malaysia; and to coordinate as well as to supervise theatre activities at state, national and international levels. The association's international efforts to date comprise sponsoring groups from the ASEAN region, especially Indonesia.

Several amateur Malay-language groups have endured over the years under committed leaders. Among the best known are Hidayah, Batek, Suara Alam, Kumpulan Teater Kuala Lumpur (Kuala Lumpur Theatre Group), Kau (in Kedah) and Tetamu (Visitors) in Terengganu. These groups function through the consensus of organizational committees.

Amateur groups, which usually perform in English and are registered as non-profit societies, such as the long-established Liberal Arts Society and the Selangor Philharmonic Society (which stages musicals), are comprised of talented members of both the Malaysian and expatriate communities. They operate under executive boards with decisions being made by committee.

A notably active promoter of cultural activities in Malaysia is the British Council, which sponsors British theatre groups, workshops, speakers, poetry readings and exhibits as well as providing a popular venue for small-scale experimental theatre productions by Malaysian companies.

There are also amateur Chinese drama groups, performing in Mandarin, Cantonese and other Chinese languages, which are energized by graduates from the Malaysian Institute of Arts, members of the Chinese-Malaysian community and guest artists from abroad. The Indian-Malaysian community also supports amateur theatre. The Temple of Fine Arts stages large-scale productions, often multicultural in theme and style. Plays are presented by other Indian religious and community groups, performing in various languages (Malayali, Tamil, Bengali).

A few theatre groups have been operating successfully as businesses: Five Arts Centre, Actor's Studio, Instant Cafe Theatre, CentreStage and Kamikasih. Although the groups rely heavily on sponsorship for productions and individual members do not depend wholly on theatre for their livelihood, these energetic companies foreshadow increasing professional opportunities for theatre artists in Malaysia.

The size of companies varies. Amateur groups tend to have large memberships, between thirty and a hundred people. Those groups operating on a commercial basis usually have a core of five to ten.

Groups generally rehearse from a month to three months, depending on the size of the production. Some performances are staged first as workshops, the participants welcoming comments from invited or public audiences; the final performance is staged later as a reworking of the initial project. Some groups have started to co-sponsor performances and to plan joint theatre seasons.

The national, state and city governments subsidize productions regularly and provide the rehearsal and performance space. They pay directors, playwrights, actors and technical crew. They often commission performances for special occasions, such as the King's coronation and birthday, Independence Day or the opening of a new building. The national government provides about 50,000 ringgit for one-act plays and 80,000 ringgit for full-length plays at MATIC (2.5 ringgit equals US$1.00).

Other sponsoring agencies include TEMA, the colleges and universities, Malaysian and multinational corporations, Dewan Bahasa dan Pustaka, newspapers, television stations and shopping malls. TEMA, in conjunction with the Ministry of Culture, Arts and Tourism, conducts a biennial theatre competition called Pekan Teater (Theatre Boroughs) among TEMA-affiliated groups from across the country. The winning play is given a showcase performance at a major Kuala Lumpur venue.

Advertisements appear in newspapers, on radio, sometimes on television, through direct mailing, by word-of-mouth, posters and banners. Although most theatre activity occurs in Kuala Lumpur and its environs, occasionally groups tour to Penang and other states, supplementing existing theatre activity, or outside groups come to Kuala Lumpur to perform.

Every two years, the national government, in conjunction with Dewan Bahasa dan Pustaka, awards a national literary prize for the best one-act play and the best full-length play. Among the recipients of the Anugerah Sasterawan Negara (National Writer Laureate Award) presented by the national government when deemed appropriate, the winner in 1993 was Noordin Hassan, the only recipient to date known solely for his playwriting and directorial work.

TEMA has, since 1993, organized a one-act playwriting competition every year in an effort to enrich the one-act play repertoire. The competition is conducted in tandem with the one-act play series sponsored by the Ministry of Culture, Arts and Tourism.

ESSO, the multinational oil company and the National Writers' Association of Malaysia (GAPENA) have organized three national ESSO-GAPENA playwriting competitions. The English-language daily, the New Straits Times, in conjunction with ESSO, has organized two national playwriting competitions in English.

Theme-specific playwriting competitions have also been held. The prime minister's department organized a playwriting competition inviting works with Islamic themes and the Persatuan Sejarah Malaysia (Malaysian Historical Society) organized a competition inviting works with historical themes.

Ticket prices for plays vary from 7 to 50 ringgit, depending on the degree of sponsorship for the performance. Benefit performances cost more, up to 100 ringgit per ticket. There is also dinner theatre, performed at major hotels by foreign touring companies, the cost of which is 80–100 ringgit per person. Since the late 1980's there has been a noticeable increase in ticket prices; many performances in the 1970s were free or cost only 1–3 ringgit. The higher prices reflect higher production costs, including artists' fees, a higher cost of living and broad-based middle-class support. The government now not only seeks to recover some of the costs of sponsored productions but also wishes to educate the public to value the theatrical enterprise so that they will support it more fully. Finally, higher ticket prices reflect a move towards greater professionalism in theatre.

It should be noted that glossy, artistically designed programmes for non-government-sponsored plays may cost 3–10 ringgit each. In the past, programmes for all performances were free and more simply designed. As a comparison, for 3 ringgit in 1997 one could go to a nearby food stall after the show and buy a hot noodle dish and *teh tarik* (pulled tea). Alternatively, for 10 ringgit, one may go to an up-market hotel and have coffee and toast.

Artistic Profile

In Malaysia, one can now attend traditional theatre, 're-fashioned' *bangsawan* and modern theatre, including music and dance programmes. Traditional theatre can be seen in mostly rural areas during special occasions (weddings, harvest times, illnesses, rites of passage, vow-fulfilling rituals, ceremonies and festivals). However, depending on the political climate in some states, particularly Kelantan, there may be restrictions placed on public performances of traditional theatre to accommodate certain religious sentiments. Traditional performances are staged in Kuala Lumpur, Penang and other state capitals and towns for special occasions as tourist attractions and for the general public's entertainment.

Bangsawan is no longer performed as a commercial venture with professional troupes touring the country. However, some state agencies and university lecturers try to keep *bangsawan* alive through their support of the few remaining performance groups. In addition, modern playwrights have sought to keep *bangsawan* visible through the incorporation of *bangsawan* theatrical elements in their dramas or by creating modernized *bangsawan* plays. The Ministry of Culture, Arts and Tourism occasionally organizes a *bangsawan* performance.

Modern plays can be viewed throughout Malaysia but most frequently in Kuala Lumpur and other major cities and towns. Dance theatre also is predominantly an urban cultural activity although it may draw its inspiration from traditional theatre and stories. Musical theatre is performed annually in the capital by the Selangor Philharmonic Symphony. Foreign touring companies stage musical performances in Kuala Lumpur, Shah Alam and Penang. Certain playwrights, like Noordin Hassan, incorporate musical theatre elements into their modern plays. Chin San Sooi stages musical reviews and dramas.

Traditional theatre still draws the local rural community and when performed in urban venues usually attracts a cosmopolitan audience as well. Also, Malaysian and other researchers will seek out and document traditional performances in original venues as well as transplanted ones. Universiti Sains Malaysia, in particular, has been known for including traditional performing artists among their drama faculty. Occasionally, special festivals are arranged by USM in Penang and the National Academy of Arts and City Hall in Kuala Lumpur. In recent years in Kuala Lumpur, the Ministry of Culture, Arts and Tourism has organized Malaysia Fest annually, a two-week cultural event featuring the dances, music, songs and traditional theatres of Malaysia. Hotels and restaurants participate in Malaysia Fest by providing a sampling of traditional Malaysian food, décor and crafts.

ASEAN countries have also begun a programme of joint tourist promotions by alternating 'tourist years' (e.g. Visit Malaysia Year, Visit Thailand Year). Traditional and other performances are planned for each year in the respective countries to cater to the tourist industry.

Bangsawan, since it is no longer performed in its original manner, draws basically urban audiences who enjoy a nostalgic entertainment. The revived, 're-fashioned' *bangsawan* is also meant to attract a tourist audience and to ensure the continued availability of *bangsawan* performers.

Modern theatre draws both urban and rural audiences. Plays from outside Kuala Lumpur are occasionally staged in the capital for competitions, festivals and showcase performances. Also, Kuala Lumpur groups occasionally tour to other states, especially to perform at Universiti Sains Malaysia in Penang and the new Universiti Malaysia Sarawak (UNIMAS), both of which have performing arts departments, as well as to Singapore for the Singapore International Arts Festival or for joint projects/workshops with Singapore artists. Music and dance theatre attract a mostly urban audience.

Wayang kulit is the best known of the traditional theatre forms. Believed to be derived from Indian shadow-puppet theatre, it has been performed in Southeast Asia for at least 500 years. The basic purpose of *wayang kulit* is entertainment, although cultural values are clearly inculcated into the performance. *Wayang kulit* is traditionally very long, lasting several nights. It is usually seen on special communal occasions or by request. Traditionally it is a rural art form but nowadays *Wayang kulit* is usually done in one evening since even rural residents have adapted to more modern time schedules.

Mak yong, another traditional form, originated in Kelantan and was also popular traditionally in Terengganu. It is performed by female troupes (clown roles are played by men) and was established as a court form (*c.*1875) that became popular with the villagers as well.

The various traditional theatre forms share several features in common. Performances are usually unscripted and are drawn mainly from stories and legends known to the community. Generally, plots are episodic and long enough to allow audience members to drift in and out during the performance. Traditional artists are also free to improvise, especially in clown

Wayang kulit (shadow-puppet theatre).

sections or in sections which relate to contemporary issues. Performers work towards the creation of recognizable character types, stylized movement, poetic language and rhythmic speech. Along with dialogue and narrated passages, music, song and dance are also incorporated into traditional performances. Serious or tragic events are intermixed with comedy. Traditional performances have a connection with ritual and the world of spirits.

There are usually ritual ceremonies prior to the start of a traditional performance to ensure its success and the safety of the performers and audience. Since the forms are regionally based, the performers use regional dialects, which may be incomprehensible to Malaysians from other parts of the country. Plays usually have an opening scene that introduces the royal or major figures. The hero encounters one difficulty after another. The play usually ends with the status quo of traditional society re-established, the hero safe and betrothed or reunited with the heroine and the kingdom secure. Also, set patterns of performance styles are transmitted from master artist to apprentice, from one generation to the next.

Chinese theatre, performed in various dialects, has had a long history in Malaysia, dating back to at least the nineteenth century. It is performed by groups for special religious and festival occasions and not as regular, commercial entertainment. Audiences are usually from urban areas.

The plot of a Chinese Opera often involves a conflict between social obligation and personal or humanistic concern. Some plays end on a cheerful note with marriage or the return of the hero to his family; others end on a sombre note with a dramatic death.

Bangsawan originated during the last quarter of the nineteenth century when a *wayang parsi* touring group from India came to Penang and influenced the establishment of similar troupes. *Bangsawan* was the first professional/commercial theatre venture in what was then Malaya and the first in which both men and women performed. *Bangsawan* troupes were also the first groups to use standard Malay (whereas traditional theatre was performed in dialect) and to use a proscenium stage with painted backdrops. At its peak, urban, town and rural audiences all enjoyed *bangsawan*. Beginning in 1987, the government tried to invigorate the *bangsawan* theatre through a special series: Manifestasi Bangsawan I–V.

Bangsawan is an improvised theatre form, using a basic plot scenario or outline. The performance entails a similar episodic plot structure to that of traditional theatre, except that interlude performances are included to entertain the audience (popular songs, dances, comic sketches, etc.). Also, *bangsawan* performances draw from a wider range of legends and tales than do the traditional theatres (Indian, Arab, Persian, Chinese, Malay and western); some also depict contemporary life. *Bangsawan* as performed in the 1990s is no longer improvised but based on written scripts and interludes are usually omitted. Also, some contemporary playwrights – Noordin Hassan, Syed Alwi, Zakaria Ariffin (b. 1952) – like to create characters who are members of *bangsawan* troupes. These characters then create *bangsawan* sketches in a play-within-a-play format as well as act the role of *bangsawan* performers in the main action of the drama. Rahman Bujang (b. 1947) in *Puteri Li Po* (*The Princess Li Po*) attempted to create a modern *bangsawan* play based on a historical figure: the story of the Chinese princess who came to Malacca in the fifteenth century to wed

Zakaria Ariffin's production of *Raja Lawak* (*King of Comedians*).

Sultan Mansor Shah, thereby establishing links between the Malaccan Sultanate and China.

Sandiwara theatre was primarily a phenomenon of the 1950s and early 1960s in Malaysia. However, the style has not totally disappeared and since the 1970s, *sandiwara* plays have occasionally been revived. As well, some contemporary theatre groups and playwrights still create in the *sandiwara* mode. Two examples are the group Hidayah, under the leadership of playwright/director Kamarulzaman and playwright/director Mohammed Ghouse Nasuruddin whose works are often performed and toured by his USM students.

The *sandiwara* repertoire includes both historical (*purbawara*) and contemporary plays. Characters are mortal beings, often of a stereotypic or symbolic nature. Stylistically, *sandiwara* playwrights were inspired by Shakespeare and the Greek tragedies and modified certain conventions of *bangsawan* and traditional theatre. At the same time, *sandiwara* reflects an overall trend toward realism. The *sandiwara* playwright of greatest repute is Shaharom Husain, who established many of the norms for *sandiwara* theatre. His plays, some of which are written in poetic verse, show figures who challenge the feudal order and colonialism by evoking democratic principles but who meet defeat due to their own shortcomings.

The heyday for realistic drama was in the 1960s. However, since the 1980s, playwrights have returned to realism to draw audiences back to the theatre. There are also occasional revivals of the 1960s plays.

The experimental absurdist style of the 1970s resurfaces only occasionally in the 1990s. The most recent example of such a 1970s-style play was Mohammed Ghouse Nasuruddin's *Kabur* (*Obscurity*, 1995).

Companies

The only national performing arts company is the music and dance troupe of the National Cultural Complex (KBN) which is the creative arm of the Ministry of Culture, Arts and Tourism. Since the 1970s, KBN has employed and trained its own troupe, working specifically with dancers. These dancers in turn train other dancers and choreographers from throughout the country at the KBN facility in Kuala Lumpur. The latter then return to their respective states and help develop state dance troupes.

KBN's national troupe performs throughout Malaysia as well as internationally. In addition, its performers are available for special occasions and have been featured in theatre productions, particularly the music dramas of Noordin Hassan. The national dance troupe gives steady employment to young artists and has provided ongoing training. There is, however, no national dramatic troupe.

The theatre companies that operate in every state, including in or near Kuala Lumpur, are therefore working on an amateur basis although since the 1980s many operate as businesses rather than as clubs or groups. The progenitor of this type of theatre enterprise was Teater Elit (Elite Theatre) formed in the late 1970s by poet/playwright Usman Awang, poet Sutong R.S. (b. 1948) and the new generation absurdist dramatist Dinsman and friends. By calling themselves Elite Theatre, these artists were making the satirical point that Malaysians could produce commercial theatre in the manner of foreign touring companies. Malaysians, too, could perform for profit and public consumption by catering to the artistic aspirations of a growing middle- and upper-class audience accustomed to seeing the foreign companies that performed in major hotels. Therefore, Teater Elit's dinner theatre, regular poetry readings and business office were hotel-based. Teater Elit operated until the mid-1980s.

Current companies include Five Arts Centre, Actor's Studio, Instant Cafe Theatre, Centrestage, Kamikasih, Suasana Dance Company and Sutra Dance Company. Five Arts Centre specializes in English-language plays by Malaysian writers and is, in fact, a major promoter of Malaysian English-language theatre, showcasing established as well as new artists. Many of their productions are presented in workshop format, inviting audience response before final productions are mounted. Lately they have also experimented with multilingual productions. In addition, they are recognized for establishing close ties with the Singapore theatre community. Krishen Jit, one of the founding members of Five Arts Centre, directs Singapore productions and also co-directs with a Singapore colleague in Malaysia. Further, as the name implies, Five Arts Centre promotes various arts besides drama, such as dance, music, painting and sculpture. Some of their performances take place in galleries and are avant-garde, multi-art events, such as *Skin Trilogy* (1995) based on a text by K.S. Maniam and performed in the National Art Gallery in Kuala Lumpur.

Suasana Dance Company under the direction of Azanin Ahmad.

Actor's Studio is known for bringing North American, Australian and British theatre to Kuala Lumpur and for mounting mainstream as well as fringe productions. Australian Joe Hasham (b. 1948), the artistic director of the group, has also adapted Irish theatre to the Malaysian context.

Instant Cafe Theatre has brought a high level of sophisticated political satire to Malaysian urban, corporate audiences.

There are other companies that perform with regularity but are not businesses. For example, the Temple of Fine Arts, which stages elaborate annual productions of dance-dramas drawn from a wide repertoire of stories and legends (e.g. the Indian Ramayana, the Malay tale of Mahsuri, the Chinese legend of Lady White Snake and Shakespeare's *A Midsummer Night's Dream* set in sixteenth-century Rajasthan). All proceeds from the Temple of Fine Arts productions go to support their health clinic and other charitable organizations.

The Liberal Arts Society remains active and is beginning to promote fringe, rather than only mainstream, productions. Selangor Philharmonic Society has begun to stage Malaysian as well as western musicals. Other companies are evolving, such as the all-women's company Kuali Works (established 1994), as Malaysian theatre in general experiences a renaissance in the 1990s.

The Dramatic Arts Society promotes theatre activities in Mandarin, sometimes in conjunction with faculty, students and graduates from the Malaysian Institute of Arts. The Malaysian Chinese Cultural Society has sponsored a major production and invited an established playwright/director as well as performers from abroad to work with the Malaysian cast. Chinese Assembly Hall members also sponsor and stage plays of relevance to their respective communities. The Chinese Opera Society is treading new ground by offering play excerpts in English as well as in Cantonese. Another experiment was the staging of a Chinese Opera based on the story of Hang Li Po, drawn from Malay history.

These various companies – whether operating as business or as amateur associations – are of importance because they provide a diverse, steady stream of high-quality theatre for Malaysian audiences, albeit mainly those living in or near the capital. The companies have made increasing efforts to cooperate with one another in offering their seasons and now provide actor training programmes, theatre workshops and a laboratory framework for new directors and playwrights. The more established members of these companies often mentor new artists.

Suasana Dance Company, for example, under the artistic directorship of Azanin Ahmad, researches indigenous theatre forms and legends and incorporates them into theatrically innovative productions. Suasana tours productions abroad, introducing a contemporary Malay dance-drama aesthetic to international audiences. Sutra Dance Company, under the artistic directorship of Ramli Ibrahim, investigates, trains in and creates from an indigenous base. The Temple of Fine Arts uses traditional dance forms drawn from a variety of cultures as a choreographic base. KBN employs traditional artists, such as the *wayang kulit* puppet master (*dalang*), Pak Hamzah, winner of the national traditional artist award, to train their music and *wayang kulit* ensemble. KBN utilizes traditional forms (mainly Malay) as a choreographic base.

Occasionally, the companies, the ministry and/or other agencies will sponsor theatre festivals and retrospectives. For example, the British Council assisted several theatre companies stage an English-language theatre retrospective in 1995, featuring Malaysian plays from the 1960s to the mid-1970s. The companies are also a means of introducing Malaysian theatre arts to the international community. Apart from the members of the KBN troupe, no one is yet making a living doing theatre, but many performances are of professional quality and there is a strong professional attitude among theatre practitioners.

Dramaturgy

Drama moden playwrights pursued a stricter course of realistic drama than found in *sandiwara*. Their works address the problematic consequences of progress during the 1960s post-independence era of nation-building. Characters are drawn from everyday life and speak colloquial Malay. The dramatic form is modelled on Indonesian and western realistic plays. Plots often involve characters who reconnect with their past in order to reaffirm cultural values that are still important for the present. Mustapha Kamil Yassin (whose pen name is Kala Dewata, b. 1925) set the guidelines for realistic drama, encouraging a realistic acting style as well as realism in dialogue, costume and setting.

Another prominent playwright whose career began in the 1960s is Bidin Subari, who writes under the pen name of Malina Manja (b. 1937). Bidin Subari pushed realism to exaggeration and dark comedy (see Solehah Ishak, *Histrionics of Development: A Study of Three Contemporary Malay Playwrights*, 1987: 61–2, 69–98).

Although model *drama moden* plays end with clear plot resolution and on an optimistic note, some realistic plays written from the mid-1960s onwards have open endings and are less optimistic in tone. Plays such as *Di Mana Bulan Selalu Retak* (*Where the Moon Always Cracks*) by A. Samad Said and *Anna* by Kemala, (the pen name of Ahmad Kamal Abdullah (b. 1941), are good examples of this attempt to demonstrate that social issues are complex and not easily resolved.

Experimental theatre of the 1970s was a reaction against realism. Themes addressed not only social issues, but also existential and universal concerns, and the nature of drama itself. Experimental playwrights evidenced an appreciation for the irrational in human behaviour. Characters were drawn from local history and legends, along with contemporary life. Dreams, illusions, fantasy, visions and symbolic deaths featured prominently in many 1970s plays. Staging was abstract or surrealistic and playwrights often experimented with traditional theatre forms. Experimental theatre reflected the 1970s era of increased governmental policy-making in the social, cultural and economic spheres of Malaysian life.

Noordin Hassan is credited with revolutionizing Malay theatre in the 1970s with his eclectic experimental approach to drama, utilizing choruses, traditional theatre elements and religious chants. Syed Alwi brought a multimedia approach to his theatre. His plays often stress character psychology more than social issues and are humanistic in tone.

A younger group of 1970s writers – Dinsman (b. 1949), Johan Jaaffar (b. 1953) and Hatta Azad Khan (b. 1952) – calling themselves Generasi Ketiga (Third Generation), established the absurd style of theatre in the 1970s. Their characters were often searching or abstract. Some were remodelled legendary figures like the fifteenth-century Malaccan warrior Hang Jebat who appeared in modern dress as a social martyr/hero, rather than as the rebel/traitor traditional literature presents him.

The 1980s witnessed renewed interest in the period prior to, during and just after World War II. These *Merdaka* (Independence) plays may have been inspired by the political changes occurring in Malaysia at the time – the split in the major political party, UMNO. Among these plays are *Pentas Opera* (*The Opera House*) by Zakaria Ariffin, *Mitos* (*Myth*) by Othman Zainuddin and *Anak Tanjung* (*Children of This Land*) by Noordin Hassan.

The first half of the 1990s witnessed a profusion of one-act plays, most performed at MATIC. The plays follow recommendations set by the Ministry of Culture, Arts and Tourism for light, comic, non-controversial entertainment meant to draw audiences back to Malay theatre. Although critics have found the MATIC plays of less substance than earlier works, these plays do have general audience appeal and have helped theatre regain audience support. Some playwrights, such as Syed Alwi and Hatta Azad Khan, adapted a neo-realistic style to suit the MATIC formula. Their newer plays have the easy comprehensibility of the realistic dramas of the 1960s but utilize multimedia effects and evidence greater multicultural awareness than encountered in *drama moden*.

English-language plays written in the 1960s evidenced mixed genres. Some plays, such as Patrick Yeoh's *The Need To Be* and Edward Dorrall's *A Tiger Is Loose in the Community* are realistic. However, other plays are experimental, such as Patrick Yeoh's first piece *Stools* and many of Lee Joo For's dramas (for example, *The Propitious Kidnapping of the Culture Hero's Daughter* and *Halter*). In the 1980s, a profusion of styles appeared: neo-realist dramas (K.S. Maniam's *The Chord*), futuristic plays (Kee Thuan Chye's *1984 Here and Now*) and musicals (Chin San Sooi's *Yap Ah Loy*). The 1980s also witnessed the beginning of an interest in monodramas, with Malaysian productions of Singaporean plays such as Stella Kon's *Emily of Emerald Hill* and Kuo Pao Kun's *The Coffin's Too Big for the Hole*.

By the 1990s, Leow Puay Tin had created her own monodrama, *A Modern Woman*, and Ramli Ibrahim wrote a trilogy of monodramas called *In the Name of Love*. There have also been recent plays with only two or three actors playing multiple roles, such as Leow Puay Tin's *Two Grandmothers* and *Three Children* and Jit Murad's *Wind, Rain and Hailstones*. These monodramas and multiple-role plays indicate the playwright's desire to reconnect with a

K.S. Maniam's *The Chord*.

storytelling tradition as well as to frame in vignette fashion particular lifestyles and eras; these plays also provide actors vehicles for *tour-de-force* performances.

Some of these plays are structured multiculturally, that is, scenes with pluralistic voices alternate with those that focus on a single voice (the Five Arts productions of *Us* and *Skin Trilogy*). There are also experimental plays that connect different years of history, such as Kee Thuan Chye's *We Could *** You, Mr. Birch*, in which the late nineteenth century alternates with the present and Syed Alwi's *I Remember … the Rest House* in which pre-World War II days are framed by a young man's return home in 1957. A 1990s Chinese drama called *Naja* also uses this technique of presenting two periods: a Chinese legendary past and the Malaysian present.

Directing and Acting

In Malay-language theatre it is rare to find an individual who is solely or primarily a director. Indeed, most playwrights have become their own directors out of necessity and some have proven themselves immensely skilled in the art.

Among the most impressive of the playwright/directors is Noordin Hassan, whose winning of the nation's highest literary award, the Anugerah Sasterawan Negara (National Writer Laureate Award) in 1993, not only marked the first time this prestigious award was given to a writer who is primarily a playwright but also was recognition of Noordin's work as a director. His landmark anti-realistic, experimental production of *It Is Not the Tall Grass Blown by the Wind* in 1970 radically altered concepts of staging for the next generation of theatre artists nation-wide. Since then, Noordin has continued to approach theatre as an eclectic, experimental art, drawing upon his theatre studies in Britain, his familiarity with traditional theatre (mainly *boria* from his home state of Penang and *bangsawan*) and his own visions of a progressive, just society, strengthened by religious tenets.

Noordin is known for his episodic music dramas that incorporate choral singing, chanting, poetry, dance, proverbs and traditional theatre elements to enrich the style of the pro-

Noordin Hassan's production of *Anak Tanjun* (*Children of This Land*).

Noordin Hassan's production of Peran (Roles).

duction. The tone of a Noordin Hassan production is reflective with moments of absurd comic relief. His *mise-en-scène* is usually symbolic, at times even surrealistic. Midway in his career to date, Noordin attempted to develop an Islamic form of theatre called *teater fitrah* (theatre of faith) in which stage design, actor groupings, chanting and dialogue are meant to lead the audience to a spiritual catharsis. (In some scenes, for example, his actors move in spiral, circular paths towards 'greater awareness'.) Two plays developed during this phase to coincide with the new Islamic century – *1400* and *Don't Kill the Butterflies* – exemplify both concrete and abstract/mystical (Sufi) approaches to religious theatre. Noorin's plays often feature ideal female characters as well as newly enlightened and transformed characters.

Syed Alwi is a second playwright/director of note whose style has influenced many others, particularly 'third generation' theatre artist Hatta Azad Khan. Syed often uses multimedia effects, such as film, slide projections and human shadows on a large side or back screen. Hatta Azad Khan has similarly exploited such techniques, even with his most recent work, *Korporat* (*Corporation*). For both directors, the multi-

media effects provide a useful vehicle for casting a satirical look at what is happening on stage.

Syed creates prominent, positive female characters and has also cast women in traditionally male roles. His plays often evoke a nostalgic atmosphere reminiscent of his favourite era, the 1950s. What also distinguishes Syed's theatre is its multiracial cast, typified by the Indian station master, a stock character appearing in many of his works, including his most recent *I Remember ... the Resthouse*.

Hatta Azad Khan is a third playwright/director and critic who established himself with his *Patung-Patung* (*Puppets*), an anthology of four plays published in 1980. Two of the plays, *Mayat* (*Corpse*) and *Setesen* (*Station*), won awards. During the same year, he wrote and directed another three plays, *Awang*, *Jebat* and *Puteri Gunung Ledang*.

Hatta's early work was absurdist in style but his later works were more realistic. His themes also changed from corruption of power to emptiness and illusion. Hatta utilizes music, poetic lyrics, mime and also experiments with certain forms of Malay traditional theatre.

During the 1980s, Johan Jaaffar left his own promising playwriting career (and the directing of his own plays) to turn to the adaptation and directing of literary works by some of Malaysia's best known authors: (*Salina* by A. Samad Said, *Zaman Gerhana* (*The Eclipsed Era*) by A. Samad Ahmad and *Rumah Kedai di Jalan Seladang* (*The Shop House Along Seladang Road*) by A. Samad Ismail.

Zakaria Ariffin is among the most talented of the country's playwrights/directors, and in the 1980s began to direct others' plays as well as his own. His well-funded productions have impressive stage action, technical expertise, ensemble groupings and the effective use of large venues.

Among Malay directors, Marzuki Ali (b. 1942) from Teater Asyik in Terengganu, is unique in his preference for directing western classics, such as the plays of Sophocles, Shakespeare and Chekhov. Marzuki Ali adapts the plays to East Malaysian settings, costumes and movements. He staged *Oedipus Rex*, for example, in *Sarawak* style and *Macbeth* in a *Sabah* style.

In the 1980s, Norma Nordin of CentreStage became known for her productions of dramatic pieces based on Malay poetry. Most often collaborating with Najib Nor, her productions are noted for their stylish flair.

In the 1990s, Zainal Latiff, who worked mostly within the university milieu (USM), staged his first off-campus production at

MATIC. *Antara* was constructed through improvisations and it later toured six major cities of Malaysia and represented Malaysia at the Fourth Asean Theatre Festival in Brunei in 1995.

Krishen Jit is unique in being predominantly a director and critic, often experimenting with traditional forms. His early work was in Malay-language theatre, but from the mid-1980s, with the creation of Five Arts Centre, he has turned his attention to the English-language stage, helping to develop new Malaysian voices, such as K.S. Maniam and Leow Puay Tin, to reflect the multicultural complexity of Malaysian life. Notable examples are his productions of *Three Children* by Leow Puay Tin, in which he and a co-director from TheatreWorks in Singapore created acting styles based on Chinese Opera techniques and tai'chi, and the collective effort *Us*, which was multilingual (Malay, English and Mandarin) and represented Malaysia at the annual experimental theatre festival in Egypt in 1993.

Chin San Sooi is a veteran director of the English-language stage, his talent initially nurtured at the Anglo-English School in Ipoh. A director since the early 1970s, he received theatre training in England under a British Council scholarship. His early work was on large-scale productions involving music. Beginning in 1973, he staged several of Stella Kon's futuristic works, Brecht's *Caucasian Chalk Circle* (1974) and *Lady White Snake*, for which he used Chinese Opera techniques. He became involved briefly in *wayang kulit* with Phoenix '61 (1976), a theatre/training group that performed at shopping centres. In *The Battles of Coxinga* (1979), he combined Chinese and Japanese theatrical elements.

In the 1980s, Chin San Sooi started writing his own plays. *Refugees* (1987) is a collection of images about Vietnamese boat people portrayed through music, poetry and ballads. He worked for an extended period of time with Leow Puay Tin, directing her – in Malaysia and Hawaii – in Stella Kon's acclaimed monodrama of Nyonya-Baba life, *Emily of Emerald Hill*. He has since returned to large-scale productions: *Yap Ah Loy*, a musical version of the life of the famous Kapitan China of Kuala Lumpur, a revival of *Lady White Snake*, a revue of the songs of the 1960s and *Reunion* (about Chinese family life at New Year's time). Chin San Sooi directs meticulously and has long rehearsal periods.

Among the more recent English-language directors to create an impact in the English-language theatre world is Joe Hasham. Hasham and his Malaysian spouse, veteran actress Faridah Merican, are co-founders of the Kuala Lumpur Actor's Studio. Hasham has staged American classics such as *A Streetcar Named Desire* and *Zoo Story*, as well as contemporary American works such as *As Is* and modern Australian, British and Irish drama. His productions touch on topical social issues like homosexuality, AIDS, mental illness and immigration. In the early 1990s, he adapted Irish playwright Brian Friel's *Philadelphia, Here I Come* to a multicultural Malaysian setting.

In Chinese theatre, Soon Chung Mae is interested in presenting not only western pieces with messages of special relevance to the Chinese community, but also new pieces using traditional forms to highlight social problems. Trained in Stanislavski realism in Taiwan, Soon also works improvisationally to create dramatic pieces relevant to her actors' lives. She has done several shows in a non-realistic, absurdist performance style.

In terms of acting, it was possible prior to the mid-1980s to speak of a Malay style on the modern stage derivative of traditional forms as well as the *bangsawan* theatre. Performers often delivered lines in an emotional declamatory manner and evidenced little interest in blocking patterns, posture and gestures. However, from the mid-1980s onward, it has become increasingly difficult to distinguish acting in Malay theatre from that of English or modern Chinese theatre. One reason is that many actors perform in both Malay and English theatre and are now trained in similar acting methods. Also, many actors have studied abroad, either on a long- or short-term basis. In addition, since the 1980s, little attention has been given to emulating traditional acting styles or to incorporating stylized acting in Malay theatre.

Occasionally, one can see traditional performances, such as *mak yong* or *menora* which utilize traditional dance-drama movements, vocal patterns and trance elements, but these elements are not as readily translated on to the modern Malay stage as they were in the 1970s. However, many recent Malay productions have included 'refashioned' *bangsawan* characters in play-within-a-play formats without relying on the melodramatic and improvised acting style of former *bangsawan* theatre. The new form does retain, however, the nostalgic, traditional melodies and *silat* (Malay martial arts). A proclivity for comic characters is still in evidence, but the absurd theatre of the 1970s and early 1980s has given way to neo-realistic drama and a more precise acting style.

Music Theatre
Dance Theatre

For a discussion of music and dance, see the opening, historical section and **Artistic Profile**.

Theatre for Young Audiences

Traditionally, children watched theatre alongside their parents at all-night performances of popular forms such as *wayang kulit*. During the first three decades of the modern theatre movement in the country (the 1950s to the 1970s), no special theatre for young audiences emerged. Since the 1980s, however, there has been increased recognition on the part of government agencies and individual theatre artists of a need to develop a public theatre for young audiences.

The pioneer in the area was Vijaya Samawickarma who taught children's theatre at USM in the early 1970s. His effort was then continued by one of his students, Zainal Latiff, who taught the same course in 1979 when he returned from the University of Hawaii. His productions *Teater Sang Kancil* and *Teater Pak Pandir*, both based on improvisations, played to children in Penang and Kuala Lumpur and in 1982 toured Brunei.

Another prime mover in this area since the 1980s has been Janet Pillai (b. 1955) who lectures in Children's Theatre at Pusat Seni (Arts Centre) in USM. Initially, under the sponsorship of the National Cultural Complex, she trained young performers, 9–17 years of age, in structured programmes that ultimately led to production. Her *Garuda* was taken on tour in Malaysia and Singapore in 1982.

Her plays are usually constructed from improvisations based on themes such as war (one piece included visiting Palestinian children) or child abuse. In her adaptation of *The Bridge* by Stella Kon, she blended traditional characters such as Rama and Sita from the *Ramayana* with modern youth problems of consumerism, video fixation and conformism.

Later, working with Five Arts Centre, her Teater Muda (Youth Theatre) project offered an adaptation of Rudyard Kipling's *Jungle Book* as a musical called *Suara Rimba* (*Voices of the Jungle*, 1993). This was the first Malaysian children's theatre production to achieve commercial success. Her productions usually feature a multicultural cast and are performed in the national language or in a mixture of languages.

Theatre for young audiences performed by adults can be seen at Dewan Bahasa dan Pustaka. Teacher trainees at the Language Training Centre in Kuala Lumpur perform plays in schools. The Memorial Library in Kuala Lumpur has its own children's theatre group and performs occasionally with the aim of inculcating reading habits among children. There is also an annual Christmas pantomime staged as holiday entertainment by members of the expatriate and Malaysian communities. Dance theatre companies, such as Suasana, Sutra and the Temple of Fine Arts, begin training children at an early age and often include them in major productions.

Occasionally children's theatre festivals occur, such as the 1994 international storytelling festival which featured children's theatre groups from Asia and the west. The recent International Puppet Theatre was also aimed for a children's audience.

The private television station in Malaysia has tried to encourage youth theatre by holding secondary school drama competitions. There is, however, no sustained national sponsorship of children's or youth theatre, as there has been for modern adult theatre.

Puppet Theatre

The major puppet theatre in this region is *wayang kulit* (shadow-puppet theatre). Historically rooted in East Coast Malaysia, notably in the states of Kelantan and Terengganu where the *Ramayana* repertoire was most popular, *wayang kulit* troupes would perform for special occasions, ceremonies and festivals. Now troupes perform less frequently due, in part, to restrictions placed on the performance of the art by home state governments who question aspects of the art form from a religious point of view. However, one may still see performances in select tourist venues or even commission a special performance oneself. It is interesting to note that at the same time the state government of Kelantan restricted public performances, the federal government awarded the first national traditional artist award to Pak Hamzah, a well-known Kelantanese *dalang* (puppet master), who, for many years, taught puppet classes at USM in Penang.

One difficulty in making *wayang kulit* more generally popular is that it is commonly performed in a dialect that people from other states cannot easily understand. Nevertheless, *wayang kulit* is regularly staged at the Central Market in Kuala Lumpur. As yet, no significant national effort has been made to carry on and develop the art of *wayang kulit*.

Traditionally, *dalang*s and *wayang* musicians-in-training learned their craft by watching and assisting established performers over a long period of time. Now, some training is given at Pusat Seni at USM, the National Arts Academy and KBN. But the fruits of such training have thus far mainly produced artists interested in using elements of the shadow puppet theatre in experimental-style productions. For instance, the shadow screen may be used with live actors, rather than puppets, to create the specific shadow effects. In a recent revival of Usman Awang's *sandiwara* classic *Matinya Seorang Pahlawan* (*The Death of a Warrior* or simply *Jebat*), the two warriors – Hang Tuah and Hang Jebat – fought much of their duel-to-the-death behind shadow screen palace walls.

Traditionally, *wayang kulit* audiences would watch the shadow plays throughout the night for several nights at a time until a story cycle was completed. Now, performances are shortened and although they may occur for several nights if there is a special occasion, usually *wayang kulit* is a one-evening event. New *wayang kulit* troupes, it should be noted, are not being established.

Wayang kulit puppet collections can be found in the performing arts museum at USM and the National Museum in Kuala Lumpur; video documentation may be found in the National Arts Academy.

Chinese puppet theatre is also performed in Malaysia, especially for the Hungry Ghosts Festival in Penang, Ipoh, Klang and other cities or towns with large Chinese populations. Chinese puppet stages are set up near temple sites and shows are held for both religious reasons and entertainment.

Traditional masked theatre includes the *selampit* storytelling art although it is now rarely seen. Masks are sometimes used in modern productions to create heightened theatricality, distancing and cultural identity. In K.S. Maniam's *The Cord*, for example, Indian masks from the Chau tradition were used for a revelatory dream/vision sequence.

Design

Traditionally, theatre was performed outdoors with simple lighting and without attention to sets. The *wayang kulit* shadow screen was originally lit by an oil lamp; now the screen is illuminated by a light bulb. These days, *mak yong* and *menora* performances are also lit by electric lights, although still usually performed outdoors. Traditional performers are costumed according to original styles, unless they are performing in restricted situations. If the performances are held in a traditional outdoor setting, one finds a simple stage area, perhaps a temporary stage, with no setting *per se*. The Central Market in Kuala Lumpur, which schedules performances of traditional theatre forms among its monthly programmes, has a permanent but simple outdoor stage.

Bangsawan, although performed outdoors at first, is now staged in indoor theatres with sophisticated modern lighting techniques. In contrast to traditional theatre, *bangsawan* was known for its six painted curtain backdrops, wings and borders which created a palace interior, a street scene, a jungle, a garden, the interior of a poor person's home and a landscape. *Bangsawan* performances were also known for *tasmat* (special effects). Heroes and heroines would be lavishly attired. Modern groups trying to replicate *bangsawan* might give attention to the typical sets, special effects and costumes. In modernized *bangsawan*, such as Rahmah Bujang's *Puteri Li Po*, the standardized sets are usually not employed.

For traditional Chinese opera, daytime outdoor performances may have electric lights if necessary; night-time outdoor shows have theatrical lighting which is meant basically to light the stage area, but not to provide special effects. Traditional costumes are worn, although they are not elaborate. Settings are kept minimal in design.

Malaysian theatre generally utilizes spectacular effects. Dry ice is commonly used in productions to cast a mysterious glow upon a scene. In a Temple of Fine Arts' production of *A Midsummer Night's Dream*, a large replica of a camel paraded on stage; later, a large replica of a horse was ridden down the aisle. Grand sets were provided for this production and the dancers wore vibrant Rajasthani costumes. In contrast, Joe Hasham's production of Edward Albee's *Zoo Story* had only the requisite park bench.

Although technical expertise is at an all-time high in Malaysia, especially in theatres located in and near the capital and at USM in Penang, designers have yet to achieve a distinctive identity in a body of work. Certain productions stand out for their design aspects but a particular designer's 'trademark' has not yet been established.

Theatre Space and Architecture

Traditional theatre performances take place outdoors. A temporary wooden stage may be built as a performance area with mats laid on the ground for audience seating. Audiences may also watch from the sides of the stage and no attempt is made to mask the changing area at the back. Audience members may even sit at the back of the stage to experience the performance from this close position. Traditional performances in Malay *kampung* areas may take place in fields, the most convenient venue for rural people. For special festivals, outdoor stages may also be erected.

Chinese theatre, when performed for religious festivals, is performed on stages erected across from temple sites. Usually for Chinese theatre, a proscenium type stage is used.

The Central Market in Kuala Lumpur has a permanent outdoor theatre space for poetry readings, traditional and modern theatre and other cultural events. Often mats are placed in front of the stage on the cement plaza so audiences can sit casually and watch the evening's performance.

In Kuala Lumpur and vicinity, there are several theatres which are well equipped with sophisticated lighting and sound facilities and which can accommodate elaborate set designs. The City Hall Auditorium which seats approximately 1,000 viewers has a proscenium stage and is technically well equipped. Dewan Bahasa dan Pustaka renovated their large hall,

proscenium stage and technical facilities. KBN's Experimental Theatre in Kuala Lumpur features a large, flexible rectangular playing space and is able to accommodate about 400 viewers seated on three sides of the stage area. The Experimental Theatre is only part of a new national theatre project still awaiting completion.

The 400-seat indoor MATIC auditorium has a proscenium stage with a large apron area and excellent technical facilities. Its large lobby doubles as a gallery space and occasional performance/rehearsal site. Adjacent to the lobby is a small amphitheatre.

The Actor's Studio is the first contemporary theatre group to operate its own theatre. Located underneath Merdeka Square in Kuala Lumpur, it has a seating capacity of about 200.

Some office buildings include a small proscenium theatre for small-scale productions that accommodate 200–300 viewers. Occasionally, theatre groups use non-theatre spaces such as art galleries to stage experimental productions.

The Petaling Jaya Civic Centre in the satellite town of Petaling Jaya, located near Kuala Lumpur, has a large hall with a proscenium stage and well-equipped lighting facilities. The Shah Alam Auditorium is similarly well furbished.

All major towns and cities have halls that can be used as theatre spaces. Usually, these venues have proscenium stages and can also accommodate flexible or thrust staging. Universities have large halls for performances and some have experimental or formal theatres as well, such as USM, Universiti Malaya (University of Malaya or UM), Universiti Kebangsaan Malaysia (National University of Malaysia or UKM), Universiti Putra Malaysia (UPM) and University of Malaysia Sarawak (UNIMAS).

Training

Traditional theatre training always featured master artists whose skills were, over time, passed on to their apprentices. This transference would usually begin when the apprentices were very young. Though such training continues, more and more of these and other skills needed for the modern Malaysian theatre are now being taught in formal training programmes.

In 1970, the Universiti Sains Malaysia in Penang opened Pusat Seni (Arts Centre), which offered the country's first academic training in the performing arts. At Pusat Seni, students can take specific courses, work towards a degree or come for a special one-year creative course offered to talented individuals not formally enrolled in the university. Pusat Seni offers theatre, music and dance programmes at the undergraduate and graduate levels.

Universiti Malaya has provided theatre arts training for many years through a student drama society called LIDRA, affiliated with the Department of English. The university has also begun a specific performing arts programme which draws upon faculty members from various departments. The new University of Malaysia Sarawak (UNIMAS) has a performing arts department geared for the professional job market in theatre, film and television.

The National University of Malaysia has staged productions through its Department of Malay Letters. Drama production classes have been taught in the School of Art and Design and the Department of Mass Communication at MARA Institute of Technology. Further training at colleges and universities has been provided by each institution's Cultural Unit which often includes theatre courses in its co-curriculum activities.

In 1994, the Ministry of Culture, Arts and Tourism funded the new National Arts Academy which offers a three-year diploma programme in drama. The programme includes courses in acting and technical theatre as well as in theatre history and performance theory. Also, at the Malaysian Institute of Art, where the medium of instruction is Mandarin, students can receive a diploma in theatre after successfully completing a three-year training period.

At government institutions, tuition fees are subsidized for qualifying students. At the Malaysian Institute of Art, students may receive special scholarships from the administration.

Some theatre companies, such as Actor's Studio and Five Arts Centre (especially through its Teater Muda project) offer acting classes for interested adults or young people. Drama Lab organizes playwriting workshops to encourage new talent. Suasana Dance Company, Sutra Dance Company and the Temple of Fine Arts all run dance training programmes for children, youth and adults.

Many theatre artists have trained outside the country, especially in Indonesia, Australia, Britain, the United States, France and India. Some Malaysians have pursued special one-year programmes in theatre to hone particular skills, while others have earned Master's and PhD degrees abroad.

Criticism, Scholarship and Publishing

Theatre research focusing mainly on Malay theatre is conducted by the staff of the Modern Literature Department and the Library at Dewan Bahasa dan Pustaka (DBP). DBP keeps up-to-date files on playwrights, productions and criticism and the agency also publishes drama books, literary magazines and journals (in Malay and English) such as *Dewan Sastera, Dewan Budaya, Dewan Bahasa* and *Malay Literature* which contain theatre articles, reviews and plays. DBP also organizes seminars and conferences which stimulate drama scholarship.

The universities are also important centres for theatre scholarship, where graduate students as well as lecturers engage in relevant research. Among major critics affiliated with universities are Rahman Bujang and Anuar Nor Arai (b. 1943) at the University of Malaya; Krishen Jit, formerly at the University of Malaya and now Head of the Drama Department at the National Arts Academy; Mohammed Ghouse Nasuruddin and Ghulam Sarwar at Universiti Sains Malaysia; Solehah Ishak (b. 1951) and Abdul Rahman bin Napiah (pen name Mana Sikana) at the National University of Malaysia; and Nur Nina Zuhra (b. 1945) at International Islamic University Malaysia. Drama criticism focuses mainly on Malaysian theatre but some attention is also given to the theatre of Asia, especially that of Singapore and Indonesia.

DBP is a major publisher of plays in single editions, as well as in collections and anthologies. The agency also commissions translations of Malay plays into English and foreign plays into Malay. Other publishing companies occasionally publish Malaysian plays and individual writers may publish their own works, having them ready for sale at the time and place a play is first performed.

Useful theatre books in English include Nur Nina Zuhra's *An Analysis of Modern Malay Drama*, Solehah Ishak's *The Histrionics of Development: A Study of Three Malay Playwrights*, Tan Sooi Beng's *Bangsawan: A Social and Stylistic History of Popular Malay Opera*, Patricia Matusky's *Malaysian Shadow Play and Music: Continuity of an Oral Tradition*, Mohammad Anis Mohammad Nor's *Zapin: Folk Dance of the Malay World*, Mohammad Ghouse Nasuruddin's *The Malay Traditional Music*, Mubin Sheppard's *A Royal Pleasure Ground: Malay Decorative Arts and Pastimes*, Rahman Bujang's *Boria: A Form of Malay Theatre*, Ghulam Sarwar's *Panggung Semar: Aspects of Traditional Malay Theatre* and Amin Sweeney's *The Ramayana and the Malay Shadow Play* and *Malay Word Music: A Celebration of Oral Creativity*.

Useful theatre books in Malay include Rahman Bujang's *Sejarah Perkembangan Drama Bangsawan di Tanah Melayu dan Singapra (The History and Development of Bangsawan in Malaysia and Singapore)* and *Seni Persembahan Bangsawan (The Art of the Bangsawan Performance)*, Krishen Jit's *Membesar Bersama Teater (Growing with Theatre)*, Mana Sikana's *Drama Moden Malaysia: Perkembangan dan Perubahan (Modern Malaysian Drama: Development and Change)* and *Di Sekitar Pemikiran Drama Moden (Thinking About Modern Drama)* and Solehah Ishak's *Pengalaman Menonton Teater (The Experience of Attending Theatre)*.

Theatre criticism, scholarship and publishing have, for the most part, tended to separate Malaysian theatre along language lines. Only recently is the idea of an integrated view of Malaysian theatre beginning to emerge. This new approach is evident in critical essays which compare works by authors or directors working in different languages or which take special note of those artists working multilingually. It is also apparent in the use of major theatre venues by groups working in different language mediums. It is seen as well in theatre publicity and programmes which aim to inform Malaysians, expatriates and visitors to the country about theatre events in languages other than that of the performance.

Solehah Ishak, Nur Nina Zuhra

Further Reading

For Chinese names, the family name is placed first; for Malay names, there is no family name. Therefore Chinese and Malay names are alphabetized according to the first word in the name as it is usually written.

Abdul Rahman bin Napiah. 'Perkembangan dan Perubahan dalam Drama Moden Malaysia'. Thesis, Universiti Kebangsaan Malaysia, 1980–1. Published under Mana Sikana (the author's pen name) as *Drama Moden Malaysia: Perkembangan dan Perubahan* [Modern Malaysian drama: Development and change]. Kuala Lumpur: Dewan Bahasa dan Pustaka, 1987.

Camoens, Cantius Leo. 'Sejarah dan Perkembangan Teater Melayu' [History and development of Malay theatre]. Thesis, University of Malaya, 1980–1.

Jit, Krishen. 'Contemporary Children's Theatre In Malaysia'. *Theatre Studies*, 1983.

——. 'Hatta Azad Khan dan Teater Kontemporari Malaysia' [Hatta Azad Khan and Malaysian contemporary theatre]. *Dewan Sastera* (March 1982): 22–3.

——. *Membesar Bersama Teater* [Growing with theatre]. Transl. Nor Azmah Shehidan. Kuala Lumpur: Dewan Bahasa dan Pustaka, 1986.

Mana Sikana. *Di Sekitar Perikiran Drama Moden.* [Thinking about modern drama] Kuala Lumpur: Dewan Bahasa dan Pustaka, 1989.

——. *Drama Moden Malaysia: Perkembangan dan Perubahan* [Modern Malaysian drama: Development and change]. Kuala Lumpur: Dewan Bahasa dan Pustaka, 1987.

Matusky, Patricia. *Malaysian Shadow Play and Music: Continuity of an Oral Tradition*. Kuala Lumpur: Oxford University Press, 1993.

Mohammed Anis Mohammed. Nor. *Zapin: Folk Dance of the Malay World*. Singapore: Oxford University Press, 1993.

Mohammed Ghouse Nasuruddin. *The Malay Traditional Music*. Kuala Lumpur: Dewan Bahasa dan Pustaka, 1992.

Mohammed Safian Hussain, Tahani Ahmad and Johan Jaaffar, eds. *Sejarah Kesusasteraan Melayu: Jilid 1* [The history of Malay literature: Volume 1]. Kuala Lumpur: Dewan Bahasa dan Pustaka, 1974.

Mustapha Kamil Yassin. 'The Malay Bangsawan'. *Traditional Drama and Music of Southeast Asia*. Kuala Lumpur: Dewan Bahasa dan Pustaka, 1974.

Nanney, Nancy K. 'An Analysis of Modern Malaysian Drama'. PhD dissertation, University of Hawaii, 1983. Published under Nur Nina Zuhra (the author's alias) as *An Analysis of Modern Malay Drama*. Shah Alam: Biroteks, MARA Institute of Technology, 1992.

Pillai, Janet. 'Malaysia'. *International Guide to Children's Theatre and Educational Theatre: A Historical and Geographical Source Book*, ed. Lowell Swortzell. New York: Greenwood Press, 1990.

Rahmah Bujang. *Boria: A Form of Malay Theatre*. Singapore: Institute of Southeast Asian Studies, 1987.

——. *Sejarah Perkembangan Drama Bangsawan di Tanah Melayu dan Singapura* [The history of the development of bangsawan in Malaysia and Singapore]. Kuala Lumpur: Dewan Bahasa dan Pustaka, 1975.

——. *Seni Persembahan Bangsawan* [The art of the bangsawan in Malaysia and Singapore]. Kuala Lumpur: Dewan Bahasa dan Pustaka, 1975.

Sarwar, Ghulam. *Panggung Semar: Aspects of Traditional Malay Theatre*. Petaling Jaya: Tempo, 1992.

Sheppard, Mubin. *Royal Pleasure Ground: Malay Decorative Arts and Pastimes*. Singapore: Oxford University Press, 1986.

Solehah Ishak. *Histrionics of Development: A Study of Three Contemporary Malay Playwrights*. Kuala Lumpur: Dewan Bahasa dan Pustaka, 1987.

——. *Pengalaman Menonton Teater* [The experience of attending theatre]. Kuala Lumpur: Dewan Bahasa dan Pustaka, 1992.

——. *Protest: Modern Malaysian Drama: An Anthology of Six Plays*. Kuala Lumpur: Dewan Bahasa dan Pustaka, 1992.

Sweeney, Amin. *Malay Word Music: A Celebration of Oral Creativity*. Kuala Lumpur: Dewan Bangsawan dan Pustaka, 1994.

——. *The Ramayana and the Malay Shadow Play*. Bangi: Universiti Kebangsaan Malaysia, 1972.

Tan Sooi Beng. *A Social and Stylistic History of Popular Malay Opera*. Singapore: Oxford University Press, 1993.

MELANESIA

(see **SOUTH PACIFIC**)

MICRONESIA

(see **SOUTH PACIFIC**)

MONGOLIA

Known from 1924 to 1991 as the Mongolian People's Republic, Mongolia is bounded on the north by Russia and on the east, south and west by China. It has an area of 1,565,000 square kilometres (604,200 square miles). Also occasionally referred to by its former name, Outer Mongolia, it had a population in 1997 of approximately 2.5 million. The capital is Ulan Bator. Kazakh and Khalkha Mongol is spoken by over 90 per cent of the population. There is no official state religion although the traditional faith in the country was Buddhist Lamaism which was suppressed by the ruling Soviet government beginning in 1929.

Mongolia as a nation was created by Genghis Khan (1162–1227) in the thirteenth century when he united the nomadic tribes of the steppes and created an empire extending from China to the Middle East. Mongolian-speaking tribes had themselves developed a pastoral existence based on raising sheep and horses, the latter supplemented by the camel in the most arid regions. Tribal warfare, however, was endemic and individuals of great personal power moved easily to positions of leadership. In the fifteenth century, after the death of the Mongol conqueror Tamerlane, unity gave way to internal unrest. Tibetan Buddhism gained popularity in the sixteenth century and in 1650 the son of the Mongol Khan of Urga (present-day Ulan Bator) was named a Living Buddha.

A combination of Buddhist theocracy and secular Mongol aristocracy ruled the country from 1696 until the twentieth century with the Manchu dynasty of China controlling Mongolia's foreign relations but allowing it

sovereign control over internal affairs. The Republic of Mongolia, established in 1924, attempted to create a more modern national culture through the sponsorship of European-style drama, art schools and a State Theatre of Music and Drama.

Traditional Mongolian culture, however, is far from European models and is based more heavily on ancient myths, proverbs, sayings, *yurol* (a poetry of good wishes), *magtaal* (a poetry of praise), blessings, tales and epics. These traditional forms, stories and songs have been passed down orally from one generation to the next, their origins lost over time. Horses – as one example – are so deeply enshrined in the Mongol culture that songs and verses written centuries ago followed the rhythm of horses' galloping hooves. Such songs remain an intrinsic element even in the more modern culture.

Buddhism in early Mongolia was promoted primarily through public festivals and expressed a uniquely Mongolian interpretation of the faith. The Maitreya Festival, for example, a significant event in the Buddhist calendar, took on particular significance in Mongolia where it became associated with the hope for a new Buddhist age and the recurring Mongol desire for the restoration of a powerful empire.

Tsam is perhaps the most compelling Mongolian Buddhist festival and another example of Mongolian creativity in religious areas. Originally from ancient India, *tsam* was brought to Tibet a thousand years ago by Padmasambhava, renowned for his victories over demons and spirits. In Mongolia, *tsam* was enriched with elements of witchcraft and the pagan traditions of Mongolia's nomadic tribes. Intended to exorcize evil forces and obstacles to enlightenment, the *tsam*'s costumes and masks, as well as stage sets, differ widely from those used in other Buddhist countries. Mongolian masks (made by monks) are painted in bold colours – red, black, yellow, white and blue – and are big enough that the audience could clearly see them from great distances. Although larger than life, the masks are nevertheless made in strict adherence to canons of religious, decorative and applied arts. Lavishly decorated and designed to inspire awe and reverence for the deities, the masks are made from papier mâché and inlaid with coral, gold, silver and precious stones. They are also decorated with gouache and mineral dyes and depict the main Buddhist deities.

During the nineteenth century, numerous monasteries were built in the country and *tsam* performances took place in them, one performance per year given at each of the 700 major monasteries. Such performances were stopped in the late 1930s, the last one held in the square in front of the Choijin-lama's monastery in Ulan Bator.

There are three types of *tsam*: the first presenting episodes from the life of Milaraiba, an Indian hermit poet of the eleventh century; the second dedicated to Khan Gessar, a folk hero; and the third, *Erlik Tsam,* depicting the struggle between good and evil. The masked performers, always monks, enact ancient ritual dances and scenes from the lives of both heros and deities. Through movement and gesture, the actors are able to convey the concept of eternal triumph of good over evil and life over death.

Long preparations were needed for these *tsam* performances. Rehearsals would begin one or two months prior to the event under the guidance of an experienced, high-ranking lama. Some scenarios have survived and one, about Gessar Khan, includes ninety-four acts. The Mongolian *tsam* also incorporated many traditional shamanistic figures who served to appease the followers of shamanism and convert them to Buddhism. These native deities were incorporated as allies or official protectors of the Buddhist faith. Thus, shamanism, although often outlawed, coexisted with Buddhism into the twentieth century.

The folk song is another of the ancient forms of Mongolia's musical and poetic art. Such songs can be classed according to function – songs of everyday life, ceremony and songs to dance to. In terms of genre, they are further separated into lyrical works, narratives, response songs, tragic melodies, humorous or festive songs. Short songs are quite popular, have sharp rhythms and are connected to daily life. The longer songs are of a more classical

Mongolian movable stage.

genre, philosophical in style, evocative of vast, open spaces. In addition, these latter works require the singer to have great skill in breathing and guttural vocal technique.

Traditional Mongolian music was strongly influenced by lifestyle and economy in addition to traditional belief systems. Many musical features – the way the sound is produced vocally, the timbre and colouring of the sound and the way the instruments are played – are determined by the close relationship of music to the natural environment and by the Mongol idea about the essence of music and its purpose, a reflection, in other words, of the relationship between people and nature. Folk legends link the origin of some instruments and Mongolian music with the sounds of nature: the wind, rivers and waterfalls or the cries of animals and birds.

The key role of horses in the Mongolian lifestyle is also reflected in legends about the creation of the most important traditional musical instrument – the *morinkhuur* or spike fiddle. According to legend, the instrument was created when a nomad rode a flying horse and the horse's mane fluttered in the wind, producing an enchanting melody which helped the nomad keep his cattle herds together. An evil witch caused the horse's wings to be cut off and the horse died. The hero, inconsolable, made the first *morinkhuur* from the horse's remains. The *morinkhuur* itself consists of a trapezoidal wooden form covered with horse's skin. A horse head is carved at the top of the wooden peg box of the fiddle. When the legend of the *morinkhuur* is performed, the singer, while playing the instrument, imitates the neighing and clattering of hoofs and reproduces the sensations of galloping and flight by using expressive melodic, rhythmical and onomatopoeic devices.

Khurchins (folk poets and singers) are the official keepers of these oral epics and ballads and their mime and expressive gesturing gave rise to popular biting, satirical, vaudeville-style productions such as *Sumya Noyon* and *Dunkher Da-Lam*.

Another category of professional singers exists as well: *Rhapsodes Ulgerchi* (rhapsodic poets) who during the long winter nights sing and recite long epic poems called *ulgers*. These singers also accompany themselves on the *morinkhuur*. Each must be able freely to compose a plot by combining and varying particular stanzas of the text while at the same time leading a vocal 'melodic party' accompanied by an instrument. It also involves improvising instrumental introductions and interludes. The performance of these traditional epic legends can last for up to three days.

The creation of a European-style theatrical group in 1922 – attached to the Central Committee of the Mongolian Revolutionary Youth League – became the basis of a modern revolutionary theatre. Starting on an amateur basis, it developed trying to utilize the joint traditions of the country's inherited folklore and the influence of the Soviet theatre.

In its professional incarnation, the State Drama Theatre, founded in 1931, first produced classical plays such as *Revizor* (*The Government Inspector*) by Nikolai Gogol (staged in 1931 and 1937) and *Fuente Ovejuna* by Lope de Vega. In 1933, the State Theatre participated in the International Olympiad of Revolutionary Theatre in Moscow and over the next few years staged a number of realistic revolutionary plays including *Among Three Hills of Sorrow* by D. Natsagdorj, *The Brave Commander-In-Chief Sukhe Bator* and *Dark Power* by S. Buyannemekh, and *Struggle* by D. Namdag. Since the 1950s, plays by Shakespeare, Schiller, Brecht, Gorky and Mikhail Sholokhov have been staged by the company.

Still another theatre started in this revolutionary period was the State Theatre of Opera and Ballet. In 1950, a Secondary School of Dance and Music was established and further extended the training of young dancers. *Our Cooperative* was the first Mongolian musical work in the Soviet style. By the end of the 1950s, the State Ballet had staged many Russian classics as well as such original ballets such as *Gankhuyag* by S. Gonchigsumlaa and *A Flower Among Sage Bushes* by E. Choidog.

Other groups emerging in Ulan Bator include the Children's Theatre, Puppet Theatre, Folk Song and Dance Ensemble and the People's Army Song and Dance Ensemble. A State Circus is hugely popular. Other major cities in the 1990s have also developed such modern drama groups.

In all theatrical forms – both traditional and modern – there is a tendency toward the epic. Rooted in songs that proclaim the valour and courage of historical heroes, early epics of the twelfth and thirteenth centuries – *Geseriada* and *Jangar* – are to Mongolia what the *Iliad* and *Odyssey* are to Greece and what *Mahabharata* and *Ramayana* are to the Indian subcontinent and southern Asia. Handed down from generation to generation, newer epics by writers such as Jiker and Parchin have enriched the repertoire and present-day epics such as *Bum Erdene*, *Khan Kharankhui*, *Daini Khurel* and *Dsul Aldarkhan* depict the prosperity of the Mongol people. The actor-singer B. Avirmed was awarded the 1991 State Prize of Mongolia specifically for his performances/recitations of these works.

A State Children's Central Theatre was founded in 1950 and performed its first play, *Snowboy* by A. Lubimova, in 1957. The focus of the theatre has primarily been to instil in children ideology, morality and aesthetics and to mould them into patriotic citizens. Until the 1990s, this philosophy was firmly upheld as only Soviet plays were staged there. Local playwrights Ch. Lodoidamba, D. Namdag, Ch. Oidor, L. Vangan and Ch. Chimig, among others, began writing for young audiences in the 1970s.

In 1981 the theatre became the Youth and Children's Theatre, an event which coincided with the Youth Union's Golden Jubilee. Since the social and political reforms in the 1990s, the theatre has been moving away from a communist ideology and finding ways to develop a more indigenous theatre for young audiences in the country.

There are several specialized periodicals in the country that report on theatre. Among them is *Soyol* (*Culture*) aimed at art and cultural workers.

WECT staff

Further Reading

Cultural Policy in the Mongolian People's Republic: A Study. Paris: Unesco, 1982. 49 pp.

Dix-huit chants et poèmes Mongols [Eighteen Mongolian chants and poems]. Paris: Librairie Orientaliste Paul Geuthner, 1937. 28pp.

'Folk Music from Mongolia/Karakorum' [sound recording]. Berlin: Internationales Institut fur Traditionelle Musik, 1993.

Haslund-Christensen, Henning. *The Music of the Mongols: Eastern Mongolia*. New York: De Capo Press, 1971. 97 pp.

'Hoomii and Urtin Duu' [sound recording]. Los Angeles: JVC, 1992.

Metternich, Hilary Roe, ed. *Mongolian Folktales*. Boulder, CO: Avery Press; Seattle, WA: University of Washington Press, 1996. 130 pp.

'Mongolian Folk Music' [sound recording]. Hungary: Hungaroton, 1967.

Namdziliin, Norvobanzad. 'Virtuosos from the Mongolian Plateau' [sound recording]. Tokyo: Seven Seas, 1994.

MYANMAR

(Overview)

Guarded to the east, north and west by mountains that have kept the country relatively isolated throughout most of its history, Myanmar – known as Burma for most if its history – is surrounded by India, Bangladesh, China, Laos and Thailand and, to the south, by the Bay of Bengal and Andaman Sea. With a land area of 676,600 square kilometres (261,200 square miles), the country had a population estimated in 1995 at just over 45 million.

Burmans, who now make up about 68 per cent of the population, first migrated to this area of Southeast Asia from the mountains of southern China around the eighth century AD. Other ethnic groups include the Chins, who live near India; Kachins in the north; Shans, a people who also settled in Laos and Thailand, in the east and who represent about 9 per cent of the population; and Karens, who live in the eastern hills and along the Irrawaddy River delta and represent about 7 per cent of the population. More than 120 different dialects are spoken in the country although Burmese is understood by most.

Though Buddhism is the official state religion since its introduction in 1056, nearly 11 per cent of the population practises other religions including Islam, Hinduism and various animist beliefs. Burmese Buddhists believe deeply in concepts such as reincarnation and *karma* and believe that one's spiritual life is at the root of both everyday reality and cultural practice as a whole. Monasteries, which dot the country, serve therefore not only as religious centres but also as community centres, schools, short-term accommodation and even as hospitals.

The country's first independent institution of higher learning was the Arts and Science University founded in 1920 in the national capital of Rangoon (now called Yangon). A second university was later founded in Mandalay. State colleges of theatre, music and the visual arts also exist in these two cities.

There are no family names among traditional Burmese. Given names are therefore often preceded by honorifics such as U (literally meaning 'honoured uncle') for a man and Daw (literally meaning 'honoured aunt') for a woman. As in many states in this part of Asia, religious and national holidays are one and the same, and are celebrated as *pwes* (full-blown festivals) with performative events a major part ranging from parades to poetry, storytelling, song, dance and theatricalized re-enactments. The two most important holidays are the Burmese New Year or Water Festival (Thingyan) celebrated in April and the Festival of Lights (Thadingyut) celebrated in October.

Burma has a cultural tradition dating back some fifteen centuries. The first Burmese kingdom, with its capital in Bagan, lasted for some two hundred years and is considered the golden age of Burman culture. Chinese records indicate that in AD 802 an ensemble of thirty-five dancers from the country was sent to China, the earliest evidence that culture during this period had reached a level high enough to be officially recognized and used for diplomatic purposes. Paintings, scrolls and sculptures from the ninth to the thirteenth centuries show that Indian-style dances were a feature of court life. Spirit dances date to at least the eleventh century AD.

Kublai Khan, the Mongol Emperor of China, captured Bagan in 1287. Records indicate that in 1336, King Ngasishin-kyaw-zwa was himself composing martial songs known as *karchin*, a word that literally means 'shield dance song'. The king not only composed such songs but also had the shield dance performed. The Konbaung kingdom, founded in the eighteenth century, claimed part of the Tenasserim (Taninthiryi) peninsula, previously belonging to Thailand (then Siam) and colonized Arakan (Rakhine) and ultimately westward towards India, attacking Bengal. During a series of wars in the nineteenth century, the British gained control of Burma and in 1886 Burma became a province of British India. In 1937 Burma was granted dominion status. In 1941, the Japanese invaded the country and occupied it until 1945. In 1948 Burma became independent.

A parliamentary democracy at that point, the army took control from 1958 to 1960 and seized power again in 1962 when the Burma Socialist Programme Party – the only legal political party – took control. Over the next few years most foreigners were expelled, the government nationalized most businesses, gave the land to the people working it and restricted imports. It was in 1989 that the name of the country was changed to Myanmar and the capital's name from Rangoon to Yangon which, according to the government, was to help refocus the modern Burmese identity.

That identity, as indicated earlier, has been very much a part of the spiritual realm and has long involved dance and music, the celebration of the many *pwes* and recognition of the country's thirty-seven *nats* (dominant spirits) in all national and individual activities. Even in the war of conquest against Siam, this aspect of the Burmese spirit was seen as whole troupes of actors and dancers were taken back to Burma as captives, there to perform for the Burmese courts.

Popular among every class of Burmese society, traditional theatrical performances are still widely attended and appreciated with both enthusiasm and direct involvement. One can, in fact, find a *pwe* of some kind or other on every full moon night in virtually every city and village. Such performances attract not only members of the community as a whole but also government officials, religious leaders, scholars, students and visiting foreigners. The most ancient of the *pwes* relate in various interdisciplinary forms tales of the life of the Buddha, some seriously, some more comically and others

mixing the two forms. In the masked play form known as *Ravana*, the villain, for example, is always treated as a comic figure no matter how wicked he may be in the plot. One can also see such styles in the centuries-old puppet theatre and even in the many dance-drama forms borrowed and ultimately adapted from India.

Always taken seriously, however, the apparent secularization of certain forms began to be seen with alarm by the late eighteenth century and it was at this time that Burma became the first country in the world to create a Ministry of Theatre. Founded in 1776, its main aim was to exercise some sort of control over the enormous number of theatrical performances taking place across the country and to try to eliminate their growing unruliness. As well, the new ministry was to ensure that performances respected both the sanctity of Buddhism and the royal court, depicting both with propriety and decorum. The ministry was also expected to stimulate the theatre along lines agreeable to the state and to keep theatre in political accord with state policies.

Clearly, artists of this period had begun to use their art to make political points while puppeteers, particularly, were airing grievances in ways that live actors could never dare. As written and spoken plays began to grow out of the British presence in Burma and as Burmese dramatists began to write their own scripts, the politicization of the theatre became even more clear. The most important script from this period was *Wizaya* (*Victory*) by U Pon Nya (1807–66). Appearing at a time when there was a clear battle for power in the country, U Pon Nya set the play in Ceylon drawing upon various Buddhist stories about usurpation and power already well known to the people. Not only was the play immensely popular but also it contributed substantially to changing public opinion. The playwright was later put to death for his support of the perceived coup.

Such connections between politics and the theatre continued well into the twentieth century with both officials and members of influential families trying their hands at playwriting and some even taking up acting as well. One such was former Prime Minister U Nu (1907–96), one of the country's most reasonable and able politicians as well as someone extremely popular with the masses. In his youth, U Nu wrote several well-conceived plays on subjects that included marriage problems and their need for equitable solutions (some written from a Freudian point of view) and religion. One of his later plays was both distinguished and controversial, *The People Win Though*, which describes the failure of communism to govern the country adequately. In 1957, U Nu visited the United States where he was able to see this play in translation at the Pasadena Playhouse.

By the beginning of the twentieth century Burma had developed its own 'star' system and at least three actors had attained such fame that they were true celebrities in the country: Aungbala (d. 1910) whose funeral occasioned both riotous behaviour and a mass expression of deep emotion; Sein Kadon who became famous for his special costumes made of hundreds of tiny electric lightbulbs that flickered on and off at dramatic moments; and the greatest of them all, U Po Sein (1882–1952) who was so famous that late in his career he had to appear on stage with bodyguards. U Po Sein demanded that actors be treated with respect and insisted that those going into the profession be themselves of good moral character. His contributions to charity were well known; during World War I he gave a number of performances to aid the Red Cross. In his later work, he managed to include popular improvised physical comedy into even the most spiritual of *pwe* performances, something which endeared him even more to local audiences. After his death, his son Kenneth continued the family's acting tradition.

Most Burmese productions give the feeling of being variety shows, last many hours and have many different segments, a play being just one element. Music and dance play a significant role in most of them and even the modern plays have full orchestras that perform appropriate backgrounds as the production proceeds. The *saing*, the traditional *pwe* orchestra, consists of about a dozen different instruments including ornately carved teakwood xylophones whose keys are made from a specially resonant bamboo and are struck with chamois-skin mallets.

The *saing* also usually has reed instruments like oboes with brass funnels loosely fitted over the bell to augment the sound. There are other various percussion instruments, some small – foot-long tubes of bamboo that crack and snap as the player shakes them – and some even smaller – square castanets and tiny thimble-size cymbals.

Another key instrument of the *saing* orchestra is a set of twenty-one extremely ornate, small graded drums set up in a circle and tuned by

Various instruments in the *saing*, the traditional *pwe* orchestra.

placing moist rice paste in the centre of the various hides to keep them taut. Tuning takes over an hour and must be repeated each time the drums are used.

To the side of the orchestra are two heavy gongs that are gorgeously decorated with animal figures, some real and some imaginary. These gongs punctuate the beat of the music and determine the orchestra's basic tuning. The music itself has tremendous variety – sometimes sensuous and sometimes like bubbling water, sometimes like jazz and other times like firecrackers.

Dancing is invariably energetic and designed to excite, agitate and stimulate. Men and women share the same stage; it can be said that the dance theatre of Myanmar is a dynamics of poses. Emotional range, however, is limited with emotions such as sorrow only superficially represented. It is said that a sad dancer simply can not dance since dance is itself an art of joy and exuberance.

To some historians, the artificiality of this theatrical dance is linked to the movements of Myanmar's puppet theatre. In dances one can clearly see the stiff, jerky walk of puppets and it is clear that the frequent jumps belong more logically to the movements of a stringed marionette than to a human body.

But it is the festivals themselves, the many *pwe* (closely related to the word *hpwe* meaning gathering or assembly) where the theatrical arts make their widest and strongest popular appeal. *Pwes* are organized to celebrate births, deaths, namings, weddings, divorces, rites of passage, entering or leaving monasteries, races, building bridges, dedicating homes or pagodas, for sowing seeds and for harvesting crops.

The *pwe* tends to take five main forms: *zat pwe* (classical show), *yo' pwe* (puppet show), *nat pwe* (spirit show), *yein pwe* (choral show) and *pya zat* (modern play). Sometimes several of these forms will be seen in the same evening. All these forms are now most easily seen in Yangon but may also be found in smaller centres as well. The word *zat* comes from the ancient Indian word *jataka* and refers specifically to the enormous body of stories and legends about the previous incarnations of the Buddha. Religious in tone, the stories used in the *zat* focus on Buddha's youth since, following his enlightenment, he is considered so holy that any representation, either in temple carvings or on public stages, is considered sacrilegious and offensive.

The *zat pwe* is therefore well known, allowing the artists, as the narrative progresses, to indulge in long dance passages. Ancient in style and subject with formal rules of structure, the *zat pwe* contains required historical and mythological dramatic sequences, many of which show the clear influence of Indian classical theatre.

The colourful Mintha and Minthani perform life-like Burmese dances.

Within this strict framework, there is sufficient latitude for each artist's creativity.

Most *pwes* will start late in the evening and continue through dawn. The play sections – newly composed for each run, are often set in the classical period of Myanmar history and deal with standard characters – kings and queens, deceitful courtiers and scheming prime ministers. They often focus on questions of succession to the throne, flights by night into woodland hideouts and concealed identities. The structure demands alternating scenes of comedy and pathos with the leading character taken from happiness to hardship and back again. During intervals, each character sings a song to emphasize the mood of the action that has just taken place.

At about the midway point between midnight and dawn, the main dance sequence begins – the *hlut-pa-thwa*, a kind of *pas de deux* in which the two foremost stars of the troupe dance their most brilliant traditional routines, unchanged through the years. Essentially an interlude without any direct bearing on the main plot, it might include a court festival, a marriage feast or something similar. The main story resumes at the end of this section.

Throughout the *pwe* the *saing* orchestra plays to announce upcoming scenes and to provide happy or sorrowful backgrounds, to establish the settings as court or forest, to establish the powers of a character and to underscore the overall mood.

The puppet-based *yo' pwe* (also called *yopshinpwe* or *yo'shinpwe*) allows even greater flights of fancy and even more outrageous quirks of humour than the *zat*. As well, the puppet theatre has traditionally been able to show activities on stage which are, by tradition, not permitted. For example, a man and a woman, unless married, are not supposed to be seen walking the street together and even the simulation of love on a stage by actors is not considered acceptable. Into such a situation steps the 60–90 cm (2–3 feet) tall puppet since it cannot be censured as a living person.

Controlled by ten to thirty strings (although the complex princess puppet could have sixty strings) enabling it to perform some sixty different types of movement, most *yo' pwe* shows are also built around the religious-based *jatakas* and sketches from the nation's history. The puppet play is announced with three beats of gong and cymbals. Very often these plays will begin with the creation of the world. The king of the spirits descends from the sky to divide the earth. A

Burmese puppetry is traditionally an adult entertainment, as a full performance may last all day.

natkadaw (spirit medium) – always in female garb, but often a transvestite – then enters and dances in praise of the four island paradises where the spirits live. The *natkadaw* later sings and dances and offers rice, coconuts and bananas to the king of the earth. A series of animal puppets then enter: horses from heaven, monkeys and eventually ogres who compare their powers and skills in a series of dances. These plays usually end with the marriage of the king's son or with the sad parting of the son.

Records indicate that the first puppet plays were written as early as 1714 when Prime Minister Padesaraja wrote a puppet play for the court entitled *Manikhet*. The minister also wrote different songs for each of the thirty-seven spirits. During the late eighteenth and early nineteenth centuries the *yo' pwe* were especially popular and the early Ministry of Theatre gave special support to the art. By the late nineteenth century, however, the art began to fall into decline and, it is argued, live actors replaced the puppets while carrying on the puppet movements.

The *nat pwe* (spirit dance) is performed only on astrologically auspicious days which can be

The maid character in Burmese puppetry.

frequent in given months. Most frequently performed during New Year celebrations and similar in many ways to Sri Lankan devil dances, the *nat pwe* allows contacts with higher spirits who can guide one's life and effect one's future. At certain moments during the dance, a candle is lit and the medium – again a woman – goes into a trance and bites into the candle. Representing the thirty-seven spirit deities, the medium is able to answer questions on behalf of the spirits. Most questions concern love such as 'Which girl shall I marry?' The answer is often equivocal. 'The one who writes you a letter.' At the end of the performance, money is collected from the audience, the collection going on until the spirit is satisfied.

In earlier periods, the *nat pwe* also offered unusual opportunities for democratic action. During particularly tyrannical periods, the mediums, falling into trances, might make contact with certain members of the audience, attributing to them godlike qualities. In such circumstances, the king was required to respect them and listen to their advice.

One of the most famous *nat pwe* stories is a moving re-enactment of the martyrdom of two young boys. The story dates back about a thousand years to a period in which a king was about to attack China. In order to ensure the success of his venture, he decreed that an enormous pagoda be constructed. Every male citizen was

required to contribute one brick toward the building. One family had two beautiful sons and they were dispatched with their bricks to make the family's contribution. But on their way, the two young boys became engrossed in playing children's games and forgot their mission. For their negligence, the king had them crucified. The people were so shocked by this caution that they deified the two boys and made them part of the pantheon of spirits (*nats*). In the performance of this story, the scene in which the mother feeds her sons for the last time, with the boys paying respect to her before departing to their doom, is regarded as one of the country's most sacrosanct pieces of theatre.

In the early 1960s, a film company shot its own version of the story. While the film was being made inside the studio, a full-scale outdoor version was simultaneously performed to ensure that no offence was taken by the secular retelling of the story.

The *yein pwe* in its turn involves a chorus of dancers and singers working without soloists. Group skill is extremely high with movements restricted to the body, head, arms, hands and fingers rather than the legs or feet. These are dances of poses and postures rather than of movement. Flexibility, grace and expressiveness are combined in high virtuosity though the restricted leg and footwork may appear static.

The *pya zat* is essentially a modern play, usually a comedy. In fact, Myanmar dramaturgy has no purely tragic plays even in its classical theatre. An evolution from the nineteenth-century and early-twentieth-century Euro-American realistic dramaturgy, these plays were particularly popular during the Japanese occupation of Burma during World War II when European and US films were banned. Since the war, their popularity has not diminished although in comparison to the classical plays they reach a far smaller audience.

In all of these theatrical styles, drop curtains are frequently used along with painted backdrops. But the major emphasis is on costume design and makeup. Kings and nobles are always robed in orange and peach satins studded with brilliant headdresses of gold and carry flashing swords of silver.

Performances of traditional pieces usually include the creation of a large altar made of bamboo and palm leaves at one end of the stage. By the time the performance starts, the altar is covered with offerings of coconuts, bananas, flowers, betel nuts, pieces of cloth, eggs, apples and bottles of wine or liquor. The orchestra locates itself at the opposite end of the stage. Such makeshift stages – often in the open air or sometimes under tents – are covered by bamboo matting in the audience seating area. A number of more or less permanent *zat yon* (theatres) exist across the country. Many play the same show for extended runs. The largest such theatres – in Yangon – hold over a thousand people who sit cross-legged either on the ground, on the mats or on the side on low-slung canvas beach chairs. A special area is reserved for the shaven-headed, bare-shouldered, yellow-robed Buddhist priests who watch such spectacles with as much secular enjoyment as the rest of the audience.

The best known permanent theatre in the country is the Win-Win in Yangon. Performances are held at the Win-Win every night of the year, mainly the *pya zat* (modern plays). The Win-Win from the outside looks much like a typical Burmese pagoda. Inside it is a modestly equipped theatre providing the essential facilities needed by any theatre company.

Many of the larger cities in the country have at least one troupe of performers and the major cities of Yangon and Mandalay each have at least three. The companies – usually numbering well over a hundred artists – work under the direction of a leading actor-manager. Up until the 1980s, the troupes toured widely but such touring has been severely cut back because of political instability in the 1990s. The best known company in the country has long been the Sein-Maha-thabin that was begun by Po Sein. Other troupes of note are the Myo-daw which stages modern plays, the Shwe-Man-thabin and the Shwe-Man.

A State Orchestra (composed of traditional Burmese instruments) began in the 1950s, as did the State Schools of Music and Drama and a School of Fine Arts. In 1997, the schools had over one hundred students studying in these fields.

Students being trained for the more classical *pwe* performances, are enrolled at an average age of 8. Initial training takes about six months during which time a dance of greeting is learned along with ten basic steps. The best students go on to work with dance and music masters.

There are a number of useful books dealing with aspects of Burmese theatre, one written in English by Maung Htin Aung called *Burmese Theatre* and published by Oxford University Press in 1937 (reprinted in 1947 and 1967).

New plays are popular reading material and some plays can sell as many as 20,000 copies within a few weeks of their first editions. Former Prime Minister U Nu in the 1940s and 1950s was involved in the establishment of the Burma Translation Society which set as its main task the translation of both national and international literary works into the Burmese language. Until this time, most Burmese works were published in English. By 1954, the society had published over 5 million copies of various titles which were being used regularly in schools at all levels.

One of the country's most widely read modern playwrights is Kodaw Kaming (b. 1875). Educated in Buddhist monasteries, Kodaw Kaming was a leading nationalist as well as a professional journalist. The author of some eighty plays and fifty other books, he won the International Stalin prize in 1954 and is known as the Bernard Shaw of Burma.

The country now has only two newspapers and both are strictly controlled by the government. At independence there were thirty-nine including five in Chinese, two in Hindi, one each in Urdu, Tamil, Telegu and Gujarati, most offering reviews of new performances and feature stories. After the military coup of 1962, the government nationalized all publishing and newspapers were licensed for only a year at a time. At the same time, a Press Registration Board and a Press Scrutiny Agency were created. In 1975, the government issued new guidelines for publishing. All published works – novels, plays, magazines and newspapers – had to promote socialism, contribute to national unity, promote national culture and spread progressive ideas from other nations.

In the years since, many writers, artists, journalists and intellectuals were jailed. In 1980, the government established a Federation of Writers with a membership of 2,377 writers and 768 journalists, another organization that was politically controlled and under party domination. The military allowed criticism only in so far as the goals of the state were not questioned. That is, performances could be criticized but not ideology. As a result, contemporary intellectual and artistic creativity has been generally stifled. This is also seen in the area of national awards that are given by the state only to those who further its political goals.

WECT staff with Ravi Chaturvedi, U Ye Htut

(The editors and authors would like to acknowledge their intellectual debt in the preparation of this article to many writers

including *Faubion Bowers for his seminal work*, Theatre in the East: A Survey of Asian Dance and Drama; *Hugh Tinker for his book*, The Union of Burma: A Study of the First Years of Independence; *and to David J. Steinberg, author of* Burma: A Socialist Nation of Southeast Asia.)

Further Reading

Aung, Maung Hin. *Burmese Drama*. London: Oxford University Press, 1937 (reissued 1947 and 1967).

Becker, A.L. 'Journey Through the Night: Some Reflections on Burmese Traditional Theatre', *Traditional Drama and Music of Southeast Asia*, ed. M. Osman. Kuala Lumpur, 1974.

Bowers, Faubian. *Theatre in the East: A Survey of Asian Dance and Drama*. New York: Thomas Nelson & Sons, 1956. 374 pp.

Brandon, James R. *Theatre in Southeast Asia*. Cambridge, MA: Harvard University Press, 1967.

Burma Handbook (An official publication of the Government of Burma in exile at Simla). Simla, 1944.

Dounison, I.S.V. *Burma*. New York: Praeger, 1970.

Khaing, Mi Mi. *Burmese Family*. Calcutta: Orient Longman, 1956.

Pe Hla. *Kaonmara Pya Zat 1* [Popular Burmese modern drama]. London, 1952.

Scott, J. George. *The Burman: His Life and Notions*. London: Macmillan, 1895. Reprinted 1963 by Norton Library (New York).

Singer, N. *Burmese Puppets*. Singapore, 1992.

Steinberg, David I. *Burma: A Socialist Nation of Southeast Asia*. Boulder, CO: Westview Press, 1982.

Tinker, Hugh. *The Union of Burma: A Study of the First Years of Independence*. London: Oxford University Press, 1961.

U Nu. *Saturday's Son*. New Haven, CT: Yale University Press, 1975.

——. *Towards Peace and Democracy in Burma*. Rangoon, 1949.

Zagrski, Ulrich. *Burma: Unknown Paradise*. Tokyo: Kodansha, 1972.

NEPAL

Lying on the southern slopes of the Himalayas, Nepal is bounded to the north by China's Tibetan Autonomous Region and on the east, south and west by India. A landlocked country, Nepal has an area of approximately 141,200 square kilometres (54,700 square miles). The estimated 1997 population of Nepal was 20 million, the majority of whom live in rural areas and make their livelihoods through farming.

The Nepali Himalayas comprise only 520 miles out of 1,500 miles of the stupendous mountain chain, yet occupy the very core of the mountain system. More than 240 peaks are above 20,000 feet and of the nine highest mountains in the world, eight are located in Nepal.

For the past 2,500 years the Nepali hills and villages have provided shelter to waves of migrants who came as refugees and pilgrims or traders from both Tibet and India. The current population of Nepal has two major strains: the Caucasoid (Indo-Aryan) and the Mongoloid with different degrees and mixtures. Politically speaking, it is the Indo-Aryan group who dominated the history of Nepal and constituted the national elites while the Mongoloid group have remained the regional or local elites. Most prominent among the Mongoloid group are the Rais, Limbus, Sherpas and Tamangs, who occupy the hills east of Kathmandu, while the Gurungs, Magars and Thakalis inhabit the hills west of Kathmandu. The Newars are another important group in Nepal who embrace people from the Caucasoid and the Mongoloid stock. Nepal's official language is Nepali, one of twenty different languages spoken in the country.

The syncretic element of Nepali culture is its most visible characteristic. This is seen in the free give-and-take of ideas between Hinduism, Buddhism and Lamaism. Officially a Hindu state, Nepali Hindu, Buddhist and Lamaistic devotees have gone to the extent of building icons and monuments of the opposing faiths in their sacred precincts as well as coining joint expressions like *Halahal Lokeshwar* and *Nilkantha Lokeshwar*, both of which embody the personality of Shiva and Sakyamuni. The marital tradition constitutes another important element of Nepali culture. The growth of the Sakti cult (cult of the Mother Goddess) is really the fusion of marital tradition into the religious sphere.

Nepal is the cradle of one of the earliest civilizations in the world and has revealed layers of culture from the stone and bronze age. For the greater portion of Nepali history, the Kathmandu Valley has been the country's historical and cultural centre. It is this valley that sets the tone, for example, of everything from Nepali hairstyles, social etiquette and manners to the evolution of new norms and values, which ultimately permeate all walks of Nepali life.

The early rulers of Nepal came from a semi-nomadic people known as the Gopalas and Mahispalas. Then came the Kirat period, which began in about the ninth century BC and lasted until the first century AD, a period of more than a thousand years. By the beginning of the Christian era, the Licchavis controlled much of Nepal and led the country into the classical period which was extremely rich in the plastic arts utilizing stone, bronze and terracotta. Hundreds of *stupas* and *chaityas* (religious and cultural buildings) were built in this period with numerous icons and epigraphs that speak of the glories of the period.

By the thirteenth century AD, the Mallas had come into prominence in Nepal, a people who left behind a very rich and powerful culture. All the monuments in the old section of Kathmandu, Patan and Bhaktapur that exist today, for example, belong to the Malla period. If the Lichchavis excelled in stone art, then the Mallas exhibited their genius in wood and bronze art. Although stone art as well as terracotta continued in the Malla period, it could not match its Lichchavi counterparts.

During the period from 1768 to 1900, the territorial unification of Nepal took place under the leadership of the Gorkhalis. However, after the death of the foremost Gorkha ruler, Prithvi Narayan, the history of Nepal becomes not the history of its kings but rather of its regents or prime ministers. From 1846 to 1951 Nepal was ruled by a line of ten Rana premiers. They kept Nepal isolated from the rest of the world and ruled Nepal with an iron fist.

Following Indian independence in 1947, the Ranas lost British support in the region. Indeed, spurred by the independence movement in India, a Nepalese independence movement emerged as well with many demanding the overthrow of the Ranas. By 1951, the political autocracy of the Ranas ended and Shah King Tribhuvan Bir Bikram Shah, the figurehead since 1911, gained political control. The relaxation of censorship that followed and the opening of the country to tourism at this point encouraged a new revival of artistic and intellectual expression. Most subsequent Nepalese art reflected this new cultural renaissance. King Mahendra, the successor to King Tibhuvan Bir Bikram Shah, a poet whose Nepalese lyrics were published in English under the name M.B.B. Shah, did much to continue this cultural revival.

Maintaining political stability, however, proved elusive during the 1950s. A general election was called in 1959 that resulted in victory for the Nepali Congress, the first popularly chosen government in Nepal. However, a dispute between King Mahendra and the prime minister led the king eventually to dismiss the government, suspend the constitution and imprison many of the Congress leaders. After declaring a State of Emergency and stating that Nepal was not ready for democracy, King Mahendra replaced the parliamentary government with a partyless *panchayat* (council) system. Although a royal amnesty freed most of the political prisoners in 1968, political parties continued to be banned. When Mahendra died in 1972, his eldest son, Birendra took the throne. Faced with riots and student unrest, he allowed a national referendum in 1980 which

supported the *panchayat* system. In the years immediately after, a modified parliamentary government was restored. Nepal now has a multi-party system with a constitutional monarchy, where the prime minister is the head of government, and the king the head of state. There are two legislative houses.

Kathmandu remains the country's capital city with other major cities including Pokhara, Biratnagar, Birgunj, Janakpur, Bhaktapur, Lalitpur and Kirtipur. Only 12 per cent of the people, however, live in urban areas. The country is still economically underdeveloped and per capita income is less than US$200. Some 42 per cent of the total population fall below the poverty line.

Few people in the world are more tradition-bound than Nepalis, so while tracing the history of theatre in Nepal one has to go into traditions of antiquity and see the ancient gods themselves as the ultimate artists. The Nepali people have always conceived Lord Shiva, for instance, as the supreme dancer; he is also known as Natyaswara, the master of 108 forms of dances. The cosmic dance that he performs is known as the *Tandava Nritya*. Thus, it is quite natural to find icons and paintings of Lord Shiva in dance schools, theatres and temples.

Two types of dances were performed in Nepali theatres in the past: *shastric* dance and the *loknritya*. In the *shastric*, one sees dances of gods and goddesses and other acolyte deities while *loknritya* constitutes dances staged by various ethnic groups during feasts and festivals. The themes conveyed by the *loknritya* are social, secular and satirical and full of irony and paradoxes. Topographically speaking, the dances in Nepal can be divided into high-mountain-belt, mid-mountain-region, the plain and the valley. Those living in the different regions perform dances specific to their own traditions and culture, for example, the *dhan nacha* of Mechi, *dheme* and *dhintami* of Bagmati, *maruni* of Gandaki, *jhamre* of Lumbini, sohara of Bheri, *salaju* of Dhaulagiri, dauda of Seti, *suranje* of Rapti, *dhumai* of Mahakali and *dhunrikheri* of Karnali.

The history of Nepali theatre dates at least to the Kirat period where the *purohit* (priest) known as Knochring was in charge of dance and music. In the medieval period, the Malla rulers not only helped in the promotion of folk dances but also gave rise to new forms of performing arts such as the *navadurga* and *narasingha* dances; trusts were created by rulers like Siddhi Narsingha Malla and Rai Malla for the promotion of such theatrics. Malla kings such as Pratap Malla and Rudra Malla were themselves also well versed in the field of dances and dramatics. Both, for example, played the role of Narsingha in the play *Narsingha Avatar* (*The Incarnation of Narsingha*). Many plays like *Bhairav Nanda* and *Natyaswara Dasaka* were also staged in the *dabalis* (open-air theatres) of medieval Nepal. Scenes from *Ramayana* and *Mahabharata* were staged in the *dabalis* and they continue to be the major location for public entertainment in Nepal.

By the close of the nineteenth century the Rana rulers began to build theatres in their palaces to stage Hindi, Urdu and Nepali plays and to entertain audiences with folk and classical songs as well as *bhajans* (religious hymns) from the *Gita Govinda*. Dances were performed during times of high emotion. Such theatres were exclusively reserved for members of the Rana family and select nobility.

In the 1940s, Nepal moved into more modern forms. A step in this direction was taken by Balakrishna Sama, who wrote plays in blank verse and chose social and secular themes for his plays. He also trained a group of Nepali artists in the field of acting. His play *Mukunda Indira*, which he staged and directed, was another step in that direction. In the play, a married Nepali youth goes to Calcutta to study and decides not to return. In the 1950s the play *Birami* (*A Sick Person*) was directed by Hridaya Chandra Pradhan and acted by Mrigendra Man Singh to great popularity. In the same decade, plays

devoted to martyrs, like *Ganga Lal Ko Chita*, were written and staged. *Ganga Lal Ko Chita* was directed by Krishna Prasad Rimal with the role of Ganga Lal played by Mrigendra Man Singh. Other directors who made the transition from religious to social and secular themes were Hari Prasad Rimal and Gopi Nath Aryal. These younger directors gave continuity to folk and classical plays while modernizing them by fusing them with social and contemporary ideas. The play *Muna Madan*, a musical drama, staged by the organization Sanskritik Samsthan was also very popular and drew full houses for a hundred performances.

In the pre-1950 period the theatregoing audience was basically confined to the aristocratic elite and the merchant community. But in the post-1950 era more and more of the middle class became part of the theatregoing audience. Immediately after World War II Premier Juddha built a theatre in central Kathmandu to stage plays for the public – the Jana Seva, a milestone in the history of public theatre in Nepal.

It should be noted that traditionally performances were almost exclusively done by men. Dancing, acting and music were not considered honorable for Nepali women prior to and during the 1950s. During the 1960s the government of Nepal also began to give support to contemporary theatre. In the 1990s, with the popularity of cinemas and a massive invasion of television, live theatre has moved to the cultural background.

Structure of National Theatre Community

So many festivals are celebrated in Nepal that the country has often been called 'the land of festivals'. Most originated centuries ago and have simply been carried on through the ages. The majority are regularly re-enacted, sometimes for reasons now blurred by the passage of time or because Nepal's recorded ancient history has been destroyed over the centuries. Many remaining documents may actually be more myth than anything else. Nevertheless, inconsistencies, omissions and embellishments in the folklore and legends are ignored by the people. Uppermost is the preservation of the communal heritage.

As Nepalese people are often isolated from one another due to topography as well as a national literacy rate of only about 28 per cent

(of that number only one-third as many women can read as men), these festivals are also seen as unifying forces for the nation. While some of the festivals celebrated are quite local, the vast majority are celebrated all across the country. In rural areas, such events are often the major recreational activities of the year. Most are financially supported by various *guthis* (religious endowments or funds) which are administered by either the public or the private sector.

There are four basic types of festivals celebrated in Nepal: religious, historical, legendary and seasonal. Religious festivals are dedicated to a deity either of the Hindu or Buddhist faith. Regardless of religious preference, all are celebrated with the same solemnity, fervour, intensity and gaiety. Historical festivals are celebrated primarily in memory of one of the national kings or to celebrate the date of a great event. Legendary festivals are rooted in certain popular beliefs or myths, while seasonal festivals hope to gain or regain the favour or goodwill of deities in time for good harvests or to thank them at the end of the harvest season.

Exact dates for the annual festivals were fixed in ancient times according to the lunar calendar, which does not conform to the solar calendar currently in use in Nepal or with the Gregorian calendar used in the west. Nepalese calendars are therefore printed with all three dates. Simply put, the lunar month is divided into two fifteen-day periods: the 'light' fifteen days before the full moon and the 'dark' fifteen days after. Even this may vary as it is necessary to add an extra month to the lunar calendar every three to four years. The hour that each festival is to start is determined by astrologer-priests who announce the time when the planets and stars are properly aligned.

Some of the most notable festivals in the Nepalese year are Buddha Jayanti Purnima, Gai Jatra, Indra Jatra, Tihar or Diwali, Shiva Ratri and Holi. All have religious, mythological or traditional roots and all involve dance, music, history and legend, the latter providing communities with ongoing contact with stories from the past.

Buddha Jayanti Punima (Full Moon of Lord Buddha's Birth) occurs in late April or early May. Also known as the Triple Blessing, this festival marks the day on which Buddha was born, the day he later received enlightenment and the day on which he passed into Nirvana (about 483 BC). The focal point of the festivities is the massive, white domed stupa which crowns Swayambhunath Hill just across from the Vishnumati River in Kathmandu, the largest, most sanctified of all Nepalese Buddhist shrines. Throughout the night, the Swayambhunath is ablaze with lights which can be seen for miles around. Devout Buddhists flock there from all over the country as well as from across this part of Asia to spend the night fasting and chanting. In the morning, the hilltop is brightly decorated with flowers and ancient religious tapestries. Innumerable prayer flags flutter from streamers strung from the temple spire. A giant, gilded figure of Buddha is displayed with hundreds of smaller images to which believers bring gifts and offerings and pray. Yellow-robed monks perform religious ceremonies which involve solemn, stylized dances. Processions, led by the monks, carry Buddha down the steps to the cloister of Naghal where rituals are performed before he is returned to the hilltop. Parading groups march through the streets with images of Buddha, prayer flags and banners.

Gai Jatra (Procession of Sacred Cows) is celebrated in August or September. The cow is a sacred animal who guides and protects the spirit of the deceased along the dangerous journey to *Patal* (the Underworld) where the God of Death decides at what level the souls of the deceased should be reincarnated. The judgement gates of *Patal* are opened only once a year, the day of Gai Jatra. On this day, many families aim to ensure, through the performance of good deeds, that a sacred cow will be in readiness to push open the gates with her horns and assist their loved one's soul to enter for judgement. Therefore, every recently bereaved family honours the soul of their dead by sending a religious procession through the streets on a historically prescribed route. The procession consists of a decorated cow (or a boy richly costumed to represent one), the family priest, a troupe of musicians and a small boy dressed as a *yogi* (holy man). After the early morning rituals at home, each parade starts on its way to join hundreds of similar groups moving past temples, idols, holy places and ancient royal palaces. When the procession returns to the bereaved household, religious ceremonies are again performed and the cloth tails of the cow-costumed boys are cut into strips and tied around family members' necks to protect them from misfortune. Gai Jatra ceremonies vary with financial status, religious inclination and locality. In some areas the entire community participates in one long procession rather than in smaller, familial ones.

The late afternoon of this day offers entertainment quite removed from the solemnity of the morning. The celebrations which begin in the afternoon may last for up to eight days. A carnival spirit pervades the air. Throughout the streets of the Kathmandu bazaar, citizens in costume burlesque Nepalese institutions, social and religious customs, the government, political leaders, the army, foreigners and sometimes the gods themselves. Men may dress as women, monsters or animals; some wear comic masks or paint their faces and parade with bands – often under the influence of home-brewed spirits – to perform for the waiting crowds. On this day, citizens are free to express themselves without fear of reprisal.

Indra Jatra opens on the twelfth day of the waning moon in September with the raising of the flag of Indra, King of the Gods, before the old palace at Hanuman Dhoka in Kathmandu and lasts for one week. The flag signifies Lord Indra has come to the valley, and peace, prosperity and unity are assured. According to myth, the flag-pole was given to Indra by Lord Vishnu; subsequently, Indra's forces were unified and he found the strength to overcome demons. It is still worshipped as a symbol of unity, victory and power.

Several days before Indra Jatra, men drag a pole made from a 15 metre (50 foot) pine tree – felled by a priest and then sanctified – into the Hanuman Dhoka square where they are given a royal feast. The pole-raising ceremony on the morning of the twelfth day draws large crowds of spectators. Court astrologers announce the moment the pole should be raised amid music and the firing of guns. Thus the festival begins. Each night of Indra Jatra the ancient palace buildings are aglow and hundreds gather around to see the elaborate costumes and painted masks worn by the performers depicting scenes, in tableau form, from the ten earthly incarnations of Vishnu. Elsewhere around the city, folk dramas are performed in the streets by the light of flaming torches. Sumptuous costumes and grotesque masks represent demons and deities and the performers wearing them dance with grace and stylized precision. In contrast to the rowdy crowd surrounding them, the dancers seem to be in a religious trance and therefore are paid great respect.

The dance-drama festival of Mani-Rimdu in May contains many popular elements associated with the Tibetan festival of Cham which itself was based on temple dances connected to exorcism rites. Basically a prayer ceremony, Mani Rimdu originally lasted three days and included the participation of dozens of performers. It now lasts only one day and utilizes a minimum of sixteen participants. Large masks are worn along with colourful costumes to represent well-known allegorical characters. The tone is humorous but the moral of the ceremony is clear. Mani Rimdu is celebrated annually at the monastery of Tengpoche located between Kathmandu and Mount Everest. Though no archival evidence exists at the monastery, it is

Masked dance, Nepal.
Photo: courtesy of the Nepal Department of Tourism.

believed that the festival has been celebrated annually since about 1930 at Tengpoche and since about 1940 at the monastery of Thami.

Tihar or Diwali, Goddess Laxmi's Festival of Lights, occurs in October or November of the year. Tihar literally means 'a row of lamps' and lighting displays are traditional, although this festival is actually a succession of significant holidays celebrated for a variety of reasons. Tihar brings the worship of Laxmi, the Goddess of Wealth, and is a day to worship one's own body or self. Also worshipped are the dog, the ill-omened crow, the sacred cow, the family money box and the brothers of every household. The God of Death is appeased, the New Year begins and throughout Nepal an avid and illicit five-day indulgence in gambling takes place. Every night for five nights every home, temple and building is lit with row upon row of lights. It is believed if the goddess is pleased with a family's display as well as the gifts and offerings made to her, she will protect their money box and grain store in addition to granting prosperity throughout the year. On the most sacred night of the festival, the third night, groups of women and children go door to door singing, asking for alms and receiving coins and sweetmeats. Children run through the streets waving sparklers and fireworks are set off.

The Shiva Ratri festival honours the Sacred Night of Lord Shiva. Shiva is a diverse god, celebrated in literature under 1,008 names and his supremacy in the Hindu faith is unquestionable. Shiva Ratri, meaning 'the night consecrated to Shiva', falls on the fourteenth day of the waning moon in February or early March. Pilgrims come from all over Nepal to the main temple in Kathmandu to make offerings and bow before the holy *lingam* (phallus) of Shiva. When darkness falls, the religious fervour intensifies. Drums and flutes drive the multitudes to move and surge in the glow of the candles and lamps. Singing and chanting can be heard from the fasting pilgrims who make trip after trip inside the temple to worship.

Finally, Holi, the Festival of Colours, runs for eight rowdy days in either March or late February when men, women and children douse themselves in red powder or liquid. The throwing of colour on passers-by is expected to be accepted with good humour. The first day of the festival is marked by the installation of a 7.5 metre (25 foot) bamboo pole, topped with three umbrella tiers draped in colourful cloth, amid a crowd of revellers. Gunfire, flutes and drums echo throughout the square. During the last

A stone bas-relief is covered in red powder during Holi, the Festival of Colour.
Photo: Don Rubin.

three days of the festival, groups of young men wander through the streets singing traditional Holi songs which praise lovely maidens and glorify romance. Often these lyrics are somewhat risqué. On the final day, as the bamboo pole is lowered, revellers grab for the colourful cloth that has adorned the pole. A strip of this fabric, worn as an amulet on the clothes, is believed to ward off disease and evil spirits. The pole is then burned and many carry away pots of the burning embers to purify their homes.

There are also half a dozen more modern theatres operating in the country and most of them are in the Kathmandu Valley. The theatres in Kathmandu are the National Dance Theatre, Theatre of the Royal Nepal Academy and Town Hall Theatre. Tribhuvan University also has theatres in its Memorial Hall and the Education Auditorium where modern plays are staged. Theatres outside Kathmandu Valley include Dafe Kala Mandir in Pokhara and Birendra Sabha Griha, Bhanu Kala Mandir and Himal Kala Mandir in Biratnagar. Though most theatres are operated either by government or quasi-governmental bodies and are subsidized and maintained by the government, Dafe Kala Mandir, Bhanu Kala Mandir and Himal Kala Mandir are privately owned and operated.

In addition to these theatres, mention must also be made of the *dabalis* in Kathmandu, Patan and Bhaktapur. Here dramas are staged during certain festivals and festive occasions like the *Gai Jatra*, *Indra Jatra* and *Durga Puja* festivals. Religious trusts organize these plays on certain occasions and the themes are social, religious or satirical; they also serve to highlight the evils in both society and the political system. Exposing the evils of society and political system through the plays staged in the *dabalis* and

theatres has become an important feature of Nepali life. The plays staged in the *dabalis* are free of charge, while tickets for plays staged in closed theatres range from 50 to 500 rupees. This can be compared with cinema tickets which range from 10 to 30 rupees.

The organizations that promote dramatics in Nepal – Sanskitik Samsthan and Royal Nepal Academy, for example – have large troupes of artists and musicians ranging from fifty to one hundred performers. Organizations in the private sector usually have a core staff of twelve or fewer on the regular payroll with part-timers or recruits hired according to need.

Artistic Profile

Contemporary theatre in Nepal can be divided into two categories: those in the Kathmandu Valley supported and nurtured by the government – like Sanskritik Samsthan and Royal Nepal Academy – and those outside the Kathmandu Valley. Within the valley, theatre companies possess a national character and thus stage plays and music belonging to different ethnic communities, whereas theatres outside the Kathmandu Valley specialize in regional and local plays, dances and music and possess a regional and a distinctly local flavour. The national theatre in Kathmandu stages classical plays, dances and musical performances.

Among specific dances to be seen are the *Tandav Nritya*, *Hallisik Nritya* and *Ras Nritya*. In the first, as the legend goes, in order to kill the demon Tarukasur, God Shiva created the Kalidevi. He found it difficult to please her so Shiva composed the *Tandava Nritya* and performed this art himself. In this dance God Shiva is the central figure but other minor deities like devis, spirits and voginis are seen dancing in full ecstasy.

Hallisik Nritya – a dance form associated with Lord Krishna and Gopinis – is performed on moonlit nights or preferably nights of a full moon. In this dance-drama Krishna is the central figure. This dance is now performed in groups. It consists of numerous female attendants with only one male figure playing the predominant role. The *Ras Nritya* dance is performed before a river, under the shade of the banyan, pipal or chestnut tree. One male dancer has two female counterparts and the dance is performed in a circle. Each dancer carries two short sticks and

the beat of the sticks gives rhythm to the dance. The origin of this dance can be traced back to Lord Krishna and the Gopinis.

The local theatres of Pokhara and Biratnagar stage more regional dances, like the solo dance of the Tamang. Here groups of male and female dancers criticize each other under the beat of the *damphu*. Though the solo dance began as a Tamang dance it has now taken on a national character. *Jhyaure* (popular songs) have a distinct local flavour and are participated in by the local people. The stage for such dramatics are either natural platforms or temporary ones erected for the purpose.

A masked performance at the Everest Cultural Society.
Photo: Don Rubin.

Nepal has two agencies, fully supported by the government, which promote contemporary theatre – the Sanskritik Samsthan and the Royal Academy. The main objective of the first is to promote classical and modern dance and drama. Employing its own artists and musicians, the organization stages plays, operas, dances and concerts of regional music; it sends troupes abroad to represent Nepal in the international arena.

The Royal Nepal Academy has a specialized department for plays, dance and music; it employs artists, musicians and playwrights and stages plays and traditional and modern Nepali dance. It organizes special shows during festive occasions like the *Gai Jatra*, New Year's Day and the anniversary of the Academy. It also represents Nepal in the international arena.

Privately owned theatres, which include Dafe Kala Mandir, Natya Sargam, Bhanu Kala Mandir, the National Centre for Dance and Himal Kala Mandir, are important in terms of promoting Nepali dramatics by staging plays, classical and modern dances, and music.

Companies
Dramaturgy
Directing and Acting

There are two types of modern plays seen in Nepal – *rup* (spoken drama) and *rupak* (action drama). For the spoken drama, the thematic content is drawn primarily from rural life. Plays about community life with music are particularly popular. The aim of these plays is to give to the audience – both children to adults – entertainment and a moral. This form of drama does not follow the *shastric* rules.

Action dramas are closer to dance works and follow the necessary *mudras* (symbolic hand gestures like the conch-shell, trident, floral design, swordfish and deer head) as well as the required design styles (headdress, jewellery, clothing, garlands and scent). Hairstyle is a very important facet in Nepali design.

According to Nepali tradition, the purpose of drama is to entertain the audience through nine different elements: arrangement, courage, melancholy, surprise, laughter, uniqueness, terror, pathos and anger. Many classical performances are associated with Hindu deities. Mention can be made of the Bhadrakali dance which is often staged in the *dabalis*. Both male and female deities take part in this dance but the female deity, Bhadrakali, occupies centre stage.

All wear a *mukuta* (headdress), ornaments, gaudy clothing and masks that represent the particular deity. This dance is performed in the *dabalis* once every twelve years. The *pachali bhairav* dance also is staged in the *dabalis* once every twelve years and in its style is theatrically similar to the Bhadrakali dance.

In this connection one can also mention the *Halechowk Bhairab Niritya* and *Naradevi Swetakali Niritya*, which are staged annually in the *dabalis*. By the eighth century AD the Buddhists of Nepal had evolved a unique dance form known as *Charya Niritya*, which is still popular. This dance displays a series of hand and leg movements to a background of soft religious melodies. In this dance the characters are five Buddhas and five female counterparts. All wear their characteristic *mukutas*, ornaments and colourful costumes. Many classical dances in Nepal are in this form.

Although there are many writers in Nepal, it is impossible to earn a living in the country through writing; therefore most writers and poets are also employed as teachers or in government appointments. As such, many remain unrecognized. The government is aware of this situation and understands the need to foster the arts through government intervention, but its efforts are limited.

Among major writers are poets Laxmi Prasad Devkota and Siddhicharan Shrestha and the dramatist Balakrishna Sama. Other writers of note include Rudra Raj Panda, Balkrishna Shamsher, Bhimnidhi Tiwari and Lekhnath Sharma.

Panda, a graduate of the University of Allahabad, was principal of Trichandra College in Kathmandu. His best known work is *Rupmati*, a novel of Nepali family life and the first book of its kind in Nepali literature. The novel was subsequently dramatized and staged both in Nepal and India.

Shamsher is Nepal's most important dramatist. He is the author of two plays, *Audhabeg* and *Prahlad*, the first a family drama about jealousy and the second, a verse drama based on local myth. *Prahlad*, an early play of Shamsher's, has been produced in Nepal as well as in both north and south India.

Tiwari achieved note with his first play, *Sahansheela Susheela* (*The Tolerant Susheela*), produced in Kathmandu. Following in the footsteps of Shamsher, the play is about daily life in the courts of the Rana family. Susheela is the traditional Hindu wife obeying her husband despite his insulting manner. The play includes a number of *jhyaure* (popular songs).

A scene from *A Plane Crash* performed at the Rastriya Nach Ghar theatre.

Music Theatre
Dance Theatre

For a discussion of music and dance, see the opening, historical section and **Artistic Profile**.

Theatre for Young Audiences

There is no theatre for young audiences in Nepal *per se*. Children are encouraged to participate in community festivals and have prescribed roles and functions to perform during many of them.

School-aged children, since 1951, have received cultural training within their formal education, from primary to secondary levels.

The development, preservation and publicity of the national language, culture, literature and art are realized through social education, language programmes and extracurricular activities including dance, music and drama. Training in the performing arts is compulsory at the primary level and schools wishing to continue it at higher levels are encouraged to do so. Inter-school competitions are held yearly. Inter-district and inter-regional competitions are held on special occasions. Trophies, certificates and prize money are awarded at these events.

The Nepalese government has also mandated the singing of national songs within educational institutions; the staging of at least one drama production per year by every school; the organization and performances of folk dances and music and competitions for such, as well as the acquisition by students of adequate knowledge of national festivals and their importance.

Puppet Theatre
Design
Theatre Space and Architecture

There are about a dozen theatres in Nepal, most located in the Kathmandu Valley. The most important theatres in Nepal are the Rastriya Nach Ghar of Kathmandu and Royal Nepal Academy Hall of Kamaladi. The theatre Rastriya Nach Ghar in Kathmandu has a capacity of 500 and Royal Nepal Academy Hall in Kamaladi is able to seat 1,500. The Town Hall of Kathmandu, with a capacity of 1,000, is frequently used by stage and dance directors. The Memorial Hall at Tribhuvan University has a capacity of 700 and the education auditorium, which can accommodate 500, are often used to stage dramas. Outside the Kathmandu Valley the Dafe Kala Mandir, which has a capacity of 500, and Birendra Shava Griha of Biratnagar, which has a capacity of about 700, are used to stage dramatic productions.

The Cloud Covered Scene staged at the Rastriya Nach Ghar theatre in Kathmandu.

The *dabalis* are square platforms of about 7.5 × 7.5 metres (25 × 25 feet) and serve as open-air theatres to stage religious, social and satirical dramas as well as dances during festivals. The technical facilities in Nepali theatres are of a simple nature: stage, lights with colours, teasers and curtains and green rooms.

Training

In the pre-1950 period, religious and social trusts served as training schools for dancers and those involved in music and dramatics. After 1950 a music college was opened where theatre was taught as a second subject. In the 1990s Padma Kanya College of Tribhuvan University has a Department of Dance where theatre is also taught.

A private organization known as Pradhan Natya Mandal (Premier Theatrical Association) was established in 1965 with the aim of providing theatre training to Nepali youth. This school is still in operation and is one of the best schools in the country giving training in theatre. Other schools like the National Centre for Dance serve the same purpose. In the 1970s and 1980s institutions like Nepal Kala Kendra and Himali Koselee came into existence to fulfil the same need.

Opened in 1958, the Royal Nepal Academy's main objectives are to produce and publish original works on the Nepali language, literature, arts and culture, to honour artists, scholars and people with unusual talent and to develop the arts at national and international levels. The king is the Chancellor of the Academy, which has three main divisions – Literature, Arts and Culture. The Culture Division deals with political, economic, social, religious and cultural history while the Arts Division deals with theatre, music, sculpture and architecture in both its modern and classical manifestations.

The Nepal Association of Fine Arts (NAFA) teaches painting, sculpture and music and hopes to produce competent artists who will in turn promote the artistic traditions of the country. At least four times a year, the institution organizes an art exhibition which also includes cultural programming. NAFA strongly believes that art education should be given from primary levels all the way through the formal education system.

Kala Nidhi Nepal Sangeet Maha Vidyalaya is a private institution which is associated with the University of Prayag in India. Students may receive an undergraduate diploma and degrees in vocal and instrumental music and dance. Graduate degrees may be obtained only from the University of Prayag.

Another programme was initiated in 1965 allowing actors and directors to receive special advanced training at India's National School of Drama in New Delhi. On their return, many of these people initiated special workshops at Tribhuvan University in Kathmandu. Discussions have been held from time to time about the establishment of regular workshops by visiting faculty from the National School of Drama in New Delhi and from other countries.

Criticism, Scholarship and Publishing

Gorakhapatra – which is published in Nepali – is the oldest newspaper in the country and was first published in 1902. It began as a weekly paper but by 1944 was increased to bi-weekly. In 1947 it began to appear three times per week and by 1961 had become a daily. The special Saturday issues always carry one or two articles aimed specifically at the country's cultural heritage. Another popular daily, *The Rising Nepal* – published in English – carries articles relating to culture in its Friday supplement and its monthly literary magazine, *Madhuparka*, has regular columns devoted to Nepalese culture and the arts.

Several institutes of higher learning have included publishing in their realm of responsibility. The Institute of Nepalese and Asian Studies conducts research on the history, culture, civilization, art and religion of Nepal and other Asian countries. This institute can be credited with numerous prestigious publications on Nepalese culture, history and language. Scholars can also earn PhDs for their research work.

In 1952 during the early post-Rana period, the Nepal-Samskritik Parishad was established to do research in Nepalese culture and architecture. It did not, however, survive for very long and has left nothing behind save a few volumes of its quarterly journal, *Nepal Samskritik Parishad Patrika*. In the same vein, a group of poets and writers banded together in 1957 and produced several issues of a literary journal entitled *Indreni* which quickly ceased publication. In 1962 Nepal Sahitya Samsthan was organized to stimulate public interest in Nepalese culture via literature. *Himani* is its quarterly magazine.

One of the mandates of the Royal Nepal Academy is to help individuals or organizations publish catalogues of books, dictionaries, encyclopedias and other literary works. They also translate works of literature from foreign languages into Nepali and from Nepali into foreign languages.

In addition to regular academic work, the Royal Nepal Academy has published several hundred volumes. Each year on the anniversary of the birth of King Mahendra, an All-Nepal Poetry Festival is held. Competition winners receive a cash prize and a medal. During the Gai Jatra festival, the academy organizes an exhibition of satiric and comical plays, poems and songs.

The artists employed in the performing arts department of the academy who contribute to, and are published in, the fields of Nepali literature, language, arts and culture are also eligible to receive cash awards and honours. The largest award is the Prithvi Pragya-Puraskar which is given every five years, the second largest is the Tribhuvan-Pragya-Puraskar given every three years and the third, the Mahendra-Pragya-Puraskar is awarded every two years. Another important honour, the Birendra-Pragya-Lankar, is granted to foreign scholars who have made distinguished contributions to Nepalese studies. Fellowships are also awarded yearly to assist scholars in their research.

The NAFA art magazine is published annually on the occasion of King Birendra's birthday and represents the ideas of contemporary Nepalese artists in both traditional and modern fields. NAFA, in realizing its mandate, has also undertaken the preparation of books and articles and has presented awards to artists and scholars who have made significant contributions.

The national Archives of Kathmandu have invaluable manuscripts concerning traditional dance and drama. Research in the late 1990s is being conducted by the Premier Theatrical Association and the Dance Department at Tribhuvan University. Among research works on Nepali theatrics, the publications of Mrigendra Man Singh Pradhan, Prachanda Malla, Sabi Shaha and Beti Bajracharya are important.

Prem Raman Uprety, Mukunda Raj Aryal,
WECT staff

(*The editors would like to acknowledge the importance of Mary M. Anderson's* The Festivals of Nepal *in the preparation of the* **Structure of the National Theatre Community** *section.*)

Further Reading

Amatya, Shaphalya. *Some Aspects of Cultural Policy in Nepal.* Paris: Unesco, 1983. 63 pp.

Anderson, Mary M. *The Festivals of Nepal.* London: Allen & Unwin, 1977. 288 pp.

Coomaraswami, A.K., ed. *Natya Darpan.* Cambridge: Cambridge University Press, 1917.

Karan, P.P. and W.M. Jenkins. *A Cultural and Physical Geography of Nepal.* Lexington, KY: University of Kentucky Press, 1960.

Lall, Kesar. *Lores and Legends of Nepal.* Ratnat Postak Bhandar: Kathmandu, 1978.

Manupuria, Trilok Chandra and Indra Majupuria. *The Complete Guide to Nepal.* India: Smt. M.D. Gupta, Lalitpur Colony, Laskkar (Gwalior), 1986. 341 pp.

Pradhan, Mrigendra Man Singh. *Avinaya Darpan.* Kathmandu: Tribhuvan University, 1976.

——. *Nepali Niritya Kala.* Kathmandu: Krishna Pradhan, 1996.

——. *Niritya Kala.* Kathmandu: Sajha Prakashan, 1980.

——. *Niritya Tatha Nirityakar.* Kathmandu: Pradhan Natya Mandal, 1994.

——. *Pancha Buddha and Dance.* Kathmandu: Royal Nepal Academy, 1966.

Sakya, Karna. *Tales of Kathmandu.* Brisbane, 1980.

Slusser, Mary Shephard. *Nepal Mandal: A Cultural Study of the Kathmandu Valley.* 2 vols. Princeton, NJ: Princeton University Press, 1982.

Note: The *Pradhan Natya Mandal* brings out commemorative issues that contain research articles on Nepali dramatics.

NEW CALEDONIA

(see **SOUTH PACIFIC**)

NEW HEBRIDES

(see **SOUTH PACIFIC** (Vanuatu))

NEW ZEALAND

Located in the Pacific Ocean at the southwestern corner of the Polynesian triangle, New Zealand comprises two main islands, North Island and South Island, and a number of smaller ones. New Zealand's nearest neighbours are Australia, nearly 2,000 kilometres (1,250 miles) to the west across the Tasman Sea, and New Caledonia, Tonga and Fiji, much the same distance to the north. With a total land area of about 270,000 square kilometres (105,000 square miles), but stretching over 1,600 kilometres (1,000 miles) north to south, New Zealand is long and narrow, characterized by a spine of rugged alpine and volcanic mountains, hilly pockets of native bush, extensive rolling pasture land, and an immensely long shoreline. The climate is maritime, and largely temperate, though becoming subtropical in the north.

The main metropolitan areas are the cities of Auckland and Wellington (the capital) in North Island and Christchurch and Dunedin in South Island, with over 300 kilometres between each one. The population, which is largely concentrated in these cities (Auckland alone holds about one-third) and a number of provincial cities and towns, is made up of about 85 per cent people of European ethnic origin (pakeha, to use the useful Maori-derived term for non-Maori), and about 12 per cent Maori, the *tangata whenua* (people of the land). In recent years there has been an increasing migrant population from the Pacific Islands and Southeast Asia. The 1996 census showed a population of just over 3,660,000, making New Zealand one of the least densely populated countries of the 'western' world of which it considers itself a part. Formerly a British dominion and now a member of the Commonwealth, New Zealand is an independent democratic constitutional monarchy (with a governor-general acting in most cases for the British monarch) governed by a unicameral parliament. English is almost exclusively the language of administration and day-to-day life, but Maori is an official language, and active steps are being taken to preserve and encourage its use.

Colonization of New Zealand (the British signed the Treaty of Waitangi with the sovereign Maori chiefs of Aotearoa in 1840) introduced theatre, in the European sense of the word, in the wake of settlers and government officials. The discovery of gold in 1861 brought expansion, prosperity and an audience sufficient to attract regular Australian, British and North American touring companies. They provided the bulk of stage entertainment until well into the twentieth century, and substantial theatres and opera houses were built to house them. Large-scale touring, however, declined in the face of silent film, radio, recessions, World War I, talkies and the Depression of the early 1930s. An amateur theatre movement became established in the 1920s, with affiliation to the British Drama League from 1932. Organizations like the Country Women's Institute were also important, and locally written one-act plays were encouraged by competitions. New Zealand literary and cultural self-expression was still very new, so theatre generally followed British fashions in choice of plays and style of presentation, although a few writers experimented with European and North American models of symbolism and expressionism.

In the towns and cities the larger amateur 'Repertory' theatres provided regular dramatic entertainment that was socially as well as theatrically acceptable for the professional and middle classes. World War II limited theatrical activity, but 'concert parties', presenting music and theatrical sketches to the troops, added to performance confidence. After the war, a very wide cross-section of the community continued to be involved in amateur theatre. In addition to the British Drama League, which maintained its support for the writing of one-act plays, the New Zealand Drama Council was formed in 1945 to support the larger amateur theatre groups.

During World War II alternatives had started emerging to the commercially successful production by the large civic repertory societies of recent successes from London's West End. But the alternatives were also based on British models. Wellington's Unity Theatre (founded 1943) was patterned on the left-wing London theatre club of the same name, although its initial commitment to socialist and Marxist plays was soon redefined to include any play of social significance. It was, from the 1940s through the 1960s, adventurous both in presenting unfamiliar new British and European plays, and new local plays.

A more literary Anglophilia permeated the Canterbury University College Little Theatre in the 1940s, where Ngaio Marsh (1899–1982) became the centre of an art theatre devoted to Shakespeare and new poetic plays. Allen Curnow (b. 1911) was already an established poet, and his verse drama *The Axe* (1948), rich in New Zealand and Pacific poetic and anthropological themes, was regarded by the Canterbury group as a high point of this movement.

The triumphant London Old Vic tour of Australia and New Zealand in 1948, in which Laurence Olivier and Vivien Leigh were idolized like royalty, added impetus to New Zealand aspirations, again following the British pattern, for a bricks-and-mortar national theatre. However, the first and only professional national company, the New Zealand Players, was a touring group. Its founders, Richard and Edith Campion (both b. 1923), were two young New Zealanders trained at the Old Vic who financed the company out of private means. The company toured the length of the country, small towns as well as cities, from 1953 till its bankruptcy in 1960. The repertoire was largely English classics and popular contemporary plays, with very occasionally a New Zealand work, such as the 1957 workshop production of *The Pohutukawa Tree* by Bruce Mason (1921–82).

A more modest pattern of touring, to rural towns and smaller communities throughout the upper North Island, was undertaken by the Community Arts Service (CAS) Theatre from 1947 until the mid-1960s. Organized by Auckland University's Adult Education agency, the CAS was modelled on British wartime cultural activities for workers' hostels and evacuee centres, with music, opera, ballet and graphic arts as well as theatre. At the other end of the country the Southern Comedy Players was formed in 1957, a Dunedin-based professional touring company which survived until the late 1960s with a seasonal repertoire of light comedy.

The New Zealand Players collapsed in 1960, ironically the year that the New Zealand government finally established an arts funding body, the Arts Advisory Council. In 1963 this became the Queen Elizabeth II Arts Council of New Zealand. Its favoured scheme for the development of professional theatre was not a centralized national theatre, but regional trusts supporting theatres on the English provincial model. Pressure in this direction resulted in short-lived Canterbury and Southern (Dunedin) theatre trusts in the mid-1960s. Their professional companies were not good enough to survive underfunding and some antagonism from amateur theatre audiences (and practitioners). Only Auckland, perhaps because of its larger population (then over half a million), was successful in establishing a trust-based, fully professional theatre on the English provincial repertory model: the Mercury Theatre, which opened in 1968 under Anthony Richardson (1926–82), formerly director of England's Belgrade Theatre, Coventry.

During the 1960s radio drama under the leadership of William Austin (1915–74) had fostered New Zealand writing and offered the only secure livelihood for the few professional actors. An alternative approach to regional theatre was also developing. Downstage Theatre was formed in Wellington in 1964 by a poet, an actor, a lecturer and a businessman. They decided to fill the vacuum left after the collapse of the New Zealand Players by creating a base for their own theatre work. Downstage grew slowly from ramshackle semi-professionalism and in due course acquired Arts Council funding. By the early 1970s Wellington as well as Auckland had a regional professional theatre. The Downstage example of starting small and semi-professional was followed by other locally based companies that sprang up throughout the country in the early 1970s, until by 1976 a network of nine subsidized professional regional theatres formed the Association of Community Theatres (ACT).

Overseas models were now as often American or European as British, and nowhere more so than in experimental and alternative theatre. New Zealand in the early 1970s had its own Living Theatre Troupe (1970–5), the Lecoq-trained Theatre Action (1972–7), the cabaret and performance art of Red Mole (founded 1974) and the more exploratory Amamus (1971–8), which moved from left-wing documentary theatre to Grotowski-style work.

The same period saw a national stocktaking in theatre and the arts. A major arts policy conference in 1970 recommended that New Zealand cultural priorities include regional development, increased funding, a theatre school and support for New Zealand playwriting. That year Nola Millar (1915–74) formed the theatre school which in 1974 became the New Zealand Drama School under the auspices of the Arts Council. In 1973 Playmarket was established as an agency to promote New Zealand playwriting.

Several universities introduced drama programmes at this time: Phillip Mann (b. 1942) in Wellington, and Mervyn Thompson (1935–92) in first Christchurch and then Auckland, had a considerable impact on theatre, as did their graduates.

Amateur theatre too was having to redefine its function. Gone were the days of hiring vast opera houses for the latest West End hit; many societies had retrenched or acquired their own small theatres, and were faced with the demands of a younger generation of members wanting to respond to the excitement of overseas theatrical revolutions of the 1960s. The New Zealand branch of the British Drama League merged with the New Zealand Drama Council in 1970 to form the New Zealand Theatre Federation.

The 1970s saw New Zealand plays finally getting on to the stage in significant numbers. In 1976 *Glide Time*, a civil service comedy by Roger Hall (b. 1939), was presented by Circa Theatre (a newly formed actors' cooperative in Wellington). It quickly transferred from the 100-seat Circa to the 1,200-seat Opera House, was subsequently performed in every centre in the country with a professional theatre, and broke all records for audience attendance for a New Zealand play. *Glide Time* became a household word, spawned a radio and television series, and proved to theatre directors that New Zealand audiences might accept New Zealand plays in preference to overseas writing. Two years later,

Hall's second comedy, *Middle-Age Spread*, was playing in London (and won the West End Theatre Managers' Comedy of the Year Award).

The next watershed was 1980, when out of Playmarket's first national Playwrights' Workshop there emerged *Foreskin's Lament* by Greg McGee (b. 1950), a funny and ferocious drama that turned New Zealand's national sport of rugby into a self-critical metaphor for the country's loss of innocence in the passage from colony to independent nationhood. What *The Pohutukawa Tree* in the amateur theatre and *Glide Time* in the professional theatre had done for acceptance of New Zealand drama as popular entertainment, *Foreskin's Lament* did for the role of playwright as social critic in the national arena.

Social critique became an increasingly common standpoint of both mainstream and alternative theatre in the 1980s. A resurgence of Maori nationalism produced specifically political theatre groups, and many pakeha writers and theatres associated themselves with Maori social protest. Alternative theatres based on a cooperative structure, and in effect subsidized by meagerly rewarded actors, put pressure on the mainstream theatres by doing rougher, more experimental productions, new local writing, and plays that appealed to feminist, Maori and Polynesian audiences, youth and the politically committed. A wider range of work was presented, often crossing traditional boundaries of arts disciplines, and incorporating increasingly bicultural and multicultural forms.

The optimism of the 1970s and early 1980s led to growth in the theatrical infrastructure as well. In particular, Playmarket formed the base for the New Zealand Centre for the International Theatre Institute, published a national theatre magazine *Act*, set up the Tasman Theatre Exchange with Australia, organized biennial playwrights' workshops and coordinated several playwrights' awards and residencies.

The decade from 1975, however, saw a drop in government funding for the arts in real terms as the New Zealand economy went through a period of very high inflation and as the Arts Council had to respond to the wider range of artistic demands. The number of ACT theatres fell from nine in 1976 to five in 1986, largely because subsidy was insufficient to maintain professional theatres, some established in population centres too small to support them, seating little more than 100, and failing to fill even those seats. In 1986 the failure of *Act* magazine, the virtual demise of ACT, and the closure of Auckland's second professional theatre (Theatre Corporate, founded 1973) emphasized just how fragile the situation was.

In the mid-1980s the Arts Council overhauled its theatre subsidy policies, and was successful in attracting substantially increased government funding. The surviving theatres were given increased operating grants and money to pay off accumulated debt. But the new funding regime reserved some of the money for incentive funding tied to targeted priorities, such as developmental, interdisciplinary and Maori and Pacific work, for which theatres had to apply separately. In addition, companies were required to meet much more rigorous planning criteria, to attract alternative income such as sponsorship, and to understand that there would be no bail-outs if they failed.

Major changes in New Zealand society reinforced this tougher environment. New Zealand had been, since the 1930s, one of the most regulated economies in the world. From the mid-1980s monetarist economic policies and New Right theories of government and management were introduced at bewildering speed, and New Zealand rapidly became one of the least regulated economies. For the Arts Council, since 1994 trading under the name Creative New Zealand, this meant testing the accountability of its arts clients according to newly overhauled strategic objectives. Survival became precarious for the producing theatres if they failed to adapt to the new criteria, and low box-office returns for even one or two productions could spell

bankruptcy. Auckland's principal ACT theatre, the Mercury, crashed in 1992, and Wellington's Downstage survived only by selling many of its assets, shedding all its production and most administrative staff, and restructuring itself as principally a venue, producing its own shows only from time to time. By 1994, only three of the original ACT theatres survived as full-time producing theatres.

For small companies with no buildings, however, and for those theatres which successfully made the change to more entrepreneurial planning, the targeted funding and slim administration required under the new regime provided opportunities. Individual companies producing new New Zealand work, for instance, were well placed to apply for project funding. Cooperatives such as Circa in Wellington, and venues presenting independent shows as well as producing their own, like Auckland's Watershed (formed 1991), became the new mainstream theatres in these cities.

The entire pattern of subsidized theatre had by the mid-1990s changed almost out of recognition from what it had been in the 1970s. Pessimists expressed genuine concern for a future in which the survival of buildings, companies and careers was based on short-term criteria and a succession of projects rather than long-established institutions. Optimists, however, pointed to the artistic vibrancy of an environment in which new creative impulses could receive immediate support, and people or theatres that had lost their spark were not allowed to drain the limited pool of subsidy.

Structure of the National Theatre Community

Subsidized professional theatre in New Zealand divides into three main categories: producer theatres (with their own buildings), producer companies (with no venue), and mixed producer/presenter venues (companies with their own building which mount some plays themselves as well as making their theatre available to outside shows). From the 1960s until the early 1990s regional producer theatres were the norm, and the Court (Christchurch, founded 1971), Centrepoint (Palmerston North, founded 1973) and Fortune (Dunedin, founded 1974) still largely adhere to the pattern. Each is controlled by a trust board and run by either an artistic director or a general manager and a

small permanent staff. Artistic personnel often move from one theatre to another, sometimes being hired just for an individual show. A loose company may be created from time to time, since the professional theatre population is very small, but none of the producing theatres has created an ensemble company. With a theatre ticket costing two or three times the price of a cinema ticket, audiences are predominantly the urban middle class.

Non-venue producer companies tend to be small and are more likely to rely on project funding than annual funding from the Arts Council. They are also likely to tour their shows to other cities, a development strongly supported by the Arts Council. Auckland's Theatre at Large (founded 1990) and the two largely Samoan companies, Pacific Theatre (founded in Auckland in 1987), and the Christchurch-based Pacific Underground (founded 1991), fall into this category. So too does the Auckland Theatre Company (founded 1992), though operating only in Auckland, which reflects its origins as a successor to the defunct Mercury Theatre.

Producer/presenter venues such as Auckland's Watershed and Wellington's Downstage not only mount some plays themselves, but also make their theatres available to independent and touring shows. They are likely to share both the risk and the rewards in presenting independent shows. Under an ever-increasing variety of financial and production arrangements, they are attempting to establish a nation-wide pattern of targeting exchanges of shows to venues. In some cases the theatre will buy an independent show and tour it after a home season, or sell it on to a theatre in another centre, or to one of a growing number of regional arts festivals.

Wellington, which has a surprising level of theatrical activity for a small city, has seen the development of the cooperative theatres Circa, Taki Rua (founded as the New Depot in 1983) and Bats (founded 1989). Circa pioneered the co-op concept, with a loose artistic collective which restricted itself to deciding on applications from co-ops for a performance slot in its hired venue, and to minimum administration. A new co-op (technically, a single-venture legal partnership between all the actors, director, designer and crew to share risk, and profits – if any) is formed for each show, and takes full artistic responsibility for the show. The theatre itself usually takes between 15 and 30 per cent of box office, depending on the overheads and costs it pays for, and the rest is divided among all the co-op members.

The financial risks are considerable for unsubsidized co-ops, and two distinct artistic tendencies result: either safe, small-cast comedies and dramas performed by established actors; or more adventurous new plays (or large-cast classics) by actors and directors prepared, in effect, to subsidize their own opportunity to work, or to gamble on the chance of success. Circa, however, moved in 1994 from a dilapidated 100-seat studio to a 300-seat purpose-built theatre, and has Arts Council and some corporate funding for a trust fund which now provides rehearsal wages and production funds for each co-op. It has virtually become a producing theatre in Downstage's place. Similarly, Taki Rua and Bats now produce their own shows as well as being available to co-ops.

All these types of theatre tend to have very similar artistic working methods, and theatre practitioners move easily among them. Rehearsal periods are usually only three or four weeks (though project-based companies, such as Theatre at Large, will sometimes plan an extended period of up to nine weeks) and the run of a play is generally four or five weeks. A play requiring more than seven actors is regarded as financially risky. The democratic basis of the co-ops has partially broken down the traditional power of the director; one result has been an increase in the number of women directors.

A few small groups offer a more physical, clown or image-based performance, and Theatre-in-Education companies tour to schools. For local or touring amateur and professional musicals and the few overseas shows, large commercially operated or civic theatres are available for hire in the main cities and towns.

Arts Council subsidy for regional producing theatres is generally about one-third of total income, with box office and sponsorship making up the rest. These theatres used to get the lion's share of Arts Council funding, but policy changes in the late 1980s and 1990s see funding targeted much more to specific plays, projects and touring which match identified national priorities such as new writing, Maori theatre and interdisciplinary developments. Arts Council money is no longer allocated on predominantly discipline lines, but through cross-disciplinary objectives. In 1994–5, the final year of discipline-dominated grants, Arts Council support for theatre was NZ$3,052,000, out of a total council budget of NZ$23,000,000. Regional producing theatres received a total of NZ$1,877,000; non-venue producers NZ$245,000; grants for new work totalled NZ$715,000; and grants for professional development and infrastructure NZ$215,000. (The largest grant was NZ$565,000 to the Court Theatre; the smallest NZ$20,000 to Pacific Underground. This excludes projects: commissions, schools touring, and staging specific new work.)

In 1996 only about two hundred actors, of a national pool probably two or three times that, were members of Actors' Equity, the actors' union (now a section of the National Distribution Union). Membership has never been an absolute requirement. Furthermore, the substantial deregulation of the New Zealand labour market in the early 1990s has resulted in most actors being employed under individual contracts rather than a union award rate. In 1996 actors could expect to earn about NZ$400 to $600 per week in the theatre, a little below the national average. Since actors can rarely work year-round, their annual income is usually significantly below average. However, some actors make substantial income from the much better paying areas of radio, television, video and film.

Playmarket, the agent representing nearly all New Zealand working playwrights, has about a hundred and fifty writers on its books, but only one or two could make their living from playwriting alone. Probably another dozen make a living from radio and screenwriting. The Bruce Mason Award was established in 1983, and is given annually in recognition of achievement by

a playwright at the beginning of a career; in 1996 its value, sponsored by the *Sunday Star Times* newspaper, was NZ$5,000.

The New Zealand International Festival of the Arts (founded 1986) is a major festival held every other year in March in Wellington. Initially it concentrated on international attractions (on the coat-tails of the Adelaide Festival), but increasingly it commissions new theatre works. It has sprouted a fringe festival, which is predominantly new New Zealand work. The Aotearoa Traditional Maori Performing Arts Festival (founded 1972), currently held alternate Februaries in a different location each time, concentrates on traditional forms. So too does the quadrennial Pacific Festival of Arts (established 1972), which moves from country to country in the South Pacific.

Artistic Profile

At first view, New Zealand presents an artistic profile immediately familiar to anyone acquainted with European or North American theatre. Both amateur and professional theatres present plays mainly from the English-speaking tradition: classics (especially Shakespeare); contemporary drama and comedy from Britain, the United States and, increasingly, Australia; musicals; and new New Zealand plays. Occasionally plays from the European repertoire are given, and overseas companies are seen at the biennial International Festival of the Arts. The urban theatres operate year-round, with generally a brief dark period during the post-Christmas (summer) holiday.

European and North American trends of the late 1980s and 1990s towards more physical and image-based theatrical styles have been reflected in New Zealand, particularly by project-based companies such as Theatre at Large. Similarly, the previously sharp distinctions between drama, contemporary dance, physical and object theatre, musical performance, opera, stand-up comedy and clowning have increasingly overlapped. These interdisciplinary trends in the 1990s have significantly changed audience perceptions of a tradition that is essentially based on spoken drama.

New Zealand differs in many ways, however, from Europe and North America and this is nowhere more evident than in the influence of indigenous Maori culture. Traditionally, because

Maori is an oral culture, performance has been an important element in all literature and formal speech as well as in music and dance. *Whaikōrero* oratory and the telling of stories are accompanied by gesture and emphatic pausation, emphasis, repetition and other rhetorical devices. Less physical in their presentation are the *mōteatea*, the traditional song-poems and laments that are particularly associated with formal occasions, but the emotion and accuracy of delivery of the words and chants is vital. *Mōteatea* and *waiata* (songs) counterbalance and add relish to sequences of oratory and debate.

Maori dance forms are now mainly associated with *kapa haka* cultural groups. *Kapa* means 'rank, row' and *haka* in Maori for dance, so *kapa haka* defines the group standing in ranks in order to perform dances to an audience, to greet guests at a formal occasion with a symbolic challenge or, in the traditional war dance form, to hurl defiance at an enemy. *Haka* has always been associated with the songs and chants which play a central part in ceremony through prescribed forms and sequences maintained from pre-European times to the present day. The words are of primary importance in all forms of *haka*, often relating a specific event or exploit. Vigorous stamping and quivering arm gestures accompany the rhythmic shouted chant. Some *haka*, particularly the battle *haka*, are reserved in most tribes for performance by men, while a few are performed only by women. Usually they perform together the *haka pōwhiri*, the danced chant of welcome to guests: men and women stand in separate rows, on occasion moving in a group through the gaps in order to take a new position at the front or back of the *haka* for a time. In the twentieth century and especially in entertainment context such as concert parties and the national competitions, most *kapa haka* groups, which may be up to seventy strong, have a roughly equal number of men and women and perform most of the *haka* jointly.

The *haka poi* (poi dance) is a uniquely New Zealand form of women's dance, employing a light fibrous ball on the end of a short or long cord. The *poi* is swung and twirled rhythmically to accompany a song. Originally a game rather than a dance, it was transformed in the 1880s into a symbol of political resistance to pakeha rule and has subsequently become enormously popular as a form of entertainment. Considerable variety and virtuosity can be displayed by the use of both long and short *poi*, by variation of speed and by changing from single *poi* to one in each hand and even to two in each hand. In contemporary concert performance, black light and other technical means are often used to emphasize the dazzling speed and intricacy of the synchronized *poi* movement presented by large groups; massed *haka poi* is often the spectacular finale to a show.

Waiata-a-ringa (literally, 'songs using the hands', frequently referred to as 'action songs') are an early-twentieth-century development, reflecting an effort to revitalize Maori culture through the teaching of cultural traditions. Usually adopting the *kapa* formation of the large group standing in rows to perform, this new form puts Maori words to popular contemporary tunes. The Maori words are not, however, a translation of the popular song, but new words for which the available tune seems appropriate. A widely quoted example is the use of the Glenn Miller favourite 'In the Mood' to carry a solemn and moving lament for the dead of the Maori Battalion at the end of World War II. The *waiata* are accompanied by graceful hand and arm movements, particularly by the women, and a gentle swaying of the body. Each action holds a particular meaning and actions are carefully matched to words. Although most of these songs adopt current western popular music, there is a respected and growing body of original music for them by Maori composers. Action songs have become exceedingly popular and now both old and new action songs provide the core of most culture groups repertoires.

Their creation has become increasingly sophisticated over the years, but they have always been presented as much for communicative purposes as for entertainment, with subjects ranging from political issues to matters of personal concern.

Kapa haka groups, or culture groups, rehearse and perform *haka* and *waiata-a-ringa* for a variety of presentational contexts ranging from informal presentation to family and friends, to formal challenges and welcomes on marae, to the more entertainment-oriented annual competitions, concert parties or professional employment in tourist hotel shows, cabaret or professional theatre. Unlike most western theatre, however, there is no gap between the cultural meaning of these traditional and developing modern forms as they function within Maori tradition and protocol, and their wider presentation as entertainment.

None of these traditional Maori forms constitutes drama in the strict western sense of actors presenting themselves as characters in imagined acts, but new research is suggesting there may have been dramatic entertainment in the pre-European period. Certainly there was an institution called the *whare tapere* (house of entertainment). There was puppetry of some sort. But pakeha theatre until recently tended to depict Maori people, if at all, in a patronizing or stereotypical way; Maori themselves seldom felt at ease with western dramatic conventions. That is now changing as distinctive Maori culture and artistic initiatives incorporate and adapt western forms.

The largely Maori cast and chorus for *Porgy and Bess* in 1965 seized the event to form the Maori Theatre Trust in 1966, with the aim of developing Maori professional theatre skills. Although the group's emphasis gradually swung towards concert party performances, it nevertheless played an important communal nurturing role. Several Maori actors went on to employment in professional theatre as well as in radio, television and film. In 1972 *Te Raukura* by Harry Dansey (1920–79), a historical play in English incorporating Maori dialogue and song, became the first play by a Maori writer to be staged.

Throughout the 1970s and 1980s Maori alternatives to mainstream theatre were also developing. Maori political activists rejected the myth of New Zealand's harmonious race relations and demanded redress of a century's grievances. For example, *The Death of the Land* (1976) by Rori Hapipi (Rowley Habib, b. 1935) not only dealt with the recurrent theme of alienation from the ancestral lands which form a vital part of the Maori spiritual context, but also was the first play presented on a marae. (Marae are the spiritual, ancestral and community centres of extended tribal families.) More recent plays by Maori writers have confronted such issues as urban dislocation of Maori from rural marae, tensions between traditional Maori customs and young Maori who have grown up in a global youth culture, and the importance of acknowledging the results of a colonial past.

Government work schemes of the 1980s were ingeniously used by several Maori practitioners to train young Maori in performance and in creating their own shows. By the early 1990s Maori and Pacific Island actors were graduating from the New Zealand Drama School in significant numbers, Maori playwrights were writing cross-cultural plays in which elements of Maori language, protocol, music and spiritual values were syncretized into essentially western dramaturgy, and increasingly Maori practitioners at Taki Rua Theatre and elsewhere were taking theatrical control into their own hands. The large Pacific Island communities in New Zealand were similarly exploring western drama as a means of expression, particularly of the immigrant experience.

Companies

Since the collapse of the nationally touring New Zealand Players in 1960, the Arts Council has nurtured professional theatre on a pattern of regional companies based principally in the four main centres (Auckland, Wellington, Christchurch and Dunedin).

The sudden bankruptcy in 1992 of Auckland's Mercury Theatre, the country's largest subsidized company, showed how fragile was the position of the established regional producing theatres. By the mid-1990s only Centrepoint, Fortune and the Court survived in their traditional form (as well as having developed from a cooperative-based theatre, Circa). The Court Theatre in Christchurch, the strongest example of the old pattern, continues to operate under long-serving artistic director, Elric Hooper (b. 1936). Production, design and acting are considerably influenced by mainstream European and North American styles, tending to modified realism. Typical programming for a year might comprise three or four successful plays from London or New York, one

or two modern classics, one or two new New Zealand plays (including commissions for Christchurch playwrights) and a Shakespeare. In addition, Hooper will usually surprise his loyal Christchurch audience at least once each year by lifting from obscurity a little-known classic from the European repertoire.

Wellington's Downstage Theatre saved itself from following Auckland's Mercury into bankruptcy only by abandoning to Circa its traditional place as the mainstream producing theatre in Wellington, and adopting instead a new role pioneered by the small co-op theatres. Like Watershed in Auckland, Downstage now mounts some shows itself, but also invites outside and touring productions to use the theatre. Rather than a traditional artistic director, it has an artistic manager, Guy Boyce (b. 1959), who cut his teeth running the small Bats co-op across the road. Downstage has started to attract a younger audience to the eclectic mix of comedy, new plays (particularly those with a physical theatre style), contemporary dance and the occasional big classic. Centrepoint and Fortune may well be moving towards a similar model.

Bats and Taki Rua, both small co-op based theatres in Wellington, now also fall into the category of mixed producer/presenter. Taki Rua is particularly significant because it is unique in the country in its commitment to Maori theatre, biculturalism and new New Zealand writing. From its 100-seat theatre its collective consensus-based managing group started in the mid-1990s not only to support individual production co-ops, but also to produce annual short seasons of new plays by Maori playwrights, and of plays largely or entirely in Maori. They also actively promote opportunities for Maori directors and other practitioners. Pacific Island culture has also been welcomed, particularly Samoan plays, as well as interdisciplinary work with dance theatres and music performance groups. In addition, the theatre has a tradition of supporting politically linked constituencies: feminist, gay, lesbian and left-wing theatre.

The other major group of companies are the non-venue producers. The Auckland Theatre Company, in some respects a successor to the Mercury, usually hires a theatre to present a repertoire similar to that of the traditional producer theatres. Auckland's Theatre at Large is more project-based and adventurous. Its directors, Anna Marbrook (b. 1966) and Christian Penny (b. 1964), have become known for the physicality and theatricality of their shows,

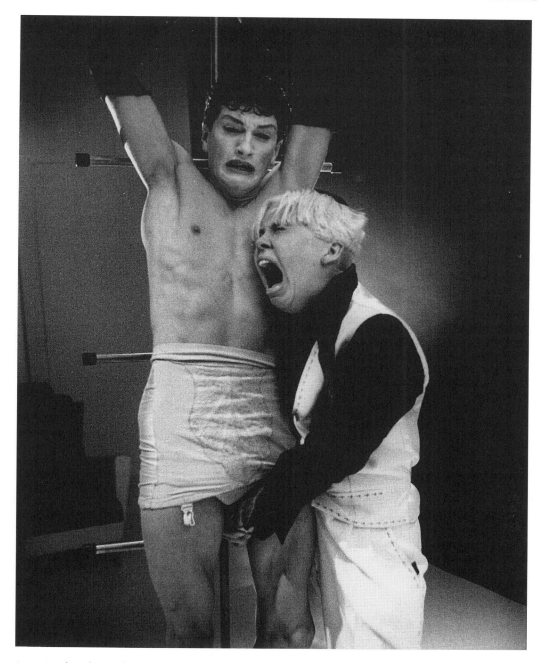

Anna Marbrook, co-director of Theatre at Large as Cardinal Wolsey and Tim Spite as Mary Boleyn in the company-devised show *Henry 8*.
Photo: Paul McCredie.

usually devised from improvisation by a company assembled for the project, or energetically reconstructed and deconstructed versions of classics. They perform in a variety of both theatrical and found spaces, and frequently tour their work to other cities. The two Samoan companies operate on a similar project basis: Pacific Theatre, formed in Auckland by director

Justine Simei-Barton (b. 1961) and her play-wright husband Paul (b. 1958); and Pacific Underground in Christchurch, in which the actor/writers Oscar Kightley (b. 1969) and more recently David Fane (b. 1966) have been central figures in presenting the Pacific Island immigrant experience in New Zealand.

Dramaturgy

A number of poets and short story writers before and after World War II ventured into playwriting, notably Allen Curnow, Frank Sargeson (1903–82) and James K. Baxter (1926–72). While none of them succeeded in developing a dramaturgy equivalent to their literary skills, Baxter in particular was influential. He provocatively explored the potential of Greek mythic and tragic structures in contemporary New Zealand settings, and brought New Zealand vernacular speech (from the subculture of alcoholic derelicts) on to the polite Anglocentric middle-class stage.

Bruce Mason was the first professional post-war playwright and a figure of importance both for his significant output and for his self-appointed role as crusader, critic and exemplar for the theatre. His earliest plays (one-act pieces for Wellington's Unity Theatre, 1953–5) were severely naturalistic, but with a sharp, satiric eye on complacency, puritanism and provincialism in New Zealand society.

Mason's first major full-length play, *The Pohutukawa Tree* (written for and given a workshop production by the New Zealand Players, 1957), introduced the formality and emotional power of Maori rhetoric as a counterpoint to the limitations of realism. Debate between Maori and pakeha values is dominated by a powerful Maori matriarch. Furthermore, Maori attachment both to the land the pakeha now own and to versions of pakeha-introduced Christianity are thematically complex. The tendency to noble-savage romanticism in content and dramaturgy is partly balanced by comedy, such as a satiric set-piece of a pakeha country wedding. *The Pohutukawa Tree* became the first New Zealand play to be placed on the schools syllabus, and as such achieved an influence considerably greater than even its many amateur and occasional professional stage productions could have generated on their own. In the absence of a professional theatre after the collapse of the New Zealand Players in 1960, Mason started presenting his own solo pieces, of

Maori matriarch Aroha Mataira, overlooked by her warrior ancestor in Downstage's 1984 production of Bruce Mason's *The Pohutukawa Tree*.
Photo: Guy Robinson.

which the boyhood reminiscences (not without social point) of *The End of the Golden Weather* (1959) were vastly popular and performed nearly a thousand times throughout the country in the two decades following; it was subsequently made into a successful movie.

The establishment of regional theatres in the late 1960s and early 1970s created new opportunities for writers. Robert Lord (1945–92) was closely associated with first Downstage and subsequently Mercury as he developed a spare, abstract style based on ambiguity of dialogue and relationships (*It Isn't Cricket*, 1971; *Meeting Place*, 1972). He attended the Australian Playwrights' Conference in 1973, and the influence of David Williamson was evident in the black farce *Well Hung* (1974; later retitled and published as *Country Cops*) in which Lord's keen ear caught a distinctively New Zealand comic idiom. His last play, *Joyful and Triumphant* (1992), progressing in a parallel time scheme through the course of a family's Christmas day over four decades, explored both a comic nostalgia for the recent past, and bitter personal despair covered by the tinsel cheerfulness of Christmas.

Joseph Musaphia (b. 1935), who had developed his craft writing for radio in the 1960s, displayed a darkly comic talent with plays such as *Victims* (1973), *Obstacles* (1974) and the enormously successful *Mothers and Fathers* (1975), all very firmly set in middle New Zealand. Comedy was starting to gain a place for New Zealand playwrights in the professional theatres.

It was Roger Hall who made that place secure. After an apprenticeship of university revues and radio and television comedy, Hall's first play *Glide Time* (1976) was an instant success which established him as the country's most significant playwright in both artistic and commercial terms. Set in an obscure government department and full of despairing humour about circumscribed middle-class lives, the play's sharp one-liners and its characters were instantly accepted as comic home truths. Many of Hall's subse-

quent plays have worked the same ground. *Middle-Age Spread* (1977), *State of the Play* (1978), *Fifty/Fifty* (1981) and *Conjugal Rites* (1990, subsequently a series on British television) all dealt in semi-comic terms with the insecurities and uncertainties of middle-aged men in marital, professional and personal life crises.

In *The Share Club* (1987) and *After the Crash* (1989) Hall satirized the entrepreneurial frenzy that followed financial deregulation in New Zealand in the mid-1980s, and the aftermath of the stock market crash. In 1996, twenty years after *Glide Time* opened at Circa Theatre, almost the same cast returned in *Market Forces*, a bleakly funny play in which the same characters face the dismantling of the public service in which so much of their audience spent their working lives.

Greg McGee eclipsed Roger Hall for a time on the basis of *Foreskin's Lament* (1980), his first and most successful play. With an intense mixture of locker-room humour and passionate soul searching, the play uses the New Zealand national game of rugby as a metaphor for the

Locker room humour in the Court Theatre's 1981 production of Greg McGree's *Foreskin's Lament*. Photo: courtesy of the Court Theatre.

loss of innocence of a post-colonial society. McGee laments the passing of the old order at the same time that he scathingly strips bare its smug hypocrisy and intolerance. The dramaturgy of the play moves from realistic comedy to an overtly theatricalist ending in which the main character demands that the audience recognize the hollowness of the myth of New Zealand as a social paradise. Most of McGee's subsequent writing has been for television and film.

Mervyn Thompson, as well as being a charismatic university teacher and an unflagging champion and director of New Zealand plays in the professional theatre, was himself a significant writer, particularly of song-plays: dramatic presentations of songs on a political theme with linking dialogue. These included *O! Temperance!* (1972) on the women's suffrage and temperance movement, *Songs to Uncle Scrim* (1976) about the Depression, *Songs to the Judges* (1980) championing Maori land rights, *The Great New Zealand 'Truth' Show* (1982) about yellow-press journalism and his one-man autobiographical shows *Coaltown Blues* (1984), based on his youth in a West Coast mining township, and *Passing Through* (1991), a retrospective view of three decades in New Zealand theatre.

Several writers of poetry and prose turned to playwriting in the 1980s, most notably Rachel McAlpine (b. 1940), Maurice Shadbolt (b. 1932) and Vincent O'Sullivan (b. 1937). McAlpine's *Stationary Sixth Form Poetry Trip* (1980) and *Driftwood* (1985) are lyrical contributions to the growing theatre for young audiences. Shadbolt's *Once on Chunuk Bair* (1982) examines the history of the Gallipoli landing in 1915 to explain the roots of New Zealand post-colonial nationhood. O'Sullivan's *Shuriken* (1983) uses a World War II incident in a New Zealand camp for Japanese prisoners of war to explore the social and racial tensions and incomprehension within New Zealand society. O'Sullivan's style in *Shuriken* and other more dramaturgically radical work is unusual in incorporating several different theatrical modes (in *Shuriken,* realism, expressionism, *Noh,* music hall and film newsreels).

Stuart Hoar (b. 1957) was an experienced writer of radio drama before turning to stage plays, and dense dialogue is perhaps not surprisingly a hallmark of his work. His stage images are strong and emblematic, however: a colonial photographer forever carried on the shoulders of his assistant as he documents the entrepreneurial 'squattocracy' who seized the great

The Mercury Theatre's production of Stuart Hoar's *Squatter*, 1987.
Photo: Michael Tubberty.

South Island sheep runs in the late nineteenth century (*Squatter*, 1987); or two Roman centurions dragging the remains of their galley across the Australian outback after a shipwreck as they return from an embassy to China in AD 169 (*The Boat*, 1992). A contemporary irony often renders historical characters difficult to place in an already complex intellectual framework, and his plays have not found easy acceptance in the theatre.

Among later writers, David Geary (b. 1963) is notable for, on the one hand, broad comedies about stereotypical New Zealand activities (*Pack of Girls*, 1991, about a rugby team – but for women; and *The Learner's Stand*, 1995, about sheep shearing), or, on the other, for astute examination of New Zealand myth, as in *Lovelock's Dream Run* (1993), which examines the legend of the famous New Zealand runner Jack Lovelock (1910–49) who won a gold medal at the Berlin Olympics in 1936. In both kinds of plays Geary comically deconstructs the national self-image, at his best with considerable seriousness of purpose. Geary, like several other young writers, brings irreverence and a strong pop music influence to his theatre work.

Women writers were prominent in amateur playwriting competitions in the period before and after World War II, but not until the 1980s did many women playwrights come to national attention on the professional stage. When they did, they attracted a new audience of younger women to the theatre. Renée (b. 1929), a socialist lesbian feminist, has been most successful with traditional naturalist dramaturgy, spare understated dialogue and numerous substantial roles for women. *Wednesday to Come* (1984) is her best known play, charting an incident in the lives of four generations of women in a small-town family during the Depression of the 1930s, with a clear implication of the political message for a contemporary audience. Two of the younger characters reappear in a sequel, *Pass It On* (1986), set twenty years later during New Zealand's savagely divisive 1951 waterfront labour dispute; Renée adopts a more Brechtian structure and style for this more overtly political material.

The final play of Renée's trilogy is *Jeannie Once* (1990), set in Dunedin in 1879 on the eve of a twenty-year depression. It provides a biography of the Irish great-grandmother from *Wednesday to Come* as a working-class immigrant in New Zealand, and uses music-hall songs of the period, with audience participation, lightly to underline the serious themes of the otherwise realist drama. Nor is this merely distant history; Renée clearly had an eye on the overheated economy of the 1980s, the collapse of New Zealand financial institutions in 1987 and the effect of capitalist boom and bust on the working-class poor then and now.

Another playwright with an overtly women's agenda is Lorae Parry (b. 1955) who serves to illustrate how writers' concerns are changing. Her early play *Frontwomen* (1988), about a suburban wife and mother discovering love, to her perturbation and then delight, with a television 'frontwoman', is televisual in its structure of short scenes of realist dialogue, and politically simple in its implicit plea for tolerance of lesbianism. Her later plays such as *Cracks* (1994), and even more so *Eugenia* (1996), are more complex. *Eugenia*'s dramaturgy involves a double structure: a historical story of an Italian immigrant woman in Wellington in 1916 who regards herself as a man (not a lesbian, a notion which initially disgusts her), and lives, works and marries in her male persona until finally discovered by a resentful male rival; and a modern school drama project in which the students and two teachers (the same actors) not only research

and create a play about Eugenia, but also engage in their own drama about the complexities of gender and power. It is a searching and compassionate examination of entrapment caused by individual and societal rigidities of thinking.

Similar gender complexities are to be found in *A Frigate Bird Sings* (1996) by Oscar Kightley and David Fane, a play by two Samoan New Zealanders about a *fa'afafine*, a man who behaves in the fashion of a woman. Added to the gender ambiguities of *fa'afafine* (and their equivalents in most Polynesian societies), the protagonist, Vili, is a first generation immigrant to New Zealand, looking after a father who becomes increasingly alcoholic after his wife's death, and a younger brother who is more New Zealander than Samoan in his culture. *A Frigate Bird Sings* achieves a new seriousness for Samoan New Zealand theatre in its careful ambiguity about gender, cultural and immigrant issues that are all too often oversimplified. It also starts to assert a real theatrical dramaturgy rather than television structure and dialogue.

Like much women's writing in the 1980s and 1990s, writing by Maori has often been preoccupied with asserting rights after a long period of oppression. Dramaturgically, Maori playwrights have faced the further challenge of establishing a syncretic form that not only develops the European-derived tradition of spoken drama, but also incorporates Maori spiritual and social values and Maori oratorical and performative modes. John Broughton (b. 1947) has written plays dealing entirely with Maori concerns, but his most successful play to date is *Michael James Manaia* (1991), a one-man show in which a veteran of the Vietnam War reveals, in a raging and desperate confession, the extraordinary strains of inheriting and living in both Maori and pakeha culture at the same time.

One of the most interesting recent developments has been adaptations by Maori writers of European classics to their own ends. Apirana Taylor (b. 1955), for instance, used Brecht's *Mother Courage* as a springboard for *Whaea Kairau: Mother Hundred Eater* (1995), an epic story of the nineteenth-century New Zealand Wars. Hone Kouka (b. 1968) recast Ibsen's *The Vikings at Helgeland* as *Nga Tangata Toa: The Warrior People* (1994), set in a coastal Maori community with a haunted veteran of World War I returning to his ancestral home. Viking heroes and sagas transmute easily to Maori warrior culture and rhetoric, and the romanticism of early Ibsen allows for formal songs and traditional protocol. Kouka has written partly in

Maori, though mainly in English; in the first production he worked with a pakeha director and a Norwegian dramaturge. The combination reflects the challenge for young Maori of establishing their own voice in contemporary New Zealand theatre.

Directing and Acting

Directors in New Zealand are usually self-taught. Most have started as actors, and have learned their craft by experience, combined with the occasional master class or overseas visit. In the absence of formal training, new directors generally get a start with semi-professional shows, and gradually prove themselves by trial and error. They tend, with a few notable exceptions, to be actor-centred, and to have developed their directing skills in small venues with severely limited budgets. Nevertheless, there is a high general level of competence, and a few directors with real conceptual and visual flair. Raymond Hawthorn (b. 1936) was particularly important in the 1970s for the influence of his training and the swirling company style of his Theatre Corporate in Aukland, as well as for his subsequent work at Mercury Theatre as an opera director. Many have been influenced by observation and experience of international styles. In addition, some are increasingly willing to incorporate Maori concepts of consensus and cultural awareness into both their working methods and their dramatic vision. A few, such as Colin McColl (b. 1948),

are in demand overseas as well. McColl is noteworthy for his recent bicultural productions with Maori playwrights such as Hone Kouka at Taki Rua Theatre, and for his striking interpretations of Ibsen in New Zealand settings.

Senior actors who entered the profession prior to the development of the New Zealand Drama School in the 1970s tend to have had an *ad-hoc* training: from amateur theatre, speech and drama teachers, or simply having a good voice and proving they could speak with the received English accent which was then a prerequisite for radio and the stage. A few attended overseas academies, usually in Britain. Actors now usually have formal training, and greater attention to physical and emotional aspects of acting than used to be the case. And they must be able to speak with a New Zealand accent.

Most young actors are familiar with Maori cultural forms; there is a growing pool of Maori and Polynesian actors well able to operate in both western and Maori theatrical contexts. With the exception of specifically Maori forms, however, the general acting style is modified realism. Only a few directors and companies encourage their actors to explore expressionism, physical theatre and other more non-naturalistic forms. Again, because New Zealand is such a small and relatively self-contained and isolated theatrical community, most actors have a high level of versatility. They earn a significant proportion of their income from radio, television and occasional film work, and take for granted the ability to work in all these media.

Music Theatre
Dance Theatre

Opera has been difficult to sustain in a country with a small population and large distances between urban centres, but its popularity is undiminished. The New Zealand Opera Group was formed by Donald Munro (b. 1913) in 1954, and for several years toured from town to town with a pianist and a handful of singers. In the late 1950s the scale enlarged, and as the New Zealand Opera Company it invited overseas singers and directors to present major works of the international repertoire in regular seasons in the main cities. Despite some creditable work, neither box-office returns nor Arts Council subsidy could sustain the massive touring costs. Various alter-

natives were attempted in the 1970s, and opera was eventually re-established in 1979 as the National Opera of New Zealand. After three years it too succumbed to high touring costs.

Regional companies now operate in Auckland, Wellington, Christchurch and elsewhere, presenting basically a nineteenth-century repertoire. New Zealand-composed operas tend to be confined to performance in the music departments of universities, although Ross Harris's *Waituhi* (1985), with text by the Maori novelist Witi Ihimaera (b. 1944), was an event of considerable cultural importance for the Maori community. The New Zealand

International Festival of the Arts commissioned Chris Blake's *Bitter Calm* (1994), an ambitious work with text by the playwright Stuart Hoar (b. 1957) based on a Maori–pakeha love story during a period of armed conflict in the 1840s.

Musicals, revues and pantomimes have a long tradition in New Zealand, both in university 'capping concerts' and in amateur and professional theatre. The most noteworthy indigenous musical since World War II has been the Roger Hall/Philip Norman/A.K. Grant show *Footrot Flats* (1983), based on Murray Ball's widely syndicated strip cartoon about a working farm dog and his loveable but incompetent owner. More experimental music theatre performance has been explored by From Scratch (founded 1979), by the Topp Twins (b. 1958), who present lesbian country-and-western songs and comedy, and by the Front Lawn (founded 1984), with a surreal integration of music and rhythm, often created from found objects, with concrete poetry, satirical sketches and storytelling.

The western traditions of both classical ballet and modern dance were initially represented by international tours to New Zealand and by private dance teachers. What is now the Royal New Zealand Ballet was formed in 1953 by Poul Gnatt (1923–95), and has established a repertoire of romantic, classical and contemporary ballets. Several modern dance companies were established in the 1970s, and dancers and choreographers increasingly worked with both the classical and contemporary forms. More recently, project-based companies such as the Douglas Wright Dance Company, which Douglas Wright (b. 1956) formed in 1984, and

the Commotion Company, formed in 1990 by Michael Parmenter (b. 1954), have achieved national and international recognition for their innovative choreography, dramatic content and expressive dancing.

In professional contemporary dance, Maori influence and participation has led to new choreography, and new companies such as Black Grace (formed 1995), which represent a uniquely New Zealand development in dance.

Traditional forms of Maori dance and song play a vital part in ceremonial and in less formal community gatherings, and are also the central core of traditional Maori performance entertainment. Culture groups continue this role of maintaining the performing arts heritage; at the same time, concert groups have proven artistically and commercially viable, particularly as part of New Zealand's tourism industry.

Kahurangi New Zealand Maori Dance Theatre, formed in 1983, works from a cultural base of Maori language and traditional *kapa haka* training at its Takitimu Performing Arts School. From this foundation it develops accessible programmes of contemporary dance and music based on traditional forms and often incorporating cabaret or other popular presentational styles. Entertainment and Maori culture are central to its ethos, whether performing for schools, festivals or commercial venues in New Zealand or overseas. One curious result is that the successful touring company that it maintains in North America, where the traditional Maori song and dance offers the appeal of the exotic, attracts larger audiences than the New Zealand company.

Theatre for Young Audiences

Educationally oriented theatre for schools was toured throughout the country from the mid-1950s to the mid-1970s by the New Zealand Players' Drama Quartet; other companies sometimes followed suit in their own particular areas. During the 1970s the Theatre-in-Education (TIE) movement from Britain was taken up by several professional theatres in New Zealand, but TIE was always the first activity to be cut in any financial crisis facing a theatre. In addition, reassessment in the early 1980s of the educational soundness and of the artistic quality and purpose of such programmes led to revised priorities in both the education sector and the Arts

Council. Support for TIE teams and performers-in-schools programmes was reduced to allow for residencies for artists of various kinds who would work in partnership with teachers, and across artistic disciplines, to encourage and assist creative work from the students themselves.

Within the education system, creative drama and improvisation have a strong place in primary schools. In secondary schools drama is being developed as an autonomous subject area within a wider arts curriculum. Play production, especially with a revival of interest in Shakespeare, is a common feature of the school year. At the same time, many schools encourage their students to write, improvise or devise their own plays for production. The New Zealand Association for Drama in Education was formed in 1984 to support teachers working in this area.

A separate youth theatre culture has developed since the 1980s, with a huge surge of interest both in school and out. Young New Zealanders participated effectively in the first International Festival of Young Playwrights (Inter Play '85) in Sydney, and subsequently. A number of youth theatres around the country provide drama classes and production opportunities for students.

Opportunity of a different sort is offered by the Young and Hungry Season run annually by Bats Theatre in Wellington as a showcase for new plays and young performers. A number of professional theatre practitioners also work with young people, such as playwright Gary Henderson (b. 1955) with plays specifically about and for performance by school-age young people.

Another significant development since the 1980s has been a recognition by professional companies that young audiences are important. Among these are Pacific Underground, Te Rākau Hua o te Wao Tapu (founded 1989) and Calico Theatre (formed 1990). All tour principally to schools with carefully researched and devised educational shows. In addition, plays for children are widely offered by amateur drama societies and professional theatres during school holidays.

David Carnegie

Puppet and Mask Theatre

The first puppets in New Zealand were created by the Maori and were known variously as *karetao, kararī* or *toko raurape*. Although examples of the puppets survive in museums in New Zealand, North America and Europe, the performance tradition, thought to have been highly ritualized, has been lost.

The first significant modern puppet theatre troupe in New Zealand was the Goodwin Marionettes (1937–63), which performed principally for adult and family audiences on its national tours. The artistic integrity of its work, high production values and commitment to serious plays had a significant influence on a number of New Zealand puppeteers. The Goodwin Marionette collection was in 1983 restored by Anne Forbes (b. 1959), who then founded the New Zealand Puppet Theatre and Museum of Puppets (1984–94). An Arts Council-funded professional company, it followed the Goodwin tradition of innovation in puppetry, experimented with a variety of styles, created work for adult audiences, and offered training for puppeteers, including master classes with Philippe Genty (France) and Richard Bradshaw (Australia). (When the Museum of Puppets closed, the Goodwin marionettes and some other puppets from the collection were acquired by the Auckland Museum.) Various other puppet companies have operated from time to time, chiefly for school audiences. Burton Theatre of Puppets, for example, toured schools from 1964 to 1981

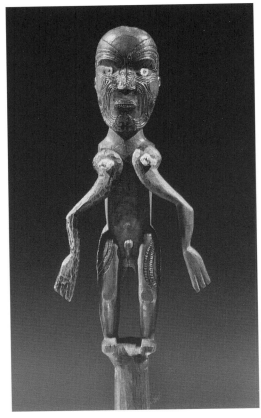

A *karetao*, a carved wooden Maori puppet. Photo: courtesy of Museum of New Zealand Te Papa Tongarewa, negative number F.1133.

with stories from a wide range of cultures. A number of practitioners continue this tradition.

In the early 1970s the influence of Theatre Action, the company formed by Francis Batten (b. 1940), reinforced journal articles and pictures of such overseas companies as the San Francisco Mime Troupe, Bread and Puppet Theatre (USA) and, later, Welfare State International (UK). A number of New Zealand groups incorporated substantial mask and puppet techniques into their theatre work. Red Mole, for instance, on occasion used both shadow techniques and very large-scale puppets to extend the impact of its experimental theatre and political cabaret. A number of its members also formed, with Rose Beauchamp (b. 1946), a glove-puppet company called White Rabbit (1975–82).

Theatre Action, whose founding members had all trained in Paris at the Lecoq school, conducted mask workshops, including *commedia dell'arte*, as well as performing, and strongly influenced the development of Red Mole, Dramadillo (1982–8), Theatre at Large and other companies. Murray Edmond (b. 1949), who worked with Batten in the early 1970s and subsequently developed an educational clown theatre, ran a mask workshop over the summer of 1978–9 leading to a substantial masked element in the first Wellington Summer City festival. Warwick Broadhead (b. 1944) has also been active in spectacular community-based mask and costume events.

Dramadillo was a touring physical theatre company founded by Nick Blake (b. 1952) after he returned to New Zealand from training at the National Circus School of France and a study of mask in Indonesia. Dramadillo members all attended mask workshops with Francis Batten, and he directed two of their shows. Batten continued to have an influence on New Zealand performers for the period he remained at his Australian school, Drama Action Centre. Also from an Australian base, John Bolton has frequently taught the use of Basle style mask in New Zealand. Others have explored Leonard Pitt's neutral mask work from the USA, and *Noh* mask from Japan.

The first New Zealand Puppet Theatre Festival, held in 1986, led to the setting up of Puppeteers in New Zealand (PINZ), which produces a newsletter and promotes communication both nationally and internationally through the International Puppeteers' Union (UNIMA). The 1990s have seen the development of several small independent companies that tour internationally, especially in the Asian region. Also following world-wide trends, the use of puppetry and mask on film and television is growing.

Rose Beauchamp, Anne Forbes,
David Carnegeie

Design
Theatre Space and Architecture

New Zealand's colonial legacy includes one Victorian and several Edwardian proscenium arch theatres and opera houses, but these are all venues for hire, not homes for permanent companies. Seating between 1,000 and 1,500, they include the St James in Auckland, another St James in Wellington, as well as the State Opera House (with the initials 'J.C.W.' in the ironwork at the end of each row of seats – a reminder of the importance of the Australian theatrical empire of J.C. Williamson in New Zealand early in the century), the Theatre Royal in Christchurch and, the sole Victorian survival, the 1899 Wanganui Municipal Opera House, built of wood. Several have been lovingly restored. More modern equivalents are usually municipal theatres seating over 1,000 people. A few smaller civic drama theatres have been built since the 1960s, usually seating in the region of 700. Like the older theatres, virtually all of these are proscenium arch theatres.

The historical accident of Downstage's beginnings in the 1960s in a café rather than a theatre building has had a significant impact on the rather different development of theatre spaces for professional companies. Low-budget performance in a flat open space intended for eating and drinking before the show led not only to non-representational and theatricalist settings, but also to expectations of flexibility in establishing the actor–audience configuration. When Raymond Boyce (b. 1928), already a well-established designer for the New Zealand Players and opera and ballet, and who subsequently exhibited at the Prague Quadrennial in 1983 and 1987, initiated the concept for the new Hannah

Playhouse (opened 1973) in Wellington for Downstage, he and architect James Beard (b. 1924) created one of the most flexible purpose-built theatre homes for a resident professional company anywhere in the country.

Theatre Corporate, Centrepoint, Circa and Taki Rua all subsequently developed flexible staging arrangements in their adapted spaces. When Circa built its new 300-seat theatre in Wellington in 1994, it effectively built a warehouse with movable seating units so as to retain this pattern of flexibility. With the growth of companies without their own theatres, there is now a greater emphasis on the use of a variety of venues. Even theatres like the Court with fixed end stages would seem to have been influenced by Downstage and Boyce in their avoidance of a picture frame proscenium.

In the 1990s the producing/presenting theatres with their own buildings (Watershed in Auckland; Centrepoint in Palmerston North; Circa, Downstage, Taki Rua and Bats in Wellington; Court in Christchurch and Fortune in Dunedin) seat between about 100 (Bats and Taki Rua) and about 300 (Circa and Downstage). As a typical example, the Court Theatre converted an old lecture theatre (in the civic Arts Centre's Gothic-revival former univer-sity buildings) to seat an audience of 291 in shallow angles around a three-sided semi-thrust stage 20 metres (65 feet) wide and 6 metres (20 feet) deep, with a rehearsal room of the same dimensions directly above. Adjacent to the stage are a sizeable props dock and dressing rooms. Lighting in the ceiling grid is controlled by a 250-channel Arri Image board, utilizing eighty-six dimmers, from a control room behind the prompt-side audience bank. The sound system comprises two main JBL 38 centimetre (15 inch) speakers and eight Bose effects speakers and sub-woofer, with input from reel-to-reel, cassette, CD, DAT and mini-disk through a Holden Series 6 16 channel mixer. The 115-seat Court II studio in the same complex has a 7 metre by 6 metre (23 feet by 20 feet) arena stage with a lighting grid above. A Theatrelight 36/72 Scenemaster desk controls twenty dimmers. Sound input is from reel-to-reel, cassette and CD through an eight-channel mixer to two 30 centimetre (12 inch) JBL speakers. The building also houses an actors' green room, additional rehearsal and workshop space and administration offices.

At the more modest end of the spectrum, Bats Theatre in Wellington, seating ninety-three people, has an open end-stage 8.6 metres (28 feet) wide by 6.5 (21 feet) metres deep with a

Hannah Playhouse, home of Wellington's Downstage theatre, in its original use as a café theatre.
Photo: courtesy of *The Evening Post*.

tiny dressing room area behind it. A scaffolding-pipe lighting grid just under the ceiling is served by a spaghetti tangle of extension cables feeding a veritable museum of old lights, but control is from a modern forty-eight-channel computerized desk. The sound system comprises reel-to-reel and cassette decks, amplifier, ten-channel mixer and two speakers.

Design, like so many theatre crafts in New Zealand, has relied largely on individuals whose primary training – graphic arts, acting, architecture – had to be adapted to theatre. Raymond Boyce was trained at the Slade School of Fine Arts in London, and a few others at New Zealand or overseas art schools, but by and large practitioners have learnt on the job. Low budgets and non-purpose-built theatre spaces have provided their own creative challenges. Iain Aitken (b. 1955) started in the tiny Theatre Corporate before widening his sphere of work; his design has twice been exhibited at Prague. Tony Rabbit (b. 1951) started as a lighting designer, an influence clearly reflected in his sets; his partnership with the director Colin McColl in transposing classics to expressionistic New Zealand settings has been particularly influential.

Some of the most interesting work has been in the adaptation of actor–audience relationships in these small spaces. Dorita Hannah (b. 1961), for instance, created in Taki Rua a transverse stage for Hone Kouka's Nga Tangata Toa: The Warrior People (1994; design exhibited at Prague 1995) that appropriately resembled both a Viking hall and also a Maori meeting house, not only of the period of the play but also as found in a Maori community now. Hannah, a theatre architect as well as a scenographer and teacher, has also been influential in continuing the New Zealand theatrical interest in flexible spaces suitable to such design, working in a consultative capacity for the Watershed adaptations of wharf sheds to theatres in Auckland in 1991 and 1992.

Training

In 1970 Nola Millar, with Arts Council support, established in Wellington a national drama school, what is now Toi Whakaari o Aotearoa: the New Zealand Drama School. During most of the 1970s and 1980s, under the direction of George Webby (b. 1925), it was the only drama school in the country. Webby had been a lecturer at the Wellington Teachers' College but was, unusually for a New Zealander, US-trained in drama; the two-year acting course he designed was therefore somewhat more exploratory and less technically based than might have been expected in a country so reliant on British models.

In the late 1980s and 1990s Toi Whakaari transformed itself into an actively bicultural school: under director Robin Payne (b. 1947) Maori and Polynesians average up to half the annual intake of sixteen students into the acting programme; Maori cultural and performance competence is an essential part of both the training and the ethos of the school. The Ministry of Education has taken over the responsibilities from the Arts Council, and subsidizes about two-thirds of actual cost; the rest is met by tuition fees. In 1992 a two-year technical theatre course was introduced with an annual intake of eight; in 1997 the acting course was expanded to three years.

Tertiary training programmes for traditional Maori performance have been established, such as the Maori Performing Arts Course at Manukau Polytechnic, the Takitimu Maori Performing Arts Trust programme (which trains performers for the Kahurangi Maori Dance Theatre in both contemporary and traditional styles of performance) and the Polynesian Performing Arts programme at Whitireia Polytechnic. The last-named fosters Maori and Pacific Island performance forms which are part of the living dance and music cultures of Samoa, the Cook Islands, Tonga, Tokelau and Niue.

In the 1990s a freeing up of the educational system has led several polytechnics (notably Auckland's Unitec, an institution with aspirations to become a university) to establish acting programmes for theatre and film; and to apply, like Toi Whakaari, to have their diplomas reassessed as Bachelor's degrees. In addition, independent performing arts schools, either complementary to or potentially competing with Toi Whakaari, have started in Wellington, Christchurch, Dunedin and elsewhere.

Directing, design and administration are, with the exception of a few individual university courses, largely learned on the job or on ad-hoc weekend or short intensive courses. University drama departments maintain close relations with professional theatre, both through staff activity and graduates moving into theatre jobs, but do not offer professional training.

Criticism, Scholarship and Publishing

A detailed survey of New Zealand drama since the colonial period is provided by Howard McNaughton (b. 1945) in his 'Drama' chapter in the *Oxford History of New Zealand Literature in English*; as well as dealing with dramatic literature, he has extensive knowledge of the theatrical context in which these works were performed. Another academic writer, John Thomson (b. 1936), pays more attention to the society reflected in the plays, in his *New Zealand Drama 1930–1980: An Illustrated History*. A general history of theatre for this period can be found in *A Dramatic Appearance: New Zealand Theatre 1920–1970* by Peter Harcourt (1923–95), who has also written about the history of musical theatre and of radio in New Zealand.

Australasian Drama Studies, published by the University of Queensland in Australia, is the only scholarly journal in the region specifically devoted to drama and theatre, and its two focus issues on New Zealand theatre (1984 and 1991) are particularly useful, both for specialist articles and, in the first, for a detailed critical bibliography by Howard McNaughton, and a brief chronology of New Zealand theatre history. The *Journal of New Zealand Literature* provides in most years a useful annual survey of production and publication of New Zealand plays.

More general magazines on theatre have come and gone, and remain a valuable resource for the period they cover. The quarterly magazine *Act* started in 1967 as a house journal for Downstage Theatre, but under the editorship of playwright and critic Bruce Mason, subsequently Nonnita Rees (b. 1944) and then Laurie Atkinson (b. 1936), it established national coverage of theatre news and reviews of record. In 1976 it was reincarnated by Playmarket as a smaller and less financially draining four-to-eight page monthly bulletin called *Act: Theatre in New Zealand* until 1986. The demise of *Act* in both its forms was a severe loss to the New Zealand theatrical community; and since the mid-1980s there has been no comprehensive national coverage of theatre or performance.

The Association of Community Theatres published *Performance*, a biennial record of the theatre and the performing arts, for 1979–80, 1981–2 and 1983–4. *Illusions*, a new quarterly magazine covering film, television and theatre from a left-wing and theoretical stance, was founded in 1986 by a group of students and former students of film theory from Victoria University. Film and television are its predominant focus, but it is useful in providing a forum for theoretically based criticism of theatre in a social and ideological context.

Theatre criticism in New Zealand is mostly, therefore, newspaper reviewing in the daily and weekly newspapers and magazines. A compilation of photocopied newspaper reviews of all professional theatre on both sides of the Tasman Sea started to appear regularly from 1988 as *The Australian and New Zealand Theatre Record*.

The principal play publisher is Victoria University Press through its New Zealand Playscripts series, although other commercial houses occasionally publish plays, as do The Women's Play Press and Playmarket.

David Carnegie

Further Reading

Atkinson, Laurie, Pat Hawthorne and Judy Russell, eds. *Playmarket 1973–1994*. Wellington: Playmarket, 1995. 38 pp.

Australasian Drama Studies 3 no. 1 (October 1984) and no. 18 (April 1991) [New Zealand focus issues]. Brisbane: University of Queensland.

Harcourt, Peter. *A Dramatic Appearance: New Zealand Theatre 1920–1970*. Wellington: Methuen, 1978. 177 pp.

Lane, Dorothy F. *The Island as Site of Resistance: An Examination of Caribbean and New Zealand Texts*. New York: Peter Lang, 1995. 181 pp.

Mason, Bruce. *Every Kind of Weather*, ed. David Dowling. Auckland: Reed Methuen, 1986. 306 pp.

McNaughton, Howard. 'Drama', *Oxford History of New Zealand Literature in English*, ed. Terry Sturm. Auckland: Oxford University Press, 1991: 269–332.

——. *New Zealand Drama.* Boston, MA: Twayne, 1981. 168 pp.

——. *New Zealand Drama: A Bibliographical Guide.* Christchurch: University of Canterbury Library, 1974. 112 pp.

New Zealand Cultural Statistics: Nga Tatauranga Whakapuaki Tuakiri o Aotearoa. Wellington: Statistics New Zealand: Te Tari Tatau; Ministry of Cultural Affairs: Te Manatu Tikanga-a-Iwi, 1995.

New Zealand Performing Arts Touring Directory. Wellington: Creative New Zealand, 1996. 75 pp.

Performance: A Handbook of the Performing Arts in New Zealand. Wellington: Association of Community Theatres, 1980 [for 1979 and 1980], 1983 [for 1981 and 1982], 1985 [for 1983 and 1984]. 33, 37, 62 pp.

Perkins, Elizabeth. *The Plays of Alma De Groen.* Amsterdam/Atlanta: Rodopi, 1994. 183 pp.

Playmarket Directory of New Zealand Plays and Playwrights. Wellington: Playmarket, 1992. 228 pp.

Robinson, Roger and Nelson Wattie, eds. *The Oxford Companion to New Zealand Literature.* Auckland: Oxford University Press, 1998.

Scotts, Neil, Lewis Holden and Jenny Neale. *Arts Facts: A Statistical Profile on the Arts in New Zealand.* Wellington: Department of Internal Affairs, 1987. 140 pp.

Simpson, Adrienne. *Opera's Farthest Frontier: A History of Professional Opera in New Zealand.* Auckland: Reed, 1996. 288 pp.

Simpson, E.C. *A Survey of the Arts in New Zealand.* Wellington: Wellington Chamber Music Society, 1961. 181 pp.

Smyth, Bernard W. and Hilary Howorth. *Books and Pamphlets Relating to Culture and the Arts in New Zealand: A Bibliography Including Works Published to the End of the Year 1977.* Christchurch: University of Canterbury, Dept. of Extension Studies in association with Unesco and Department of Internal Affairs, 1978. 103 pp.

Tait, David. *New Zealanders and the Arts: Results From a Survey of Attendance and Interest Patterns in the Performing and Visual Arts.* Wellington: Queen Elizabeth II Arts Council of New Zealand and Department of Internal Affairs, 1983. 64 pp.

Thompson, Mervyn. *All My Lives.* Christchurch: Whitcoulls, 1980. 185 pp.

Thomson, 'Bibliography: Drama', *The Oxford History of New Zealand Literature in English*, ed. Terry Sturm. Auckland: Oxford University Press, 1991: 621–3.

——. *New Zealand Drama 1930–1980: An Illustrated History.* Auckland: Oxford University Press, 1984. 108 pp.

NORTH KOREA

(see **KOREA**)

NOUVELLE CALEDONIE

(see **SOUTH PACIFIC** (New Caledonia))

OUTER MONGOLIA

(see **MONGOLIA**)

PAKISTAN

The Islamic Republic of Pakistan – the centre of one of the oldest civilizations in the world – is located in south Asia on the Arabian Sea between India and Iran. It is bordered to the east by Afghanistan and to the north by China. With a total land area of 803,900 square kilometres (482,400 square miles), it had a 1995 population estimated at 131.5 million of which 95 per cent were Muslim (Sunni 75 per cent, Shia 20 per cent) and 5 per cent Christian, Hindu, Zoroastrian and other minorities. Composed of four provinces, each with a distinct language and culture, a tribal territory and a capital area, Pakistan's national capital is the city of Islamabad (Place of Islam) with a population of some 250,000. Its major industrial and financial centre is Karachi, the country's largest city with a population of over 12 million. Pakistan's cultural centre is Lahore, a city of just over 6 million people and the capital of Punjab, the country's most populous province. The official language of Pakistan is Urdu though Punjabi is the most widely spoken language. English is widely understood and extensively spoken among well-educated people. In the mid-1990s, only about 25 per cent of the population was literate.

The River Indus, which flows through the length of the country from north to south, was the centre of the Indus Valley civilization, c. 2500 BC. The area's cultural heritage also owes much to subsequent invasions by central Asians, Greeks (Alexander the Great), Persians, Huns and Mongols including Timur (Tamerlane). Islam made inroads through the arrival of the Arab general, Mohammad bin Qasim who led a punitive expedition against pirates and left his governor behind in Sind in AD 711.

In 1524 Zahir ud-din Babur invaded the Indian subcontinent from central Asia and set up a new Mogul Empire. A British East India Company was established in 1600 and by 1784, the British had instituted the post of governor-general of India, which then included Pakistan.

Complete British authority was established after a bloody war for independence in 1857.

In 1947 India finally gained its independence from the British, and Pakistan was carved out as an independent state for Indian Muslims. Divided into two territories – West Pakistan and East Pakistan – and separated from one another by 1,600 kilometres (1,000 miles) of Indian territory, the new country saw 3 million non-Muslims leave Pakistani territory for India and more than 5 million Muslims leaving India to live in Pakistan. A shaky peace with India subsequently led to three wars between the two nations. The last one, in 1971, ended with East Pakistan formally seceding from the union and declaring independence as the new nation of Bangladesh. Pakistan now refers only to the former West Pakistan.

In the years after the war, Zulfikar Ali Bhuto, the prime minister, did much to restore Pakistan's confidence and economy but political turmoil led to a military coup in 1977, led by General Mohammed Zia ul Haq who suspended the National Assembly and the constitution. Bhutto was subsequently arrested and, in 1979, executed. In 1985 parliamentary government was re-established, the constitution restored with several amendments and martial law ended. In 1988, Benazir Bhutto, the Oxford and Harvard-educated daughter of Zulfikar Ali Bhutto, was elected the first woman prime minister in a modern Muslim state. Dismissed in 1990, she was re-elected prime minister in 1993 but lost office again in 1996.

The region's complicated politics have also been reflected in its theatre history. Linked for most of its history to the oral storytelling tradition of the Bhands, Nautanki and Tamasha people who flourished long before the British arrived, performances by itinerant storytellers and performers were extremely popular especially in what is now the Pakistani province of Punjab. Secular for the most part, these stories were designed to provide entertainment across the entire divide including religion and caste. Performances, usually held during rural festivals, drew entire towns, could often be quite bawdy and particularly appealed to male audiences.

From the storytellers grew more and more complicated enactments. In Hindu areas these were based on tales from the *Ramayana* – the so-called *Rāmlilās* (plays about Lord Ram) and the *Rāslilās* (plays about Lord Krishna). Most involved music and dance and developed clear links with the classical Indian theatrical forms such as *kathakali*. It was these forms that were

supported by the Mogul emperors who had a very enlightened view of art and culture and delighted especially in the arts of poetry, music and dance. They did not, however, have any particular interest in a western-style spoken theatre. This, combined with the fact that Islam itself does not encourage human representation, made the development of a literary theatrical tradition in what is modern Pakistan very slow to arrive.

Among the first successful attempts at the creation of a written play in the Urdu language was in 1855 by Mirza Amanat (1816–59), an aristocrat at the Lucknow court of Wajid Ali Shah. The play, *Indar Sabha* (*Rajah Indar's Assembly*), was a lavish court spectacle in verse with elaborate costuming and music. Unfortunately, before any specific tradition could develop at the court, the shah was deposed by the British and, following his exile, further attempts at an indigenous literary style all but died.

With British influence in India growing, however, British art forms were inevitably making their way across the subcontinent as well, most particularly the Victorian melodrama. During the 1870s, perhaps inspired by the success of *Indar Sabha*, a number of Parsi (Zoroastrian) entrepreneurs set about creating Urdu language productions on a commercial basis, mixing in traditional music and dance with a British-style melodramatic flavour. Among these early Parsi producers were Pestonji Framji and Khurshidji Balliwala who produced a number of shows which became so popular that they found audiences from across India and as far away as Sri Lanka.

Though published credits did not start to be given to writers until 1880, early dramatists working in this form included Raunaq Benarsi (1825–86), Mian Zarif (1810–93), Vinayak Parased Talib, also known as Talib Benarsi (1852–1922), Ahsan Lucknowi, Narayan Prasad Betab (d. 1945) and Agha Hashra Kashmiri (1879–1935), all of whose careers spanned the decades just before and after 1900. Talib Benarsi was the first to write in prose and to introduce Urdu songs. Among the groups of note at this time were the Victoria Theatre Company, Alfred Company and New Alfred Company.

As the commercial viability of this Parsi theatre grew, several writers tried to push it further by bringing social issues into the work. This was short-lived, however. In 1876, the British decided to control theatre activities by instituting a Dramatic Performances Control Act requiring approval of each script by the District

Police Commissioner (see also INDIA). The scripts quickly reverted to their original musical melodramatic style. The continuing existence of this Act – the law was still in force in the 1990s – has continued to have ramifications in Pakistan.

In the first decades of the twentieth century, the Parsi companies continued to grow, tours extended their popularity across the country and profits were considerable. In the 1930s, two events took place in INDIA which had a significant impact on the development of Pakistani theatre. One was the development of the talkies in an already active Indian cinema industry; the other, the founding of an Indian People's Theatre Association (IPTA), an offshoot of the Indian Progressive Writers' Association. The emergence of the new art of cinema effectively killed the popular Parsi theatre and audiences swiftly shifted their allegiances to the screen.

Adapting to the times, most of the Parsi companies switched from theatrical production to film production. Some smaller theatre groups emerged, however, playing mostly in the countryside and eventually establishing themselves as full-time touring groups. As films became more and more popular, actors, musicians and even dancers were drawn away from the Parsi forms toward the new cinematic arts. The theatre's loss, however, helped to define the somewhat theatrical style of modern cinematic art in the country. Gradually, most of the Parsi-style theatrical companies ceased regular operations. Two of the few groups remaining in production are the Watan and Gaman Theatres which manage to retain some of their old popularity among a faithful core of spectators.

Nevertheless, dramatic writing in a more European style was being supported and encouraged by the left-wing Indian People's Theatre Association which had branches across the subcontinent including two in Karachi and Lahore. The IPTA style, inspired by Soviet experience in artistic creation and support, encouraged a more socially rooted theatre. Aimed at creating and staging plays which challenged the social status quo, IPTA leaders were primarily interested in the country's continuing struggle for independence from the British. IPTA plays were less concerned with literary qualities than they were with their ultimate impact on people's thinking. They were often short and were usually presented as part of a longer programme of song, dance and even mime. While some productions were done indoors, most were done on street corners, in parks and even at bus stops, usually on Sundays. IPTA productions attracted large audiences

of young people and especially the young intellectuals, many of them socialists. Among the Pakistanis working closely with IPTA was Safdar Mir (b. 1922) who, in 1945, left Lahore for Bombay to work more closely with IPTA leaders. With independence in 1947, most of the active IPTA people in West Pakistan (the majority of them non-Muslims, Hindus and communists) left Lahore and Karachi for political and religious reasons, taking most of the serious theatre with them to India where IPTA formed the foundation for India's modern theatre movement.

Mir, however, returned to Pakistan in 1948 and eventually took up a teaching position at Government College in 1951. There he helped to reorganize the Government College Dramatic Club (GCDC) which had been founded in 1887 and had staged a play a year throughout its history including works by Shaw, Rattigan, Goldsmith, Shakespeare and Gogol. Training actors, writers and directors, the Dramatic Club also introduced many younger people to the committed IPTA style of dramatic art. Among those who worked with Mir at Government College and who would later go on to make a significant contribution on their own to the Pakistani modern theatre were director Fareed Ahmed (1935–93), actor-director Zia Mohyuddin (b. 1931, acclaimed for his work in the film *A Passage to India)* and writer-director Shoaib Hashmi (b. 1939). Others from GCDC who went on to become prominent in the performing arts included director Madiha Gohar (b. 1956), actor-director Shahid Nadeem (b. 1950) and playwright Sarmad Sehbai (b. 1945), to name just a few.

In the years after independence the political and social turmoil resulted in the lack of a clear policy on the development of the arts in the new Pakistan. Since some interpretations regard all the performing arts (music, dance, film and theatre as well as painting of human forms) as un-Islamic, there was a certain amount of confusion in the official policy to the arts. The performing arts were never actively promoted and each conservative or martial law regime has made full use of the censorship laws that were available to it. By the early 1950s the Pakistani Communist Party was banned and its leaders arrested. Since many of the communist leaders were active in the evolution of political theatre in Pakistan, the revised political situation left a vacuum in the country which was not filled until the 1970s.

Political instability simply added to the situation. One of the few attempts to restart the movement was initiated by IPTA veteran Ali Ahmed, who created a new group called Natak. Working until the early 1990s, Ahmed created many original works such as *Sheeshay Kay Admi* (*Men of Glass*) and trained many actors but his attempts to politicize western classics such as Beckett's *Waiting For Godot*, Camus's *Caligula* and Molière's *Bourgeois Gentleman* failed to attract a following.

In Lahore a privately operated Pakistan Arts Council was created in 1948 for the promotion of the arts since the government was preoccupied with establishing other national institutions. Among the founding members were the poet Faiz Ahmed Faiz, writer Imtiaz Ali Taj, Justice S.A. Rahman and painter A.R. Chughtai. The Pakistan Arts Council produced its first play *Mera Qatil* (*My Killer*) in 1955 written by Imtiaz Ali Taj. In a very short while the Pakistan Arts Council became a centre of theatrical and artistic activity in Lahore. In the 1960s plays were being performed every night with each play running for a month. It was in the late 1960s that the trend started to change and the plays began to drift from the more intellectual to the more standard comedies.

In Karachi the major group was the Drama Guild founded in 1952 by writer-director Khawaja Moenuddin. A satirist, his plays attacked the lack of any real change in values and attitudes in the new Pakistan. Many of his works also dealt with the problems of those newly arrived from India. Among the important plays written and staged by him were *Zawal-e-Hydrabad* (*The Fall of Hydrabad*), *Laal Qilay se Laloo Khaith* (*From the Red Fort to Laloo Khaith*, 1953), a play dealing with partition which was performed over 200 times (once in a stadium before 10,000 people). In 1954 he wrote *Naya Nishan* (*New Mark*), a play about the situation in Kashmir written during negotiations between India and Pakistan about Kashmir's future. The play, however, proved too politically sensitive for the government which banned its production.

One of the more unusual initiatives during the 1950s – albeit totally non-professional – was the appearance of several Islamic theatre groups in Peshawar. Qamir Ali Qamar Sarhadi formed the Socrates Dramatic Club and staged productions each year on themes of significance to Islam and national pride. Among them were *Nure-e-Islam* (*The Light of Islam*), *Qurbani* (*Sacrifice*) and *Shan-e-Islam* (*The Greatness of Islam*). Another Peshaar group was the Afghan Dramatic Club which only allowed men to perform in public.

The late 1960s saw a popular movement for democracy and the creation of a relatively large number of new plays. Major Ishaq Mohammed, a leftist leader, wrote *Mussali* (*The Sweeper*) in Punjabi. The play had many performances in lower-class neighbourhoods in Punjab province including several performances by street sweepers themselves. Sarmad Sehbai, an important writer in the 1960s, wrote *Dark Room, Too Kaun* (*Who Are You*) and *Panjwan Chiragh* (*The Fifth Lamp*), all depicting the spirit of rebellion that characterized this period.

Through the 1970s, it was the colleges and universities which maintained the more serious theatrical activity in the country. In 1974, the promised creation of a series of arts councils across the country began to generate new life in Pakistan's theatres but the reality was that most of it was limited to Lahore. With the declaration of martial law in 1977, alternative methods of political protest began to be sought to fight very real repression and it was in the months and years that followed that an active political theatre movement emerged known as the 'parallel' theatre. The imposition of martial law, in fact, stopped most public theatrical activities for the better part of a decade but these parallel groups – many of them working on the streets and passing the hat around after each performance and often calling themselves private clubs – remained active until the restoration of democratic freedoms in 1988. A few of them were still operating in the late 1990s, having shifted their focus from political repression to social problems and awareness.

In Karachi during this period there was only a single professional theatre group that remained active – Theatre Walley (Theatre People). Created by Rahat Kazmi, the group – despite its name – was neither controversial nor politically motivated. The company was composed of well-known professionals from television and the commercial theatre. Of genuine aesthetic quality, the Walley's plays, however, were always quite safe, most of them adaptations of West End and Broadway successes. The group disbanded in 1988 due to the lack of a suitable venue.

A number of new commercial ventures in the major cities of the country began to be seen once again in the late 1980s and 1990s along with regular work produced by the arts councils. Throughout, the old storytelling traditions remained, continuing to provide a base upon which more modern theatrical activities were able to thrive.

Structure of the National Theatre Community

The Arts Council Act of 1974, approved by Prime Minister Zulfiqar Ali Bhutto, created a structure in which the national government would take responsibility for arts activity across the country through the creation of a series of provincial, divisional and district arts councils.

The federal government created the Pakistan Nation Council of the Arts (PNCA) in Islamabad to nurture artistic activity at a national level and act as a coordinating body between all the various provincial and district arts councils that were to be created. The PNCA currently owns the Liaqat Hall in Rawalpindi, which is rented out to commercial producers. The PNCA sponsors one or two productions every year; it also invites foreign directors to come and work with Pakistani actors.

Punjab province was the first to follow the new legislation and to create a provincial arts council along with several divisional arts councils. Unfortunately, other provinces did not follow suit. In the North West Frontier Province, the already existing Abasin Arts Council in Peshawar was brought under government control. Unlike the Punjab councils, though, the Abasin council did not produce any theatre work nor provide funding. Rather it limited itself to renting out its facilities at a subsidized rate. In Sind, the Karachi Arts Council founded in 1956 remained a private body. The PNCA created the Mehran Arts Council in Hyderabad after the restoration of democracy in 1988. Beyond these federal, provincial and divisional efforts, little occurred. No district councils ever came into being and the arts council programme overall was never fully developed nor realized.

In the late 1990s, only the Lahore Arts Council (which had changed its name from the Pakistan Arts Council) was funding and operating regular subsidized seasons of theatre and producing three to four plays annually. All other arts programmes in the country were simply renting out facilities primarily to commercial productions. As a result of this, there is no funding or subsidy of any kind to groups

Lahore Arts Council's 1994 production of *Talismati Tota* directed by Madiha Gohar.

operating on an independent basis or to individuals. Independent productions are therefore seen only sporadically. Commercial producers, however, have made a comeback and produce regular work with relatively stable companies of about ten or twelve well-known actors.

For most Arts Council and 'parallel' productions, rehearsals generally last three to four weeks, a bit less for the commercial theatres. In the Arts Council theatres, plays usually run for no more than sixteen nights, commercial productions run as long as possible while 'parallel' theatre groups generally play for between five and ten nights. Productions are often remounted by both commercial and 'parallel' groups.

Most productions are actively promoted via public banners stretched across streets and through newspaper advertising. Posters have been a late addition to the promotional arsenal. Ticket prices tend to be relatively expensive for urban theatres (up to 240 rupees or about nine times the cost of a cinema ticket) while the 'parallel' theatres charge up to 50 rupees (about twice the cost of a cinema ticket). Theatres outside the cities usually charge about the same as a film or even slightly less.

The few groups that have toured internationally have tended to play mostly in the United States and Europe, especially in countries which have a significant Pakistani expatriate population. Commercial productions have also toured extensively in the Gulf States, particularly in the United Arab Emirates. 'Parallel' theatre groups have been invited to festivals in Bangladesh, Nepal, Korea, Egypt and Norway.

The country's longest-running theatre festival is the Alhamra Festival sponsored by the Lahore Arts Council. A national festival, it invites seven groups to play there each year for two weeks in late October or early November. The Pakistan National Council of the Arts held its own festival for the first time in 1994 and invited some thirty groups to play in Islamabad over a ten-day period. Traditional storytelling, music and dance forms were seen along with performances by contemporary companies with well-established performers serving as adjudicators and commentators. An International Drama Festival is privately organized by the Raffi Peer Theatre Workshop every two years. The first festival was held in 1996 with over forty foreign and local groups performing.

The highest award for achievement in the arts is the national Presidential Pride of Performance Award.

Artistic Profile

Companies
Dramaturgy
Directing and Acting

Since the 1950s, four distinct types of theatre have existed in terms of style, content and audience. The folk or *lok* tradition goes far back into the history of the region while the 'parallel' theatre with its socio-political agenda is the newest. In between are the Punjab commercial theatre and various attempts at creating a western-style drama.

The *lok* theatre has long been an essentially non-urban phenomenon. Still seen on special occasions especially in Punjab province, it is a mix of what can be called Indian classical traditions (especially *kathakali*) with its music, dance, stylized costumes and gestures, and various kinds of music and dance forms which developed into the Parsi commercial theatre at the beginning of the twentieth century. Based on well-known tragic love stories, myths and legends, *lok* performances tend to be seen at festival periods, especially festivals commemorating the lives of saints. *Lok* performances still can draw large crowds. In the late 1990s, two companies were operating which specialized in such performances – the Watan Theatre and Gaman Theatre in Multan – which tour widely.

As opposed to the *lok* theatre, there is a spoken theatre tradition begun by the many British-oriented amateur and semi-professional little theatre groups operating in the major cities during the nineteenth and twentieth centuries. Later adapted by universities, it continues to focus on educated audiences. These plays are now done in Urdu but English-language productions are not unusual. Works by well-known European and North American dramatists are still popular. Kamal Ahmed Rizvi (b. 1930) is an important writer and director who adapted many western plays into Urdu as well as creating original works from the 1960s to the present day. His original works include *Hum Chor Hain* (*We Are All Thieves*) and *Kis Ki Bivi Kis ka Shohar* (*Whose Wife, Whose Husband*). During the 1980s, this type of theatre was attacked by both state officials and religious leaders but has made a resurgence in the 1990s. Spoken dramas can regularly be seen at the Alhamra Art Centre in Lahore and at the Finance and Trade Centre in Karachi. The Lahore Arts Council, for example, staged a notable production at the Alhamra of Ibsen's *A Doll's House* in 1992.

Commercial producers became involved in the 1970s and the plays tended to become more lightweight in content. Such commercial plays became more improvised and ad-libbed than other spoken drama. They also became more explicit and lewd. This form of theatre remains the dominent type in the major cities, attracting a predominantly male audience.

During the 1980s, the 'parallel' theatre devel-

oped as an alternative to both the commercial theatre and to the literary but generally non-political spoken theatre traditions. The new 'parallel' companies were composed of younger artists and the scripts were strongly critical. The first important group to work in this way was Dastak (Knock), started by Aslam Azhar (b. 1935) in 1982. The first group of note in Lahore was Ajoka (Today) created by Madiha Gohar and Salman Shahid in 1983. Another important 'parallel' group is the Punjab Lok Rehas (Punjab People's Theatre) in Lahore, formed in 1985.

Most of these groups began with plays by Brecht but quickly moved on to writing their own scripts. Dastak, for example, staged Brecht's *Exception and the Rule* (1984), *Galileo* (1985), *He Who Says Yes, He Who Says No* (1985) and *Saint Joan of the Stockyards* (1986). The groups have experimented with a variety of styles including elements of the folk theatre. Their audiences tend to be young and are

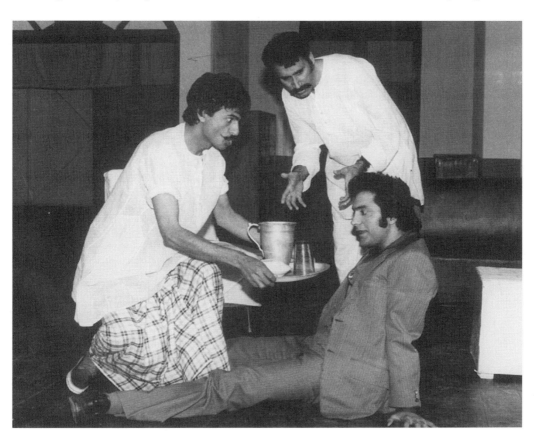

The Inquiry Officer directed by Khalid Saeed Butt, 1983.

composed mostly of students, artists and intellectuals. At various points through the 1980s and 1990s, the activities of these groups came under political fire. In response, groups performed unannounced on street corners and then disappeared. Other performances were much more public and have been sponsored by individuals, groups and even foreign cultural centres such as the German Goethe Institute. Many of the groups have toured and some have even been seen at international festivals.

Ajoka was particularly important because of its commitment to the production of new Pakistani plays dealing with contemporary social problems as well as women's issues. Its very first production was *Jaloos* (*Procession*), by the Indian dramatist Badal Sirkar. Staged on a lawn, the play was performed in the round. Three other original plays of note produced by the group in the 1980s were *Barri* (*Acquittal*, 1987) by Ajoka's resident playwright Shahid Nadeem (b. 1947), a play about prison conditions for women; *Jhali Kithay Jaway* (*Where Should the Mad Woman Go?*) and *Lapar* (*Slap*), two collective creations dealing with the abuse of women and women's rights. Among

the Brecht plays produced by Ajoka have been *Caucasian Chalk Circle* (1985), *The Good Person of Setzuan* (1988) and *Threepenny Opera* (1989).

Another company dealing with women's issues is Tehreek-e-Niswan (Women's Movement), a Karachi group founded in 1981 by Sheema Kirmani. The company grew from a feminist discussion group. In the beginning, few in the group wanted to appear on stage, partly out of a lack of experience but even more because of Islamic tradition in which women are sheltered and any public show by a woman is considered immodest. Nevertheless the company began to operate despite public threats against its members. At a 1983 International Women's Day event at Karachi University, for example, fundamentalists warned them they would open fire on the actors the minute a woman stepped on stage with a man present. The threat turned out to be just that and nothing actually happened. Among this group's major productions was an Urdu version of Jean Anouilh's *Antigone*, Safdar Hashmi's *Aurat* and Vijay Tendulkar's *Anji*. In 1988, the group staged its own adaptation of García Lorca's *La casa de Bernarda Alba* under

Ajoka-Goethe Institute, Lahore's 1989 production of *Takay da Tamasha*, an adaptation of *The Threepenny Opera*.

the title *Birjees Qadar Ka Kumba* (*The House of Birjees Qadar*).

The Punjab *lok* Rehas company is particularly important for its commitment to preserve traditional culture and particularly the Punjabi literary heritage by staging plays in the Punjabi language. Between 1985 and 1988, the group staged an impressive eight productions of Punjabi works including *Andherhay Da Pandh* (*Path of Darkness*), a play which dealt with the psychological, existential and political problems afflicting the urban middle classes; *Dhroo* (*Oppression*), about the death of a trade union leader and a farcical police investigation, and *Zanani* (*Woman*), an adaptation of Safdar Hashmi's Indian street play *Aurat*, both by Lakht Pasha; and *Takht Lahore* (*The Throne of Lahore*) by Najam Hussain Sayed (b. 1936), a historical play about Punjabi nationalism in the sixteenth century. The company was founded in 1985 by Mohammed Wasim and Nisar Mohyuddin, two Ajoka actors who broke with the older company after disputes over politics, language and artistic approach. The group operates on a collective basis with each member given opportunities to act, direct, write and design. The company has close ties to the Punjab Padjar Committee, a cooperative of local progressive writers.

Sanj (Unity) was the only theatre group in the country with a direct link to politics. Connected with Benazir Bhutto's Pakistan People's Party, the group was formed in 1986 to stage a fictional account of Bhutto's last few days in prison – *Bandiwan* (*The Prisoner*). Over the next few years, Sanj staged Brecht's *The Exception and The Rule* and Safdar Hashmi's *Machine* as well as an original play for the Family Planning Association of Pakistan. The company broke up in 1988.

Another addition to the 'parallel' groups is Naya Theatre (New Theatre), formed in 1991 by Rana Fawad and Aslam Rao. Made up of graduates of the Lahore Drama School, the group's productions have included *Kuttay* (*Dogs*), a play about urban terrorism; *Taleem-e-Balighan* (*Adult Education*), a satire by Khawaja Moenuddin on social attitudes; and *Tasadum* (*Conflict*), a play by Imran Aslam about student life in a system that demands conformity.

Among the commercial theatres Tamaseel is important since it was the first post-1988 private theatre in Lahore. Built by Afzal Ahmed, Tamaseel was the first theatre to invest in spectacular sets, lights and costumes. *Janam Janam ki Maili Chaddar* (*The Dirty Shawl of the Generations*), premièred in 1995, is the longest running play in Pakistan, still continuing in the late 1990s.

In terms of style, the urban theatres tend to be rooted in realistic forms while the *lok* theatre is much more melodramatic. The 'parallel' theatre groups, strongly influenced by Brecht, have engaged in a number of experiments involving the use of *lok* forms (most often the use of music and a narrator). Commercial theatres tend to be the broadest in style and many productions abound in physical comedy.

Two directors of note are Shoaib Hashmi (b. 1938) and Salman Shahid (b. 1951). Hashmi was trained at the Royal Academy of Dramatic Art in London and brings a strong aesthetic sense and exceptional detail to his work. His best productions have been comedies and satires. Shahid received his training in film in Moscow and has worked extensively with the 'parallel' groups. His work is slightly more absurdist in style and his best productions have a dynamic dramatic edge to them.

Music Theatre
Dance Theatre

For a discussion of music and dance, see the opening, historical section and **Artistic Profile**.

Theatre for Young Audiences

Pakistan has only a single company for young audiences – the Grips Theatre in Karachi, named after the well-known German company. Founded in 1979 by actor-director Yasmin Ismail, its productions are mostly Urdu adaptations by Imran Aslam of plays from the repertoire of the German

Grips company. The company, sponsored by the Goethe Institute, performs one play a year at the Pakistan-American Cultural Centre Auditorium in Karachi. Plays are usually performed for seven to ten nights. The company has toured within Pakistan.

Prior to the founding of Grips, there was little activity aimed specifically at young audiences in Karachi. Among those who made earlier attempts to establish such groups in the 1970s in Lahore were Perin Cooper and Jamil Bismil who set up a theatre performed by children.

Puppet Theatre

Puppetry has existed in Rajisthan, central and southern Punjab and Gujrat for many centuries and when this area of Asia became Pakistan the tradition continued. This was a family art with the husband and children normally manipulating the puppets and the wife singing an accompaniment to the performance. To get an audience, the puppeteers would enter a neighbourhood or a village wearing bright turbans and holding their marionettes in their hands. Sometimes they would knock on doors and the puppet would speak to members of the family. On festival occasions – religious or communal – puppet companies would also perform to even large audiences.

Such performances were entertainment for the entire family, young and old. Quite often, it was the puppet show which provided news of the region and even commentary on current events.

After the creation of Pakistan and its attendant political problems, however, the old-style puppeteers were often discouraged from commenting on the politics of the day and eventually puppet performances – indeed, all performances – had to have a No Objection Certificate from local authorities. Essentially, this certificate meant that

a performance would not cause a problem to the community but in reality it became a way to stop political debate. It was at this point that many traditional art forms, including puppetry, began to fade away.

Since the 1970s, however, puppetry has had a rebirth in Pakistan and though perhaps now much less political, it can be seen regularly and still is a part of public debates. Over the decades, several names have stood out for their work in this form. Perhaps the best known is Farooq Qaisar, the creator of the popular Uncle Sargam character seen for years on television. Qaisar, a graduate of Bucharest University in Romania, began his puppet career in the 1970s with a weekly television show. Since that time, he has staged more than 300 public performances as well across Pakistan, India and as far away as Norway and Germany.

Rafi Peer Puppet Theatre is part of the Rafi Peer Theatre Workshop, the oldest continuous independent theatre group in Pakistan. Founded in 1947 by Rafi Peerzada (1898–1974) as the Pakistan Drama Marka, the group, like Peerzada, was keenly interested in politics. Peerzada began his own playwriting in the 1920s having grown up on the Parsi Theatre styles. He later studied in Britain and Germany working with Max Reinhardt and coming to know Bertolt Brecht. Returning home, he started an Indian Academy of Dramatic Arts in 1930, wrote stage and radio plays as well as feature films. After his death in 1974, the Drama Markaz was renamed the Rafi Peer Theatre Workshop and it has staged innumerable productions in all genres of the theatre including puppetry.

The puppet company began its work in 1978 and produces everything in-house from puppets to costumes to scenery. Operated by Rafi Peerzada's sons – Faizaan, Sadaan and Imran – the group has work with rod-puppets, marionettes, glove-puppets and shadow-puppets. The company has also been the chief organizer of the Pakistan International Puppet Theatre Festivals

Alhamra Puppet Theatre.

held alternate years since 1992 without government support. Plans are currently underway by the company to organize a National Museum of Puppetry in Lahore. Already on file are some 200 hours of video material documenting the work of puppeteers from more than thirty countries.

Other puppet groups of note in Pakistan include the National Puppet Theatre which operates under the Pakistan National Council of the Arts, was founded in 1975 and has its own 200-seat theatre in Rawalpindi; Alhamra Puppet Theatre which operates under the Lahore Arts Council, was founded in 1986, is directed by Samina Ahmed and has a 250-seat theatre in Lahore at the Alhamra Arts Centre; and the puppeteers of the National College of Arts in Lahore, a group founded in 1992 by Nadeem ul-Hassan.

Salmaan Peerzada

Design
Theatre Space and Architecture

Design is mostly undertaken by theatre directors themselves although painters are occasionally brought in to realize the work. Most commercial productions use standard drawing room sets, dating back to the 1960s when British farces were popular. Often the only thing that varies in these shows is the colour scheme.

Lok theatre productions are usually performed in front of painted backdrops that tend towards the fantastic.

The best equipped theatres in the country are found in Lahore. Four are owned and operated by the Lahore Arts Council – two at the Alhamra Art Centre (one with 750 seats and

Alhamra Arts Centre, Lahore.

another with 450 seats) and two others at the Alhamra Cultural Complex (a 3,000-seat open-air theatre and a 350-seat theatre). Another open-air theatre – the Bagh-e-Jinnah – is owned by the Punjab Arts Council and seats 1,000. There are also three commercial theatres – Tamaseel, Rabia and Lahore Theatre which seat between 700 and 800 people.

In Rawalpindi, the major theatre space is the Liaqat Hall which seats 900 while in Islamabad two cinemas are used for dramatic performances, one seating 500 and the other 300. As there is no purpose-built theatre auditorium in Karachi, most of the theatrical activity there is concentrated at the Finance and Trade Centre Auditorium (seating 400) and at the Pakistan-American Cultural Centre which seats 200. There is also an open-air theatre owned by the Karachi Arts Council but it is virtually unusable because of traffic noise. A converted cinema hall, the Rio, is an alternative venue for Karachi's commercial theatre producers and seats 700.

The Abasin Arts Council owns one theatre in Peshawar, an auditorium that seats 500. Most universities and colleges across the country also have small theatres. Touring groups have played in town halls, cinemas and even in stadiums.

Training
Criticism, Scholarship and Publishing

Lahore Drama School, founded in 1990, provides instruction in acting. It is the only theatre school in the country. The teachers are mostly working actors or directors and the curriculum tends to vary according to the interests of each instructor. Other than this one school, theatre professionals mostly learn through observation and experience.

Relatively little formal research has been done in the area of Pakistani theatre history although there is some research on pre-independence Urdu theatre by Indian scholars. The Dutch scholar Eugene Van Erven has done some good research particularly on the 'parallel' theatre movement. A few less well researched books exist in Urdu.

Most English language dailies – the most prominent being *The News* in Lahore and *The Dawn* in Karachi – carry reviews of performances in their weekly arts editions. Such reviews vary widely in quality. Among the few journalists with theatre background are Sarwat Ali and Safdar Mir.

Samina Ahmed, Zain Ahmed,
Salmaan Peerzada

(*See also* **INDIA**)

Further Reading

Erven, Eugene Van. *The Playful Revolution: Theatre and Liberation In Asia.* Bloomington, IN: Indiana University Press, 1992.

Hussain, Mohammad Shahid. *Folk Tradition and Urdu Theatre* (in Urdu). New Delhi: Husnain, 1992.

Javaid, Inam-ul-Haq. *Punjabi Drama* (in Urdu). Islamabad: Idara-e-Saqafat, 1986.

Sohail, Ahmed. *Jadeed Theatre* [Contemporary theatre]. Islamabad: Idara-e-Saqafat, 1984.

PAPUA NEW GUINEA

(Overview)

The independent Pacific nation of Papua New Guinea occupies the eastern half of New Guinea island along with numerous offshore islands. The western half of the island is a province of Indonesia, Irian Jaya. With a land area of 462,800 square kilometres (178,700 square miles), Papua New Guinea's rugged topography is mostly thickly forested mountains (about 320,000 square kilometres covering much of the centre of the country) with lowlands along the coast. There are an estimated 1,400 smaller islands (including the Bismarck Archipelago and North Solomons group of islands) including the Admiralty Islands, New Ireland, New Britain and Bougainville. In 1994, Papua New Guinea had an estimated population of 4.2 million.

There are over 700 languages spoken in Papua New Guinea, making it probably the most linguistically complicated nation in the world. These languages are often divided into Austronesian (or Melanesian) languages related to those spoken over a wide area in other parts of Oceania, and non-Austronesian (or Papuan) languages. In contrast to Austronesian languages, non-Austronesian languages are not part of a single group and are often very diverse from one another. Austronesian languages are typically found in costal areas with very few major incursions inland, suggesting a much more recent arrival for these languages. English, Tok Pisin (New Guinea Pidgin) and Hiri Motu (a pidginized form of a local language) are all official languages and have played a very important part in allowing interaction between distant groups.

A constitutional parliamentary democracy with the British monarch as head of state, Papua New Guinea's highest official is the governor-general though the effective head of government is the prime minister. There are nineteen provinces, each with its own governor, and a national capital district which contains the national capital, Port Moresby.

Human habitation dates back at least 39,000 years with evidence found near Bobongara, northwest of Finschhafen, on the Huon Peninsula. The finds at Bobongara are, in fact, the earliest evidence of human settlement in New Guinea or Australia. Successive waves of people probably entered the country from Asia.

European visits date from the sixteenth century but European land claims did not seriously begin until the nineteenth century when the Dutch took control of the western half of the island, Irian Jaya. The southern half of present-day Papua New Guinea was claimed by Britain in 1884 but was transferred to Australia in 1905. The northern half was claimed by Germany also in 1884 but was captured during World War I by Australia, which was then granted a League of Nations' mandate and later a United Nations' trusteeship over the area. The two territories were administered jointly after 1949 and granted self-government in late 1973. Papua New Guinea became independent on 16 September 1975.

Although many parts of the country have experienced drastic changes since European colonization, there are still very strong indigenous performative traditions in many regions. Papua New Guinea's songs, dances and legends, for instance, have been handed down from one generation to another in a rich oral tradition. Storytelling kept alive many of the beliefs of the people, and the oral tradition, during the last decades of the twentieth century, was being retrieved and documented. Also being studied were the island's traditions in mask, pageantry, procession and religious dance. These latter were examined by F.E. Williams, a government anthropologist, who documented the elaborate dance performances of the Orokolo and Orokaiva peoples. In his 1940 book, *Drama of Orokolo*, Williams set down in detail aspects of Orokolo social and ceremonial life describing three major kinds of ritual performance: the *hevehe*, *kovave* and *eharo*.

The *hevehe* was a performance cycle spanning twenty-five years. A re-enactment of the creation myth, the central feature was the communal construction of an *eravo*, a men's longhouse. This ritualized performance was staged in large-scale style, involving substantial material and human resources which had to be maintained over the extended cycle period. The *hevehe* involved not only the host village but also the surrounding villages over a relatively wide area. Utilizing masks, dance and music, the various connected performances united the different tribes as well as the peoples around them, attempting in the process to expand the social horizons of the participants. For Williams, the *hevehe* was a means of expression 'for the group spirit ... a school for the development of mutual support and loyalty'.

Like all such rituals, the power and significance of the work was to be found in both the preparation as well as the realization; in the creation of masks and in the building of costumes; even in the use of the physical space during performances. The mask was particularly important for it allowed contact with the ancestral spirits. Among the extant sacred masks are not only animal figures but even some representing sea monsters. During the enactment phase, such monsters could be seen rising out of the sea in the night, the dancers wearing dazzling costumes and elaborate makeup. In the formal procession of masks – an important part of the cycle – the oldest men in the host village would act as author-directors collectively supervising rehearsals that could last for a week at a time. All the masks were made under the cover of secrecy.

The *kovave* and *eharo* rituals, in contrast, were shorter. In fact, they could be staged within the *hevehe* cycle. The *kovave* was an initiation event; the *eharo* was a community competition. Williams suggested that when a girl was to marry, her family might organize a *kovave* in celebration of the occasion. Other *kovave* might be organized around the initiation of male children with the village elders going into the bush to cut cane for the making of masks while the young initiates grew their hair long in readiness for their coming of age ceremony. When the masks were ready, the initiates would be taken into the bush where the masks were put on each of them. Later led back into the village, the event concluded with dancing, rejoicing and much feasting. In the *kovave* of the Orokolo people, the period of seclusion of the initiates was quite extended, heightening the expectation of the audience waiting in the village.

The *eharo* in its turn was a competitive festival involving dance, music and masks. The competitors would come from many villages and parade along the beaches each with their own village drummers and supporters. Attracting

The Warma Sing-Sing group from Enga Province with black painted faces and human hair wigs that sway to the beat of the drums.
Photo: courtesy of *Paradise*.

large crowds, individuals would follow whichever *eharo* group interested them. Clowns would also follow the various groups and delight audiences with their lapses into obscene gestures and songs providing comic diversion from the quite serious competitions of the day.

Still another performance form – this one reported by missionary J.H. Holmes in 1924 working in the Purari delta to the west of the Orokolo – involved the telling of traditional folk tales by men while older women from the community would mime the events being related.

In all these forms, innovation was discouraged and the success of the performances was judged on how closely established tradition was followed. Masks, it should be noted, could be used only once in all these forms.

Dance and music in modern Papua New Guinea is still rooted in many of these early traditions. Although the large rituals are all but gone in some areas, there remains an abundance of dance, music and storytelling modes which clearly emanate from them and which are still to be seen in more extended forms in ceremonies, celebrations and festivals as well as at ceremonial feasts at which large quantities of foodstuffs and valuables are exchanged with neighbours.

With the advent of Christianity and a cash economy, most of the old forms faded as converts would often demonstrate their new faith by destroying family masks and even by exposing the secrecy of traditional performance spaces. Nevertheless, a desire for public performance remained and, as Christian missions emerged in Papua New Guinea, church groups replaced the *hevehe* with enactments of events such as the arrival of the first missionaries to the villages. Some of those enactments even included scenes of violence – one notable example dealing with the 1901 killing of the missionary James Chalmers at Dopima on Goaribari Island. Other such shows included traditional scenes from the Bible and one included the staging of a Hiri legend about Motuan trade expeditions to the Papuan Gulf. All became part of the modern cycles of village entertainment.

The performance of European written drama did not begin until European expatriates living in Port Moresby and Rabaul began to form amateur groups in the mid-twentieth century, eventually competing for annual awards. One of the first local plays in the new style was Leo Hannet's (b. 1941) short sketch, *Em Rod Bilong Kago* (*The Route to Development*), which was staged by the Arts and Drama

Society of the University of Papua New Guinea in 1963. The play was also published in the pilot issue of the university's cultural magazine, *Kovave*. A German-born lecturer at the university, Ulli Beier, was instrumental in encouraging the writing, production and publication of much early creative writing at this time. Schools (especially the University of Papua New Guinea, Goroka Teachers' College and the national high schools) also contributed with religious as well as non-religious dramatic performances.

A number of other plays followed that were also written in Pidgin. The first indigenous production of a local play was in 1969 at Goroka Teachers' College when two student plays were staged. The 1968 publication of Albert Maori Kiki's book, *Kiki: Ten Thousand Years in a Lifetime* – one of the first books written by a New Guinea-born author – kindled still greater interest in writing among young people. Written before independence, many writers followed his example, clearly in search of their own and the nation's modern identity.

Among the notable playwrights to have emerged since that time have been Nora Vagi Brash (one of the country's few female writers), John Waiko, Rabbie Namaliu and John Kolia (né Collier, born in Australia, naturalized at independence). Radio drama became a later way of reaching audiences, particularly under the direction of Australian-born Peter Trist. A National Literature Competition was begun at this time with categories for both stage and radio plays.

In 1974, a grant of A$5 million from the Australian government laid the ground for a National Cultural Development Act. Its main feature was the establishment of a National Cultural Council which ultimately created several institutions including a National Museum, an Institute of Papua New Guinea Studies, Creative Arts Centre (later called the National Arts School), National Theatre Company, the Raun Raun Theatre and Skul Bilong Wokim Piksa, a film-making school. This Act also determined the functioning and mandate of all the national cultural services and remained, with amendments, the country's main cultural legislation until 1990.

Specifically, the National Theatre Company and Raun Raun were established to promote national culture through the performance and teaching of dramatic arts. The National Theatre, based in Port Moresby, ran classes, staged shows in the capital and toured, establishing

Sing-Sing Festival performers.
Photo: courtesy of CIDA.

theatre centres across the country in the larger towns. Raun Raun, with its home at Goroka in the Eastern Highlands province, had a similar mandate but focused more on the Highlands region. Both groups were given direct government subsidies.

Among the provincial theatre groups established during this period were the Raun Isi Theatre in East Sepik, Dua Dua Theatre in Morobe, Orobondo Theatre in Oro province, Tipuke in Manus, Alotau Provincial Theatre in Milne Bay, and San Kamap in North Solomons.

Most began as offshoots or direct initiatives of the National. In 1982, the National Theatre began a new Cultural Awareness Programme in the provinces which resulted in the establishment of still more provincial theatres funded totally by local governments. The experiment was short-lived, however, and by 1986 that specific funding was gone.

The National Cultural Council's initial goal in establishing both the National Theatre and Raun Raun was the preservation, promotion and development of Papua New Guinea's traditional culture. Over the years, however, the National Theatre became known primarily for its repertoire of western-style plays by contemporary Papua New Guinea authors. Its first major production was Peter Kama Kerpi's *Voices From the Ridge*, directed by US-born Oliver Sublette, which was taken to the South Pacific Festival of Arts in New Zealand in 1976. Raun Raun, in contrast, grew into a more traditional-style populist theatre devoted to the performance of a kind of folk opera usually based on traditional legends. The group travelled widely, both inside and outside the country.

At its inception, the National Theatre was connected to the Drama Department of the National Creative Arts Centre, which in its turn was closely associated with the University of Papua New Guinea. Its three original staff members were Arthur Jawodimbari (artistic director), Oliver Sublette and John Kaniku. The National Theatre later grew to thirty artists.

Raun Raun began its life with a troupe of nine actors and eleven apprentices each receiving an allowance of 30 kina (about US$21) per fortnight and free housing. The actors took regular classes in performance, dance, mime and improvisation. During production, rehearsals would last well into the night. Its annual budget generally matched that of the National Theatre. One of Raun Raun's original mandates was to perform at the Market Raun (a government project aimed at decentralizing social and market activities) staging sketches in market-squares. Intended to educate as well as entertain audiences, such circuit performances highlighted social issues including malnutrition, diarrhoea, scabies and venereal disease. Similar programmes were later undertaken on the effects of coffee cash-cropping and family planning.

The successful work of Raun Raun led to the development of a government-sponsored national Popular Theatre Campaign involving up to seventy-two annual performances along a regular circuit of villages. The work soon spread to other provinces where audiences not only watched these performances – often free-of-charge – but also could comment on them and contribute to the action. Even when ticket prices were charged they were low – 5 kina for adults and 2 kina for students, a reasonable price when compared to a loaf of bread (1.50 kina) or a bottle of beer (2 kina).

Raun Raun's folk opera productions stimulated new interest in Papua New Guinea traditions of song, dance and drama. The company established links with Goroka Teachers' College (now a branch campus of the University of Papua New Guinea) and other technical colleges within the Goroka area and assisted with various community arts projects. Over the years, Raun Raun developed a repertoire of performances based on traditional legends and local dances.

Raun Raun Theatre's work in music and dance long reflected the approach of its director Greg Murphy. At its best in such shows as *Nema Namba* (*Mother of the Birds*) for the Papua New Guinea independence celebrations in 1975, this work was dance-drama treating the theme of independence in an allegorical form. Based on a poem by Henginike Riyong called *The Dead Hunter*, the piece is about two birds representing the forces of chaos and evil who fight against order and social harmony. Still another Raun Raun show of note was *The Legend of Jari* (1978) which toured the provinces and later played in Sydney and New York. This dance-drama was based on a story from the Murik Lakes area of the Sepik and made use of songs, dances and musical instruments from the Siassi Islands, Manus Islands and Highlands areas. Based on a creation legend, it dealt with a young woman trying to relate to the world of men and spanned the cycle from birth to death. Two important folk operas by John Kasaipwalova were also staged – *Sail the Midnight Sun* by Raun Raun and *Sana Sana* by the National Theatre Company.

Comic sketches too were part of Raun Raun's programme. The best known of these were the Kainantu snake dance and a comic dance drawn from the Kainantu area of the Eastern Highlands. Raun Raun even created a folk opera based on the *hevehe* cycle, a re-enactment of the creation myth by the deities of the environment and the people of the Gulf area.

In 1996, under the new National Performing Arts Troupe, Milne Bay Provincial Theatre staged one of its largest productions – *Kumwakalakedakeda* – based on a Tewala Island legend. The show was directed by Robson

Shirley Tauwaigu as Kasabwaibwaileta's mother in the Milne Bay Provincial Theatre Group's production of *Kumwakalakedakeda*.
Photo: courtesy of *Paradise*.

Ubuk and Kilori Susuve with choreography by Norman Toru. After its initial presentation it toured local schools and surrounding communities and then played in and around the capital. Wherever it played, it drew full houses. Among its Port Moresby venues were the open-air theatre at the University of Papua New Guinea, the Waigani Arts Theatre, St Joseph International School Hall in Boroko, Don Bosco Secondary School Hall, and the Teachers' College Hall. It later played at the 1996 Festival of Pacific Arts in Western Samoa.

In 1994 the National Theatre and Raun Raun were united into a new National Performing Arts Troupe. The new troupe – operating from four regional centres – included the best talents from both companies. Like the two disbanded groups, the new troupe was mandated to organize theatre workshops and to train artists as well as to perform. By 1997 the troupe was still without its own theatre performing in a variety of community sites, usually outdoors.

The National Performing Arts Troupe began with a company of thirty-nine including staff and a first-year budget of 1.8 million kina. Its first director was William Takaku (b. 1952), a graduate of the National Institute of Dramatic Art (NIDA) in Sydney, Australia.

One other group of note is the Malabo (Flying Fox) Theatre Group established in 1992 and housed at the Madang Cultural Centre or, as it is popularly known, Haus Tumbuna (House of the Ancestors). A major initiative of the Madang Visitors and Cultural Bureau, it was under the direction of Simon Labon (b. 1968), who trained with Raun Raun. The first major production of Malabo was the collective *Stori Bilong Madang* (*The History of Madang*), an epic that traces the history of Madang from traditional creation stories (Manub and Kilibob) to modern times – with scenes about traditional life, the arrival of the Europeans, the Siar uprising, World War II and independence. The play finishes with a look at modern Madang and looks into the future, asking the question: 'What future do we want and are we prepared to work for it?' Many important issues are raised in the play: national identity and unity, cultural heritage and rapid social change.

There are also several village-based and non-profit theatre groups in Papua New Guinea that developed independently of the main government-financed National Theatre Company and Raun Raun. The largest is Awareness Community Theatre (ACT), a network that was formed in 1992 to disseminate social and health information to the general public. A loose affiliation of about twenty-one theatre groups from all but three provinces, ACT offers free Theatre-in-Education training, administrative and financial support. ACT's first programme coordinator was Yasmin Padamsee (b. 1967); artistic trainers included George Aisa (b. 1968), Vincent Orea (b. 1966), Elizabeth Asimba (b. 1965) and Allan Serembari (b. 1970). In 1996, ACT's repertoire included twenty basic storylines built around local social and health issues.

Dance group in Madang wearing traditional face masks.
Photo: courtesy of Yasmin Padamsee.

As a result of ACT's work, many new theatre groups have emerged including Tiffy Theatre in Morobe province, Sumung Central Theatre in Southern Highlands province, Lasela Palu Theatre in Enga province and Bena Neheya theatre in Eastern Highlands province. ACT has also worked with more established groups such as Malabo Theatre and Orobondo on awareness campaigns.

Such initiatives involving education through theatre have been especially important in rural Papua New Guinea where television and radio are not readily accessible and only 52 per cent of the adult population is literate (*Human Development Report*: Oxford University Press, 1993). Street theatre in this light has become a logical communication choice. A typical market performance, for example, draws between 500 and 1,000 people. After the play, the audience is invited to ask questions of local health experts who accompany the troupe.

On the other side of the spectrum is Market Raun (Travelling Market), a non-government, travelling performance group that is taking 'commercial' theatre to the interior of the New Guinea Highlands. This group is contracted by multinational companies seeking to advertise their products throughout Papua New Guinea. Market Raun usually travels along the Highlands region from village to village advertising tinned meat, soft drinks and detergents to villagers. The group has added in community education and has dramatized family planning issues in rural areas. Market Raun is a project of Human Resource Development (HRD) Advertising, a marketing agency based in Port Moresby.

With so few troupes in the country, there are no performing arts unions in Papua New Guinea though in the 1980s several attempts were made to set one up. Connections, however, do exist with various Australian groups, most notably with the Playbox Theatre Centre in Melbourne and NIDA in Sydney.

Listings of most drama and dance performances in Papua New Guinea are published in the National Cultural Commission's annual calendar of events. Among the notable dance festivals that form part of the calendar is the one at the Port Moresby Agricultural Show where traditional dances from different provinces are shown each June. Such performances have become the focal point at other agricultural

A drama on immunization and child health staged by a village theatre group from Mile Bay Province. Immunization 'caps' designed by Awareness Community Theatre (ACT).
Photo: courtesy of Yasmin Padamsee.

shows as well and prizes have been awarded. Performances generally take place in a huge open-air arena (about the size of a football pitch) with bleachers on one side. Groups tend to be made up of provincial dancers resident in Port Moresby.

The annual Hiri Moale Festival, staged in Port Moresby every September, coincides with independence celebrations and is a three-day festival consisting not only of traditional dances (such as those of the Motu-Koitabu peoples of the Central Province), but also of re-enactments of legends (such as the Hiri trade with the people of the Gulf Province). The highlight of the festival is always the arrival of the *lagatoi* (large trading vessels) and the crowning of the Hiri Moale queen. One popular dramatization during the festival is the coming of the Christian missionaries to the Papuan coast in their white clothes. Confronted by spear- and axe-wielding villagers bent on killing them, the missionaries form a tight circle and proceed to sing spiritual songs oblivious to the dangers. Just as tragedy is about to strike, however, they are saved by the village women, who form a human shield around them.

These activities are generally organized under the aegis of the municipal government of the national capital district. The performance area for this event includes the whole of the Ela Beach in central Port Moresby which is garlanded during the festival. While awaiting the arrival of the *lagatoi*, various dance groups perform on the beach. A raised stage is used for the parade of the Hiri Queen contestants.

In the provinces, Mount Hagen Agricultural Show attracts other local groups from different parts of the Highlands for an impressive massed display of traditional dance. It too offers prizes for the best group.

Aside from festival performances, groups on tour generally use village performance spaces known as *haus sing sing*. Large round buildings made from bush materials and roofed only above the audience area, these spaces are important year-round community centres.

Academic theatre training is supplied by the Faculty of Creative Arts at the University of Papua New Guinea, at Madang Teachers' College and at Goroka Teachers' College.

An important examination of the work of early modern Papua New Guinea playwriting was completed by Kirsty Powell – a doctoral dissertation called 'The First Papua New Guinean Playwrights and Their Plays' (University of Papua New Guinea). Journals which have published plays include *Kovave*, *New Guinea Writing*, *Gigibori* and *Bikmaus*.

Anthony Adah, Esohe Veronica Omoregie

Further Reading

Beir, Ulli, ed. Introduction to *Five New Guinea Plays*. Milton: Jacaranda Press, 1971.

Eri, Vincent. *The Crocodile*. Brisbane: Jacaranda Press, 1970.

Gillison, Gillian. *Between Culture and Fantasy: A New Guinea Highlands Mythology*. Chicago: Chicago University Press, 1993.

——. 'Living Theatre In New Guinea's Highlands'. *National Geographic* (August 1983): 146–69.

Goroka's Travelling Players. Theatre Raun Raun, Report to the National Cultural Council, April 1975–June 1976.

Hannet, Leo. 'Em rod bilong kago'. *Kovave* (pilot issue June 1969): 47–51.

Holmes, John H. *In Primitive New Guinea*. London: Seeley & Service, 1924.

Inimgba, S.O. *Concepts of Dance: A Review of Papua New Guinea Point of View*. NCC Discussion Paper, 1995.

Kaniku, John Wills. 'Cry of the Cassowary; and Turuk, Wabei, Kulabob'. *Two Plays from New Guinea*. Melbourne: Heinemann Educational, 1970.

Kiki, Albert Maori. *Kiki: Ten Thousand Years in a Lifetime*. Melbourne: F.W. Cheshire, 1968.

Murphy, Greg. 'Kainantu Farces and Raun Raun Theatre'. *Gigibori* 4 no. 1 (February 1978): 28–39.

Paradise: In Flight With Air Niugini. Port Moresby: Morauta and Associates (March–April 1997).

——. 'Nema Namba: A Dance Drama by the Raun Raun Theatre'. *Gigibori* 3 no. 2 (April 1977): 13–18.

Powell, Kirsty. 'The First Papua New Guinean Playwrights and Their Plays', PhD dissertation, University of Papua New Guinea, n.d.

Schwimmer, Erik. 'Aesthetics of the Aika'. *Exploring the Visual Art of Oceania* (1979): 287–92.

Williams, F.E. *Drama of the Orokolo: The Social and Ceremonial Life of the Elema*. Oxford: Clarendon Press, 1940.

——. *Orokaiva Society*. Territory of Papua, Anthropology Report 10. Oxford: Clarendon Press, 1930.

PEOPLE'S REPUBLIC OF CHINA

(see **CHINA**)

PERSIA

(see **IRAN**)

PHILIPPINES

The Republic of the Philippines, an archipelago of 7,100 islands covering a total area of 300,000 square kilometres (115,800 square miles) in Southeast Asia with a population of about 65 million, has a centuries-old, Malay-type indigenous culture that gradually assimilated diverse influences from the outside, evolving to its present state through 333 years of Spanish colonization, 48 years of US rule and 50 years of independence.

Each period in the country's history produced its own traditions in theatre. From the indigenous tradition comes rituals, mimetic dances and mimetic customs; from the Spanish colonization, the *komedya*, *sinakulo* religious playlets, *sarswela* and *drama*; from the US colonial period, the *bodabil* (vaudeville) and plays in English; and from the contemporary, original plays, in representational or presentational styles, inspired by modern theatres of the world or local traditional genres. All these forms coexist in the late 1990s in urban or rural areas, in various stages of development and decline.

Indigenous rituals, dances and customs are still performed by a few cultural minorities to mark life-cycle events, such as birth, baptism, circumcision or first menstruation, wedding, sickness and death, or to underscore the importance of tribal activities, such as rice-planting, hunting, fishing or going to war. In most rituals, the shaman dances and goes into a trance as the spirit being called takes possession of the shaman. While entranced and acting as the spirit, the shaman kills a sacrificial animal which represents the supplicant.

Mimetic dances imitate either the movements of familiar fauna – hawks, monkeys, butterflies, lizards and flies – or the motions of rice cultiva-

tion from planting to winnowing. Others mime fighting with shield, sword or spear, hunting for honey, deer or wild pigs or fishing with baskets and nets. Mimetic customs include courtship jousts, like the Cebuano *balitaw*, where a man and a woman outwit and outperform each other through an exchange of verses, songs and dances; wedding rites, like those of the Bilaan *samsung*, where the bride and groom execute symbolic motions, such as the bride standing beside the groom and putting a heavy foot on his shoulder and vice versa; and burial customs, such as the Aeta *baraning usa*, where a deer is represented with a banana stalk body, and legs of twigs and is pursued in the bushes, shot with a real arrow and placed in the grave as food and for companionship for the deceased in the afterlife.

As a whole, indigenous dramas draw their matter and motive from nature and tribal life

An Aeta hunting dance *c*.1970.

itself, even as they legitimize among young and old alike the activities which contribute to the economic and political survival as well as the social cohesiveness of the community. Created by the collective, these dramas are invariably communal in their concerns.

The Spanish period (1565–1896) introduced and popularized new dramatic genres, many of which still continue to be performed today among some of the Christianized lowlanders who constitute the majority of the Philippine population, specifically, the Tagalog, Cebuano, Ilocano, Bicol, Ilongo, Pangasinan, Pampango and Waray. The most popular religio-secular play is the *komedya*, a verse play depicting either the stories of Christian saints – usually the patron saint of the town – or, as is more common, the conflicts in love and war between royal characters of medieval European kingdoms (Spain, Portugal, France, Italy, Germany) and their Middle Eastern antagonists (Persia, Turkey, Arabia). Staged for about five hours every night for three or more nights during the town fiesta, this spectacle delights audiences with its colourful costumes, elaborate marches, choreographed battles between individuals or armies and magical artifices representing divine miracles or enchanted phenomena (for example, goddesses materializing from giant flowers or predatory birds swooping down from a tower). Costumes clearly identify the camps (blue/black for Christians, red for Moors) and the hierarchy of authority (kings have crowns and capes, princes have three-cornered hats, soldiers have plumed felt hats). Favoured by Spanish priests, the *komedya* helped to lure distant villagers into the Spanish pueblo.

In the pueblo, Catholic catechism was conducted not only through sermons and masses but especially through the religious playlets that visualized episodes in the life of Jesus Christ following the liturgical calendar. The Christmas season witnessed the *panunuluyan* (search for lodging), a street procession depicting the search for an inn by Mary and Joseph on the first Christmas eve; the *pastores* (a group of thirteen males and females in shepherd attire, dancing and singing in Spanish); native *villancicos* (carols from house to house); and the *tatlong hari* (three kings), a short play dramatizing the journey of the three kings in search of Bethlehem and their encounter with Herod.

The Lenten season is enlivened with Holy Week playlets like the Palm Sunday *osana* (hosanna), a procession with the priest and twelve apostles re-enacting Christ's triumphal entry into Jerusalem; the Holy Tuesday *via crucis* (way of the cross), an evening procession showing Christ carrying the cross and which stops to meditate at the altars enshrining the Stations of the Cross; the Holy Thursday *paghuhugas* (washing of the feet), a church ritual where the priest, representing Christ, washes and kisses the feet of twelve male parishioners dressed as apostles; the Holy Thursday *huling hapunan* (last supper), which is an actual lunch or dinner consumed by the priest and twelve apostles in commemoration of Christ's Last Supper; the Good Friday *siete palabras* (seven words), a series of sermons delivered before the faithful in church from 1 to 3 p.m., where a lifesize wooden image of Christ hanging on the cross, moves its head generating 'thunder and lightning' when one of the seven words is spoken; the Easter Sunday *salubong* (encounter), which dramatizes in song and dance the meeting of the Risen Christ with the Virgin Mary on the dawn of the first Easter Sunday and features an angel descending from heaven to remove the Virgin's mourning veil; the *hudas*, a ritual performed after Easter Sunday mass, where the effigy of Judas Iscariot is eaten up by black birds and exploded with firecrackers; and the *moriones* (helmets), an Easter morning street drama showing the pursuit, arrest and beheading of the Roman soldier Longinos, who witnessed Christ's resurrection and proclaimed Christianity to everyone.

A full-blown religious drama is the *sinakulo*, a verse play depicting the history of salvation, from the creation of the world to the coronation of the Virgin in heaven, with special emphasis on the life, suffering, death and resurrection of Jesus Christ. Staged near the barrio chapel for about five hours every night from Palm Sunday to Easter Sunday, the *sinakulo* follows a convention of marches (one-step for the holy people, a double-step for the *hudyo* or villains), chants (laments for the good, lively for the *hudyo*) and special artifices to represent miracles (for example, the storm at sea, the ascension and assumption). Costumes are often derived from the images of Christ and the saints in religious processions and in the *pasyon* (verse narrative on the life of Jesus Christ or, in a more modern vein, biblical films like *Jesus of Nazareth*).

Theatre clearly underwent a drastic reorientation under Spain. Dramatic matter had turned from the life of the people and the environment to the life of Christ and the saints. Still later it changed to the adventures of Charlemagne and

Sinakulo performance in Malolos, Bulacan, 1967.

the Twelve Peers of France, Gonzalo de Cordoba and other heroes of medieval European romances. Rather than answering any of the needs of the immediate community, the *komedya* and *sinakulo* succeeded in shaping the natives into good colonials with minds that looked up to the Europeans as a race superior in mind and body to their own, into Christians as God's favoured and invincible soldiers, into subjects of the king and his representatives as authorities who were somehow ordained by God and fate to rule over them, and into people with wills moulded after the church's version of Christ: a model of passivity, blind obedience and resigned to their suffering.

In the last two decades of the nineteenth century, Spanish troupes performed Spanish *zarzuela* and *drama* in Manila and other cities of the country. Later, Filipino artists indigenized these forms, popularizing them during the American period from 1900 to the 1940s. The *sarswela* (Spanish *zarzuela*; see SPAIN) is a play with prose dialogue, songs and dances, revolving around a love story between characters of different social classes. It is spiced with comic scenes between amorous servants and with topical themes like usury, westernized manners, corrupt politicians, greedy landlords, cruel step-

mothers, husbands or wives addicted to cock-fighting and card games respectively, and recently, drug addicts and recruiters who take advantage of migrant workers.

Probably the most popular Tagalog *sarswela* is *Dalagang Bukid* (*Country Maiden*, 1919), by writer-impresario Hermogenes Ilagan and Maestro Leon Ignacio, which is about the young love between a pretty flower girl, Angelita, and a handsome law student, Cipriano, which is almost thwarted by the money and machinations of rich, old Don Silvestre.

Like the *sarswela*, the *drama* is also a play in prose, but it has no songs or dances. Whether comic or tragic or a combination of both, the *drama* also uses the framework of a romantic love story to comment on social issues, like the divorce bill which raised a controversy among the Catholic population; socio-religious topics, like abusive priests and their fanatical followers; or social contradictions, like the conflict between landlords and peasants, capitalists and workers.

In the early 1900s, nationalist Filipinos, defying arrest and imprisonment, allegorized the *drama* to expose The United States' betrayal of the Philippine revolution and to exhort the people to unite against the new colonizer. Typical of these *drama simboliko* (allegorical

A scene from the popular Tagalog *sarswela Dalagang Bukid* (*Country Maiden*) in Manila, 1987.

dramas) is Aurelio Tolentino' *Kahapon, Ngayon at Bukas* (*Yesterday, Today and Tomorrow*, 1903), about the love between Liwanag (a free Filipino) and Kaulayaw (a revolutionary Filipino), which is frowned upon by Liwanag's uncle, Maimbot (representing the US colonizer).

In all, the *sarswela* and *drama* represent an important breakthrough in the history of Philippine theatre because they pioneered in the portrayal of real characters and conflicts in Philippine society, especially in the early American occupation. The portraits they painted were as vital as they were true, making them immensely popular with their audiences. Because these plays were primarily written to proselytize against social vices, they also tended to typify, not individualize, characters, and to manipulate plots through coincidences, accidents and other *dei ex machina* to come to a 'correct ending', in which the social offenders are, with the stroke of a facile pen, transformed into defenders of establishment morality and law.

The American half-century (1900–46) introduced other new theatrical forms and styles into the Philippines. The earliest of these was vaudeville, brought in by US travelling troupes in the 1900s. By the 1920s, Filipinos had created their own *bodabil*, which competed with and slowly edged out the *sarswela* from Manila theatres in the decades before World War II. Not a play *per se*, *bodabil* was a variety show which featured popular, mostly North American, songs and dances, comedy skits which were more often than not slapstick, circus acts with animals (dogs leaping over blazing hoops or monkeys dancing the *cha-cha*), and magical acts (swords being swallowed and women being sawn in half). During the Japanese occupation (1942–5), the *bodabil* appended the *drama* or short play in prose as its last and main event, to accommodate and capitalize on popular movie actors who lost their jobs when the Japanese confiscated all film equipment. This expanded version, called the stage show, continued to pack audiences into the theatres two decades after the war. By the 1970s, to compete with the cinema, the stage show added jamborees or singing contests (to choose the pop star of the week/month/year) as well as beauty contests or parades of beauties in different stages of undress. Such stage shows now survive in a few dingy theatres or in provincial fiestas.

As *bodabil* dished out popular entertainment to the common folk, the plays in English were analysed as literature and mounted in parts or as a whole as speech laboratories for the learning

An example of a *bodabil* act.

and practice of English in high schools and universities all over the country, where the language had come to be equated with education, class and opportunity. These plays, which were either originally written in English or were translated into English, included the major plays of the western stage – Greek classics such as Sophocles' *Oedipus Rex,* Euripides' *Medea,* Aeschylus' *Oresteia* and Aristophanes' *Lysistrata*; Shakespeare's *Romeo and Juliet, Merchant of Venice, Hamlet, Macbeth* and *Julius Caesar,* among others; as well as other European classics, such as Goldoni's *The Fan,* Molière's *The Miser,* Rostand's *Cyrano de Bergerac*; and the classics of the modern theatre, such as Ibsen's *A Doll's House,* Strindberg's *Miss Julie,* Chekov's *Uncle Vanya,* Hauptmann's *The Weavers,* Wilde's *The Importance of Being Earnest,* Shaw's *Arms and the Man,* Brecht's *Caucasian Chalk Circle, Galileo* and *The Good Person of Setzuan,* Ionesco's *The Bald Soprano,* Dürrenmatt's *The Visit,* Lorca's *La casa de Bernardo Alba,* Miller's *Death of a Salesman,* Williams's *A Streetcar Named Desire,* and Beckett's *Waiting for Godot*; and Broadway plays, such as Simon's *Barefoot in the Park,* and musicals, like *My Fair Lady* and *Jesus Christ Superstar.*

Through the decades of direct US rule and long after, *bodabil* and the plays in English

shifted the Filipino's eyes to US pop culture and to the dramaturgy of western theatre, transporting local audiences to the American dreamland either through pop songs, dances and comedy skits (in the case of *bodabil)* or through productions of the 'legitimate theatre'. Having set the American as ideal and as some sort of world standard, they strove to sing, dance, talk and act like the American originals, flaunting the dubious honour of being the 'Elvis Presley of the Philippines'. But even as Filipino artists were Americanized in thought, speech, manner and taste by these plays, so were they introduced to a range of dramatic theories and styles which opened new directions for growth and expanded the vocabulary of theatrical expression and practice for playwrights, directors, actors and designers. Such plays became the training ground for the original Filipino theatre of the post-independence generations.

In the contemporary period (1946 to the present), Filipino artists have created original plays in the representational style which seek to elicit emotional response from the audience by creating an illusion of reality through three-dimensional characterization and realistic sets and costumes; in the presentational style which aims to make audiences analyse the social issues being dramatized by the play through the use of narrators, choruses, songs, dances, mime, symbolic sets and costumes and other dramatic devices which encourage critical enjoyment of the performance; and in the revitalized style which revives and transforms selected traditional forms for the communication of timely and urgent ideas.

The representational style is equated with western-type realism, which in Philippine theatre follows two tendencies: the psychological, which dwells on the problems of individuals describing and diagnosing their anguish and joy, ambition and frustration, hope and despair; and the social, which contextualizes personal problems and conflicts within the wider framework of social contradictions – especially class conflict. The psychological is exemplified by Nick Joaquin's *Portrait of the Artist as Filipino* (1952), later translated into Filipino as *Larawan*, which revolves around two spinsters living in an old pre-war mansion in the decaying walled city of Spanish Manila who refuse to capitulate to US commercialism and pragmatism. The social is typified by Alberto Florentino's *The World Is An Apple* (1955) which depicts the tragedy of the urban poor in the post-World War II slums of Intramuros who are 'cornered by an unjust system into a life of crime in order to survive'.

The presentational style has been influenced to a great extent by Brecht's *Theatre of Instruction* and later to a lesser extent by Boal's *Theatre of the Oppressed*, and the plays of Samuel Beckett. This style blossomed during the regime of Ferdinand Marcos (1972–86) when realistic portrayals of poverty and political oppression were promptly met with censorship or arrest. Speaking indirectly, playwrights used history, folklore, radio plays, *bodabil*, the old *drama simboliko* and Brechtian-type musicals to expose and protest about the plunder of the economy and tortures by the military. To this style belong the documentary plays like Al Santos' *Mayo A-Beinte Uno* (1977), which traces the life of freedom fighter Valentin de los Santos from the period of revolution against the Spanish to the war with the Americans and later the Japanese, and the development of his millenarian group, many of whose members were massacred by Marcos's military in 1967.

With the realization that the majority of Filipinos were reared on traditional forms and a different philosophy and aesthetics of theatre, many contemporary playwrights have studied and used these genres to reach a wider rural audience. Virgilio Vitug's *Sinakulo ning Belen* (*Passion Play of the Country*, 1982) reinterprets the Christ of the *sinakulo* as a champion of the poor who condemns everyone from the empty words of non-believing religious recruiters to candle-sellers who help to commercialize religion. Amelia Lapeã-Bonifacio's *Ang Bundok* (*The Mountain*, 1976) is a modern *sarswela* which dramatizes a mountain people's resistance against the mining company which would displace them from their land. Rene Villanueva's *Sandaang Panaginip* (*A Hundred Dreams*, 1981) uses the *komedya* prince and princess to expose and satirize the frivolity and luxury of the Martial Law elite.

Although such a variety of styles might seem to negate the possibility of the country ever evolving a homogenous Philippine theatre, postwar artists have proved that these traditions can be enriched by relevant foreign influences to create a theatre that can express and respond to the needs of contemporary Philippine society. Slowly but surely, the country's most innovative artists are creating and defining a theatre that is multicultural in origin but national in perspective and commitment.

Structure of the National Theatre Community

To produce Philippine theatre, performers and aficionados have formed organizations that are community-based, church-based, school-based or sector-based, or they have moved into the realms of the professional or the semi-professional. The community-based are rooted in specific villages, *barrios* or towns, drawing their members, supporters and audiences mainly from this area. Such groups come together primarily for the staging of a *komedya* during the a town fiesta or a *sinakulo* on Holy Week, but also for social gatherings or to help members in times of need.

One community-based example is the *Komedya de San Dionisio* (KSD) of Barrio San Dionisio Rizal. Composed of a group of elders and an association of young actors, the KSD oversees the performances of the *komedya* during fiestas. The elders choose the *hermano* and *hermana* (sponsors) who provide the sets, costumes, lights, sounds, brass band and all the meals for actors and musicians on the days of the fiesta. To help the sponsors, the elders go from house to house collecting donations, while some *barrio* folk build the stage. Since all participants join the play to fulfil a social obligation or a personal vow to the patron saint, no one can be forced to do anything. Because of this, the fact that the *komedya* happens only once a year and that there are new recruits every year, performances cannot go beyond the amateur level, which of course is no obstacle to their being thoroughly enjoyed by a *barrio* audience. In community-based performances, the preservation of social harmony takes precedence over all other considerations, artistic or otherwise.

School-based companies are composed of students and teachers in a particular high school, college or university, whose main activity is the production of an annual play or season of plays, usually in a school venue. Funding for such productions comes from the school itself, which often has a small budget for extracurricular activities provided by government grant-giving agencies such as the National Commission for Culture and Arts (NCCA) or the Cultural Centre of the Philippines (CCP) as well as from outside sponsors who may give donations in cash or in kind, such as cosmetics and makeup or snacks for rehearsals and performances.

Church-based organizations are usually run by the parish council. Composed of the parish priest and elected parishioners, the council takes charge of the activities (masses, processions, shows) for the town fiesta during Christmas and Holy Week, including traditional playlets based on the church liturgy or, since the 1970s, even socially relevant productions which serve as communal social conscience and unite members of Basic Christian Communities (BCC) on issues affecting the people – such as militarization, abusive officials and election fraud. In Kawit Cavite, the pastoral council elects the *hermanos* who fund and manage the most important town event – the *maytinis* – which dramatizes the history of Christian salvation in a procession of twelve huge floats.

Sector-based groups started to proliferate during the Marcos dictatorship to protest the repression of human rights. Founded and supported by particular sectors of the community (e.g. farmers or workers) these groups draw members and target audiences from the same sector. Their expenses are kept to a minimum because they often do not need costumes (their plays are about themselves) and because they have to keep their plays portable (no sets and an absolute minimum of props). To maximize their efforts and project their issues, they often belong

A 1983 street performance of *Kalayaan* (*Freedom*) in Manila to protest the Aquino assassination.

to theatre networks whose members have a similar persuasion.

Typical of these groups are Teatro Pabrika of the workers' sector, which dramatizes issues related to wage increases, workers' benefits, management and government policies towards labor; the Tanghalan ng Maralitang Taga-Lungsod of the urban poor, which focuses on the problems of unemployment, poverty, lack of housing facilities, demolition of slums and government policies towards the urban poor; and Gabriela Cultural Group, which discusses feminist issues such as anti-woman management policies in factories, equal opportunities and responsibilities for men and women and women's liberation from patriarchal values and practices. Sector-based groups are formed primarily for political education and mobilization, so they often have no time for training or rehearsals and members often have to rely on their commitment to certain issues to make a performance work.

Professional or semi-professional troupes must also be based in theatres that are accessible to their target clientele. Professional companies pay salaries to trained artists and stage productions that are of a high artistic quality, while semi-professional are those that not only pay honoraria on a per-production basis, but also stage regular productions. These companies are financially sustained through subscriptions, walk-in tickets and pre-sold performances (bought by schools for their students as well as by corporate sponsors), local and foreign development groups and government institution. Budgets are drawn up on an annual basis. Expenses include production costs and artists' honoraria or salaries.

Artistic Profile

Music is found in most Filipino traditional forms but musical theatre *per se*, or theatre whose principal medium of expression is music, makes its appearance in three main forms: the opera, the *sarswela* and in modern musicals. Introduced in the second half of the nineteenth century, the western opera has been patronized mainly by the middle and upper classes. To this day, productions of *La Traviata, Aïda, Carmen, Lucia di Lammermoor, Madame Butterfly* and *La Bohème*, in their original languages or in Filipino translation or adaptation, continue to be mounted in Manila. Less often produced are original Filipino operas, like Felipe Padilla de Leon's adaptations of Jose Rizal's novels, *Noli Me Tangere* (*Touch Me Not*, 1957) and *El Filibusterismo* (*Subversion*, 1970); Jerry Dadap's *Andres Bonifacio, Ang Dakilang Anak Pawis* (*Andres Bonifacio, the Great Plebian*, 1979) and Francisco Feliciano's *La Loba Negra* (*The Black Wolf*, 1984).

More popular than the opera, the *sarswela* was introduced by Spanish actors to Manila audiences about 1880. Dominating the theatre scene in the first half of the twentieth century, the *sarswela* was edged out of the stage by *bodabil* and the movies, but revivals of classic *sarswela* have proved that the musical can draw sizeable crowds even among young audiences. Revived successfully in the 1980s was *Sa Bunganga ng Pating* (*In the Shark's Jaws*, 1921). Because contemporary Filipinos continue to delight in this musical, modern *sarswela* have been written and produced with equal success, as proved by Domingo Landicho-Rey Paguio's *Sumpang Mahal* (*Sacred Vow*, 1976), Bienvenido Lumbera-Lucio San Pedro's *Ang Palabas Bukas* (*Tomorrow's Show*, 1979) and Nicanor G. Tiongson-Lutgardo Labad *et al.'s Pilipinas Circa, 1907* (1982).

Finally, exposure to Broadway musicals as well as rock and pop music has led Filipinos to create original modern musicals which use Philippine folklore and ethnic music motifs, such as Rio Alma-Tito Climaco's *Bernardo Carpio* (1976) and Bienvenido Lumbera-Jim Paredes' *Bayani* (*Hero*, 1977). Other musicals are inspired by contemporary life, personalities and issues, such as Gines Tan's *Magsimula Ka* (*Begin*, 1983), Ryan Cayabyab's *Katy* (1988), Al Santos-Joey Ayala's *Nukleyar É and II* (1982 and 1984 respectively).

Dance theatre, which uses dance and music to dramatize a narrative or to interpret individual emotion, includes a range of styles. Folkloric dance theatre has adapted for the stage folk dances gathered by researchers from the ethnic and lowland rural communities and is exemplified by the productions of Bayanihan Dance Company (founded 1957), the Ramon Obusan Folkloric Group (founded 1971) and the scores of smaller folk dance companies in the country. Folkloric ballet, which uses classical ballet techniques for folk materials, is exemplified by Agnes Locsin's *Igorot* (1987), an ingenious work combining classical and modern dance techniques to interpret an authentic Cordillera chant.

European classical ballet, introduced early in the twentieth century, continues to be popular among the upper-middle class. Ballets like *Giselle, Sleeping Beauty, Swan Lake* and *Nutcracker Suite* are produced mainly by Ballet Philippines (founded 1969) and Philippine Ballet Theatre (founded 1986). Works in modern ballet, which employ classical ballet techniques to interpret contemporary material, include Leonor Orosa-Goquingco's *Nolé Dance Suite* (1955), with music by Antonio Molina and others.

The largest number of dance theatre works, however, belong to the genre of modern dance, which draws from, interprets, adapts, experiments with or builds on contemporary approaches, techniques and styles of dance expression developed by twentieth-century choreographers like Martha Graham, Doris Humphrey, Merce Cunningham, Jose Limon, Paul Taylor, Twyla Tharp, Mark Morris and Pina Bausch, among others.

Modern dance pieces have been mostly commissioned and performed by Ballet Philippines. Alice Reyes choreographed *Amada* (1970) based on Nick Joaquin's story about a woman's defiance of macho supremacy in Spanish Philippines; *Tales of the Manuvu* (1970) with Bienvenido Lumbera and Nonong Pedero, which enacts myths of one Philippine ethnic group; and *Rama Hari (Rama King*, 1980), with Bienvenido Lumbera and Ryan Cayabyab, which is a contemporary rendition of the ancient Asian tale of the *Ramayana*. Denisa Reyes did *Diablos (Devils*, 1989) with Al Santos and Ronnie Quesada, about a Bagobo woman who is hunted down by the Evil Bird because she is about to give birth to the saviour of the land; and *Siete Dolores (Seven Sorrows*, 1988), with Nicanor G. Tiongson and Fabian Obispo, which dramatizes the condition of youth, women, politicians, artists, peasants, military and workers in contemporary Philippine society.

Other notable examples of modern dance include Agnes Locsin's *Hinilawod* (1992) with Edwin Duero, based on the native epic of the Sulod of Panay; *Encantada (The Enchanted One*, 1992), with Al Santos and Joey Ayala, about the clash between the natives who lived in harmony with nature and the Spanish colonizers who destroyed the land; *La Revolucion Filipina (The Philippine Revolution*, 1996), about the struggle between the two leaders of the 1898 Revolution; Gener Caringal's *Ang Sultan (The Sultan*, 1973) with Lucrecia Kasilag, which dramatizes the tragedy of a sultan who opposes the love between his daughter and a commoner; Basilio's *Ang Babaylan (The Shaman*, 1988) with Edward Defensor and Taga-Aton, which treats of the clash between the native shamans and the Christian conquerors; and Steven Patrick Fernandez's *Sarimanok*, which is based on a Maranao folk tale.

Of all the forms of dance theatre, modern dance has proven to be the most adaptable for the interpretation of Philippine materials and the affirmation of Filipino identity.

(See also the opening, historical section for a discussion of other theatre forms.)

Companies

In Metro Manila, some of the most active school-based groups are the Dulaang University of the Philippines Company, UP Repertory Company, Anak-Tibawan of the University of the Philippines, Tanghalang Ateneo Dulaang Sibol and Ateneo Children's Theatre of the Ateneo de Manila University, Harlequin Theatre of De La Salle University, Sininglahi of Polythecnic University of the Philippines, Teatro Tomasino of the University of Santo Tomas and Adamson Company of Talents of Adamson University.

In the provinces notable theatres include Teatro Umalahokan of UP Los Baños, Dagyaw Dance and Theatre Company at Iloilo National High School, Integrated Performing Arts Group at Mindanao State University in Iligan and Sining Kambayoka Marawi, the University of San Carlos Theatre Guild in Cebu, and Teatrong Lungsudnon of Xavier University. Due to budget limitations, fast turnover of members and the absence of honoraria, school-based productions are categorized as non-professional. Because these productions are not commercial, good directors and talented actors can come up with outstanding productions. One should note as well here that during periods of political repression, it is mostly those organizations based in state universities that can mount critical plays under the mantle of academic freedom.

Professional and semi-professional groups include Repertory Philippines, a company founded by Zeneida Amador which now has its own theatre, a regular season of only western plays in English and an upper- and middle-class audience from Makati; Tanghalang Pilipino, a professional resident theatre company of the Cultural Center of the Philippines which stages regular seasons of original Filipino plays as well as translations/adaptations of foreign classics; Philippine Educational Theatre Association (PETA), a company founded in 1967 by Cecile Guidote-Alvarez and based at the open-air Raha Sulayman theatre in the ruins of the walled city of Intramuros (the company's season is composed of original Filipino plays as well as translations/adaptations of foreign classics); Bulwagang Gantimpala Theatre Foundation, a group founded by the Cultural Centre of the Philippines in 1978 that rents different theatres for its performances and produces mainly original Filipino plays for student audiences; and Teatrong Mulat ng Pilipinas, a semi-professional company founded in 1977 by Amelia Lapeña-Bonifacio that presents Filipino children's plays.

Dramaturgy

Indigenous dramas require no scripts but follow movements and patterns in dance and music that have been set for centuries. Dramaturgy, therefore, begins with formal theatre under Spain – for the *komedya*, *sinakulo*, religious playlets and later the *sarswela* and *drama* scripts now used for these traditional forms are mainly those from the past. In *Tikay*, Malolos Bulacan, for example, the same *Original ng Cenacolo o Pasion Ymuerte* (*Script of the Sinakulo or Passion and Death*, 1948) by Hermenegildo de Guzman, has been presented every Holy Week since the 1950s with only minor changes. Similarly, no substantial changes have been made in the *pastores* of Camalig, Albay, the *tatlong hari* of Gasan, Marinduque and the *salubong* of Angono, Rizal. Sometimes scripts are edited to tighten the performance for a modern audience. In a few cases like that of the *moriones* in Gasan Marinduque, new scripts have commissioned since the mid-1970s to beef up the play for tourist purposes and later, to give it social relevance.

A few scripts of forms that have long bowed out of the stage like the Tagalog *sarswela* and *drama* have been revived because a strong wave of nationalism in the 1970s drove Filipinos to 'look back to their roots' in order to create an identity of their own. Successfully revived were the *sarswela Walang Sugat* (*No Wounds*, 1902) by Severino Reyes (1861–1942) and *Fulgencio Tolentino* and *Paglipas ng Dilim* (*After the Darkness*, 1921) by Precioso Palma and Leon Ignacio, as well as the *drama Mga Santong Tao* (*People As Saints*, 1901) by Tomas Remigio and R.I.P. (1901) by Reyes. Sometimes old scripts, like those of the anti-American *drama simboliko*, have been updated to include present conditions. *Kahapon Ngayon at Bukas* (*Yesterday Today and Tomorrow*) by Tolentino was restaged by PETA in 1990.

In the few areas where the traditional *sarswela* and *komedya* still live, new scripts have been written such as the Ilocano *sarswela Ippes a Bukel* (*Bad Seed*) by Barbaro Paat of Bantay Ilocos Sur. Contemporary *bodabil* follows not a script but a formula for creating a show of popular songs and dances, comedy skits and beauty contests. Even its drama follows no script but improvises dialogue on a given topic according in the old *bodabil* tradition.

Playwrights of the modern stage wrote mainly in English from the 1920s to the 1960s, then in Filipino from the 1960s to the present. Outstanding Filipino plays in English have also been translated into Filipino since the mid-1970s. In the provinces, playwrights have used Cebuano, Ilongo, Ilocano, Bicol and whatever language is understood by the audience. Subject matter has been drawn from history, like Bonifacio Ilagan's *Katipunan, Sigaw ng Bayan* (*Katipunan, Cry of the Country*, 1978) about the 1899 revolution against Spain; folklore, like Rudolfo Galenzoga's *Maranatha* (*Make Haste, Lord*, 1974) about an ancient kingdom in Lanao, victimized by a huge black bird; literature, like Tony Perez's *Florante at Laura* (*Florante and Laura*, 1988) about contemporary characters inspired by Francisco Baltazar's (1788–1862) nineteenth-century *awit*, (romance); famous personalities, like Manuel Pambid's *Canuplin* (1979) about the career of a *bodabil* comedian; and contemporary life, like Nonilon Queaño's *Alipato* (*Embers*, 1975) about the struggle for survival in Manila's slums.

Whatever language they have used, playwrights have employed a range of genres and styles: comedies, tragedies or tragicomedies, straight plays or musicals, or plays influenced by western realism, Brechtian theatre, Theatre of the Absurd, Chinese revolutionary plays, Japanese *noh*, *kyogen* and *bunraku*, local radio plays as well as traditional *komedya*, *sinakulo*, *sarswela*, *drama* and *bodabil*.

Contemporary playwrights were introduced to realism through literature courses and the translations/adaptations of European and American plays on the Filipino stage. Adapted to the needs of their society and the changing times, realism developed with two marked tendencies – the psychological and the social. Pioneering psychological studies of character are first seen in Wilfrido Ma Guerrero's *The Forsaken House* (1940) about the conflict between an autocratic father and his rebellious children; Severino Montano's *Sabina* (1944) about the tragedy of a barrio maiden who commits suicide when her American boyfriend abandons her in her pregnancy; and Nick Joaquin's *Portrait of the Artist as Filipino*. From these beginnings sprung the psychological dramas of the 1970s, 1980s and 1990s: Orlando Nadress's *Paraisong Parisukat* (*A Square Piece of Paradise*, 1974) about a salesgirl who buries her life and love in the stuffy stockroom of a city-centre shoe store; Bienvenido Noriega's *Bayan-Bayanan* (*Little Country*, 1977) about the personal dreams and frustrations of Filipino expatriates in Switzerland; Rene Villanueva's *Hiblang Abo* (*Strands of Grey*, 1980) about the

A 1985 production of Tony Perez's *On North Diversion Road* in Manila.

tragic dreams of four senior citizens in the home for the aged; Tony Perez's *Biyaheng Timog* (*Journey South*, 1985) about a landlord-patriarch who destroys the lives of his children; and Elsa Coscoluella's *In My Father's House* (1987) about the disintegration of a Cebuano family during the Japanese occupation of Negros Oriental in the 1940s.

Social realism was first exemplified by Albertos Florentino's *The World Is An Apple* (1955). Later examples include Rogelio Sicat's *Moses, Moses* (1969) about a middle-class family's fruitless search for justice in a small town; Marilou Jacob's *Juan Tamban* (1978) about a poor boy who eats roaches and lizards; Jose Dalisay's *Sugatang Lawin* (*Wounded Hawk*, 1979) about heroism and cowardice during the Japanese occupation; Chris Millado's *Buwan at Baril sa E♭ Major* (*Moon and Gun in E♭ Major*, 1985) about the politicization of a farmer, worker, socialite, priest, ethnic woman, student activist and teacher; and Reuel Aguila's *In Dis Korner* (*In This Corner*, 1979) about boxers fighting the system of fixing in the ring.

Non-realistic plays have been influenced principally by Brecht's epic theatre or theatre of instruction, which discourses on social and political issues and adopts a presentational style using folklore, history and other non-realistic sources as well as songs, dances, mime, music, slides, stylized sets and costumes. Inspired by texts or productions of Brecht's plays are: Paul Dumol's *Paglilitis ni Mang Serapio* (*Trial of Old Serapio*, 1969) about a federation that exploits beggars; Frank Rivera's *Mga Kuwentong Maranao* (*Maranao Folktales*, 1974) about frivolity and militarization during the Marcos dictatorship; Al Santos' *Ang Sistema ni Propesor Tuko* (*The System of Professor Gecko*, 1980), an absurd treatment of authoritarianism under Martial Law; Bonifacio S. Ilagan's *Pagsambang Bayan* (*The Country's Worship*, 1977), a mass that conscientizes its audience about the plight of workers, peasants, fishers and other sectors under the Marcos regime; Rolando Tinio's *May Katwiran ang Katwiran* (*Right has Reason*, 1981) about a landlord who enslaves his tenant through specious logic; Dong de los Reyes's *Bien Aligtad* (1985), about a real-life gangster who is depicted as product and victim of an unjust society; and Anton Juan Jr's *Death in the Form of a Rose* (1992) about the execution of rebel Pier Paolo Pasolini by the 'establishment'. The same philosophy of theatre informs cause-oriented plays, like Tanghalang Bayan's *Hukumang Tuwad* (*Kangaroo Court*, 1971),

Bien Aligtad by Don de los Reyes, directed by Joel Lamangan.

Peryante's *Ilokula, ang Ilocanong Drakula* (*Ilokula, the Ilocano Dracula*, 1980), Negros Theatre League's *Sakada* (*Seasonal Worker*, 1983) and Kaliwat Theatre Collective's *Siak sa Duha Ka Dango* (*Crack in Two Dreams*, 1992).

Committed to the exposition of Filipino characters, situations, issues and conflicts from the lowest to the highest rungs of society and responding sensitively to the major political, economic and social upheavals of post-war Philippine society, contemporary plays have developed unique dramatic styles that draw from the traditions of international and local theatre in order to communicate insights more effectively to both urban and rural audiences. Thus is Philippine theatre slowly coming into its own and beginning to fulfil the most basic expectations of a national theatre.

Directing and Acting

Two kinds of directors may be distinguished in Philippine theatre: the traditional and the modern. The *komedya*, *sinakulo*, *sarswela* and *drama* director may be looked at together because in all cases they choose scripts, work with the principal sponsors, identify the lead actors and run the whole production with a crew of friends, relatives or *barrio* mates. This type of director does not interpret the play in any real way but simply stages it. The director teaches the actors how to deliver the *komedya dicho*, *sinakulo chant* or *sarswela/drama*

dialogue, how to execute the marches and what gestures and movements to do on stage. The director also oversees the building of the sets, the painting of *telones*, the acquisition of props, the creation of magical artifices and the rental, placement and handling of lights and sounds. The director chooses or approves the designs of costumes. During the performance, the director checks on all backstage requirements, gives cues to the *telonero* for the changing of backdrops and props and to the band for the marches to be played or to the orchestra for the start of another song. Often he also prompts from behind a curtain or in a *concha* (shell) in front of the stage. The director may also be the author of the play, the impresario-producer or an actor as well as the head of the actors' organization and counsellor-friend to its members. This director then is a transmitter of tradition rather than an artist expressing a personal vision, a pillar of the community fulfilling an annual social commitment to the *barrio*.

With the advent of modern plays in urban centres, especially after World War II, a new kind of director took over the helm of play production. Schooled in theatre or art institutions in the west (most often in the United States) or trained in local workshops and performances, these directors became recognized as the principal artists in a production, controlling visionaries who create their own interpretations of plays, and who conceptualize and orchestrate all elements of the play to express their own vision and emotion. Often autocratic, they decide on the editing or rewriting of a script, cast the play, supervise every stage of rehearsal, approve the design of sets, costumes and lights, and pull the play together before opening night. In school productions, they even have to plan and check on the content of the program and talk to possible sponsors.

Among the important modern directors and the companies they founded are Severino Montano and his Arena Theatre, Wilfrido Ma Guerrero and his UP Dramatic Club and UP Mobile Theatre, James B Reuter, S.J and the Ateneo Players Guild, Lamberto V. Avellana and Daisy Hontiveros-Avellana and their Barangay Theatre Guild, Nick Agudo and his Chamber Theatre (from the 1950s to the 1960s), Onofre Pagsanghan and Dulaang Sibol, Zeneida Amador and Repertory Philippines, Cecile Guidote-Alvarez and PETA, Rolando Tinio and the Teatro Pilipino, Behn Cervantes and UP Repertory Company, Tony Mabesa and the Dulaang UP, Tony Espejo and Bulwagang Gantimpala, Amelia Lapeña-Bonifacio and Teatrong Mulatng Pilipinas, and Nonon Padilla and Tanghalang Pilipino from the 1960s to the 1990s.

The 1970s and 1980s witnessed the directorial débuts of Jonas Sebastian, Anton Juan, Jr, Lutgardo Labad, Joel Lamangan, Soxy Topacio, Chris Millado and Jorge Ledesma in Manila; and Leo Rimando, Joonee Gamboa, Frank Rivera, Karl Gaspar, Nestor Horfilla, Ed Defensor, Amiel Leonardia, Rudolfo Galenzoga and Steven Patrick Fernandez in the regions.

Acting for traditional dramas implies mastering a set of fixed conventions for the *bida*, (hero/heroine) and *kontrabida* (villain/antagonist). In the *sinakulo*, the *banal* (holy people) chant in lamentative tones, march to funeral beat and move like lambs, while the *hudyo* (Jews and Roman alike) perform a crisp chant, swagger to a lively *pasadoble* and move pompously about. In the *komedya*, the Christians and Moors alike walk grandly to the *marcha* or buoyantly to a *pasadoble* and deliver the *dicho* in sing-song manner with appropriate gestures. Christians, however, are distinguished for their chivalry and fairness while the Moors are despised for their tyranny and cowardice. In the *sarswela* and *drama*, the heroine is invariably pure, obedient and all-suffering, the hero kind, gentlemanly and self-sacrificing, while the villains are modern, scheming and selfish. Comedians in traditional plays (e.g. the *komedya*, jester, the *sarswela* servant) are devoted to wit, wine and women. In all, traditional acting is the external manifestation of thought and emotion through the correct execution of gestures and movements.

In modern theatre, one major style of acting that came with realistic plays was the naturalistic style evolved by Stanislavski, which was later developed in Lee Strasberg's method-acting and Eric Norris's *Acting is Being*. This is the type of acting employed for all realistic plays, whether it be Tennessee Williams's *Glass Menagerie* in Filipino or Nick Joaquin's *Portrait of the Artist as Filipino*.

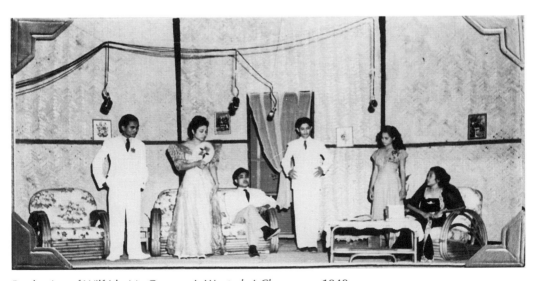

Production of Wilfrido Ma Guerrero's *Wanted: A Chaperone*, 1948.

For non-realistic styles, the Brechtian style of acting has been adopted, requiring actors to play a character, not become the character, so that they can maintain a critical distance between them, the audience and the ideas propounded by the play. Not absolute, the Brechtian style has been adapted to the many genres of pedagogical theatre. Sometimes the style is pushed towards the absurd as in *Propesor Tuko*, or towards Broadway-type showmanship as in *Bien Aligtad*, or towards Greek choral seriousness as in *Pagsambang Bayan*, or to *bodabil* mountebank vociferation as in *Ilokula*.

Music Theatre
Dance Theatre

For a discussion of music and dance, see the opening, historical section and **Artistic Profile**.

Theatre for Young Audiences
Puppet Theature

Children's theatre includes both the plays performed by children for children and plays mounted by adults for children. The first may be done by school, community or professional groups. School-based groups are organizations like the Ateneo Children's Theatre, which has produced annual plays for children for decades, and St Scholastica's College-Manila's Children and Teachers Theatre, which uses theatre as a medium of instruction for social studies courses in the different grades. Community-based groups are those found in urban poor areas, like Smokey

PETA Metropolitan Teen Theatre League's 1993 Mobile Theatre Season production of *Ambon ng Kristal*. Photo: Bing Concepcion.

Mountain, which educates audiences of all ages about children's issues, and those sponsored by non-government organizations, like Children's Rehabilitation Programme which helps children victimized by political and social violence.

Run by a professional theatre group, the PETA Children's Theatre Workshops held in summer teach children creative movement, dance, visual arts, writing and drama improvisation. These activities are aimed at dramatizing themes from history and contemporary society, using legends, games, radio plays and other cultural forms. Plays mounted by adults for children may be school-based or professional. Inside and outside the University of the Philippines, UP Repertory has staged Amelia Lapeña-Bonifacio's *Ang Manok at ang Lawin* (*The Hen and the Hawk*) and *Kung Paano Pinatay ng mga Ibaloé ang Higante* (1974), while UP's Sining Kabataan has done productions like *Tikbalang* (1989) and *Munting Mithi* (*Small Wishes*, 1990).

Professional companies like Tanghalang Pilipino, Teatrong Mulat ng Pilipinas, Black Theatre and Anino-Papet Collective combine actors and puppets in their productions. Tanghalang Pilipino has produced and toured children's plays based on folklore, like Bienvenido Portugal's *Korido* (*Metrical Romance*, 1987) and *Bidasari* (1988). Amelia Lapeña-Bonifacio's Teatrong Mulat uses puppets inspired by *wayang kulit*, *wayang golek* and *bunraku* to dramatize Philippine folk tales, like *Abadeja, ang Ating Sinderella* (*Abadeja, Our Cinderella*, 1977), *Ang Pagong at ang Tsonggo* (*The Turtle and the Monkey*, 1980) and *Si Suan, si Suan* (*Suan, Suan*, 1983) as well

Papet sa Pasko (c.1980) by Amelia Lapeña-Bonifacio.

as long narratives, like the *Papet Pasyon* (*Passion Puppets*, 1985), which adapts both the passion play and the *pasyon* (verse narratives on the life of Jesus Christ).

Black Theatre is a black light company which uses hand-puppets, string, puppets and muppets for works like *Bernardo Carpio*, *Awit ng Adarna* and *Mariang Alimango*. Being part of the Philippine Information Agency, the company, directed by Lolit Aquino, usually works with developmental themes, like responsible parenthood and good dental care.

ANINO-Shadow Play Collective of the Philippine High School for the Arts is an experimental group that creates a wealth of images through rear-projection, candle-shadows, hand and body movements or overhead projectors, as well as muppets and puppets to interpret music like Yoyoy Villame's *Buchikik*, *Magellan* and other songs.

Design
Theatre Space and Architecture

Indigenous rituals and dances have never required a special stage and were simply performed on the ground, in a house, in a field or near a river with the community either following the performers or just gathering around them. Even in Spanish period pueblos, religious playlets were dramatized on the streets, like the *panunuluyan* and *via crucis*, or in church, like the *paghuhugas* and *siete palabras*, or in front of or near the church, like the *osana* and *salubong*.

Formal dramas, however, demanded a special place for performance. The *komedya* needed a big stage, with acting area in front and

dressing area at the back, divided by a permanent structure of bamboo or wood. The structure, which has one or two levels, is usually designed on stage to represent a castle and has an entrance on stage right for Christian characters and another stage left for Moors. On the second level is a balcony, from which the royalty watches the tournament which is part of the production. On this set, scenes are identified through props; a carved chair at the centre indicates a throne room, a potted plant in a corner a garden, a free-standing cage a prison, an opening at centre ground level a cave in a forest.

Teatro de Binondo, a Spanish period theatre in Manila, c.1855.

The stage for the *sinakulo*, *sarswela* and *drama* is framed by a series of side panels or tormentors with matching teasers, going all the way back to the final and permanent backdrop which divides the acting from the dressing area. From behind the teasers roll down the *telones* or cloth backdrops painted with different settings; for the *sinakulo*, the interior of a palace, a mountain, the façade of a house, the city gates of Jerusalem; and for the *sarswela* and *drama*, the interior or exterior of a rich man's mansion or a poor man's hut, a country landscape. Props match the different telons, while a front curtain masks scene changes.

Illumination in all traditional stages is not so much for effect as for visibility. The modern theatre has experimented with different types of stages, among them the proscenium, the thrust and the arena. Most commonly used for the past century by school or commercial companies is the proscenium stage, with a front curtain, tormentors, teasers and cyclorama. Such is the Cultural Centre of the Philippines, Tanghalang Nicanor Abelardo and Tanghalang Aurelio Tolentino and Repertory Philippines' Shaw Theatre. The thrust stage is exemplified by the open-air Dulaang Raha Sulayman of the PETA, which is a T-shaped platform of cement surrounded by the ruins of old Fort Santiago. The arena theatre was popularized by Severino Montano who presented his plays in the round – in halls or rooms or the open air.

The arena style is often used by cause-oriented groups for performances in communities, strike areas and other open spaces. Some theatres, like CCP Tanghalang Huseng Batute, may be converted into an arena or thrust stage. On all these types of stages are built sets and props of different styles: realistic or stylized, elaborate or minimal, conventional or experimental. Like sets and props, costumes and lighting are designed to match the style and interpretation of individual plays.

Among the most creative contemporary set and costume designers are Rolando Tinio, Salvador Bernal, Amiel Leonardia, Ogie Juliano and Brenda Fajardo, while notable lighting designers include Teddy Hilado, Monino Duque, Katsch Catoy and Dennis Marasigan.

Training

In indigenous theatre and traditional dramas, performers are taught their craft simply by exposure to the rituals and dances. In the *komedya*, *sinakulo*, *sarswela* and *drama*, artists or technicians learn to declaim or chant verses, march and do battle, dance and sing, direct and write plays, paint backdrops and build mechanisms for magic by apprenticing with senior practitioners or at month-long rehearsals before a performance. Thus a young man may join the *komedya*, learn the techniques of verse-delivery, marching and fighting through many years of performing, become an assistant director or prompter, and eventually, upon the death or resignation of the old director, take over as director and manager of the group.

In modern theatre, there are more ways to train theatre artists. Campus or community theatre actors used to get their training only at rehearsals for specific productions. But now there are more opportunities for learning the art and craft of theatre. Theatre workshops, held for one to two months in summer and covering all aspects of productions: from writing to directing to acting to set and costume, lighting and music design are held regularly by theatre groups like PETA and Tanghalang Pilipino for basic, intermediate and advanced levels. Sometimes foreign artists like Fritz Bennewitz, Brooks Jones and Alex Moncleart visit the country to direct a production and conduct special workshops.

Formal training in the theatre has been instituted in academe. The College of Arts and Letters at the University of Philippines campus in Diliman now gives a BA, an MA and a

Certificate in Theatre Arts, with courses in directing, acting, stage management, voice, production work, stagecraft, scene design, stage lighting, makeup, playwriting, production design, technical theatre as well as Philippine theatre Asian theatre, western theatre and world theatre.

On the secondary level, the Philippine High School for the Arts has a programme in theatre arts which offers courses in acting, stagecraft, stage and production management, directing, history and theory. In all theatre schools, actual theatre practice is emphasized in almost all courses.

Criticism, Scholarship and Publishing

Drama criticism or the evaluation of the script and performances of plays by professional critics does not have a long or strong history in the country. At the turn of the century, journalists who were also creative writers would make short impressionistic comments on *komedya* or *sarswela* performances in newspaper articles or columns or even argue on the validity of these forms, as Severino Reyes and Isabelo de los Reyes did *c.*1904. In the English magazines of the 1920s and 1930s, university-bred Ignacio Manlapaz, Jean Edades and Francisco Icasiano reviewed plays and other cultural events held in mainly Manila's venues. In the 1950s and 1960s, performing arts critics included Morli Dharam, Jose Lardizabal, J. Zulueta di Costa and Rodrigo Perez III.

Since the 1980s, drama critics of note who have published reviews in newspapers and magazines include journalists Rosalinda Orosa and Mauro Avena, academicians Bienvenido Lumbera, S.V. Epistola, Doreen G. Fernandez and Nicanor G. Tiongson, and artists Leonor Orosa-Goquingco, Nestor U. Torre, Steve Villaruz, Pio de Castro III and Behn Cervantes. Because critics are often artists themselves and because most theatre artists know each other personally, criticism tends to be taken personally rather than objectively. Thus, critics have to walk a tightrope – to be honest without hurting feelings, to be encouraging without being familiar, to be fair without being cold.

Nicanor G. Tiongson

Further Reading

Aguila, Reuel Molina. *Ligalig at Iba Pang Dula*. Manila: Kalikasan Press, 1989.

Buenaventura, Cristina L. *The Theatre in Manila: 1846–1946*. Manila: De La Salle University Press, 1994.

Chua, Soo Pong, ed. *Traditional Theatre in Southeast Asia*. Singapore: SPAFA and Centre for the Arts of the National University of Singapore, 1995.

Cruz, Isagani, ed. *A Short History of Theatre in the Philippines*. Manila, 1971.

Fernandez, Doreen G., ed. *Contemporary Theatre Arts: Asia and the United States*. Quezon City: New Day Publishers, 1984.

——. *The Iloilo Zarzuela 1903–1930*. Quezon City: Ateneo de Manila University Press, 1978.

——. *In Performance*. Quezon City: Vera-Reyes, 1981.

——. *Palabas, Essays on Philippine Theatre History*. Quezon City: Ateneo de Manila University Press, 1996.

Florentino, Alberto S. *The World Is an Apple and Other Prize Plays*. Manila: Cultural Publishers, 1959.

Frenandez, Steven Patrick C. 'The San Miguel Fiesta Rituals of Iligan City: Correlations of Form, Function and Values'. MA thesis, University of the Philippines, 1985.

Guerrero, Wilfrido Ma. *My Favourite 11 Plays*. Manila: New Day Publishers, 1976.

Joaquin, Nick. *A Portrait of the Artist as Filipino*. Manila: Alberto Florentino, 1966.

Lapeña-Bonifacio, Amelia. *Ang Bundok at Iba Pang Dula*. Manila: De La Salle University Press, 1994.

Manlapaz, Edna Zapanta. *Aurelio Tolentino: Selected Writings*. Quezon City: University of the Philippines Press, 1975.

Mojares, Resil B. *Theatre in Society, Society in Theatre (Social History of a Cebuano Village 1840–1940)*. Quezon City: Ateneo de Manila University Press, 1985.

Noriega, Jr, Bienvenido M. *Bayan-Bayanan at Iba Pang Dula*. Manila: National Book Store, 1982.

Philippine Drama: Twelve Plays in Six Philippine Languages. Quezon City: NSTA-Assisted UPS Integrated Research Progress 'A', 1987.

Ramas, Wilhelmina Q. *Sugbuanon Theatre from Sotto to Rodriguez and Kabahar (An Introduction to Pre-War Sugbuanon Drama)*. Quezon City: Asian Center, University of the Philippines, 1982.

Realubit, Lilia F. 'The Bicol Dramatic Tradition'. *Philippine Social Science and Humanities Review* 31 (March–July 1976).

Riggs, Arthur Stanley. *The Filipino Drama [1903]*. Manila: Intramuros Administration, 1981.

Sebastian, Federico. *Ang Dulang Tagalog*. Manila: BBS Silangan Publishing House, 1955.

Sikat, Rogelio *et al. Tatlo sa Tanghalau*. Manila: Kalikasan Press, 1990.

Tiongson, Nicanor G. *Kasaysayan at Estetika ng Sinakulo at Ibang Dulang Panrelihiyon sa Malolos*. Quezon City: Ateneo de Manila University Press, 1975.

——. *Kasaysayan ng Komedya sa Pilipinas: 1706–1982*. Manila: De La Salle University Press, 1982.

——. *Pilipinas Circa 1907*. Quezon City: Philippine Educational Theatre Association, 1985.

——. *What is Philippine Drama?* Theatre Studies 1: Quezon City: Philippine Educational Theatre Association, 1983.

——. ed. *Modern ASEAN Plays: Philippines*. With scripts in English translation of Al Santos' *Sistema ni Propesor Tuko*, Rene O. Villanueva's *Hiblang Abo*, Tony Perez's *On North Diversion Road* and Malou Jacob's *Juan Tamban*. Manila: ASEAN COCI, 1992.

POLYNESIA

(see **SOUTH PACIFIC**)

POLYNESIE FRANÇAISE

(see **SOUTH PACIFIC** (French Polynesia))

REPUBLIC OF CHINA

(see **CHINA**)

SIAM

(see **THAILAND**)

SINGAPORE

(Overview)

An island nation of 640 square kilometres (250 square miles) located between the South China Sea and the Indian Ocean south of the Malaysian mainland and east of Indonesian Sumatra, Singapore in 1945 was not a separate political entity but rather the capital of the British Straits Settlements, which had become a crown colony in 1867. In 1946, Singapore became a crown colony in its own right, yet was not to acquire its own civil service until 1954.

Granted internal self-government status in 1959 under the leadership of Prime Minister Lee Kuan Yew, Singapore gained independence as part of the Federation of Malaysia in 1963, and two years later, following its withdrawal from the Federation of Malaysia, became a fully independent republic. The country now has four main and very independent language communities – English, the most dominant; Mandarin with its cultural roots in China; Tamil with its roots in India; and Malay, once dominant but with independence, now a minority. The 1995 population of Singapore was 2.9 million.

Any attempt at an historical overview of the Singapore theatre must perforce begin with a recognition of the multifarious complexities that such an enterprise confronts. In his widely respected study of the history of Singapore, C.M. Turnbull (1977) notes:

It is difficult to see that any 'standard' history of Singapore can be written for some time to come, since the diversity of cultural background and experience is so great that no foreigner or Singaporean of any one community can speak for the society as a whole.

It is precisely these diversities – cultural, religious, ethnic, linguistic – that problematize the study of Singapore theatre and its history.

To begin with, it is unhelpful to speak in terms of a Singapore 'theatre', for theatrical activity has taken place over the island nation's history, and continues to take place, in each of Singapore's main languages. In addition, as the prominent English-language dramatist and critic Robert Yeo (1982) has noted, theatrical activity and enterprise within each of the language streams has been firmly compartmentalized:

While some exchange of production and acting talent takes place between groups in the same language, there is little or none between languages. The staging of plays in the Malay, Mandarin and Tamil languages goes on separately in terms of acting/production personnel and audience. For example, a Tamil dance drama engages largely Tamil producers, cast and audience, unrelieved by the fact that the Tamil producer, actor or member of the audience may also speak another language.

This 'other' language to which Yeo refers is, typically, English – the language of the colonial power, the language of administration, the professions and, almost exclusively, the language of education, with a specific and relatively limited number of hours a week allotted for instruction in the 'mother' tongues. English is thus taking on an increasing cultural importance and is rapidly becoming an adoptive 'first' language for an increasingly large number of Singaporeans. Thus we have the case that, while theatrical activity in the other languages is predominantly local and confined to specific ethnic groups, theatre in English takes place across language and ethnicity, bringing together Singaporeans of all races and including, in addition to English-speaking and English-educated Singaporeans, an expatriate contribution stemming largely from the British and United States communities in Singapore.

Given this complex scenario, it is more precise therefore to speak, not of a Singapore 'theatre' but rather of Singapore 'theatres'. As an extension of this situation, it is simply not possible, both in view of the necessarily synoptic nature of this article as well as of the diversities outlined by Turnbull, to attempt a history of theatrical activity in Singapore that provides fair and comprehensive coverage of all the available traditions and histories.

What will be essayed, therefore, is a concise overview of the English-language theatre in Singapore with some additional information added to provide a greater sense of context. There are a number of factors that render this choice, given the limits of the present volume, ineluctable. First, while recognizing the solid achievements of theatrical work in other language streams, it is the English language theatre that has travelled the furthest afield and, on the current record, achieved the widest degree of international exposure. Given the status of English as an international language, it is this theatre, bringing together as it does Singaporeans of all ethnicities and creatively harnessing the nations' cultural diversity, which is likely to have the most impact in future and break through to the international scene.

Second, whatever the historical suspicions directed against English as a non-indigenous tongue, the language of a former colonial oppressor, and as an agent of certain western values perceived as inappropriate, even perniciously subversive of Asian identity, the fact of the matter remains that English has long functioned as the 'link' language connecting Singapore's different ethnic and cultural groupings. Further to this, the government's commitment to and establishment of English as the language of education at all levels has made it inevitable that English will eventually become the adoptive 'first language' for the majority of Singaporeans and therefore, in the spirit if not in the letter of the phrase, a 'native tongue'. The necessary corollary of this is that in the contexts of poetry, fiction and the drama, that is to say in

those areas of the imaginative and creative life of the nation dependent on language, English will come to play an increasingly prominent role.

A final consideration that has impelled the choice of focus on the English-language theatre is that the relatively meagre historical source material and documentation that exist tend to favour the English-language theatre. While some materials are available for the historical study of theatre in other language streams, the dependence on oral history in this latter connection would be severe. There exist, in the Malay, Mandarin and Tamil language streams practitioners – critics, dramatists, directors and actors – capable of reaching out to a collective memory; but to do justice to all of them would involve a time-frame and demand a space that the exigencies of this framework render inoperable. It is important to recognize at the outset, however, that important work has been done and continues to be done in the other language streams. And the one way in which this can be recognized is to direct the interested scholar or reader to the important figures in these streams.

The early history of the Singapore theatre in English c.1945 and through the fifteen years that followed is, in large part, a prehistory. English-language drama meant, primarily, the amateur theatrical activities of British colonial residents and members of the British armed forces service clubs. Among these groups were the Island Players, active in the 1950s, and the Royal Air Force Seletar Theatre Club. The longest lasting, the most eminent and prolific of the expatriate theatre groups, however, was the Stage Club, which was still active in the late 1980s. Formed in 1945, shortly after the end of World War II, the Stage Club was active in amateur theatricals till the end of 1949, when it suspended operations under its own banner to assist a newly formed but short-lived group called Singapore Repertory. Reactivated in 1951, the Stage Club commenced production and has maintained a steady stream of dramatic performance.

The club's productions for the 1945–9 period included Shakespeare's *Twelfth Night*, George Bernard Shaw's *Pygmalion*, *Arsenic and Old Lace*, Oscar Wilde's *The Importance of Being Earnest* and Agatha Christie's *And Then There Were None*, as well as regular Christmas pantomimes – works that are a useful index to the group's aesthetic and ideological preferences. The productions centred, and continue to centre, on the classic repertoire: Shakespeare,

Restoration drama, Wilde, Shaw, Terrence Rattigan, J.B. Priestley, Noël Coward, Christopher Fry, Christie mysteries, farces, pantomime and musical comedy. Forays have been made into more experimental work but the results have usually been uncomfortable.

This is, of course, not Singapore drama, but prehistory. If locals participated at all, their characteristic positions would be as backstage help, general factotum, and the occasional token stage presence: the local in a minor role, analogous to the presence of the working classes in British drama in the 1940s and 1950s prior to the emergence of John Osborne in 1956. Production, direction and major roles remained firmly in the hands of expatriate talent. It is a situation that persists into the 1990s. The Island Players are also usefully illustrative of the state of play during this period. In 1956 the group presented, at the Victoria Memorial Hall, *Princess Chrysanthemum: A Japanese Operetta for Children, with Ballet.* Playing the title role was, of course, an expatriate: Kitty McGinlay.

Such conditions were perhaps inevitable, given the historical and political circumstances. And naturally enough, audiences were largely expatriate. The legacy of such groups has been complex: they gave the English-educated Singaporeans of the time their shaping, formative exposure to theatre. They provided 'role models', as it were, for the possibilities of theatrical art and enterprise. Crucially, they entrenched conventions of structure, dramatic language, speech register and accent, norms of action, setting and characterization, which historically have generated the central critical and creative problems confronting all those working for the development of an indigenous English-language theatre for Singaporeans and by Singaporeans, a theatre that negotiated in English with the particularities of indigenous reality and experience.

It is within this early matrix of a theatre largely catering to the tastes of, serving and serviced by, a colonial expatriate community, with locals essentially a marginalized presence, that the first stirrings of and movements towards an authentically Singaporean theatre may be detected. While the general perception is that the Singapore theatre has its beginnings in the early 1960s, the fact is that the breaking of ground, the laying of the first foundations had already begun in the late 1940s and continued into the 1950s.

The most important early work, on all available evidence and documentation, was carried out by Singaporeans working in the education service. Two crucial bodies in this connection were the Singapore Teachers' Union and a related organization known as the Teachers' Repertory. The importance of the Singapore Teachers' Union can hardly be overstressed, as it was responsible for initiating and nurturing the growth of drama in Singapore schools. It sponsored the first of Singapore's Youth Drama and Music Festival, which are now a feature of the current scene. This first festival was inaugurated in 1950 at the Victoria Theatre. As early as 1950, therefore, we find the organizing committee noting in the festival programme 'we believe that the foundations of Malayan Drama and Music have to be laid in our schools, and Youth Groups'. Entries for the drama section of the festival were dominated by foreign works, but they did include some of the earliest documented examples of indigenous writing for the local stage: *Christmas in Endau* by Seah Yun Chong was performed as the Raffles Institution senior play, *Getting a House* by W.H. Ponniah as the St Andrew's School intermediate play and David Tan's *The April Fools* as the Presbyterian Boys' School entry in the senior section.

The body known as Teachers' Repertory was an offshoot organization of the Singapore Teachers' Union, founded in 1947 and run by the drama section of the union. It defined itself as 'a non-profit cultural organization which gives special attention to developing interest in the theatre among students', and its membership included a 'junior repertory' section for students. The group ran practical drama classes in 1947 and 1948, providing local students with training in production, stage management and acting. Their programme also envisaged the establishment of a costume wardrobe, a library of acting editions of plays and stocks of props and fittings, with the intention of making these available to schools and drama clubs. Among the most active in Teachers' Repertory were Tung Muh Shih, H. Hochstadt, Leslie Woodford, Seow Cheng Fong, C.V. Devan Nair and Philip Liau, many of whom went on to positions of prominence in education, politics and the civil service. The more prominent include Liau, for many years principal of Raffles Institution and the inspiration behind what remains the most eminent of school drama groups, the Raffles Players; and perhaps most notable, Devan Nair, a past president of Singapore. Probably the most steeped and professionally equipped in the craft of theatre, however, was Tung, a teacher at St Andrew's

School, who became chair of Teachers' Repertory in 1947. Tung received his early training with the Crocker Company, Bourton-on-the-Water, UK, and took part in the Bath Drama Festival in 1939, which was disrupted by the outbreak of the war.

There were predictable limits, however, to the achievements of Teachers' Repertory, and to its vision of a Singaporean theatre. The record of its activities outlined above speaks eloquently for its significance, and it was perhaps the first indigenous body to articulate the need for the infrastructural development of the theatre and for a coordinating body to facilitate inter-group cooperation, the pooling of resources and the establishment of an umbrella grouping that could speak on behalf of all groups to the government. In a message printed in the programme for its 1948 production of *Macbeth*, Teachers' Repertory noted

> it is plain that theatre is an important living art form here. It lives however under difficulties, which might be made less if there was a recognized body able to speak on behalf of those who work for the growth of this living Malayan drama.

In practice, however, 'living Malayan drama' was largely confined to English-educated locals performing Shakespeare and the classic British repertoire, with no exposure being given to indigenous dramatic writing. This was despite the fact that the inaugural Youth Drama and Music Festival also included, in its programme, a playwriting competition with the express purpose of gathering 'new plays with Malayan background suitable for use in Malayan schools and on the Malayan stage'. In addition, major productions, although performed with local actors occupying all major roles, were regularly directed by David Lyttle, a Briton with professional theatre experience working as a broadcaster in Singapore.

In addition to the Singapore Teachers' Union and Teachers' Repertory, no account of early efforts to indigenize the English-language theatre can ignore the pioneering work of the Raffles Society of the University of Malaya (in Singapore) and the University of Malaya in Singapore Dramatic Society. Founded in 1950, the Raffles Society displayed a strong awareness of the problems facing the development of a theatre in English in Singapore. In 1952, it mounted a Festival of Drama, which ran from 25 to 28 February, at the university's Oei Tiong Ham Hall. In the festival programme, the society's president, Jamit Singh, argued that the festival represented 'the first time a serious attempt is being made to foster interest in and promote local drama'. He went on to note, 'by drawing attention to plays with Oriental setting we are giving expression to and stimulating interest in the cosmopolitan richness of our country. It is by efforts like these that a Malayan drama will evolve; for out of the contact with drama of this nature will our young writers be carried into Malayan life and spurred into creating drama that is relevant to cultural synthesis'.

Whatever qualifications need to be made to the society's claims to being 'first', Singh's introduction to the festival offerings articulates an embryonic ideology for a truly indigenous theatre and bears implicitly the conviction that it is the English-language theatre that functions as a vehicle for a unified national culture. The festival gave centre stage, literally and metaphorically, to work in Asian traditions, but performed in English. Items included Rabindranath Tagore's *Sacrifice*; a Chinese drama entitled *Mulan (The Warrior Woman)*, *Laksamana Hang Tuah*, a Malay drama based on the exploits of quasi-legendary Malay warriors and heroes, and *Pathmini*, an original drama in English written by Tse-Kwang Hsu and directed by Lam Khuan Kit. The programme's description of this latter work describes the drama as 'a play of symbols. Its characters represent entities beyond themselves. They stretch far beyond the confines of this stage to embrace the wider realms of a new Malayan ideology – the concept of nationhood'.

The University of Malaya Dramatic Society, that is to say the student drama group of the university, which later came to be known as the University of Singapore Drama Society and then as Varsity Playhouse, took up preoccupations and themes similar to those of the Raffles Society. As its contribution to the Variety Concert held in conjunction with the golden jubilee celebrations of the University of Malaya in 1955, the University of Malaya Dramatic Society presented perhaps the earliest example on record of the adaptation of a foreign text to indigenous settings in search of a theatre of relevance. The play was entitled *Medicine Without Effort*, and described as 'a Malayanized version of Molière's *Physician in Spite of Himself*'. In 1958, the group broke more new ground with the staging of excerpts of a locally written piece by Lloyd Fernando entitled *Strangers at the Gates*, which offers a study of Singaporean society on the eve of its achievement of internal self-government.

Taken together, the groups and their various activities outlined might be said to represent the first phase of the Singapore theatre in English, a transitional period in which prehistory gradually starts to be challenged by history. What was developed by the end of the 1950s was an initial, tentative momentum which, as Singapore turned the corner into the 1960s, was seized upon and consolidated by three groups: Centre '65, the Experimental Theatre Club and the University of Singapore Society. Taken together, these three groups harnessed the most active and potent energies of a nascent tradition and made the most significant contributions to the identity of the Singapore theatre in its second phase – that of the 1960s and 1970s.

Inaugurated in 1965, Centre '65 described itself as a multiracial organization dedicated to nurturing the growth of a national culture and of the arts in Singapore. In a programme note to its production of Arthur Miller's *A View From the Bridge* held at the Cultural Centre in September 1965, the society's president, Lim Kok Ann, wrote 'we are striving towards establishing a group comprising our own playwrights, writers, directors, actors, artists, set designers'. A shaping principle was the need to get beyond traditional performance venues such as the Victoria Memorial Hall, Victoria Theatre and Cultural Centre (all three still in operation, with the last refurbished and renamed the Drama Centre) and to mount productions in schools, community centres and other available public spaces.

The group's activities were diverse, and not confined solely to drama. It held talks, readings of poetry by local writers, forums on such subjects as 'The Role of the Malaysian Writer In Our Society', exhibitions of paintings by local artists, as well as drama productions. In this latter context, plays performed by Centre '65 included work by Miller, Santha Rama Rau's adaptation of E.M. Forster's modernist classic novel, *A Passage To India* and, most importantly, brought to the stage the work of one of the pioneer writers of English dramatic writing in Singapore, Goh Poh Seng, including his plays *When Smiles Are Done* and *The Elder Brother*, the former presented in 1965 and the latter in 1966. While admittedly flawed in structure and style, and bearing the obvious marks of an apprentice playwright, Goh's full-length pieces courageously placed the particularities of local experience upon the stage and helped bring into focus one of the dominating themes of dramatic writing in the 1960s and 1970s: the conflict between Asian traditions and values on the one hand, and the forces of western modernization and liberal individualism on the other, as exemplified in the motif of the English-educated Singaporean, struggling to cope with a sense of increasing isolation and deracinating within a still largely traditionalist socio-political matrix. Goh's programme notes to the 1966 production of *The Elder Brother* give a clear account of his position. He argued:

A nation which ignores and does not encourage its theatre is, if not culturally dead, culturally pitiable; just as the theatre which ignores the drama of its people and fails to register their trials as well as their triumphs, their tears and their laughter, has little right to call itself a national theatre, but merely an amusement hall, a place for those who attend merely to kill time.

Goh's firm commitment to the evolution of an authentically national theatrical movement was not, in fact, the first voice to be heard in the 1960s. That distinction, historically speaking, belongs to Lim Chor Pee, who worked under the aegis of the Experimental Theatre Club, which was founded in 1961 with an express commitment to new and experimental work, to the presentation of modern Asian theatre, and the nurturing of a Singapore theatre in English. Following its inaugural production, in 1962, *Thunderstorm*, by the Chinese playwright Cao Yu, the club went on to present two plays by Lim, the first of these being *Mimi Fan*, mounted in 1962 and the second entitled *A White Rose at Midnight* in 1964. Robert Yeo's description in 1982 of these plays as 'probably the first conscious attempts to demonstrate that it was possible to create a Singaporean theatre in English' may overstate the case slightly, but Lim's status as a major pioneering figure is unquestionable, and in addition, the protagonists of both his plays exemplify and incarnate, in their struggles, the themes of psycho-cultural conflict that Goh Poh Seng was later to refine. Lim Chor Pee's search, as Yeo (1982) notes, was for 'a relevant theatre – a theatre that thematically reflects Singapore concerns, and whose characters and castings reflect the multi-racial Singapore reality'. Yeo continues:

As a playwright, he created in *Mimi Fan* (1962) and *A White Rose at Midnight* (1964), with varying success, Singaporean characters:

the bar-girl Mimi Fan, the night club singer Wong Ching Mei, the disillusioned Chan Fei Loong, summoned home from England to manage the family business, the materialistic playboy Wong Fook Seng, the dilettante Baram, the idealistic student leader Muthu ... the bar-hopping colonial Tony Maxwell, the gung-ho Voice of America correspondent Dan Heyworth, to mention just these.

And the playwright himself (Lim Chor Pee 1964) went on record to argue that

One of the factors that has retarded the establishment of an English-speaking theatre in this country is that almost every play that is produced here is some superficial piece of western drawing-room drama. After awhile it gets very boring because theatre is essentially a reflection of truth and not the false and unattainable dreams of the western middle-class.

With the presentation of Lim's plays by the Experimental Theatre Club commencing in the early 1960s, it is clear that a new phase was beginning for the indigenous theatre, for Lim was the harbinger not merely of a more aggressive ideological thrust directed against a dominating anglo-centricity; he also ushered in a period when the full-length play written by a Singaporean would begin to stake a claim to the Singapore stage. The Experimental Theatre Club complemented its work on behalf of an indigenous output with productions of work drawn from the modern European and United States theatre. But it also continued to do important work, as the 1960s gave way to the 1970s, with indigenous dramatic writing. In 1972 it presented Ron Chandran-Dudley's *Trace the Rainbow Through the Rain* and Kiru Joseph's *No Waitresses*, and also presented three plays by one of the most eminent of the Malaysian dramatists writing in English, Lee Joo For, *Do You Know That Jesus Was Black?*, *Bread and Blood* and *Chabaran: The Challenge*. But perhaps its landmark production for the 1970s was *The Sword Has Two Edges*, by Li Lien Fung (Mrs R.H. Ho). A prominent novelist, poet and essayist writing primarily in Chinese with a readership extending to Hong Kong and Taiwan, Li wrote the play in English, though its setting is ancient China, developing it from a story in the classical Chinese epic *The Romance of the Three Kingdoms*. The play, exploring the themes of passion, political intrigue and divided loyalties in the imperial Chinese court, was directed by D. Murugan and performed at the Cultural Centre in 1977. It also broke new ground in its fusion of elements of classic Chinese theatre – settings, costumes and subject matter – and the techniques of western realism in acting, dialogue and the probing of individual psychology. The production played to packed houses and was an important refutation of the prejudice, still current at the time, that audiences for indigenous drama were limited to coterie groups.

Consolidating the challenge of the indigenous theatre in the 1960s and 1970s was the University of Singapore Society, the organization for graduates of the university. In the 1960s the society concentrated primarily on experimental work in the Anglo-American theatre, but in the 1970s brought Robert Yeo, the third of Singapore's pioneer dramatic figures, to the fore. Yeo's *Are You There, Singapore?*, the title of which succinctly suggests the play's concern with identity and the search for rootedness, was presented at the Cultural Centre in 1974. Directed by Prem Kumar, the play broke all box-office records for a theatre performance in Singapore. Yeo's *One Year Back Home*, the second play in what the dramatist projected will be a dramatic trilogy of Singaporean life, developed the themes of the first work and included a satire on politics in Singapore. The play was directed by Max Le Blond and was performed, again to a packed house, at the Development Bank of Singapore Auditorium in 1980.

Looking back from this distance, it may be seen that the 1960s and 1970s were crucial, 'breakthough' decades for the English-language theatre in Singapore. They witnessed the emergence of dramatic and cultural groupings that provided a sustained focus for the energies dedicated to an indigenous theatre and which, while welcoming and accommodating expatriate talent, broke away from the dependence on expatriate leadership. It was in these decades that an ideology of Singapore theatre – a theatre for Singaporeans and by Singaporeans – was articulated and explored with greater thoroughness and depth, and the constrictive potential of allegiance to western convention confronted. And most importantly, these were the decades of the emergence of full-length drama by Singaporeans on to the local stage. Audiences were created; the first serious challenges to colonialist and neo-colonialist assumptions about valid theatre were raised; and playwrights, engaged with the concrete task of transferring the words of their scripts into enacted, performance art were learning first-hand about the insidious power of long-established conventions of dramatic language, valid accent and thematics.

If the foregoing suggests a roseate hue to the image of the Singapore theatre entering the last two decades of the millennium, the impression should be corrected immediately. Though the output of dramatic writing has increased, the Singapore theatre continues to be dominated and sustained largely by productions of foreign plays. Centre '65 is defunct; the Drama Committee of the University of Singapore Society, now renamed the National University of Singapore Society, has devoted its energies to the production of European operettas, at a cost of roughly US$100,000 per production; while audiences are increasing they remain to a significant extent the preserve of a middle-class intelligentsia whose standards and images of success tend towards the West End or Broadway 'smash hit'.

The Experimental Theatre Club, under the directorial leadership of Chandran K. Lingam, who first came to prominence as an undergraduate director working out of the University of Singapore Drama Society in the early 1970s, has continued its commitment to experimental work. With Lingam at the helm as its major creative and directorial energy, the club has produced most of the finest work available in Singapore theatre, productions such as *Boesman and Lena* and, in 1986, Mtwa, Ngema and Simon's *Woza Albert!* If there are regrets, they lie primarily in what appears to be Lingam's constitutional inability to apply and exercise his formidable creativity in any engagement with local material. The result of this is that the club's later experimental work has largely taken place in connection with non-indigenous material.

On the positive side, consciousness of the possibilities of indigenous material has definitely been established and needs now to be consolidated and sustained. Both Goh Poh Seng and Lim Chor Pee have been silent in theatrical terms for several decades, and while Robert Yeo is still working, younger, newer writers have been productive. Interest in playwriting has markedly increased as witnessed by the entries to drama writing competitions organized in the late 1970s and early 1980s by the Ministry of Culture. Work by Singaporean dramatists has also begun to travel. In 1986, for example, Yeo's *One Year Back Home* was performed as a staged reading in New York under the auspices of the La MaMa Experimental Theatre Club. Also in 1986, a satiric dramatic monologue

entitled *No Parking On Odd Days* by the writer-dramaturge Kuo Pao Kun was performed at the Hong Kong Festival of Arts. Stella Kon's *Emily of Emerald Hill: A Monodrama*, first prize winner of the Ministry of Culture's drama writing competition for 1983, became the hit of Singapore's 1985 Drama Festival, went on to represent Singapore at the Commonwealth Arts Festival in Edinburgh in 1986, and was subsequently invited to perform at the Edinburgh Festival Fringe the same year.

The Singapore theatre of the 1990s has also witnessed the emergence of a fledgling professional theatre, and three groups warrant notice in this connection. In 1984, the first group to commit itself to professional careers in theatre emerged. This was Act Three, originally comprised of three members, as their name suggests: R. Chandran, Jasmin Samat Simon and Ruby Lim-Yang. Act Three, now enlarged to a core group of five members, specializes in children's theatre, performing regularly in schools as well as in private homes as part of their concept of 'living-room theatre'.

The second of a total of three professional groups is Singapore Theatre's American Repertory Showcase (STARS). Led by Maria Wheeler, Roger Jenkins and Christina Sargent, STARS was active in the amateur theatre in the early 1980s, working to a large extent with expatriate talent with input from a number of Singaporeans. Since turning professional in late 1986, the group has done valuable work providing training in the theatre arts for Singapore youth, and has conducted a series of drama workshops which they hoped would lead to the setting up of a national youth theatre.

The third professional group, by far the one with the greatest potential contribution to make to the Singapore theatre is Theatreworks, established in 1985 by a group of Singaporeans with the principal objective of mounting 'fully-fledged as well as financially self-sustaining productions for the stage'. Another aim as defined in the programme of the company's first production, *Be My Sushi Tonight*, an adaptation to local contexts of British dramatist Mike Leigh's *Goosepimples*, held at the World Trade Centre Auditorium in 1985, is 'to sow the seeds for truly relevant and meaningful English-language drama'. In practice, however, the decision to earn a living through full-time commitment to professional theatre imposes limits on its ability to take risks with new, experimental, indigenous materials. While Theatreworks commands some of the best acting, production and technical talent, including professionally trained actor-directors Lim Kay Tong and Lim Siauw Chong, it has yet to work out a fully convincing strategy for the second of its stated objectives. What remains to be said as the Singapore theatre moves into the closing years of the 1990s is that despite the sizeable increase in interest and activity, there is still too much skirmishing on the peripheries of an indigenous theatre, too much of the best energy and talent committed to foreign work, and inadequate long-term infrastructure building and consolidating strategy and effort placed in the area where it is most needed: the development of an indigenous, creative and dramatic tradition. It is symptomatic of this situation that at the present time, there is only one group concentrating on workshopping and devising new indigenous material for the stage. That distinction belongs to Third Stage, founded in 1983 by Wong Souk Yee, Lim Soon Neo and Tay Hong Seng.

A recent breakdown of registered cultural organizations in Singapore, undertaken by the Ministry of Community Development (the reorganized structure replacing the Ministry of Culture) identified a total of forty drama groups across the language streams.

Support comes largely from government funding and is administered by the Cultural Affairs Division of the Ministry of Community Development. There are six major support schemes currently in operation. The first is a project grant scheme, introduced in the mid-1970s and covering all the arts. These are individual grants, primarily for those groups organizing cultural events or productions on an occasional basis.

The second type of support is the annual grant scheme, introduced in 1985. It provides support for groups that demonstrate a more sustained level of activity, with a minimum of two major events or productions a year.

The third type, the drama promotion (play production assistance) scheme, was introduced in 1975. It provides one-time grants to groups for specific productions.

The Semi-Residential Status in Theatres Scheme, the fourth support mechanism, began in 1987. It caters to the needs of the emerging professional and semi-professional groups with open eligibility. Groups are selected on the basis of artistic standard and past production record. Chosen on an annual basis, groups under this scheme must stage at least four productions totalling not less than twelve performances. They are assigned to specific auditoriums, with up to one year priority booking of the perfor-

mance space for their productions. Charges for equipment, overtime allowances for auditorium staff are waived and free use of the auditorium for the four productions as well as for three pre-production rehearsals for each production is provided. Two of the minimum four productions should be new additions to the group's repertoire, and should preferably be Singaporean in origin. For these two productions, clerical support is provided and entertainment licences and taxes are waived. Groups are expected to maintain a high standard of performance and to be innovative and experimental both in staging techniques and repertoire. A minimum 75 per cent attendance should be achieved for all performances.

Currently, six groups participate in the scheme: STARS, the Chinese Theatre Circle and Sriwana (a Malay group) are assigned to the Victoria Theatre, while Act Three, Theatreworks and the Practice Performing Arts School (a Chinese stream group) work in the Drama Centre.

The fifth type of support comes from the Singapore Cultural Foundation. This is an ancillary body established in 1978 to give private firms and individuals a channel for private sector contributions to the arts and cultural activities in Singapore. The foundation operates under a board of trustees, chaired by the Minister for Community Development. It helps finance the promotion of cultural projects or activities organized or sponsored by the ministry, provides scholarships and study awards in any field of the arts, finances visits by professional groups from abroad, and assists individuals, local cultural groups and organizations in undertaking artistic pursuits and overseas performances.

Private funding is the final method of support. In addition to the traditional and major source of support – government funding – groups often seek and are rendered assistance by individuals, private companies and corporate sponsors.

While there are annual drama festivals and biennual arts festivals that include dramatic performance, as well as an annual festival of young people's theatre mounted by the Ministry of Community development, there are no schools of theatre design and architecture nor national schools of theatre training in English.

As of 1994, a Chinese Opera Institute has begun operation offering specialized training in Chinese opera techniques. The first director of the school is the distinguished dancer-scholar Chua Soo Pong.

The National University of Singapore, while supportive of the performance arts, has neither a department of theatre studies nor a curriculum element incorporating formal instruction in practical theatre. Movements in this direction are likely to be cautious in the foreseeable future. At the ministry level personnel from STARS are currently conducting workshops in practical theatre for students in schools and junior colleges. The privately run Practice Performing Arts School has since 1983 conducted successful directing workshops in English and Mandarin, under the leadership of Kua Pao Kun. Of interest as well was the first Retrospective of Singapore Plays in English held in 1990 under the direction of Ong Keng Sen, a director of Theatreworks.

This discussion cannot in good faith conclude without a reminder of the valuable work being done in other language streams. Among the key figures are Kuo Pao Kun, an Australian-trained playwright-director who later became director of the Practice Performing Arts School in the Mandarin community and who in the late 1980s wrote a series of effective one-man shows evoking the Chinese storytelling tradition; Nadi Putra, director of Teater Nadi in the Malay theatre (itself a dominant theatre until the separation of the country from Malaysia in 1963); and N. Narathan, a member of the Drama Advisory Committee of the Ministry of Community Development for the Tamil theatre. Among the theatres of note in these communities, one must mention the Malay theatre Sriwana led for many years by Kalim Hamidy and the more experimental Teater Kemuning led by Lut Ali. Mention should also be made of the privately funded arts centre called the Substation founded in 1990 by Kuo Pao Kun which has tried to bridge the gap between the various ethnic communities and of William Teo's Asian Theatre Research Circus.

M. Le Blond

Further Reading

Birch, David. 'The Life and Times of Singapore English Drama: Loosening the Chains, 1958–63'. *Performing Arts* 3 no. 1 (1986): 28–32.

——. 'The 1981 Singapore Drama Festival'. *Commentary* 5 nos. 3–4 (August–September 1982): 100–3.

Le Blond, M. 'Drama in Singapore: Towards an English Language Theatre'. In *Discharging the Canon: Cross-Cultural Readings in Literature*, ed. Peter Hyland, 112–25. Singapore: Singapore University Press, 1986.

Lim Chor Pee. 'Is Drama Non-existent in Singapore?' *Tumasek* 1 (January 1964): 42–4.

Seet Khiam Keong. 'Waiting in the Wings: A Critical Look at Singapore's Playscripts from the 1960s to 1980, Part 1'. *Commentary* 5 nos. 3–4 (August–September 1982): 47–55.

Yeo, Robert. 'Towards an English Language Singaporean Theatre'. *Southeast Asian Review of English* 4 (July 1982): 59–73.

SOLOMON ISLANDS

(see **SOUTH PACIFIC**)

SOUTH KOREA

(see **KOREA**)

SOUTH PACIFIC

(Overview)

Difficult to aggregate, the vast area known loosely as the South Pacific covers a breadth of sea five times the size of South America and includes such cultural diversity that fully one-fifth of all the world's languages have developed there. Yet, if one excludes the larger rim-lands of Australia, New Zealand, Hawaii and Papua New Guinea, the region sustains a population of no more than 2 million people, scattered over thousands of islands (Fiji alone contains over 800 islands) and some twenty states and territories. The region also encompasses economies as relatively affluent as that of Fiji, classed 'lower-middle income' by the World Bank, and as impoverished as those of Tuvalu, Western Samoa and Kiribati. Some of its people live in cities as technologically advanced as Fiji's capital, Suva; others live in a subsistence environment without electricity, piped water or frequent visits by ships. Some live on the largely volcanic and fruitful high islands; others on the more barren coral atoll low islands.

The configuration of these scattered demographic units into colonies and then nations has often created curious national constructs, too small to be viable economies, yet too ethnically divergent and geographically distant to consolidate into larger administrative and political units. It is this apparently inescapable pattern of dependency which has proved to be the greatest inhibitor of development in the modern Pacific.

The earliest settlers arrived in the western Pacific by canoe from Southeast Asia perhaps as early as 37,000 BC. In an epic migration that covered millennia, these travellers – pushed on by war, famine and territoriality – gradually fanned out across the sea, reaching the tiniest and most remote islands and extending almost to the coast of South America in the east and as far south as the cold regions of New Zealand's South Island.

Isolation and adaptation to their widely varied environments generated an extraordinary variety of cultures that have been constructed by external scholars into the broad categories Polynesian, Melanesian and Micronesian. The very names suggest the superficiality of the distinctions, as the size and number of the islands inhabited by two of these groups are contrasted with the melanin content of the complexions of the third.

None the less, some general characteristics may perhaps be suggested. The Polynesians of the eastern Pacific tend to have highly centralized societies, with powerful chieftaincies; the Melanesians of the southwestern Pacific have decentralized societies, dominated by those whose power arises from acquired wealth; and the Micronesians of the north-central Pacific have small-scale societies, with a variety of traditional structures.

The western notion of the South Seas began to be constructed as early as 1528; by 1599 Shakespeare was writing, in *As You Like It*, of a hazardous 'South-sea of discovery'. By the nineteenth century, two equally invalid essentialized ideas of the region had congealed – that of the 'noble savage' (from Tacitus, via Dryden and Rousseau) and that of the 'duplicitous native' (a perceptual transfer from Europe and America's experience of the slave trade).

The intervention of traders, adventurers, colonists and missionaries from Europe commenced in the mid-sixteenth century, with the arrival of Alvaro de Mendaña in what are now the Solomon Islands and the Marquesas. Over the next two centuries, voyagers from the Netherlands (Abel Tasman, Jacob Roggeveen), Britain (Samuel Wallis, Philip Carteret, James Cook) and France (de Bougainville, La Pérouse, d'Entrecasteaux) began to draw externally defined borders of colonial power around the region. Although there was much resistance to foreign annexation throughout the region, European domination was firmly in place by the 1890s.

The arrival in Tahiti of the London Missionary Society in 1797, marked the beginning of the spread of the various forms of Christianity currently active in the Pacific, and the erosion, indeed, at times the total obliteration, of traditional belief systems. Missionaries, in tandem with the burgeoning colonial authorities, exerted a powerful influence over social behaviour, effecting the eventual cessation of the practice of cannibalism, a massive revision of perceived history, a fundamental restructuring of local power relations, and the abandonment or alteration of many ancient performance modes. Christian churches are now the most powerful social forces in many of the region's societies, closely allied to political interest groups.

Despite Germany's short-lived Pacific empire (1899–1914) and Japan's administration and occupation of various parts of the Pacific between the 1930s and the end of World War II, foreign control has largely been exerted by France and the anglophone industrialized world (Britain, the United States and latterly, Australia and New Zealand). The colonial policies implemented by them have not always been very prescient. The almost random delineation of borders has yoked the island of Bougainville, culturally aligned with the Solomon Islands, to Papua New Guinea, resulting in a secessionist war in the 1990s. The New Hebrides (now Vanuatu) was bizarrely administered by France and Britain as a condominium, with parallel legal systems, postal services, police departments and taxation governing constituencies which could be distinguished only by the acquired language they used. Indentured workers were recruited from India to work the sugar plantations of Fiji between 1879 and 1916, creating an ethnic-political mixture which the colonial administration intentionally kept divided, guaranteeing instability for generations to come. France unevenly developed its Pacific territories, encouraging the Polynesians of Tahiti, because of their perceived picturesqueness, to retain many of their traditional practices and their social hierarchy, while entirely marginalizing the Melanesians of New Caledonia and assuring that the control of nickel mining and commercial agriculture would remain in the hands of French settlers (Caldoches) and business interests in the metropole. Bougainville, in 1769, baldly articulated this hierarchy of prejudice: 'The black men are much more ill-natured than those whose complexions are nearer to white.'

The declaration of Western Samoa's independence from New Zealand in 1962 began the *de jure* decolonization of the anglophone Pacific. But the fragility of most island economies has meant that, in most countries and territories, the GDP is massively supported by external government aid and by remittances from relatives overseas.

POLYNESIA

French Polynesia (Polynésie Française)

Although the written record is sparse – the accounts of early European travellers are often obscured by ignorance and prejudgment – and the testimony of oral tradition has been transmuted over time by cultural change, it is very clear that substantial performance cultures, including dramatic forms, were prominent in the pre-colonial societies of the Pacific basin. Not only were there vibrant enacted storytelling traditions (like the informal folkloric *fagogo* and the *tala* origin tales of Samoa), elaborate narrative dances, gestural songs and chants, but also fully developed dramatic enactments, involving character creation and sustained action.

The most comprehensively documented of these pre-contact theatrical cultures is that of the Maohi *arioi*, in what is now French Polynesia. In their several accounts of visits to the islands of Raiatea and Tahiti, in 1769 and 1773, Captain Cook, his naturalist Joseph Banks and astronomer William Wales describe in some detail performances of what Cook calls 'a Comedy or Dramatick Heava (*heiva*)', presented by companies of high-born travelling players. As recounted, the plays, both comic and melodramatic, dealt with social and domestic issues like theft, divided lovers and elopement, and may have included satirical comments on the British visitors, which their lack of familiarity with the language rendered them unable to understand. As Cook reports of a two-hour enactment at Point Venus, 'it was not possible for us to find out the meaning of the Play, some parts of it seem'd to [be] adapted to the present time as my name was mentioned several times'.

Such *heiva* were a combination of pre-established scenario and topical improvisation. As Cook notes admiringly, 'These people can add little Extemporary pieces to their entertainments whenever they see occasion.' But not all travellers were as sympathetic. J. Forster, in 1778, described the *arioi* 'nocturnal festivals' (which he had not witnessed), as 'indecent and lascivious'. In 1801, a minister of the London Missionary Society (LMS) wrote of the performers' movements as like that of 'so many lunaticks'. In 1837, J.M. Moerenhout recorded his shock when 'performers and spectators alike seemed to lose themselves in a mad frenzy, and not infrequently ... would perform actions of such depravity as to prohibit our description of them'.

It seems likely that the *arioi* were, in fact, an exclusive and perhaps aristocratic Maohi religious sect, the members of which sustained themselves through the gifts awarded for their public performances. Also likely is that there was a strong erotic presence in both their beliefs and their practices. It was undoubtedly because of its incompatibility with Christianity, that *arioi* was eventually eradicated and there appear to be no first-hand accounts of *arioi* performances after the 1840s.

In Tahiti, traditions of dance and music continue in the 1990s, but now distanced from their philosophical origins and shaped by a more gallic aesthetic. Little remains of *arioi* playmaking. Perhaps the most active Tahitian producer is John Mairai, whose *Maro Putoto*, a free rendering into the Maohi language of *Macbeth*, transposed into a pre-contact Polynesian setting, was mounted on the thrust stage of the Te Fare Tauhiti Nui theatre in the territorial capital Papeete in 1987.

Western Samoa

In Samoa (now artificially divided into the independent nation of Western Samoa and the Unincorporated Territory of American Samoa), several vestiges survive of what must have been a dynamic pre-Christian religious theatre. The comic sketches known as *fale aitu* (literally, house of spirits) are little more than farcical amusements, often featured in the annual Christian celebration of *Lotu Tamaiti* (White Sunday), each October. The successful entertainer Petelo, leader of the best known of the *fale aitu* groups, designs programmes of music, dance and stand-up comedy, which he has toured to overseas Samoan communities in New Zealand and the United States.

The name, however, suggests a more important social function, now lost. An *aitu* was a guardian spirit, and the celebrations of and homage paid to such forces probably, as in *arioi* practice, involved some sort of dramatic enactment, perhaps both moralistic and erotic. As late as 1884, George Turner describes Samoan 'theatricals', in which 'illustrations would be given of selfish schemes to take things easy at the expense of others'. But, as in Tahiti, missionary hostility was great. In the memoir of his mission for the LMS in Samoa during the 1840s, John B. Stair justifies the suppression of such performances: 'Regrets are often expressed at the manner in which these obscene dances have been discouraged by the missionaries; but such sentiments can be uttered only in ignorance of oblivion of the true character of the dances and their tendency'.

Modern Samoa has produced fewer playwrights than it has poets and writers of fiction, perhaps because, while musical performance is given great emphasis in the school curricula, drama remains no more than a literary study. In the 1960s, Albert Wendt wrote and produced several unpublished one-acts. His *Sons for the Return Home* (1973), Samoa's first novel in English, was adapted to the screen by Television New Zealand in the early 1980s, but was largely an overseas production. In 1990, his novel *Flying-fox in a Freedom Tree* was similarly produced in New Zealand. More recently, newspaper editor Fata Sano Malifa has published a political satire, *A Kava Bowl Called Paranoia* (1992), as an afterpiece to a collection of his verse.

Tonga

Cook, who visited the Kingdom of Tonga's island of Ha'apai in 1777, records a sung and acted performance at which the local audience appeared to derive great 'pleasure ... from the sentimental part, or what the performers delivered in their speeches. However, the mere acting part, independently of the sentences repeated, was well worth our notice both with respect to the extensive plan in which it was executed, and to the various motions'.

While this specific form was probably eventually subsumed in formal dance, Tonga, as elsewhere in the Pacific basin, has maintained a strong tradition of comic performance, the *koniseti*. Farcical, often satirical and parodic, these sketches probably lie behind the bizarre, indeed surrealistic fictive vision of Tonga's best known contemporary writer, the anthropologist Epeli Hau'ofa (*Tales of the Tikongs*, 1983; *Kisses in the Nederends*, 1987). Like the Samoan 'court buffoons' described by Turner, the *koniseti* performers greatly resemble the jesters of medieval Europe's Feasts of Fools, licensed for an occasion to invert the hierarchy and openly to criticize their class superiors, serving to effect a periodic release of social tension and, ultimately, a conservative support for the existing power structure.

More directly influenced by the west, the 'Atenisi Institute, founded in Tonga's capital Nuku'alofa by classical scholar Futa Helu, on the model of Plato's Athenian Academy, has mounted several elaborate productions of ancient Greek tragedies, in Tongan translation.

Cook Islands

Cook Islands' oral history tells of the small fleet of canoes which set forth from the main island Rarotonga and began the settlement of New Zealand. Certainly, the varieties of Maori spoken in both countries and in Tahiti suggest a common origin. Rarotongans, with their direct contacts with relatives in Auckland and their joint New Zealand citizenship, are far more urban in outlook than their rural small-town environment would suggest. With Television New Zealand beamed in each evening, indigenous performance has become largely reserved for national festivals. The annual Constitution Week (August) sees amateur drama competitions, with scripted plays on historical themes. The church-sponsored national Gospel Day (October) involves a similar competition for plays on biblical themes. Performances often exploit the rich Cook Islands repertoire of energetic dance, slit-drumming, ukulele music and song.

MICRONESIA

Kiribati

The tiny island communities of Micronesia, speaking Malayo-Polynesian languages and largely dependent upon subsistence fishing, although lacking the critical population mass to generate and sustain extended dramatic forms, have developed arresting and highly stylized mimetic dances.

Most striking of these are the *inwaie* (dances) of Kiribati, formerly the Gilbert Islands and independent since 1979. Among the i-Kiribati *kaimatoa* (standing dances, as distinguished from the *bino* or sitting dances), are those which imitate and celebrate the frigate-bird, in which the silent dancer, accompanied by a mixed chorus and mat-beating percussionists, evokes the jerky head and wing movements of the rapacious sea-bird. Fast disappearing, however, are the intense *ietoa* (war dances) which, having lost their original social functions, remain too aggressive to be mere entertainment.

In his account of a visit to the Gilberts in 1889, Robert Louis Stevenson, who was to spend his last years in Samoa, describes several performances to which he refers variously as 'drama', 'opera' and 'ballet': 'Already this is beyond the Thespian model [i.e. a single-actor recitation], ... it is the drama full developed although still in miniature'.

In 1994, the newly formed Itibwerere Theatre group travelled to Vanuatu to train with the well-established Wan Smolbag company (see **Vanuatu**) and in the following year Wan Smolbag conducted a production and training tour to Kiribati.

Significantly different in culture and history from the islands of the eastern and north-central Pacific, Melanesia has been the site of the harshest colonial excesses and neglect in the region. Because there are no strong chieftaincy structures, the colonial powers were unable to conclude agreements with local surrogates, as they had in Polynesia, and imposed often draconian direct authority. The nineteenth-century practice of 'black-birding' – kidnapping men to work on farms elsewhere – is the origin of the Solomon Islands communities in Fiji and Australia.

The consequent anger was most clearly evident in the university-based theatre of Papua New Guinea in the period immediately preceding and just after independence in 1975 (see PAPUA NEW GUINEA). The establishment of the National Theatre in Port Moresby and the Raun Raun travelling theatre in the Highlands, and the emergence of young playwrights, many of whom rose to significant political and economic power in the first years of national government,

would eventually influence theatre development in neighbouring Vanuatu and the Solomon Islands.

Vanuatu

A country of some 80 islands and 115 discrete languages, the former French-British condominium (1906) of the New Hebrides became the independent Republic of Vanuatu in 1980. It is here that perhaps the most exciting Pacific theatre project of recent decades, a full-time professional theatre, has developed.

In 1989, Peter Walker, an alumnus of Joan Littlewood's East 15 Acting School in London and a former teacher of English and drama in Zimbabwe, established what has become the Wan Smolbag Theatre, initially involving six untrained actors. The group's name suggests Grotowski's 'poor theatre', one for which all the stage paraphernalia can be carried in 'one small bag', for the sake of economy and mobility. Like

A nineteenth-century 'black-birder' tries to trick ni-Vanuatua into being kidnapped as slave labour. *The Old Stories*, Wan Smolbag Theatre, Vanuatu, 1991.

A traditional pan-piper (Timothy Andrew). *The Old Stories*, Wan Smolbag Theatre, Vanuatu, 1991.

the numerous community theatres in sub-Saharan Africa, Wan Smolbag has worked in crucial development areas, with plays on AIDS and sexually transmitted diseases (STDs), family planning, clean toilets, deforestation, disability, family violence and the causes of crime, as well as the history and cultures of Vanuatu. Most plays have been presented in the local pidgin, Bislama, but actors are also able to perform in English and French. Best known of the group's stage productions is *The Old Stories* (1993) which animates some of the more wrenching episodes in Vanuatu's past, and was performed twice-weekly for several years in the Chief's Nakamal, the elaborately ornamented meeting-house of Vanuatu's Council of Chiefs in Port Vila.

With funding from Britain and Australia, and earnings from productions commissioned by government ministries and international agencies, Wan Smolbag was able by the mid-1990s to lease its own theatre space, in a former warehouse to the west of the capital, where workshops for school and community groups could be held. They also began a series of performance tours and training courses in neighbouring regional countries. As well, they branched out into radio, mounting a seven-part AIDS serial on Radio Vanuatu, *I No Save Happen Festaem* (*I Didn't Know It Could Happen the First Time*). Several of their major productions have been televised and are available on video. These include *Like Any Other Lovers*, on STDs (English, 1962); *Pacific Star*, a comedy with music questioning the role of tourism in development (English and Bislama versions, with Pasifika Communications (Fiji), 1993); *Storian Blong Angela* (*Angela's Story*), exploring attitudes towards family planning (Bislama, 1993); *George and Sheila*, dealing with domestic gender relations (English and Bislama versions, 1994); *On the Reef*, a poignant musical about a group of sea animals preparing for a reef band competition (English, with Handspan Theatre (Melbourne, Australia) and Pasifika Communications (Fiji), 1995); *Things We Don't Talk About*, a play about physical disability featuring a disabled member of the acting company (English, 1996); and *Kasis Road*, a feature-length film on population and family issues (English, 1996).

Wan Smolbag have also produced two documentaries on their methods (*The First Five Years*, English, 1994; *Another Week, Another Workshop*, English, 1995) for the instruction and encouragement of other theatre groups in the region.

Puppeteer Willine Toka and one of the characters in the puppet musical *On the Reef*, Wan Smolbag Theatre, Vanuatu.

Solomon Islands

In the neighbouring Solomons, with eighty-seven languages spoken over a chain of some thirty-five large islands and groups, traditional performances include witty animal mimicry, hunting simulations and warrior dances, accompanied by song and a range of pan-pipes which are often of great size – made of mature bamboo and struck at the ends with a broad-surfaced object (these days, often a plastic sandal).

Modern Solomons theatre emerged well before independence from Britain in 1978. During the 1950s, in the capital Honiara, monthly plays in the local Pidgin *lingua franca* were being produced by various groups, including the police, in abandoned United States Army quonset huts erected during the Guadalcanal campaign (1942–3). The plays, predominantly comic while none the less dealing with grave themes such as bravery and death, often revisited the traumas of the war.

By 1969 Francis Bugotu, who was later to become his country's Permanent Representative to the United Nations, had written the screenplay of what was to be the first dramatic film shot in the Solomons, *This Man*, which deals with the social problems created by westernisation and was developed for the consecration of the new Cathedral of the Anglican Diocese of Melanesia in Honiara.

In the early 1970s, the radio became drama's most vibrant and effective medium, allowing new plays a national audience otherwise unachievable in such a scattered population. Among the pioneers of Solomons's radio theatre was a forceful personality who would later emerge as the country's longest serving prime minister, Solomon Mamaloni. He and Bugotu, with the then head of the Central Bank, Tony Hughes, mounted – for radio, stage and, later, cinema – *Borokua Stori*, which was followed by an adaptation of *Oedipus Tyrannus* in Pidgin.

In the late 1970s, Mamaloni began writing a weekly series, *Aedo* (literally the burnt remains of a traditional rolled-tobacco cigar), which, in Pidgin and with often Rabelaisian humour, charted the life and times of the eponymous government factotum. *Aedo* was enormously popular and reflected increasing anxiety about urban drift and the hazards of the quickly expanding towns. It included the acting talent of Ashley Wickham and the production skills of Patteson Mae, each of whom would become, in turn, chief executive of the Solomon Islands Broadcasting Corporation (SIBC). Eventually, however, the explicitness of

the realism and the raciness of the dialogue – much of which was improvised on air – led to the programme's cancellation and Mamaloni's departure from the project. As, however, Mamaloni was by then the Leader of the Parliamentary Opposition, the demise of *Aedo* was generally seen as politically motivated.

With the audience of radio theatre now firmly established, the SIBC continued to offer drama programming, although, unlike Papua New Guinea's National Broadcasting Corporation (NBC), it never created a dedicated Drama Department. In the early 1980s, under the influence of the BBC's long-running agricultural soap opera, *The Archers*, the SIBC began *Kirori*, the partly scripted adventures of a Ministry of Agriculture adviser who propagated farming information while getting into complicated social and domestic difficulties. The programme, heavily reliant upon the microphone presence of the main actor, continued well into the 1990s.

Also in the early 1980s, a new live theatre took shape, the Lukluk Wantok group (literally 'Look, look, people of one language' or 'Come and see, fellow Solomon Islanders'), which began with topical improvisational plays, progressed through writing workshops to scripted plays, and was able to attract support from the Australian South Pacific Cultures Fund. In the 1990s, a team of social workers established a travelling theatre, probably influenced by the success of Vanuatu's Wan Smolbag, with which they hoped to encourage public debate about community development issues. This popular theatre model, begun in Africa and effectively transplanted to Papua New Guinea, Vanuatu and the Solomons, has become dominant in Melanesia, earning support from both funding sources and a broad range of audiences, rural and urban.

Few Solomon Island plays have been published, for while there is a keen audience for performance, there is a very small potential readership in such a precarious economy. One text by Mamaloni, however, is available: *The Census Day* (1978), a nativity play, somewhat localized, but in standard English, with numerous clearly intentional anachronisms, rather resembling the more comic and secular of the medieval Townely cycle texts, *The Second Shepherds' Play* or *Noah's Flood*.

New Caledonia (Nouvelle Calédonie)

The territory of New Caledonia was annexed by France in 1853 and has, despite a history of

Dancers celebrate the Volcano 'Yasur', in the opening segment of *The Old Stories*, Wan Smolbag Theatre, Vanuatu, 1991.

resistance, been governed externally ever since. The original Melanesians, known as Kanaks, now constitute less than 45 per cent of the population and have become, unlike the Maohi of French Polynesia, a permanent social and economic underclass. For most of the period of French occupation, Kanak culture was devalued and relegated to rural communities, while in the capital Noumea an almost exclusively metropolitan culture prevailed.

In 1975 as a forceful statement of national identity, Jean-Marie Tjibaou, the popular nationalist political leader who would be assassinated fourteen years later, produced his epic *Kanaké* as part of Melanesia 2000: The First Festival of Kanaka Arts. Acted, narrated and danced – part play, part ceremony, part pageant – *Kanaké* involved 2,000 participants in an impressionistically rendered history of New Caledonia's people. At the centre of a vast arena, with an audience of 50,000, a narrator stands atop a Y-shaped tree and declares, in the Patyi language, 'This is Tee Kanaké. / This is the story of the one who is your chief. / He is strong and will bring you victory! / He is good and will help the less fortunate. / He is wise and knows his ancestry!'

But the play is not driven by a simplistic cultural nationalism, acknowledging the difficult contradictions faced by the colonized: 'They came / in huge canoes. / Strangers, / leave on the boats / which brought you / we do not want / your animals / we do not want to destroy / our cultures / which our fathers made / they suffice to feed us. / The white man of today / replied / who are the real men of Kanaké? / those who weep / over the past / or those who are prepared to face / tomorrow?'

Fiji

Fiji is the major anomaly of the Pacific. Indigenous Fijians are Melanesians who, over generations of invasion by Tonga into their eastern islands, acquired a Polynesian chiefly culture, which is unevenly distributed over the country. The arrival of indentured sugar workers from India in 1879 radically redrew the demography, so that, by the mid-1990s each group represented just under 50 per cent of the population, the balance being made up of those with Chinese, European, Kiribati, Solomons and combined ancestries.

Traditional Fijian *meke* (dance-song) performance is, like that of courtly cultures elsewhere, highly regimented with precisely coordinated movements of the head, hands, arms and upper torso. It is usually narrative and employs a highly stylized gestural language to animate the words. In his *Dance Theatre of Fiji*, which has performed daily at the Pacific Harbour Cultural Centre since the mid-1980s, Manoa Rasigatale choreographs the ancient *meke* form into narrated plays about Fiji's pre-contact history, for a predominantly tourist audience.

In the Indo-Fijian communities, the cultures of India are, to some extent, preserved in classical music and dance and in the occasional production of spectacular dramatizations of episodes from *Ramayana* and *Mahabharata*. Several commercial films have been produced in both standard (*Shudh*) Hindi and the local dialectal mixture, Fiji *Baat*. Beginning in the late 1970s, with *Kalaank*, and continuing through the 1990s with the work of Vishwa Naidu and VTC. Films (*Kanoon Se Rista*; *Qayamat Ki Zindagi*, 1995), local actors have been combined with Indian musical performers from Australia and elsewhere in formula films designed to resemble as closely as possible the love-crime-music-dance products of Bombay's 'Bollywood'.

Spoken theatre in the western sense was introduced in the schools and churches of Fiji fairly early in the colonial period but has never found a place in the educational curriculum and has not received institutional encouragement in recent years. Suva's Fiji Arts Club performed western plays with largely expatriate casts and audiences until local playwrights began to appear in the early years of independence. Jo Nacola, whose short sketches on social themes are collected in *I Native No More* (1976), taught drama at the University of the South Pacific (USP) and encouraged several writers and performers, including Joseph Veramu, whose two-act mythological play *Killers of Turukawa* (1980) began as a workshop project.

Indeed, theatre in English has been largely the province of the USP which, while serving twelve of the region's states, has its main campus in Fiji's capital, Suva. If Pacific theatre in the 1960s was dominated by playwrights produced by the University of Papua New Guinea, the major theatre writers working in 1990s' Pacific are or have been attached to the USP. Of these, the best known have been Vilsoni Hereniko and Larry Thomas (b. 1954).

Hereniko was born on the Polynesian island of Rotuma and educated at the USP and in Dorothy Heathcote's Theatre-in-Education programme at the University of Newcastle upon Tyne (UK). After teaching at the USP and completing doctoral research on the *han maneak su* (the traditional Rotuman female clown), he joined the staff of the University of Hawaii.

Hereniko's plays present characters in ethical and social conflict, reflecting the ethnic and economic tensions in contemporary Fiji. He has published four full-length plays and mounted several one-acts. In *Don't Cry, Mama* (1977), box-set realism written as an undergraduate, Hereniko offers a study of the newly urbanized whose acquisitiveness comes to rule their judgments. *A Child for Iva* (1981) examines ethnic and generational differences, arranged marriages and infanticide. In *Sera's Choice* (1986), two university students – a Fijian woman and an Indo-Fijian man – decide to marry against both convention and family hostility but are unable to transcend fully Fiji's firmly delineated ethnic topography. *The Shadow* (1987) again explores the domestic and the marital in the predicament of a woman whose husband has just returned from an extended stay as part of the United Nations peace-keeping force in the Middle East. In *The Last Virgin in Paradise* (1991), Hereniko satirizes the misperceptions and distorted assumptions of both tourists and anthropologists in Polynesia. Like much of Hereniko's earlier work, this play presents an internal contradiction, for while it challenges western preconceptions, it promotes equally illegitimate stereotypes of the west. Few of Hereniko's characters emerge from cliché and much of his plotting is mechanical or melodramatic. An exception to this is the disturbing one-act *The Monster*, written in 1982 but revised in the shadow of the two ethnically divisive 1987 miliary *coups d'état* that overthrew a recently elected multi-ethnic government in the name of indigenous Fijian cultural nationalism. In an effective reworking of Beckett's *Waiting for Godot*, two friends, a Fijian and an Indo-Fijian, are assailed and find their relationship threatened by a demonic militaristic figure whom eventually they defeat and whose death allows them again to draw together.

With *Just Another Day* (1988), Suva playwright Larry Thomas emerged as an important new voice of uncompromising social realism in Fiji's contemporary theatre. A richly observant and clear-eyed commentary on the despair and the humanity of Fiji's urban working class, its vision is fully as bleak as its dialogue, an arrestingly accurate rendering of Suva's street English. In the tradition of naturalism, the play, while replete with action, lacks conventional plot and anatomizes an uncommitted life of boredom, conflict and violence, a tension which arises out of the hopelessness of poverty.

Women, in Thomas's world, bear the brunt of much of this violence, both physical and verbal. But their social entrapment renders them unable to devise strategies for self-protection. In *Outcasts* (1989), Thomas's second major stage production, his study of the victimization of women is extended to a broader array of the marginalized, including homosexuals, prostitutes and the desperately poor, living in a row of flimsy corrugated iron squatter shanties. They, and the young men and women from the neighbouring alleyways, constitute a kind of randomly assembled family whose poverty and shared need obliterate the more superficial distinctions of ethnicity. The claustrophobic congestion of their dwellings denies them both privacy and the freedom to fool themselves as they alternate between cruelty and supportiveness of one another: 'In this place you can't hide anything, even if you wear a mask.' Although *Outcasts* relies more upon plot than does *Just Another Day*, it is essentially structured around a series of confessional monologues in which the harried and frustrated souls of this vividly conceived hell reveal both their hopeless ambitions and the social forces which make those dreams unrealizable.

Indeed, the play could be seen as lying in that strong international theatre tradition which includes Maxim Gorky's *The Lower Depths* and Eugene O'Neill's *The Iceman Cometh*. But while O'Neill, and to some extent Gorky, present their characters' destinies as determined by their own personalities, Thomas sees the distorted lives of his outcasts as the products of an unsympathetic society. *Outcasts* gives voice to a world which for too long huddled in the shadows.

In the two-hander *Yours Dearly* (1991), Thomas again centralizes women's sensibilities, although in a rather slighter domestic vehicle. More complex, if not entirely successful, is *Men, Women and Insanity* (1991), which interrogates the relationships between personality and environment through a group of excluded young people who spend their days in the back yard of a factory.

In 1993, poet and USP academic Sudesh Mishra offered his densely imagistic *Feringhi*

for production at the Fiji Arts Club, as a response both to the military coups and to ethnic exclusivity in Fiji.

The South Pacific has for decades been a popular setting for the commercial cinema, which, virtually without exception, has romanticized or demonized the region's people. The Hollywood back-lot loin-cloth and *lavalava* 'B' films of the 1940s and 1950s, often starring Dorothy Lamour or Jon Hall (*South of Pago Pago*, 1940; *On the Isle of Samoa*, 1950), are depictions of the Pacific no more valid than the images of Africa in the same period's film adaptations of Edgar Rice Burroughs's *Tarzan* novels. African-American actors, or whites in brown-face, were frequently employed to play islanders.

As early as 1929, F.W. Murnau, best known for his silent expressionistic vampire tale *Nosferatu* (1922), directed his last film, *Tabu*, on location in Tahiti. This was followed by such films as John Ford's *The Hurricane* (1937), *Return to Paradise*, with Gary Cooper (1953), John Banas's Australian feature *Emma: Queen of the South Seas* (1988), all shot in Western Samoa; *Return to Blue Lagoon* (1991), the remake of *The Swiss Family Robinson* (1996), and several Australian television series (*Voyage of the Seaspray*, 1966; *Embassy*, 1990), filmed in Fiji; and the much-publicized *Mutiny on the Bounty* (Lewis Milestone, 1962), with Marlon Brando, shot on the French Polynesian island of Moorea. Of these, only Robert Flaherty's 1925 silent documentary *Moana*, shot on the Samoan island of Savai'i, could be said to demonstrate any appreciation of island societies.

Besides the Solomon Islands, Vanuatu and Fiji films already noted, few cinematic productions have originated in the islands. Limitations of both funding and audiences have discouraged this expensive dramatic mode. Despite the advent of video recorders and then television in most of the region, it is radio that remains the most effective venue for theatre in the South Pacific. Since just after World War II, most of the larger radio services have offered some sort of locally produced drama or storytelling programming. In the 1980s and 1990s, USP Professor Andrew Horn, with the support of the PacBroad Pacific Broadcasting and Training Project of Germany's Friedrich-Ebert-Stiftung, offered a series of radio drama workshops which abandoned scripting in order to avoid the woodenness of many read productions. Plays were developed from group-generated scenarios, expanded into improvised and carefully rehearsed scenes, and carried into final recording and editing within hours. Broadcast productions included several plays devised in Solomons, Vanuatu and Papua New Guinea pidgin – *Bird Blong Dai* (*Bird of Death*), a mystical murder mystery; *Kissem*, a series of comic sketches on failures of communication, 1987; and *Pepa blong Mared* (*The Marriage Bond*, 1991); plays in English, syndicated throughout the region (*The Runaways*, about urban drift, 1987; *Expectations*, about a school drop-out, *Tonumaipe'a: The Decision of the Flying Foxes: A Legend from Samoa*, 1988; *By Chance or Choice*, on family planning, and *Hot Dogs!*, a variety entertainment, 1993); as well as numerous plays in others of the region's languages. The minimal cost of radio drama, the enormous flexibility of setting and atmosphere it affords and the large audiences it can reach in extremely widely scattered populations suggest that radio will continue to be the most popular medium for dramatists in the Pacific.

Andrew Horn

Further Reading

Dorras, Jo and Peter Walker. (Vanuatu) *The Old Stories: A Play About the History of Vanuatu*. Port Vila, Vanuatu: n.p. [Wan Smolbag Theatre], n.d [1993].

Hereniko, Vilsoni Tausie. (Fiji) *A Child for Iva: A Three-Act Play*. Auckland: Heinemann, 1981.

——. (Suva, Fiji) *Don't Cry Mama*. *Mana: A South Pacific Journal of Language and Literature* 1977. Reprinted in *Chinese Journal of Oceanic Literature* 2 (1981). Excerpts reprinted in *Creative Writing from Fiji*, ed. Stanley Atherton and Satendra Nandan, Suva: Fiji Writers' Association, 1985.

Hereniko, Vilsoni Tausie and Teresia Teaiwa. *The Last Virgin in Paradise: A Serious Comedy*. Suva: Institute for Pacific Studies, 1993.

——. *The Monster and Other Plays*. Suva: Mana, 1989.

——. *Two Plays* [*A Child for Iva* and *Sera's Choice*]. Introduction by Andrew Horn. Suva: Mana, 1987.

Malifa, Fata Sano. (Western Samoa) 'A Kava Bowl Called Paranoia'. *Song and Return*. Apia: Samoa Observer, 1992: 79–104.

Mamaloni, Solomon. (Solomon Islands) 'The Census Day'. *Mana: A South Pacific Journal of Language and Literature* 1979. Reprinted in *Chinese Journal of Oceanic Literature* 3 (1982).

Manoa, Pio. *Rachel*. Fiji English Teachers' Journal 7 (November 1973): 33–56.

Nacola, Jo. (Fiji) 'A Few To Go'. *I Native No More: Three Drama Sketches*. Suva: Mana, 1976.

——. *Gurudial and the Land*, Mana 3 no. 1 (October 1978): 17–99.

Racule, Raijele. (Fiji) *Lasawalevu and Lasawalai*. *Pacific Voices*, ed. Bernard Gadd. Albany: Stockton House, 1977. 78–83.

Thomas, Larry. (Fiji) *Just Another Day: A Play*. Suva: Fiji Centre, University of the South Pacific, 1989.

——. 'Outcasts', 'Yours Dearly', 'Men, Women and Insanity'. *3 Plays*. Suva: University of the South Pacific, 1991. Revised edn 1995.

Tjibaou, J[ean-] M[arie]. (New Caledonia) *Kanaké*. See *Kanaké: The Melanesian Way*. Trans. Christopher Plant. Papeete, Tahiti, French Polynesia: Les Editions du Pacifique, 1978.

Veramu, Joseph C. (Fiji) *Killers of Turukawa*. Suva: South Pacific Creative Arts Society, n.d. [1980s].

Wan Smolbag Theatre. (Vanuatu) *George and Sheila*. Video. Port Vila, Vanuatu: Wan Smolbag Theatre, 1994.

——. *Kasis Road*. Video. Port Vila, Vanuatu: Wan Smolbag Theatre, 1996.

——. *Like Any Other Lovers*. Video. Port Vila, Vanuatu: Wan Smolbag Theatre, 1992.

——. *On the Reef*. Video. Port Vila, Vanuatu: Wan Smolbag Theatre, Handspan Theatre (Melbourne, Australia) and Pasifika Communications (Fiji), 1995.

——. *Pacific Star*. Video. Port Vila, Vanuatu: Wan Smolbag Theatre and Pasifika Communications (Fiji), 1993.

——. *Storian Blong Angela* [Angela's story]. Video. Port Vila, Vanuatu: Wan Smolbag Theatre, 1993.

——. 'The Tale of Mighty Hawk and Magic Fish'. *Sacred Earth Dramas*. London: Faber, 1993.

——. *Things We Don't Talk About*. Video. Port Vila, Vanuatu: Wan Smolbag Theatre, 1996.

——. *Three Plays for the Pacific*. 'The Tale of Mighty Hawk and Magic Fish', 'The Invasion of the Litter Creatures', 'On the Reef'. Port Vila, Vanuatu: Wan Smolbag Theatre, n.d. [1994].

Additional Sources

Banks, Joseph. *The 'Endeavour' Journal of Joseph Banks, 1768–1771*. 2 vols. 2nd edn. Edited by J.C. Beaglehole. Sydney: Angus & Robertson and Public Library of New South Wales, 1963. 1: 290, 324–5, 351–2, plates 12 and 13.

Cook, Captain James. *The Journals of Captain James Cook on His Voyage of Discovery …* Vol. 1: *The Voyage of the 'Endeavour',*

1768–1771. Edited by J.C. Beaglehole. 4 vols. Revised edn. Cambridge: Cambridge University Press and Hakluyt Society, 1968: 148–9.

——. *The Journals of Captain James Cook on His Voyage of Discovery ...* Vol. 2: *The Voyage of the Resolution and Adventure, 1772–1775*. Edited by J.C. Beaglehole. 4 vols. Revised edn. Cambridge: Cambridge University Press and Hakluyt Society, 1969: 223–4.

Dunlop, Peggy. 'Samoan Writing: Searching for the Written Fagogo'. *Pacific Islands Communication Journal* 14 no. 1 (1985): 41–69.

Forster, George. *A Voyage Round the World in His Britannic Majesty's Sloop, 'Resolution'*. 2 vols. London, 1777.

Forster, Johann Reinhold. 'Journal of a Journey from London to Plymouth and a Voyage on Board His Majesty's Ship the 'Resolution', Captain Cook Commander, 1772–75'. MS in Staatsbibliothek Preussischer Kulturbesitz, Berlin.

——. *Observations Made During a Voyage Round the World on Physical Geography, Natural History and Ethic Philosophy ...* London, 1778: 473–5.

Langdon, Robert. *The Lost Caravel*. Sydney: Pacific Publications, 1975: 123, 126–7, plate 5 (facing 112), 302.

Maka'a, Julian and Stephen Oxenham. 'Writing in Solomon Islands: The Voice in the Shadow'. *Pacific Islands Communication Journal* 14 no. 1 (1985): 12–23.

Martin, John. *An Account of the Natives of the Tonga Islands in the South Pacific Ocean, With an Original Grammar and Vocabulary of Their Language*. 2 vols. London: John Murray, 1817, 2: 304–52.

——. *An Account of the Natives of the Tonga Islands, in the South Pacific Ocean ...* London: John Murray, 1817. Reprint. Farnborough, England: Gregg International, 1972: 309–23, 329–33.

Mead, Margaret. 'The Role of the Dance'. *Coming of Age in Samoa*, 1928. Harmondsworth: Penguin, 1943: 92–101.

Moerenhout, J.A. *Voyages aux îles du grand océan* [Voyages to the islands of the great ocean]. 2 vols. Paris, 1837. I: 499 ff. Reprinted Paris, 1959.

Moyle, Richard, ed. and trans. *'Fangogo' Fables from Samoa in Samoan and English*. Auckland: University of Auckland Press, 1981.

Nacola, Jo and T. Vunibola. 'Fijian Meke'. *First*

Mana Annual of Creative Writing. Suva: South Pacific Creative Arts Society, 1973.

Oliver, Douglas. *Ancient Tahitian Society*. 3 vols. Honolulu and Canberra: University Press of Hawaii and Australian National University Press, 1974. 3: 913–64.

Pacific Islands Communication Journal 14 no. 1 (1985). 'Pacific Writing and Publishing' special issue.

Pacific Islands Communication Journal 14 no. 2 (1985). 'The Written Word: Writing, Publishing and Information in the Pacific Islands' special issue.

Parkinson, Sydney. *A Journal of a Voyage to the South Seas*. London, 1773: 74–5.

Pearson, Bill. *Rifled Sanctuaries: Some Views of the Pacific Islands in Western Literature*. Auckland: University of Auckland Press and Oxford University Press, 1984: esp. 12–13.

Pillai, Raymond and Ruth Finnegan, eds. *Essays on Pacific Literature*. Suva: Fiji Museum, 1978.

Stair, John. 'Amusements, Trades and Employments of Samoa'. *Old Samoa, or Flotsam and Jetsam from the Pacific Ocean* (1897). Papakura, NZ: R. Macmillan, 1983: 131–9.

Stenderup, Vibeke. *Pacific Islands Creative Writing: A Selected, Annotated Guide for Students, Librarians and the General Reader*. Hojbjerb: Vibeke Stenderup, 1985.

Stevenson, Robert Louis. *In the South Seas*. London: Chatto & Windus, 1900. Reprinted Honolulu: University of Hawaii Press, 1971: 253–6.

Subramani. *South Pacific Literature: From Myth to Fabulation*. Suva, Fiji: University of the South Pacific, 1985.

Tiffin, Chris, ed. and Introduction. *South Pacific Images*. Brisbane: South Pacific Association for Commonwealth Literature and Language Studies, 1978: 1–10.

Turner, George. 'Amusements'. *Samoa: A Hundred Years Ago and Long Before*. London: Macmillan, 1884. Reprinted Suva, Fiji: Institute of Pacific Studies, University of the South Pacific, 1984: 124–6, 132.

Wan Smolbag Theatre. *Another Week, Another Workshop*. Documentary video. Port Vila, Vanuatu: Wan Smolbag Theatre, 1994.

——. *The First Five Years*. Documentary video. Port Vila, Vanuatu: Wan Smolbag Theatre, 1994.

Williamson, Robert W. *Essays in Polynesian Ethnology*, ed. R.O. Piddington. Cambridge: Cambridge University Press, 1939. 113 pp.

SRI LANKA

(Overview)

An island nation located in the Indian Ocean some 30 kilometres (19 miles) southeast of India, Sri Lanka – known as Ceylon to the British – has a history dating back to the sixth century BC when, according to Sinhal legend, the north Indian Prince Vijaya arrived with 700 supporters and married an indigenous Sinhala. It was from this marriage that the Sinhalese Dynasty is said to have grown with its kings controlling the island for the next 2,300 years. Long known to the Chinese, Arabs, Greeks and Romans, Sri Lanka became a Buddhist state in the third century BC but its cosmopolitan nature made it home to numerous other races and religions. While the Sinhalese still form the largest ethnic group in Sri Lanka – some 74 per cent of the population – Tamil people (mostly Hindu) are also a large community representing about 18 per cent of the population and Muslims and others constitute 8 per cent. In 1996, Sri Lanka – a country with one of the highest literacy rates in East Asia – had some 17.8 million people living on the island.

Shaped like a pear, Sri Lanka is 435 kilometres long (272 miles) and approximately 220 kilometres (140 miles) wide with an overall land area of 65,600 square kilometres (25,300 square miles). Connected historically and culturally to India, Sri Lanka was nevertheless visited by many Europeans including, in the thirteenth century AD, Marco Polo, and by Portuguese explorers beginning in 1505. Portuguese influence quickly grew as did the spread of Roman Catholicism. Sri Lanka soon became a Portuguese colony and elements of the Portuguese language entered the Sinhala language.

In 1658, the Portuguese were driven out by the Dutch; in 1796 the British began exploring the area and trading on the island. By 1815, the Kandyan Kingdom was ceded to the British and Sri Lanka – by this time called Ceylon – became a crown colony. The fact that Buddhism remained the state religion, however, was formally opposed by the Church of England and church policy eventually dominated. Despite social unrest over colonization, religion and culture for some two centuries, the British remained in control until 1948 when the country adopted its own independent constitution and became a self-governing member of the British Commonwealth. In 1972 it became an independent republic and severed its formal ties to the British Crown. During the same year, the island returned to its more ancient name, Sri Lanka, and moved toward socialism. During the last four decades of the twentieth century, Sri Lanka was torn by both political and economic debate as well as bloody rivalry between the Sinhalese and the Tamils. The Tamil Liberation Front, formed in 1976, began to demand a separate Tamil state. As the political situation in the late 1990s became increasingly unstable, all public activities in the country – including theatre – began to face a new range of problems.

Such a mix of religion and politics also created in Sri Lanka a mix of cultural styles in religion, the arts and even dramatic representation. Buddhist traditions, for example, have always been enormously theatrical. Of particular note in this regard are the various levels of ordination ceremonies within Buddhism, rituals connected to the different seasons, seven-day rituals of Pirit Chanting, what are known as

Participants in a Buddhist religious drama sequence called *Dorakada Asna* (*Invitation To the Dieties*).
Photo: Tisara Munasinghe.

is a depiction of the collection of rice and other ingredients for an offering of alms to the maha guru while the *boru yakkama* is a scene in which false utterances are made as to where the ritual is being performed. The *maha yakkama* is a depiction of the ritual's origins and its connections to Sri Lanka's ancient kings. Always performed outdoors, usually on a slightly raised threshing floor, these plays use dialogue, impersonation, makeup, props, costumes, mime and a wide range of other standard theatrical techniques.

Other traditional folk forms – many now fading from view – are rooted in a more satiric narrative style, the *kolam*. These masked dance dramas satirized recognizable local figures. Similar elements can be seen in *yakun natanavaa*, also known as *tovils* (devil dances) such as *Suniyam Kapilla* (*Destruction of the Sorcery*), *Rata Yakuma* (also called *Riddi Yagaya*, or *Seven Barren Queens*), *Sanni Yakuma* (*The Demon Sanni*), and even in communal celebrations performed in honour of the goddess of chastity, Pattini. Many of these forms are actually closer to public healing rituals than they are to public entertainments. In the 1990s, *tovils* and *kolams* tend to be performed in Colombo only for tourists.

Among the Tamil population, a folk drama emerged as well, the *nadagama*. Popular particularly in the northern and eastern regions of Sri Lanka, the *nadagama* was based in great measure on the south Indian dramatic form of *natakam*, a form introduced to the island in the late eighteenth century by Indian touring players. Utilizing south Indian *karnatic* music, *nadagama* are almost always done in Tamil. The first written and printed *nadagama*, credited to a Roman Catholic blacksmith, Phillippu Singho (1770–1840), was called *The Sinhaley Nadagama* and written about 1824. It dealt with the surrender of the last king of Sri Lanka to the British in 1815. Janchi Singho also later scripted *nadagama* works in Sinhala.

An English visitor to Sri Lanka in 1830, J.W. Bennett, described one of the *nadagamas* he saw at that time. He pointed out that they

invariably take place in the open air, generally in some spacious compound or garden, where abundance of jak, bread fruit, and other trees can be made available to the purpose of illumination, and where also, from the quality of the ground, a natural amphitheatre is easily fitted for the purpose.

The erection of booths, covered with white cloths and ornamented in a very tasteful style

twin-seat discourses, homages to past Buddhas, sermons on many hells, rituals called the taming of the untamed and confessions of monks. All are intensely dramatic and all are still practised by Sri Lankan Buddhists.

Even a folk play tradition dating back to the fifteenth century supports and in some ways encourages Buddhism's unique sense of ritual and other-worldliness. These early ritualistic events rooted in healing deal with Buddhism's pantheon of divine beings (including the demon *yakshas* and *pethas*), usually as dramatized battles between good and evil. One of the most popular is *Kohomba Yak Kankariya*, performed as part of a ritual in the Kandy region, which seeks prosperity. Each event has five episodes called *yakkam*. The first is always the *vedi yakkama*, an invitation to the thirty-six Vedda demons (those who cause illness) to eat and drink before they are sent away and purification is obtained. The second section, *ura yakkama*, is a depiction of the stalking and killing of a wild boar and the apportioning of meat among those who participate in the ritual. The *naya yakkama*

Nalukeerit Sabha's folk drama production produced by Dayananda Gunawardena.

for which the natives are celebrated with mosses, wild flowers, ... fruits of all sorts in clusters, interspersed with the white flowers and olas or leaflets of the coconut palm, ... add to the beauty of the scenery and give an air of richness and luxuriance to the whole.

Tragedy alone is worthy of native attention, the everlasting subject of it being kingly depravity or virtue, the latter of which is still more rare in Asia than in European record. After multiplied scenes of bloodshed, there is the usurper's destruction and the lawful sovereign's restoration (he being the chief character of the native dramas) all done in pantomime.

A tragedy occupies several consecutive nights in the performance. All the avenues, trees and booths are illuminated with coconut oil, in lamps made with the shells of green or water coconuts stuck upon stakes. ...

The plays are very well attended and the order ... is invariably maintained without the intervention of police or constables. The music is extremely barbarous, and monotonous to an European ear. ...

The dresses of the actors are very gaudy being set up with every possible variety of foil and tinsels. There are no actresses. The admissions are gratuitous, the costs being defrayed by collections from the native audience.

Most *nadagama* were introduced by a narrator who identified the time, place and action of the story and, from time to time, explained those incidents that were not, by convention, ever shown. The narrator was supported by a chorus of singers and two drummers. A harmonium was added at a later date.

The *nadagama* stories almost always revolved around royalty – kings, queens, princes, ministers – and their foreign equivalents which included characters from both Europe and Asia. The central conflict often arose out of a romance between a youthful aristocrat and a royal princess and the opposition of their parents or some other agency. The problems were always resolved and the lovers united but not before intrigues of various sorts, often involving murders, poisonings, kidnappings, disguises and mistaken identities, ran their course. Plots, music and even movement tended to be nearly identical in many plays. Even the styles of recitations – *keertanam, viruttam, venpa* and even rhyme schemes – were restricted to accepted forms. The movements of royalty, for example, were always stereotypically stylized and often modelled on foreign rulers.

Costumes, on the other hand, always had to glitter under the lights, usually torchlight since

Villagers of Homagama in a community ritual called *gammaduwa* in praise of the goddess of chastity, Pattini.

the plays were most often done in outdoor arenas before the entire village. The spaces used were enclosed by *cadjan*, temporary walls made of dried and woven coconut leaves. On some occasions, large sheds were constructed instead. Audiences would always sit on the ground but only those in front had to pay an admission charge. Eventually, everyone was asked to pay.

The four-part *nadagama* was usually performed over five days with the third day taken as an extended interval. Traditional performances would begin at 8 p.m. Actors playing non-royal figures would often appear on stage before the production to welcome audiences. Immensely popular in the nineteenth and early twentieth centuries, *nadagama* can still occasionally be seen in parts of Chilaw, Nattandiya, Negumbo and Wattala.

Performance traditions, however, began to change in 1877 when the Hindusthan Dramatic Company – a commercial endeavour supported by the Zoroastrian Parsees of Bombay – made a tour to Sri Lanka and played for a week in Colombo. Staging an immensely popular Indian fairytale, *Inder Sabha*, with a cast of twenty and performed in Urdu, the production boasted colourful costumes and a new style of dance and

song. Dealing with a love affair between a mortal young man and an immortal fairy woman with earth and heaven as the background, its spectacular effects included flying clouds and earthquakes, things that *nadagama*, for example, only reported and did not show. Adding in very specifically created stage settings, the production also included women in its cast (something never before seen), used gas lighting instead of torches and earthen lamps and was done indoors on a proscenium stage.

The production spawned many local copies, all quite far from traditional forms which maintained their own autonomous existences. The most interesting combined the new style with *nadagama*. *Rolina*, one of these experiments, was written and produced in late 1877 by C. Don Bastian Jayaweera Bandara (1852–1921). With a running time of less than three hours, rather than five days, *Rolina* was an instant success. Bastian Jayaweera Bandara was soon working on other plays, some utilizing plots from foreign mythology. The new combined genre, known as *nurti*, was always about youthful lovers who were impeded by someone or something in their desires to be together. Very often, the blocking character would be a wizard who would force them to go in opposite directions, their journeys taking them through forests, caves and rivers and they would very often be abducted by spirits. In these *nurti* plays, trees and flowers would speak, the lovers would encounter sages and hermits and, in the end, all would work out and the lovers reunited.

One of the more unusual *nurti* productions was an adaptation by Bastian of *Romeo and Juliet*. Utilizing painted scenery in the Italian style, which established a more European rather than Asian feel, the playing style was broad, closer to grand opera than *nadagama*.

Audiences responded positively to *nurti* not only because of its novelty but also because of its new styles of music and dance (north rather than south Indian), its short duration, its realistic backdrops, the use of indoor stages and especially its use of actresses.

Another writer who worked in the *nurti* style was Makalandage John De Silva (1857–1922), a lawyer who from 1886 presented *nurti* versions of *Julius Caesar, Measure for Measure, Merchant of Venice* and *Othello* as well as adaptations of well-known Sanskrit plays such as *Nagananda, Ratnāvali* and *Shakuntala*. Other productions by De Silva included plays about ancient Sinhala royalty.

With the *nurti* style establishing itself as the dominant form by the beginning of the twentieth century and with new playhouses being built to accommodate it, *nurti* drama groups began to be established and new means of promoting and producing plays set in motion. Perhaps the most active of the *nurti* producing groups at this time was the Tower Hall company in Colombo. This group began its existence in 1911 with a production of the play *Pandukabhaya* written by lawyer Charles Dias for the new 1,500-seat Tower Hall theatre.

As for *nadagama*, though the occasional production could still be seen through the first half of the century, the form had all but breathed its last by the 1950s. Indeed, *nadagama* elements had simply blended seamlessly into the new *nurti* style in plays by dramatists such as Charles Silva Gunasinha (d. 1962).

The coming of motion pictures to the island not only ensured the disappearance of *nadagama* but also came close to wiping out *nurti* as well. In 1932, as if to underscore this point, Tower Hall became a cinema.

World War II saw laws imposed against assemblies of all large groups of people as well as curfews. This affected the large film audiences but left the way open for smaller state productions. Once again, a number of theatre groups emerged, many doing dramatizations of well-known English and Tamil films. Some even contained elements of social criticism. Groups such as the Minerva Amateur Dramatic Club managed to combine several film plots in its productions. One plot, for example, involved both a middle-class story and a story of the lower classes (a maid and butler fall in love in one plot while the mistress of the house has a relationship with a gentleman admirer in another). Such plays included a significant mix of comedy and music.

In such productions many new stars were created, among them Rukmani Devi (Daisy Daniels, d. 1968), the Minerva's leading lady and later a well-known screen actress; Eddie Jayamanne and Jemini Kanta. Eventually Minerva's interests led it to produce its own films and in 1946 the group moved to the Chitrakala Studio in India. A year later Minerva completed its first film in Sinhala, *The Broken Promise*. A commercial success, *The Broken Promise* led Minerva and other groups to embrace cinema production enthusiastically; by the mid-1970s some 600 Sinhala films had been produced, most of them shot and edited in India. Not until the 1960s did film production begin to take place regularly in Sri Lanka (thanks mostly to the commercial interests of playwright and producer Sirisena Vimalaweera (1901–63) and his Navajeevana Studio at Kiribatgoda). In 1972, a State Film Corporation was established. Throughout the decades from the 1930s to the 1970s, film rather than live theatre dominated the island. By 1979, film itself was being challenged by a newly emerging television industry.

Despite the dominance of film, western-style plays continued to be produced by such groups as The Thespians, headed by Lucian De Zoysa. Focusing on Shakespeare in its early productions, during the 1950s it began to stage dramatizations of national historical stories. Among these were *Fortress in the Sky* (1956), *Parakramabahu, Vijaya and Kuveni* (1968) and *Princess of the Lonely Day*. Even plays by Sartre and J.B. Priestley were produced by the company. There were also productions at the University of Ceylon (now the University of Peradeniya), an institution founded in Colombo as an affiliate of the University of London in 1921 and which became autonomous in 1942.

Western-style Sinhala drama also began to emerge after World War II at the University of

Ceylon's Drama Society, a student venture under the auspices of the Department of English. Though other universities came into being including Vidyodaya University and Vidyalankara University (both 1959), University of Moratuwa (1972), University of Jaffna (1974), University of Ruhuna (1979), the Eastern University (1986) and Sabaragamuva and Rajarata Universities (both established in 1996), none had the impact in theatrical circles of the original University of Ceylon Drama Society.

From 1933 to 1956, for example, one play a year was produced on the Colombo and Peradeniya campuses by E.F.C. Ludowyke of the Department of English. A graduate of Cambridge, Ludowyke introduced a number of major dramatists – both classical and modern – to Sri Lanka and built up a discerning audience for spoken drama as well as a nucleus of talented amateurs. Among the playwrights he introduced were Sheridan, Molière, Goldoni, Shaw, Shakespeare, O'Neill, O'Casey, Pirandello, Ibsen, Pinero, Plautus, Brecht and Anouilh.

Ludowyke also produced a number of students keenly interested in directing who would, after him, continue the spoken drama tradition. Foremost among these were Ranjini Obeysekera, Ashley Halpe and Cuthbert Amarsinha. His first production in Sinhala came in 1945 when he produced an adaptation of Gogol's The Marriage.

An alumni group was responsible for yet another university-based group – Stage and Set, a company which produced such dramatists as Arthur Miller (Death of a Salesman and The Crucible were both produced in the 1960s) and even Brecht (Caucasian Chalk Circle and Mother Courage).

The founding of the Arts Council of Sri Lanka in 1952 was perhaps the most significant step in the overall development of public support for theatre activity on the island. Modelled on the Arts Council of Great Britain, the Sri Lankan Arts Council by 1959 began focusing attention on Sinhala-language drama although many English-language groups continued to operate along with others working in Tamil. Eventually three different Arts Council drama panels were established for the three different language groups along with other Arts Council panels for traditional music, western music, dance, visual arts and puppetry.

In the spoken drama areas, the first major problem facing the council was the perceived lack of quality scripts. A series of annual competitions was launched for new plays as well as adaptations into Sinhala and Tamil and the council became involved in supporting productions of the winning scripts. Annual new play festivals soon became part of the theatrical landscape. Most of these scripts dealt with contemporary social problems although a fair number turned to national history for subject matter. While most were fairly conservative in style, some writers did begin to experiment with form as well as content. Crossover forms involving elements of older and ritual forms also began to be seen within the new written dramas.

Among the most impressive of the Sinhala scripts was Ediriweera Sarachchandra's (1914–96) Maname, written in 1956. A landmark in the history of Sinhala drama, the play is based on a Jataka tale and combines nadagama with the well-made-play form. In 1961, he created a second important work in this style, Sinhabahu, a piece dealing with the origins of the Sinhalese and conflicts between young and old. Other writers who followed this style were Gunasena Galappatti, Dayananda Gunawardena (1934–94), Henry Jayasena

The Sinhala Drama Circle's 1956 production of Maname written and produced by Ediriweera Sarachchandra.

(b. 1931) and Bandula Jayawardhene (b. 1928). These plays found new audiences for theatre and led to the creation of still other groups and the emergence of other writers.

Among these new dramatists were Sugatahapala De Silva (b. 1928) whose play *Tattu Geval* (1962) dealt with sex, marriage and the urbanized middle class; R.R. Samarakoan (b. 1939) and Jayasekera Aponsu (b. 1954), both of whom wrote about life in the slums; and Felix Premawardhene (b. 1926), Premaranjit Thilakaratna and Dhamma Jagoda (d. 1988), all trained in the west and all authors of Sinhala adaptations of western plays.

By the 1970s several new purpose-built theatre spaces came into being. Among them were Navarangahala Royal College Hall, the 200-seat Sudaharshi Hall, the Ramakrishna Hall and John De Silva Memorial Hall, all in Colombo. The older Tower Hall, again being used for theatre, remained the largest and best equipped of the theatre spaces.

A new enthusiasm, especially for Sinhala drama, could be seen in the 1970s especially among the young, bilingual and well-educated. During this decade, provincial cities began to see some of the prize-winning plays from the Colombo Festivals, a tradition that began in 1967 on World Theatre Day (27 March), a Unesco-supported event organized by the International Theatre Institute each year.

During the late 1970s and early 1980s political satire began to be seen in the works of Simon Navagattegama (b. 1939), especially his *Subha Saha Yasa* (1974) and more commercial plays began to be seen in the works of writer Nihal Silva. The plays of Nedra Vittachchi, particularly *Smart Ass* and *Knots*, wry studies of middle-class love, sex and marriage, also attracted wide attention. A number of writers turned to television, however, which robbed the live theatre of some of its most promising dramatists.

The 1970s and 1980s also saw a number of foreign theatre professionals – mostly British, US and German – invited to Colombo to offer workshops of various sorts including some in musical theatre and some in theatre for young audiences, the latter with the assistance of the German Cultural Institute. As a result, a Children's Drama Panel was added to the Arts Council in 1975 headed by Tissa Kariyawasam. Among the writers and directors to emerge from these workshops were Karen Brekenridge, Irene Wanigaratne, Rohan Wadugodapitiya, Leticia Boteju and E.M.W. Joseph.

Two of the more active groups in the 1990s have been the Colombo Amateur Dramatic Society which has done regular productions of mostly light comedies, and the Young Players founded by Richard De Zoysa (d. 1989). Among

Jackson Anthony in Ape Kattiya (Our People)'s 1986 production of *Marat/Sade* produced by Sugatahapala De Silva.

notable actor-directors in Colombo in the 1990s are Jit Pieris, Indu Dharmasena, Chitranga Kariyawasam, Sakuntula Dharmatilaka, Rudi Corens and Steve De La Silva.

Despite such activity by the Arts Council, the notion of state subsidy was still the exception rather than the rule in Sri Lanka in the 1990s. Nevertheless, professionalism was growing, thanks in part to the support of the Tower Hall Theatre Foundation and National Theatre Trust. The National Theatre Trust was an arm of the Arts Council dedicated to the development of Sri Lankan drama in the 1970s. It selected the best plays of the year and toured them to various cities at a subsidized admission. The manager of the trust was Gamini Wijesuriya, an actor. From 1965, the National Theatre Trust urged that playwrights, directors and actors be paid at least nominal sums for their work. Even so, Sri Lankan theatre artists remained unable to live on their work in theatre and government discussions about the establishment of a professional 'national' company remain unfulfilled. The National Trust was abolished by the party that came to power in the 1970s.

In the 1990s, a number of businesses began to support individual productions. Combined with the various activities of independent and university-related groups each season, Colombo now sees more than a hundred performances annually. The most successful groups tour (usually by bus) to smaller cities including Kandy, Galle and Anuradhapura. There are many annual drama festivals in Colombo, including a festival of children's theatre, a festival of puppetry (both sponsored by the Arts Council) and a youth theatre festival (sponsored by the Ministry of Youth Affairs, Sports and Rural Development).

Festivals of traditional music and dance and the many public healing rituals most often take place in communities outside Colombo. Looked at broadly, three basic styles can be seen at these events: a hill country style, a low country style and a Sabaragamuva style. All three styles are directly connected to ritual and are aimed at such things as propitiating gods and demons or, as indicated, curing illness. Each has its own system of hand and body movements and each mixes segments of Sri Lankan classical movement with folk dance. Among the latter are sword dances, stick dances and the popular yak tail dances. All three styles are performed to the accompaniment of drums with both the drums themselves and drumming styles unique to the different dance forms.

The State Dancer's Ensemble depicting supernatural mythical birds (*gurula*) and the cobra (*naga*) in a *kolam*. Directed by W.B. Makuloluwa.

A more modern Indian-style of dance-drama was introduced to Sri Lanka in 1934 when dramatist-director Rabindranath Tagore visited the country with his acclaimed production of *Shap Mochan* (*Redemption*). Many young Sri Lankans became interested in this approach which combined both classical Indian and more modern western dance forms. Sri Lankans who studied the form in India were further influenced by Uday Shankar. Many later offered performances in the new style which they tended to call ballet though it was far from the western meaning of the term. Such Sri Lankan ballet currently involves the presentation of a story through dance and song narration. From this movement emerged a School of Dance and Ballet which now has university-level status.

In general, rehearsal periods are short for all styles of Sri Lankan theatre and technical rehearsals almost non-existent. It is rare that a group gets into a theatre more than a day or two prior to its opening. As a result, improvisation is a much appreciated technique.

One last form that needs to be mentioned is Sri Lankan puppet theatre which has the longest history of any form and is even mentioned in ancient literature. Unfortunately, no concrete examples of the art exist prior to the mid-nineteenth century. Among the major scholars and practitioners in the field is G. Podi Sirina, a puppeteer from Ambalangoda – one of two coastal cities in which the ancient styles of puppetry are still practised. At the same time that the *nadagama* was declining in importance early in the twentieth century, Podi Sirina began to create brilliant puppet versions of the original stories. Later his puppets were used for the telling of a wide variety of historical tales. Evidence exists indicating that puppetry was even utilized by Buddhist monks and Roman Catholic missionaries.

During the last half of the twentieth century, puppetry was popularized by Jayadeva Tilakasiri (b. 1921). Utilizing European forms as well as introducing glove-puppets, Tilakasiri was the major organizer of the first Sri Lankan Puppet Festival in 1975, an event that included both modern and traditional performances. During later festivals, puppet troupes from Czechoslovakia, Belgium, the United States and Australia participated. It was Belgian puppeteer Rudi Corens who helped to develop rod and glove puppetry in the country. Jim Henson-inspired Muppets are now used as well in various education programmes.

In the area of theatre for young audiences, a relatively extensive survey was written by Somalatha Subashinghe for Lowell Swortzell's *International Guide to Children's Theatre and Educational Theatre* (1990). This study notes that:

In the 1960s two women, Eileen Sarachchandra and Soma Kiriella, gave impetus to the creation of real children's theatre. Their work with children, using creative dramatics and child drama based on current pedagogical and philosophical theories of children's theatre, reawakened interest in the field.

In the late 1960s the faculty of education at the University of Peradeniya, headed by Professor Premadasa Udagama, formed the Lama Natya Mandalaya (Children's Drama Circle). This move was initiated by Bandula Jayewardena and Wimaladharma Diyasena, theatre artists and educators. With the cooperation and support of the Department of Education, the two set up a project in the Kandy schools in which they promoted children's theatre. Seminars and discussions, supported and attended by educators, artists, intellectuals, and the media, were followed by children's theatre competitions that stressed various forms of theatre for children: performances for and by children, Theatre-in-Education, and creative dramatics. Although the project was well received within the educational and theatrical community, the population at large was not yet convinced of the validity of children's theatre.

In 1967 Gamini Wijesooriya, an actor and teacher attached to the Ministry of Education, organized a Drama-in-Education workshop for teachers under the sponsorship of UNESCO (United Nations Educational, Scientific, and Cultural Organization) and the Ministry of Education. The workshop was run by Professor David Kemp, a drama-in-education specialist from Canada. The workshops were offered annually through 1972, when they ended because of the lack of funds. Nevertheless, they helped to create an awareness of and interest in contemporary children's theatre, and the Interschool Drama Competitions that followed revealed evidence that ideas investigated and discussed in the workshops had made their way into the classroom.

Of the first group of workshop participants, many (including Chandrasena Dassanayake,

Lionel Ranwela, Piyasena, Daya Alwis, Sriyananda, Sunethra Sarachchandra, Gamini Samarakoon, Gamini Haththotuwa, and Somalatha Subashinghe) made significant contributions to the advancement of children's theatre in Sri Lanka. Popular artists such as Vajira Chitrasena in dance and Nanda Malini in music also made valuable contributions in their specific fields.

Meanwhile folktales such as *Rattaran* and *Elova Gihin Melowa Awa*, by E.R. Sarachchandra, *Nari Bena* and *Goraka Yaka*, by Dayananda Gunawardena, and *Thawath Udesenak*, by Henry Jayasena, which began as plays acted by schoolchildren, were now being presented by adult companies. These works were considered suitable for young audiences and became accepted successes in their new incarnations.

Sri Lanka has no drama schools. Courses at high school level are offered but are often taught by people without adequate training in the field. Despite this, such courses are popular and the government regularly speaks of establishing more advanced programmes. To date, however, little has happened in this area.

In terms of scholarship, comparatively little has been published on Sri Lankan theatre and virtually nothing on its history. One of the more useful texts is Ediriweera Sarachchandra's *The Folk Drama of Ceylon* (1952). Originally published in English, it was translated into Sinhala in 1968 and reissued in 1992. Another valuable history of Sinhala-language dramatic literature can be found in Tissa Kariyawasam's three volumes on Sinhala drama, which cover the period from 1867 to 1956. He also did a study of Sri Lankan university theatre focusing on the period 1921–81. Scholar Mudiyanse Disonayke has published four important volumes on theatrical traditions in the hill country and Vanniya areas.

Tissa Kariyawasam

Further Reading

Goonethillaka, M.H. *Kolam Nataka Sahitya* [Kolam: A traditional drama]. Colombo: Ratna Publishers, n.d. 165 pp.
——. *Nadagam*. New Delhi: Satguru, 1991. 93 pp.
Hapuarachchi, D.V. *Sinhala Natya Itihasaya* [A history of Sinhala drama]. Colombo: Lakehouse Publishing, 1983. 220 pp.
Kariyawasam, Tissa. *Gan Madu Puranaya* [Community rituals]. Colombo: Library Services Board, 1985. 220 pp.
——. *Sinhala Natakaye Vikashanaya 1867–1911* [A history of Sinhala drama 1867–1911]. Colombo: Pradeepa, 1979. 260 pp.
——. *Vishva Vidyala Natya Vamsaya 1921–1981* [A history of university drama 1921–1981]. Colombo: S. Godage & Bros., 1983. 104 pp.
——. *Visi Vasaraka Natya Ha Ranga Kalava 1912–1931* [Twenty years of Sinhala drama and theatre 1912–1931]. Colombo: S. Godage & Bros., 1981. 178 pp.
——. CC. *Visipas Vasaraka Natya Ha Ranga Kalava 1932–1956* [Twenty-five years of Sinhala drama and theatre 1932–1956]. Colombo: S. Godage & Bros., 1983. 200 pp.
——. *Yak Thovil Ha Inhala Samajaya*. [Demon rituals in Sinhala society]. Colombo: Ministry of Cultural Affairs, 1975. 172 pp.
Sarachchandra, Ediriweera. *The Folk Drama of Ceylon*. Colombo: The Government Press, 1952; reprint edn, 1968; reissued 1992. 180 pp.
Subashinghe, Somalatha. 'Sri Lanka'. In *International Guide to Children's Theatre and Educational Theatre: A Historical and Geographical Source Book*, ed. Lowell Swortzell, 290–6. Westport, CT: Greenwood Press, 1990.
Tilakasiri, Jayadeva. *Puppetry in Sri Lanka*. Colombo, 1961.

TADJIKISTAN

(see **TAJIKISTAN**)

TAIWAN

(see **CHINA**)

TAJIKISTAN

(Overview)

Formerly the Tadzhik Soviet Socialist Republic (SSR) of the Union of Soviet Socialist Republics (USSR), Tajikistan has been an independent republic since 1991. Bordered on the north and west by Kyrgyzstan and Uzbekistan, on the east by China and on the south by Afghanistan, Tajikistan also includes the region previously known as Gorno-Badakhshan Autonomous Oblast, which occupies 44.5 per cent of the country. Tajikistan is extremely mountainous and settlement is concentrated in the lowlands. The total land area is 143,100 square kilometres (55,200 square miles).

Dushanbe, built by the Soviets after Stalin ceded the cities of Samarkand and Bukhara – the major centres of Tajik culture and history – to Uzbekistan, became the Tajik capital and largest city. In 1990, it had a population of about 602,000. Khojand (formerly Leninabad) is the country's second largest city with about 163,000 inhabitants. The least urbanized republic of the former USSR (more than two-thirds of its population live in rural areas), Tajikistan's largest economic sector remains agriculture.

Tajiks, an Iranian people with a Sunni Muslim heritage, constitute about 62 per cent of the country's population, which was estimated in 1994 to be 6 million. Uzbeks, the largest minority with nearly one-quarter of the population, live primarily in the Fergana Valley and in the vicinity of KIliab in south central Tajikistan. Russians constitute about 8 per cent of the population. Other minorities include Kyrgyz, Ukrainians, Germans, Turkmen and Koreans. Some 10 per cent of the population are Pamiris who practise Ismailism and are thus Shia

Seveners (believers in the succession of seven imams after Muhammad). In 1992, civil war broke out and Uzbeks and Russians began leaving the country in large numbers. This massive emigration of technically skilled workers has contributed to the country's economic decline in the mid-1990s.

With independence, Tajikistan faced the worst and longest running political crisis among all the former Soviet Central Asian republics. Fighting between pro- and anti-communist forces broke out in Tajikistan in 1992 and eventually led to the ousting of President Rakhmon Nabiyev, former chief of the Communist Party of the Tadzhik SSR in the early 1980s. Afghanistan and Iran supported the Islamic democratic side, but with the aid of Russian and Uzbek arms, pro-communists took power and established a new government headed by Imomali Rakhmonov, gaining control of the entire country in the process. Opposition groups were banned in 1992, activities of the press severely constrained and all opposition newspapers were closed. Many journalists and prominent independent leaders were arrested and some killed. This civil war forced government officials, most of them former communists, to suspend economic reforms. Tajikistan continues to be a member of the Commonwealth of Independent States (CIS).

Tajiks have lived in the area of present-day Tajikistan since approximately 1000 BC, when Persian tribes moved northwards into central Asia and Afghanistan. The word *taj* was used by early Arab invaders to describe those who spoke Persian. Over the course of its history the area has been invaded by Macedonians, Arabs, Mongols and others. By the thirteenth century the area was part of the Mongol Empire and became part of the Bukhara Khanate in the sixteenth century. Russian control was established in 1868. In 1916 many Tajiks and others in central Asia rebelled against the Russian government when it attempted to enlist them in the Tzarist army.

Following the Socialist Revolution of 1917, nationalist and Islamic movements spread. Local Basmachi guerrilla groups resisted Russian rule and Soviet power, but were defeated in 1921. The area then became part of the Turkestan Autonomous Soviet Socialist Republic (ASSR) which also included portions of present-day Kazakhstan, Turkmenistan and Uzbekistan. In 1923 a famine caused by the civil war was followed by massive epidemics. In total, these events wiped out half a million Tajik families and helped the Bolsheviks finally to overthrow the resistance. In 1924 the area of present-day Tajikistan was made an autonomous republic within the Uzbek SSR and a distinct Tajik political entity was formed for the first time in the 1920s. In 1927 Arabic script was replaced by Latin and in 1940 it was changed to Cyrillic.

Throughout these changes, national, religious, cultural and historical values were all but ignored. By the end of 1992, political, religious and ethnic tension continued to lead to civil war. Thousands of Russians were evacuated at this point, many others escaping to Afghanistan. In the late 1990s the overall economic and political situation was still extremely strained.

Theatrically, Tajikistan boasts centuries-old traditions in the national arts dating back to the Hellenic period. By the twelfth century, Omar Khayyam reported on the existence of a popular puppet theatre, *zochabozi*. Certain theatrical elements can be found in peasant songs connected with popular customs and traditions, such as the spring festivals of flowers, and in pantomimes. *Maskharobozes* (buffoons) performed utilizing music, dance and storytelling became very popular for their comic and sharply satiric art. Welcomed at weddings and Muslim holidays such as Ramadan and Qorban, their art reached its developmental peak in the late nineteenth and early twentieth centuries. The Grotesque, exaggeration and buffoonery were major components of the *Maskharabozes'* acting.

Other indigenous forms included comic sketches, humorous stories, fairytales, fantasies and songs as well as poems by such classic Tajik authors as Bedil, Khafid, Saadi, Jami and Khiloli. In addition, actors would also play musical instruments, dance, perform acrobatics and improvise pantomimes for audiences of several hundred at a time.

The evolution of theatre and drama in Tajik culture also has much in common with Uzbek tradition (see UZBEKISTAN) and, during the twentieth century, with Russian theatrical art. The first modern amateur groups appeared in Dushanbe in 1927. Their repertoires consisted of propagandistic plays about life after the 1917 Russian Revolution. The first Tajik State Theatre was opened in 1929. In the beginning, the state theatre staged mainly Russian plays in translation. The first play by a Tajik dramatist to be performed was *Struggle*, a drama about the Red Army. Written by the actor A. Usmanov, it was produced in 1933. The première of Schiller's *Perfidy and Love* (1937) was the first attempt to stage a world classic. Other early landmark productions included *Men With Red Batons* by Satim Ulugzade, *Rustam and Sukhrob* by Abdushukur Pirmuhammadzoda and Shakespeare's *Othello*, staged during the ten-day Festival of Tajik Arts and Literature held in Moscow in 1941.

Realistic acting, based on the Stanislavskian identification of each actor with the dramatic character played and the creation of true-to-life images, came to predominate in the theatre by the late 1930s. The years of the Great Patriotic War (1941–5) saw a number of modern national plays infused with a fervent patriotic feeling. *Nadir's House* (1943) by Jalal Ikrami and Alexei Faiko, *Mother's Heart* (1942) by Ikrami and *In the Flames* (1944) by Ulugzade exemplified the hard work and mass heroism of the battlefields and reflected the image of a multinational Soviet people.

Tajikistan, as in other Soviet Asian republics during the war, became a home for theatres from other parts of the USSR. Leningrad Theatre of Comedy, headed by Russian director Nikolai Akimov, worked in Dushanbe throughout this period of occupation. A more heroic style of work was seen in productions such as *Fuente Ovejuna* by Lope de Vega, mounted by Leningrad director V. Kantsel with Sofiya Tuiboieva in the main role and Shamsi Qiyomov as Frondoso.

However, comedy, rooted in *maskharoboz*, remained closer to the Tajik nature than realism or heroic-romantic pathos. Such comedies as

Maisara by Uzbek author Khamza and the lyric-satiric *The Five Ruble Bride* by Mamed Ordubady were major successes. Tajik theatre also continued to develop in the area of musical drama using domestic characters, farcical motifs and a lively sense of humour, and such plays remained in the repertoire of many companies during the war years. Meanwhile, Molière's *Imaginary Invalid* (1944) shaped the national taste for more classical comedy. The State Theatre production socialized the story with Argan becoming an egoistic and careless bourgeois.

In the post-war years the State Theatre – now known as the Lahuti Theatre – turned to foreign and Russian classics, staging such plays as Schiller's *The Robbers*, Shakespeare's *Hamlet, Romeo and Juliet* and *Othello,* with Mohammadjon Qasymov in the title role, and *Revizor* (*The Government Inspector*) by Gogol. Also seen were plays rooted in folklore and historical productions such as *Alisher Navoi* (1949) by Uzbek playwrights A. Uighun and I. Sultanov.

In the early 1950s national playwrights attempted to reflect contemporary life in plays such as *Iskateli* (*Searchers*) by Ulugzade about geologists but most such works met with the disapproval of critics. Since that time, most Tajik playwrights have rejected plays whose conflicts are too clear or sharp. The result has been many conflictless plays about farmers and the *intelligentsia*, all without action or interesting characters. One of the few new themes had to do with the fight of Tajik women for equal rights and the prosperity of collective farms, both seen in *Woman's Will* (1962) by A'zam Sidqi.

In the 1960s, dramatists began to reflect a more private life and to focus on the individual within the larger social unit. Domestic comedies proved popular and included *Cost: 30 Kopeks* (1961) by Qiyomov and Muhyiddin Farhat and the extremely optimistic *Sparkling Pearls* (1962) by Ulugzade which used young people as main characters. Plays about the Revolution and the Great Patriotic War with their larger-than-life heroes and stereotypical images of enemies were also in the repertoire.

The documentary play *Storm* (1967) by Ghani Abdullo and Qiyomov dealt with opposition to the Red Army by the *basmachi* bands during the 1922 civil war in central Asia. It was a large-scale performance by director Evgeni Mitelman and focused on counter-revolutionary resistance to Soviet power. The play was dedicated to the forty years of Soviet presence in Tajikistan and was more a dramatized report to authorities than a work of art.

The isolated Tajik theatre after 1956 and into the 1960s could barely keep pace with contemporary tendencies in political, social and artistic life taking place in the Soviet Union, the years of Khrushchev's thaw. The cult of Stalin's personality was unmasked at this time, condemned and soon became part of the country's tragic history. More democratic tendencies, however, encouraged all Soviet nations in the 1960s and gave them the hope of long expected societal changes for the better. No noticeable achievements in artistic life reached or directly impacted the Tajik theatre, however. None the less, the period saw the restoration of many national names which had been wiped out by Stalinism during the 1930s and 1940s. Tajik scholarship also corrected and rehabilitated falsified biographies of older poets, philosophers, humanists and thinkers charged with being Tajik nationalists. New, more objective research by orientalists also became very important in the new evolution of a strong national identity.

This in turn led to a number of biographical plays devoted to prominent people of Tajik heritage – Hafiz Rudaki, Abuali Sina, Jami, Omar Khayyam and Bedil. *Rudaki* (1958) by Ulugzade, devoted to the 1,100th anniversary of Abu Abdullo Rudaki, founder of Tajik-Persian classic literature, was the first in this genre. Mounted at the Lahuti Theatre by Mitelman with a spectacular set design, the play, with Asli Burkhanow in the title role, focused in poetic language on the social and religious conflicts of the time revealing the tragic history of Rudaki as poet and humanist. Even Shakespeare's *King Lear* (1957) with Qasymov in the title role, was produced by the Lahuti Theatre as a poetic Tajik fairytale about a father whose madness and hard heartedness led to his tragic fall. The production was successful despite its old-fashioned, declamatory performing style and its attempt to reflect socialist realism as demanded by the Communist Party in 1946.

In 1959 the Lahuti Theatre company was reinvigorated by a new group of graduates from the Tajik Studio of GITIS (State Institute of Theatre Arts, now the Russian Academy of Theatrical Arts in Moscow) led by Olga Pyzhova and Boris Bibikov. In 1958 a Youth Theatre was established by a group of Tajik students graduating from the Shchepkin School in Moscow. Within a short time, however, this group merged with the Lahuti company. This new generation of actors and their more restrained acting style demanded a new repertoire that was more poetic, psychological and intellectual. One of their first successes was the exotic, Italian theatrical fairytale *The Stag King* by Carlo Gozzi, a production influenced by Evgeni Vakhtangov's famous production of *Princess Turandot*. For the audience it was a meeting with an unknown, spectacular world full of love, envy and brave fantasy. The young actors were skilled in mime, rhythm and gesture and to some it was a reincarnation of the ancient Tajik *maskharoboze* tradition.

The production *Rustam and Sukhrob* (1967) by Abdullo, mounted by F. Alexandrin and Kh. Abdurazzakov, became a sample of the possible fruitful cooperation of different generations. This was not a remount of the theatre's 1941 production but rather a new interpretation of the heroic-tragic stories from Ferdowsi's *Shakhnamae* epic emphasizing anti-war themes. Tajik theatre at this time also tended toward the poetic as in *Gorianka* (*A Mountain Girl*, 1961), a translated drama by Dagestan poet Rasul Gamzatov. Director Mitelman combined romanticism with realism, comedy and tragic tension.

The 1960s marked a period of interest in Indian dramaturgy; *Oblation* (1959) by Rabindranath Tagore set the tone. Later *Woman From Punjab*, *Sonni* and *Makhival* by B. Garga were all staged, as were translated plays from the other Soviet republics.

By the early 1980s, there were eleven theatre companies in the republic staging dramas, musical comedies, opera, ballet (Aini Opera and Ballet Theatre in Dushanbe) and a theatre for young audiences.

Perestroika, however, barely reached Tajikistan even by the early 1990s. With the dissolution of the USSR, state-supported theatres suddenly had to look for sponsorship. Some succeeded; some did not. Since 1988, the annual theatre festival *Parastu* (*Swallow*) has helped energize theatre life in the republic. The festival has also encouraged new groups to be formed and has led to the decentralization of theatre life, earlier concentrated in the capital. The Fourth Festival in 1991 – on the eve of the USSR's dissolution and of Tajik independence – had even greater cultural significance than usual.

Economic misery and political polarization did not prevent a cultural revival in Tajikistan during the first year of independence (1991).

Tajikistan found itself in a unique cultural paradox: the more the political and economic situation in the republic worsened, the more various and interesting the theatres' work became. In 1989 Malika Djurabekova opened an experimental folk-ethnographic theatre-studio. Shortly after, *Nowruz*, a central Asian theatre festival, became an annual event. By the mid-1990s a new direction was clear. For decades the official position was that the smaller republics received their theatrical cultures from 'elder sister' Russia. This influence was obvious and the best national artists were graduates of Moscow theatre schools. But this cultural policy simply led to the creation of hundreds of similar, pseudo-national productions throughout the central Asian region.

By 1995 – with a rise in national self-consciousness – the most interesting productions were turning back to indigenous traditions and were opening up newer aspects of national culture. This process was occurring in all the former Asian Soviet republics.

A production by Tajik director Farukh Qasymov of *Yusuf the Lost Will Return to Khanaan Again* was awarded the Grand Prize at *Nowruz '90*, and was probably the starting point for this widespread trend. It is impossible to overestimate the significance of this event. It assimilated earlier pre-theatrical forms, rituals, folklore, poetry and other elements of national art and culture. The metaphoric language of these forms was transformed into modern theatre language and became part of a reconstruction of the national spirit. Rich in Tajik-Persian poetry, this performance told of the loss of spirituality and beauty. It encompassed not only art, but also real life.

The Rudaki Khorogh Theatre in the mountain town of Khorogh was ruined in 1991 after an earthquake but the company continued to work under extreme conditions without theatre premises. Despite this misfortune, the group took part in *Parastu '91* in Kulob with a new production, *Zir O Bam* (*Sound and Rhythm*). Director M. Mazabshoyev – utilizing primitivism as well as theatrical minimalism – created a musical-dramatic poem celebrating a culture born through an unbreakable connection between humanity and nature.

At the touch-point between indigenous music-dance traditions and later styles of national dramaturgy has come a new type of performance tending towards the recognition of problems utilizing parable or a pointed grotesque. *Fishor* (1989) by S. Ayubi, staged by Mirzovattan

Small Apartment With a Big Balcony by Sh. Shamanadze.
Photo: courtesy of *Teatr*.

Mirov at the Valizade Kuliab Theatre of Musical Comedy is a good example. Its aesthetics were innovative in the country as well as fruitful as later productions proved.

A sharply dramatic play, *I Am a Murderer* (1991) by Nurullo Abduloyev, revealed a range of national characters and relationships in both their domestic and ethical aspects. The director and main performer, Ato Mukhamedjanov, effectively mined this rich psychological material and successfully mounted it at the Lahuti Theatre.

In the 1990s theatres suffered a great number of problems. Unfortunately, the civil war terminated what promised to be the beginning of a real theatrical revival. Lost were theatres such as the Akhorun – headed by Farukh Qasymov, famous for his production of *The Firebugs* (1989) by Max Frisch – a theatre that fought to save national traditions and freedom of consciousness. Also lost was the Theatre Studio Poluostrov (Peninsula) of director Borzu Abdurazzakov, who had been praised by critics for his productions of *Glass Menagerie* (1989) at the Lahuti Theatre and *Antigone* (1990) by Jean Anouilh. He was a winner of *Parastu-90*. A graduate of GITIS and a student of outstanding theatre masters such as Maria Knebel and Anatoly Efros, he developed the tradition of highly psychological theatre. His work examined personality through conflicts and the realities of the time, while resisting spirituality. In his extremely theatrical production of *Sultan Is Sultan* (1991) by Syrian playwright S. Vannus, at the Valizade Kùliab Theatre of Musical Comedy in the city of Kùliab, he utilized the method of 'theatre in theatre' wherein the actors played a comedy about the impersonality of power and highlighted the joyful absurdity of collisions emphasized by carnival elements in the performance – the theatre's way of laughing and speaking ironically about the people and their rulers. This director's style produced various results in family stories. In *Small Apartment With a Big Balcony* by Georgian author Sh. Shamanadze staged in the Poluostrov, the director sympathized with the exhausted people in the play who, forced by circumstance to live together and share their hard routine, was too familiar to millions of families. These productions were events of social significance.

Natasha Rapoport

Further Reading

Istoriya sovetskogo dramaticheskogo teatra [History of Soviet dramatic theatre]. 6 vols. Moscow: Nauka, 1966–71.

Nurdzanov, N.H. *Istoriya tadzikskogo sovetskogo teatra* [History of Tadjik soviet theatre]. Dushanbe: Donis, 1990. 408 pp.

Rashid, Ahmed. *The Resurgence of Central Asia.* London: Oxford University Press, 1994.

Rozanova, Evgenia. *Pod krylom kuliabskoy lastochki* [Under the wing of Kuliab swallow]. *Teatr* 10 (1991).

TASMANIA

(see **AUSTRALIA**)

THAILAND

(Overview)

One of the few countries in Asia never to have been colonized, Thailand, known until 1939 as Siam, is a Southeast Asian kingdom bordered by Myanmar (Burma), Laos, Cambodia and Malaysia. With a total land area of 198,100 square kilometres (513,100 square miles) the country had a 1995 population estimated at 60.2 million, 77 per cent of whom lived in rural areas. Its largest city and capital is Bangkok. Thai, a Sino-Tibetan language, is spoken by virtually the entire population but English is also used in commerce and government.

The Thai people are thought to have emigrated to Southeast Asia from southwestern China in the first century AD. Thailand's period of greatest cultural development was the Sukhotai period (1238–1378) when the Thai absorbed elements of various civilizations including the Indian and Chinese. In 1350 a unified Thai kingdom was established by a ruler known posthumously as Rama Thibodi, who founded the kingdom of Ayutthaya and made the city of Ayutthaya his capital. This kingdom flourished over the next four centuries conquering the Khmer (Cambodian) Kingdom of Angkor in 1431 and, in the process, adopting many Cambodian court dance and music styles. Contacts, some friendly and some not, were made over the next four centuries with the Portuguese, Dutch, British and Chinese.

In 1767 Burmese troops captured and destroyed Ayutthaya. Burmese control was ended quickly, however, with an uprising led by General Pya Taksin, who proclaimed himself king. On his death, the crown passed to General Pya Chakri, founder of the present dynasty of Thai kings. He ruled as Rama I from 1782 to 1809. A commercial treaty was signed with the British in 1826 and British influence expanded in Thailand through the nineteenth century.

Though the country's independence was maintained, it did give up some territory during this period.

The Thai government entered World War I on the side of the Allies in 1917. Later becoming a founding member of the League of Nations, Thailand tried to get back some of its former territory by supporting the Japanese during World War II. After the war, it signed a treaty with India and Britain renouncing its land claims.

In 1947 a military junta seized control of the government and retained tight control – except for a very brief period – until 1957. In 1954 Thailand became a founding member of the Southeast Asia Treaty Organization (SEATO) with headquarters in Bangkok. A series of coups in 1957 and 1958 led to the banning of all political parties. A new constitution was put forward in 1968 and parliamentary elections were held a year later with the United Thai People's Party winning a majority and the Democratic Party winding up as the official opposition. Through the 1970s, 1980s and into the 1990s, the pattern continued with military coups, new constitutions and new elections taking place on an almost regular basis.

Classic Thai art and literature is based heavily on the *Ramakien*, the Thai version of the Hindu epic, *Ramayana*. Its many court forms of dance have been strongly influenced by Indian dance styles, and its music by both India and China. Thai peasants have traditionally expressed their joys and sorrows through music, dance and storytelling. These arts have long formed an integral part of popular pastimes as well as of religious ceremonies. Also used to communicate and inculcate community values across the generations, public performative events relate to birth, death, healing, celebrating harvests and acknowledging various rites of passage among other things.

At the root of this popular oral tradition is *plaeng puen muang* (folk song), which varies according to the locality, the seasons and the reasons for the particular event. Some fifty different styles of *plaeng puen muang* have been noted by cultural anthropologists. Among these are *plaeng rua* (boat song) which dates to before 1450 and involves a song and movement exchange between a young man and woman and is always done in a boat; *mohlam*, a type of song and dance involving up to three people who perform on an open platform; and *mohlam moo*, performed on a decorated stage utilizing performers acting out the roles of various individuals in traditional stories. There are many sub-genres of *mohlam*.

The most typical traditional performance in the south is *norah*, a dance-drama believed to have evolved from hunting rituals and other ancient ceremonies. Influenced by both Indian and Javanese cultures, the *norah* dance – among the best known of Thai dances – is highly sophisticated, clearly defined and emotionally powerful. *Norah* is intended to express the beauty, gentleness and softness of the Thai people as well as their strength and power. Its rhythms and melodies are loud and forceful yet they have a warm and natural charm. Known also as *manorah*, performances involve three actors – a prince, a princess and a clown – and a traditional orchestra composed of drums, gongs and double reeds. Mystical at its roots and done for the entertainment of the spirits as well as the community, *norah* can now be performed by both men and women. *Norah* and other traditional performances had other functions: to unite the community, to provide a rhythmic background for work or leisure activities, to entertain, to inculcate beliefs, to transmit information, and to reflect emotions.

Palace-based performances did many of these same things but were more formalized, refined and set standards for artistic skills. They also set in motion an ongoing model for royal and state patronage of the arts in Thailand. One also needs to understand the interrelationship of *baan* (village), *wang* (palace) and *wat* (temple) to appreciate the complexities of traditional Thai life. With both royalty and the people going to the temples, religious ground becomes a key place for interchange on both the political and cultural levels. As Mattani Mojdara Rutnin (1988) has stated,

Classical performing arts have always been associated with the monarch. Training of classical dancers started in the royal palace in the Ayutthaya period in the late sixteenth century under the supervision of royal princesses. Traditionally, these royal dancers performed only for the King and the royal family as an important part of the royal ceremonies, celebrations and entertainments. Female court dancers, many of whom were consorts, sisters, daughters, nieces or granddaughters of the King and Queen, were confined within the Inner Court. They performed celestial dances and dance-dramas which glorified the King as Vishnu-Avatar (Incarnation of the god Vishnu) such as the *Ramakien* and *Unarut*. These *nang nai* (ladies of the Inner Court) represented Nang Apsorn (celestial dancers and musicians) and therefore were protected by royal permission from other royal prerogatives of the King. There were many political incidents in which Thai kings did not give royal permission to other royal princes or rulers of states ... to train or possess *lakhorn nang nai* (female royal troupes) as this could be regarded as an attempt to rival the King and his absolute monarchy.

Royal performances can be divided into two types: *khon* (a masked dance performed mostly by men) and *lakorn* (dance-dramas performed without masks). *Khon* has no dialogue and can also be classified as a genre of mime with all *khon* stories based on the *Ramayana*. *Lakorn* is the Thai version of the Javanese word *lakon* or perhaps the Malay word *lakan*. Some believe that the word was derived from the name of Nakornsritammarat province, often abbreviated to Nakorn. Whatever its genealogy, it is agreed that there are two types of *lakorn*, the *lakorn nai* (performed exclusively within the palace) and *lakorn nork* (outside drama and the folk counterpart of the indoor palace style). The stories in both styles deal with love and tragedy.

Lakorn nai, though considered as sung drama, is actually not sung by its principal performers. The players rather mime and dance to words sung by an accompanying chorus. Strictly performed within the walls of the palace and done only by women, its main purpose was to support the glory of the king as symbol as well as to continue the traditional dances and movements. Unlike *lakorn nork*, it stressed values of exquisite beauty rather than entertainment. Originally based on religious themes and stories, performances often went on over three days and nights.

The traditional puppet forms must also be mentioned here – *nang yai* and *nang talung*, for *khon* (dating to at least the sixteenth century) derives part of its uniqueness from puppetry. Done by male dancers with a traditional orchestra to the chanting of a storyteller, *khon* has four main types of characters which the performers specialize in – the young male or female, the antagonist-demon and the athletic and usually comic monkey figure. The actors wear brightly coloured masks which cover their entire faces and the dancing is usually quite athletic. The posture of the dancers is square and their goal is to appear puppet-like in respect for the still older form, *nang*, a shadow-puppet genre.

Nang yai is the court form of this ancient puppet art and utilizes large, coloured, leather figures manipulated by two poles of varying lengths. The puppets are danced by their manipulators behind large screens to the stories sung by narrators and to the music of, once again, the traditional orchestra. On occasion, the puppeteers and puppets dance out from behind the screen to reveal their corporeal forms to the delight of the audience. *Nan talung* is the non-court version done with smaller figures and in a much more casual social environment with a smaller orchestra. Performances can go on for an entire night. A three-dimensional puppet, the *hun*, also exists and seems based on Chinese rod and string marionettes.

Over the course of the past 250 years or so, all these forms gradually secularized and lost their essential religious significance. One can divide this change into five basic periods. The first may be termed the classical period, a period of direct royal patronage, and goes from King Rama I (whose reign began in 1782) to King Rama VI (whose reign ended in 1925). Rama I actually created several of the early classical works although he did so with the aid of many poets of the period. These include the first dramatized versions of *Ramakien, Dalang* and *Unarut*. The popularity of *lakorn* dance-dramas was very high during these centuries.

King Rama II was also a poet and played a major role in supporting *lakorn* performances – both royal and popular. He and his team of poets created many masterpieces in the form including *Inoa*, considered by many to be the greatest of these dance-dramas. King Rama III, for his part, discouraged and eventually abolished performances of *lakorn* within the courts but continued to encourage the popular *lakorn nork*. King Rama IV again revived the royal form and made many literary contributions to it during his reign. He also permitted women to take part in the *lakorn nork* style, a major departure from tradition. During the reigns of Rama V and VI, Thai drama reached its zenith. Kings and princes jointly created many important pieces, some of which began to include spoken dialogue and more contemporary themes.

In 1904 the first public theatre was built in Thailand. Known as the Prince's Theatre, the work shown on its stage displayed a blending of the two *lakorn* forms and an integration of the stories used as their base. So popular was the new *lakorn* that new stories were demanded. Clearly, one way to meet the demand was to blend the forms even more. Royalty continued to remain involved with Prince Narathip founding his own troupe, Preedalai, and allowing his daughter, Princess Laxami Lawan, to run it.

Other groups founded at this time were the Mae Boonnak Troupe and Mae Chamoi Troupe.

By about 1935 during the reign of Rama VIII, dance-drama of this new style was so well established that many more theatre buildings opened, among them the National Theatre, Chalerm Nakorn, Chalerm Thai and Chalermkrung, all used at one time or another for films as well. At the same time the original versions of most of the stories had become secularized to the point where they were clearly no longer seen as classical *lakorn* but rather romantic comedies, the second category in this historical cataloguing. Chanropas Troupe under the direction of Pran Boon was among the most popular during this time. His production of *Laerd Supan* (*Blood of Supanburi*) at the government's new National Theatre was a landmark of the period. Other groups of note from the 1930s to the 1950s were the Sivarom Troupe, Thepasilp Troupe, Pakavalee Troupe and Asavin Karn Troupe, the latter supported by Prince Panuphanyukol.

Stories used in the new romantic comedy *lakorns* came mostly from popular novels or even original tales written for the groups. Most were simply love stories based on fictional or historical backgrounds. The advent of film and television in the 1960s caused a severe decline in interest yet the style still has its following as proven by the success of two troupes in particular, which have inherited its mantle, Monthienthong Theatre founded in 1984 and Dass Entertainment founded in 1986. Monthienthong Troupe performs at and takes its name from the Monthien Hotel where it stages even more modern romantic comedies for its sophisticated and generally wealthy audience. The theatre has become a symbol of socially respectable entertainment for the people of Bangkok. Among the famous directors who have worked there are Patravadee Sritairat, Seri Wong Montha, M.L. Panthevanob Thevakul and Kris Attaseri.

Dass Entertainment, also commercially oriented, began as a musical theatre for children and staged one major show a year during 1986, 1987 and 1988. In 1990, the group committed itself to providing quality professional entertainment on a regular basis to Bangkok audiences and since that time has staged five or six plays each year. It has also produced orchestral concerts, performances of western ballet and even of modern dance. In 1992, the company was also producing a weekly television comedy show. The first privately owned theatre to be built in Thailand, the 650-seat Bangkok Playhouse, was built by Dass in 1993. In 1995, the company was given control of the Sala Chalermkrung Theatre, which is now run by a subsidiary of Dass Entertainment, Dass Creative Productions.

The royal family had much to do with the emergence of western-style spoken-drama in the country. In 1904 Prince Vajiravudh (later King Rama VI) staged one of the earliest western style productions seen in Thailand in a 100-seat theatre he had built on his return from studying in Europe. As King Rama VI, he wrote over 100 plays, mostly melodramas and light romances, most of them trying to instil essential Thai values. Primarily linked to the upper classes and the court, such plays successfully blended Thai music and dance with the more melodramatic elements of spoken plays.

But real western-style playwriting was not to emerge until the 1960s when professors and students of English literature departments at Chulalongkorn and Thammasat Universities began translating a range of western-style plays from Shakespeare through Ibsen to the absurdists. At Chulalongkorn University it was Sodsai Puntumkomol who led this work while at Thammasat University it was Mattanee Ruttanin. It was at the universities also that the third period in Thai theatre history can be noted – a socio-political period. During these decades students particularly began to search for self, social justice and personal freedom. Many western plays were translated and/or adapted into Thai, enabling students and local audiences to understand both their styles as well as their politics. Mattanee also translated western plays – among them Arthur Miller's *Death of a Salesman*, Tennessee Williams's *A Streetcar Named Desire*, the musical *My Fair Lady* and even *Macbeth* and *Midsummer Night's Dream*.

With some of these works and many later ones as models, students at these two universities quickly brought the new western-style protest theatre of the 1960s and 1970s to Thailand. The consequent student uprising of 1973 led to a new awareness of political and social issues as well as awareness about how to use theatre forms – along with literature, poetry and music – to bring such issues to public attention.

At Thammasat University, Prachansiew (Crescent Moon Theatre) was among the leading groups to stage these plays. Among them *Mr. Apaimanee, I Wanted to Be Out* and *The Party*. All expressed the inner struggle of this generation to be free from cultural conditioning as well as from the old political controls.

The founders of this movement went on to become Thailand's best known directors and

The Haunted House, 1995.

producers of both stage and television plays. The following waves of socially conscious artists have gradually decreased in number and by the late 1980s and 1990s, each of the new waves was concentrating on more and more specific social issues. Prominent among the later socially conscious theatre groups – the fourth in our grouping of historic categories – has been Maya, founded by a group of university students in 1981. This group, typical of many in the 1990s, focuses its artistic energies on the plight of children, especially those living in slum areas. Among the group's most interesting works have been *Fifty Ways to Torture Children*, *Siddhartha* and *The Glass Mask*. Founded as a not-for-profit organization, the company has played throughout Bangkok and in remote villages outside the capital, utilizing a van for its mobile theatre programmes. The company has been run for many years by Santi Chitrachinda. Partly as a result of Maya's success, children's theatre courses are now given at two universities – Chulalongkorn and Thammasat.

Other new theatre groups such as the White Line of Nattree Tirarojanapong stage plays that deal with AIDS and prostitution while the Honey Bee group stages educational plays for prostitutes in the Pat Pong area. Krachokngoa (Mirror) and Makarmpom work with non-governmental organizations to help children in both Bangkok and rural areas. During the late 1980s and into the 1990s, a number of these groups have attempted to link collective creation with traditional Thai dance-drama forms leading to the beginning of a fifth main movement, one which may be called integration/revival. Some of these experiments have proven effective but most have not. Through such experiments, new styles have begun to emerge. Among the more challenging linkings have been those that have tried to connect Thai and international, modern and classic, Greek and Sukhothai, pantomime and gymnastics.

A very clear example can be drawn from the female director and playwright Patravadee's *Singhakraipob* (*Temple Tale*). The production combines aspects of the Broadway musical, traditional *kaon*, pantomime, various traditional forms and the Greek chorus. Her production attracted tremendous attention. In 1992, Patravadee set up her own outdoor theatre (called the Patravadee Theatre) in her home area of Bangkok and within a year developed a loyal audience which attended virtually all of her new productions. She continues to be one of the few directors in Thailand who continues to make full use of the possibilities presented by the integration/revival approach.

Other contemporary groups of note include Group 28 and Tia Thien Hiang. The former was established in 1989 as a collective for young professionals and has experimented with various production styles. Two of the group leaders are director and playwright Rasamee Paoluangthong who has a strong interest in German theatre (particularly in Brecht) and Yuthana Mukdasanikt, well known as a film director. The company has staged plays by Brecht and Dürrenmatt as well as an adaptation of a work by Kafka.

In the area of indigenous playwriting, new work has begun to be produced in the 1990s by Rasamee Paolunagthong, Somporn Thopunya and by Pattravadee as well as by various collective groups including Group 2 (*Nippan Electric*) and Maya Group (*Fifty Ways to Torture Children*, 1991).

As for theatre space, traditional performances always took place outdoors. In 1902 the indoor, proscenium arch theatre was introduced in Bangkok and by 1921 it had become the standard for most new spaces. Early spaces were small. The Chalermnakhon and Weongnakhonhasem Theatres, for example, held only 80 seats each. Later theatres, such as the Chalermkrung, expanded the number up to 700. Many traditional *khon* performances are held in this space.

The most important of the country's modern theatre spaces is the National Theatre in Bangkok, constructed in the 1930s and rebuilt in 1967 to accommodate new technology. The Thailand Cultural Centre, built in 1993, is the most up to date of Thailand's theatre spaces with three different theatres – a main hall

To Fight!, 1995.

holding up to 3,000 with a picture frame stage; a 600-seat auditorium with flexible seating; and an outdoor theatre which holds some 2,000 people.

A number of Bangkok's small groups often utilize modest venues such as the Arts Theatre which holds 300. A basic black box, the space can be adapted to almost any type of production. Among the most effective of the mid-sized spaces in and around Bangkok are the AUA Auditorium which holds 800; the 600-seat Bangkok Playhouse which has been used for Broadway-style productions; the Phoebus Amphitheatre which holds 5,000, and the Vajirawoodthanusorn Auditorium.

Since 1932, the government's Department of Fine Arts has been responsible for the support of theatre, music and dance; in 1934 it aided in the creation of a school of classical dance, Witthaylai Natasin. The top students at the school have been regularly invited to join the National Theatre company which presents work in all of the aforementioned classical styles.

In the 1990s, Thai theatre was able to offer audiences a range of experiences from the most traditional dance-dramas to Broadway-style productions, from western-style experimental spoken drama to historical epics. But though the theatre is clearly well established, it also faces many continuing problems: a lack of quality directors and playwrights (the best ones are quickly hired away by television and film), a less-than-enthusiastic response from mass audiences to spoken drama and an almost total lack of government support for innovative ventures from the state.

Marisa Saenkulsirisak
With Sulaiman Wesyaporn, WECT staff

Further Reading

Association of Southeast Asian Nations. *The Cultural Traditional Media of Asia*. Manila, 1986.

Brandon, James. *Theater in Southeast Asia*. Cambridge, MA Harvard University Press, 1967.

Carkin, Sary Bryden. 'Likay: The Thai Popular Theatre Form and Its Function Within Thai Society'. PhD dissertation, Michigan State University, 1984. 292 pp.

Kullman, C.H. and W.C. Young, eds. 'Thailand'. *Theater Companies of the World*. Westport, CT: Greenwood Press, 1986.

Rutnin, Mattani Mojdara. *Modern Thai Literature*. Bangkok: Thammasat University Press, 1988.

——. *The Siamese Theatre*. Bangkok: Sompong Press, 1975.

Virulrak, Surapone. 'Theatre in Thailand Today'. *Asian Theatre Journal* (Spring 1990): 95–104.

Yupho, Dhanit. *Khon Masks*. Bangkok: Fine Arts Department, 1989.

TIBET

(see CHINA)

TONGA

(see SOUTH PACIFIC)

TURKMENISTAN

(Overview)

Formerly the Turkmen Soviet Socialist Republic of the USSR and the southernmost of the former Soviet republics, Turkmenistan, a republic in central Asia, is bordered on the north by Kazakhstan and Uzbekistan, on the east by Uzbekistan and Afghanistan; on the south by Afghanistan and Iran, and on the west by the Caspian Sea. Its land area totals 448,100 square kilometres (188,500 square miles).

With an estimated 3.9 million inhabitants in 1994, Turkmenistan is also the least populated of the former Asian Soviet republics. Settlement is concentrated along rivers, canals and other waterways. Ashkhabad, established by the Soviets, is the capital and largest city with 517,200 inhabitants in 1993. Other important cities include Chardzhou, with 164,000 inhabitants and Dashowuz, with 114,000 inhabitants in 1990. More than half of the population still lives in rural areas.

An ethnically homogeneous country, Turkmenistan's Turkic-speaking people have a Sunni Muslim religious heritage and are the largest ethnic group with 73 per cent of the population. Russians and Uzbeks constitute the remainder of the population in about equal numbers. In contrast to most of the other former Soviet republics, Turkmenistan did not suffer a massive emigration of minorities in the 1990s. At the same time the Turkmen government has launched several large-scale ventures involving foreign partners to explore, develop and export natural gas. Other industries include food processing, textile manufacturing, and carpet weaving. Nearly all economic activity is still state-controlled. Turkmenistan is officially a member of the Commonwealth of Independent States (CIS).

The structure of political power in Turkmenistan is the most antiquated of the former Soviet republics and resembles the politics of the Soviet era before the reforms launched by leader Mikhail Gorbachev between 1985 and 1991. Political decisions are taken by a single person, President Saparmurad Niyazov, who is the only political leader in central Asia who was in power before *perestroika* began. As a result, most political freedoms as well as the right of dissent have been suppressed and freedom of the press has been officially removed from the country's constitution.

The original Turkmen population migrated from the Altai region, in eastern Turkestan, to the Caspian Sea during the tenth and eleventh centuries, as part of a larger migration of the Oghuz Turks. The whole history of Turkmen, who built a reputation as warriors in ancient times, is connected to political resistance: to Persians, to Russians and to Soviets. Arabs converted the local population to Islam in the seventh and eighth centuries and the oases of Tedzhen and Merv were prominent agricultural and trade centres at the time. The region was included in the Mongol empires of Genghis Khan in the thirteenth century and of Tamerlane in the fourteenth century. The last central Asian territory to come under Russian control, the Turkmen stronghold of Geok-Tepe fell in 1881 with the loss of some 150,000 Turkmen lives.

After the Russian Revolution of October 1917, the Turkmen population briefly achieved independence from Moscow, resisting the Bolshevik armies until 1918. Shortly after, the republic was incorporated into the Turkestan Autonomous Soviet Socialist Republic. With the help of British forces, Turkmen nationalists soon overthrew the Bolsheviks and established a brief, independent state but the area was soon recaptured and by 1924 was reincorporated in the new USSR. It joined the United Nations as the independent republic of Turkmenistan in 1992.

A Turkmenistan theatre was officially born after 1917 but earlier artistic forms such as music and poetry performed by *bakhshi* (itinerant singers) and *gohende* (storytellers and folk tale narrators) as well as rituals with spectacular theatrical elements existed for centuries. In the early 1920s these forms were joined by a more European style of written theatre and numerous amateur theatrical groups began to spring up. Most such groups, using a clearly agitprop style, actively propagandized for the new Soviet rule.

During the First All-Turkmenian Congress of Soviets in 1925 a resolution was passed calling for the creation of a Turkmen theatrical company. In accordance with this resolution, a Turkmen Drama Studio for training actors was opened in Ashkhabad in June 1926. An all-male school with men trained to perform the female roles, the school provided the company for the Turkmen State Drama Theatre when it was established in 1929. By that time women were allowed to join the company.

By the early 1930s the theatre had a varied repertoire consisting mainly of propagandistic plays by Turkmen and Soviet authors. World classics were represented by productions of *Il Servitore di due padroni* (*The Servant of Two Masters*) by Carlo Goldoni, *Les Fourberies de Scapin* by Molière and the widely popular *Fuente Ovejuna* by Lope de Vega, which was considered, in the Soviet theatre, a revolutionary play.

When the Turkmen State Drama Theatre performed in Moscow during the 1930s, it took advantage of its visits to hold meetings, discussions and classes with outstanding Russian directors and actors. Such tours also set off a period of new development in acting, directing, and playwriting based on the Stanislavski system. Many important productions in this style were mounted over the next decade including *The Rise* by Berdy Kerbabayev (directed by A. Atayev), *Aina* by A. Karliyev (by the same director) and *Dzhuma* by A. Kaushutov. A production of Shakespeare's *Othello* with Aman Kulmamedov in the title role became proof of the company's artistic maturity. At the same time a permanent studio was set up at the theatre to train future generations of Turkmen actors.

Developing too was a new generation of amateur companies, the best of which later would be granted professional status. By the early 1940s several such theatres had emerged in regional centres such as Tashauz, Chardzhou, Kerki as well as in Ashkhabad. Just before the Great Patriotic War (1941–5), a group of graduates from a special Turkmen studio at GITIS (State Institute of Theatre Arts in Moscow) joined the State Drama Theatre with a new repertoire that included Molière's *Doctor in Spite of Himself* (1942) and Ostrovsky's *Poverty Is No Disgrace* (1943), both staged by studio directors Olga Pyzhova and Boris Bibikov. During the war years, local dramatists wrote new plays with themes of war and patriotism including Kerbabayev's *Love for the Motherland,* an episodic play about a *kolkhoz* (collective farm) and *Kurban Durdy,* a documentary. All the plays of this time stressed the mass heroism of relatively ordinary people. The writers also used historical events, seen in Kerbabayev's *Makhtumkuli* in 1941 (directed by J. Feldman), a play about a Turkmen thinker and poet of the eighteenth century and again in *Khorezm* (1944) by Kh. Shukurov and *Soltan Sandjar* (1945) by Bazak Amanov. Plays by Ostrovsky, Gogol and Schiller were also staged.

In the late 1940s and 1950s the State Drama Theatre staged many translated Soviet plays: *For Those in the Sea* by Boris Lavrenev, *Days and Nights* (1947) and *Russian Problem* (1948) by Konstantin Simonov (directed by P. Kharlip) and *People of Good Will* by Gregory Mdivani to name just a few of the most important productions.

In October 1948 Ashkhabad was struck by a severe earthquake that destroyed the entire city and killed two-thirds of its population. The leader of the USSR, Joseph Stalin, however, hid the news from the world and refused to accept foreign aid. Turkmen still relate the backwardness of the republic to that earthquake, for it demolished the intelligentsia and educated middle class of the city and much of the intellectual potential of the nation.

The post-war years saw national dramaturgy here – as in the entire Soviet Union – fighting the official doctrine of socialist-realism. As a result, the repertoire of the state company continued to idealize Soviet reality and the socialist system. Among those productions that stood above this tendency were Ostrovsky's *The Profitable Place*

(1950) and *Guilty Without Guilt* (1951) with Aman Kulmamedov as Yusov and T. Gafurova as Kruchinina; Gogol's *Revizor* (*The Government Inspector*) with Kulmamedov as Gorodnichy and Alty Karliyev as Khlestakov, a role he played for almost twenty years.

In the mid-1950s the annual Ten-Day Festival of Fraternal Republics in Moscow was a popular forum for examining 'ideological maturity'. That is to say, the festivals examined both loyalty to the system and to socialist realistic principles in the arts. The Ministry of Culture itself was able to criticize, correct and praise, to award medals, give honorific titles and prizes to a variety of companies and artists. During the 1955 Festival, held in Moscow, the Turkmen State Drama Theatre presented *Allan's Family* by Gusein Mukhtarov (directed by Murad Seitniyazov) about 'communist morality' and a new type of Soviet family relationship, *Revizor* by Gogol and Shakespeare's *Othello* (directed by I. Gromov), interpreted as a tragedy of racial inequality. These productions received high praise from critics, especially the works of actors A. Kulmamedov as Othello, M. Checkezov and Sonia Muradova; soon after the festival, the theatre was named after the Turkmen classical poet Mollanepes and received the official title of Academic (classical) theatre.

Shortly after this festival, a second group of graduates (the Second Turkmen Studio) from GITIS reinvigorated the company still further with a repertoire of four new productions – *Meshchane* (*The Bourgeois*) by Gorky, *Poverty Is No Disgrace* by Ostrovsky, *Servant of Two Masters* by Goldoni and *Funny Guest* by Mukhtarov.

After the death of Stalin in 1953, the breakdown of his dictatorship, the twentieth Congress of the Communist Party of the Soviet Union and then the beginning of the Khrushchev thaw in 1956, people in the Soviet Union looked forward to the possibility of new political reforms and greater democratization of society. Censorship and ideological strictures were relaxed and freedom of speech and creation seemed to be a greater reality than ever before. Positive changes in many fields, including culture, were seen during this time in the European part of the USSR, but were slow to arrive in the Asian republics. The mandatory principles of socialist realism, proclaimed in 1946 by the Communist Party of the Soviet Union (CPSU), for example, continued to operate until the 1980s. The theatre of Turkmenistan, in fact, seemed committed to maintain all earlier principles, themes and performance styles. As well, repertoire policy remained unified under strict government control and Turkmen dramaturgy continued to show idealized reflections of local problems.

Most typical of this style were productions such as *The Decisive Step* by B. Kerbabayev in 1957, a play about the Turkmen people's struggle for power and their recognition as new national heroes born within the crucible of revolution and civil war, the Turkmen's real resistance to the Bolsheviks in the 1920s. An official point-of-view at the time proclaimed that 'people are the driving force of history in the struggle for a bright communist future'. Theatres promoted such ideas and the Turkmen State Theatre was praised for plays such as *The 1930s* by Mukhtarov (1958), part of a trilogy about the 'inevitable victory of collectivization' in the countryside. A highly ideologized repertoire, such plays were filled with 'class enemies' and were more a product of media manipulation than fact. The last part of this trilogy, *Important Operation* (1959), billed itself as the first modern socialist psychological drama. All three plays focused on the relationships between individuals and society. Such theatre seemed to be interested only in large-scale problems.

The profile of the Turkmen theatre of this period could not be discussed without mentioning *Kremlin Chimes* by Nikolai Pogodin (directed by I. Gromov), *The Kushka Fortress* by A. Adzhanov (1964) and *The Emir's Ambassador* by K. Kuliyev (1970), all plays about Lenin's life. These productions reflected the Turkmen theatre's desire to create propagandistic art, an art directed by the local communist party and its cultural leaders rather than by artists. There were nevertheless a few effective plays in this style based on historical national material: *Destiny* (1962) by Khidyr Deryaiev (directed by M. Kulmamedov) and the biographical *Mollanepes* by Bazak Amanov (1963) about the founder of Turkmen literature.

Mukhtarov's *Who Is the Offender?* with its optimistic pathos, was staged by Feldman in 1963 and was the first successful foray into a contemporary theme. In this play, absolutely positive heroes are in conflict with a corrupt and narrow-minded bureaucracy. Though still one-dimensional and limited, it marked a change but still only very roughly resembled reality. In 1965 the Turkmen State Academic

Drama Theatre returned to Moscow and this opportunity to visit the capital proved revivifying. The next season, *Love* (1966), based on a poetic novel in verse by A. Kekilov, was a success. A new performance was staged by O. Khadjumuradov in a lyric-heroic style and dealt with happiness, love, good, evil, war and peace. At once epic and domestic, the play was close to the people and very national in its nature. This was the first production that allowed serious discussion of the issues of national playwriting based on traditional Turkmen literary traditions, original directing and acting.

Certain productions from this period remained in the State Theatre's repertoire until the early 1980s including *Kremlin Chimes* and *Destiny*. Years later, however, they looked anachronistic, especially in comparison with the theatre's rare new productions.

Through the 1970s, the problem of establishing a contemporary repertoire persisted.

Resolutions of Party Congresses and annual festival competitions proved unhelpful. Attempts in the 1980s were mostly linked to the work of the theatre's new director, A. Alovov. His interpretation of Shakespeare's *Richard III* reflected a new trend leading to many innovative productions of world classics. The production of *Richard III*, designed by Kulmamedov, for example, saw the stage transformed into a huge prison. Cells symbolized the mechanism of tyranny with the scenic space dictating the entire style of production. However heroes were too heroic and villains too villainous. In A. Kurbandurdyiev's interpretation, Richard was the essence of vice, cruelty his sole obsession. Such tyranny could only be destroyed.

During this period, newspaper culture sections also promoted Soviet-style criticism and ideological language in their responses to the theatre. It was politics rather than art that controlled all reactions.

Richard III directed by A. Alovov at the Mollanepes State Drama Theatre in Ashkhabad.
Photo: courtesy of *Teatr*.

Seen for the first time in the mid-1980s was the work of director Kakadjan Ashirov. Heralding *perestroika* and *glasnost* in the Turkmen theatre, he staged Shakespeare's *Taming of the Shrew* and *Chuzhoy* (*The Stranger*) by A. Mamaliyev at the new Theatre for Young Audiences in an absolutely new style: deeply psychological, heartfelt and not realistic. Ashirov continued his experiments in *Yashcheritsa* (*The Lizard*, 1987) by Russian playwright Alexander Volodin. Again he broke from principles of socialist realism and this spectacular and poetic production about misunderstanding and love between people brought him to national attention. But his daring was too much at this point and shortly after all the participants in the production were fired.

But the State Theatre showed its interest in change by hiring Ashirov. One of his first successes at the theatre was *Djan* (*Soul*) based on A. Platonov's novel. Shortly after, Ashirov found himself in a unique situation, having been offered back control of his original theatre as well. Now simultaneously controlling both a large state company and a youth theatre, he renamed the latter company Djan after this very successful early production. Eventually, Ashirov united the two companies, also taking in a group of graduates from the Turkmen Studio of Shchepkin Theatre School in Moscow. His work and vision changed the theatre situation in Turkmenistan and made it a centre of a general theatre renaissance in this part of central Asia.

A national theatre festival *Elemgoshar-1992* in Ashkhabad, creative and competitive with new life in scenography and performance, reinforced this opinion. A sense of achievement in national theatre art began to be felt. Ashirov's vision was aesthetic while paying careful attention to national styles. His production of Oghuz's fifteenth-century epic, *Korkut aga* (*The Book of My Grandfather*), a symbol of Turkmen national identity and forbidden for years for its 'nationalism', was staged by both companies, the State Theatre and Djan, each doing different sections. He wrote and staged two quite different plays based on the same folk material. These two works – *Igry Oguzov* (*Plays of Oghuzes*) about tribal conflicts between the Oghuzes and the Giaurs, their war and peace, and *Bezumnyi Domrul* (*Insane Domrul*), a tragi-farce focusing on the opposition of life and death, paganism and Islam – produced a new genre he called 'didactic parable'. With its theme of the search for harmony within the human soul, magnificent costumes,

Bezumnyi Domrul (*Insane Domrul*) by K. Ashirov at the Djan in Ashkhabad.
Photo: courtesy of *Teatr*.

the acting talents of Aore Annaberolyiev and G. Ashirova and a stage design by Biashim Karadjayev, it won the Grand Prize at the *Elemgoshar-1992* festival.

In the early 1990s the theatre's repertoire was reinvigorated once more with *Sheherezada* (1991) by the Yugoslavian author Ivo Svetin, a play based on the oriental epic fairytale *A Thousand and One Nights*. A dark, post-Chernobyl variation on the Scheherazade story, its hero is an obsessed and sick power-figure, full of jealousy and vengeance. Existential influence was clear. Staged by Tatchmammet Mammetveliev with the actors from the Young Audience Theatre, the production focused on the contradictions within the human soul. Designed by Andris Freiberg, the action was transferred to the auditorium and the audience was placed on stage. Determined to break up the indifference of Turkmen audiences, Mammetveliev injected a more modern and dynamic theatre style into the Turkmen theatre through the use of a familiar story. Indeed, the

Igry Oguzov (*Plays of Oghuzes*) by K. Ashirov at the Mollanepes State Drama Theatre in Ashkhabad. Photo: courtesy of *Teatr*.

author had defined his play as an 'eastern—western opera'. It is exactly this point of intersection that remains vital for the future of the contemporary Turkmen theatre and its future relationship both to Asia and Europe.

Natasha Rapoport

Further Reading

Aboukova, FA. *Turkmenskaja opera: puti formirovanija, Ozanrovaja tipoligija* [Turkmenian opera: Its paths of formation, genre typology]. Aschabad: Ylym, 1987. 162 pp.

Istoriya sovetskogo dramaticheskogo teatra [History of Soviet dramatic theatre]. 6 vols. Moscow: Nauka, 1966–71.

Ivanovskaya, Polina. *Staroye i novoye* [Old and new]. *Teatr* 3 (1981).

——. *Zhiviot takoy tiuz* [Such Tiuz lives]. *Teatr* 7 (1978).

Miagkova, I. *Da ne pokochnetsia dom vash!* [May your home not totter!]. *Teatr* 6 (1992).

Rashid, Ahmed. *The Resurgence of Central Asia.* London: Oxford University Press, 1994.

UZBEKISTAN

The most populous state in Central Asia, Uzbekistan is a landlocked country covering 447,000 square kilometres (172,800 square miles). It is bordered on the north and northwest by Kazakhstan, on the east and southeast by Kyrgyzstan and Tajikistan, on the southwest by Turkmenistan and on the south by Afghanistan. Of the country's 22.2 million people, roughly 71 per cent are Uzbek, 8 per cent Russian and other Europeans and almost 9 per cent Tajik and Kazakh, 2 per cent Tatar, 2 per cent Karakalpak and 7 per cent other. Tashkent is the capital of Uzbekistan and, with a population of 2.2 million, it is the largest city in central Asia as well as the country's cultural centre. Other major cities include Samarkand, Andijan, Bukhara, Fergana and Kokand.

On 31 August 1991, the Republic of Uzbekistan proclaimed its independence from the Soviet Union. Uzbek, a Turkic language, was declared the official language in 1992. Prior to incorporation into the USSR in 1924 as the Soviet Socialist Republic of Uzbekistan, the region was known as Turkestan. Because it lies between the Amu Darya and Syr Darya rivers – known in antiquity as the Oxus and Jaxartes – the area was called Transoxiana or 'the land beyond the Oxus'. The first urban settlements in the region appeared c.1500 BC.

Uzbekistan's geographical position at the heart of the ancient Silk Road exposed the area to influence from Greek, Arab, Chinese, Persian, Turkic and Hindu cultures through trade and conquest as well as pilgrimage and the quest for knowledge that activated groups to traverse the region. The armies of Alexander the Great invaded the region in the fourth century BC and Genghis Khan conquered it in the thirteenth century. Shamanism, Zoroastrianism, Buddhism, Nestorian Christianity and Manicheanism were all practised in this part of central Asia. Arab invasions during the seventh and eighth centuries brought Islam to the inhabitants.

The medieval period in central Asia witnessed major achievements in science, literature, architecture and music. The ninth-century mathematician Al-Khwarizmi (literally of Khiva) gave his name to the term algorithm. Ibn Sina (980–1037), known to the west as Avicenna, wrote on medicine, philosophy and the science of music – *ilm-l musiqi*. In the fourteenth century, Tamerlane made his capital in the ancient city of Samarkand, gathering architects and artisans from throughout the east to build mosques, medrassahs and tombs. The astronomer prince Ulugbek grandson of Tamerlane, built the world's largest sextant at his observatory in Samarkand. Ulugbek's calculations were so accurate that his star charts were used in Europe for centuries after his murder in 1449. The profoundly spiritual poetry of the Sufi saint Bahauddin Naqshband (d. 1389/90) is still revered over 600 years later and his tomb near Bukhara is a place of pilgrimage.

Early in the 1700s, czarist troupes began to launch attacks on central Asian khans as the Russian empire pushed its borders eastward. At that time the region was dominated by three distinct principalities: the Khanate of Kokand (in the Fergana valley), Khanate of Khiva (in the Khorezm region) and Emirate of Bukhara. Each had developed its own distinct cultural traditions. Russia expanded into central Asia in the mid-nineteenth century, conquering Tashkent in 1865, Khiva in 1873 and Kokand in 1876.

Native traditions went largely undisturbed during the Russian colonial period although

Russian Orthodoxy was introduced into this predominantly Sunni Muslim territory. The Governor of Turkestan resided in Tashkent and the city became divided into two sections: the Old City, inhabited by native residents, and the New City, the Russian or European section. The European population brought with them their forms of entertainment, including theatre. Professional Russian artists performed in Turkestan and the celebrated actress Kommisarzhevskaya died after falling ill while on tour, having purchased contaminated clothing in Samarkand.

Prior to the twentieth century, the Uzbeks did not have professional theatre as known in the west. Indigenous central Asian theatre included puppetry, described a thousand years ago in the poetry of Omar Khayyam. Entertainers performed outside in open-air courtyards and bazaars. The remains of the earliest theatre in Turkestan is located on the banks of the Amu Darya river in present-day Afghanistan and dates back to the time of Alexander the Great. Legends and tales, especially the exploits of the folk hero Mulla Nasreddin, were popular themes. Groups of itinerant minstrels known as *maskharoboz* wore clown-face makeup; they improvised performances noted for their biting humour. Tightrope walkers and stilt walkers performed in open-air squares and in the bazaars. The tightrope walkers especially were contacted by those who had special wishes, it being thought that they occupied a holy place as they walked through the air. Another traditional entertainment, *askia*, was a humour competition requiring participants to improvise jokes and verses to challenge the sharp wittedness of their opponents.

A movement known as *Jadidism* (renewal) came to Turkestan from the Crimea where it had been founded by the Tatar educator Ismail Bey Gaspirali (1851–1914). The first Jadid school was established in Tashkent in 1901 with the goal of teaching a modern curriculum within a Muslim framework. These educational reforms served as a bridge between traditional central Asian culture and the secular ideas of other peoples. The reform movement used theatre or *janli surat* (living picture) to bring their message to an illiterate population. The nucleus of Uzbekistan's first modern theatre company is linked to the Jadid cultural organization Turon. Created in 1913, its activities included publishing journals, newspapers and the works of Uzbek poets. Turon also formed an amateur theatre group in 1914 under the leadership of Abdulla Avlony which was called the Turkestan Company.

Jadid plays were performed by an all-male cast and emphasized the need for reform by depicting all sorts of moral and social ills: alcoholism, theft, wife-beating, adultery, ignorance, pederasty and murder. In 1914, the company presented *Padarkush* (*The Patricide*) by Mahamud Khoja Bekhbudii, which premièred in Samarkand and revealed how the immorality of a son led to the death of his father. Later in 1914, *Padarkush* was performed in Tashkent at the Coliseum theatre.

Other plays in Turkestan's repertoire included *Zakharli Khayot* (*Poisonous Life*) by Khamza and *Leyli and Majnun* by U. Khojibekov. The theatre company changed its name in 1918 to the Karl Marx Uzbek Drama Company. After the death of poet and playwright Khamza in 1929, the company assumed his name and is known by it to this day.

The power vacuum created in central Asia by the fall of the Romanovs and the Provisional Government provided the opportunity for several short-lived attempts at self-determination. At the same time, the Basmachi movement openly opposed the new Soviet power in favour of local autonomy. In April 1918, Moscow attempted to quell the growing insurgency by declaring the formation of the Turkestan Autonomous Republic which initially welcomed participation by Jadids and other Muslim organizations. Enver Pasha (1881–1922), one of the Young Turk leaders, came to central Asia at the request of Soviet authorities. Arriving in Bukhara in 1921, he switched sides to join forces with the Basmachis in the hope of creating a central Asian Muslim state.

The new Soviet government soon brought an end to the Jadid movement in Turkestan because its Islamic focus conflicted with communist ideology, although some Jadids initially cooperated with the new regime. The Jadid's use of theatre as a propaganda tool led to the development of professional theatre in Uzbekistan. According to Soviet sources, the literacy rate in Turkestan at the time of the Bolshevik Revolution was only 2–3 per cent. Stage plays made socialist ideology accessible to the masses. For example, the 1929 play *Khujum* was named for the unveiling campaign designed to liberate central Asian women. The glorification of labour was also acceptable material; the first Uzbek dance-pantomime, *A Red Caravan*, was created in 1932 by Mukarram Turgunbaeva and devoted to the theme of cotton growing.

Talented young people from Turkestan were sent to Moscow to attend the Uzbek drama department of the Moscow Studio Theatre School during the 1920s. One of the first student productions was Gogol's *Revizor* (*The Government Inspector*) in 1926. Some of these actors excelled in European classics which they studied in Russia; Abror Hidoyatov gained fame for his interpretation of Shakespearian roles. In 1935, the Uzbek Academic Drama Theatre presented *Hamlet*.

The Tashkent People's Conservatory, which later became the Tashkent Conservatory, was founded in 1918, training students in both European and Uzbek musical traditions. In 1920, Lenin signed a decree which promoted higher education in Turkestan and a state university opened. Prominent intellectuals and educators came from Russia to work at the new institution.

The first ensemble of music and dance in post-revolutionary Turkestan was founded by folk singer Mukhiddin Kari-Yakubov and included one woman, Tamara Khanum. Born in Margelan in 1906, Tamara Khanum was one of the first women to defy tradition and perform unveiled, often courting death at the hands of reactionaries. In 1924, she performed Uzbek dance at the World Exposition in Paris, marking the first time in modern history that central Asian dance had been seen in the west. One of Tamara Khanum's female colleagues, a young dancer named Nurkhon, was murdered by her own brother for dishonouring the family by dancing in public. Nurkhon later became the subject of a musical drama by Kamil Yashin.

During the Soviet era, the performing arts received significant government sponsorship. The goal of bringing art to the masses resulted in a significant building campaign; nearly all of Uzbekistan's major theatres were constructed during this period. In 1939, performing artists were enlisted to entertain labourers at the building of the Fergana Canal, a massive works project which was accomplished in forty days.

Traditionally, the social status of performing artists in Islamic cultures is low but the Soviet government not only provided wages and pensions for professional entertainers, but also raised their prestige by awarding titles such as Honoured Artist and People's Artist. Along with these acknowledgments of excellence went social privileges. But conformity to ideology was expected in return. Stalin's dictum, 'national in form, socialist in content', meant that while artists could use native languages and cultural traditions in their works, the underlying message had to adhere strictly to Marxist-Leninist ideology.

During World War II, Tashkent became a temporary home for Russian evacuees, including prominent intellectuals, making Tashkent an artistic mecca. Uzbekistan's First Secretary Usman Yusupov used his close relationship with Stalin to assure the continued construction of Tashkent's Opera House even during the war years. Yusupov also managed to prevent leading Uzbek singers and musicians from serving at the front. The Muqimi Theatre of Uzbek Musical Drama became the focal point of Tashkent's artistic life, although female roles were still played by male actors. Theatre artists aided the war effort by entertaining troupes and performing at fundraising concerts. Tamara Khanum herself earned enough money through her concerts to purchase a tank to send to the front.

The Tashkent earthquake of 26 April 1966 brought death and destruction, damaging thirty theatres. Workers came from all over the Soviet Union to help repair the devastation, including a significant number of Ukrainians. By the late 1980s, Uzbekistan had twenty-eight repertory theatres, two opera houses, nine philharmonic societies and over nearly four thousand community centres. Theatre reached an even wider audience when Uzbek State Television created a special drama division devoted to the broadcast of plays in their entirety. Productions from regional theatres, as well as Tashkent companies were aired throughout the country; dance performances could be seen several times a week.

Even after independence, the performing arts remain somewhat under government control, with decisions concerning the content of performances and the directorship of theatres extending to the presidential office. Art still serves the state. The Ministry of Foreign Affairs opened a Department of Culture, Education and Exchanges in the mid-1990s furthering government supervision of artistic activities. All invitations to Uzbek artists to tour abroad must be approved by this office before performers can receive a visa which permits them to leave Uzbekistan.

Once amply supported by the government, independence has brought uncertainty to the artistic world. Economic restructuring has forced many theatres and dance companies to reduce their size. Government salaries are no

Bakhor Dance Ensemble dance *Bayot*, choreography by Mukarram Turgunbaeva.

longer adequate and some artists have left their profession to go into more lucrative fields. Some theatres and ensembles now search for private sponsorship to underwrite the expense of productions. The Navoi Theatre of Opera and Ballet has found private sponsors for overseas tours but while abroad presents familiar classics of the nineteenth-century Russian repertoire rather than lesser known native ballets with Uzbek choreography and music. Even the appropriateness for funding western art forms such as opera and ballet has been debated in the press. Other groups which specialize in indigenous central Asian forms, like the celebrated Bakhor Dance Ensemble, has cut its dance corps of forty by nearly 50 per cent and curtailed its once extensive tours.

Structure of the National Theatre Community

Of Uzbekistan's three dozen professional theatre companies operating in the mid-1990s, about one-third of them are located in Tashkent. Other drama and puppet theatres are scattered throughout the country, in cities such as Andijan, Bukhara, Samarkand, Kokand, Margelan and Urgench. In addition to professional theatres and dance companies, a large number of amateur ensembles exist throughout the nation, especially at large factories and collective farms.

During the Soviet period, professional companies were state subsidized and came under the jurisdiction of the Ministry of Culture. Salaries of employees were comparable to the average national wage of about 150 rubles with certain favourites earning as much as 500 rubles. Performers were given a stipend upon retirement. During the years immediately following independence, the salaries of theatre artists did not keep up with inflated prices and some performers added to their income by performing at wedding or in nightclubs or leaving the profession altogether.

In spite of government reductions, many theatres still have large companies, including actors, directors, administrators and production staff. Tashkent's Navoi Theatre has about 600 employees; the Khamza Uzbek Drama Theatre has approximately 450; Gorky Russian Theatre

Gulsara with Khalima Hasirova and Mukarram Turgunbaeva.

has 350; Theatre for Young Audiences (TYUZ) and Tashkent Puppet Theatre have 150 each.

Uzbek theatres operate on a repertory system often requiring that daily rehearsals be devoted to material different from that presented in evening performances. Performers must master several roles simultaneously. At the Navoi Theatre, the schedule alternates daily between opera and ballet with as many as twenty different productions staged each month. The average length of a rehearsal for a new play is two to three months, but in rare cases this can be extended to over a year. Once introduced into a company's repertoire, a production may be performed for several years, even decades.

Major professional companies prior to independence toured annually throughout the Soviet Union, often using these summer tours to première new material. As part of a reciprocal agreement, an Uzbek company performed in cities such as Kiev, Tallin, Riga, Tbilisi, Erevan or Vladivostok, while a company from another Soviet republic would use the vacant theatre space in Tashkent. Upon returning to Tashkent, local companies would present the productions that were first presented on the road.

Soviet theatre festivals were also held before independence on a regular basis, involving participants from all fifteen republics. The newly independent Republic of Uzbekistan now organizes annual festivities involving theatre, music and dance around the spring equinox holiday of Navruz and the Independence Day celebrations that begin on 31 August and last several days. Other major performing arts festivals have been conducted in connection with the observance of historical events, such as the 1996 commemoration of Tamerlane's 600th birthday and the 2,500th anniversary of the founding of the cities Samarkand and Bukhara, celebrated in 1997.

The Union of Theatrical Workers (STD) was established in Uzbekistan in 1947 as a non-governmental organization to provide support to artists as well as to create theatre festivals, master classes, tours and other creative efforts. In 1989, Uzbekistan's STD invited a thirty-member delegation of theatre workers from the United States, marking the first time that home stays were allowed for such an exchange. In 1993, the Uzbek STD organized the first East–West International Theatre Festival in Tashkent, which included participants from around the world. A major fire at STD's Tashkent headquarters in 1996 severely damaged the Union's main office but the archive of 70,000 negatives from the history of theatre in Uzbekistan survived.

Theatre schedules are published in local newspapers and posters also announce performances. Each major theatre has a press liaison and STD also assists in promoting theatrical events. Prior to the demise of the Soviet Union, theatregoing was a popular form of entertainment with the larger theatres playing to full houses. In the first years after independence, the public exhibited a reluctance to go out after dark; many theatres moved their curtain times up to as early as 5 or 6 p.m. Even with such measures, theatre attendance has dropped significantly, especially for the opera, provoking discussion as to the expediency of underwriting this European art form. Ticket prices also have gone up but are relatively inexpensive for foreigners. In 1997, ticket prices in Tashkent ranged from 25 sum (roughly equivalent to the price of a loaf of bread) for a matinée performance at the Republican Puppet Theatre to 100 sum for admission to the opera or ballet. In contrast to these state-sponsored theatres, the independent Ilkhom Theatre charged nearly 350 sum, the same as 1 kilogram of high-quality meat, for their best seats.

Artistic Profile

Uzbek culture contains a fascinating amalgam of traditional and modern, occidental and Oriental. Within Tashkent, traditional and contemporary forms of European theatre exist alongside more indigenous genres such as puppetry. Classical ballet and Soviet-style folk dance are included in the annual Independence Day celebrations. Nightspots present variety shows modelled after Las Vegas – on a modest scale. Tightrope walkers still perform in the bazaars where the latest pirated cassettes of western rap music can be purchased. Wedding celebrations – which take several days – run the musical gamut of ancient traditions and electrified ethno-pop songs. As the new nation searches for an identity free from Soviet constraints, it remains to be seen how much of the western legacy will survive and which of the older central Asian forms may be revived.

In Uzbekistan, 61 per cent of the population is rural so that while Tashkent is cosmopolitan, the outlying regions retain more traditional tastes. Productions of European forms at Samarkand's Theatre of Opera and Ballet are poorly attended. Traditional entertainment, such as puppetry and dance or Uzbek-language productions based on themes from central Asian history, enjoy greater popularity.

Music and dance play a central role in the lives of Uzbeks; petroglyphs and artefacts left by ancient tribes depict dancers and musicians. Before the advent of Islam, the Chinese court sent to central Asia for dancers and horses. The Arab invasion of the region led to the practice of veiling and sexual segregation. Since professional dance had primarily been the realm of women, troupes of *batchas* or dancing boys dressed and made-up as women became the only public dancers, although there were female court dancers.

Women entertained each other at gatherings, sometimes dressing up as men to sing and dance. A few professional female dancers still perform male dances, donning men's clothing and false beards. Although dancing boys were still common in the early 1900s, they have all but disappeared from present-day Uzbekistan. Men played women's roles in theatrical productions until the mid-twentieth century but there are still occasional references to this practice on stage. The celebrated ethno-pop group Yalla included a piece in their repertoire about an old

Petty Bourgeois Wedding by Brecht.

married couple with one of the male singers performing the woman's role in a *paranji* (veil).

The surviving dance heritage of the Uzbek people includes both folklore and professional traditions. Uzbek folk dances grew from pre-Islamic rituals associated with the cycles of nature, daily chores or important events such as weddings. The Baysun Ensemble has preserved these ancient dances. Also still performed in the *zikr*, a Sufi ritual in which dancers travel in a circle with repetitive movements accompanied by chanting and percussion.

Classical Uzbek dance is characterized by intricate arm and hand movements, a variety of spins and turns, backbends, shoulder isolations and animated facial expressions. Prior to its incorporation into the Soviet Union, three separate political entities which existed in Turkestan developed the distinct Fergana, Khorezm and Bukhara dance styles.

Although Russia conquered Turkestan in the mid-nineteenth century, local traditions went largely undisturbed until 1924 when the region became incorporated into the USSR. The Bolshevik campaign to eliminate the custom of veiling soon led to public performances of dance by women, although early performers were stoned by fundamentalists.

The Uzbek Ethnographic Company was established in 1926 to create concerts staged by masters of traditional dance. In the 1950s, several Uzbek folk song and dance ensembles were formed. Long established as the leading Uzbek dance ensemble since its inception in 1957, Bakhor (Spring) toured extensively, bringing Uzbek culture to every corner of the world. Lazgi (created in 1958) specializes in the unique and challenging dances of the Khorezm region. Zarafshan presents dances from the Bukhara area, which includes Tajik influences. In 1988, a new company called Tanavar was created, performing more modern stylized versions of traditional Uzbek dance. In 1997, these four ethnic dance companies lost their sovereignty and fell under the directorship of a new governmental agency, Uzbekraqs. Another ensemble, Shodlik (founded 1936), was renamed the Ozbekistan Company. The Uzbeknavo association organized concerts and tours for Uzbek performing artists.

The first contemporary dance studios were founded between 1927 and 1932. Isadora Duncan performed in Tashkent and Samarkand in 1924 and later her adopted daughter taught special classes at the Tashkent Choreographic Institute. Modern dance is currently not taught or performed in Uzbekistan.

The first Uzbek musical theatre, Muqimi, was established in 1939. Combining folk dance forms with classical elements, two new productions were introduced. *Pakhta (Cotton)* was staged there in 1933, with choreography by Konstantin Bek, Usta Kamilov and Mukarram Turgunbaeva. Politics made its way into *Shakhida* (1938), a depiction of the struggle against the reactionary *Basmachi* choreographed by Kamilov, Turgunbaeva and Alexander Tomsky. In 1939, the State Academic Theatre of Opera and Ballet named for Alisher Navoi opened in Tashkent. Two of Uzbekistan's first native ballerinas were Galia Ismailova and Bernara Karieva, who performed both traditional Uzbek dance as well as classical ballet. Uzbek choreographers have created their own oriental-influenced ballets – such as *Amulet of Love*, *Poem of Two Hearts* and *Tomiris* – set to scores by native composers. A Korean music and dance ensemble founded by Elizabetta Kim in 1989 has toured abroad. This self-supported company is drawn from Tashkent's Korean population, which first came to Uzbekistan in 1937.

Popular western dance forms now flourish in Uzbekistan, including ballroom dance, breakdance, aerobics and hip-hop, especially among young people. Ballroom and hip-hop competitions are well attended.

Uzbekistan annually celebrates its independence with a major concert of music, dance, poetry and gymnastics performed by thousands of professional and amateur entertainers. The ancient celebration of the spring holiday of *Navruz* has also enjoyed a renaissance in the post-Soviet era with numerous concerts and a competition between professional dance companies for the best new festival programme. Televised dance performances also enjoy great popularity, giving leading dancers celebrity status.

Companies

Uzbekistan has professional theatres operating in virtually every genre of theatrical art. These include drama, opera and ballet, satire, theatre for young audiences, puppetry, operetta, experimental theatre and musical dramas and comedies. Tashkent is also home to a permanent circus and six professional ethnic dance ensembles.

Like most Uzbek groups, Navoi Theatre operates on the repertory system and presents four different operas and three ballets each week. Dancers sometimes rehearse as many as four ballets in one day. The company's repertoire includes European classics such as *Carmen*, *The Barber of Seville*, *Madame Butterfly*, *Eugene Onegin*, *Swan Lake*, *Sleeping Beauty* and *Don Quixote*. Uzbek operas such as *Dilorom* (M. Ashrafi, 1958) and *Alisher Navoi* (M. Burkhanov, 1990) along with ballets like *Tomaris* (U. Musaev, 1984) and *Ikki Dil Dostoni* (*Tale of Two Hearts*, O. Melikov, 1982) depict themes from central Asian history and legend. The ballet has now found private sponsors for overseas tours.

Khamza Drama Theatre performs in Uzbek but includes European works in its repertoire. During the Soviet years the company enjoyed great success and was known for the brilliance of its actors. Classics by Shakespeare, Gorky, Chekhov, Tolstoy and Pushkin, as well as works by Uzbek authors translated into Russian, are presented during its seasons.

Muqimi Theatre, established in 1939, performs exclusively in the Uzbek language and specializes in musical dramas and comedies. Much newer, the Operetta Theatre was created in 1971 and has a repertoire of European works by composers like Strauss and Ferenc Lehár.

The Russian language Theatre for Young Audiences presents fairytales such as *Puss in Boots* and *The Little Match Girl*, along with plays by Molière and even *Fiddler on the Roof*. Productions by the Uzbek TYUZ include works by western and Uzbek authors.

The Ilkhom began in 1976 as an independent studio theatre created to give actors an opportunity to experiment with contemporary, highly political material not acceptable in government-run companies. Professional actors would come to perform without pay after finishing their evening shows at state theatres. Although Ilkhom's ticket prices are much higher than at state-subsidized theatres, the company continues to play to full houses and frequently tours abroad. While the Ilkhom may be Tashkent's smallest theatre, it is the best attended.

Alisher Navoi by M. Burkanov, 1990.

Khazma Drama Theatre's 1928 production of *Nuchum*.

Ilkhom Theatre's production of *Firebird*.

Dramaturgy

Until the Jadidist efforts of the early twentieth century, Uzbek literature, although rich in poetry, had no tradition of dramatic writing. Among the first playwrights to emerge was Khamza. In an attempt to encourage the development of Uzbek theatre, Russian cultural workers enlisted poets such as Khamza to work as playwrights. Khamza's works were highly political; he was a dedicated activist for women's rights, participating in the public burning of veils. He was killed by an angry mob of fundamentalists in 1929. Tashkent's Uzbek Drama Theatre and Institute of Fine Arts both bear his name.

In the 1920s, theatre became a weapon of Bolshevik propaganda, especially against the old social order. Rich landowners, the Muslim clergy and the oppression of women came under attack. A martyr to these early days of Uzbek theatre was Nurkhon, a young Uzbek girl who ran away from home to perform in a theatre company founded by Russians. Her life and subsequent murder at the hands of her brother was chronicled in the musical drama *Nurkhon* by Kamil Yashin, who also wrote *The Dawn of the Revolution*.

Iron Woman by Sharaf Mashbekov.

The professional theatres of Soviet Uzbekistan included European classics in their repertoire along with works by Russian writers such as Chekhov, Gogol, Ostrovsky and Turgenev. Since gaining independence, dramas focusing on central Asian history have been popular. *Nodira Begim*, poetess and ruler of Kokand, was the subject of a 1992 Uzbek language production by the Muqimi Theatre. *Alexander the Great* (1993) at the Abror Hidyatov Theatre was also in Uzbek although the title role was played by a French actor who delivered his lines in his native tongue. *Tamerlane* was produced at the Khamza Theatre in 1992.

Throughout Uzbekistan there are ten professional theatres of musical drama and comedy. Musical dramas are an extremely popular genre since they are closely linked to traditional Uzbek songs, which often contain lyrics focusing on unhappy love, the human struggle and the role of fate.

On the lighter side are comedies such as Mashrab Babaev's *Guest from Tashkent*, Sharaf Mashbekov's *Iron Woman* and Said Akhmat's *Revolt of the Daughter-in-Law*, the latter of which was made into a film. Many Uzbek actors perform both in film and on stage.

Directing and Acting

The heritage of Turkestani theatre with its strong improvisational and comedic elements can be seen in contemporary Uzbekistan. Native actors are known for their excellence in mime, movement and voice. Directors encourage actors to improvise while in rehearsal giving less instruction than what, by comparison, an American actor may expect.

Director Mark Weil of Tashkent's Ilkhom Theatre has won international recognition for his work which rejects the conventional storytelling approach of Soviet theatre. His productions employ urban, contemporary, media-influenced images from which politics are never absent. Physical humour, music and dance are hallmarks of Weil's work. His highly visual style is well represented by *Clamadeus*, a piece in the eastern European clown tradition which uses virtually no dialogue, with the exception of a word game based on the alphabet.

Bakhodir Yuldashov, director of Tashkent's Abror Hidoyatov Theatre, excels at large-scale Soviet-style productions which require the skilful manipulation of large numbers of actors, dancers and musicians on stage, as in his 1995 productions of *Ulugbek* and *The Great Silk Road* (1997) – both of which were performed in Samarkand's historic Registan Square. Like Weil, he incorporates traditional and contemporary music in his work. Yuldashov's painterly style groups actors into constantly changing and visually arresting tableaux. He frequently collaborates with scenic designer Giorgii Brim.

Music Theatre
Dance Theatre

For a discussion of music and dance, see the opening, historical section and **Artistic Profile**.

Theatre for Young Audiences

Uzbekistan has four professional theatres for young audiences – two in Tashkent and one each in Andijan and Karakalpakia. Known by the acronym TYUZ, Tashkent's Theatre for Young Audiences was established in 1927 and is housed in two separate buildings. The Russian TYUZ, which has both Russian and Uzbek productions, is located near Metro station Navoi. The Uzbek TYUZ is near the Old City and presents only Uzbek language performances.

Performances for young audiences are usually weekend matinées with a strong musical content. Plays aimed at teenagers are performed in the evenings. Vladimir Bagramov, an actor, writer, composer and singer, is especially noted for his children's plays. Actors from Tashkent's other theatres occasionally take part in TYUZ productions.

The Children's Folklore Studio Tomasha was founded in 1988 by artistic director Nadira Kurbanova. Her company is not government sponsored and any interested child is welcome to participate. Company members range in age from about 4 to 14. All productions involve singing and dancing. Tomasha's performances have been aired on Uzbek television and the ensemble has toured abroad.

Puppet Theatre

Puppetry enjoys a long tradition in central Asia. The earliest puppets were very simple – two sticks tied together at right angles and covered with rags. Performances took place in public squares and market-places. A single actor manipulated many different *qugirchoq*

Traditional Uzbek puppeteer.

(puppets) using a special device to imitate women's voices. The puppeteer's performances were always accompanied by music, especially the *doire* (traditional Uzbek drum). Another actor, known as the *korformon*, served as the master of ceremonies, summoning people to watch the performance and commenting on the action in the play.

Two kinds of puppets were used. The *chodirhayol* (marionette show) took place only in the evening so the strings on the puppets would be less likely to be seen. Hand-puppets were used for the *chodirjamol*, which could be performed at any time. The leading hero of the Uzbek puppet theatre was Kachalpavlan and his wife Bichekhon. Their domestic life was the subject of humorous anecdotes. Puppet theatre performances were geared primarily to adult audiences and were often severely critical of political leaders, judges, doctors and *mullahs*.

Under Soviet influence, Uzbekistan was introduced to European puppetry and abandoned much of the central Asian traditions, taking performances out of the bazaars and into theatres. Since independence, Uzbekistan's puppet theatres are again expressing an interest in their roots.

Contemporary puppet theatres use a variety of puppets, including marionettes, shadow-puppets, planchettes, hand-puppets and occasionally large muppet-like creatures with actors inside. Puppets vary in size from finger-puppets to larger-than-life figures that require two puppeteers to operate. Sometimes the actors are hidden from view, but also popular are the 'live plan' productions in which the actors sing, dance or play a musical instrument as part of the story or to provide brief interludes.

Tashkent's Puppet Theatre has a repertoire of more than thirty plays. Each year they present four new productions, two in Russian and two in Uzbek. In addition to elaborate productions designed for the theatre, daily performances are given by travelling actors who visit schools with more portable shows. Although there have been some productions created for adult audiences, as was traditional in central Asia, puppet theatres currently cater to children since adult

Tashkent Republican Puppet Theatre.

attendance for all kinds of theatre performance has dropped significantly.

Every two years, the Republican Puppet Festival gathers all the professional puppet theatres in a nation-wide competition. Puppet theatres from neighbouring republics and foreign guests from outside central Asia are invited to participate.

Tashkent's Theatrical Institute offers a four-year programme in puppetry. During the first year of classes, students are not allowed to work with puppets but instead develop acting and improvisational skills. The training theatre where puppetry students gave free concerts was demolished by government order in 1993 and has not been replaced by other facilities.

Design

Theatre in Turkestan was primarily performed out-of-doors with no formal sets or costumes. Actors relied on mime, gesture and imagination to turn everyday objects into props needed for a particular story. Jadidist plays performed at the beginning of the twentieth century employed simple costuming and sets; major theatrical design dates from the Soviet period. While some early productions in post-revolutionary Uzbekistan reflect the influence of Russian constructivist art, most design was realistic. Later, Soviet and Eastern bloc designers introduced the

Happy Beggars.

possibility of using set décor to reveal the emotional content of a play rather than simply depicting architectural structures.

Scenic design in most of Uzbekistan's theatres is still dominated by realism. When productions are based on eastern themes from history or legend, Oriental architectural motifs and visual elements from miniature paintings are used. One of Tashkent's leading contemporary designers, G. Brim, employs both European and central Asia architectural forms as well as signs and symbols in his works. Zinaida Kuryshch, designer at the Navoi Theatre of Opera and Ballet for several decades, creates costumes for European classics along with folk dress and historical garments for productions based on themes from Uzbek history and legend. Although major theatres such as the Navoi and the Khamza have their own design departments, factories specializing in the construction of costumes, jewellery and footwear cater to the numerous dance ensembles.

Theatre Space and Architecture

One of Uzbekistan's first theatres was built during the colonial period in Turkestan. Khiva Theatre, located in the Russian sector of Tashkent, was designed by Georgy M. Svarichevsky, who became the chief architect for the Turkestan region. The theatre was constructed between 1910 and 1912 and incorporated elements of central Asian architecture in the design; the walls were decorated with painting of Khivan caravans. The building burned in 1916 and was rebuilt as the Great Khiva.

The theatre most associated with the development of theatre in twentieth-century Uzbekistan was designed by architect E.F. Kaufman and built in Tashkent's New City in 1903. It was named for G.M. Tsintsadze. After remodelling in 1913 to include a central cupola, the theatre was renamed the Coliseum. For a few months it was used for circus performances but soon became Tashkent's major theatre. Turon theatre company rented it for performances, including the historic 1914 *Padarkush*. In 1918 the building was nationalized after the Bolshevik Revolution and in 1919 was named for Ya. M. Sverdlov. Until the completion of the State Academic Theatre of Opera and Ballet named for Alisher Navoi in 1947, the Sverdlov served as Uzbekistan's first opera house and was renowned for its outstanding acoustics. After its opening, the Sverdlov became the home of the Philharmonia, an association of Uzbekistan's professional musical and dance ensembles. In the mid-1980s the theatre was closed for major renovations and reopened in 1996 as Tashkent's new stock exchange building.

Uzbekistan's major theatres were constructed during the Soviet period and most feature European proscenium stages. Although the design for the Alisher Navoi Theatre of Opera and Ballet was the subject of an architectural competition the project was turned over to architect and archaeologist Alexei Shusev (d. 1949) who, along with many other prominent Russians, was evacuated to Tashkent during World War II. Most of the labour on the opera house was done by Japanese prisoners of war. Completed in 1947, the building is an amalgam of neo-classical and central Asian elements. One of the lobbies within the theatre is decorated with murals painted by the celebrated Uzbek artist Chinghiz Akhmarov. The Bukhara lobby is decorated with traditional *ganch* (stucco) designs in elaborate arabesques, created by Shirin Muradoghli. The auditorium accommodates 900.

Tashkent's circus, named for tightrope walker Toshkanboev, is housed in a large circular structure near the Chorsu Bazaar in the Old City. Designed by G. Alexandrovich and G. Masyagin, the building opened in 1975 and has a capacity of 2,597. In addition to the performance space, dressing rooms and large buffet, the circus also houses the animals, which include Bactrian camels, lions and tigers. In 1997, the building underwent major renovations.

Khamza Theatre of Uzbek Drama was originally built in 1939 as the Rodina Cinema and was designed by A. Sidorov and N. Timofeev. The interior was reconstructed in 1967 to create a proscenium stage with a hall capacity of 776. The experimental Ilkhom Theatre occupies a converted space in the basement of a youth hostel. This black box space seats between 135 and 200 people, depending on the configuration of the stage.

Bakhor Dance Ensemble occupies a large neo-classical building on Mustaqillik Maidoni (Independence Square). Designed by architect

S. Poupanov, the building became the home of the dance company in 1969 with rehearsal rooms and a 500-seat performance hall. In 1997, the building was closed for major renovations.

Designed in 1979 by V. Kulianov, Tashkent's Puppet Theatre features an outdoor tower from which mechanical figurines appear to announce performances. A child-sized miniature Oriental city decorated with ceramic figures from fairytales embellishes the spacious lobby. Another large room contains a puppet museum. The hall seats 350.

With a capacity of 4,000, the Palace of People's Friendship is Tashkent's largest hall and is used for major concerts and conferences. Designed by a committee of seven major architects, the structure features stylized interpretations of eastern arches on the exterior. The lobby has glazed tile work of local origin, imported chandeliers and Florentine mosaics. The ceiling of the auditorium is decorated with representations of the *karnai*, a long trumpet-like Uzbek folk instrument. The stage's heavy velvet curtain is embellished with traditional gold-thread embroidery for which the city of Bukhara is famous.

In 1993, Tashkent's Turkestan Palace opened, complete with state-of-the-art light and sound equipment. While the auditorium seats only 900, the building itself houses numerous offices and rehearsal rooms. Originally intended as a new home for Tashkent's Gorky Theatre, the Turkestan now caters to *estrada* or popular music concerts. The so-called 'summer hall' located on the grounds of the Turkestan is an amphitheatre with laser light equipment and is admirably suited to Tashkent's dry, sunny climate.

Most of the theatres used regularly by dance companies have stages warped and splintered from the practice of sprinkling wooden surfaces with water to provide better traction.

Training

Central Asia's major training school is Tashkent's State Institute of Art named for Mannon Uighur. Established in 1946, the institute has three faculties: acting, puppetry and arts education, and radio and television. New courses in arts management and pop music were added to the curriculum in 1997. After completing their secondary education, potential students audition each summer by preparing pieces in several genres – song, pantomime, dance, prose, fable and monologue. After three rounds of auditions, approximately twenty-four pupils are selected annually for each faculty from hundreds of applicants. Acting and puppetry are both four-year programmes, while directing takes five years. Courses include world theatre traditions, Russian and Soviet literature, art history, stage movement, fencing, pantomime, acting, dialects, dance, foreign languages and the history of theatre. Actors are trained for both theatre and film work. Students are apprenticed to Tashkent theatres while at the institute and participate in productions. The institute also provides training for the ethnically distinct Ulghur and Karakalpak regional theatres. Upon graduation, students are guaranteed a placement at professional theatres throughout Uzbekistan. Government-sponsored institutes of culture in major Uzbek cities also provide acting, directing and dance courses.

Tashkent's Ilkhom Theatre runs a private training programme.

Dancers begin training at an early age. While still in primary school, students are accepted into Tashkent's Higher School of Choreography and National Dance based on criteria such as body type, musicality and flexibility. In addition to several hours of dance classes six days a week, pupils also study a curriculum similar to other school children. Although ballet, character dance and cental Asian dance are taught to all, students specialize in either ballet or Uzbek dance. Final examinations take place in front of a panel of experts who grade students on their performance in barre and centre floor exercises and group and solo dances. According to their final scores, graduates are offered work in professional dance companies throughout Uzbekistan, with the most talented students receiving placement in Tashkent's most prestigious ensembles. In Soviet times, the most coveted position was with the Bakhor Ensemble since not only was it considered the finest, but also it provided members with the opportunity to tour world-wide.

Criticism, Scholarship and Publishing

During the Soviet period, a system developed under which each theatre company had its own literary manager who also served as its resident critic. Only Moscow, Leningrad and Tashkent offered training in theatre criticism. Stalin's 1948 'anti-cosmopolitanism' campaign forced many theatre workers to leave Russia for the more remote regions of central Asia, among them actors, stage designers, directors, theatre historians and critics. From the period of Khrushchev's thaw to *perestroika*, preview performances of new works were followed by public discussions which sometimes ran as long as two hours.

Khamza Institute of Fine Arts Studies, located in Tashkent, serves as a major research centre for central Asia. Specialists study diverse theatre topics, including the history of the circus in Uzbekistan. Noted specialists are Liubov' Avdeeva on Uzbek national dance and ballet, Tulkin Obedov on the circus in central Asia and Muksin Qadirov, Tashpulat Tursunov and Mamajon Rakhmanov on the history of theatre.

During the Soviet period, the government-run Gafur Gulyam Literature and Art Publishing House printed works on theatre and dance. Books on leading actors and dancers like Abror Hidoyatov and Tamara Khanum were available hardbound editions lavishly illustrated with colour photographs, but in extremely limited quantities. Popular performers graced calendars and postcards. Post-Soviet inflation has sharply curtailed the number and quality of books published.

Laurel Victoria Gray, Natasha Rapoport

Further Reading

Abdullaeva, Salomat, ed. *Abror Hidoyatov*. Tashkent: Gafur Gulam Literature and Art Publishing House, 1985.

Allworth, Edward A. *The Modern Uzbeks: From the Fourteenth Century to the Present: A Cultural History*. Stanford, CA: Hoover Institution Press, 1990.

Avdeev, Boris. *Povest' o tantsovshchitse* [Legend of a dancer]. Tashkent: Gafur Gulam Literature and Art Publishing House, 1987.

Avdeeva, Liubov Aleksandrovna. *Tanets Makarram Turganbaeva* [The dances of Mukarram Turganbaeva]. Tashkent: Gafur Gulam Literature and Art Publishing House, 1989.

Cohen, Selma Jeanne. 'Report from Tashkent: East Meets West in Central Asia'. *Dance Magazine* (July 1990): 45–8.

Gray, Laurel Victoria. 'Dancing Boys'. *Arabesque* (May–June 1986): 8–11.

——. 'Living Legacy: Women's Dances of Uzbekistan'. *Arabesque* (January–February 1983).

——. 'The Splendor of Uzbek Dance'. *Habibi* [three part series] Part I: Khorezm, vol. 14, no. 2; Part II: Fergana, vol. 14, no. 3; Part III: Bukhara, vol. 16, no. 3.

——. 'Uzbeks Adapt To Independence'. *Dance Magazine* (August 1994): 22–3.

Kadyrova, S.M. 'Svoeobrazie uzbekskoi Komedii i principy ee sceniceskogo voploscenija v semi-desiatye i v pervoy polovine vosmidesiatykh godov.' [The distinctive qualities of Uzbek comedy and the principles of its stage realization, seventies to first half of eighties]. Synopsis, PhD dissertation, Tashkent: In-t iskusstvoz-nanija, 1986. 21 pp.

Karimova, Rozia. *Buhkarskii tanets* [Bukharan dance]. Tashkent: Gafur Gulam Literature and Art Publishing House, 1978.

——. *Ferghanskii tanets* [Fergana dance]. Tashkent: Gafur Gulam Literature and Art Publishing House, 1973.

——. *Khorezmskii tanets* [Khorezm dance]. Tashkent: Gafur Gulam Literature and Art Publishing House, 1975.

——. *Tantsy ensemblya 'Bakhor'* [Dances of the Bakhor ensemble]. Tashkent, Khamza Hakim-zade Niyazi Institute of Fine Art Studies, 1979.

——. *Tanovar*. Tashkent, 1993.

——. *Uzbekskie tantsy v postanovke Isakhara Akilova* [Uzbek dances staged by Isakhar Akilov]. Tashkent: Gafur Gulam Literature and Art Publishing House, 1987.

Khamidova, Marfua. *Akterckoe iskusstvo uzbek-skoi musikal'noi dramy* [Actor's art of Uzbek musical drama]. Tashkent: Khamza Hakim-zade Niyazi Institute of Fine Arts Studies, 1987.

Levin, Theodore. *The One Hundred Thousand Fools of God: Musical Travels in Central Asia (and Queens, New York)*. Bloomington, IN: Indiana University Press, 1996.

Mirchazdarova, Z.M. *Muzyka v dramatickom teatre Uzbekistana* [Music in the dramatic theatre of Uzbekistan]. Tashkent: Izdetelstvo literatury i iskusstba im. G. Guljama, 1986. 102 pp.

Shirokaya, O.I. *Al'bom Tamara Khanum* [Album of Tamara Khanum]. Tashkent: Gafur Gulam Literature and Art Publishing House, 1973.

Sosnovskaya, Alla Georgievna. *Puti razvitiya teatral'no-dekoratsionnovo iskusstva Uzbekistana* [The path of development of the art of theatrical decoration in Uzbekistan]. Tashkent: Khamza Hakim-zade Niyazi Institute of fine Art Studies, 1989.

Tulyadjaeva, M.T. and T.I. Yuldashov. *Uzbekskaya dramaturgiya na stsene teatr (60–80–e godyi)* [Uzbek dramaturgy on the stage (1960–1980)]. Tashkent, 1989.

VANUATU

(see **SOUTH PACIFIC**)

VIETNAM

(Overview)

Located in Southeast Asia and extending some 1,100 square kilometres (700 square miles) from China in the north to the Gulf of Thailand in the south, Vietnam shares extended borders on the west with Cambodia and Laos. Divided for much of the twentieth century into a North and a South Viet Nam, this now united country has a land area of 329,600 square kilometres (128,400 square miles) and in 1995 its population was estimated at 74.3 million.

Settled by the Viet people, a southern Chinese tribe, in the third century BC, the area was under Chinese control by 111 BC. Ruling the territory for more than a thousand years, the Chinese lost their control in AD 939 to an indigenous army led by Ngo Quyen. Vietnamese power gradually expanded southward as far as the Mekong River and by the eighteenth century most of what is modern-day Vietnam had come under its influence. But with transportation between the north and south difficult through most of its history, the two parts of the country developed quite differently.

The Portuguese began to trade with Vietnam as early as the sixteenth century and over the next hundred years Catholic missionaries began to visit the country. In 1858, France developed interests in the territory and by 1883 Vietnam had become a French colony. Towards the end of the nineteenth century, Vietnam, Cambodia and most of present-day Laos were incorporated into what became French Indo-China.

During World War II, the Japanese invaded and occupied the country. Within a year, an active opposition emerged (led by Ho Chi Minh) seeking Vietnamese independence. Known as the Vietminh, the opposition seized power in August 1945, declared the independence of Vietnam and established the Democratic Republic of Vietnam in September to become a free state within the French Union in early 1946 as the French returned to claim control over their old colony. France, however, insisted on maintaining control of the southern part of the country and war broke out in December of the same year. In 1954, the Vietnamese captured the northern fortress of Dienbienphu from the French and effectively ended the French colonial regime in Vietnam.

Officially divided at that point into two territories by the Geneva Agreements of 1954 and with an election in both parts of the country expected to unite Vietnam in 1956, the north, under Ho Chi Minh, embraced communism while in the south communist sympathizers were forced underground. When the South Vietnamese leader Ngo Dinh Diem refused to allow the 1956 elections, communists in the south, with the aid of North Vietnamese, organized their own political movement (National Liberation Front of South Vietnam) and their own liberation army commonly known as the Viet Cong. The Ngo Dinh Diem regime, which had been politically and financially supported by the United States, was overthrown in a coup in 1963 but US aid – now strengthened by military involvement – continued. During the next decade, over 50,000 US soldiers would lose their lives along with hundreds of thousands of Vietnamese in the bloody and, for many Americans, senseless Vietnam War. In 1975, the government of South Vietnam was finally forced to surrender to the North and a year later the country was reunited. Over the next decade, Vietnam was rebuilt and cultural activities – some traditional and some with a clear eastern European influences – began to play a role once more in national life.

Compared with other countries in Southeast Asia, Vietnam was one of the earliest to have established and recognized theatrical activities. Not even considering the many performative events involved in early religious rituals – spirit dances and songs performed by mediums, and the many story-songs chanted by *xam xoan* (blind singers) – more formal performances such as the *hat cheo* have taken place for over a thousand years. Rooted in the plains of Bac Bo (North Vietnam), a *hat cheo* group could be made up of only a few artists who would begin their work by laying down a thin mat and a trunk full of musical instruments in front of an audience. Performed before the houses of mandarins, in community spaces or even in the front yard of communal houses on festive occasions, the key principles of this theatrical form were outlined in a 1501 book, *Hi Phuong Pha Luc* by the scholar Luong The Vinh. Storytelling is at its root with the plot always told by a narrator in the prologue. Other actors would in turn then take the stage, enacting in recitative and song the essential story. Characterization was always based on recognizable character types with little attempt at illusion. Rather than mimesis, it was the actor's job to find an interior reality for each character presented. *Hat cheo* has hundreds of recognizable songs attached to it along with a defined system of body movement. Few texts, however, actually exist and those that do reveal little. Among the most popular of the traditional pieces are *Quan Am Thi Kinh, Truong Vien, Luu Binh-Duong Le, Kim Nham, Chu Mai Than* and *Tu Thuc. Hat cheo* is still performed regularly in the Hanoi area.

Just as *hat cheo* has been passed down, so too has the Vietnamese classical opera and dance style known as *hat boi* (also known as *tuong* in the north). Originally growing from the royal courts – tradition has it that the form was, as believed by certain scholars, brought to Vietnam by a captured Chinese actor in 1285 – it was particularly popular in the north. The form attained its height in the eighteenth century starting in the royal palace but eventually spread to the countryside. Sung in a falsetto voice, *hat boi* performances also took place outdoors although a theatre was specifically built for *hat boi* performances in the nineteenth century at Hue, then the capital. Over the centuries, Chinese actors were imported to add new elements to the Vietnamese version. Phuong Nha Tro, an official court troupe, operated until 1946, witness to *hat boi*'s continuous popularity. Again utilizing song and dance, *hat boi* also uses specific musical instruments. More than five hundred texts exist with some having as many as one hundred acts, one act traditionally done each evening over several months. *Hat boi* is generally divided into two main forms: *tuong pho* and *tuong do*. The *tuong pho* form of *hat boi* deals with affairs of state and royal personages, often borrowed from Chinese tales while *tuong do*, more comic in tone, deals with lower officials and more average people.

In the central zone of Vietnam, *hat boi* and the *ca hue* styles are also popular and traditional. Other regional sung forms include *vi dam* in the Nghe Tinh province, *quan ho* in the Bac Ninh province, *ca hue* in the Binh Tri Thien province, the *du ke sung* form of the Khmer minority and the *kich cham* of the Cham minority.

Developing alongside these forms in the early part of the twentieth century was *cai luong* (literally, reformed theatre). Particularly popular in the 1920s in the southern part of the country, *cai luong* includes response songs, clowning and sung monologues. Over the first half of the century, elements of *cai luong* were added to some of the older forms and certain amounts of social criticism also crept in. By 1980, more than a dozen troupes were specializing in *cai luong*.

Design is not part of any of these traditional forms of theatre. Actors describe the space much as Elizabethan actors did, utilizing words and movement. Costume and makeup also clearly express character, rank and even temperament. In all these traditional forms, dance plays a major part and is done to beats of a drum, adding to the beauty of gesture, word and tune. In such traditional forms, people find understanding within, in communion with the actor – far different than from the social and ideological problems manifested in the more modern drama.

As for *kich noi*, spoken theatre of the European style, early performances in the 1920s – mostly of Molière and Corneille – were done by French colonials for officials and those who could speak French among the local citizenry in the major cities. Later performed by educated Vietnamese themselves – first in French and later in the vernacular – after nearly half a century of development, this type of theatre has become an important component in Vietnamese theatre life, particularly in the post-Vietnam War period. Indeed, it is the European Stanislavski system which is currently taught at the country's major theatre school, the Institute of Theatre and Cinema in Hanoi. As a result, an important group of spoken theatre dramatists and directors has developed. Even designers are now emerging though they are still doing mostly painted backdrops.

The first spoken drama in Vietnamese was *Chen thuoc doc* (*A Cup of Poison*) by Vu Dinh Long (1901–60) in 1921. Another early dramatist of note was Nguyen Huy Tuong (1912–60), author of *Vu Nhu To* (1943), a famous classic dealing with the complexity of people – power, creativity and love – in a play so controversial that it was able to be produced only in 1995; and *Bac Son* (1945) dealing with revolution. Among the other modern dramatists to be published is Luu Quang Vu (1948–88) who wrote *Truong Ba da hang thit* as well as a series of plays that shook

A production of *Friendship with Angels*.
Photo: courtesy of ASSITEJ Japan.

A production of *Yrit and Wolf-mother*.
Photo: courtesy of ASSITEJ Japan.

Vietnam during the late 1980s. Other play-wrights include Xuan Trinh, Nguyen Dihn Thi and Nguyen Huy Thiep, author of *Con Lai Tinh Yeu* (*Love Remains*, 1990).

In total, more than 150 theatre groups exist in Vietnam. In Hanoi, the most important theatre during the 1960s to the 1980s was the Central Theatre. In the 1990s, the Youth Theatre and Hanoi Drama Theatre hold the same impor-tance as the Central Theatre in terms of spoken drama. Although the spoken theatre groups are all following western traditions – particularly important have been Russian plays and play-wrights – some of the more modern directors have been trying to blend Vietnamese traditional theatre forms with spoken drama forms. Though such crossovers have borne little fruit to date, they do continue on an occasional basis.

State policy officially encourages all these styles and is particularly concerned with the preservation and maintenance of the traditional in national culture. Since reunification in 1975, Vietnam has passed into a period of active con-struction in an all socio-economic domains creating very favourable conditions for development in the arts. Every city of any size has at least two or three theatre, music or dance

troupes, some (like the major groups in Hanoi) are committed to performances of all the traditional forms as well as spoken theatre. A performing artists' union, – the Association of Theatre Artists, represents 3,000 actors, over 150 dramatists and 60 directors.

Many companies tour to other areas of the country after completing their own home seasons. Since 1975, a national theatre festival has been held every five years bringing together the best performances from across the country. These festivals not only introduce and encour-age new talents but also become real festive occasions for the city in which they are held.

As for puppet theatre, one of the world's unique forms of the art, *mua roi nuoc* (water puppetry), has existed in Vietnam since at least the twelfth century. First performed in rice paddies and now in more accessible ponds and, when on tour, in specially created pools, the form offers simple, traditional stories for amuse-ment and basic morality. The puppeteers stand behind a bamboo curtain, several metres away from the wooden animal or human puppets (some of which measure up to a metre high) which they manipulate with long wooden poles that are kept at all times under water. The water puppets are extremely popular in Vietnam and have attracted wide attention when they have toured outside the country despite the difficulty of trying to re-create something of the original integrity. Nevertheless, for those who are able to put what they see into a Vietnamese context, the experience is unforgettable.

Other puppet forms, generally based on Russian models, have also become popular since 1975 with ensembles for both adults and children founded in Hanoi and in Ho Chi Minh City. Another dozen or so such ensembles exist in larger cities as well as in the many Child and Youth Culture Houses that now exist across the country.

A Youth Song and Dance Ensemble exists in Ho Chi Minh City which has done some very good work in the field of theatre for young audiences. Founded in 1980, it has some thirty artists in its company. Its counterpart in Hanoi is the Youth Theatre, which is equally important in the field. There is a Vietnamese branch of the International Association of Theatre for Children and Young People (ASSITEJ) which since its founding in Vietnam in 1985 has regularly been involved in the organization of a youth theatre festival each June and August. It has fourteen group members and thirty individual members (mostly writers). Exchanges have been held with the Leningrad Youth Theatre and with theatre groups in Germany, France, Czechoslovakia, Japan and Australia.

In the area of training, the Hanoi Institute of Theatre and Cinema, founded in 1980, was one of the earliest evidences of the new cultural growth seen in the country after 1975. Unfortunately, the economic downturn of the mid-1980s has negatively affected all areas of culture – including training – right into the mid-1990s. Spoken theatre now no longer has the novelty it once did and traditional forms are not supported by the young. Too many spoken plays are thrown together hastily and too much pressure is coming from film and television to keep young people interested in these earlier forms.

Economically, state subsidy has remained the same or been even higher for state groups. However, the box office, a very important source of income for actors, has declined for many companies. In turn, companies without audiences lose state subsidy. The number of companies has been reduced from 150 to approximately 100 through merging together.

Hoang Su
With additional material from Pham Thi
Thanh and WECT staff

Further Reading

Brandon, James R. *Theater in Southeast Asia.* Cambridge, MA: Harvard University Press, 1967. 370 pp.

Durand, M. and Nguyen Tran Huan. *An Introduction to Vietnamese Theatre.* New York: Columbia University Press, 1985. 213 pp.

Jones, Margot A. 'Mua roi nuoc: The Art of Vietnamese Puppetry. A Theatrical Genre Study'. PhD thesis, Honolulu. 1996. 280 pp.

'Le Théâtre vietnamien' [The Vietnamese theatre]. *Les Théâtres d'Asie,* ed. J. Jacquot. Paris, 1968.

Mackerras, Colin. 'Theatre in Vietnam'. *Asian Theatre Journal* 4 no. 1 (Spring 1987).

Nguyen Ba Khoach, trans. *Vietnamese Water Puppets* [video recording] 1982.

Nguyen, Duk Kon. *Ot istokovtradicii do sovremennosti (ob osnovich osobennostjach I priemstvennosti v rezvitisj vjetnamskogo tradicionnogo teatra): Avtoref* [From the roots of tradition to the present (on the major characteristics and acceptance in the development of Vietnamese traditional theatre): Dissertation abstract]. Moscow: VNII Iskusstvozinanija, 1989. 23 pp.

Nguyen Huy Hong and Tran Trung Chinh. *Vietnamese Traditional Water Puppetry.* Hanoi: The Gioi, 1992. 79 pp.

Le Théâtre vietnamien [The Vietnamese theatre]. Brussels: Van-Tiën, 1985. 23 pp.

'Vietnamese Water Puppets'. *Performing Arts Journal* 9 no. 1 (1985).

WESTERN SAMOA

(see **SOUTH PACIFIC**)

FURTHER READING

Reference Works/Dictionaries/Encyclopedias/Bibliographies

Brandon, James R., ed. *The Cambridge Guide To Asian Theatre*. Cambridge: Cambridge University Press, 1993. 254 pp.

——. *The Performing Arts of Asia*. Paris: Unesco, 1971. 168 pp.

——. *Theatre in Southeast Asia*. Honolulu: University Press of Hawaii, 1976.

Brandon, James R. and Elizabeth Wichmann, eds. *Asian Theatre: A Study Guide and Annotated Bibliography*. Theatre Perspectives no 1. Washington, DC: American Theatre Association, 1980.

Buzo, Alexander. *The Young Person's Guide to the Theatre and Almost Everything Else*. Ringwood, Victoria: Penguin, 1988. 164 pp.

Chua Soo Pong, ed. *Traditional Theatre in Southeast Asia*. Singapore: UniPress for SPAFA [and] the Centre for the Arts, National University of Singapore, 1995. 150 pp.

Johnson, Sheila, J. *Non-Western Music: A Selected Bibliography*. 2nd edn. Sacramento, CA: Sacramento Library California State University, 1973. 40 pp.

Lal, P. *An Annotated Mahabharata Bibliography*. Calcutta: Writer's Workshop, 1967. 31 pp.

McLean, Mervyn. *An Annotated Bibliography of Oceanic Music and Dance*. 2nd edn. Warren, MI: Harmonic Park Press, 1995. 502 pp.

Yousof, Ghulam-Sarwar. *Dictionary of Traditional South-East Asian Theatre*. Kuala Lumpur: Oxford University Press, 1994. 327 pp.

Theatre History

Davidson, Clifford and John C. Stroupe, eds. *Early and Traditional Drama: Africa, Asia and the New World*. Kalamazoo, MI: Medieval Institute Publications, 1994. 165 pp.

Dzarylgasinova, R.S. and M.V. Krukov, eds. *Kalendarnyje obycai i obriady narodov Vostocnoj Azii: Novyj God* [Calendar traditions and rites of the people of East Asia: New Year]. Moscow: Nauka, 1985. 264 pp.

Kim, N. *Narodnoje chudozestvennoje tvorcestvo Sovetskovo Vostoka: ocerki istorii massovovo teatralnova iskusstva Srednej Azii* [People's art of the Soviet East: Historical essays on popular theatrical forms of Middle Asia]. Moscow: Nauka, 1985. 197 pp.

Criticism and Aesthetics

Afro-Asian Theatre Bulletin. American Educational Theatre Association.

Asian Theatre Journal. Honolulu: University of Hawaii Press, founded 1984.

Asian Theatre Reports. [Honolulu] Asian Theatre Organization of the University of Hawaii.

Barfoot, C.C. and Cobi Bordewijk, eds. *Theatre Intercontinental: Forms, Functions, Correspondences.* Amsterdam/Atlanta, GA: Rodopi, 1993. 224 pp.

Brandon, James. 'Theatre East and West: International Congress'. *Asian Theatre Journal* 2 (fall 1985).

Foley, Kathy, ed. *Essays on Southeast Asian Performing Arts: Local Manifestations and Cross-Cultural Implications.* Berkeley, CA: International and Area Studies, Centre for South and Southeast Asian Studies, University of California at Berkeley, 1992. 139 pp.

International Theatre Institute. *World of Theatre 1988–1990: Essays on Theatre Seasons Around the World.* Moscow: Culture Publishing, 1991. 172 pp.

Kinderman, Heinz, ed. *Einfuhrung in das ostasiatische Theater* [Introduction to the oriental theatre]. Maske und Kothurn, Beiheft 7. Vienna/Cologne/Graz: Bohlau, 1985. 426 pp.

Marotti, Ferruccio. *Il volto dell'invisibile. Studi e ricerche sui teatri orientali* [The face of the invisible. Studies and research on oriental theatre]. Rome: Bulzoni Editore, 1984. 180 pp.

Moore, Albert C. *Arts in the Religions of the Pacific: Symbols of Life.* London/New York: Pinter, 1995.

Ottaviani, Gioia. 'L'Attore e lo sciamano: esempi d'identita nelle tradizioni dell' Estremo Oriente' [The actor and the shaman: Examples of identity in the traditions of the Far East]. *ThR* 10, no. 3 (1984).

Pronko, Leonard C. *Theatre East and West: Perspectives Toward a Total Theatre.* Berkeley, CA University of California Press, 1967. 230 pp.

Scott, A.C. *The Theatre in Asia.* London: Weidenfeld & Nicolson, 1972. 289 pp.

Tatlow, Anthony. *The Mask of Evil: Brecht's Response to the Poetry, Theatre and Thought of China and Japan: A Comparative and Critical Evaluation.* Bern/Las Vegas: P. Lang, 1977.

van Erben, Eugène. *The Playful Revolution: Theatre and Liberation in Asia.* Bloomington, IN: Indiana University Press, 1992. 304 pp.

Varadpande, Manohar Laxman. *Religion and Theatre.* New Delhi: Abhinav, 1983. 148 pp.

Williams, David. *Peter Brook and the Mahabharata: Critical Perspectives.* London/New York: Routledge, 1991.

Theatre Arts

Ahn, Mim-Soo, Suk-Kee Yoh and Taw-Ju Lee. *Yeun-ki* [Acting]. Seoul, 1988. 267 pp.

Awasthi, Suresh. *Drama: The Gift of the Gods.* Tokyo: Institute for Study of Languages and Cultures of Asia, 1983. 134 pp.

Belich, Margaret, ed. *Performance.* Wellington: Association of Community Theatres, 1985. 62 pp.

Fernandez, Doreen G., ed. *Contemporary Theatre Arts: Asia and the United States.* Quezon City: New Day Publishers, 1984. 78 pp.

Fitzpatrick, Tim. *Performance, From Product to Process.* Sydney: University of Sydney, 1989. 253 pp.

Fluekiger Bukhalter, Joyce and Laurie J. Sears, eds. *Boundaries of Text: Epic Performances in South and Southeast Asia.* Ann Arbor, MI: Centre for South and Southeast Asian Studies, University of Michigan, 1991. 161 pp.

Goji, Hamada. *Bee Honey Honeycomb: Document of Performance Art.* Perth: Pica, 1994. 163 pp.

Staveacre, Tony. *Slapstick! The Illustrated Story of Knockout Comedy.* North Ryed, NSW: Angus Robertson, 1987. 189 pp.

Anthologies/Playwrights' Studies

ASEAN Committee of Culture and Information. *Modern Asean Plays*. (Individual volumes of plays from Thailand, Malaysia, Philippines and Indonesia.) Thailand, 1994.

Winther, Barbara. *Plays from Folktales of Africa and Asia*. Boston, MA: Plays Inc, 1976. 274 pp.

Puppet and Mask Theatre

Contractor, M.R. *Creative Drama and Puppetry in Education*. New Delhi: National Book Trust, 1984. 100 pp.

Kumar, Sunil. *Puppetry: A Tool of Mass Communication*. Varanasi: National Council for Development Communication, 1989. 77 pp.

Shah, Anupama. *Puppetry and Folk Dramas for Non-Formal Education*. New Delhi: Sterling, 1992. 174 pp.

Tilakasiri, J. *The Puppet Theatre of Asia*. Colombo: Department of Cultural Affairs, 1968. 166 pp.

Vanni Menichi, Carlo, ed. *Le maschere dell'uomo: Segni plastici da oriente as occidente* [The masks of man: Plastic signs from east to west]. Pistoia: Tellini, 1986. 80 pp.

Wisniewski, David. *Teaching with Shadow Puppetry*. Englewood, CO: Teacher Ideas Press, 1997. 225 pp.

Music and Dance Theatre

Bharatha, Iyer, K. *Dance Dramas of India and the East*. Bombay: Taraporevala, 1980. 73 pp.

Bloch, Stella. *Dancing and the Drama East and West*. New York: Orientalia, 1992. 13 pp.

Bowers, Faubian. *Theatre in the East: A Survey of Asian Dance and Drama*. New York: Thomas Nelson & Sons, 1956. 374 pp.

Carell, Beth Dean. *Three Dances of Oceania*. Sydney: Sydney Opera House Trust, 1976. 96 pp.

——. *South Pacific Dance*. Sydney: Pacific Publications, 1978. 108 pp.

Chesterman, Colleen and Virginia Baxter, eds. *Playing With Fire: Women Writing For Performance*. Darlinghurst: Playworks, 1995. 139 pp.

Dance and Music in South Asian Drama: Chhau, Mahakalipyakhan and Yakshagana/Report of Asian Traditional Performing Arts, 1981. Tokyo: Tokyo Academia Music, 1983. 354 pp.

Folk Songs of Asia and the Pacific: Guidebook. Tokyo: Asian Cultural Centre for Unesco, 1988. 115 pp. and three sound cassettes.

Gamo, Satoaki, ed. *Nihon no Ongaku Asia no ongaku* [A study of Japanese music and Asian music]. Tokyo: Iwanami shoten, 1989. 314 pp.

Ginn, Victoria. *The Spirited Earth: Dance, Myth and Ritual from South Asia to the South Pacific*. New York: Rizzoli, 1990. 191 pp.

Island Music of the South Pacific [sound recording]. Los Angeles: Nonesuch, 1981.

Jowitt, Glenn. *Dance in the Pacific*. John Hart and Kath Joblin, eds. Auckland: Longman Paul, 1990.

Kaeppler, Adrienne L., Judy Van Zile and Carl Wolz, eds. *Asian and Pacific Dance: Selected Papers from the 1974 CORD-SEM Conference*. New York: Committee on Research in Dance, 1977. 173 pp.

Malm, William P. *Music Cultures of the Pacific, the Near East and Asia*. Englewood Cliffs, NJ: Prentice Hall, 1967. 169 pp.

Miettinch, Jukka O. *Classical Dance and Theatre in Southeast Asia*. Singapore/Oxford/New York: Oxford University Press, 1992. 175 pp.

Monographs on Music, Dance and Theatre in South East Asia. New York: Asia Society Performing Arts Program, 1979– .

Music and Dance of the Silk Route. Society for Preservation and Propagation of Eastern Arts, 1987. 53 pp.

Osman, Mohammad Taib, ed. *Traditional Drama and Music of Southeast Asia*. Kuala Lumpur: Dewan Bahasa dan Pustaka, 1974.

Palmer, Bruce and Beth Dean. *South Pacific: Islands Art and Dance*. Suva, Fiji: Fiji Times and Herald, 1972.

Sakakibara, Kiitsu. *Dances of Asia*. Chandigarh, India: Abhishek, 1992. 218 pp.

Shawn, Ted. *Gods Who Dance*. New York: E.P. Dutton & Co., 1929. 208 pp.

Van Zile, Judy. *Dance in Africa, Asia and the Pacific: Selected Readings*. New York: MSS Information Corp., 1976. 177 pp.

Zarina, Xenia. *Classical Dances of the Orient*. New York: Crown, 1967. 232 pp.

See also *The Drama Review* which has regularly published a wide variety of material on Asian theatre, including several special issues.

INTERNATIONAL
REFERENCE

SELECTED BIBLIOGRAPHY

The following is a list of significant theatre books that have been published since the early 1950s. For a larger listing of world theatre publications, see volume 6 of this encyclopedia, *World Theatre Bibliography/Cumulative Index*. This section was prepared with the collaboration of the Belgian scholar René Hainaux and the Centre de Recherches et de Formation Théâtrales en Wallonie with the assistance of collaborators from Europe, North and South America, Africa, the Arab World and Asia.

Reference Works/Dictionaries/Encyclopedias/Bibliographies

Attisani, Antonio. *Enciclopedia del teatro del' 900* [Theatre encyclopedia of the twentieth century]. Milan: Feltrinelli, 1980. 598 pp.

Bailey, Claudia Jean. *A Guide to Reference and Bibliography for Theatre Research*. 2nd edn. Columbus, OH: Ohio State University Libraries, 1983.

Banham, Martin, ed. *The Cambridge Guide to World Theatre*. Cambridge: Cambridge University Press, 1988. 1,104 pp.

Brauneck, Manfred, and Gérard Schneilin, eds. *Theaterlexikon: Begriffe und Epoche. Bühnen und Ensembles* [Theatre lexicon: terms and periods. Stages and ensembles]. Hamburg: Rowohlt, 1986. 1,120 pp.

Bryan, George G., ed. *Stage Lives: A Bibliography and Index to Theatrical Bibliographies in English*. Westport, CT: Greenwood Press, 1985. 368 pp.

Cao, Yu, and Wang, Zuo Ling, eds. *China's Great Encyclopedia of World Theatre and Drama*. Beijing/Shanghai: China's Great Encyclopedia Press, 1989. 583 pp.

Carpenter, Charles A. *Modern Drama Scholarship and Criticism 1966–1980: An International Bibliography*. Downsview, ON: University of Toronto Press, 1985. 650 pp.

Cohen, Selma Jeanne, ed. *International Encyclopedia of Dance*. New York: Oxford University Press, 1998.

Corvin, Michel. *Dictionnaire encyclopédique du théâtre* [Encyclopedic dictionary of theatre]. Paris: Bordas, 1991.

Couty, Daniel and Alan Rey, eds. *Le Théâtre* [Theatre]. Paris: Bordas, 1980.

Cruciani, Fabrizio and Nicola Savarese, eds. *Teatro* [Theatre]. Milan: Garzanti, 1991. 353 pp.

Dahlhaus, Carl. *Pipers Enzyklopädia des Musiktheaters* [Piper's encyclopedia of music theatre]. 5 vols. Munich: Piper, 1986– .

D'Amico, Silvio, ed. *Enciclopedia dello spettacolo* [Encyclopedia of the performing arts]. 11 vols. Rome: Le Maschere, 1954–66.

Esslin, Martin, ed. *The Encyclopedia of World Theater*. New York: Scribner, 1977.

Fielding, Eric, gen. ed. *Theatre Words: An International Vocabulary in Nine Languages*. Prague: Publication and Information Exchange Commission of OISTAT, 1993.

Gassner, John, and Edward Quinn, eds. *The Readers' Encyclopedia of World Drama*. New York: Thomas Y. Crowell, 1969. 1,030 pp.

Giteau, Cécile. *Dictionnaire des arts du spectacle: Théâtre-Cinéma-Cirque-Danse-Radio-Marionettes-Télévision-Documentologie* [Dictionary of the performing arts: Theatre-Film-Circus-Dance-Radio-Puppetry-Television-Documentation]. Paris: Dunod, 1970. 430 pp. In French, English and German.

Gregor, Josef, and Margret Dietrich. *Der Schauspielführer: der Inhalt der wichtigsten Theaterstücke aus aller Welt* [The play guide: Synopses of the most important plays from the whole world]. 15 vols. Stuttgart: Anton Hierseman, 1953–93.

Hainaux, René, ed. *Stage Design Throughout the World*. 4 vols. London: Harrap; New York: Theatre Arts Books, 1956–75.

Hartnoll, Phyllis, and Peter Found, eds. *The Concise Oxford Companion to the Theatre*. 2nd edn. New York: Oxford University Press, 1992. 586 pp.

——. *The Oxford Companion to the Theatre*. 4th edn. London: Oxford University Press, 1983. 934 pp.

Hawkins-Dady, Mark, ed. *International Dictionary of Theatre*. Vol. 2: *Playwrights*. Detroit/London/Washington, DC: Gale Research International/St James Press, 1994. 1,218 pp.

Hochman, Stanley, ed. *McGraw-Hill Encyclopedia of World Drama*. 2nd edn. 5 vols. New York: McGraw-Hill, 1984.

Hoffmann, Christel, ed. *Kinder- und Jugendtheater der Welt* [Children's and youth theatre of the world]. 2nd edn. Berlin: Henschelverlag, 1984. 276 pp.

Kienzle, Siegfried. *Schauspielführer der Gegenwart: Interpretation zum Schauspiel ab 1945* [A guide to contemporary plays: An interpretation of plays since 1945]. Stuttgart: Alfred Kröner Verlag, 1978. 659 pp.

Koegler, Horst, ed. *The Concise Oxford Dictionary of Ballet*. Oxford: Oxford University Press, 1987. 458 pp.

Kullman, Colby H. and William C. Young. *Theatre Companies of the World*. 2 vols. New York/London: Greenwood Press, 1986.

Leleu-Rouvray, Geneviève and Gladys Langevin, eds. *International Bibliography on Puppetry: English Books 1945–1990*. Paris: Institut International de la Marionnette/Associations Marionnette et Thérapie, 1993. 281 pp.

Matlaw, Myron. *Modern World Drama: An Encyclopedia*. London: Secker & Warburg, 1972. 960 pp.

Mikotowicz, Thomas J., ed. *Theatrical Designers: An International Biographical Dictionary*. Westport, CT: Greenwood Press, 1992. 365 pp.

Mokulski, S.S., and P.A. Markov, eds. *Teatralnaia Entsiklopedia* [Theatre encyclopedia]. 6 vols. Moscow: Sovietskaia Entsiklopedia, 1961–7.

Molinari, Cesare. *Storia universale del teatro* [Universal history of the theatre]. Milan: Mondador, 1983. 358 pp.

Ortolani, Benito, ed. *International Bibliography of Theatre*. 7 vols. New York: Theatre Research Data Center, 1985–93.

Pavis, Patrice. *Dictionnaire du théâtre: termes et concepts de l'analyse théâtrale* [Dictionary of the theatre: Terms and concepts of theatrical analysis]. 2nd edn. Paris: Editions Sociales, 1987. 477 pp.

Philpott, A.R. *Dictionary of Puppetry*. London: MacDonald, 1969. 291 pp.

Quéant, G., ed. *Encyclopédie du théâtre contemporain* [Encyclopedia of contemporary theatre]. Paris: Olivier Perrin, 1959. 211 pp.

Rischbieter, Henning. *Theater-Lexikon* [Theatre lexicon]. Revised edn. Zurich-Schwäbisch Hall: Orell Füssli, 1983. 484 pp.

Sadie, Stanley. ed. *The New Grove Dictionary of Opera*. 4 vols. London: Macmillan, 1992.

Salgado, Gamini and Peter Thomson. *The Everyman Companion to the Theatre*. London: J.M. Dent & Sons, 1985. 458 pp.

Schindler, Otto G. *Theaterliteratur. Ein bibliographischer Behelf für das Studium der Theaterwissenschaft* [Theatre literature. A bibliographic guide for theatre studies]. 3 vols. Vienna: Institut für Theaterwissenschaft, 1973.

Shemanski, Frances. *A Guide to World Fairs and Festivals*. Westport, CT/London: Greenwood Press, 1985. 309 pp.

Shigetoshi, Kawatake, ed. *Engeki Hyakka Daijiten* [Encyclopedia of world theatre]. 6 vols. Tokyo: Heibonsha, 1960–2.

Swortzell, Lowell, ed. *International Guide to Children's Theatre and Educational Theatre. A Historical and Geographical Source Book*. Westport, CT: Greenwood Press, 1990. 360 pp.

Trapido, Joel, ed. *An International Dictionary of Theatre Language*. Westport, CT: Greenwood Press, 1985. 1,032 pp.

Veinstein, André and Alfred Golding, eds. *Performing Arts Libraries and Museums of the World/Bibliothèques et musées des arts du spectacle dans le monde*. 4th edn. Paris: Centre National de la Recherche Scientifique, 1992. 773 pp.

Wilcox, R. Turner. *The Dictionary of Costume*. New York: Scribner, 1969. 406 pp.

Theatre History

Anderson, Jack. *Ballet and Modern Dance: A Concise History*. 2nd edn. Princeton, NJ: Princeton Book Company, 1992. 287 pp.

Arnott, Peter. *The Theatre in its Time*. Boston, MA: Little, Brown, 1981. 566 pp.

Aslan, Odette. *L'Art du théâtre* [The art of theatre]. Verviers: Marabout, 1963. 672 pp.

Award, Louis. *Al masrah al âlami* [World theatre]. Egypt, 1964.

Brockett, Oscar G. *History of the Theatre*. 6th edn. Boston, MA: Allyn & Bacon, 1990. 680 pp.

Calendoli, Giovanni. *Storia universale della danza* [General history of dance]. Milan: Mondadori, 1985. 288 pp.

Dumur, Guy, ed. *Histoire des spectacles* [History of the performing arts]. Encyclopédie de la Pléiade Collection. Paris: Gallimard, 1965. 2,010 pp.

International Theatre Institute. *World of Theatre 1988–1990*. Moscow: Culture Publishing, 1991. 172 pp.

——. *World of Theatre 1990–1992*. Bangladesh: ITI, 1993. 275 pp.

Jurkowski, Henryk. *Dzieje teatru lalek: Od wielkiej reformy do współczesnośi* [History of the puppet theatre: From theatre's reform to today]. Warsaw, 1984.

——. *Ecrivains et marionnettes: quatre siècles de littérature dramatique* [Writers and puppets: four centuries of dramatic literature]. Charleville-Mézières: Institut National de la Marionnette, 1991.

Kuritz, Paul. *The Making of Theatre History*. Englewood Cliffs, NJ: Prentice-Hall, 1988. 468 pp.

Kybalova, Ludmila, Olga Herbenova, and Milena Lamarova. *The Pictorial Encyclopedia of Fashion*. New York: Crown, 1968. 604 pp.

Londré, Felicia Hardison. *The History of World Theatre: From the Restoration to the Present*. New York: Continuum, 1991. 644 pp.

Molinari, Cesare. *Teatro* [Theatre]. Milan: Mondadori, 1972.

——. *Theatre Through the Ages*. New York: McGraw-Hill, 1975. 324 pp.

Mordden, Ethan. *The Fireside Companion to the Theatre*. New York: Simon & Schuster, 1988. 313 pp.

Nagler, A.M. *A Sourcebook in Theatrical History*. New York: Dover, 1952. 611 pp.

Nicoll, Allardyce. *The Development of the Theatre: A Study of Theatrical Art from the Beginnings to the Present Day*. 5th edn. London: George G. Harrap, 1966. 318 pp.

Niculescu, Margareta. *Teatrul de păpuşi in lume* [Puppet theatre in the world]. Berlin: Henschelverlag; Bucharest: Meridiane, 1966. 230 pp.

Nutku, Ozdemir. *Dünya Tiyatrosu Tarihi* [A history of world theatre]. 2 vols. Ankara: Ankara Universitesi dil ve Tarih Coğrafya Fakültesi Yaylonlan, 1973.

Ottai, Antonella, ed. *Teatro oriente/occidente* [Oriental/occidental theatre]. Biblioteca Teatrale no. 47. Rome: Bulzoni, 1986. 565 pp.

Pandolfi, Vito. *Storia universale del teatro drammatico* [World history of dramatic art]. 2 vols. Turin: Unione Typografico-Editrice, 1964. 1,626 pp.

Pronko, Leonard C. *Theater East and West Perspectives Toward a Total Theater*. Berkeley, CA: University of California Press, 1967. 280 pp.

Roose-Evans, James. *Experimental Theatre: From Stanislavksi to Peter Brook*. 2nd edn. London: Routledge, 1989. 224 pp.

Sallé, Bernard. *Histoire du théâtre* [History of the theatre]. Paris: Librairie Théâtrale, 1990. 320 pp.

Wickham, Glynne. *A History of the Theatre*. New York/ Cambridge: Cambridge University Press, 1985. 254 pp.

Zamora Guerrero, Juan. *Historia del teatro contemporáneo* [History of contemporary theatre]. 4 vols. Barcelona: Juan Flores, 1961–2.

Criticism and Aesthetics

Appia, Adolphe. *Oeuvres complètes* [Complete works]. 3 vols. Ed. Marie L. Bablet-Hahn. Lausanne: L'Age d'Homme, 1983–8.

Artaud, Antonin. *Oeuvres complètes* [Complete works]. 25 vols. Paris: Gallimard, 1961–90.

Barba, Eugenio. *Beyond the Floating Islands*. New York: PAJ Publications, 1986. 282 pp.

——. *The Floating Islands*. Holstebro, Denmark: Thomsens Bogtrykkeri, 1979. 224 pp.

—— and Nicola Savarese. *The Secret Art of the Performer. A Dictionary of Theatre Anthropology*. Ed. and compiled by Richard Gough. London: Routledge, 1991. 272 pp.

Bawtree, Michael. *The New Singing Theatre*. Bristol, UK: Bristol Classical Press; New York: Oxford University Press, 1991. 232 pp.

Beckerman, Bernard. *Dynamics of Drama*. New York: Drama Book Specialists, 1979. 272 pp.

Bentley, Eric. *The Dramatic Event*. Boston, MA: Beaucou Press, 1956. 278 pp.

———. *The Life of the Drama*. New York: Atheneum, 1964. 371 pp.

———. *The Playwright as Thinker*. New York: Reynal & Hitchcock, 1946. 382 pp.

Bharucha, Rustom. *Theatre and the World: Performance and the Politics of Culture*. London/New York: Routledge, 1993. 254 pp.

Birringer, Johannes. *Theatre, History and Post-Modernism*. Bloomington, IN: Indiana University Press, 1991. 240 pp.

Boal, Augusto. *Theatre of the Oppressed*. New York: Theatre Communications Group, 1985. 197 pp.

Brecht, Bertolt. *Kleines Organon für das Theater* [A little organum for the theatre]. Frankfurt: Suhrkamp Verlag, 1958.

———. *Schriften zum Theater* [Writings on the theatre]. 7 vols. Ed. Werner Hecht. Berlin: Aufbau Verlag, 1963–4.

Brook, Peter. *The Empty Space*. London: MacGibbon & Kee, 1969. 141 pp.

Brustein, Robert. *The Theatre of Revolt*. Boston, MA: Little, Brown, 1964. 435 pp.

Carlson, Marvin. *Theories of the Theatre: A Historical and Critical Survey, from the Greeks to the Present*. Ithaca, NY/London: Cornell University Press, 1984. 530 pp.

Clark, Barrett H. *European Theories of the Drama*. New York: Crown, 1965. 628 pp.

Craig, Edward Gordon. *On the Art of Theatre*. London: Heinemann, 1911, 1968. 295 pp.

———. *Towards a New Theatre*. London: J.M. Dent, 1913.

Dort, Bernard. *Théâtre en jeu* [Drama in performance]. Paris: Seuil, 1979. 334 pp.

———. *Théâtre réel* [Real theatre]. Paris: Seuil, 1971. 300 pp.

Epskamp, Kees P. *Theatre in Search for Social Change: The Relative Significance of Different Theatrical Approaches*. The Hague: Centre for the Study of Education in Developing Countries, 1989.

Esslin, Martin. *The Field of Drama*. London: Methuen, 1987. 190 pp.

———. *The Theatre of the Absurd*. Garden City, NY: Doubleday, 1961. 364 pp.

Frye, Northrop. *Anatomy of Criticism*. Princeton, NJ: Princeton University Press, 1957. 383 pp.

Goodman, Lizbeth. *Contemporary Feminist Theatres*. London: Routledge, 1992. 272 pp.

Grotowski, Jerzy. *Towards a Poor Theatre*. New York: Simon & Schuster, 1968. 262 pp.

Innes, Christopher. *Avant-Garde Theatre, 1892–1992*. London/New York: Routledge, 1993. 262 pp.

Ionesco, Eugène. *Notes et contrenotes* [Notes and counternotes]. Paris: Gallimard, 1962. 248 pp.

Kidd, Ross. *The Performing Arts, Non-Formal Education and Social Change in the Third World: A Bibliography and Review Essay*. The Hague: Centre for the Study of Education in Developing Countries, 1981.

Kott, Jan. *Shakespeare Our Contemporary*. Garden city, NY: Doubleday, 1964. 241 pp.

———. *The Theatre of Essence*. Translated by Michael Kott. Evanston, IL: Northwestern University Press, 1984. 218 pp.

MacAloon, John J., ed. *Rite, Festival, Spectacle: Rehearsals Toward a Theory of Cultural Performance*. Philadelphia, PA: Institute for the Study of Human Issues, 1984. 280 pp.

Mackintosh, Iain. *Architecture, Actor and Audience*. London/New York: Routledge, 1993. 184 pp.

Mitchell, Arnold. *The Professional Performing Arts: Attendance Patterns, Preferences and Motives*. 2 vols. Madison, WI: Association of College, University and Community Arts Administrators, 1984.

Pavis, Patrice. *Theatre at the Crossroads of Culture*. London: Routledge, 1991. 256 pp.

Quadri, Franco. *Il teatro degli anni settanta: Invenzione di un teatro diverso* [The theatre of the seventies: Invention of a different theatre]. Turin: Einaudi, 1984. 298 pp.

River, Julie, and Germaine Dellis. *L'Enfant et le théâtre* [The child and the theatre]. Brussels: Labor, 1992. 155 pp.

Schechner, Richard. *Between Theatre and Anthropology*. Philadelphia, PA: University of Pennsylvania Press, 1985. 342 pp.

———. *Environmental Theatre*. New York: Hawthorne. 1973. 339 pp.

———. *Performance Theory*. London: Routledge, 1988. 320 pp.

Schutzman, Mady and Jan Cohen-Cruz, eds. *Playing Boal: Theatre, Therapy, Activism*. London/New York: Routledge, 1994. 246 pp.

Seltzer, Daniel. *The Modern Theatre: Readings and Documents*. Boston, MA: Little, Brown, 1967. 495 pp.

Stanislavski, Konstantin. *The Collected Works of Konstantin Stanislavski*. Ed. Sharon Marie Carnicke. 10 vols. London: Routledge, 1993– .

———. *Sobraniye Sochinenii* [Collected works]. 7 vols. Moscow: Iskusstvo, 1954–60.

Strehler, Giorgio. *Per un teatro umano: pensieri scritti parlati e attuali* [Towards a humanized theatre: contemporary written thoughts and discussions]. Milan: Feltrinelli, 1974. 363 pp.

Turner, Victor. *From Ritual to Theatre: The Human Seriousness of Play*. New York: PAJ Publications, 1982. 127 pp.

Ubersfeld, Anne. *L'Ecole du spectateur* [The school for theatregoers]. Paris: Editions Sociales, 1981. 352 pp.

——. *Lire le théâtre* [Reading performance]. Paris: Editions Sociales, 1977. 280 pp.

Wandor, Michelene. *Carry On, Understudies: Theatre and Sexual Politics*. London: Routledge, 1986. 224 pp.

Theatre Arts

Bablet, Denis. *Les Révolutions scéniques du XXième siècle* [Scenic revolutions of the twentieth century]. Paris: Société Internationale d'art XXième siècle, 1975. 388 pp.

Barba, Eugenio and Nicola Savarese. *The Secret Art of the Performer: A Dictionary of Theatre Anthropology*. Transl. Richard Fowler. New York: Routledge, 1991. 272 pp.

Barton, Lucy. *Historic Costume for the Stage*. London: A. & C. Black, 1961. 609 pp.

Bellman, Williard F. *Scenography and Stage Technology*. New York: Thomas Crowell, 1977. 639 pp.

Braun, Edward. *The Director and the Stage: From Naturalism to Grotowski*. London: Methuen, 1982. 218 pp.

Cole, Toby, and Helen K. Chinoy. *Actors on Acting: The Theories, Techniques and Practices of the Great Actors of all Times as Told in Their Own Words*. New York: Crown, 1970. 715 pp.

Currell, David. *The Complete Book of Puppet Theatre*. Totowa, NJ: Barnes & Noble, 1985. 312 pp.

Duerr, Edwin, ed. *The Length and Depth of Acting*. New York: Holt-Rinehart & Winston, 1962. 590 pp.

Gaulme, Jacques. *Architectures scénographiques et décors de théâtre* [Scenographic architecture and theatre design]. Paris: E. Magnard, 1985. 144 pp.

Gillibert, Jean. *L'Acteur en création* [The actor in creation]. Toulouse: Presses Universitaires du Mirail, 1993. 206 pp.

Gorelik, Mordecai. *New Theatres for Old*. New York: Dutton, 1962. 553 pp.

Grebanier, Bernard. *Playwriting*. New York: Thomas Y. Crowell, 1961. 386 pp.

Institut del Teatre de Barcelona. *El teatre d'ombres arreu del mon: Les grans tradicions* [Shadow puppets of the world: the great traditions]. Barcelona: Institut del Teatre, 1984. 192 pp.

Izenour, George C. *Theater Design*. New York: McGraw-Hill, 1977. 631 pp.

Jones, David Richard. *Great Directors at Work: Stanislavsky, Brecht, Kazan, Brook*. Berkeley, CA: University of California Press, 1986. 290 pp.

Machlin, Evangeline. *Speech for the Stage*. New York/London: Routledge/Theatre Arts Books, 1992. 254 pp.

Malkin, Michael R. *Traditional and Folk Puppets of the World*. New York: A.S. Barnes, 1977. 194 pp.

Mello, Bruno. *Trattato di scenotecnica* [A treatise on scene design]. Novara: G.G. Gorlich, Istituto Geografico de Agostini, 1979.

Niccoli, A. *Lo spazio scenico: storia dell'arte teatrale* [Scenic space: a history of theatre art]. Rome: Bulzoni, 1971.

Pilbrow, Richard. *Stage Lighting*. New York: Drama Book Specialists, 1979. 176 pp.

Quigley, Austin E. *The Modern Stage and Other Worlds*. New York/London: Methuen, 1985. 320 pp.

Saint-Denis, Michel. *Theatre: The Rediscovery of Style*. London: Heinemann, 1960. 110 pp.

——. *Training for the Theatre*. New York: Theatre Arts Books, 1982. 242 pp.

Sherzer, Dina and Joel Sherzer, eds. *Humour and Comedy in Puppetry: Celebration in Popular Culture*. Bowling Green, OH: Bowling Green State University Popular Press, 1987. 151 pp.

Spolin, Viola. *Improvisation for the Theatre: A Handbook of Teaching and Directing Techniques*. Evanston, IL: Northwestern University Press, 1963. 397 pp.

Tidworth, Simon. *Theatres: An Architectural and Cultural History*. New York: Praeger, 1973. 224 pp.

Warthen, William B. *The Idea of the Actor*. Princeton, NJ: Princeton University Press, 1984. 269 pp.

Watson, Lee. *Lighting Design Handbook*. New York: McGraw-Hill, 1990. 458 pp.

WRITERS AND NATIONAL
EDITORIAL COMMITTEES

AFGHANISTAN

Writers: Khan Agah Soroor (Actor; Independent Scholar), *WECT* staff

AUSTRALIA

Writers: Gordon Beattie, Richard Bradshaw, Katharine Brisbane (Publisher, Currency Press), Michael FitzGerald, Richard Fotheringham, Derek Nicholson, John Senczuk, Jill Sykes, Ross Thorne, John West
Readers: Geoffrey Milne (La Trobe University, Melbourne), Helen Thomson (Senior Lecturer, English Department, Monash University, Melbourne; Senior Theatre Critic, *The Age*, Melbourne), Joanne Tompkins (Department of English, University of Queensland)

BANGLADESH

Writer: Kabir Chowdhury (President, Bangladesh Centre of the ITI)
Reader: Rudraprasad Sengupta (Director, Nandikar Theatre, India)

BHUTAN

Writers: Ravi Chaturvedi (Professor, Department of Dramatics, University of Rajasthan, Jaipur), *WECT* staff

BRUNEI

Writer: Zefri Ariff (Senior Script Editor, Deksyen Drama TV)
Reader: Furrukh Khan (Doctoral Candidate, Centre for Colonial and Post-Colonial Studies, Rutherford College, University of Kent, UK)

CAMBODIA

Writers: *WECT* staff
Readers: Pich Tum Kravel (Ministry of Culture and Fine Arts, Cambodia; Director, Actor, Playwright and Independent Scholar), Toni Shapiro (Visiting Scholar, Department of Dance, Mills College, Oakland, California; Research Associate, Centre for Southeast Asia Studies, University of California at Berkeley)

CHINA

Writer: Rong Guangrun (President, Shanghai Theatre Academy, Shanghai)
Readers: Bernard Luk (York University), Ren Sheng Ming (Professor, Shanghai International Studies University, Shanghai)

INDIA

Writers: Ravi Chaturvedi (Professor, Department of Dramatics, University of Rajasthan, Jaipur),

Sunita Dhir, Jasmine Jaywant (Independent Scholar), Anjala Maharishi, Ranbir Singh, Prakash Syal, G. Kumar Verma
Readers: Arun Agnihotri (Artistic Director and Consultant, The Playhouse, Vadodara, India; Centre Correspondent, ASSITEJ India), Anatol Schlosser (Associate Professor, Department of Theatre, York University)

INDONESIA

Writer: Saini K.M. (Professor, Department of Theatre, Academy of Performing Arts)
Readers: Jody Diamond (American Gamelan Institute, Lebanon New Hampshire)

IRAN

Writers: Farrokh Gaffary (Film Director; former Director of Iranian Film Archives; former Director of Centre for Rituals and Traditional Performing Arts, Tehran), Arby Ovanessian (Independent Scholar; Former Artistic Director, National Theatre of Iran), Anthony Shay (Artistic Director, Avaz Dance Theatre), Laleh Taghian (Theatre Critic; Independent Scholar; Editor, *Theatre Quarterly*, Tehran)

JAPAN

Writers: Imamura Osamu, Koshiro Uno, Kuniyoshi Kazuko (Theatre Critic; Scholar), Odagiri Yoko (Stage Designer), Ogawa Nobuo, Ozasa Yoshio (Professor; Editor, *History of Modern Japanese Theatre*), Senda Akihiko (Senior Staff Writer, Drama Critic, Asahi Shimbun, Tokyo), Tanokura Minoru (Theatre Critic, Asahi Shimbun)

KAZAKHSTAN

Writer: Natasha Rapoport (Theatre Researcher, GITIS Institute, Moscow)
Reader: Michael Witta (Director, Triune Arts Company, Toronto)

KOREA

Writers: Kim Eui Kyung, Lee Du Hyun, Yoh Suk Kee (Professor, Department of English, College of Liberal Arts, Korea University, Seoul), Yoo Min Young
Reader: Kyung-Hee Lee (Founder, UNIMA-Korea)

KYRGYZSTAN

Writer: Natasha Rapoport (Theatre Researcher, GITIS Institute, Moscow)

LAOS

Writers: *WECT* staff

MALAYSIA

Writers: Solehah Ishak (Associate Professor, Department of Malay Letters, National University of Malaysia, Selangor), Nur Nina Zuhra (Professor, Department of English Language and Literature, International Islamic University of Malaysia, Selangor)
Reader: Zainal Abdul Latiff (Lecturer in Drama and Theatre, Centre for Distance Education, Universiti Sains Malaysia, Penang)

MONGOLIA

Writers: *WECT* staff

MYANMAR

Writers: Ravi Chaturvedi (Professor, Department of Dramatics, University of Rajasthan, Jaipur), U Ye Htut (Chief Stage Director, Fine Arts Department, Myanmar), *WECT* staff
Reader: Alfred Birnbaum

NEPAL

Writers: Mukunda Raj Aryal (Professor, Central Department of Culture, Tribhuvan University), Prem Raman Uprety (Head, Department of History, Tribhuvan University), *WECT* staff

NEW ZEALAND

Writer: Rose Beauchamp, David Carnegie (Professor, Department of Theatre and Film, Victoria University, Victoria), Anne Forbes
Reader: Laurie Atkinson

PAKISTAN

Writers: Samina Ahmed (Artistic Director, Lahore Cultural Centre; Independent Scholar), Zain Ahmed (Independent Scholar), Salmaan Peerzada (Artistic Director, Rafi Peer Theatre Workshop)
Reader: Solmon Piazado

PAPUA NEW GUINEA

Writers: Esohe Veronica Omoregie (Dean, Faculty of Creative Arts, University of Papua New Guinea, National Capital District), Anthony Adah
Readers: Don Niles (Institute of Papua New Guinea Studies, Boroko), Yasmin Padamsee (former Awareness Community Theatre Coordinator and NGO Facilitator, German Technical Assistance, Papua New Guinea; Independent Theatre Consultant, New York), William Takaku (Director, National Performing Arts Troupe, Papua New Guinea), George H. Ulrich (Curator, African and Pacific Ethnology, Milwaukee Public Museum)

PHILIPPINES

Writers: Nicanor G. Tiongson (Cultural Centre of the Philippines)
Reader: Amelia Lapeña-Bonifacio (Professor Emeritus, University of the Philippines; Artistic Director, U. P. Teatrong Mulat Ng Philippines)

SINGAPORE

Writer: M. Le Blond (Professor, Department of English, National University of Singapore, Kent Ridge)

SOUTH PACIFIC

Writer: Andrew Horn (Head, Department of Literature and Language, University of the South Pacific, Suva, Fiji)

SRI LANKA

Writer: Tissa Kariyawasam (Professor, Institute of Aesthetic Studies, University of Kelaniya, Nugegoda)
Readers: Michael M. Ames (Professor; Director, Museum of Anthoropology, British Columbia) Vandasanda Rathapala (Professor, University of Sri Jayawardhenepura); Ediriweera Sarachchandra (Professor Emeritus, University of Ceylon, deceased)

TAJIKISTAN

Writers: Natasha Rapoport (Theatre Researcher, GITIS Institute, Moscow)
Readers: Soleiman M. Kiasatpour (Instructor, Department of Political Science, University of California)

THAILAND

Writers: Marisa Saenkulsirisak, Sulaiman Wesyaporn, WECT staff
Reader: Mattani Rutnin (Professor, Drama Department, Thammasat University, Bangkok)

TURKMENISTAN

Writer: Natasha Rapoport (Theatre Researcher, GITIS Institute, Moscow)

UZBEKISTAN

Writers: Laurel Victoria Gray (Uzbek Dance and Culture Society, Washington, DC), Natasha Rapoport (Theatre Researcher, GITIS Institute, Moscow)
Reader: Resul Yalcin (PhD candidate, International Relations, University of Exeter, UK)

VIETNAM

Writer: Hoang Su (Dean, Faculty of Drama, Hanoi Institute of Theatre and Cinema, Hanoi)
Readers: Pham Thi Thanh (PhD; People's Award Artist; Development of Performing Arts, Ministry of Culture and Information, Vietnam); Truong Buu Lam (History Department, University of Hawaii)

INDEX